Bruce Robinson is the director and screenwriter of *Withnail and I*, *How to Get Ahead in Advertising*, *Jennifer 8* and *The Rum Diary*. He has also written the screenplays for *The Killing Fields*, *Shadow Makers* (released in the US as *Fat Man and Little Boy*), *Return to Paradise* and *In Dreams*. He is the author of *The Peculiar Memories of Thomas Penman* and *Paranoia in the Launderette*, and of two books for children, *The Obvious Elephant* and *Harold and the Duck*, both illustrated by Sophie Windham. *They All Love Jack* was longlisted for the 2015 Samuel Johnson Prize for Non-Fiction.

ALSO BY BRUCE ROBINSON

FICTION
The Peculiar Memories of Thomas Penman
Paranoia in the Launderette

FOR CHILDREN
The Obvious Elephant
Harold and the Duck

They All Love Jack

BUSTING THE RIPPER

BRUCE ROBINSON

4th ESTATE • London

4th Estate
An imprint of HarperCollins*Publishers*
1 London Bridge Street
London SE1 9GF
www.4thEstate.co.uk

First published in Great Britain by 4th Estate in 2015
This paperback edition first published in 2016

A catalogue record for this book is
available from the British Library

ISBN 978-0-00-754890-3

Printed and bound in Great Britain by
Clays Ltd, St Ives plc

MIX
Paper from
responsible sources
FSC
www.fsc.org FSC® C007454

In memory of Sergeant T. J. Hageboeck
of the Los Angeles Police

Contents

Author's Note xi

1 All the Widow's Men 1
2 A Conspiracy of Bafflement 59
3 The Mystic Tie 102
4 The Funny Little Game 119
5 The Savages 162
6 On the Square 181
7 The Ink-Stained Hack 210
8 The Double Event: Part Two 249
9 Rotten to the Core 279
10 'They All Love Jack' 323
11 On Her Majesty's Service 358
12 The Mouth of the Maggot 405
13 A Gentleman's Lair 449
14 'Orpheus' 487
15 'The Ezekiel Hit' 516
16 'Red Tape' 551
17 'The Spirit of Evil' 611
18 'The Maybrick Mystery' 627
19 Victorian Values 690

Appendix I: The Parnell Frame-Up 761
Appendix II: A Very Curious Letter 791
Acknowledgements 803
Sources 805
Picture Credits 833
Index 835

Power, like a desolating pestilence,
Pollutes whate'er it touches, and obedience,
Bane of all genius, virtue, freedom, truth,
Makes slaves of men, and, of the human frame
A mechanised automaton.

Shelley, 1813

Author's Note

There is an aphorism. When you see a giant, make sure it isn't a dwarf standing in a favourable light. Thus we approach 'the mystery of Jack the Ripper'.

He's in a house of smoke and shifting mirrors. There are glimpses of amorphous faces. Many Jack the Rippers are in here, feeding off what historical fragments their keeper can throw into the pit.

Middle-aged men with disturbing expressions lean over the safety rail, clutching files. These are the Ripperologists. They are waiting for the Rippers to come out.

'There he is!' bellows one. 'It's the wall-eyed onanist from Zadonsk! Look at him, he's playing with himself! Can't you see him? He's got a satchel of wombs!'

Nobody can see him. Attention migrates to another man, and he's just seen somebody else. 'There, *there*,' he barks, shuffling his Metropolitan Police files. 'The Jew! The Jew!! *Mark the Jew!!*'

An inflamed, bespectacled authority fights his way to the front. 'Shut this farce down!' he demands. 'You are all duped!' He struggles to get a pedometer past a pack of egg sandwiches. 'I've measured his routes,' he charges, thrusting his instrument as proof. 'I challenge you all with the *routes*!'

Insults begin to fly, and argument breaks out between him and a man with a compass. But the lights have already started to dim, and the shutters have gone up. It's time for the Ripperologists to go home and save their arguments for another day.

This book has no interest in the house of mirrors, and despite selective admiration for some, no interest in Ripperologists. I don't believe this collective could catch the object of its aspiration in a thousand years, and furthermore, I don't believe in 'the mystery of Jack the Ripper' either.

*

We all know the story, at least the blurb on the paperbacks.

> It is the autumn of 1888. The cobbled streets of Whitechapel echo
> to the chilling footsteps of a ruthless killer … Out of the foetid
> darkness came this subhuman nemesis of blood-hungry evil.
> Taunting the frantic police, he visited merciless death on five
> desperate women, nothing to speak as his witness but their hide-
> ously mutilated remains. He left no clue, but went as silently as he
> came, leaving nothing but a name that will forever be etched into
> the annals of criminal infamy: 'Jack the Ripper'. Ah! Jack the
> Ripper. (Fog to taste.)

This book is a repudiation of virtually everything Ripperology has
ever written. Anyone who wishes is welcome to have their Ripper
back, and retire with him to the nearest gaslit alley. I tend towards
a cynical point of view. In politics I expect the worst, and usually
get it. But I had no idea of what I was in for with this. Buried in the
'mystery' of the Ripper atrocities is a scandal that ain't much short
of incredible. Exploring it was like pulling at a small, wizened root
that as it disinters is discovered to be connected to an enormous
root-system, deeper and more protectively concealed than I could
ever have imagined.

I've spent rather a while enquiring into this 'mystery', and incre-
mentally I have learned to loathe much of what was the Victorian
governing class. Wealth was a deity in Victorian England, and
everything was subservient to the maintenance of it. Underpinned
by their 'right to rule', their cupidity and institutionalised hypocrisy,
these defects constituted a potent amalgamation of the forces that
conspired to turn this monster into a 'mystery'.

There's a perverse, almost heroic status that has evolved around
this prick, as though he were someone special, rather than the epi-
tome of all that is cruel, and a God-damned repugnance. His only
claim to the extraordinary is his anonymity, his so-called 'mystery';
and even that doesn't belong to him, but was the gift of others.

There's a hybrid of Ripperology responsible for a dizzying variety
of publications over the last half-century. By a process of attrition
and endless industry, this coterie of authors has come to 'own' this
history. They are self-appointed 'experts' and guardians of flat-earth
thinking. Under constrictions of the herd (and by some by design)

they have constructed a formidable camouflage around this criminal. It is necessary to break through it before there is any possibility of discovering the identity of our Victorian psychopath.

Busting Jack entails an unravelling of the root-system that is way beyond the constipated strictures of Ripperology.

During the Second World War there was an interrogator for Army Counter-Intelligence by the name of Lieutenant Colonel Oreste Pinto. It was his task to break the cover of enemy spies, and he's one of my weirder heroes. In 1942 Pinto had a man at the other side of his desk who instinct told him had to be an enemy agent. Before arriving at the Colonel's office (just off The Strand in central London), this suspect had been through many searing investigations and survived them all. Notwithstanding that, the authorities continued to harbour suspicions; but nobody could break him. So what did Pinto think?

Pinto interrogated his man over a period of days. The suspect had an impeccable Oxford accent, excellent socio-geographic knowledge, backed up by documentation that was as good as it gets. Down to the last little parochial nuance, he had an answer for everything, and seemed totally and utterly kosher.

Even so, Pinto was convinced he was dealing with an exceptionally talented spy whose true provenance was Berlin. But he couldn't crack him, so he invited him out to lunch. Ten minutes later they were walking up The Strand, about to cross it to go to the chosen restaurant when, as they stepped off the kerb, Pinto screamed, 'Look out!' – and he got his German because the bastard looked the wrong way.

'We drive on the *left* in England, old boy.'

That is an expert in action. In that one inspired moment, all the lies, all the carefully contrived subterfuge, and all the mystery fell to bits. I'm afraid my narrative will take rather longer to make its point than that flash of inspiration from Pinto. But I believe that the Ripper is just as vulnerable. Nailing this aberration means looking beyond the masquerade and requires but a single word. So look out, Jack! We're stepping off the kerb, and I'm going to bust your arse.

B.R.
2 May 2015

1

All the Widow's Men

We must return to Victorian values.

Margaret Thatcher, 1983

Reactionary nostalgia for the proprieties of Victorian England is unfortunate, like a whore looking under the bed for her virginity. Thatcher was perhaps confused because there were no drug busts in nineteenth-century England, few prosecutions for cruelty to children, and little recorded sex crime.

But who needs to force his attentions, with twelve hundred harlots on the streets? There was sex aplenty, at prices all could afford. At the bargain end you could fuck for the price of a mug of tea.

As far as narcotics were concerned there was even less of a problem, because getting smashed wasn't illegal. Any toff on his way to the Athenaeum could stroll into Harrods and demand half an ounce of their finest cocaine. There was no 'war on drugs'. The only drug wars in the Victorian epoch were those conducted by Englishmen in soldiers' uniforms trying to get the Chinese hooked. If they refused to become junkies, they murdered them. Hundreds were strung up outside their own homes. When Victoria's Prime Minister Lord Palmerston had finally achieved stability of the market, the dealers moved in, shipping their opium out of British Calcutta – 5,000 tons a year by 1866. What today are quaintly called 'street values' were astounding, and the revenues to the Crown require no less a word. British 'administrators', i.e. pushers, computed that in Fukien province eight out of ten adults were addicted, and nine out of ten in Canton. A complete marketing success.[1]

One of the outstanding paradoxes of the Victorian age was its obsession with morality, when morality there was none. When it came to sex, Victorian hypocrisy rose to the very ether. The age of consent (determined by an all-male Parliament) was twelve. More often than not, however, consent didn't come into it. Children were regularly sold into upmarket brothels as a leisure facility for gentlemen (little girls sometimes having their genitals surgically repaired to sustain the fiction of fresh goods). Champagne on the house, of course, padded chambers available on request. The beating of a common child into bloody insensibility with a whip may not have gained you the epithet of a 'good egg' at the club, but it wouldn't have put you into prison either.[2] It was men like W.T. Stead who got banged up for trying to do something about it.

William Thomas Stead was one of the great Victorians, a powerful and influential journalist, frequently vilified by the midgets of his trade who were anxious of his sincerity and success. He and Bramwell Booth, of Salvation Army fame, attempted to expose upper-class depravities by going out and buying a thirteen-year-old girl for a fiver. He published a full report of it in the *Pall Mall Gazette*, titled 'The Modern Babylon'.[3] This didn't go down at all well with the Establishment (many politicians being punters), and the pair of them ended up in the dock at the Old Bailey.

'Nothing less than imprisonment', farted *The Times*. Mr Justice Lopes got on with it. 'William Thomas Stead – I regret to say that you thought it fit to publish, blah, blah ... and that you deluged our streets and the whole country with an amount of filth, blah, blah, blah ... and I don't hesitate to say, will ever be a disgrace to journalism.'[4]

Three months' hard labour.

In 1888 you could fuck a child for five shillings, but you couldn't read Zola. What the Establishment didn't like about Emile Zola was his treatment of the working class, who he had the French neck to represent as human.

In his novel *Germinal*, for example, a coalminer not only falls in love with a girl Capital has reduced to an animal, but he also forms an embryonic trade union. Good God, two horrors in one! The Right Honourable's wig must have lifted six inches into the air. Like Stead, Ernest Vizetelly (the British translator and publisher of Zola) got three months.

But there was a darker, deeper fear abroad in Zola's mines, indeed in the minds of the Victorian Establishment. It was the voice from the abyss, the voice of Socialism, howling, 'Enough, enough. Get off your all fours in the darkness, and stand on two feet like men.'

London was the richest city on earth. Bar none. A Baedeker guide of the period wrote: 'Nothing will convey a better idea of the stupendous wealth of London than a visit to its docks.' Eighteen months after an unprecedented working-class riot in Trafalgar Square in November 1887, London's docks were hit by a cataclysmic strike.[5] A Mr Norwood, for management, put it down to 'dark deliberations of a Socialist Congress in Switzerland'. He was believed then, and might even be now. But I think the strike was more likely to have been caused by the habitual agony of three hundred men fighting over one job, the 'most ravenous, that is, potentially the cheapest', getting it. The rest could crawl off and die. And many did, one man actually starving to death on Cannon Street Road.

Enquiries were made into his accommodation:

> In it is a woman lying on some sacking and a little straw, her breast half eaten away with cancer. She is naked but for an old red handkerchief over her breast and a bit of sail over her legs. By her side a baby of three and three other children. Four of them. The eldest is just nine years old. The husband tried to 'pick up' a few pence at the docks – the last refuge of the desperate – and the children are howling for bread. That poor woman who in all her agony tries to tend her little ones ...[6]

The Queen sent a bunch of posies to the East End – not for the dying woman, but for the Sisters of Jesus, who were teaching girls to sew. In 1888, at Swan & Edgar, Piccadilly, you could order an evening gown and have these scrofulous, albeit industrious little Whitechapel fingers make it for you to wear at the *soirée* that very night. That very year, the Earl of Dudley threw a party for his ever-hungry but already overfed friend Edward, the Prince of Wales. The dinner service was specially made for the occasion by Sèvres. It had the royal glutton's crest on it, and cost £22,000.

At about the time of the description of the dying woman in Whitechapel, historians liked to kid the British that they went to war over such outrages. Victorian schoolchildren were informed of one such escapade. It featured a stinking cellar full of men, women and children, and was colloquially known as 'the Black Hole of Calcutta'.

I've read extensively about this 'hole', but details of its myth needn't trouble us here. I raise it merely to point out that if Victorian educators wanted a hole to get uptight about, they could have had as many as would satisfy their indignation without the inconvenience of sending an army to India. A penny ride on a London omnibus would have taken them to Aldgate (Jack's nearest and frequently used underground station), east of which were thousands of black holes more permanently frightful than anything in Bengal.

Here, the sub-British ate, slept and wiped their arses in cellars full of vermin and promiscuous death. It was a state of affairs nobody in government got into a particular tizz about, making one wonder if the outrage over sanitary conditions in Calcutta wasn't something of a theatrical overreaction to get at something else.

In 1877 Victoria became Empress of India, but not of London's East End. There was no money in it. Thus the Victorians managed to persuade themselves that this suburb of hell was nothing to do with them, and that poverty was somehow engendered by evil. Poverty was portrayed as a lack of morality, rather than a byproduct of greed. These bastards were conniving, thieving, degenerate, congenital criminals, born sinners, and if they'd only stop fucking each other, cherry blossom would sprout spontaneously up the Mile End Road.

One West End Nazi offered businesslike solutions to deal with the maggot-coloured infants sullying London's streets. The following is from an elegantly produced little guidebook for tourists published by the Grosvenor Press in the 1880s, at the height of Victoria's reign.

Observe the East End streets, and you will notice hundreds, and thousands of little children wandering about in mobs. Their food is scant and they come ten in a family. Like the wretched Hindus, whom a famine, *that is really well deserved*, has overtaken, and who supinely breed up to the last pound of rice, these Hindus of the East End take no thought for the morrow, and bring into existence swarms of children for a life of barbarism, brutality, and want in the midst of plenty. Yet our civilisation prates at the sanctity of this human life, and in the same breath speaks of the mercifulness of putting a horse with a broken leg 'out of its misery'.[7]

In other words, kill them. Was the writer of the above mentally ill, or simply inured to the cruelties of his time? His words are quoted verbatim (only the emphasis is mine), but they give a kind of perspective. Of course there were giants of the philanthropic trades who fought against such 'values'. But this book isn't about the genius of Victorian England. It's about the bad guys, and even the bad side of the good guys.

The nineteenth century was on its famous roll, and the name of the game was gain. Glittering times for those at the top, not so cosy for those pushing the juggernaut. A confederacy of enterprising Englishmen fought their way up – heroes and cowards, saints and shysters – dragging buckets for the gold. 'I would annex the planets if I could,' said Cecil Rhodes, staring up at Africa's stars. On a more prosaic level, the common herd were required to stand behind cordons of policemen and wave little flags at the passing millionaires.

From time to time they were also required to shell out. Somehow the Victorian elite had managed to amend the mythological affection the peasants had for Robin Hood. It will be remembered that he robbed the rich and gave to the poor. The richest family on earth had turned that on its head. In advance of a Royal Wedding – 'the Fairest Scene in all Creation' – the nuptials of the Queen's grandson George, Duke of York, the mob were instructed to buy the bride a present.

> Dockyard labourers, longshoremen, river boat men, village peasants, mechanics, miners, parish school children, cottagers, weavers, carpenters, bricklayers – the whole, in a word, of the poorest and hardest worked members of the nation – were bidden, in terms which admitted no denial, to give up a day's wage or the price of a week's meals to assist in purchasing some necklace, bracelet, or other jewel for a young lady who is to be the future wearer of the crown jewels of Great Britain. Royalty in England makes a nation of snobs and sycophants out of a nation that otherwise would be sturdy and self-respecting.[8]

Not from my pen, but from that of a brilliant, now neglected writer of the time, 'Ouida' (Marie Louise de la Ramée), who couldn't be dismissed as a horrid Continental republican, because she was

British. She continues, under the subheading 'Physical Defects of the Royal Breed':

> Given their consanguinity in marriage, their hereditary nervous maladies, their imprisonment in a narrow circle, their illimitable opportunity of self-indulgence, the monotony, the acquisitiveness, which lie like curses on their lives, we must give them the honor that they remain as entirely sane as some of them do. They are, moreover, heavily and cruelly handicapped by the alliances which they are compelled to form, and the hereditary diseases which they are thus forced to receive and transmit. The fatal corporeal and mental injuries of the royal families due to what the raisers of horses call 'breeding in and in' cannot be overrated, and yet seem scarcely to attract any attention from the nations over which they reign. Mental and physical diseases are common to them, and so are certain attitudes, moral and political. They are almost all great feeders, and tenacious of arbitrary precedence and distinction. No one ever tells them the truth, they are surrounded by persons who all desire to please, that they may profit by them.[9]

Needless to say, this piece was never published in England, but in the American edition of *Review of Reviews*. If I were obliged to agree with only one phrase of it, it would be the last: 'that they may profit from them'.

Victorian royalty was a gigantic conjuring trick, pomp and pretty circumstance designed to keep your eye off the ball: precisely the reason conjurors use a blonde with big tits. The trick was mother love (and love of mother). Victoria loved her people, and 310 million people loved her.

But this proposition sweats a bit under analysis. Her family feared her. Half the world feared her armies and her avarice – young men flocking to heaven in a brainwashed patriotic stupor at the bugle-call of her greed.

'We must with our Indian Empire and large Colonies,' wrote the Queen, 'be prepared for *attacks* and *wars somewhere* or *other* CONTINUALLY.' Her emphasis, but not her blood.[10]

By 1887 Victoria had been queen for fifty years. At her Jubilee celebrations she wept joyously at the battalions of young soldiers, but got a bit fraught when asked to contribute to the cost of the festivities. Marching feet might bring a sting of imperial hubris, but underlying it was the sentiment of a clapped-out cash register. It was made clear to ministers that if she had to pay, she'd never celebrate again.

She didn't want to pay for her swarm, either. Victoria had twenty-two grandchildren, and by the time of her death, thirty-seven great-grandchildren.[11] That's fifty-nine junior royals with their hands in the till. By the late 1880s this regal cavalcade of indulgence at public expense was stretching political and fiscal credibility to breaking point. It had become too much even for the Conservatives. In an attempt to navigate cross-party dissent, the government quietly suggested that the Palace might want to police its own finances. Nothing radical, you understand: Fat Ed would still get his £128k a year; but could not the Queen herself see a way to appoint a committee that might, very delicately, 'recommend economies, which, without interfering with your Majesty's personal comfort, state, or dignity, [the loyal throat was cleared] might be made available as a fund out of which provision could be made either wholly or in part for the young members of the Royal Family?'[12]

In other words, can you cough up a bit for the kids?

This was construed by the Queen as a piece of common insolence, as was made pretty evident by the tone in which she batted it back. Clearly she thought it iniquitous that she should be expected to shell out. Her Prime Minister, Viscount Lord Salisbury, was the recipient of the bleat. It was 'most unjust', wrote the Queen, 'that she, in her old age, with endless expenses, should be asked to contribute'. Furthermore, she considered herself 'very shamefully used in having no real assistance for the enormous expense of entertaining' (at her own Golden Jubilee). Did not Salisbury realise what all this guzzling cost?

Next day she had another seethe at the ingratitude of the masses, via their Parliament. 'The constant dread of the House of Commons is a bugbear. What ever is done you *will not* and cannot conciliate a *certain* set of fools and wicked people who will attack *whatever* is done.'[13]

These 'fools and wicked people' were actually the taxpayers, a large number of whom were living in abject poverty – which in Her Majesty's view was about all the excuse they had for not understanding the price of Cristal champagne. Is this letter not as illuminating as it is astonishing? The richest woman on earth considered poor people who wouldn't give her money 'wicked'.

'Oh, but she was a wrenching, grasping, clutching covetous old sinner, and closed as an oyster.' I vandalise Dickens's Christmas masterpiece, but his description of Ebenezer Scrooge is appropriate here. I think Dickens found his Miss Havisham in Queen Victoria – his creation a bitter old woman in white, and his muse this caustic old broken heart in endless black. Since the death of her husband Albert in 1861 she had lived in a perpetual funeral, grieving for her lost love and cut off from reality like Havisham in her rotting wedding gown.

The Victorians were subjects of this wretched widow, and in her presence kept a straight face. You had to polish your boots, assume a stiffened aspect, and pretend that everything in the world was serious. Fun was behind her back. In my view, Victoria's permanent grief invented Victorian hypocrisy. You couldn't get your hand up at an endless funeral, and had to pretend outrage if somebody else did. This ethic of counterfeit rectitude survives in not a few British newspapers to this very day.

But then, the name of the game is expediency: what do you want to make people think? Politics is reducible to that last defining question: who do you prefer, our liars or theirs?

I reproduce the following because they save me writing a paragraph (and also because they serve as a vivid metaphor for the so-called official 'Ripper Files' of the Metropolitan Police). They come from the same newspaper, on the same day, but for a different audience. I always imagined a 'balanced view' at Mr Rupert Murdoch's *Sun* meant a big pair of tits given equal prominence towards the camera. But this demonstrates that it too is capable of a little political sophistication. These two front pages concern the introduction of the euro. The one on the left is for the British reader, whose government is anti-European, and that on the right is for the Irish, whose government is pro.

The problem for the Victorians (and some of the wilder of the Ripperologists) was that they equated 'evil' with 'insane'. In terms of nailing our Whitechapel monster, this is a mistake; but the Victorian public were conditioned to think in this direction by the police and by the newspapers.

Jack the Ripper was no more 'insane' than you or me. A psychopath, yes, but not insane. Was Satan insane? I don't think so. For a while he was part of the in-crowd, a dazzling angel, Lucifer, the Bringer of Light. God didn't kick him out of heaven because he was a nut, but simply because he was a nasty piece of work. During his reign, Henry VIII had 72,000 people put to death, and he also liked to cut ears and noses off. Was Henry insane? Probably not, just a Tudor despot who was intolerant of Catholics and others who didn't subscribe to his theological *diktat*.[14]

Is Iago insane? Not noted for his difficulty with words, the greatest writer who ever lived gave this infinitely evil bastard but one line of explanation: 'I hate the Moor.' What if it's as simple as that? With all reverence to Shakespeare, I will change one word: 'I hate the Whore.'

Jack wasn't the first, or the last, to make women a target of hate.

He went over there, ripped her clothes off, and took a knife and cut her from the vagina almost all the way up, just about to her breast and pulled the organs out, completely out of her cavity, and threw them out. Then he stooped and knelt over and commenced to peel every bit of skin off her body and *left her there as a sign for something or other.*

The italics aren't mine, but Jane Caputi's, whose book *The Age of Sex Crime* this comes from.

'Left her there as a sign for something or other'.

As with much in Caputi's book, her judgement here is precise. Although her description echoes aspects of the Ripper's crime scenes, she's actually writing about a squad of American soldiers who have just beaten and shot a Vietnamese woman to death. The perpetrator here is a representative of USAID. 'Such crimes are indistinguishable from the crimes of Jack the Ripper,' writes Caputi; 'both are meant to signify the same thing – the utter vanquishment and annihilation of the enemy.'[15]

You don't have to be 'insane' to cut people up, no matter how fiendishly you do it. You just have to hate enough. The Whitechapel Murderer was a beast who hated women (one young American woman in particular), but no way was he insane.

In 1889 an American lawyer wrote about the Ripper scandal in a Boston legal journal called the *Green Bag*. Considering his piece is contemporary, it is quite remarkable in its perceptions, and is not remotely taken in by the forest of nonsense being put out at the time. It's far too long to reproduce in its entirety. This edited version therefore is mine, as are the emphases.

> It is surprising that, in the present cases, there has been a failure to discover the perpetrator of the deeds; for they have not been ordinary murders. Not only are the details as revolting as any which the records of medical jurisprudence contain; they are also *marked by certain characteristics* which at first sight would seem to afford a particularly strong likelihood of the crimes being cleared up. The very number of the crimes, the almost exact repetition of the murderer's procedure in each, the similarity of hour and circumstances, the elaborate mutilation of the bodies … these things might not unnaturally be expected to give some clue.[16]

My kind of lawyer. I couldn't agree more, exploration of the words 'marked by certain characteristics' being the aspiration of this book.

> Yet this abundance of circumstance gives none. So far from giving a clue, *they would seem to conspire to baffle the police.*

The writer goes on to dismiss the theory of a 'homicidal maniac' as an unreliable proposition:

It is the very atrocity of the Whitechapel murders that gave rise to the theory of their being the work of a madman. It is not a novel line of reasoning, this. Only let the deed be surpassingly barbarous, and the ordinary mind will at once leap to the conclusion that it was a maniac who wrought it. Now, the inference is quite fallacious. Some of the most barbarous murders on record have been perpetrated by admittedly sane men – men on whose perfect soundness of mind no doubt has ever been cast. The mutilation of the bodies of these wretched women in East London, taken by itself, is no indication whatever of insanity on the part of the perpetrator of the deeds. The craft and the cunning evinced in the murders seems little to consist with insanity. The rash and uncalculating act of the lunatic is not here. No doubt there are on record a few isolated cases of considerable caution being shown on the part of insane homicides; but we are not acquainted with any which approach to the present display of prudence and circumspection. The craftiness of these deeds is astounding; and the highest tribute to it is the fact that all attempts at detection have been made in vain hitherto. The actual execution of his foul deeds must have been swift and dexterous, and shows coolness of hand and steadiness of purpose. These things are all markedly in the direction of disproving insanity.[17]

But that wouldn't do for the hierarchy at Scotland Yard; it was not even up for consideration. For mischievous reasons that will explain themselves, the authorities needed a maniac, preferably a foreigner or a Jew.

Havelock Ellis's hysterically funny but apparently serious book *The Criminal* (1890) gives a thumbnail sketch of the kind of thing the Metropolitan Police were trying to sell. The following is a description of one such murderer in the dock:

Imagine a sort of abortion, bent and wrinkled, with earthy complexion, stealthy eyes, a face gnawed by scrofula, a slovenly beard framing a yellow bilious face of cunning, dissipated and cruel aspect. The forehead is low, the hair black and thrown backwards, the muscles of a beast of prey. His repellent head was photographed on my memory, and lighting up the sinister features with a sinister gleam, two small piercing eyes of a ferocity which I could scarcely bear to see.[18]

This perceived horror and 'lair-dweller' – as widely prescribed for our world-famous gent – was an unquestioningly well-enjoyed camouflage, relished and accepted not only by the press and public, but by a majority of experts (the Ripperologists of their day): Jack was a Hebrew frightener with the eyes of a ferret, a sort of Elephant Man with no laughs, and on a moonless night his complexion approached hues of the earth from a freshly violated grave:

> The eye of the habitual criminal is glassy, cold, and fixed; his nose is often aquiline, beaked, reminding one of a bird of prey. The jaws are strong, the canine teeth much developed, the lips thin, nystagmus frequent, also spasmodic contractions of one side of the face, by which the canine teeth are exposed.[19]

Now, I don't know about you, but if I was a hardened, streetwise East End whore, half-sloshed and desperate for fourpence or not, I would definitely avoid going up an alley with this man. Forget the canine teeth, it's the spasmodic contractions of one side of the face that would do it for me.

No whore in Christendom is going to entertain it. But just in case she does, there's more. Let's overlook Talbot and his 'degenerate ear' (1886), and move straight to Ottolenghi (1888), who described the 'extraordinary ape-like agility noted in criminals', a characteristic sometimes accompanied by 'unusual length of arm'; he also drew attention to the prevalence of the 'prehensile foot'. In 1886 Giovenale Salsotto apparently found 'abundant hair round the anus'. So you knew what to look out for.[20]

What the Victorians feared in their Ripper was a manifestation of their own prejudices, and it was rubbish like this that got women killed. 'Your suspect, ladies, is an anthropophagite goon, and local Israelite. Avoid large noses and hair round the anus and you'll be all right.'

It all kicked off with this, fly-posted and hawked all over the East End immediately after the murder of Annie Chapman, with no complaints from the police.

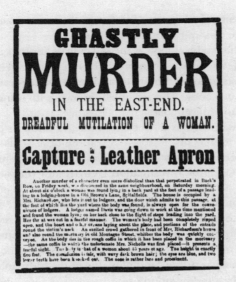

Another murder of a character even more diabolical than that perpetrated in Buck's Row, on Friday week, was discovered in the same neighbourhood, on Saturday morning. At about six o'clock a woman [Chapman] was found lying in a back yard at the foot of a passage leading to a lodging-house in Old Brown's Lane, Spitalfields.

The hunt was now on for a man called John Pizer, a.k.a 'Leather Apron', who was 'known to carry knives'. This was not entirely unreasonable, since his trade was as a boot-finisher – which is presumably why he also wore an apron.

Pizer was a Jew, well known to the police in Whitechapel. In the light of what was to evolve, it is noticeable that the authorities showed little care for Hebrew sensibilities. When they weren't accusing Jews, the police were destroying potential vital evidence in the ridiculous pretence of protecting them from anti-Semitic attack. As will be seen, from various schools of Ripperology there's been a catalogue of excuses for the police concerning the obliteration of some writing on a wall at Goulston Street, near the scene of one of the murders. (Ripperology calls this writing 'graffito'. This unhelpful sobriquet has attracted a good deal of explaining away and very little explaining.) But, as is my intention to demonstrate, not a few senior policemen had a vested interest in the maintenance of bafflement and the dissemination of fairy tales.

Let's just have a brief look at the sad case of another utterly innocent little Jew, called Kosminski. His star rose when certain Ripperologists gave credibility to a bit of worthless moonshine in the margins of a book. This scribble is known, with some reverence, as 'the Swanson Marginalia'.

Donald Swanson was a Met cop, and the book in question, in which he proffered his note, was a volume of reminiscence by Sir Robert Anderson, who at the time of the Ripper crimes was the head of the Criminal Investigation Department (CID) at Scotland Yard.

Hearts got in a flutter at the discovery of this 'marginalia'. Amongst other non-starters, one of the names endorsed as a possible suspect by Swanson was the aforementioned Kosminski, who, according to the later Assistant Commissioner Sir Melville Macnaghten, was a prime candidate due to his addiction to 'solitary vices' – in other words, jerking off.

Here's what a Victorian expert on jerking off has to say:

> The sin of Onanism is one of the most destructive evils ever practised by fallen man. It excites the power of nature to undue action, and produces violent secretions which necessarily and speedily exhaust the vital principles. Nutrition fails; tremors, fears and terrors are generated; and thus the wretched victim drags out a miserable existence, till superannuated, even before he has time to arrive at man's estate, with a mind often debilitated, even to a state of idiotism, his worthless body tumbles into the grave, and his guilty soul (guilty of self-murder) is hurried into the presence of his Judge.[21]

To give credibility to Macnaghten (and Swanson too), one must give credibility to this. Kosminski may have been a local imbecile, but if he was creating pathological history by masturbating himself into a froth of homicidal lunacy, surely these sessions would have taxed his imagination to something beyond a bunch of toothless, half-drunk hags? We can't know what Kosminski was tossing off about, but I can't believe it was over Annie Chapman in her underwear.

More often than not, sexual killers seek to destroy the object of their attraction, a phenomenon corroborated by some notable contemporary criminologists. 'I only shoot pretty girls,' said David Berkowitz, a.k.a. 'the Son of Sam'. By any modern understanding, the Ripper wasn't a masturbator. It was hate rather than sex that attracted him to whores. As a matter of fact, we might question whether he was any more sexually motivated than Jane Caputi's charmer. What he unequivocally was, was a powerful, cunning, intelligent man, attributes confirmed by one of the more objective voices of the time, police surgeon Dr Thomas Bond, who wrote: 'The murderer must have been a man of physical strength and great coolness and daring.'[22]

In Kosminski's case, I imagine the tossing arm must have been highly developed, engendering a formidable bicep, and this speaks in his favour. But other than fitting the loony Yid stereotype, Kosminski is just about as likely a Ripper as the man with the involuntary spasmodic contractions exposing his canine teeth.

If the Ripper got hold of you, you were dead. He overwhelmed an entire society, let alone his victims. Apart perhaps from Mary Jane Kelly (and that's a big perhaps) there were no defensive injuries, not even a moment to hurl a scream at the night. He owned you. You were dead. This nineteenth-century psychopath could have snuffed anyone he liked, anywhere he liked – men, women and children – and indeed he did kill all three.

Kosminski was a ninety-eight-pound simpleton, living off crusts in the gutter, with the physique of an underfed ten-year-old. How do we know this? Because people watched the sad little idiot: the police watched him, he was a face in the East End, as was that other maligned Israelite John Pizer, who incidentally successfully sued at least one newspaper for defamation.

In respect of suspects, the opinions of Assistant Commissioner Sir Melville Macnaghten are not to be taken too seriously; any more than are those of his governor, the notable anti-Semite Sir Robert Anderson, or for that matter the man at the coalface of this débâcle (the washer-off of the so-called 'graffito'), the Commissioner of Metropolitan Police, Sir Charles Warren.

These individuals' peculiar judgements and selective certainties were designed for the Victorian mob. They are opinions from the world of banjo-playing niggers and patent medicines, where the same sugar-coated dose of chalk and arsenic cured asthma, cancer, tuberculosis and piles.

And that's my tiff with the Ripperologists. They think like Victorians, and they think like each other. If a supposed 'authority' said it, irrespective of any possible agenda, they gobble it up like the universal quack remedy Fowler's Solution.[23] (Written on a wall, it's 'graffito', written by a copper, it's 'Grail'.) I can only speak for myself, but I decline to swallow such nostrums. The baseline for me is simple: if some greased unguent 'for coughs, colds, sore holes and pimples on your dick' is now considered obsolete, and if masturbation doesn't drive you screaming to the grave, why cling to this hotchpotch of Victorian propaganda and misinformation, when today we're dealing with something we can discover something about? I'm frankly not interested in what some ludicrous copper has to say about 'solitary vices'. The Victorians' hypocrisy was like a self-induced blackmail of their own intelligence, and that was how the proles were conditioned into deference: work your arse off, wave a flag, and go to heaven. Are we to suppose that we are to function at the discretion of such fictions today?

The Jew myth takes a close second to the most preposterous Ripper assumption of them all, the 'no Englishman could commit such a crime' myth.[24] Very popular in its day. From whence this quaint homily originated it is hard to tell, but it was commonly agreed amongst the newspapers, and the Empress herself was known to share it. Anyone with sufficient IQ to get out of bed should decline to give it a moment of credibility.

Jack the Ripper was a killer in a killer state, and in my view more likely to have been an Englishman than a citizen of any other nation on earth.

Between 1870 and 1900, the British were involved in 130 wars. 'Pax Britannica' was an oxymoron. The only Pax was *in* Britannica; the rest got the blade. Englishmen were killing foreigners to the limits of their maps; barging into Australasia, Afghanistan, Africa, slaughtering them in Mashonaland, Nyasaland, Matabeleland. They were wading through swamps to kill them in Burma, climbing mountains to kill them in Tibet. So rank was the avarice, so organised the homicide, they had to put a user-friendly label on it. 'Bring Christianity and Civilisation to the poor savage,' said the Great White Queen. And that's what they got, although not in that order. Bullets first, Bibles delayed. British imperialism was an enormous bulldozer of Christian murder, its participants wringing goodness

The Wild Beast Abroad.

out of genocide. It could find excuses to kill people in places it had never heard of, to pick fights with Hottentot, Watusi, Zulu, Masai, find justification to wreak vengeance on Maori at the opposite ends of the earth. Hundreds of thousands were murdered as the Christian soldiers marched on, their insatiable God barking to the fore.

In South Africa the starvation of women and children became British government policy. It was here during the Boer War that the British invented the concentration camp – literally a camp in which to concentrate your enemies: in this case the families of the Boer army whom the Brits were having some difficulty trying to defeat in battle. So they went for the wives and kids. Thousands died like the child in the snap overleaf. Meanwhile, Boss Officer Field Marshal Lord Roberts ordered the destruction of all animals and the burning of all crops and farms within ten miles on either side of any railway line the enemy had attacked.

I include this picture because it is as shocking as anything our 'mystery man' in Whitechapel ever did, and for me it pretty much sums up the calling card of nineteenth-century Christian imperialism. Such hideous cruelties did not receive the press coverage or the

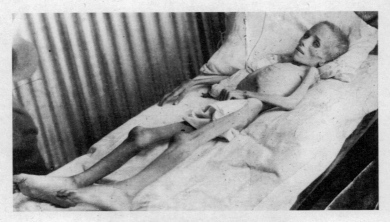

Bloemfontein concentration camp, c. 1900

public notoriety of Jack's atrocities, even though by imperial standards he was barely an amateur.

Nowhere was the imperial narrative more wretched than in the
maintenance of England's first overseas conquest: Ireland.

Salisbury called the Irish 'Hottentots' in response to their aspirations for Home Rule. 'I decline,' he lathered, 'to place confidence
in a people who are in the habit of using knives and slugs.' No
filthier cant ever came out of a human mouth. The English had
been unwelcome occupiers of Ireland for seven bloody centuries,
their tenure secured only by indiscriminate use of the bullet and the
blade. Generations took English lead, and thousands more their
bayonets.

In 1649 the mother of them all had arrived. He was the fifty-year-
old commander of the New Model Army, Oliver Cromwell. Ugly as
a tortoise and clad like one in a corset of steel, he brought his God
with him and shipped into Dublin with a zealous commitment to
the Almighty's work: 'The sword without, the terror within.'
Intoxicated with Biblical fervour and high on his own juice,
Cromwell took his Protestant militia from city to town, town to
village, exterminating Catholics as he went.

Like the Victorians after him, this monster purported to believe
that his colonial enterprise was ordained by God, and it was a God
'who would not permit His wrath to be turned aside'.

The massacres were fêtes of blood, down to the last innocent baby. Those who weren't immediately put to the sword were stripped and left to starve. Some women had their hands and arms cut off, 'yea, jointed alive', wrote one contemporary observer, '*to make them confess where their money was*' (my emphasis).

Those who were spared were shipped out in bondage, 50,000 of them in all. The first slaves in the British West Indies, at Barbados, were Irish men, women and children.

According to Victorian academic James Allanson Picton, the most effective piece of artillery in the English army was the name 'Oliver Cromwell': 'He made it a terror, and it has remained a curse.' A curse it was, a damnation visited upon Ireland that would endure for another 272 years.[25]

'Without exception', wrote Her Majesty's most despised journalist, Henry Labouchère MP, the British were 'the greatest robbers and marauders that ever existed'. Their plunder, said he, was 'hypocritical', because 'they always pretended it was for other people's good'.

One exponent of this benevolence (and never mind the bollocks) was Field Marshal Viscount Wolseley, Commander in Chief of the British Army. 'War,' he opined, 'is good for humanity':

> Wherever we hoist our flag, there we honestly strive – not always, I confess, with complete success – to establish those immutable principles of even-handed justice, and of improved morality … As a nation, we can point with pride to territories once barbarous but now civilised, in every corner of the globe. The wars which extend our frontiers bring new territory under the influence of missionary work, of our laws, and civilisation.[26]

An alternative view of this 'missionary work' was recorded by a Swedish cleric called Charles Lumholtz in Victoria in 1888: 'To kill a native of Australia is the same as killing a dog in the eyes of the British colonist.' Expanding his critique, Lumholtz writes: 'Your men made a point of hunting the Blacks, every Sunday [presumably after church] in the neighbourhood of their cities … systematically passing the whole day in that *sport,* simply for *pleasure's sake* [his emphasis].'

And what a pleasure it must have been: 'A party of four or five horsemen prepare traps, or driving the savages into a narrow pass, force them to seek refuge on precipitous cliffs, and while the unfortunate wretches are climbing at their life's peril, one bullet after another is fired at them, making even the slightly wounded lose their hold, and falling down, break and tear themselves into shreds on the sharp rocks below.'[27]

Cracking shot, Johnny! Thank you, sir!

'Although local law (on paper) punishes murder,' continues Lumholtz, 'it is in reality *only the killing of a white man* which is called murder' (again, his emphasis).

Just who did these Christian civilisers think they were kidding? From which of their Ten Commandments did they consider themselves exempt? You can stuff all that twaddle, old boy. They're infidels with a different god.

Which unquestionably was true. All tanned foreigners in receipt of British lead were subject to the delusion of a different god (it was only their gold that was real). In India they had one god with three heads, and in England we had three gods with one head: the Father, the Son, and the Holy Ghost. Consequently, it's quite likely that God looked more like a British officer with half a bear on his head than a man with a bone through his nose.

Twenty-five thousand black bears a year were slaughtered to make hats for the British Army, and fashionable London ladies liked their hummingbirds skinned alive, a technique which apparently added lustre to the *chapeau*.[28]

Meanwhile, back in Africa, where the degraded races wore fur and feathers, white men were endlessly hacking at jungle to get at the loot. This was dark and dangerous territory; the continent was still largely unexplored. It was therefore always possible to face sudden confrontation with wild and dangerous men. There was a high chance, for example, of Sir Cecil Rhodes, or Major R.S. Baden-Powell, suddenly springing upon you from the thicket.

Baden-Powell was one of Wolseley's breed of chaps, 'an ambitious little man' who on the side 'enjoyed dressing up at concert parties and singing in a falsetto voice'. He was also known to enjoy the company of Boy Scouts.

Powell marched his column of fighting men from the beaches of the Gold Coast into deep up-country, his task once again 'to bring back the gold' and to destroy the religious practices of the Ashanti. When they got to their destination, a town called Kumasi, the King of the Wogs was asked to produce 50,000 ounces of gold, and spare us the mumbo-jumbo. Only six hundred ounces were forthcoming, creating a bit of a letdown amongst the visitors, who were already half-dead from the march. Baden-Powell concluded that the King and his mother should be taken back to the coast in default.

No one in Kumasi liked the idea of this, because 'The Queen Mother, as with many African peoples, was an extremely important figure in the hierarchy.' Obviously a peculiar lot. Notwithstanding that, Baden-Powell and his boys set about the business of teaching these heathens a history lesson of the type untaught in British schools. In their rage for gold they battered their way through temples and sacred mausoleums, pillaging anything of value in an 'orgy of destruction that horrified the Ashanti who witnessed it'.

With their royal family as prisoners, the Africans stood by 'like a flock of sheep'. There was not much for the civilisers to do before bidding their farewells except to 'set fire to the holiest buildings in town'. 'The feeling against the niggers was very intense,' wrote Powell, 'and the whites intended to give them a lesson they would not forget.'[29]

Some of them haven't.

The other side of the continent was of no less colonial interest, but here things weren't going so well. All the ingredients of a major imperial cock-up were *in situ*, focusing on a city in the southern Sudan called Khartoum. The Sudan had been annexed by the British, but now they wanted out. On paper this looked relatively easy: bring in the camels, evacuate all the people on our side, get them back to Egypt, and we'll sort out the details later.

George Eliot's brilliant aphorism, 'Consequences are without pity' – or words to that effect – proved its fidelity here. Before anyone knew it, Khartoum was under a siege that was to last 317 days. An army of 30,000 religious fanatics under the messianic Mahdi, a sort of Osama bin Laden of his day, wanted to kill everyone in Khartoum and take the city back into the bosom of Mohammed. But unhappily, they faced the indomitable might of the British Empire, which in this case was one man. His name was Major General Charles George Gordon.

From time to time I agree with the dead, even with a reactionary conservative politician. After Gordon's death amid the disaster of Khartoum, Sir Stafford Northcote got on his feet in the House of

Commons and told nothing less than the truth. 'General Gordon,' he said, 'was a hero among heroes.' I find nothing to contradict that. Gordon was a hero, no messing with the word. 'If you take,' continued Northcote, 'the case of this man, pursue him into privacy, investigate his heart and mind, you will find that he proposed to himself not any idea of wealth and power, or even fame, but to do good was the object he proposed to himself in his whole life.'

Gordon's government betrayed him. As far as the Conservatives were concerned – and again they were probably right – the villain in the whole affair was an irascible old Liberal the serfs had made the mistake of re-electing. Prime Minister William Gladstone was a man of compassion and large mind, but he couldn't make it up over the Sudan. 'God must be very angry with England when he sends us back Mr Gladstone as first minister,' wrote Lord Wolseley. 'Nothing is talked of or cared for at this moment but this appalling calamity.'[30]

Wolseley doubtless felt his share of guilt. It was he who had sent Gordon, at the age of fifty, to sort out the problem of the southern Sudan. Throughout the searing heat of that dreadful autumn of 1884 Gordon wrote frequently to London: send us food, send us help, send us hope. Despite the headlines and the Hansards full of unction, the dispatches went unheeded, and Gladstone's vacillations became the tragedy of Khartoum.

The infidel was closing in, at least to the opposite bank of the Nile. This didn't cost Gordon any sleep: he had a better God than theirs, and more balls than the lot of them put together. 'If your God's so clever,' he taunted, 'let's see you walk across the Nile.' Three thousand tried it, and three thousand drowned. The rest kept an edge on their scimitars, waiting for the word of the Almighty via the Mahdi. They were a particularly fearsome, in fact atrociously fearsome, mob. According to British propagandists they didn't give a toss about death, because heaven was its reward. They apparently believed that saucy virgins were going to greet them in Paradise, handing out the wine and honey. I have to say, it doesn't sound much different from the Christian facility, although our corpses don't get the girls.

January 1885 baked like a pot. The 14,000 inhabitants left in Khartoum had eaten their last donkey, and then their last rat. Nothing was left to constitute hope but relief from the British, and failing that, death.

'I shall do my duty,' wrote Gordon. And he did. There are various accounts of his death, and though this one's untrue, it's the first I ever read, in the *Boy's Own Paper* fifty years ago. He deserved so romantic an obituary. Death came on the night of 26 January, when thousands of infidels breached the city walls. Upstairs in the palace that was serving as government house, Gordon changed into his dress uniform, combed his hair and donned polished boots. With a revolver in one hand and a sword in the other, he came downstairs to meet them.

They cut off his head and carved him to ham, and we're back into reality. With his head on a stick they ran around the screeching streets, while the rest of their fraternity went berserk. Just in case there were any shortages in heaven, girls as young as three were raped and then sent to the harems for more. Infants were disembowelled in their mothers' arms, then the mothers were raped, and their sons were raped. Four thousand were massacred. A piece of human hell. There was no merciful God in Khartoum that night.[31]

Twenty years later a statue to General Gordon was put up in Khartoum. He may well have smiled at the irony. He was a Victorian hero who hated the Victorians. A few months before his death (irrespective of his fate in the Sudan) he had made up his mind that he would never return to England, writing to his sister: 'I dwell on the joy of never seeing Great Britain again, with its horrid, wearisome dinner parties, and miseries … its perfect bondage. At these dinner parties we are all in masks, saying what we do not believe, eating and drinking things we do not want, and then abusing each other.'

In another letter, having delineated his view of the difference between 'honour' and 'honours', he wrote: 'As a rule, Christians are really more inconsistent than "worldlings". They talk truths and do not act on them. They allow that "God is the God of widows and orphans", yet they look in trouble to the Gods of silver and gold. How unlike in acts are most of the so-called Christians to their founder! You see in them no resemblance to him. Hard, proud, "holier than thou", is their uniform. *They have the truth,* no one else, it is *their* monopoly' (Gordon's emphasis).[32]

The Queen never forgave Gladstone, 'that wretched old madman', for Gordon's death, and it was a day of royal celebration when he resigned his office six months later, to be replaced by something more to Her Majesty's taste.

The man in question was a born aristocrat, a master of chicanery and scandal-management, a barefaced liar – a sort of Margaret Thatcher with class. His name was Viscount Lord Salisbury, and apart from a brief hiatus, he will remain Conservative Prime Minister throughout this book.

The Victorians did nemesis very well. Salisbury didn't like what had happened in the Sudan any more than Victoria did, and both were prepared to spend whatever it cost for revenge.

It came a few years later, in uniform of course, in the shape of a forty-seven-year-old man called Kitchener. Although born in Ireland, Herbert Kitchener was a British soldier from the spurs up, fanatically committed to his Queen and country and the death ethic of his time.

'General Kitchener, who never spares, himself, cares little for others,' wrote a fresh-faced young soldier who had served under him, igniting fury amongst various old farts in the service clubs. The dispatch had come back to London from Egypt. Its author was a cavalry officer, an incredibly brave young fellow called Winston Churchill, who was augmenting his thin military income as a part-time war correspondent.

'He treated all men like machines,' wrote Churchill, 'from the private soldiers, whose salutes he disdained, to the superior officers, whom he rigidly controlled. The comrade who had served with him and under him for many years, in peace and peril, was flung aside as soon as he ceased to be of use. The wounded Egyptian and even the wounded British soldier did not excite his interest.'[33]

Kitchener was an imperious bully even when he didn't need to be. On a previous expedition into British Egypt, he'd been present when some Arab had been tortured to death. He hadn't liked the look of it, so from then on he carried a handy vial of strychnine in his pocket. He was a weird cove, and a very formidable foe.[34]

In 1898 Kitchener went up the Nile like a dose of salts, crossed the Nubian desert on a thousand camels and arrived in the Sudan with every intention of sorting the matter out. His army was better equipped than perhaps any other on earth, sporting a relatively new invention of Sir Hiram Maxim, a true masterpiece of homicidal innovation. It was a .303 machine gun capable of firing six hundred rounds a minute, and it was to cost a great number of 'astral virgins' their credentials. Kitchener was utterly ruthless towards the enemy, his men, and himself. His campaign ended in a place not too distant from Khartoum, where after savage fighting he took a desert city called Omdurman.

It was here that the Mahdi, responsible for Gordon's death, was himself interred. Oh, my lord, can you imagine the power of a victorious British General standing in the sun of the Sudan? 'Why man, he doth bestride the world.' And like all megalomaniacs, dizzy with the toxins of his own ego, he was about to lose the plot. Like Baden-Powell in his pink bit of Africa, Kitchener freaked out.

Eleven thousand Dervishes lay dead or dying on the battlefield, but there was one man Kitchener wanted to kill again. Despite the years that had passed since Gordon's death, hate for the man who had caused it still gnawed Kitchener's heart. The Mahdi's successor the Khalifa, an 'embodiment of the nationalist aspirations of the people over whom he had ruled', had built a magnificent tomb for his predecessor. Though now riddled with Sir Hiram Maxim's bulletholes it was the full Arabian works, tiled like an astonishing bathroom and topped with a golden dome.

With Allah far from his mind, it was to this shrine that Kitchener went. He dug up the corpse of the Mahdi, and bashed his bones to bits with a hammer he'd brought specially for the purpose. This must have been quite a sight. When the buckets, or whatever, were full, Gordon's nephew, Major W.S. Gordon, supervised the slinging of this infidel garbage into the Nile, an event the diplomatic language of London described as 'Removal of the body to elsewhere'. By then, Kitchener had razed the Mahdi's mausoleum to the ground.[35]

When news of this retribution seeped out, it didn't light up the day at Windsor. 'The Queen is shocked by the treatment of the Mahdi's body,' wrote Lord Salisbury, to which the recipient of this telegram, the former British Consul-General of Egypt Lord Cromer, replied that while Kitchener had his faults, when all was said and done, it was a glorious victory, and 'No one had done more to appease those sentiments of honour which had been stung to the quick by the events of 1885.'

Yes, yes, yes, said the Queen. She liked all that, and was going to hand out some ribbon, but it was getting a terrible press. She felt it was very 'un-English', this destruction of the body of a man who, 'whether he was very bad and cruel, after all, was a man of *certain importance*'. In her view, it savoured of the Middle Ages: 'The graves of our people have been respected', and so should 'those of our foes'.[36]

It seemed that filling graves didn't bother Victoria, it was taking bodies out of them she didn't like; and it was the *trophy* of the Mahdi's skull that particularly flustered her – plus, she'd caught the back end of a rumour that Kitchener had turned it into some sort of flagon, or inkwell, with gold mounts. Kitchener offered various placatory explanations. His original intention, he wrote, was to send the skull to the Royal College of Surgeons (which had apparently gratefully received Napoleon's intestines). Then he had changed his mind, and for religious reasons he'd rather not go into, had buried the offending cranium in a Muslim cemetery in the middle of the night. The inkwell and the flagon were merely vindictive gossip.

Except they weren't. I have good reason to question Kitchener's veracity, and would put serious money on the true destination of the skull, and its purpose.

My explanation will wait.

The question here is, was Kitchener insane? Dragging a putrescent corpse from its grave and bashing what's left of it to bits with a hammer isn't normal, except to certain Victorian politicians. In the House of Lords, Lord Roberts said that any criticism of Kitchener was 'ludicrous and puerile', which makes one wonder what he would have thought of a gang of Arabs turning up at Canterbury Cathedral with crowbars to heave out the body of St Thomas à Becket.

The Victorian Establishment always had it their own way, and therein lies the answer to my facetious question. Of course Kitchener wasn't insane. He was one of the most revered officers in the British Army, and would go on doing what he did for another twenty years. He was a *Boy's Own* hero, rewarded with a peerage, as Lord Kitchener of Khartoum. A top-hole chap and an intimate of the elite, he *was* the ruling class. Like his boss Lord Wolseley, and indeed like his King to be, he was an eminent Freemason.

There was no deficiency in this man's faculties – the exhumation and destruction of the Mahdi's corpse wasn't mad cruelty in the passion of battle, it was a calculated and premeditated act. What motivated Kitchener to dig up and violate that stinking cadaver was hate. Hate.

With that hammer in his hand, Kitchener belonged to Satan.

Satan, wrote Milton, 'was the first That practised falsehood under saintly shew, Deep malice to conceal, couch'd with revenge'.

In the autumn of 1888, no less a personage than Milton's fearful inspiration was about his business of revenge in London's East End. Like Kitchener, his intent was premeditated (he too carried a weapon of extreme suitability – not a hammer, but a knife). Unlike the revered soldier, the Ripper's hate wasn't so easily satiated. He rehearsed it again and again. And unlike Kitchener, the Whitechapel Fiend had a witty and macabre sense of fun.

There are three things, even at this juncture, that can be stated with reasonable confidence about our 'Simon-Pure', as Sir Melville Macnaghten calls him in his monkey-brained book.[37]

1) He was not a 'madman'.
2) He was physically and emotionally strong.
3) And the one thing we can be absolutely certain of is that 'Jack the Ripper' did not look like 'Jack the Ripper'.

No fangs. No failures.

Although complaints about underfunding and undermanning were endless, Whitechapel had not a few policemen on the beat. They were in plain clothes and in uniform, and they weren't up to much. 'The Chiefs of the various divisions, who are, generally speaking, disgusted with the present arrangement, will sometimes call one of these yokels before him to see how much he really does know. "You know, Constable, what a disorderly woman is?" "No," said the Constable. The officer went through a series of questions, only to find that the man was ignorant of the difference between theft and fraud, housebreaking and burglary, and his sole idea of duty, was to move everyone on, that he thought wanted moving on.'[38]

Constable Walter Dew, though perhaps smarter than most, was one of the above. He was a young beat copper at the time of the Ripper. Many years later he published an honest, if occasionally inaccurate, autobiography recalling his memories of the crisis. 'Sometimes,' wrote Dew, 'I thought he [the Ripper] was immune. Was there something about him that placed him above suspicion?'[39]

You nearly hit the nail on the head, Mr Dew, but it was more fundamental than that. It wasn't something about the Ripper; I'm afraid it was something about *you*.

When the Empress proclaimed that 'No Englishman could commit such crimes,' there was an implicit corollary. What she actually meant was, 'No English *gentleman* could possibly commit such crimes.'

'The London police regard the frock coat and the silk hat as the *appenage* of the gentleman, and no one so dressed is ever likely to be roughly handled, even if he forgets himself so far as to dispute a member of the force.'[40]

Walter Dew couldn't have seen Jack the Ripper if he had been standing on his big toe. Like a dose of curare, the lethal anaesthetic of class could stop a London copper in his tracks. Murderers and fiends, in this hierarchy of delusion, did not include anyone of a superior social position. Gentlemen only went to the East End to slum it, for a bit of a lark.

Here's a contemporary description of one such toff: 'The most intense amusement has been caused among all classes of the London world by the arrest last week of Little Sir George Arthur on suspicion of being the Whitechapel Murderer. Sir George is a young

Baronet holding a captaincy in the Regiment of Royal Horse Guards, and is a member of the most leading clubs in town.'

He was also, just in case we haven't quite got the picture, 'a great friend of the late Prince Leopold, Duke of Albany'. Anyway, one night – and I'm so tickled I can hardly write it – Sir George joined the 'scores of young men, who prowl around the neighbourhood in which the murders were committed, talking with the frightened women and pushing their way into overcrowded lodging houses'.

This was obviously topping fun, and providing 'two men kept together and do not make a nuisance of themselves, the police do not interfere with them'.

It was all a heady wheeze, and now comes the quite delightful dénouement:

> He put on an old shooting coat and a slouch hat, and went down to Whitechapel for a little fun ... It occurred to two policemen that Sir George answered very much the popular description of Jack the Ripper. They watched him, and when they saw him talking to women they proceeded to collar him. He protested, expostulated and threatened them with the vengeance of Royal wrath. Finally, a chance was given to him to send to a fashionable Western [i.e. West End] club to prove his identity, and he was released with profuse apologies for the mistake. The affair was kept out of the newspapers. But the jolly young baronet's friends at Brooks's Club considered the joke too delicious to be kept quiet.[41]

In other words, you only had to flash the Victorian equivalent of a Platinum Amex to get an apology and be on your way. The French Sûreté, infinitely superior to its British equivalent at Scotland Yard, suffered no such upper-crust delusions. 'Handcuffed Though Clearly a Gentleman' is the title of the cartoon overleaf from 1892. Some English con artist called Ferguson Purdie had been arrested on a charge of pickpocketing at the Auteuil races. The French police had him in 'cuffs', and the *Illustrated London News* went into shock. He was Clearly a Gentleman! All the elements of British class absurdity and wooden-headed xenophobia are encapsulated in this little sketch.

HANDCUFFED THOUGH CLEARLY A GENTLEMAN: "Mr. Ferguson Purdie, who was arrested at Auteuil Races on a charge of pocket picking, has a real grievance against the French police. Though clearly a gentleman, he was marched through the streets handcuffed, and it was four days before the Embassy could effect his release. No explanation is forthcoming"

You couldn't have got more 'gentleman-like' than the regal son of that most regal gentleman Edward, Prince of Wales. Prince Albert Victor, Victoria's grandson and later the Duke of Clarence, one of England's most eminent Freemasons, used to frequent a male

brothel at the house of Charles Hammond, in Cleveland Street in the West End of London. It cost a guinea to sodomise a boy, and as befitted the Prince's rank, the clientèle were strictly top nobs.

The police had had an eye on the place for some while, keeping a discreet record of the aristocratic comings and goings. Among the officials assigned to this unsavoury calendar was Detective Inspector Frederick Abberline. (He was also on the streets with the Ripper enquiries, and was thus a busy man, of whom we shall be hearing more.)

My interest in Cleveland Street isn't limited to the sordid activities within, but includes the almost inconceivable criminal activity without. By the late 1880s the Victorian Establishment had become so profligate, so craven, that scandal was hissing everywhere, rupturing through the upper classes like air from a perished ball. Home Office staff were forever being rushed off their feet in a frenzy of patching, and repackaging black as a very dark shade of white. The rules had to be violated, manipulated, cheated and debased. In this case the law had to be made a whore to save the royal arse.

This industry of unworthiness was the responsibility of the Home Secretary, Henry Matthews QC, commandant of the legal machine and its venal army of brown-nosed lawyers, lackeys and High Court judges. Like the military in their ursine headwear, these medieval-looking potentates under three and a half pounds of horsehair gurgled the draconian enactments of Victoria's statutes.

One such judge, James Fitzjames Stephen, who in due course will feature at the extreme peripheries of his paymaster's wickedness, had an oblique connection with Cleveland Street. His son, James Kenneth Stephen, was tutor and off-peak lover to the Duke of Clarence. He was also a publisher of verses. As Oscar Wilde remarked when bitching about a similar talent, 'He has nothing to say, and says it.' Wilde was referring to Henry Somerset, an aristocratic second-rate melodist whose brother and co-buggerer Lord Arthur Somerset is to have some prominence in this story.

Somerset was a close pal of the Prince of Wales,[42] and the Prince's son, the Duke of Clarence, was a pal of Commissioner of the Metropolitan Police Sir Charles Warren. The Commissioner was actually a house-guest at Sandringham Palace in Norfolk for the celebrations of Clarence's twenty-fourth birthday in January 1888.[43] I don't know if J.K. Stephen was there, but when Edward inadvertently got busted at an illegal gambling den, the police were chastened, and J.K.'s father was on hand to clarify what 'illegal' actually meant.

'It is occasionally said,' observed Judge James Fitzjames Stephen, 'that the law as it stands exhibits practical partiality in the odious form of undue leniency to the rich in comparison with the poor. How can it be just, it is said, that the Prince of Wales and other people of the highest rank should go to Mr Wilson's [gambling house] and play baccarat with impunity, whilst the newspapers are continually filled with accounts of raids upon gambling houses which do not do a tenth part of the harm? The answer, of course, is plain. There is all the difference in the world between keeping a house in which everyone may gamble, and private gambling which no one can share in without special invitation.'[44]

In other words, a gentleman may 'invite' another to break the law, and be within the law by doing it, but if the culprit is not a gentleman and was not 'invited', the law must make a very necessary social adjustment.

'It is true,' hawked Justice Stephen, 'that under 36 and 37 Vict. s. 3. that any man who plays or bets in any street, road, highway, or other public place with any cards or instruments of gaming … is a rogue and vagabond, and as such may be imprisoned by a magistrate for three months.'

A king to be gets a cartoon, and a common man a cell. This apparently went down all right in West End drawing rooms and the more affluent Freemasonic lodges, but didn't cut it so favourably for Masons in the United States.

Edward, Prince of Wales was Grand Master of the Grand Lodge of England, and thus the most powerful Freemason on earth. But omnipotence did not faze the Yanks. They'd got rid of kings and kingdoms almost everywhere, except in their Bibles: 'The Prince of Wales, as Grand Master of the Grand Lodge of England, should, in the opinion of many, be charged with conduct unbecoming in a Mason.' That was from the *Rough Ashlar*.[45] Another title, the *Masonic Constellation*, threw an even bigger rock: 'What will the Masons do in the matter? Cringe at the feet of such an unworthy person; lick the spittles that fall from such unworthy lips? … The Fraternity in America should take some decisive steps in the matter of the disgrace that he had brought upon the Craft … A common gambler and rake … Strip the tarnished jewels from his breast, try him for gambling and adultery, and expel him from their halls.'[46]

All I can say to that is, dream on. The hysteria from the colonies was not only disingenuous, it was naïve – the intention of the British Masons being precisely the opposite. This American seemed to have forgotten who was running the place. He had even more to say, but he was wasting his time: 'It is the duty of Masons in England to guard with jealous care the purity and high standing of our loved order. There is no palliation or mitigation in such cases, and those who shield or protect are equally guilty.'[47]

You can say that again. But nobody ever did. The 'equally guilty' responsible for shielding and protecting fellow criminals in the matter of scandal (at Cleveland Street, for example) were, almost to a man, eminent members of the 'loved order'.

Condemnation of the Prince of Wales was not restricted to American Freemasons. It also came from the British public. They wrote letters to the authorities, the newspapers and the police. There was irate criticism even from a famous murderer – the following came from 'Jack the Ripper', or at least from a correspondent signing himself thus: 'A word of warning, beware, and protect your low immoral pot-bellied prince. God has marked him for destruction and "mutilation".'

Not exactly an echo of the popular press, though Fleet Street wasn't friendly either. All in all, it was another lousy day in utopia.

But this little fracas for Edward was as nothing – wasn't even a pimple on the bum – to the truly awful scandal that had come down the pike but twelve months before, and threatened to destroy his son.

An oppressive fact about the Victorian ruling estate was its isolation. You were in it, or you were not. Its encircling walls weren't entirely visible until you ran into one. Then they were high and hard. The upper classes could slam a door in your face that you couldn't even see. It is another fact, similarly invisible, that perhaps as few as 10,000 members of this class ran the affairs of 310 million people.

Reading its contemporary journals and dainty lady-press, the claustrophobia (I want to say incestuousness) of the Victorian elite seems remarkable. It seemed that everyone knew everyone, and everyone knew everyone else. The upper classes gave an illusion of living in one enormous mansion, residing there like superior strangers, and existing only for garden parties and fireworks around the lake. Blood (no matter how thin) or money (and a lot of it) were the only ways in. Though from time to time, of course, the System absorbed those on whom its survival relied: the bishops and lawyers, the judges and generals, and Commissioners of the Metropolitan Police.

Plus, there were those it slept with or who otherwise amused it, people toys, like Lillie Langtry or Oscar Wilde.

Edward, Prince of Wales was a philistine who didn't give much for their product, but loved the company of artists. Two of the most celebrated of the age were close personal friends: the little composer with his peculiarly British talent Sir Arthur Sullivan, and a true giant of his epoch, the painter Sir Frederick Leighton.

Both of these complimentary-ticket holders of the upper class (like Oscar Wilde) were Freemasons, as were a staggering number of the class they entertained.

Unlike Freemasonry today, the Craft had its own class hierarchy, centralising like everything else in London, and above all at its gentlemen's clubs. Forget the histrionics over Parliament – that was just a floor show for the proles. In the clubs they were all players in the same game, and it was at White's, Pratt's, the Athenaeum and their like that political business was actually done.

Lord Salisbury, the Prime Minister, was a member of the Athenaeum, as were Home Secretary Henry Matthews, Judge James Fitzjames Stephen, Arthur Sullivan and Frederick Leighton. And so, for the record, were two other gentlemen we shall be hearing a great deal more of, Sir Charles Russell QC MP and London's Boss Cop, Metropolitan Police Commissioner Sir Charles Warren.

Just before it hit the fan at Cleveland Street, Prince Albert Victor had a night out. It was one of many such *soirées* organised to celebrate the sovereign's birthday: 'Prince Albert Victor dined with the First Lord of the Treasury, among other guests being Bros ["Bro" means Brother in the Freemasonic vernacular] the Marquis of Hertford, the Earl of Crawford and Balcarres, the Earl of Carnarvon, the Earl of Zetland, the Earl of Londesborough, Lord Randolph Churchill, M.P., Sir Hicks Beach, Bart, Lord Harlech, Sir John Mowbray, Bart, and Sir W. Hart-Dyke, Bart, M.P.' Other distinguished Masons feasting in honour of their monarch that week were Bros 'Lord George Hamilton, M.P., as First Lord of the Admiralty, the Duke of Portland, as Master of the Horse, the Earl of Mount Edgecombe, as Lord Steward, and the Earl of Lathom, as Lord Chamberlain.'[48]

I do not mention these names without purpose, nor seek to make an idle point. Many of the Freemasons here mentioned will acquire a specificity as the narrative proceeds.

At another banquet at Arlington Street, Lord Salisbury entertained the Prince of Wales and his ever circulating phalanx of toadies and mattress-muck: the toast, a décolletage of diamonds in the waxy light, was the same all over London: 'To Her Majesty the Queen.'

It was at about this time Verdi became popular with London's window-cleaners, whistling while they polished to the air of '*La Donna è mobile*' lyrics courtesy of the fellows of their class.

> Arseholes are cheap today
> Cheaper than yesterday
> Little boys are half a crown
> Standing up or lying down
> Bigger boys are three and six
> They are meant for bigger pricks …

Henry James Fitzroy, Earl of Euston, was a six-foot-four-inch aristocrat, who in his top hat must have cleared seven feet. His close
friendship with Edward and Albert Victor says something about all
three. Euston was a classic pile of shit, squandering family money in
pursuit of endless good times. Decadence appeared to be his life's
ambition, and was one of the few activities at which it could be said
he excelled.

'Of distinctly Bohemian tastes,' wrote an early biographer, 'he
soon got into a "set" that was anything but a desirable one. A host
of parasites looked upon him as their prey, to be exploited and
sucked dry. Nor did the women ignore him. His women friends,
however, were not of the description who would have been
welcomed in Belgravian drawing rooms. Not that they, for their
part, had any desire to be in them. They were much more at home
in the green rooms of the lesser theatres and the Haymarket night
houses.'[49]

It was at one of these dives that Euston fell for the wide eyes and
rosewater of Kate Smith, a well-known West End slut. He had
married and abandoned her by the age of twenty-four. His career in
debauchery then flourished. There were plenty of other pretty faces
in lipstick, although not all of them belonged to girls. It took a while
for Euston to work out what kind of sex he liked, and he ended up
liking all of it. By the late 1880s this enormous ex-Guards officer was
a not uncommon sight in the nancy shadows of Piccadilly.

On a late afternoon of May or June 1889, a youth emerged out of
them proffering the Earl a card: '"Poses Plastique", Hammond, 19
Cleveland Street. W.'

According to Euston, when called to explain himself at a subsequent magistrates' court, his interpretation of the term 'Poses
Plastique' meant no more than a glass of champagne and the pleasant scrutiny of a little girl's genitals. He went along to Cleveland
Street and was, he claimed, surprised to find no girls.

He would be more easily believed, at least by this writer, had he
said he was surprised to find so many of his aristocratic friends.
There was, for example, Lord Arthur Somerset ('Podge'), a fellow
intimate of the Prince of Wales. That very year, the Prince had travelled with Podge to Paris in a railway compartment shared by their
musical pal Sir Arthur Sullivan.[50] Was Podge – a notorious homosexual – another innocent victim bamboozled by some scoundrel in

Piccadilly? And then there was dear Lord Beaumont, and Lord Ronald Gower, and dozens of other guileless aristocrats, all of whom had traipsed to Cleveland Street only to discover (with corporate shock) that it was a homosexual brothel.

The secret machine was shoved into gear. When Prime Minister Benjamin Disraeli said, 'Royalty cannot survive without Freemasonry, and Freemasonry cannot survive without Royalty,' he spoke nothing less than the truth. It is what Masonry called 'the Mystic Tie'.

Not a year before, the Earl of Euston had been installed as Provincial Grand Master of Northants and Huntingdonshire, and the following day he and the Duke of Clarence were star guests at the laying of a foundation stone at the New Northampton Infirmary. Having promised in his inaugural speech to do all he could 'to advance the interests of Freemasonry', Euston positively sweated unction in his address of thanks to the Duke:

> We recognise with pride the honour done to our ancient and honourable fraternity by so many members of your Royal House, who have entered its Lodges, and done excellent work of brethren of the mystic-tie, and we trust that that connection, so intimate and so valued in the past, may have a long continuance in the future. More especially we beg your Royal Highness to convey to his Royal Highness, the Prince of Wales, our most Worshipful Grand Master, the assurance of our dutiful submission and obedience.[51]

Euston practised his Masonic submission under a multiplicity of disciplines. He was a member of Studholm Lodge, St Peter's Lodge, Lodge of Fidelity, De La Pre Lodge, Bramston Beach Lodge, Royal Alpha Lodge, Stour Valley Lodge, Grafton Lodge, Fitzwilliam Lodge, Military Lodge, Pegasus Lodge, Foxhunter's Lodge, North and Hunts Master's Lodge, Studholm Chapter, London, and Grafton Chapter, London.[52]

There is, however, one Chapter that you will not find in his obituaries, nor in his official CV at Freemasons' Hall. It is an order of the Knights Templar – a Christian adjunct of Freemasonry that claims its genesis from the time of the Crusades – called 'the Preceptory of Saint George, the Encampment of the Cross of Christ'. Amongst its august membership was another 'Christian' degenerate and friend of Euston, and he is the subject of this book.[53]

Meanwhile, on the morning of 5 July 1889, Chief Inspector Frederick Abberline went to Great Marlborough Street police court seeking a warrant for the arrest of Charles Hammond, the owner of the establishment in Cleveland Street, and others involved in the 'Poses Plastique'. The instrument was granted, charging that Hammond 'did unlawfully, wickedly and corruptly conspire, combine, confederate and agree to incite and procure George Alma Wright, and diverse other persons to commit the abominable crime of buggery against the peace of Her Majesty the Queen'.[54]

A novel way of putting it, but the game was up for Cleveland Street. One or two of its adolescent tarts were already in Abberline's custody. A postboy called Newlove thought it most unfair that he and other lads should be isolated for blame. 'I think it's hard,' he told Abberline, 'that I should get into trouble while men in high positions are allowed to walk free.'

Meaning precisely what?

'Why,' replied Newlove, 'Lord Arthur Somerset goes regularly to the house at Cleveland Street, so does the Earl of Euston and Colonel Jervois.'[55]

A cell door slammed on Newlove, but it didn't shut the mouths. A disturbing rumour was beginning to do the rounds, and it wasn't long before Hamilton Cuff, the Assistant Public Prosecutor, was writing to his boss.

'I am told,' wrote Cuff, 'that if we go on a very distinguished person will be involved,' a man then identified only by the glittering initials of 'P.A.V.'.[56]

Prince Albert Victor's father, the Prince of Wales, was in Berlin at the time, hobnobbing with relatives. On receipt of the news he roared back into London – first stop, the offices of Henry Matthews, the Home Secretary. The matter was reported coast to coast in the United States, although somehow the British press overlooked it. The *Washington Evening Star* wrote: 'The Prince of Wales is as much concerned about the matter as anybody else, for he went personally to the Home Office this week to see Secretary Matthews … the police can show him the name of Albert Victor, among those the telegraph boys mention as having visited the house.'[57]

Matthews' legal machine, already haemorrhaging under pressure from the man who was now asking even more of it, was nevertheless at the ready. Two things had to be done, and quick. 1) Dangerous mouths had to be silenced, and 2) Somebody had to be found to blame. The law simply couldn't tolerate postmen backing their anuses onto whoever they felt like. Whatever happened, however it was managed, and whoever was to suffer, Prince Albert Victor was not at that house, on any night, or ever.

> The Government will go to all lengths to secure convictions of the men it wishes to punish just as it will go to all lengths to shield the men that it desires shall escape punishment.
>
> If the reader can believe this is a statement born of partisan bigotry, I can only refer him to the exposures which are now rending 'respectable' London in twain, where all the great resources of the 'greatest empire of the modern world' are being used to save the heir to the crown, and his worthy associates, Lord Ronald Gower, and the rest of the Marlborough House set, from exposure, their crime being, as all the world knows, the same as that for which Sodom and Gomorrah were destroyed, if Holy Writ is to be believed.
>
> If the real information can be got, Scotland Yard is willing to pay for it at the market rates; under any circumstances there is always a supply to meet the demand; and if the real article cannot be had the bogus is always forthcoming.[58]

As the scandal ran for cover, the public were largely kept at a distance. Newspapers murmured, but Fleet Street didn't need any instructions in deference. As with the crisis of Bro Edward VIII and Mrs Simpson some fifty years later, British newspapers declined to print what the whole chattering world was talking about. In the 1880s, as in the 1930s, it was the American press that forced their hand. A London special to the *New York World* elaborated:

> The English newspapers are at length beginning to do something more than throw out dark hints as to the existence of a great scandal. Labouchère, without mentioning the names of the criminals, charges with complete accuracy, that the Home Office has fettered [Warren's successor] Police Commissioner Monro's hands, and he threatens to make things warm for Secretary of State Matthews when Parliament reassembles ... The names known and generally talked about thus far in connection with the case are those of Lord Arthur Somerset, Lord Beaumont, Lord Euston, Lord Ronald

Gower, and one official of high rank, now in India [i.e. Prince Albert Victor].[59]

As soon as the danger hit, Clarence was put on a boat heading for Hyderabad, so he could waste some tigers and any elephants he didn't happen to be sitting on. This regal AWOL wasn't his decision. Like everything else in this wretched creature's life, it was the System that decided: they knew what colour the incoming was, but they didn't yet know the size of the fan. The *Washington Evening Star* continued: 'Mr Labouchère talked about the scandals at a crowded meeting in Lincoln Saturday night, remarking that the hideousness was so much the subject of general comment that London conversation was becoming almost as horrible as London vice.'[60]

It was indeed a circumstance inviting not only public revulsion at the unquenchable lawlessness of the royal mob, but potentially also a dozen years in jail.

For a few breathtakingly terrible weeks the scandal seemed to be spiralling out of government control, the duration of Clarence's sojourn overseas increasing in direct proportion to the crisis. At its inception it was announced: 'With respect to the proposed visit to India of Prince Albert Victor, it has been arranged that his Royal Highness shall arrive in Bombay early in November.' To which *The Freemason* added on 5 October 1889: 'It has been decided that Prince Albert Victor shall extend his visit to Burmah, the newly acquired territory of the Empress Queen. This will so considerably prolong the trip, that His Royal Highness will not be able to return to England for at least six months.'

And it might require longer than that. On 19 November the *Washington Evening Star* reported: 'Ten days ago, it looked as though official pressure was going to succeed in hushing up the tremendous aristocratic scandal … there was a general feeling it would never get into the courts. Now the prospect is different.'

The public were becoming truly disgusted with this charade, particularly in light of an announcement that 'costly apartments being fitted up for Prince Albert Victor in St. James Palace' were to be funded at the pleasure of the taxpayer. 'It has become obvious,' summarised the *Washington Evening Star,* that there has come to be in the past few days, a general conviction that this long-necked, narrow-headed young dullard was mixed up in the scandal, and out of this had sprung a half whimsical, half serious notion, which one hears now proposed about Club Land, that matters will be so arranged that he will never return from India. The most popular idea is that he will be killed in a tiger hunt, but runaway horses or a fractious elephant might serve as well. What this really mirrors is a public awakening to the fact that this stupid, perverse boy has become a man, and has only two lives between him and the English Throne.[61]

And the seat of kings was what it was all about. Nobody gave a toss for this effete little useless pederast – that wasn't the point. It wasn't Albert Victor caught with his trousers down in Cleveland Street, it was an entire ruling ethic, the thing you waved your flag at – a class of the few enjoying unspeakable privilege at the expense of the many they despised. The Establishment didn't give a monkey's who P.A.V. buggered, they'd known about Cleveland Street for years. It was the fact that it had leaked out that freaked them, and they were stupefied with anxiety at the damage this could do to the world's greatest conjuring trick.

If anything happened to Edward, his son was what they got. His tutor, John Neale Dalton, had described 'an abnormally dormant condition of mind'. At Cambridge University, to which the dope was sent, one of his instructors doubted whether he could 'possibly derive much benefit from attending lectures', as he 'hardly knows the meaning of the word, to read'.[62]

However, at all costs, the absurdity of reverence for this twerp had to be maintained. A sudden coronary for his father, Fat Ed, was very much on the cards. Gluttony was his pleasure, and his pleasure was out of control. When he sat down to eat it was a virtual suicide attempt. 'He is a very dangerous guest,' complained a Permanent Secretary. 'He once got into Lord Cairns' dining-room, and ate up the Judge's luncheon.'[63] Trained handlers in Marienbad and Baden Baden had failed to solve his gut. Plus, there was the fornicatory urge in the groin whose onslaught he could not negotiate – men got swindled of their wives in the bedrooms of their own country houses. But it was in Paris that Edward got into full adulterous stride. Fluent in several languages, he spoke German better than English (he had a thick German accent[64]), adored all things Parisian, and had a keen interest in French furniture.

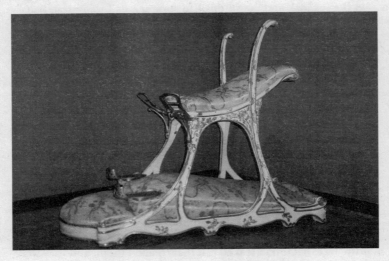

Known as the '*siège d'amour*', this contraption was manufactured to suffer the enormous regal bulk while His Majesty guzzled vintage and shagged two at once. The future Edward VII was never a 'Victorian', he simply waited for history to catch him up. Like a sort of cement-mixer in a top hat, he risked apoplexy on a daily basis, and the whole fucking lot of them could have been up the Mall in black crêpe next Saturday.

Prince Albert Victor wasn't a person, but a 'thing' to be protected. Without a king you couldn't have a queen, and without either you couldn't have viscounts, dukes, duchesses, knights, barons, earls, lords, ladies, high sheriffs, and 10,000 other unctuous little dogs-bodies walking backwards in buttons and bows. Master of the Horse, Master of the Rolls, Mistress of the Robes, Groom of the Stole, Grand Order of the Bloat and Most Noble Star of the Transvaal Murderer, all gone, all as shattered crystal without a king. A dozen centuries would go up in smoke, and history would be the property of people like Gladstone – 'this most dangerous man', wrote Victoria. 'The mischief Mr Gladstone does is *incalculable*, instead of stemming the current and downward course of Radicalism, which he could do *perfectly*, he *heads and encourages it*.'[65]

Nobody understood this better than the Prime Minister, Lord Salisbury. The right to rule was his blood's ingredient, its lineage fermenting backwards for half a thousand years. Salisbury disliked democracy, considering property 'in danger' from it, and all 'social legislation was necessarily a change for the worse'.

Victoria was very happy with Salisbury, and Salisbury would have done anything, anything, to protect the Crown. He would lie for it, cheat for it, empower the wicked to trample the innocent; he would incarcerate for it and, if necessary, put to death for it, exercising the full might of that pliable little strumpet he owned, called law.

> It is rumoured in London that Sir Charles Russell has given up his brief for Lord Euston in the libel action connected with the Cleveland Street scandal and accepted one from the Prince of Wales. He will watch the case on behalf of Albert Victor, whose name has been persistently dragged into the affair. It is evidently Lord Euston's tactics to cripple Editor Parke by heaping up costs by means of legal motions and other expensive processes.[66]

The above is a not inaccurate summary of developments (we will come to editor Parke and the 'libel' shortly). In escalating panic the government brought in its most enthusiastic Gunga Din. He was a society barrister and a personal friend of the Prince of Wales, the aforementioned Sir Charles Russell QC MP.

Russell had defended Euston before, and lost, and Edward before, and won. He was a formidable courtroom operator whose arrogance and ambition had modified his grasp on reality. I don't know if barristers have to swear an oath to uphold what is true, any more than do prime ministers, but Russell had little care for truth, other than when it could act as a servant to himself. There was nothing Russell wouldn't do for Russell. His entire career was a dedication to heaving his corpulent Belfast frame up to and beyond the next rung. Consequently, there was nothing he wouldn't do for the rabble fighting for their Crown, including appearing for the prosecution in the matter of a dangerous journalist.

Although this was the age of the telegraph and the fledgling electric light, it must be remembered that in certain areas we may still be supposed to be in the age of King Richard III. The mechanics were as crude and as transparently ugly: 'Plots have I laid, inductions dangerous' – as indeed had the top-hatted heirs of Shakespeare's villainous hunchback.

The Parke referred to was Ernest Parke, a bit of a firebrand reporter on the *Star* who would later evolve into its most famous editor. At the time of the scandal Parke was thirty-one, and the *Star* less than two years old. Loud and radical and no friend of the Establishment, he was a new kind of journalist, in the vanguard of a new breed of mass-circulation newspaper. Like its proprietor, first editor and legend of Fleet Street, the great T.P. O'Connor, the *Star* was always ready to offer a hand to the underdog and a boot up the arse to his oppressor.

More often than not, it was Parke who put it in. His style was uncompromising and to the point. 'The Metropolitan Police is rotten to the core' was but one of his journalistic pronouncements (which doubtless endeared him to those he accused).[67] Parke was passionate and enterprising, and worked at two newspapers to prove it. In parallel with his efforts at the *Star*, he was sole editor of a new evening newspaper called the *North London Press*. It stood apart from Fleet Street in more than just its title. Parke claimed to have the name of every pervert who had ever gone through the door at Cleveland Street, and, against the advice of men like O'Connor, declared that he would publish them.[68] Such infatuation with what he perceived as justice may well have been admirable, but it was also dangerous, and Parke was rapidly moving out of his depth.

In another London postal district, ominous voices were murmuring. The owners of not a few of them were in possession of regular armchairs at clubs like the Carlton and Athenaeum: 'The social position of some of the parties will make a great sensation, this will give very wide publicity and consequently will spread very extensive matter of the most revolting and mischievous kind, the spread of which I'm satisfied will produce enormous evil.'[69]

It's hard to believe that this opinion was coming from the supreme officer of law in the land. It was the contribution of Lord Halsbury, the Lord Chancellor, giving his view on the contempt held for his own statutes by a certain class of upmarket bugger. In other words, 'enormous evil' did not reside in the illegality of sodomy, only in the dissemination of the news of it. As with gambling, a different law must apply. Halsbury was by now committed to the perversion of the course of justice, and was thus himself an accessory.

The facts are in the hands of the Home Office and of Scotland-yard, but as some of the greatest hereditary names of the country are mixed up in the scandal, every effort is being made to secure the immunity of the criminals. Indeed, I am credibly informed that

THE HOME OFFICE

is throwing obstacles in the way of prompt action on the part of Scotland Yard, and trying to get the persons concerned out of the country before warrants are issued. Very possibly, our Government of the classes is of opinion that the revelations which would ensue, were the criminals put on their trial, would deal a blow to the reign of the classes, and to the social influence of the aristocracy. Let them, however, understand that they will not be allowed to protect their friends. It would be really too monstrous if crimes, which, when committed by poor ignorant men, lead to sentences of penal servitude, were to be done with impunity by those whom the Tory Government delights to honour.[70]

When the maggots started spilling out of Cleveland Street there was a rush for the coastal ports. Prime Minister Lord Salisbury personally tipped off Lord Arthur 'Podge' Somerset (via Sir Dighton Probyn, Treasurer to the Prince of Wales) that, with great regret, Her Majesty's Government was no longer able to bury a warrant for his arrest, and that it would be issued immediately – that is, immediately he was on the boat.

The gangplanks were bottlenecks of panicking homos. They cleaned out the lot. Charles Hammond, lessee of the brothel, was allowed to salvage his furniture before scuttling circuitously to Belgium with a youth. As soon as he was safely ensconced there, Permanent Secretary to the Home Office Sir Godfrey Lushington strolled out of the Athenaeum to procure a warrant for his arrest.

The Yard headed off to the Continent, forcing their quarry out of non-extraditable France, only to discover in Brussels that the British government had no enthusiasm for such extraditions. The Home Secretary, Matthews, was informed by the Prime Minister that he didn't 'consider this a case in which any official application could be made'. The Liberal MP and publisher Henry Labouchère had an alternative point of view. 'If it had not been intended to extradite

Hammond,' he asked, 'what was their object in hustling this man from France to Belgium?' A good question, and while no one was answering it, Hammond and his boy took off for America with further judicial pretence in hot pursuit.

But no one was actually interested in arresting Hammond – he was the last thing the Establishment needed in court. Instead it was Inspector Abberline who was put up to take the flak. 'Coming to the facts of the case,' reported *The Times*, 'the police had received all the information it was possible to obtain in this matter. Inspector Abberline had on that date [July 1889] all the information in his hands. But for some reason he did not act. Counsel considered that the whole cause of the mischief that had arisen through the spread of these disgraceful scandals, was the conduct of Inspector Abberline in allowing the man Hammond to leave the country. A more remarkable introduction to a prosecution in which it was suggested that the course of justice had been perverted never could be imagined.'[71]

Such sentiments were of course dwarfed by the concurrent scandal of the Ripper. Abberline was perverting the course of justice in precisely the same way 'justice' was made laughable in respect of Jack. Both the Fiend and the Arse-Seller were immune from Victorian law. What the authorities wanted from Hammond – and the only thing they wanted – was a clutch of letters he kept about his person, acquired no doubt through his connections with the Post Office trade. Having lost his income as a brothel keeper, the fear was that he'd create a new one through blackmail. These letters contained the goods on Somerset, Euston, P.A.V. et al., and were worth a good deal of money. They were also of inestimable value to anyone trying to prove the case.

A detective called Partridge was dispatched from London with instructions to 'secure the letters at any price and at all hazards'. He at last caught up with Hammond in California, and got hold of the letters in the name of justice, at a price unknown. On his way back to England he ran into a man in San Francisco who introduced himself as 'Tyrell', and stated that he had been 'sent out from London to aid Partridge'.

With the letters now in his possession, what aid Partridge might have needed is unclear. But after presenting 'credentials and testimonials', Tyrell gained Partridge's confidence and the keys to the 'zealously guarded' box containing the letters, which mysteriously 'disappeared one night', along with Tyrell.

Like so many bits and pieces of unwanted history, Mr Tyrell and his stolen letters were never heard of again. His evaporation meant, of course, that those for or against the accused at Cleveland Street had either lost or secured irreplaceable evidence, depending on whose side you were on.

It was at about this time that someone walked into the *Star* offices and presented Ernest Parke with the journalistic equivalent of a Mickey Finn. The informant told him that, like 'Podge' Somerset, the Earl of Euston had made a run for it. This was sensational news, exclusive to the *Star*. But when editor T.P. O'Connor heard it, and more importantly, who had offered it, he declined to have anything to do with the story. Parke, however, fell for it, and published it in his own newspaper, informing his readers that Euston had fled for South America, and was heading for Peru.[72]

For Salisbury's government this was manna from heaven – no seraphim could have dealt better news. By any standards, something remarkable had happened. Suddenly, it wasn't a question of Euston raping boys, but the *unspeakable outrage* of a newspaper accusing him of going to Peru! A storm of indignation raised itself inside the political Establishment. Lethal nonentities reached for their wigs. How dare any man accuse another of going to Peru? He hadn't even been to Ramsgate!

In reality, the only place Euston had been was to Boulogne, to visit fellow arse-artist Somerset, and coordinate their story.

Literally overnight, Parke was a pariah, a dangerous little North London Zola, menacing the freedoms of an unfettered press and clean sheets in general. Peru? The ignominy of it! The man must be crushed with the full wholesome mechanism of pure Victorian law.

Parke had been set up, sold a pup, conned by a breed we shall be hearing more from. I was certain that this bum steer could be sourced back to Scotland Yard, but it wasn't until the 28 January 1890 edition of a conservative magazine called the *Hawk* turned up that I could confirm it:

It may be remembered that Parke said he had certain evidence to prove that he acted in good faith (as I believe he did), which, however, he could not bring forth without sacrificing confidences. I have no confidences placed in me, and so I am sacrificing nothing. It is alleged that the way the information reached the *Star* was by an officer employed at Scotland Yard. It is also said that having promised to supply Parke with proof when the time arrived, when called on by Parke to fulfil his promise, the officer said he was instructed by his superiors to give no more information.[73]

Scotland Yard made no comment. Euston sued Parke for criminal libel, and the guilty were back in business. It's hard to believe that this actually happened. Even the sanctimonious voice of conservative Fleet Street could hardly believe it. 'We have no sort of sympathy with the prosecutor, Lord Euston,' wrote the *Standard*, virtually inviting prosecution itself, 'who admitted quite enough about his own tastes and pursuits to show that he has very little claim to the respect of persons of decent life.'

(Not a lot of irony there, then? Euston was a bosom pal of the future King, actually becoming Edward VII's aide de camp in 1901. But then, the *Standard* wasn't in line for the throne, so nobody bothered with twaddle like that.)

The judge initially selected to hear the case was kicked off, and replaced by another of more ferocious disposition. Out of the Athenaeum shuffled yet another intimate friend of the Prince of Wales, the Honourable Mr Justice Hawkins, later Baron Brampton, a vengeful seventy-two-year-old Catholic with a profound affection for coin.

Hawkins was notorious for his greed. 'On the make' was what they said of him, this disagreeable feature of character ameliorated only by his fondness for the oiled rope. He was known as 'Hanging Hawkins', although he was said to have a quite energetic fear of death himself.[74]

On this mercifully non-hanging occasion, Hawkins was to represent the apogee of institutionalised corruption for and on behalf of the Victorian ruling elite. Never mind what Albert Victor and his homosexual associates had been up to, this was the judge who had recently put a schoolboy into prison for five years for doing the same thing. 'I was horrified by the apparent brutality of the sentence,' wrote an official who had been present at the Old Bailey, 'and the thought that if the youth had belonged to a different class in society his offence would have been treated quite differently and never have been made public at all.'[75]

And that's what this venal pantomime was all about. As far as Hawkins was concerned, it was making upper-class buggery public that was the very grave offence. Parke stood before this ancient bigot to hear what Disraeli had described as 'Truth in Action' – in other words the process of British law.

Ernest Parke, you have been convicted of an offence which deserves the most condign punishment. I must say that I think a more atrocious libel than that of which you have been guilty has never been published by any man in circumstances than those in which you have published this libel ... You had nothing before you but the idlest rumours, suggesting to you that amongst other persons Lord Euston had been guilty of this abominable crime ... This was a wicked libel, published without any justification whatever ... I feel it my duty to pass upon you a sentence which I hope, besides being a punishment to you, will be a warning to others.[76]

Those last six words being the salient point. Twelve months for telling the truth, the whole truth, and nothing but the truth.

The elation of the government was as spiteful as it was predictable. A reactionary weekly, the *Saturday Review*, positively levitated with glee: 'The man Parke's clients lust, first, for personal news, secondly, for dirty personal news, thirdly, for dirty personal news, if possible about persons with titles. He gives it to them; and the law has given him twelve months imprisonment. This is excellent. This man Parke is one of a gang.' But not all were so partisan, and not a few knew exactly what this was about. 'As we expected,' wrote the editor of *Reynold's News*,

the result of the trial of the young journalist Parke, has raised a storm of indignation not only at home, but abroad. The whole affair is considered part and parcel of the plan intended to whitewash the police and government from all participation in the frightful miscarriage of justice that has taken place ... In his virulent address to the jury, and when passing what we can but consider *a most vindictive sentence* on the accused, Judge Hawkins emphatically declared that the libel was one of the grossest ever published without a single extenuating circumstance, and Mr Parke was made an example to others who dare tamper with the name of our virtuous and noble aristocracy. What, then, is the conclusion come to? Why, that the authorities were more anxious to conceal the names of those who patronised the horrible den of vice, than punish the principal patrons of the hideous place. Why were the wretched telegraph boys taken to the Old Bailey, whilst Lord Arthur Somerset, being duly warned of what had occurred, made his escape? All this requires, but we suspect will not obtain, satisfactory explanation.

This was the only part of this journal's outrage that history confirmed. When the scandal finally bloomed into ritual debate at the House of Commons, it had already been controlled. By now Somerset had dissolved into the south of France, never to return. But here come all the Right Honourable Pecksniffs to yak it all over.

For the government, Attorney General Sir Richard Webster QC MP, also of the Athenaeum, spoke the only words of truth to come out of his mouth that night. 'No good is done,' he reminded the House, 'by reporting cases of this description, and it is generally to the credit of reporters of the press, that they almost invariably refrain from reporting them.'[77]

Please bear this statement in mind.

In this instance, Webster was not alluding to Parke, but to the jailing of a pair of Cleveland Street victims, two boys hustled off in secrecy to serve relatively short terms of incarceration in exchange for keeping their traps shut.

Henry Labouchère, the aforementioned Member for Northampton, known to Queen Victoria as 'that horrible lying Labouchère', and to her son Edward, Prince of Wales, as 'that viper Labouchère', wasn't so easily silenced. He'd come into that neo-Gothic marquee of duplicity burning with indignation at the jailing of Ernest Parke; and more than that, he had something to say about the Prime Minister, Lord Salisbury.

My first charge is that Lord Salisbury and others entered into a criminal conspiracy to defeat the ends of justice. Instead of making every effort to punish offences, as far as I can see, every effort has been made to hush up the matter ... Two boys have been sent to prison. Salisbury, and several other gentlemen ought also to be

> prosecuted. We have heard a good deal lately about criminal conspiracy. What is this case but a criminal conspiracy by the very guardians of public morality and law, with the Prime Minister at their head to defeat the ends of justice?[78]

You can't really say it any clearer than that.

Labouchère's use of the term 'criminal conspiracy' is interesting. It's worth noting that not all conclusions of 'conspiracy' in respect of the events of 1888–89 are figments of modern imagination. This famous Victorian politician was arguing at the coalface of one such 'conspiracy', and it is his choice of word. Salisbury's administration was in permanent 'criminal conspiracy', and as with the 'nuclear industry' of our day, telling the truth was not an option – it had to lie to survive.

Labouchère rehearsed his points, including the unusual protocol of a British Prime Minister tipping off a wanted criminal. 'The importance of the point here,' he said, 'is why did Lord Salisbury interfere in the matter? Was it the responsibility of a Prime Minister and a Foreign Secretary to mix himself up in such matters? If he knew a warrant was going to be issued, surely the last thing a man in his official position should have done, was to communicate the fact to a friend of Lord Arthur Somerset?' Then there was the associated peculiarity of the two boys, sentenced covertly and whisked away from the Old Bailey in secret.

Well, it was nothing of the sort, rejoined Webster: 'The charge against Her Majesty's Government is that it was agreed between the prosecuting and defending counsel with the knowledge of the Treasury Solicitor, that the accused should have light sentences as the price of silence, and that corrupt bargain was made with the knowledge of those in authority. I think the house will agree that, if true, more infamous conduct was never charged against persons in authority.'[79]

It was true. Half the Conservative House did agree, and the other half didn't. Webster had, in fact, succinctly summarised the case he was put up to argue against (something he would do with less success in the 'criminal conspiracy' against the Irish Nationalist leader Charles Parnell*). With an appearance of 'almost celestial virtue' he

---

* See Appendix I, 'The Parnell Frame-Up', page 761.

repudiated the existence of this supposed 'wicked and corrupt bargain' between the courts and the Conservative government, at which a variety of Members rose, Ernest Parke's boss T.P. O'Connor among them:

> The Attorney General assumes an air of the most virtuous indignation because my Honourable Friend (Mr Labouchère) spoke for an arrangement between the prosecution and defence. The Attorney General is an experienced lawyer of many years practice, and he knows that arrangements of this kind are common ... these arrangements between one side and the other are as common almost as criminal trials. In spite of all the Attorney General says, I maintain that there was such an arrangement here, and the object and meaning of it was to close the mouths of the persons in gaol, and in that way to save the criminals who their confessions might have exposed.[80]

The essence of the response from Sir Richard Webster was basically, 'Not guilty, but I promise you we won't do it again.' It is axiomatic amongst lawyers that you do not propose a question to which you do not know the answer, and here Webster slipped. Referring to brothel-master Charles Hammond and his boy, who had come in for their share of invective, Sir Richard had this to say: 'As to the circumstances under which Hammond did go to America, my own mouth is closed. I should be perfectly willing, and some day I shall be allowed, to state them. The Honourable and Learned Gentleman, the Member for South Hackney, knows them as well as I do.'[81]

The Honourable and Learned Gentleman in question was Sir Charles Russell, who immediately professed complete ignorance of the matter. 'I know nothing about them,' he said.

This was too ridiculous a falsehood for even Sir Richard Webster to swallow, and although Russell was on the same bent agenda, he replied, 'The Honourable and Learned Gentleman's memory misleads him,' which is another way of saying, 'You are lying like the label on a bottle of snake-oil.'

Indeed he was. Russell had appeared for a man called Newton (this on behalf of the Prince of Wales). On the application to move the case to the Queen's Bench, Newton's affidavit stated 'that he had been a party to getting Hammond to go away on account of the blackmail he was levying on people in England'.

Who might these 'people in England' be? And rather than the police sending Partridge (and the mysterious Tyrell) to America with wads of cash, why wasn't Hammond extradited from Belgium and prosecuted for the very serious crime of blackmail? It was a question for which the Establishment didn't require an answer; and anyway, it was all over bar the shouting, the business of the House complete except for the ritual expulsion of Labouchère.

He was finally ordered out of the pantomime by means of a parliamentary device enforced from time to time against Members who persisted in telling the truth.

> LABOUCHÈRE: I am obliged to speak frankly and truly in this
> matter. I assert, if I am obliged to do it, that I do not believe Lord
> Salisbury.
> THE SPEAKER: I must call on the Honourable Member to
> withdraw the expression.
> LABOUCHÈRE: I decline, sir, to withdraw.

And as a matter of fact he repeated it. The First Lord of the Treasury, the successful newsagent W.H. Smith, got to his feet.

'It is my duty to move that Mr Henry Labouchère be suspended from the service of this House.'

MPs call themselves 'Honourable' because nobody else would. The House divided. There was a vote. Ayes 177, Nos ninety-six. The Ayes had it, and out Labouchère went.[82]

The End.

The Scandal of Cleveland Street affords an opportunity to take a look at the Victorian ruling class on the run. With survival in mind, extremes of criminal behaviour were no problem. It was ruthless as Herod. After a breather of two or three weeks, on 3 March 1890 Salisbury got up in the Lords and fibbed like a slut, and that was just about that. As his recent biographer Andrew Roberts tells us, 'He shrugged it off.'

The thrust of Salisbury's speech was immediately to raise the matter over which his conduct 'had been called into question': 'My Lords, it is said that I met with Sir Dighton Probyn, with the view of enabling a person who was exposed to a serious charge to escape from justice.' He then went on to describe how he had done precisely that, while insisting that he hadn't. He'd just come back from France, he said, where at Dover, he found a telegram from Probyn, asking if he could meet Salisbury in London.

> I had no notion what it was about ... I replied that I should be passing through town, and that he would find me at the Great Northern Railway Station in time for the 7 o'clock train ... Sir Dighton Probyn came to see me there. He then informed me what he wanted to do was to ask whether there was any ground for certain charges which had been made in the newspapers against sundry persons whom he named. My reply was, that so far as I knew, there was no ground whatever for them ... I think I added – but of that I am not quite certain – that rumours had reached me that further evidence had been obtained, but I did not know what its character was. My Lords, I am not ashamed to say that is all I recollect of a casual interview for which I was in no degree prepared, to which I did not attach the slightest importance ... and I may add that I can aver in the most confident manner that the suggestion which has been made that a man of Sir Dighton Probyn's character and career could have appointed an interview with me for the purpose of worming out matter which he might use for the purpose of defeating the ends of justice is the wildest and most malignant imagination that has ever been conceived.[83]

Note how this most expert liar transfers the accusation onto Sir Dighton Probyn. Is this not the most astonishing casuistry? Salisbury had deflected criticism of his own propriety into a question of the honour of Sir Dighton Probyn.

Except, that same night, Probyn had tipped 'Podge' Somerset off, and he had quit London with the alacrity of a rat up a drainpipe. The next day, Probyn had written to the Prime Minister, 'I fear what you told me last night was all too true,' a mystery of circumstance confirmed by a letter to Probyn from the Prince of Wales: 'Your interview with Somerset must have been a very painful one.'

In reality, Sir Dighton Probyn and the Prince's Private Secretary, Sir Francis Knollys, had been rushing around like a pair of hysterical waiters for months, battling for the homosexual corner in the wildest and most malignant way to defeat the ends of justice.

Salisbury's fiefdom was intoxicated with corruption, poisoned with its own iniquity. A year before, the Liberal leader Gladstone had put his knuckles on his hips and surveyed the Conservative benches opposite. His contention was 'that no government during the past half century had shown so unblushing and unscrupulous a contempt for the law as had that of Lord Salisbury'.

He was alluding here to another great and concurrent scandal, the conspiracy to defame and destroy Charles Parnell. The Parnell scandal featured government perjury, forgery, slander, bent courts and imprisonment of the innocent, establishing new benchmarks of political deceit by what Gladstone called 'the foulest and wickedest means'.

The Cleveland Street and Jack the Ripper scandals were from the same stable, and were managed with no less *élan*, requiring little more from the ruling elite than instinct. If the Crown was under threat – be it from a nancy prince or a Monster with a Blade – it was a threat to them all. And they all knew – every baron, every earl, every duke – that, provided the monarch remained supreme, then so did its most ardent beneficiaries, this to include Queen's Councillors, Most Honourable Judges, senior policemen and arse-licking MPs. They were the *Royal* Courts of Justice, not the people's courts, and I do not exaggerate when I say they were almost exclusively staffed by Freemasons.

In respect of Cleveland Street, the *victims*, low-class working boys, went to prison, and the perpetrators, guilty as it got, walked free. Bro Euston, Bro Clarence and his dad, Bro the King-to-be, were all Freemasons, and that was not without significance. To join the Masons in the nineteenth century wasn't like signing up at the golf club, because Victorian golf clubs didn't exercise the power of the state. Golf clubs couldn't hang people, or incarcerate them for life. In the matter of Clarence, we are talking about the ability of Freemasonry to seriously interfere with the administration of the law. The most senior Law Lord in England, the Lord Chancellor Lord Halsbury, was a Freemason. The man who framed charges on behalf of the government, the Solicitor General Sir Edward Clarke QC MP, was also a Freemason. In his memoir, Bro Clarke tells us: 'I kept up my Masonic work until I became a Member for Plymouth. Then I practically abandoned it for twenty years.'[84]

And why was that?

'Because I wished to avoid the slightest possibility of it being connected with politics.'

In which case, he must have had less sentient aptitude than the three famous monkeys. By the late nineteenth century Freemasonry and politics were inextricable, the Houses of Parliament resembling an enormous and permanent Freemasonic lodge. To vote Conservative in the late 1880s was to vote for the Conservative (Freemasonic) and Unionist Party. Without effort, I was able to identify 338 Freemasons in the Parliament of 1889. You could safely add another fifty.

Freemasonry likes to kid itself, or perhaps others, that it is apolitical, a bit like Henry Ford's dictum concerning the colour of his cars: 'Any politics, providing it's Conservative.' From its invention in the early eighteenth century, Freemasonry has been a deeply reactionary proposition, clandestinely linking the authorities of state. It isn't necessary to read between the lines to understand this – just read the lines themselves: 'Freemasons have always shown an unshaken devotion to the Crown'; 'Loyalty to the King is an essential principle of Freemasonry.'[85] Thus, when Labouchère told his certain truth, there might well have been a fraternal tendency to squash it and kick the Honourable Member out. To lie on behalf of the royals had become a noble requisite, a means by which one demonstrated one's 'loyalty', not to the British people, but to the ruling system; and that included Prince Albert Victor, the Duke of Clarence.

'In order to serve in the Commons and Cabinet, I had to tell eighteen lies under oath,' wrote ex-Labour Cabinet Minister Tony Benn in 2003.[86] He says he found this 'deeply offensive'. 'Above all,' he continued, 'the existence of an hereditary monarchy helps to prop up all the privilege and patronage that corrupts our society; that is why the Crown is seen as being of such importance to those that run the country – or enjoy the privileges it affords.'

One of the founders of Mr Benn's party had a not dissimilar point of view, although his was posted over a century before. 'In these modern days,' wrote Keir Hardie, 'there is nothing for a King to do except to aid in the work of hoodwinking the common people. The role assigned to him is that of *leading mime in the pantomime* in which the great unthinking multitude is kept amused while it is being imposed upon. A King is an anachronism, and is only kept in being as a valuable asset of the ruling class.'[87] Like Mr Benn, Mr Hardie had difficulties with his sovereign oath.

Now let's add another one. It's the Masonic oath:

I do solemnly promise, vow, and swear, that I will always and at all times love the Brotherhood heartily and therefore will charitably hide and conceal and cover all the sins, frailties and errors of every Brother to the utmost of my power.[88]

It doesn't come clearer than that, and at least half of Queen Victoria's Parliament had sworn to this. One can either believe that these promises were useful to the state, or one can believe that they were not. For those inclined to the latter opinion, the question must surely be, what then was the purpose of them? Why take such an oath if the corporate intention was to dishonour it?

Was Bro the Duke of Clarence not in trouble? Was Bro the Earl of Euston not in the same boat? Had not these parliamentary Brethren taken their Freemasonic oath? Did they not 'hide and conceal and cover, all the sins, frailties and errors of every Brother' to the utmost of their power? And if not, why not? If they did not, their treachery is doubly compounded.

Courtiers Bro Sir Francis Knollys and Bro Sir Dighton Probyn had taken this oath, as had a ruling executive with supremely vested interests in making it stick.

When His Royal Highness the Prince of Wales first heard of Euston's complicity in the Cleveland Street scandal, he wrote, 'It is really too shocking! A married man whose hospitality I have frequently accepted!' So shocked was he that he invited him to dinner. On 13 March 1890, Euston was a guest of His Highness at a banquet celebrating one hundred years of the Prince of Wales Freemasonic lodge.[89] Some interesting names were present, including many we shall be hearing more of. They included the Chamberlain to the Queen the Earl of Lathom, and Colonel Thomas Henry Shadwell Clerke, Secretary to the English Freemasons and Masonic Secretary to Edward himself. Like Euston, Shadwell Clerke was a personal friend of my candidate, both enjoying membership of the Knights Templar 'Encampment of the Cross of Christ'.

Bro the Prince of Wales and Bro Lathom were to be found once again at another Masonic celebration at the very heart of the English law, in Lincoln's Inn. The evening was devoted to the consecration of a new lodge, the Chancery Bar, its membership restricted to the legal profession. The other guests included the Lord Chancellor, Bro Lord Halsbury, and the First Lord of the Admiralty, Bro Lord George Hamilton, plus a galaxy of wigs: Bro Judge Sir H. Lloyd, Bro Sir Forrest Foulton, Bro Sir Frank Lockwood QC MP, Bro Mr Staveny Hill QC MP, Bro Mr Jones QC MP, Bro E.H. Pember QC, Bro D.R. Littler QC, Bro F.A. Philbrick QC, and Bro Colonel Le Grande Starkie.

Bro the Prince of Wales, who had just been made an Honorary Member of the Chancery Bar, said in a speech of thanks: 'I am a Mason. I am glad to think that on this occasion the great legal profession and the great Masonic Brotherhood are more intimately connected tonight than perhaps they have ever been before. (Cheers from all.)'[90]

Arsonists in charge of the firehose.

Which brings us to our last esteemed guest at that occasion, a man of whom it was written, 'Englishmen are far from purists in judging the manners and life of their aristocracy. What they cannot tolerate is the sight of names which they have been accustomed to regard with respect surrounded by low and contaminating associations.'[91] The guest was, of course, Bro the Earl of Euston.

The function of the Establishment was to look after the Establishment. Prying journalists could be jailed, and lippy MPs shown the door. Cleveland Street was a rank perversion of the course of justice, its puppet-masters senior Freemasons, and its puppets the Masonic herd.

'The Mystic Tie'.

We must move on from Euston and his brothel, leaving the final comment on Cleveland Street to a journalist of the day: 'The determination of men of rank to stand by scoundrels of their order, no matter what their crimes are, and the certainty with which they can count upon men who have merely a brevet claim to associate with them to help them out.'[92]

I think that is precisely put, and worth repeating. 'The determination of men of rank to stand by scoundrels of their order, no matter what their crimes are' is a statement of inestimable importance when trying to come to terms with the scandal of Jack the Ripper.

2

A Conspiracy of
Bafflement

Customary use of artifice is the sign of a small mind,
and it almost always happens that he who uses it to
cover one spot uncovers himself in another.

La Rochefoucauld, *Maxims*

It is impossible to understand 'the mystery of Jack the Ripper' without an understanding of the Freemasonry. Masonry permeates every
fibre of this conundrum, both as its inspiration and its stooge. To
acquiesce to the proposition of this scandal as an impenetrable
mystery is to prostrate one's intellect before the savageries of Victorian
spin. The 'mystery' is a manipulation, a piece of propaganda, like
calling Nixon's great felony 'the Watergate mystery', as I'm sure many
among that gentleman's associates would have been pleased to do.

'We are all the President's men,' said Henry Kissinger, and no less
were England's ruling elite 'all the Widow's men'.

The degree of control this unique criminal exercised is indicated
by the efforts of those who would still seek to protect him. Like
courtiers from beyond the grave, they are essentially blameless, but
also fools. Freemasonry may never have asked for Jack the Ripper
(it certainly did not), but a combination of circumstance and moral
turpitude made it his stupefied guardian.

Concealing the Ripper was *not* a Masonic conspiracy, but a
conspiracy of Her Majesty's executive, who almost without exception were Freemasons. In other words, it was a conspiracy of the
System. The man they were required to be baffled by was 'in house',
and unquestionably revelling in the security he'd spun about
himself. The Ripper was smart, but not that smart. It is simply an
insult to the Victorian police to believe that detectives like Moore,
Reid and Abberline couldn't have caught this prick in their sleep.

It goes without saying that there was nothing illaudable about being a Victorian Mason, any more than it was improper to enjoy membership of a tricycle club. But as I have said, this narrative is about the bad guys, and about one in particular who went rotten, and what that did to the rest of the barrel. Beyond that, I have no opinion on Freemasonry, no animosity towards it, no motive to wish it ill. My interest in Masonry is only inasmuch as it relates to 'the mystery of Jack the Ripper'.

By the late nineteenth century this quasi-religious, highly conservative society was a power in the land, perhaps the most powerful, because of its ability to insinuate itself into powerful institutions – Parliament, the police, the press, the judiciary and the Crown. It's worth reiterating that the heir to the throne, Bro Edward, Prince of Wales, was the most powerful Freemason on earth. His Chancellor, Bro Lord Halsbury, was the most powerful Law Lord, and Bro Sir Charles Warren the most senior copper in the Metropolitan Police. Excepting Home Secretary Matthews (and possibly Salisbury himself), every man at the Viscount's cabinet table had sworn the Masonic oath.

The Prime Minister's organic antipathy to democracy was generally well served by this cabal. In parallel with the elected government, the hidden constructs of Freemasonry facilitated a clandestine executive underpinning the power of the ruling class. 'A government within a government', as the American historian Henry Austin called it. At its head were the royals and estate-owning aristocrats, with their House of Lords – its laws, bishops and judges – at its servile root, an army of Pecksniffs: the town councillors, provincial chief constables, coroners, aldermen, magistrates and mayors. Throughout the kingdom, Freemasonry had managed a truly breathtaking infiltration of municipal and political representation, the Provincial Grand Master more often than not an area's MP. Thus, from the remotest little town to the grandest of cities, the English political system was inalienably connected to a terminus of power of which the electorate knew nothing, and nobody was saying anything about. It was the *secrecy* of Freemasonry that allowed this occult telegraph to survive, which at the time of Jack the Ripper was hard-wired into the nucleus of government.[1]

*

It is a paradox of this narrative that before investigating a murderer, we must investigate the policeman who was pretending to hunt him.

London's Commissioner of Metropolitan Police, Sir Charles Warren, was a forty-eight-year-old ex-military man and a Freemasonic obsessive. He was a lousy cop and a worse soldier;[2] his God inclined to the hard right – probably something like Kitchener in freshly laundered clouds. Warren was an aggressive authoritarian who imagined all social ills could be solved with a truncheon. If you were superfluous to the System – sick, unemployed or Irish, for example – then you weren't much better than a wog. In 1887 he went berserk on the back of a horse in London's West End, and shafted the riff-raff as if he was up a delta in Matabeleland.

In was in Africa only two years before that Warren had lost the plot. The Prime Minister didn't have a lot of time for ethnics, but so alarmed was Salisbury at Warren's 'overzealousness' in Bechuanaland Protectorate that in September 1885 he personally recalled him. 'His continuance in power was a real danger,'[3] Salisbury wrote, and this 'danger' returned to London to be appointed Commissioner of the Metropolitan Police.

Like many in politics with energetic mouths, the Establishment had created the very circumstance it most feared. Without enough war to soak up the rabble, the plebs were getting frisky. On Sunday, 13 November 1887 a huge contingent of the *Untermenschen*, the starving and exasperated underclass, had descended on Trafalgar Square.

Warren's intention was to kick them back to the slums where they belonged. Twelve hundred troops and sabre-wielding cavalry supplemented an army of truncheon-wielding cops. 'I've never seen such police brutality,' recalled Karl Marx's daughter – but then, she would say that, wouldn't she. Notwithstanding that, Warren's subsequent replacement as Police Commissioner James Monro summed up the inevitable consequences of trusting anything on the street to his colleague. 'I am bound to say,' he wrote, 'Sir C. Warren was just the man to have injudiciously, in some way or other, caused the very panic I was anxious to avoid.'[4] Dozens were injured, and at least one man lost his life.

Warren managed to close down Trafalgar Square, but it's perhaps worth noting that just a year later, in the dead of night, with not a mouse about, he was to claim that he couldn't shut down a doorway in the East End. We shall be coming to the lamentable events of Goulston Street by and by.

The Establishment lauded Warren for his violence, and he went down on a knee for his Queen in May 1888. 'Among the recipients of honours,' beamed the weekly *The Freemason*, 'were … Bro Sir Charles Warren, who was invested with the insignia of KCB [Knight of the Bath].'

Not everyone was quite so delighted. 'In a single twelvemonth,' reported the *Daily News*,

the martinet whose record of meddling and muddling extends over a good part of the British Empire, has destroyed the good feeling between the London police and the public, and replaced it by a feeling of bitter antagonism. It is not a case of Trafalgar Square only; that would be bad enough. But what the Square did wholesale, Sir CHARLES's men, under the brutal initiative from Scotland Yard, have done in detail. During the last few weeks hardly a day has passed when some constable has not been convicted of gross insult and harshness to some peaceful inhabitant, supported by still grosser perjury. The London Magistrates have for the most part given up the police and rejected their evidence as worthless. The moral Miracle has become the Miracle of Lying ... Major General Sir CHARLES WARREN, K.C.B., G.C.M.G., was far too lofty a personage to look after petty larcenies and street inebriates. His first Pyrrhic victory in bludgeoning the people out of the Square intoxicated him, and henceforth we have had nothing but a carnival of perjury, violence and discontent.

This condemnation of police 'perjury' and 'lying' was published on 1 September 1888, only a matter of days before Jack got his show on the street. We shall see how the perjury and lying escalated by increment as the assassin got into his stride.

I haven't got much in the way of compliments for Warren as a policeman, but he must sincerely be celebrated in the arena in which he excelled. All too often he is characterised as an authoritarian disaster. Although merit attaches to the vignette, it is ultimately shallow, hawked by authors who interminably reiterate the content of each other's books. By this corporate myopia they miss a fundamental that all but defines motive in the Ripper's thinking. Warren was a 'martinet', sure, as Ripperology never tires of telling us. But he was also a talented and undeniably brave archaeologist, and it was Warren underground that was of subliminal interest to Jack.

As a young man, Captain Warren of the Royal Engineers was motivated by a duo of passions. It distorts neither to construe them as one. They were, as he saw them, the complementary sciences of Biblical and Freemasonic research. He was driven to prove that Freemasonry was of similar stuff to the Bible, and that by investigation of one, the other could somehow be validated. Such wishful thinking came together in the Holy Land, and here Warren is, in his own words, exploring a 3,000-year-old subterranean conduit in the guts of Jerusalem:

> The water was running with great violence, one foot in height, and we, crawling full-length, were up to our necks in it, one hand necessarily wet and dirty, the other holding a pencil, compass, and field book, the candle for the most part in my mouth. Another fifty feet brought us to a place where we had to run the gauntlet of the waters, the passage being only one foot four inches high, we had just four inches of breathing space.[5]

Warren was digging his way into the Old Testament under the auspices of the Palestine Exploration Fund. The PEF had been funded by various worthies and religious executives, including the Freemasons, as 'a Society for the accurate and systematic investigation of the Archaeology, the Topography, the Geology and Physical Geography, the Manners and Customs of the Holy Land, for Biblical instruction'. Founded in 1865, its membership grew rapidly, with signatures that would include a roll-call of notables, including the Archbishop of Canterbury and the great sculptor/painter Sir Frederick Leighton.

From its inception the Society had an advocate of 'burning enthusiasm' in its co-founder and first secretary, the forty-four-year-old George Grove. Trained originally as an engineer, Grove emerged as one of the Great Victorians, a man capable of transforming enthusiasm into practicality in whatever area his humanity pleased. He was said to have known much of the Bible by heart, thus it was natural for him to write a Concordance, plus about 1,000 pages of the *Standard Bible Dictionary*. If it interested him, Grove got it done. 'His work from first to last,' wrote the novelist and historian Walter Besant, 'was literally a labour of love.'

Knighted in 1883, Sir George Grove comes out of the nineteenth century like an engine of benevolence. His infatuation with all things musical brought London its Royal College of Music, and his *Dictionary of Music and Musicians* (1879–89) is still internationally recognised as the standard work on the subject. 'I have always been a mere amateur in music,' he claimed with customary modesty. 'I wrote about symphonies and concertos because I wished to try and make them clear to myself and to discover the secret of the things that charmed me.'

Short on charm but full of secrets were the vast underground ruins of what some believed were the remains of Solomon's Temple at Jerusalem. In 1866 Grove approached the War Office on behalf of the PEF for archaeological assistance, and got twenty-six-year-old Captain Warren in response. It was a fortuitous liaison. The following year, together with his wife and little daughter and a handful of NCOs, Bro Warren and his party set sail for the Holy Land.

'It was somewhat in the role of a Crusader that Warren accepted the charge,' wrote his grandson and biographer Watkin Williams, 'as he was stirred by a longing to reveal to the Christian world those sacred places hidden in the debris of many a siege and jealously guarded by the Turkish Mussulmans.'[6] More accurately, Warren's eagerness was in no small part because he was a member of the Knights Templar.

The story of that body's godforsaken origins at the time of the Crusades needs little retelling here. For about two hundred years in the Middle Ages, the good guys (Christians) fought the bad guys (Muslims) for possession of the Holy Lands around Jerusalem. In the eleventh century the Turks had usurped control of Palestine and put their god in charge. Christian pilgrims were no longer welcome, and the proposition of liberating 'the birthplace of the cross from the thraldom of the crescent' began to resonate as a good idea. A mentally abnormal priest called Peter the Hermit went about Europe inciting a Holy War. 'It's the voice of God!' he shrieked, when in fact it was the voice of the Pope, Urban II in Rome. The result was misery without end for a God that didn't give a monkey's. Urged on in atrocity by religious fanatics called Popes, the insanity went on and on. Tens of thousands would bleed their lives away, suffering every conceivable inhumanity. In 1099, under the banner of a French knight called Godfrey de Bouillon, the Muslims were temporarily driven from the Holy City, and the real estate returned to Christ.

Great congratulation and instant myth were bestowed upon the Soldiers of the Cross. After the usual protocols of butchery and rape, a barracks was constructed in their honour on the site of Solomon's Temple, the exalted House of the Lord, and the 'fame of the Knighthood of the Temple of Solomon began to spread through the enlightened [i.e. Christian] world'.

It was primarily in Europe, most especially France, that the returning knights evolved into the Templars. Initially received as heroes, but later reviled, outcast, imprisoned, and sometimes burnt to a cinder by papal *diktat*, the Knights Templar had to put up shutters to survive. They became a secret society, and over the centuries they developed into what is understood (in the higher degrees) as Christian Freemasonry.[7]

Overleaf is the Earl of Euston, resplendent in his Knights Templar togs. Given his brush with the law, it was perhaps a happy circumstance that from the first, English jurisprudence shared an embryo with this cabal of covert Masonic tradition.

The Inner and Middle Temples at the ancient Inns of Court (off Fleet Street in the City of London) take their names from the House of the Lord in Jerusalem. 'Within these precincts have lived and toiled many of our great statesmen,' wrote barrister at law Colonel Robert Blackham, 'to say nothing of a long unbroken line of eminent lawyers who in their turn succeeded in the illustrious order of the Knights Templars of Medieval fame.'[8]

That Freemasonry and the law should conflate so intimately is no accident. By the time of Victoria it would take a very long day to discover any member of the judiciary who wasn't heir to that not entirely impartial root.

Captain Warren became a Templar in 1863, installed in the Cape Preceptory (60) while he was at Gibraltar with the Royal Engineers. Four years later, on the morning of 17 February 1867, he climbed to the summit of Mount Moriah (better known today as the Temple Mount) and looked across the city of Jerusalem from where the Crusaders had gasped their first short breath of victory. His guide would have told him what he already knew, that the plateau had been 'flattened by centuries of disaster and detrition', and that the mosque of Qubbat as-Sakhra now stood on the site of Solomon's glorious temple. It was here that de Bouillon had raised his banners to Jesus Christ, and that the mysteries of the Templars had begun.

But it was a legend of deeper antiquity, almost 3,000 years before, that was predominant in Warren's thoughts. Under his feet was the place of the Great Secret, from whence Freemasonry had come, but where no Freemason had ever been. Warren must have looked about him, wondering how he was going to get at it.

'The Dome of the Rock' at Haram el Sharif was sacred to whoever held it – Christian, Jew, Mohammedan alike – and once again it was under the flag of the Crescent Moon. Its holy places were forbidden to Christians, and it was second only to Mecca itself among the sacred sites of Islam. It is not surprising, therefore, that Warren and his diggers ran into immediate difficulties. They weren't invited and they weren't welcome. 'The result,' according to his grandson, 'was that Warren had to work on the peripheries of Jerusalem and could reach few of the places he wanted.'

This is a distracting synopsis, and in no way correct. Watkin Williams was also a Freemason, which makes his account of his grandfather's underground activities in Jerusalem somewhat circumspect. The reason is to attempt to diminish the reality of Warren's Masonic expertise. The motive behind this subterfuge will soon explain itself. When Bro Williams writes that his grandfather 'could reach few of the places he wanted', he neglects to clarify that among the few was one of the only places he really wanted, and that was deep in the foundations of Solomon's Temple. For so zealous a Freemason there could be no more enthralling place on earth. Such mystery, such occult romance was there, all waiting to be dug out. It couldn't have been more exhilarating – nor more pertinent to my point. Here was something Masonry condemns with such venom in others, but congratulates in itself: a desire to penetrate 'mystery', and a compulsion to find the truth.

Truth is not biodegradable, even after 3,000 years. Nor did it evaporate from late Victorian England. Truth was what had brought Warren to Jerusalem, and it was what, in Masonic terms, he found. But in that terrible darkness there was a caveat that none could have anticipated, and if it reads a little melodramatic, it reads just about right. For in the undisturbed mysteries of this building lay the seeds of the Whitechapel Murderer.

While sojourned in Jerusalem, Warren's life was at risk on an almost daily basis, both above and below the ground. Just as the rock threatened to crush him, the Muslims would quite literally have

VOUSSOIR OF AN ARCH FALLEN THROUGH ROOF OF ROCK-CUT CANAL.

killed him had the extent of his excavations been known. 'Our work was of such a nature,' wrote Warren, 'that, I may say, every week Sergeant Birtles had to act in such a manner as would, on active service, have assured him the Victoria Cross.'

Faced as they were with hostile Turks, catastrophic roof falls and causeways choked with antediluvian filth, this was no exaggeration. Everything in this alien place conspired to want them dead. But Warren triumphed. When the pit props ran out, he did without, and when the money ran out, he spent his own.

It isn't possible to equate Warren's dynamism here with his vacillating idiocy as a Police Commissioner twenty years later. To read of Warren in Jerusalem, and then of the neutered pomp of his failure in Whitechapel, is like reading about two different men. 'His [archaeological] reports were being published in the English press,' wrote Williams, 'and causing intense interest.' It is without question that these few Englishmen, clawing their way through thirty centuries of darkness, were men of justified fame. Warren's resolve was indefatigable, his courage unkind to no one but himself. He earned his place in the history of Jerusalem, it's his forever, and no one would ever wish to make ill of it.

But there was a psychopath who tried.

In terms of intellect, the Ripper was utilitarian, with no more sophistication than a spoiled child. Irrespective of the boundless efforts to swaddle him in cosmetic 'mystery', it is by his spite for Warren that he is betrayed. What a piece of work was this man, and what men were they that stood in his shame.

We are about to explore the Masonic, archaeological and deeply personal significance of this catastrophe for Warren. But before journeying into the 'black night of the abyss', we need to hear briefly from a voice of contemporary Masonry. It belongs to an initiate by the name of Bro McLeod, a Masonic authority we shall be hearing more of. Of Warren's archaeological adventures in Palestine, he writes, 'there are slight traces of Masonic activity in the Jerusalem interlude'.[9]

This is so dishonest you might want to call it bullshit. Warming to his topic, McLeod quotes Warren himself: 'Whilst engaged in excavating among the ruins of the Temple of King Solomon, I had the pleasure of assisting at the holding of a Lodge, almost directly under the old Temple.'

'Presumably,' suggests Bro McLeod, 'this must have been one of the projects of the American entrepreneur, Rob Morris, P.G.M. of Kentucky.'[10]

He presumes right.

But these 'slight traces of Masonic activity' can be compared with the slight traces of alcohol in Gordon's gin. So slight were they that there's actually a detailed architectural plan of their location, Warren memorialising the world's most exclusive Masonic lodge with his very own name.

Consecrated as 'the Reclamation Lodge of Jerusalem', Warren amended its title to 'Warren's Masonic Hall', a shift that could hardly be described as 'slight'. This slight trace is the Christian equivalent of consecrating a church under Calvary, for it was above this very spot that the three wretched assassins Jubela, Jubelo and

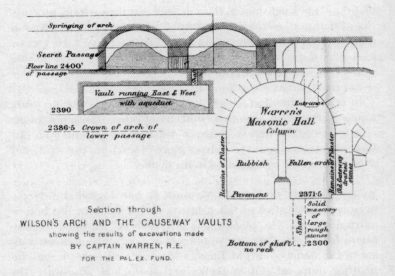

Section through
WILSON'S ARCH AND THE CAUSEWAY VAULTS
showing the results of excavations made
BY CAPTAIN WARREN, R.E.
FOR THE PAL. EX. FUND.

Jubelum were supposed to have put Freemasonry's first Grand Master, Hiram Abiff, to death.

Quite a significant environment for a young Freemason, wouldn't you say? And even if it wasn't, it was to become so, because it was here that Warren and his companions claimed to have brought Freemasonry back to the Holy City of Solomon for the first time in seven hundred years. It was Warren and his associates who participated in the establishment of the first and only Masonic lodge in Jerusalem since the time of Saladin and the Knights Templar. Only a dissembler with the disingenuousness of McLeod could call this 'slight traces of Masonic activity'. It was in fact the apogee of Masonic aspiration, a spellbinding experience fraught with considerable danger. Islam had no truck with Freemasonry – to Muslims it was an infidel perversion, the stuff of heathen wizards – and had the Brethren been discovered there was an unexceptional risk of them losing their heads. But it was a dream, and would be one of the most indelible memories of Bro Charles Warren's Masonic career.

At Goulston Street in the East End of London, it was to become his Marley's Ghost. Jack was a complicated psychopath, from the Iago school of gentlemen. An ingredient of his amusement was the persecution of Warren, and it would hardly take an Alan Turing to decipher the word 'Juwes' that, as we will see, he wrote upon a wall.

We need to stroll a little further down memory lane, and we can start with Robert Morris. To nullify Charles Warren's Masonic credentials, it's also necessary to diminish those of Bro Morris. McLeod's description of him as an 'American entrepreneur' is somewhat less than adequate. In reality he was a Masonic poet, author and lecturer, and one of the most celebrated Freemasons on earth. After his death the Brotherhood erected a shining monument to his memory at La Grange, Kentucky.[11]

Morris published many revered Masonic books, one of them detailing his sojourn in Palestine. 'While in Jerusalem,' he relates, 'I held two Masonic meetings at the Mediterranean Hotel, near the Damascus Gate, in which assemblies several officers of the British warships lying at Joppa were present; also the venerable Brother Petermann, Prussian Consul, and Captain Charles Warren RE, who was in charge of the explorations. Nothing can exceed the zeal of our English Brethren upon such occasions.'[12]

The lodge numbers and names of the five Brits present are given, but the only Freemason of specific interest here is Warren, 'the learned and zealous officer who has charge of the excavations going on here under the Palestine Exploration Fund'.[13]

It is of note that Morris describes Warren as 'learned', while McLeod dismisses him as 'only a novice', a falsehood that conveniently renders him incapable of understanding Jack's message on the wall at Goulston Street. No such handicap is recorded in Jerusalem, where the translation of potentially Masonic hieroglyphs was a cause for excited enquiry all round. Indeed, the walls of Solomon's Temple were scrutinised for any sign of them, Warren recording one such example in his own book, *Jerusalem Underground* (1876). And here he is (overleaf), in happier darkness, intrigued by a Masonic signature.

GALLERY AT SOUTH-EAST CORNER OF SANCTUARY.

Warren's description of the symbols on the wall is more precise than in the woodcut: 'A gallery was also driven,' he writes, 'where the rock was found to rise very rapidly, cutting the fourth course at 15 feet from the angle. On this course *two* red paint-marks were found, L's overturned and reversed.' An approximation of their size is given by the woodcut and in Warren's description. A pair of 'L's overturned and reversed':

Representing one of the archetypal symbols adopted by Freemasonry, the 'squares' discovered by Warren at Solomon's Temple caused hearts to flutter and an exchange of correspondence in Freemasonic journals. In 1884 an American Brother wrote to the *Philadelphia Keystone* proclaiming that 'Lieutenant Colonel Warren [the] energetic explorer, had made discoveries of the highest significance,' and insisting that such symbols were indivisible from the 'whole crux of the Masonic Legend [and] thus bear silent and unconscious witness to the loyalty and reality of our ancient Masonic traditions'.[14] This 'silent witness' meant a lot to Freemasons, even if loyalty didn't mean much to one rampaging through Whitechapel with a vengeful knife.

But I digress, and must return to Bro Morris and his Masonic rendezvous at the Mediterranean Hotel: 'This gentleman [Charles Warren] in some extremely happy observations, expressed his pleasure at this meeting, called together under such singular circumstances, and was equally impressed with the importance of introducing Freemasonry, though cautiously and judiciously, into the Holy Land.'[15]

It wasn't many days before the dream became a reality. On the afternoon of Wednesday, 13 May 1868, as a matter of fact. Setting off from outside the Jerusalem walls, Morris, Warren and the chosen few disappeared into the excavations: 'Entering with a good supply of candles, we pushed southwards as far as we could penetrate, and found a chamber happily adapted to our Masonic purpose. An upright stone in the centre served us for an altar. About ten feet above the Master's station there was an immense opening in the wall, which led, for aught I know, to the original site of the Temple of Solomon. We felt as we had never felt before,' wrote Morris. 'How impressive is a place that none but the All-Seeing-Eye can penetrate. Leaving my Bible open on the central stone, three burning candles throwing their lustre upon it, and the trowel, Square, etc., resting nearby, a few opening remarks were made by myself, to the effect that never, as far as I knew, had a Freemasons' Lodge been formed in Jerusalem since the departure of the Crusading hosts more than seven hundred years ago; that an effort was now making to introduce this, the mother country of its birth; that a few of us brethren, providentially thrown together, desired to seal our friendship by the associations peculiar to a Masonic Lodge.'[16]

This would be heady stuff for anyone, never mind a bunch of enraptured Freemasons.

'To break the long stillness of these ancient quarries by Masonic utterances, we had now assembled, and would proceed to open a Moot Lodge, under the title of Reclamation Lodge of Jerusalem. This we now proceeded to do in a systematic manner. A prayer was offered, echoing strangely from that stony rock that had heard no such sound for centuries, and the other ceremonies proceeded.'[17]

The ceremony over, there were ancillary delights, confirming that they were doing the right thing in the right Freemasonic place: 'The vast quarry thus consecrated by Masonic forms shows at every point the marks of the chisel as well-defined as the day the workmen left it. Slabs of stone partially dressed are lying upon the floor, others partially cut out of the wall stand where a few more blows would detach them. Many emblems of crosses, Hebrew characters, etc., remain, and the next visitor will see among them the Square and Compasses, as cut by our hand.'[18]

We know what a couple of squares looked like. How about a couple of compasses? They would look like this:

These were the symbols cut by Warren and his party into the walls of 'Solomon's Temple'. Both ancient and modern, sacred and trivial, the compasses are as readily to be found in the twenty-first century as they are in the earliest Masonic documents. No less than the cross for Christians, the compasses can justly be characterised as an icon of Freemasonry. The tool of T.G.A.O.T.U. (The Great Architect of the Universe), they are wherever Masonry is – in paintings, engravings, etched into drinking glasses; and carved by Jack the Ripper into Catherine Eddowes' face.

They are literally a Mason's 'Mark', what Bro historian J. Fort Newton describes as 'a mark by which his work could be identified'. The 'trademark', if you will, of Freemasonry.[19]

*

The 'mystery' of Whitechapel starts here, in Solomon's Temple in Jerusalem, as it must for all Brethren on their metaphoric journey in the footsteps of Hiram Abiff. 'The road which we shall follow,' writes Masonic historian J.S.M. Ward,

> is like the Masonic pavement, checkered with black and white, and like that used in the RA [Royal Arch] it is flecked with crimson. We must descend into the black night of the abyss itself – the abyss of savagery and fear, and the lower we descend, the further back in time we venture, the blacker becomes the darkness, lit only by a glimmering ray – the unfaltering faith and quiet heroism with which man accepted the high office and the grim fate which savage and primitive ideas had assigned to them. Hiram, indeed, may be a real man of flesh and blood, who like thousands before and after him, has been sacrificed in the false belief that thereby the corn will be made to grow and the building to stand firm forever. That Hiram was not the last architect who was sacrificed on the completion of the building on which he had toiled these pages will show, and even today, in the dark corners of the earth humble, yet valent, representatives of our Master still follow the same bloodstained path that he once trod.[20]

Hiram Abiff was the First Master of Freemasons, and the architect of Solomon's Temple. According to Masonic fable, he was murdered and buried underneath it. As Bro Ward says, he wasn't the first or the last to pay with his life in this way: it is rumoured the architects of the Taj Mahal were either blinded or beheaded on completion of their task, a certain way of preventing them from ever building anything else that rivalled its magnificence.

Bro Ward's pavement into the abyss takes us back to about 967 BC, the fourth year of King Solomon's reign, when the husband of three hundred, father of seven hundred, and murderer of his brother Adonijah, began to build 'the House of the Lord' at Jerusalem. Its purpose, apart from self-celebration, was as a repository for the Ark of the Covenant (the chest containing the tablets on which God inscribed the Ten Commandments), wherein the cult of Yahweh could find a fixed place of worship. Details of its construction are to be found in the Book of Kings (6–7), and a good deal of this description found its way into the traditions of Freemasonry – indeed, every Masonic lodge ever built owes its symbolism to this mysterious pile. We learn that cedar was culled from the forests of the Lebanon, and monster stones said to be dressed with such fantastic precision in the quarries that no further hammer, saw or chisel was used. Hence, no metal tools were required at the building site. In deference to this fable, no metal – buttons, boxes or coins – is ever tolerated about a Freemason during induction: a tradition given full mischievous attention in the deadly Masonic games of Bro Jack.

It was a famed artisan in metal who became the first Grand Master of Masonic legend. All Freemasons are designated as 'Sons of the Widow', and Hiram Abiff was the first. 'He was a widow's son of the tribe of Nephtall,' says the Bible, 'a worker in brass; and he was filled with wisdom, and understanding, and cunning to work all works in brass.' These were qualifications enough for King Solomon, who 'sent and fetched Hiram out of Tyre', hiring him to set about the business of adorning his temple by forging the biggest artefacts in metal yet seen on earth. 'For he cast two pillars of brass,' recounts the Book of Kings, 'and he set up the pillars in a porch of the Temple; and he set up the right pillar and called it Jachim; and he set up the left pillar and called the name thereof Boaz.'

And it is here that Freemasonry integrates itself with the story of Solomon, adapting the Book of Kings to construct a mythology of its own.

The next picture, of a coffin, is a typical example of Hiram's migration out of the Old Testament and into the mind-boggling eclecticism of Masonic symbol. The artwork comes from a third-degree (Master Mason) tracing board, and I reproduce it because it alludes to much of the great legend, including both the murder of Hiram and the skull-and-crossed-bones logo shared by the Knights Templar.

It's in the essence of Masonry to conceal, and here (with the compasses above) we have Hiram's name and accompanying date hidden in cipher. The letters above the skull read 'H.A.B.', for Hiram Abiff, and the date is in that curious Masonic calendar of Anno Lucis (year of light) 3000, about a thousand years before Christ. On either side of the plaque are the letters 'T.B.', representing the Biblical metal-worker Tubal Cain, an enigma we can do without. Distributed about the coffin are symbols of more pertinence.

At its centre is Bro Ward's chequered pavement, inviting our gaze into the mysteries of the temple where, according to Masonic legend, Hiram met his assassins. The tools of their trade, both manual and murderous, are also depicted. There are the square, the gavel and the rule. Above is a frond of acacia that sprang up like magic from the dead man's ignoble grave.

We approach the murder of Hiram Abiff needing but one more player of antiquity to set the stage. An icon of Masonry, he is Ezekiel, a flaming mouth of the Old Testament whose sexual hang-ups read like a prognosis for the criminally insane. Big on revenge, Ezekiel was a sulphurous prophet of merciless righteousness, and of no small importance to the Ripper's narrative.

The Temple of Solomon is manifest in the symbolic orientation of every Masonic lodge. But we need to travel via a hallucination to arrive at the place where Hiram met his death.

Into the endless violence that was Jerusalem came a Syrian king called Nebuchadnezzar, who flattened it yet again. Ezekiel was carried off in chains, and while a prisoner in Babylon he had his famous reverie of the reconstruction of 'the House of the Lord'. 'In the five and twentieth year of our captivity,' he records, 'in the visions of God brought He me into the land of Israel, and, behold, there was a man, whose appearance was like the appearance of brass, with a line of flax in his hand, and a measuring reed, and he stood at the gate. And the glory of The Lord came into the House by the way of the gate whose prospect was towards the East. So the spirit took me up, and brought me into the inner court; and behold, the Glory of the Lord filled the House.'

Ezekiel's vision is full of measurements of such precision that twenty-five centuries later theologians were able to interpret it like an architect's plan. Models were made and pictures drawn, presenting a romanticised idea of what the crime scene might actually have looked like. Hiram had built this sacred place, where the lamps flared on walls of pure gold. He had erected Jachim and Boaz, cast the bronze sea that stood outside on the backs of gargantuan bronze oxen, and jealous men, subservient to his genius, wanted to know how he'd done it.

They were Jewish craftsmen, Jubela, Jubelo and Jubelum, latterly known as the Three Ruffians, but originally called the Three Assassins.

On the day of his murder Hiram was alone in the building – at least, according to the legend he believed he was alone – when three figures emerged from three sides.

At the south gate he is accosted by the first of the Assassins. 'Give me the Master Mason's word,' demands Jubela, 'or I will take your life.'

'I cannot give it now,' protests Hiram. 'But if you will wait until the Temple is completed, and the Grand Lodge assembles at Jerusalem, if you are worthy, you shall then receive it, otherwise you cannot.'

'Talk not to me of Temple or Grand Lodges! Give me the word, or die.'

Thereupon, Jubela strikes Hiram across the throat with a twenty-four-inch gauge. In fear for his life, Hiram retreats to the west gate, where once more he is waylaid.

'Give me the grip and word of a Master Mason,' demands Jubelo, 'or die.'

Again Hiram refuses, and Jubelo strikes him across the breast with a square. In desperation the Grand Master seeks exit via the east gate, only to find his way blocked again, by the last of the Assassins.

'Give me the grip and password of a Master Mason,' demands Jubelum, 'or die.'

At the east gate threat becomes reality. Jubelum strikes Hiram a fatal blow to the forehead with his gavel, and the great architect falls dead to the temple floor.

It isn't long before Solomon realises Hiram is missing, and a search party is sent out. Later in the day a crude grave is discovered, marked by an incriminating sprig of acacia. Soon after, the Assassins themselves are found, hiding like curs in a cave. With much lamentation and contrition, they are bound and brought back to face the wrath of Solomon. The severity of his judgement and subsequent punishments constitute the acme of revenge in Masonic ritual. All three murderous Jews are sentenced to die by the King, put to death in the following horrendous manner.

JUBELA: Vile and impious wretch, hold up your head and hear your sentence. It is my order that you be taken without the walls of the Temple, and there have your throat cut across from ear to

ear, your tongue torn out by the root, your body buried in the
rough sands of the sea, where the tide ebbs and flows twice in
twenty-four hours.

JUBELO: Vile and impious wretch, etc., etc. It is my order that you
be taken without the gates of the Temple, and have your left
breast torn open, your heart and vitals taken from thence and
thrown over your left shoulder, and carried to the valley of
Jehosaphat, there to become a prey to the wild beasts in the field,
and vultures of the air.

JUBELUM: Vile and impious wretch, etc. It is my order that you be
taken without the walls of the Temple, and there have your body
severed in two, and divided to the north and south, your bowels
burnt to ashes in the centre, and scattered to the four winds of
heaven.[21]

Pretty stringent even by Biblical standards. Mix it with a psychopath
and you're well on your way to Whitechapel. Permutations of these
horrors can readily be identified in all of the Ripper's victims. One
was severed in two ('the Scotland Yard trunk'), one had her bowels
burnt to ashes (Mary Jane Kelly), more than one had her 'vitals'
thrown over her shoulder (Annie Chapman, Catherine Eddowes),
and all had their throats cut across. The vengeance and ritual execution is the story of the 'Three Ruffians', and to his profound amusement, it is the story Jack the Ripper was telling.

Infantile attempts to present Commissioner Warren as a Masonic
novice, and thus incapable of recognising these horrors, is to wilfully
misrepresent what all Masons knew, and who Warren actually was.
In the year of the consecration of his Lodge of Masonic Research
(1886), Warren's fellow founding member Professor T. Hayter Lewis
read a paper entitled 'An Early Version of the Hiram Legend', to
which Warren replied in amused understatement, 'I think I do know
something about the Temple at Jerusalem.'[22]

Most certainly he did. He had its dirt in his fingernails, and scars
on his back, and was probably better informed about Hiram Abiff
and his Three Jewish Assassins than any other man on earth.

An almost endearing characteristic of Ripperology is its enthusiasm
for taking some of the greatest liars of the nineteenth century at
their word. They've got it into their heads that policemen like Sir

Charles Warren and Assistant Met Commissioner Sir Robert Anderson are on their side, and that they're all 'mucking in together' in the great conundrum of detection. Personally, I wouldn't give the servants of so perfidious a System the benefit of a modest doubt. The subordinates of that exalted crowd were no more likely to have anything to do with the truth than their political paymasters.

They almost blew it at Cleveland Street, but nothing less than the same machine, and for much the same reasons, was at work to secure the anonymity of London's 'mystery fiend'.

The prostitutes of Whitechapel were under threat from more than just the hazards of their trade. There was also the constant virus of official disinformation. The bogey of 'Leather Apron' was speedily superseded by the truly awful prospect of 'the Womb-Collector'. This extraordinary gent, whose provenance must wait, had no more substance than a whiff of scent from a passing tooth fairy. He was a figment of panicked imagination, and about as credible as Kosminski and his dazzling wrist. 'The Womb-Collector' was just one of many fabulous creatures invented by the authorities; he would later pupate into 'the Insane Medical Student', metamorphosing as and when required.

I'm not going to trouble the reader just yet with a roll-call of also-rans, who at this juncture are best left in their lairs. However, there is one ludicrous suspect (albeit of profound ancillary importance) that we need to haul into the light before returning him to his state-funded mausoleum at Frogmore in Windsor. He was a member of the very upper classes indeed, a Freemason, and far from the usual lairs, this one lived in a palace. He was, of course, none other than Queen Victoria's dissolute grandson, Prince Albert Victor, the Duke of Clarence.

Problems for the fans of Clarence as Jack the Ripper get into the queue on page one. The least of them is that he was out of town, and provably so, when he needed to be in London murdering. The folly of perusing this effete little half-wit almost spares his inclusion in my list of no-hopers, but Clarence carries important luggage in which I have a more than casual interest.

Nobody could take this unfortunate royal as a serious contender, yet in his book *The Final Solution* (1976), an otherwise intelligent journalist called Stephen Knight did. His is a well-presented dissertation of comprehensive nonsense. Every facet of it is ridiculous. It is a twerp history.

So where did he get it? Well, without beating a way through the camouflage, like Kosminski (Robert Anderson), and 'the Womb-Collector' (a Masonic coroner), the Duke of Clarence originates courtesy of the System – to wit, the Metropolitan Police.

The theory promoting Clarence is so absurd it falls apart even as you tell it. But I'll try to deal with its mechanics as quickly as I can. The gist is something like this.

Despite being a practising homosexual, and of a class that considered working people as shit, the Duke of Clarence, in a moment of regal amnesia, forgets all this and puts a bun in the oven of a whore called Annie Crook. We know he got her pregnant, because he hired future Ripper victim Mary Jane Kelly as a nursemaid. This compelling scenario is compounded by the fact that Crook is a Catholic, which was something up with which Buckingham Palace would not put. But being the decent chap he is, Clarence does the right thing and marries her in a secret ceremony, possibly over Hoxton way.

A major ingredient of this twaddle has already gone into the toilet. It seems implausible that Clarence should clandestinely marry a Catholic prostitute at a time when he was concurrently, and quite openly, attempting to marry a Catholic princess. The Palace wasn't the problem. It was the Princess's Catholic father, the pretender to the French throne the Count of Paris, who didn't like the idea.

But back to the newlyweds. Marital bliss was rapidly soured by the nursemaid, Miss Kelly, who told her fellow Ripper victims Martha Tabram, Mary Anne Nichols, Annie Chapman, Elizabeth Stride and Catherine Eddowes that it was her intention to blackmail the royal family with her royal secret. This had the potential of a cataclysmic scandal, and obviously required careful handling from the authorities, who decided the best way to deal with it was with a spree of ritualistic disembowelling.

It's here the narrative gels. Because Clarence wasn't well known for his intellect, a 'brain' is brought in to implement the plan. This was the property of Sir William Gull, erstwhile physician to Her Majesty, and a Freemason, although he didn't know it. Further empiricisms militate against Gull in his role as the world's most famous co-murderer. Not only are his Masonic credentials unproven, he was also so ill he could hardly get out of bed. Theorists tend not to entangle themselves in unwelcome technicalities, so Gull's well-publicised infirmities could have been a cunning subterfuge to draw attention away from the reality of a seventy-one-year-old half-paralysed homicidal maniac suffering multiple strokes.

A driver called Netley was hired, disguises may well have been worn, and off they went to the East End. Absolute secrecy was paramount, of course. If this had got out it would have been as shattering a scandal as the one they were trying to conceal. But the plan already creaked under inherent weaknesses that had apparently gone unnoticed. If your desire is to maintain anonymity, it probably isn't a good idea to excite the attention of 13,000 policemen and half the world's press. But we can put this lapse down to Gull's stroke. He also suffered from epilepsy, an attack of which would not have been ideal in the middle of trying to cut someone's throat.

Nothing of this absurd chronicle, subsequently expanded to include the artist Walter Sickert (a relative of Annie Crook's), has anything whatsoever to do with the Ripper. I read somewhere that a Sickert canvas has been interfered with in the hope of matching his DNA with the Ripper correspondence. I imagine this was fruitless, particularly as those letters have been handled by the equivalent of the entire Third Reich.

At a glance, this Clarence/Gull nonsense has all the ingredients of a transparent ruse (not from Knight, but from those who put him up to it). It reads like something set up so someone else can knock it down. There's an air of Br'er Rabbit about it – 'Please don't throw me in the bramble patch,' when in the brambles is exactly where our crafty rabbit most longed to be. In other words, 'Please don't accuse me of being the Ripper,' when that's precisely what certain not entirely impartial individuals most wished for.

When I set about researching this book I wasn't thinking, 'How can I have a go at Freemasonry?' Nothing could have been further from my mind. I knew no more about it then than I knew about the Ripper himself. Had I discovered that virtually every name associated with my research had been a Jehovah's Witness, I would have read every scrap I could find on Jehovah and whoever had witnessed what on his behalf. Had the history suggested a Seventh Day

Adventist, a Catholic, Hindu, atheist or Jew, the procedure would have been the same. But everything I read escalated my consideration of Freemasonry.

There's a website on the internet that proffers instructions for the Freemason on 'How to field questions implicating Freemasonry in the crimes of Jack the Ripper', or something like that, and that's where I think Masons show a little too much ankle. I get it for the Victorians, but why is anyone bothered today? We're talking about a time when Stanley was still in Africa, Utah wasn't yet a state, and the Eiffel Tower was but three-quarters built. Isn't it time to open the curtains?

Christianity is full of assassins. I could name a dozen Jesus monsters without leaving my chair. In my view, if anyone should have a defensive website, it's the British Council of Jews. More Jews have been denigrated, slandered and falsely accused of these crimes than any other group on earth. I am not Jewish any more than I am an enemy of Freemasonry. My point is that modern Masonry is no more to blame for the crimes of Jack the Ripper than is the Catholic Church for the horrors of Gilles de Rais. Nobody ever treated Freemasonry with more contempt than Jack the Ripper. He is an ulcer in its belly. He made good men into fools and took joy at the doing, made liars out of everyone, and made Freemasonry his ridiculous dupe.

An ethos of institutionalised deceit serves to shroud this aberration. The website poses potentially hostile questions, and gives guidelines of suitable responses for the flustered Freemason.

1) Every allegation of Masonic involvement in the Ripper murders is based entirely on a story that Stephen Knight claims he was told by Joseph Sickert [the painter's illegitimate grandson, so the story goes]. But in the *Sunday Times* on 18 June 1978 Sickert said of this story, 'It was a hoax, I made it all up, it was a whopping fib,' and pure invention.

2) Those who are familiar with Masonic ritual know that the mutilations of the Ripper murder victims' bodies do not reflect any Masonic practices, rules, ritual, or ceremonies. Any seeming similarity is only slight, inaccurate, and circumstantial. And, contrary to Knight's story, neither rings nor coins were removed from any of the murder victims.

3) Knight said Masonic penalties (which in any case are purely symbolic, not actual) mention having the heart removed and thrown over the *left* shoulder. But he admits it was the intestines, not the heart that were placed over some of the Ripper victims' *right* shoulders. And it is questionable if Masonic ritual referred to *any* shoulder.

4) Whatever was meant by the 'Juwes' message found on a wall near one of the murder scenes, that the term has never been used in Masonic rituals and ceremonies, and the story of the 'Three Ruffians' had been removed from Masonic ritual in England [but not in the United States] seventy years before the Ripper murders took place.

5) The erasure of the 'Juwes' message near a murder site could have been a well-meaning attempt to prevent anti-Semitic mob violence against innocent people, since some were already thinking of blaming Jewish immigrants for some of these murders.

6) Even more significantly, the baby girl said to have been the child of Prince Eddy (Duke of Clarence) was born on 18 April 1885, so she had to have been conceived during a time when Prince Eddy was in Germany, while Annie Crook, the alleged mother, was in London.

7) Stephen Knight's story says that Eddy and Annie met in Walter Sickert's studio. But that building had been demolished in 1886; and a hospital was built on the site in 1887.

8) Dr Gull is supposed to have been the key man in the Ripper murders. But he was seventy-two [sic] at the time and had already suffered one heart attack and possible [sic] a stroke. Yet he is alleged to have brutally murdered five young and reasonably strong women in a carriage on public streets and discarded their mutilated bodies in public areas, all without anything being seen or heard by the large number of Londoners who were looking for and hoping to catch 'Jack the Ripper'.

9) British laws, then and now in effect, say that any marriage of a member of the royal family can be set aside by the monarch, and any who marry a Catholic cannot inherit the crown. So, no murders were necessary even if the story of Prince Eddy's marriage to Annie Crook were true. In any case, research shows that Annie Crook was not a Catholic.

10) Stephen Knight's story is based on the theory that the British public would have been so scandalised by the story about Prince Eddy that they would have rebelled against the royal family and the British governing class.

11) The supposed police cover-up was probably simply due to lack of experience with murders such as these, as well as some degree of police and government incompetence. Most likely, these factors, not a Masonic conspiracy, prevented the capture of 'Jack the Ripper', whose identity will probably always remain unknown.

Points 1 to 5 are tosh, points 6 to 11 irrelevant. It's not even a clever try; even its sequence is contrived.

'Even more significantly,' gushes the writer at point 6, when attempting to reduce the importance of the 'Juwes' message to less than that of Annie Crook's 'baby'. This represents a common and disreputable technique of trying to associate one disparate thing with another (in this case, fact with fiction), dismissing one in an effort to get rid of both. We are enjoined *not to suspect Bro Clarence*, as though Clarence were the only Freemason in London; and that proving Clarence had nothing to do with Jack the Ripper also proves that Freemasonry had nothing to do with Jack the Ripper either.

Clarence and Gull are patsies, straw men stuck up to be shot down at the funfair. In what brain could this ridiculous fable have germinated? Or rather, by what means could it have been disseminated? It came from what Mr Knight describes as an 'impeccable source', brokered by an official at Scotland Yard.

Our informant is a man who 'can't be named', of course. He's a man in the shadows, his intelligence dispensed on scraps of paper and sourced to 'one of our people', like something in a crummy B movie; or, more pertinently, like something that entrapped Ernest Parke eighty years before.

Knight fell for it, and wrote his book. 'The contact,' he explains in his introduction, 'was anxious to be assured that the treatment of the subject was to be conscientious in the extreme, and that they genuinely hoped to provide a definitive account of the Ripper murders.'[23]

Why?

Why, after all that time, would Scotland Yard or its clandestine associates have wanted to provide a 'definitive account' of Jack the

Ripper? They'd been sitting on files inaccessible to the public for almost a century. If openness was their intention, why not provide a definitive account themselves, or simply open the files to everyone at the National Archive? And why would Scotland Yard, or its associates, want to give currency to so scandalous a revelation as the Masonic involvement of a royal prince? After all, there isn't the thinnest whiff of Masonry in connection with the Jack the Ripper murders in the entire Metropolitan Police archive. Apparently no copper on the ground in 1888 ever even considered it (except, most curiously, in those specially released secret files).

If they really exist, why are these declassified documents not in the National Archive at Kew? We don't get so much as a scribble in respect of Clarence, Gull, Netley or Freemasonry. Why wasn't even a scintilla of this material included when the body of proscribed Ripper files was finally released into the public domain in 1992?

Mr Knight might well have done better to have reserved his judgement and considered an alternative scenario. This was in 1975, which meant that the hundred-year rule classifying all things Ripper was rapidly running out. Could it be that certain 'impeccable sources' thought it might be in their interest to leak a bit of a bum steer (an inoculation), thus pre-empting further Masonic enquiry?

This claptrap attached to Clarence would certainly qualify, effectively neutering enthusiasm for further Masonic investigation.

Knight, and anyone who took him seriously, was made to look like an idiot. A cult of the narrow-minded evolved, abetted by 'Ripperology', and the beneficiary, of course, was Masonry. 'At risk of seeming to dabble in sensationalism,' writes the aforementioned Bro McLeod, 'I touch on another matter that sheds some light on the scholarly competence and the intellectual honesty of such propagandists as the late Stephen Knight.'

The shameful excoriation of Knight that follows was published in 1986 (two years before Jack's centenary in 1988) in the *Ars Quatuor Coronatorum*, a journal of Masonic research founded a century before by Commissioner of Metropolitan Police Sir Charles Warren, and thereafter Masonry's most prestigious periodical. With Knight as his target, McLeod sets out his stall:[24]

Soon after 1.30 in the morning of 30 September 1888, the fourth Whitechapel murder took place. The victim was Catherine Eddowes, also known as 'Kate Kelly'. Within hours a policeman found a bloodstained scrap of her apron five hundred yards away, in a passage off Goulston Street; on the wall of the adjoining staircase he discovered a chalked message, 'The Juwes are not the men that will be blamed for nothing.' Commissioner Warren appeared on the scene before dawn, and ordered the words erased: indeed, he may have rubbed them out himself. The reason he later gave was to prevent anti-Jewish riot. But anti-Masonic writers assign an ulterior motive, that is, to protect the Freemasons; the word 'Juwes', they tell us, alludes to the three ruffians who murdered Hiram Abif, and were themselves later executed. Any such hypothesis meets more than one obstacle. (1) There is no indication that the graffito had any connection with the murder, or that it was written by the Ripper.[25] (2) If he did write it, what on earth did he intend it to mean? Whether we take 'Juwes' to mean 'Jews' or 'Ruffians', the inscription makes no sense as a signature or a warning. (3) There is a decisive argument to exonerate Sir Charles from any charge of 'covering up' for the Masons. Admittedly certain pre-Union exposures name the Ruffians as Jubela, Jubelo and Jubelum, and with a certain amount of good-will one might imagine they could be referred to as the three 'Juwes' (though I have never encountered a Masonic source that did so). But they vanish from most English rituals at the Union, and by a generation later they would not have been recognised by an English Mason as Masonic allusions at all, let alone as specific references to vengeance, punishment or ritual execution – unless the Mason happened to be excessively antiquarian in his interest. And *that* [McLeod's emphasis] Sir Charles Warren was not.[26]

There's a bit of a *faux pas* here, to wit: 'they would not have been recognised by an English Mason … unless the Mason happened to be excessively antiquarian in his interest'. In other words, a Mason who did happen to be excessively antiquarian might well recognise the Masonic significance. Otherwise, what's the point of such an observation? It's either Masonic, or it isn't. If the 'graffito' has nothing to do with Freemasonry, why would it matter whether Bro Warren was an expert or not?

We have at least obtained an interesting clarification from Bro McLeod: a Freemason who was 'excessively antiquarian in his interest' might indeed conjugate the Masonic significance of the writing on the wall (what he and Ripperology call 'graffito').

Although conceding that the 'graffito' is possibly Masonic, Bro McLeod insists, with emphasis, that Sir Charles Warren had no such expertise. Which is presumably why he and Walter Besant had struggled from as far back as 1872 to inaugurate a Lodge of Masonic Research, finally succeeding with the establishment of the 'Quatuor Coronati' in 1886. At a meeting of that lodge in 1887, Sir Charles is quoted as saying 'how amidst his active career, he had always kept up the study'.[27]

In a subsequent chapter it will become clear that Bro Warren was indeed 'excessively antiquarian in his interest'; which ineluctably brings us back to internet fib number 4.

> ... the story of the Three Ruffians had been removed from Masonic ritual in England [but not in the United States] seventy years before the Ripper murders took place.

'They would not have been recognised by an English Mason as Masonic allusions at all,' says Bro McLeod, 'let alone as specific references to vengeance, punishment or ritual execution.'

In reality, as all Masons know, the Jewish Ruffians hadn't vanished from Masonic ritual at the Union (in 1813), but were actually as much a part of it in 1888 as they were in a Masonic lodge near you until 1987. All that had happened was that the 'vengeance and ritual execution' had been converted into a primitive alphabetical cipher. Masons like codes and conundrums ('Juwes' for example), and it was Police Commissioner Warren's flagrant dissembling over what was written on a wall at Goulston Street that gives the Masonic game away.

This modern version of the Jubela, Jubelo, Jubelum myth, making specific reference to vengeance, punishment and ritual execution, comes from *Notes on Ritual and Procedure*, published in 1976 (that's nineteen hundred and seventy-six). It features Solomon's judgement on Jubela, Jubelum and Jubelo, incorporated into the First, Second and Third Degree Obligation (oath), as practised until 1987:

EMULATION RITUAL as demonstrated in the EMULATION LODGE OF IMPROVEMENT ϗ⨳ϩ Compiled by and published with the approval of the Committee of the Emulation Lodge of Improvement A LEWIS (Masonic Publishers) LTD Terminal House, Shepperton, Middlesex TW17 8AS IAN ALLAN GROUP © *All rights Reserved* 1 9 7 6	*First Degree* 49 power to prevent it, on anything, movable or immovable, under the canopy of Heaven, whereby or whereon any letter, character, or figure, or the least trace of a letter, character, or figure, may become legible, or intelligible to myself or any- one in the world, so that our secret arts and hidden mysteries may improperly be- come known through my unworthiness. These several points I solemnly swear to observe, without evasion, equivocation, or mental reservation of any kind, *(For Lodges using traditional form of Obl.)* under no less a penalty, on the violation of any of them than that of having my t. c. a., my t. t. o. b. t. r. *(singular)* and b. i. t. s. *(singular)* o. t. s. at l. w. m., or a c.'s l. f. t. s., where t. t. r. e. a. f. t. i. 24 hs., *(For Lodges using permissive alternative form of Obl.)* ever bearing in mind the traditional penalty on the violation of any of them, that of having the t. c. a., the t. t.o. b. t. r. *(singular)* and b. i. t. s. *(singular)* o. t. s. at l. w. m., or a. c.'s l. f. t. s., where t. t. r. e. a. f. t. i. 24 hs., *See Notes on Ritual and Procedure.*

These several points I solemnly swear to observe ... under no less a penalty, on the violation of any of them than that of having my t.c.a., my t.t.o.b.t.r. and b.i.t.s.o.t.s. at l.w.m., or a c's l.f.t.s., where t.t.r.e.a.f.t.i. 24 hs. ...

Which translates today exactly as it translated in 1888: 'under no less a penalty, on the violation of any of them than that of having my t(hroat) c(ut) a(cross), my t(ongue) t(orn) o(ut) b(y) t(he) r(oot) and (my body) b(uried) i(n) t(he) s(and) o(f) t(he) s(ea) at l(ow) w(ater) m(ark) or a c(able)'s l(ength) f(rom) t(he) s(hore), where t(he) t(ide) r(egularly) e(bbs) a(nd) f(lows) t(wice) i(n) 24 h(our)s'.

So what's all this 'vanished in 1813' tosh? The names may have been omitted, but the penalties remain the same. By the late 1960s there was a growing antipathy inside Freemasonry itself towards these verbal savageries. Many wanted rid of them, and (led in part by Churchmen) arguments for and against their abolition culminated in a packed debate at Grand Lodge in 1986. A summary of these proceedings by Bro Harry Mendoza was published in the *Ars Quatuor Coronatorum*. 'There was a feeling of repugnance,' wrote Mendoza, 'felt by the candidate while his hand is on the volume of the sacred law [the Bible] to give a faithful promise to observe an Obligation which contains a barbarous and unenforceable penalty clause. Indeed, some have argued that by taking such an Obligation, they are taking the name of God in vain and thus violating the third of the Ten Commandments. Second,' he continues, 'it is a known fact that there are some brethren who have refused to participate any further in the Craft because they felt that what they had been asked to repeat was puerile, offensive or wholly out of keeping with what they understood to be the principles of Freemasonry. Third' – and bearing the misguided Mr Stephen Knight in mind – their abandonment 'would take a potent weapon from the hands of our adversaries'.[28] Ha ha.

Mendoza then moves on to the arguments for their retention: 'We've been using these Obligations for years, and there's no good reason for changing them. The ritual was good enough for my father, grandfather, and great-grandfather, and it's good enough for me.' Moreover, 'You are forbidden to alter the ritual,' a rule that didn't vanish with the Articles of Union, but actually *predicates* upon it: 'There shall be the most perfect unity of Obligation, until time shall be no more.'

In the end the abolitionists won the day, and on 11 June 1986 'Grand Lodge resolved that "All references to physical penalties be omitted from the Obligations taken by Candidates in the three degrees."' 'The Board,' wrote Bro Higman, summing it up, 'sees it as important that the resolution is put into effect as soon as possible, particularly in so far as it affects initiations. In any event, the change should be implemented not later than June 1987.' That's June, nineteen hundred and eighty-seven.[29]

Thus, from the summer of that year, there were to be no more throats cut across, no more vitals flung over shoulders, bodies cut in half or burnt bowels. But let me not impede Bro McLeod in his flow. This malevolent junk is to have all too short a shelf-life.

'The estimable Mr Knight,' he froths, 'professes to have found "many Freemasons" who were willing to talk to him, and he alleges that he has consulted the works of such notable authorities as Father Hannah and Mr Dewer,[30] and yet he seems to be blissfully unaware of the facts that I cite. I can only conclude that he was either incompetent or a liar. Is there some other possibility?'[31]

Yes, Bro McLeod, there is, and seeing as you introduce the word, how about that you are lying, that your invective, like the website referred to earlier, is a tribute to dishonesty, and that you are about as ingenuous as some ventriloquist's dummy of a politician bewitched by his own propaganda.

Two questions require answers here. The first is, what happened to the 'impeccable source' who tipped Knight off? Where did *he* source this ludicrous Clarence twaddle, and why didn't he speak up in Mr Knight's defence? And second, why isn't Bro McLeod directing some of his sanctimonious venom at that same source? The Metropolitan Police were given Knight's manuscript before publication. On 28 August 1975, under an official Scotland Yard letterhead, the Departmental Record Office wrote to Mr Knight: 'Thank you for sight of your draft typescript about Jack the Ripper, *where you have clearly drawn on the contents of our Metropolitan Police files*' (my emphasis).[32]

You don't have to be Sherlock Holmes to see through a camouflage like Bro McLeod's. It's perfectly obvious. Mr Stephen Knight was set up. In his investigations of Bro the Duke of Clarence and Bro the Earl of Euston eighty years before, another misguided but honest journalist, Ernest Parke, got shafted by a contrived 'leak' out of Scotland Yard. Mr Knight was simply a victim of a similar contrivance. Clarence was (and is) a greasy mirror put up between Masonry and the Ripper, a clumsy contrivance to warn others off. Nobody wants to look like a banana, so everybody (most especially Ripperology) stays away, the Masonic baby duly disappearing with the royal bathwater.

I've got no brief for Stephen Knight, but he didn't wake up one wet weekend with a headful of malice towards some forgotten royal he'd never even heard of. Malice was there, but it didn't originate with him. We know some official introduced Mr Knight to 'one of our people', a gent who became the primary source for the matter of his book. But who was this man, and where did *he* get it? From whence did this putrescent fairy tale emerge?

More than a dozen years before anyone had heard of Stephen Knight, a well-known and very excellent writer, Mr Colin Wilson, was invited to lunch at the Athenaeum. His host was an affable seventy-year-old retired surgeon named Thomas Eldon Stowell, CBE MD FRCS DIH. As well as a lot of letters after his name, Mr Stowell had a secret under his arse 'that he'd been sitting on for thirty years'.

Over gulls' eggs and claret, Stowell plunged into his topic, so stimulating Mr Wilson that he ignored every word of it. Wilson had written a series of articles for the London *Evening Standard*,[33] Jack the Ripper being the theme. The crafty septuagenarian attempted to solicit the younger man's complicity by informing him that 'they were thinking in a very similar way regarding the murderer's identity', and that the assassin 'was the Duke of Clarence'. This surprised Mr Wilson, because he'd been thinking of no such thing; indeed, he 'had not even heard of that particular Duke'.[34]

It sounded like manure then, and it sounded worse sixteen years later, when Mr Wilson was commissioned to write a review of the same nonsense in Mr Stephen Knight's recently published book. 'What we are being asked to believe,' wrote Mr Wilson,

> is, basically, a far taller story than any of the other theories about the Ripper – the mad surgeon, the sadistic midwife, and so on. We are asked to believe, first of all, that Eddie, the Duke of Clarence, became a close friend of Walter Sickert. This is unsupported. We are asked to believe that he became sufficiently involved with a shop assistant to actually marry her – although like everyone else in the family, he was terrified of Queen Victoria, and knew that he might – almost certainly would – be King of England one day. We are asked to believe that the Queen's physician, Sir William Gull, was party to the kidnapping of the shop assistant, and that he probably performed some grotesque operation on her to make her lose her memory. And then that Gull, with the approval of the Prime Minister, went around Whitechapel killing prostitutes with appalling sadism (when, after all, a single stab would have done the trick). Moreover, that Gull was a Freemason, and committed murders according to Masonic ritual. (The Prime Minister and Commissioner of Police were also Masons.) Mr Knight admits that Gull had a stroke in the year before the murders, but insists that he was still spry enough to wield the knife.[35]

Had Mr Wilson swallowed the bait, it would doubtless have been he who wore Mr Knight's baleful mantle, and who would have been vilified in Freemasonic journals. But Wilson was too astute; Stowell was going to have to find himself another patsy.

In 1962 the allegations against Clarence had emerged in Paris, published by Hachette in a biography of Edward VII by Phillip Julian: '*La mauvaise reputation du jeune homme se répandit dans l'opin-*

ion. Le bruit courait qu'il était Jack l'Eventreur.' (And for those who don't:) 'The young man's evil reputation soon spread. The rumour gained ground that he was Jack the Ripper.'[36]

The French leak went nowhere. If Stowell wanted it out, he was going to have to publish it himself. This he did, his revelation appearing in the *Criminologist* magazine in November 1970: 'Jack the Ripper: A Solution?' – a virtually identical title to that used by Knight for his book six years later: *Jack the Ripper: The Final Solution.*[37]

Though more appropriate to the *National Enquirer*, Stowell's effort caused a flutter amongst the cognoscenti. 'Did the Ripper Have Royal Blood?' asked a wide-eyed *Sunday Times* that same month.[38] Clarence barely had a brain, so the question isn't even academic. The question is: what was this deceitful old man actually up to? If Stowell hadn't opened his idiot mouth, there would have been no 'one of our people', and Knight wouldn't have written his idiot book.

If Bro McLeod wants to condemn anyone for what he calls 'scurrilous journalism', he might want to consider redirecting his invective at Bro Thomas Eldon Stowell.

We have at last arrived at the source of this unsavoury fable. It came out of the mouth of a distinguished Freemason.

Bro Stowell's association with Freemasonry was more than casual (a detail he might not have shared with Mr Wilson at the Athenaeum). The doctor with the 'secret' was a Worshipful Master as early as 1918, Provincial Grand Deacon (Cheshire) by 1928, and rose through Masonic ranks to become a Companion of the Holy Royal Arch (eighteenth degree) by the beginning of the Second World War. He was Most Excellent Zerubbabe in the Cornubain (450), and wrote its history.[39]

By the tenets of Masonry, Stowell was a scoundrel, caring not a rat's arse for the oath he had sworn. 'One of the most notable features of Freemasonry – one, certainly, which attracts, more than anything else, the attention of the profane world – is that veil of mystery – that awful secrecy, behind which it moves and acts. From the earliest periods this has invariably been a distinctive characteristic of the institution; and today, as of old, the first obligation of a Mason – his supreme duty – is that of silence and secrecy.'

And yet Stowell blows the whistle on Clarence?

It might therefore be as well for Masonry to amend the website, replacing any reference to Mr Stephen Knight with the name of Bro Stowell. Contemptuous of any tradition, it was a *Freemason* who dished the dirt on Bro the Duke of Clarence. Stowell's corrosive but artful fantasies led in turn to the mind-numbing and outrageous accusations levelled against a genius called Walter Sickert, and it's at that point I've got to let this nonsense go.

While Bro Stowell was occupied with trying to push Bro Clarence into the limelight, there were others just as anxious to get Bro Sir Charles Warren out of it.

As is established, Warren was Boss Cop, supreme authority (excepting the City) over about a dozen Metropolitan Police jurisdictions, which included an area of East London encompassing Whitechapel, known as H Division. His tenure in office from 1886 to November 1888 is an indisputable fact. Any Victorian newspaper, irrespective of its political bias, will tell you that while Jack was amusing himself, Warren was the policeman enjoined to catch him. I'd go so far as to say that anyone with even a passing knowledge of the Whitechapel Horrors would know that Bro Sir Charles Warren was concurrently Commissioner of the Metropolitan Police.

We now come to a man who was in apparent ignorance of it. As far as he's concerned, Warren had absolutely *nothing* to do with the world's most famous assassin – no crisis, no panic, no connection. Such idiosyncrasy of opinion is made remarkable by the fact that this individual worked at Scotland Yard, had access to classified files, and published a book purporting to be some kind of history of the Metropolitan Police.[40]

He is former Assistant Commissioner Major Maurice Tomlin, and Maurice thinks the most startling highlight of Warren's career was the arrest of a girl in Regent Street. Since Tomlin is a source of such distinction, I quote him in full.

Sir Charles Warren's administration would have gone forward, perhaps, without very much to make it in any way noticeable, had it not been for what is known as the 'Cass' affair. In this case, a 'young person', as she would have been called, was taken into custody by a Constable of the 'C' Division in Regent Street, on a charge of soliciting. Suspicious as her actions may have been, it was not considered proved that her motives were wrong; and the case was dismissed. The arrest therefore aroused considerable public agitation: as a result, not only the Commissioner of Police but the Home Secretary were involved in the censure. It was certainly open to doubt whether the action of the Constable was as wrong, and the conduct of the lady as correct, as was made out at the time: when the Constable was tried for perjury on account of the evidence he gave in the case he was acquitted without any blame whatever being attached to him, and he was reinstated in the force. The real history of the affair is that the behaviour of the defendant certainly gave the Constable ample grounds for acting as he did, and the defendant was very lucky to be able to convince the magistrate of her innocence in the matter. Except for the two unfortunate people concerned, it was not really such a very important case, but as we of our generation know, these apparently unimportant cases, arising out of the daily work of the Police, may, at any moment, develop into a 'Sensation'; as a result, the administration of Sir Charles Warren was rather suspect by the public, and it is not to be wondered at that after a very short time he resigned in 1888.

So there we have it, a potted history of Warren's exciting tenure at the Yard. He possibly also issued a few parking tickets to the odd horse and cart. This assessment of the Commissioner's career was published in 1936, almost fifty years after the Ripper sensation.

Tosh like this is as fatuous as anything out of Bro McLeod. While he attempts to deodorise Warren's Masonic competence, others try to diminish his role as Commissioner altogether. Predicated on quasi-official histories (almost always written by ex-policemen), we are invited to believe that it was James Monro, and not Bro Warren, who was Boss Cop at the time of the Ripper murders.[41]

It wasn't only Tomlin who advertised this mirage. It was also pushed by another Assistant Commissioner, Sir Basil Thomson KCB, who incidentally 'wrecked his career and reputation on being arrested for public indecency with a prostitute in Hyde Park'. Such regretful adventures up a whore's skirt didn't preclude him from writing *The Story of Scotland Yard*, published in 1935. According to Thomson, Bro Warren had just about evaporated as Jack got active, and it was Monro who was put up to take the Whitechapel flak. With quaint indifference to reality, Thomson writes this: 'Mr James

Monro, who had lately resigned from the C.I.D. was recalled to succeed Sir Charles Warren. He [Monro] had shown great ability in unearthing the perpetrators of the dynamite outrages, but the dynamite outrages had been suppressed, and the "Jack the Ripper" outrages had filled the public mind to the exclusion of all other questions.'[42]

What exactly is he trying to sell here? Monro was in enforced 'resignation' throughout the period in question, and had virtually nothing to do with the Ripper outrages. Anyone reading Thomson would get the impression that Monro had 'succeeded' Warren, and that it was he who was in charge when the Ripper 'filled the public mind to the exclusion of all other questions'.

'Feelings ran very high against the C.I.D.,' continues Thomson, 'for its failure to arrest the murderer.' He neglects to point out that the Criminal Investigation Department was at that time managed by Robert Anderson. But so what for facts. This was James Monro's scandal, not Bro Sir Charles Warren's.

Not a newspaper in England was blaming Monro for failing to catch Jack the Ripper, and this isn't surprising, because he wasn't reappointed as Commissioner until Tuesday, 4 December 1888.[43] He was barely mentioned in that context, if he was ever mentioned at all. But everyone with a newspaper to open was blaming Sir Charles Warren. No one could understand how such an abundance of clues 'would seem to conspire to baffle the police'.

It's curious that these two policemen, Thomson and Tomlin, both ex-Assistant Commissioners, could be so misinformed when it comes to their most infamous murderer. Maybe we'll get a more accurate picture out of J.F. Moylan CB CBE, whose *Scotland Yard and the Metropolitan Police* was published in 1928. According to its preface, 'The aim of the Whitehall Series [of which this was one] is to provide accurate and authoritative information, and this book has been written with the idea of giving such information about the Metropolitan Police. In 1888 "Jack the Ripper" caused crime to take the place of disorder as the mutual preoccupation of police and public. Great importance also attached about this time to that side of police work which is represented by the Special Branch and C.I.D. It was therefore not surprising that Sir Charles Warren's place was filled by the return of Mr Monro, an expert on crime and creator of the Special Branch.'[44]

This artfully constructed paragraph is preposterous. By the time Monro got back to Scotland Yard, Jack the Ripper was officially, incorrectly and secretly declared dead. As far as the authorities were concerned, the problem had 'committed suicide' by drowning itself in the River Thames.

What does any of this have to do with Monro? Anyone of a cynical disposition might imagine there was someone (or something) out there trying to disassociate Bro Warren from Whitechapel, and to pretend that an entirely different policeman was sharing that never-to-be-forgotten relationship with Jack. But let us leave the last word to Assistant Commissioner Tomlin, who sums up my argument without inhibition: 'A new Commissioner was, on this occasion, taken from serving Police Officers in the person of Mr Monro. His services in London had been with the C.I.D. since 1884. He had to cope with the dynamite campaign ... He had also to deal with a very anxious time during the "Jack the Ripper" murders.'[45]

There it is, word for word. It was all down to James Monro, and Warren doesn't even get a look-in.

'I suggest that it's very doubtful whether Warren took any active part in the Jack the Ripper investigation, as he had no control over the detective force.'

Who's this?

It's another voice hollering off the pages of the *Ars Quatuor Coronatorum*. Bro Brigadier A.C.F. Jackson is most happy to agree with Tomlin. 'Such a reality would not have worried Knight,' froths the Brig. 'The personal communication between Knight and Bro Hamill is clear proof that the former was prepared to twist the facts to prove his anti-Masonic spleen.'[46]

Let's hear one last gasp of condemnation for Mr Knight before abandoning this cardboard armour to the memory of Bro Thomas Eldon Stowell. I leave it to the above-named Bro J.M. Hamill, Master of the Quatuor Coronati Lodge, who in 1986 got up the following: 'One point I would comment on' – and one irresistible to Bro Hamill – 'the treatment afforded to our First Master [Sir Charles Warren], by the late Stephen Knight in his *Jack the Ripper: The Final Solution* (London, 1976), a scurrilous piece of sensational journalism masquerading as historical research. Knight claims that the Whitechapel murders were a Masonic plot to cover up an indiscretion on the part of HRH Albert Victor, Duke of Clarence (son of the

Prince of Wales, later King Edward VII, Grand Master 1874–1901).'[47]

For certain individuals of this 'Lodge of Historical Research', history is not something to be explored, but something to be *owned*. 'The truth,' as General Gordon wrote, 'is theirs' – and more often than not, it's self-serving bollocks.

Freemasons habitually insist that their institution has nothing to do with Jack, yet by paralipsis they seek to control the *mythos* surrounding him. Anyone with the temerity to question it is reflexively branded 'anti-Masonic', as though that is the end of the argument. This is the bluster of bullies. By definition, a 'mystery' is in want of explanation. If nobody knows who the Ripper is, please stop telling me who he isn't.

The predisposition to look at this material as 'mystery' is beguiling, but only if one accepts the police point of view. An avenue of books either promote or have fallen for the same old ramshackle tale. If a policeman wrote it, it's enshrined, axiomatic amongst Ripperologists as a sacrosanct truth. There's Swanson and his 'marginalia', Macnaghten and his 'memoranda', Littlechild and his 'letter'. Ripperology is constipated with this junk. The policemen who never caught him are apparently to be construed as oracles after the event. The *only* senior policeman without an opinion on Jack the Ripper is the man who dared not give one, and that is the Commissioner of Metropolitan Police, Bro Sir Charles Warren.

It's noticeable that of his many books, Warren never got his pen dirty for the Whitechapel Murderer. We shouldn't be surprised. What could he write? Of his determination to impede every facet of the investigation? Muse perhaps over the destruction of evidence by his own hand? Or reminisce over tactics to discredit honourable witnesses, no effort spared?

If a witness contradicted the police, he was by definition unreliable, mistaken, a kind of Walter Mitty character, too old, too confused, or all and any of the above that could be manipulated as a means to discredit him.

For the most part, Ripperology gives unqualified credence to the Victorian police. This is at odds with Victorian newspapers, which did not. For myself, I have no inclination to accept anything put about by Boss Cops, because all too often the police were lying. Theirs is a litany of disinformation, misinformation, contradictions, missing documents and bent coroners' courts. I do not trespass beyond what I can prove. What we have here is an Establishment conspiracy – not some half-witted nonsense out of Stowell, but an agenda to conceal a Freemason, a 'Mystic Tie' wherein otherwise honourable men were coerced into becoming criminals in order to protect a criminal in their midst. I shall prove that Jack the Ripper was a Freemason, that what he called his 'Funny Little Game' was a perversion of Freemasonic ritual, and that its symbolism and traditions were the naked vernacular of these horrendous crimes. I shall prove, in fact, that Masonic symbol was Jack's 'calling card', contemptuously left at every crime scene and displayed so flagrantly in the mutilated remains of Mary Jane Kelly that there was barely anything else. What is incredible, and ultimately disastrous for Warren, is that not only did this effervescent psychopath play his 'Funny Little Games' with Freemasonry, he played them with Warren himself. Warren was an inspiration to the Ripper, and the Commissioner's past an ingredient of his malice.

The Ripper was on Warren's case. It's the big secret.

Jack hated Charlie, hated his rectitude and his evangelical hypocrisy. Most of all, he hated his authority. The more Warren tried to cover up, the more the Ripper raised the ante. You'd have to sit down and think about it to come up with a bigger piss-take than to secrete the body parts of a murdered girl in the foundations of the Boss Cop's new building at New Scotland Yard.[48] But then Jack sat down and thought, ever ruminating over new 'larks' with which to persecute old Charlie. Enormous effort was made to disassociate this particular outrage from the hand of 'Saucy Jacky', because the Ripper was doing his best to outrage Warren. It was a personal thing (he visited Scotland Yard twice). The cops couldn't keep up, and were barely able to cover up. By this point they were on automatic pilot, laundering in the Ripper's wake like a bunch of traumatised accomplices.

Isolating Charlie from Jack, in respect of the headless and sawn-in-half body at New Scotland Yard, was successful. Both the conned Victorian public and later Ripperology bought into a pantomime of two independent maniacs abroad who happened to share the same homicidal signature. And that signature was Freemasonry.

It is manifestly untrue to try to claim that 'The story of the Three Ruffians had been removed from Masonic Ritual seventy years before the Ripper murders took place.' With its vengeance, revenge and vicious punishment, that legend was still in place ninety-nine years after them. In other words, Bro McLeod's 'decisive argument exonerating Warren from a Masonic cover-up' becomes a decisive argument in favour of investigating one.

We shall now be looking at the cover-up.

3

The Mystic Tie

You shall be cautious in your words and carriage, that
the most penetrating stranger shall not be able to
discover or find out what is not proper to be intimated;
and sometimes you shall divert a discourse, and
manage it prudently for the honour of the worshipful
fraternity.

Colonel T.H. Shadwell Clerke,
Masonic Constitutions (1884)

In chronological terms, Annie Chapman was the third in the series, but it was the most shocking yet in terms of Masonic signature. Mrs Chapman was a forty-seven-year-old nothing with progressive lung disease that would probably have killed her if the Ripper hadn't. In the early hours of Saturday, 8 September 1888, in want of four pennies for a bed, she went out hawking the only thing she had. Just before six o'clock that same morning, her grotesquely mutilated body was discovered in the back yard of 29 Hanbury Street, Whitechapel.

Her killer had clearly performed some kind of postmortem ritual. Her throat was cut across, her abdomen had been slashed open and her intestines removed, and deposited on her left shoulder. A ring or rings had been wrenched from her fingers, and together with her womb were missing from the crime scene. The assailant had also cut her pockets open, making a neat display of their contents at her feet. Amongst 'other articles' these consisted of a piece of muslin and a pair of combs. 'There was also found,' reported the *Telegraph*, 'two farthings polished brightly' – coins soon to be named 'the Mysterious coins', and to become the subject of trivial controversy.

A little over a week before Annie Chapman, a forty-three-year-old dipso called Mary Anne ('Polly') Nichols had suffered a primitive version of the same penalty. She had her throat cut across, her entrails hauled out and a worthless ring purloined from her finger. It is very probable that her murderer took it.

As has been mentioned, the removal of metal is axiomatic in Masonic ritual – 'What ever he [or she] has about him made of metal is taken off,' order the statutes of lodge initiation, 'as buckles, buttons, rings, boxes, and even money in his pocket is taken away.'

No chance of any leap in forensic thinking here, then? It seems worth thinking about to me, particularly in the context of Scotland Yard's comic mantra, 'No clue too small.'

Bearing 'clues' in mind, and as a consideration, is it not possible that the assassin was indulging in some kind of postmortem compulsion that dictated entrails on a shoulder and the removal of metal? No need to get off one's perch about it – just consider it along with a cut throat, cut pockets and coins as part of a broadening debate.

The following enquiry, in respect of metal, is one of the first put to an Entered Apprentice on Masonic initiation:

WORSHIPFUL MASTER: Brother, your Conductor thinks you have money about you. Search yourself. (Candidate feels in his pockets and insists he has none.)

SENIOR DEACON: I know the Candidate has money and if he will suffer me to search him, I will convince you of it.

In the above example, the Senior Deacon surreptitiously supplies the coins, and it's my view that Jack supplied the farthings that were found near Annie Chapman's body. Although these coins were described in contemporary press reports, a stalwart voice with special historic insight raises conjecture. Boss Ripperologist Mr Philip Sugden denies that they were there, citing Dr Phillips (who conducted the autopsy) as impeccable support for his argument. Because neither Phillips nor Inspector Chandler mentions coins at the inquest, hey presto, they couldn't have been there. But Bro Dr Phillips is no more reliable than Bro McLeod, and both occasionally suffer the tribulations of amnesia. Memory loss is a shared phenomenon among certain Masons that will grip the corporate brain as we progress with this narrative. In the meantime, if the metaphor can be forgiven, I'd like to argue the toss of these coins in a later chapter, leaving the politics of metal until then.

On Wednesday, 26 September 1888, presiding over Chapman's inquest, the coroner, Mr Wynne Baxter, said this: 'But perhaps nothing was more noticeable than the emptying of her pockets and the arrangement of their contents with business-like precision in order near her feet.'

These murders were part of an evolving homicidal signature, the significance of which would have been as clear to Charles Warren as the nose on his face. For the sake of illustration, I'd like to consider Chapman's demise from a different perspective. Let us create and evaluate an alternative battery of mutilations. Instead of a throat cut across, let us suppose the fatal wound was a deep gash, as might be caused by a spear or something similar thrust into her side. And let us imagine, subsequent to death, that her killer had opened her arms into the position of a crucifixion, and had taken the time (and the risk) to drive rusty nails through the palms of her hands, then positioned these nails at her feet before he fled. Would you not expect that someone of even moderate intelligence might hazard the possibility that the murder was the work of a 'religious nut'? A one-eyed vicar up for the day could put it together. Yet of inquisitiveness over a similarly glaring distortion of Masonic ritual there was none. Warren and his detectives were positively stumped. There were no clues whatever, they said. No scream, and nothing to go on. 'So far from giving a clue,' comes a perceptive echo, 'they would seem to conspire to baffle the police.' 'It exemplifies their worst fault,' agreed the *Daily News*: 'they cannot put two and two together.'

Maths was not a problem for a journalist by the name of George Sims, who wrote a weekly column for the *Referee* under the title 'Mustard and Cress'. Sims' derisive comments don't do a lot for the idea that nobody said anything about Freemasonry in connection with the murders until the arrival of Mr Stephen Knight.

On 9 September 1888, the day after Chapman's death, Sims wrote this: 'The police up to the moment of writing are still at sea as to the series of Whitechapel murders – a series with such a strong family likeness as to point to one assassin or *firm of assassins*' (my emphasis).

'Assassins' and 'ruffians' are interchangeable in the mythos of Freemasonry. Notwithstanding that, what did Sims have in mind when he wrote of a 'firm of assassins'? Is it the same question posed in a pamphlet dedicated to Bro Sir John Corah, published in Anno Lucis 4954? 'What is this drama of Assassination?' he asks. 'And whence is it derived?'[1]

Sims needed no explanation. He was a Freemason himself, and on 16 September 1888 he returned to his theme. 'The police may be playing a game of spoof [swindle, humbug or fraud, according to *The Oxford English Dictionary*], but the fact remains that in no suggestion made by the authorities up to the present is the slightest technical knowledge of the "speciality" of the Whitechapel atrocities shown.'

Bro Sims doesn't elucidate what he means by 'speciality',[2] but that didn't prevent him adding a bit of cynical doggerel to underline his drift:

> The Summer had come in September at last,
> And the pantomime season was coming on fast,
> When a score of detectives arrived from the Yard
> To untangle a skein which was not very hard.
>
> It puzzled the Bar, and puzzled the Bench,
> It puzzled policemen, Dutch, German and French,
> But 'twas clear as a pikestaff to all London 'tecs,
> Who to see through a wall didn't want to wear specs.

'Clear as a pikestaff' it was, to Bro Sims as it is to me. But the Metropolitan Police didn't want to see anything, through spectacles or anything else. Warren and his ''tecs' would have seen nothing worth investigating if they'd been staring at the Ripper in action through an open window.

During the stalled Chapman inquiry, Inspector Abberline of H Division, Whitechapel, consulted with Detective Inspector Helson of J Division, CID, an officer who was (or should have been) still working on the Nichols horror at Buck's Row in Whitechapel. There were clear similarities between the two cases, and Abberline was palpably having a problem with his. According to the *Daily Telegraph* on 15 September, 'Inspector Abberline himself says that the Police Surgeon [Bro Dr George Bagster Phillips] has not told him what portions of the body are missing.'[3]

Is this not extraordinary – that a police surgeon should hoard evidence to himself? If true, it means that Abberline was in the dark, riding around on flat tyres. 'From independent testimony,' continues the *Telegraph*, 'it has been gathered that the description of them [body parts] would enable the jury, if not the public, to form some idea of the motive of the singular crime, and at the same time it would perhaps enable the police to pursue their investigations on a wider basis, and probably with the object of showing that the guilty man moves in a more respectable rank of life than that to which the larger proportion of the inhabitants of Spitalfields and Whitechapel belong.'

At this point, then, the mutilations peculiar to Chapman had not yet been revealed to the public, nor apparently to one of Whitechapel's most senior detectives. Astonishing as it seems, we have a police surgeon withholding evidence crucial to Abberline's investigation. Hence the Inspector's liaison with Helson. No progress there, either. Joseph Helson was no more forthcoming than, and just as baffled by it all as, Bro Dr Bagster Phillips. 'They have nothing to suggest,' was the sum total of it, according to the *Daily News*, 'and in the case of Nichols, to judge by an observation of Inspector Helson on Saturday, they have no hope of any further evidence.'[4]

In which case we may as well look at a photograph to pass the time. Inspector Joseph Helson is the Freemason with the beard on the right.

So that's that, then. Bro Helson doesn't know any more than Bro Dr Bagster Phillips. Meanwhile, Phillips was poised to show equal reticence in a coroner's court.

The coroner in question was a forty-four-year-old solicitor, fond of elegant clothes and his own opinions. By any definition, and certainly his own, Wynne Baxter was a man of importance. He had written one of the standard works on the coroner's trade, *Judicature Acts and Rules*, and, never shy of his stature in the Victorian scheme of things, his telegraph address was 'Inquest London'. Conservative to the marrow but of sincere social conscience, Baxter had risen inexorably through Establishment ranks, becoming Junior High Constable in 1880 and first Mayor of his home town, Lewes, the following year. In 1887 he'd been elected as Coroner for East Middlesex (Whitechapel included), and in that capacity almost all of Jack's outings became the business of his court. He presided over inquests into Polly Nichols, Annie Chapman, Elizabeth Stride, Rose Mylett, Alice McKenzie and Frances Coles.

Baxter was Establishment to his manicured fingertips, but he was no Establishment stooge. Minions of the state were no less immune to his searching invective than stupid witnesses (the cops got a crisp bollocking over allowing Nichols to be removed to the morgue without noticing she'd been disembowelled).

An adjournment in respect of Nichols meant that Baxter's summing-up was delivered in concurrence with the inquest following it. He was thus able to compare the postmortem atrocities she had suffered with those of Chapman. 'The similarity of the injuries in the two cases was considerable,' he observed. 'There were bruises about the face in both cases, the head nearly severed from the body in both cases.' It was at this point that his perceptions diverged from those of the police surgeon assigned to Nichols: 'Doctor Llewellyn seemed to incline to the opinion that the abdominal injuries were inflicted first, and caused instantaneous death; but, if so, it seemed difficult to understand such desperate injuries to the throat. Surely it might well be that, as in the case of Chapman, the dreadful wounds to the throat were first inflicted and the abdominal afterwards?' 'That was a matter of importance,' he remarked, 'when they [the jury] came to consider the possible motive there could be for all this ferocity.'

A matter of importance indeed; and but for the intervention of the System via Bro Dr Phillips two days later, a matter that would doubtless have been explained. Phillips was a Pecksniff of classic self-delusion whose misguided loyalties would debase Baxter and turn his court into a national laughing stock.

The inquiry into the death of Annie Chapman began on 12 September 1888 at the Working Lads' Institute, Whitechapel. It was a virtual rerun of Nichols. A string of witnesses and protracted testimony over who, what and where led to the inevitable verdict 'Wilful murder against some person or persons unknown'.

The hearings lasted over five sessions. In my view there was only one witness of real significance, and he was the one who didn't want to talk. Bro Dr Phillips arrived on day three. His evidence was punctilious and comprehensive, until he came to the tender question of the mutilations. There was then a change of tone. These horrors, he insisted, had been performed after death, and therefore had no relevance to the cause of it.

Predicated on such vacuous nonsense, it was of no importance that, for example, John George Haigh dissolved his victims in acid after shooting them through the head.[5] It was a .45 bullet that killed them, and the carboy brimming with H_2SO_4 was merely a bit of local ephemera. There was nothing left of Haigh's last victim but a couple of gallstones and a pair of dentures. Teeth with no face, but what a story they chattered. You don't need to be William Shakespeare to hear whispers from the throats of the dead. But according to *The Times*, Phillips 'thought that he had better not go into further details of the mutilations, which could only be painful to the feelings of the jury and the public'.

The jury weren't here for a lullaby, and this was tosh. Baxter formulated this view with more diplomacy. 'The object of the enquiry,' he reminded Phillips, 'is not only to ascertain the cause of death, but the means by which it occurred. Any mutilations which took place afterwards may suggest the character of the man who did it.'

'The character of the man who did it' was precisely what Phillips was trying to avoid. While feigning concern for the sensitivity of others, his posture was actually obscene, of utility to no one but the bloody outrage rampaging around Whitechapel. Phillips was covering up, cynically playing the same shabby card Warren was about to pull from his sleeve in Goulston Street.

Stand by for the obligatory dose of fairy dust, courtesy once again of Mr Philip Sugden. 'Phillips was not party to an Establishment

hush-up of any royal scandal,' he soothes. 'He was simply conform-
ing to the code of practice that Howard Vincent had bequeathed to
the CID, a code that required the utmost discretion on the part of
police officers in all cases in which the identity of the culprit has not
been established.'[6]

Irrespective of the fact that Bro Dr Phillips was not a police
officer, this is one of the most singularly ridiculous sentences in Mr
Sugden's book. I shall be returning to 'Vincent's Code', and the
contempt in which Warren held it, in the following chapter.
Meanwhile, to evoke Vincent here is to reduce his 'Code of Practice'
to the musings of Donald Duck.

Are we supposed to believe that Phillips was withholding information for the public good, that 'caution' was somehow the bedfellow
of impending forensic breakthrough? Was he poised – together with
the indefatigable efforts of Scotland Yard – for a triumphant expo-
sition that would make sense of Vincent and shortly reveal all? I'm
afraid not. In fact, nothing could be more distant from reality. At
Elizabeth Stride's inquest some few weeks hence, Bro Phillips would
dissemble like a common delinquent, and at the shameful 'inquest'
into the death of Mary Jane Kelly he attempted not to show up at
all.[7]

Vincent's Code? The only man laughing was a psychopath. Plus,
I'd like to know to which code Mr Sugden refers. I have a copy of
Vincent (1881), and in the context of homicide he properly makes
no reference to a coroner's court. He had no jurisdiction in such a
place – its procedures were conducted under the Rules of the
Coroner. I suggest some other excuse for Phillips's obfuscation must
need to be hammered to fit. Nor should we forget the superannu-
ated nonsense riding pillion: 'Phillips was not party to an
Establishment hush-up of any royal scandal.' Well, thanks for that,
but I think we've already got the gist, which I believe appears as
points 6 to 11 of Instructions to a Freemason under interrogatory
distress.

But at least there's something over which Mr Sugden and I can
agree: Phillips was *not* party to a hush-up of any royal scandal (Bro
Stowell hadn't yet invented it), and the Duke of Clarence had nothing whatsoever to do with Jack the Ripper. Clarence was *not* Jack.
And let it be understood that by hauling this hapless royal idiot back
from the grave to dismiss 'royal scandal' does not by a process of

osmosis dismiss an 'Establishment hush-up'. No, Phillips was not covering up for the royal family. But yes, he was covering up for Freemasonry.

A week later he was back on the witness stand, and this time Baxter wasn't in the mood for waffle. Once again he wanted to know about the mutilations, and once again Bro Phillips didn't want to tell him.

> BAXTER: Whatever may be your opinions and objections, it appears to me necessary that all the evidence that you ascertained from the postmortem examination should be on the records of the court for various reasons which I need not enumerate. However painful it may be, it is necessary in the interests of justice.
>
> DR PHILLIPS: I have not had any notice of that. I should be glad if notice had been given me, because I should have been better prepared to give evidence.

This pretence hit the deck when Baxter offered another postponement. Such delay was worthless if it meant returning to the issue, and Phillips declined. What exactly did Phillips think he was there for? He was a police surgeon called to give evidence at a coroner's court, and 'notice' of his requirements was surely implicit in his summons. Shuffling his notes, he tried to get away with a rehash of the evidence he'd already given: 'I think it is a very great pity to make this evidence public. Of course, I bow to your decision, but there are matters which have come to light now which show the wisdom of the course pursued on the last occasion, and I cannot help reiterating my regret that you have come to a different conclusion.'

How Baxter was supposed to arrive at a conclusion over matters he was unaware of isn't explained. He was just as much in the dark as everyone else. Phillips then went on to rehearse his descriptions of the bruises on Chapman's face, as though this were the information everyone sought. Both Baxter and the jury had heard it before, but apparently it was all they were going to get.

> DR PHILLIPS: When I come to speak of wounds on the lower part of the body I must again repeat my opinion that it is highly injudicious to make the results of my examination public.

BAXTER: We are here in the interests of justice and must have all
    the evidence before us.

Exasperated with this obstruction, Baxter ordered that 'several
ladies and [newspaper messenger] boys in the room should leave'.
Phillips had now run out of excuses, but still flapped about like
something the tide had left. Shifting from jurors' sensibilities, he
had a go at the 'ends of justice': 'In giving these details to the public,
I believe you are thwarting the ends of justice.'
    Baxter had had enough, and so had the jury.

BAXTER: We are bound to take all the evidence in the case, and
    whether it be made public or not is a matter for the responsibility
    of the press.
FOREMAN: We are of opinion that the evidence the doctor on the
    last occasion wished to keep back should be heard.

Several jurymen endorsed this with cries of 'Hear, hear.'
    'I have carefully considered the matter,' ruled Baxter, 'and have
never before heard of any evidence requested being held back.'
Considering that during his long career Baxter was to preside over
thousands of such hearings, this was quite a statement. Doing to
death by unpleasant means was the stock in trade of a coroner's
court, and he had *never before* heard of any evidence being held back.
So what was the game, doc?
    'I have not kept it back,' whined Phillips. 'I have only suggested
it should not be given out' (which to the average ear sounds remarkably like keeping it back). Presumably he was defending the police's
claim that there was 'not the slightest clue to the murderer'. Well, if
he never left a clue, why withhold it?
    In reality the mutilations didn't represent anything as mundane
as a 'clue', but were the *essence* of what these murders were, duplicated with escalating symbolic ferocity time after time. They were
irrefutable evidence of ritualistic murder, and the only question
outstanding was: What was the ritual?
    Baxter had skated into dangerous territory, insisting on his court's
rights even as the ice cracked under his feet.

BAXTER: We have delayed taking this evidence as long as possible, because you said the interests of justice may be served by keeping it back; but it is now a fortnight since this occurred, and I do not see why it should be kept back from the jury any longer.

DR PHILLIPS: I am of opinion that what I am about to describe took place after death, so that it could not affect the cause of death you are enquiring into.

BAXTER: That is only your opinion, and might be repudiated by other medical opinion.

DR PHILLIPS: Very well, I will tell you the results of my postmortem examination.

The newspapers declined to print his description, which was 'totally unfit for publication' according to *The Times*. Seekers of sensation would have to make do with the medical journal the *Lancet*, which limited itself to précis: 'It appears that the abdomen had been entirely laid open; that the intestines, severed from their mesenteric attachments, had been lifted out of the body and placed by the shoulder of the corpse.'[8]

Chapman's shocking list of injuries must have chilled the court, and especially the coroner who had demanded it. As the doctor enunciated each telling word, Baxter must have realised what all the reticence was about. Bro Phillips was describing a ritualised enactment of Freemasonic penalty, something any Freemason would have recognised immediately. Bro Wynne Baxter was a Freemason, and recognise it he surely did.

I have no doubt that (with the exception of the case of the Ripper) both Phillips and Baxter were men of integrity. But, like Shelley's pestilence, Jack poisoned the very soul of all that was honourable, and with Baxter we can actually see the process of enmeshment in action. Cue the 'Mystic Tie'. By tradition it is juries that are nobbled. In this case the process was reversed. At the next and last session of Chapman's inquest, this seasoned coroner, of previously unimpeachable repute, concocted one of the most ridiculous lies ever told in a coroner's court.

Baxter had put his foot in it, and it was now incumbent upon him to conjure up something that might serve to explain away Jack's Masonic surgery in the back yard of 29 Hanbury Street. As the finale to his deliberations, the compromised Bro Coroner implanted a preposterous fiction in the jury's mind. The Ripper had made off with Chapman's uterus, and this, according to Baxter, was the crux of the matter. Repugnant as this act was, monstrous as it was, there was no reason to suspect that anything other than market forces was at play, 'For it is clear,' he shitmouthed, 'there is a market for the object of the murder.'

The object of the murder had become the financial value of a body part. Mrs Chapman was the victim of a commercial enterprise.

Would you now please welcome 'the American Womb-Collector'.

'Within hours of the issue of the morning papers,' opined the newly accredited zombie, 'I received a communication from an officer of one of our great medical schools, that they had information that might or might not have a distinct bearing on our enquiry. I attended at the first opportunity, and was told by the sub-curator of the Pathological Museum that some months ago an American had called on him, and asked him to procure a number of specimens of the organ that was missing from the deceased. He stated his willingness to give 20 pounds for each, and explained that his object was to issue an actual specimen with each copy of a publication in which he was engaged.' (His publishers must have been well pleased that the projected dissertation wasn't upon the pathology of testicles.) 'Although he was told that his wish was impossible to be complied with, he still urged his request. He desired them preserved,' continued the unlikely entertainer, 'not in spirits of wine, the usual medium, but in glycerine in order to preserve them in a flaccid condition, and he wished them sent to America direct. It is known that this request was repeated to another institute of similar character.'

It was proved almost immediately by newspaper enquiry that no prominent medical school had ever received such an application. But the jury couldn't know that, and Bro Baxter was hardly interested. Without pausing for breath, he deftly linked author with assassin. 'Now,' he said, 'is it not possible that this demand may have incited some abandoned wretch to possess himself of a specimen?'

At last the jury was party to the classified forensics Bro Phillips had so assiduously tried to hide behind. It must have all sounded so obvious when you knew it. Jack the Ripper was working for a publisher! What Baxter would have had the jury believe was that 'some abandoned wretch', converted into an entrepreneur by something that was never said at a non-existent medical school, had then set about terrorising East London, burgling uteri, which he would post to America, where they would be packaged with a book. A sort of 'buy one get one free'.

'I need hardly say,' confided Bro Baxter, 'that I at once communicated my information to the Detective Department at Scotland Yard. Of course I do not know what use has been made of it.'

I'm happy to supply the answer. None. None, because it was diversionary junk for public consumption; and none, because the Detective Department was busy doing what *you* were now doing, Coroner Bro Baxter, and that was covering up.

As far as the 'Fiend' was concerned, Baxter had learned his lesson the hard way. He would never again make the same mistake. At the Stride inquest he would preside over an 'in-house' conspiracy that should have put him in prison. Baxter had joined the automaton, and what a pitiful little maggot Jack had made of him. He all but blew it with 'the Womb-Collector', stretching credulity into a backlash of press ridicule.

'Of all the ludicrous theories,' mocked Henry Labouchère's *Truth*, 'the theory of the coroner is assuredly the most grotesque. I don't know if there is any way of getting rid of a Comic Coroner, but if any machinery does exist for the purpose, it ought without a moment's delay be put into force.' *Truth* wanted Baxter 'retired summarily and quickly', lest 'the bibulous gentlemen about Pall Mall might get their livers torn out and offered with some number of a temperance magazine'.[9] Baxter's theory was 'altogether preposterous', according to the *Observer*.

But much more damning for 'the Comic Coroner' was the reaction of his peers in the medical profession. 'My purpose in writing,' intoned one eminent croaker, Sir James Risden-Bennett, 'was simply to demonstrate the absurdity of the theory that the crimes were being committed for the purpose of supplying an American physiologist with specimens. It would be extremely easy, here or in America either, for a physiologist to secure this portion of intestines. The notion that they were wanted in order that they might be sent out along with copies of a medical publication is ridiculous; not only ridiculous indeed, but absolutely impossible of realisation.'[10] In other words, you don't have to go through the perversions of obvious Masonic ritual to publish a non-existent book.

No one agreed more than the world's most respected medical journal. 'The whole tale is almost beyond belief,' judged the *Lancet*, 'and if, as we think, it can be shown to have grown in transmission, it will not only shatter the theory that cupidity [twenty quid] was the motive of the crime, but will bring into question the discretion of the officer of the law [Bro Baxter] who could accept such a statement and give it such wide publicity.'[11]

Baxter was no more believed than had he proposed Jack's disappearance from Hanbury Street up a beanstalk. His artful little fairy tale had backfired. The *Lancet* hadn't finished: 'And what is equally deplorable, the revelation thus made by the Coroner, which so dramatically startled the public last Wednesday evening, *may probably lead to a diversion from the real track of the murderer, and thus defeat rather than serve the ends of justice.*'[12]

Or, put succinctly, it was a resounding success. Diversion and defeat of the ends of justice were what it was all about. The felony that terminated inquiries into the death of Annie Chapman shows just how easy it was for bent officials to corrupt justice. It was 'preposterous', it was 'deplorable', it was 'comic', it was a false lead that could only serve to assist the criminal. But it was also an unaccountable system in action. Bro Baxter kept his job. The only individuals with the authority to get rid of him were those who needed him most.

The hostile reaction to his desperate lying, however, panicked the authorities, who realised that some urgent news management was required. Feeble as it was false, the conservative *Standard* delivered a wriggling little effort, attempting to portray Baxter's flight of fantasy as the result of a 'mistake' by a 'minor official'. Dismissing the £20 as an unhappy nonsense, the paper went on to dismiss the very notion of the American quack and his fabulously laughable book. 'The person in question was a physician of the highest respectability,' assured the *Standard*, 'and exceedingly well accredited to this country by the best authorities of his own, and he left London fully eighteen months ago. There was never any real information for the hypothesis, and the information communicated, which was not at all of the nature which the public had been led to believe, was due to an erroneous interpretation by a minor official of a question which he had overheard, and to which a negative reply was given. This theory may at once be dismissed, and is, we believe, no longer entertained even by its author.'[13]

It wasn't. But never mind what 'the public had been led to believe' – what about the jury? It got the same despicable earful of Establishment camouflage. If 'the Womb-Collector' was a 'theory that may at once be dismissed', should not the court have immediately reconvened under an honest (non-Masonic) coroner to examine the true nature of Chapman's mutilations? Was not Bro Dr Bagster Phillips withholding a reality, converted by Bro Coroner Wynne Baxter into a comic fantasy? Such patent rubbish had now been rejected, so what exactly were the pair of them hiding?

Such questions were emotive, and remained bereft of answer. But let no one fret – we'll soon be back in the gaslight, a sedative is on its way. 'Baxter's integrity is not in doubt,' writes Mr Sugden from his usual altitude, 'but it would be instructive to learn just how much truth there was in the information he was given.'[14]

As in, how brown is this shit? The tenor of this sentence is breathtaking. If Baxter's integrity is not in doubt, might we please know Mr Sugden's definition of integrity?

Baxter's 'integrity' was shot to bits, and all subsequent evidence reveals him to have been a Masonic dupe. He should have been summarily fired, and prosecuted for misfeasance of office. And he would have been, had he not been protecting the Establishment that owned him.

The answer to the second part of Mr Sugden's sentence is *none*. There was no truth in 'the information he was given', because he was never given it. It was merely a contribution to what the *Telegraph* called 'the scandalous exhibition of stupidity revealed in the East End inquests'. In short, it was a confection of diversionary twaddle, and once it had served its nefarious purpose, Bro Baxter (like Bro Stowell after him) denied it.[15] There was no American in London seeking uteri in glycerine. There was no medical school that could confirm such an approach. There was no £20 on offer for the merchandise, and there was no mind-numbingly ridiculous book to go with it. The 'minor official' referred to by the *Standard*, incidentally, was almost certainly Bro Phillips himself. In apparent ignorance of the impending backtrack, he turned up at Baxter's court with ambitions to confirm the theory. The witness who previously hadn't wanted to say anything was now canvassing the ear of any reporter who would listen.

Baxter, meanwhile, was in full mendacious flight on the bench. The Masonic doctor had not been called that day, and was present at the court on his own account, claiming that he had 'attended the inquest for the purpose of answering further questions, with a view to elucidating the mystery; but he arrived while the Coroner was summing-up, and thus had no opportunity'.[16]

Phillips was there in order to confirm what everyone else was about to deny. 'When told by a reporter of the startling statement in the coroner's summing up [the Womb-Collector], he [Phillips] said he considered it a very important communication, and the public [and, in time, Mr Sugden] would now see the reason for not wishing in the first place to give a description of the injuries. He attached great importance to the applications which had been made to the Pathological Museum, and to the advisability of following this information up to a probable clue.'[17]

To 'follow this information up' was to pursue an utterly false lead, and Phillips knew it as surely as did the *Lancet*. This creepy little profferer of deceit had no business to be at this court, talking up such junk. 'The American Womb-Collector' had about as much credibility as Robert Anderson's 'Ink-Stained Journalist', who was about to make his entrance, poised with his quill, in anticipation of the Ripper's correspondence. The American Womb-Collector was never to be heard of again, soon to be replaced for the duration by a character of no less fabulous provenance: to wit, 'the Insane Medical Student'. Their differences were few, but while 'the Womb-Collector' gathered in human organs, 'the Insane Medical Student' handed them out.

Nothing happens by accident. Bro Baxter didn't invent his nonsensical theory by accident, and it was no accident that Bro Phillips reappeared at his court to support it. Both were lying, and the Ripper was on a win–win. They knew he was a Mason (or someone pretending to be one), but they didn't yet know who he was. Was he someone close to the System, or even a part of it? Until this was found out, he had to be accommodated.

Evidence was therefore manipulated, degraded and distorted, and in the case of the imminent outrage at Goulston Street, literally wiped out. When Sir Charles Warren finally got his silly arse down to Whitechapel, he found the vernacular of the 'Three Assassins' flaunted like an advert for Freemasonry. In a crazy onslaught, the crime scenes were saturated with it. But Jack's extravaganza was also his immunity. 'The feeling,' accused the *Bradford Observer*, 'is that the helplessness of the police is the most discreditable exhibition of their incapacity that has been witnessed for many years.'

Discreditable it was, but they hadn't seen nothing yet. Under Warren, detectives regarded the office of a Freemason as superior to that of a serving police officer. Dispensing with any sense of duty to the public who paid them, they got into line like something out of a Gilbert and Sullivan comic opera. 'He never left a clue, lads! He never left a clue! Keep those truncheons up, lads! Not a one! Not a one! Not a one!'

What they actually meant was that he left far too many of the sort of clues they didn't want to know about. 'Sir Charles Wakes Up' was the headline in the *New York Herald*.[18] Warren had just had the kind of door-knock in the dead of night that presages dismay. When he left his home in Westminster at about 4.15 a.m. the last thing he wanted was any further intimation, be it overt or oblique, of Freemasonry. A carriage was waiting outside in the drizzle. This was the Bro Commissioner's first ever trip to the East End in respect of these murders. He must have rattled out of the Establishment heart of London expecting the worst. And he got it.

4

The Funny
Little Game

Ignorance worships mystery, reason explains it.

Robert G. Ingersoll

In the early hours of Sunday, 30 September 1888, the Ripper made two hits. The first was an aborted liaison at a place called Dutfield's Yard, off Berner Street in Whitechapel, where he attacked and murdered a forty-four-year-old part-time whore, Elizabeth Stride. It seems his postmortem activity was interrupted by the arrival of a young coster, Louis Diemschutz, with his pony and cart. Sensing something untoward, the animal shied in the darkness, and it was probably in the few moments of ensuing confusion that the assassin made himself scarce.

Like an Argentine toad – touch the bastard and die – our Purger must have been almost toxic with homicidal adrenaline. For him, murder wasn't even half the story. What motivated him was ritual. He wanted body parts, trophies, wanted to leave his 'mark', a pleasure denied him at Dutfield's Yard by the arrival of Diemschutz and his nag.

The hunt for more action took him west, into the City – over the state line, so to speak, and therefore into a location that made some sense. Stride had been slaughtered on Charles Warren's patch in Whitechapel. Jack was now out of there, relatively safe in an entirely different police district, a part of London under the aegis of another ex-military man, Assistant Commissioner Major Sir Henry Smith.

At about 1.30 a.m. the killer ran into his next victim, a forty-six-year-old drunk called Catherine Eddowes. The encounter tells us something about the Ripper's extraordinary credentials as a psychopath. Not an hour before, he'd cut so deep into a woman's throat that he was down to the vertebrae, yet here he clearly manifested no sign of physical or mental duress beyond that of a man taking a leisurely stroll. A blood-drenched cliché scuttling for a 'lair' he was not. There could have been no blood, no exposed canines – nothing to alert this streetwise woman at all. Jack was clearly a man in complete control, and within minutes he had control of Eddowes. The unfortunate woman had just got out of a police cell, where she'd been banged up for a few hours to sleep off the gin. 'I shall get a damned good hiding when I get home,' she told the copper who released her. She never made it, but became world-famous instead.

Mrs Eddowes was murdered in Mitre Square, Aldgate, at about 1.45 a.m., suffering horrendous mutilations which probably included Elizabeth Stride's share too. For it seems very likely that the disturbance at Dutfield's Yard put in its invoice here. The killer cut her throat, then flayed her in sexual insult, creating a classic Ripper atrocity.

'The throat was cut across to the extent of 6 or 7 inches,' recorded City Police surgeon Dr Gordon Brown. 'The intestines were drawn out to a large extent and placed over the right shoulder – they were smeared with some feculent matter. A piece of about two feet was quite detached from the body and placed between the body and the left arm, apparently by design. The lobe and auricle of the right ear were cut obliquely through … Several buttons were found in the clotted blood after the body was removed.'

No clues, of course, except for the usual cornucopia. It's a virtual repeat of Chapman, although in Eddowes' case the intestines were placed on the right, rather than the left, shoulder. Brown's autopsy was comprehensive, and I'll get back to it. Meanwhile, I want to concentrate on the injuries inflicted upon the face. Much hatred was lavished there, with apparently random mutilation. But as with everything else in Jack's signature, there is always a message for Charlie Warren:

> There was a deep cut over the bridge of the nose, extending from the left border of the nasal bone down near to the angle of the jaw on the right side of the cheek. This cut went into the bone and divided all the structures of the cheek except the mucous membrane of the mouth. The tip of the nose was quite detached from the nose by an oblique cut from the bottom of the nasal bone to where the wings of the nose join the face. A cut from this divided the upper lip and extended through the substance of the gum over the right lateral incisor tooth. About half an inch from the top of the nose there was another oblique cut. There was a cut on the right angle of the mouth as if the cut of a point of a knife. The cut extended an inch and a half, parallel with the lower lip.

This is crazy stuff, an uncoordinated frenzy of spite. However, the last cuts Brown describes are very different from the rest, and were almost certainly the last the Ripper made on this occasion. 'There was a cut on each side of the cheek,' he notes, 'a cut which peeled up the skin, forming a triangular flap about an inch and a half.'

Complementary of each other, these are the only duplicated injuries to the face. No slashing here: rage has given way to balance and control. Irrespective of the darkness and the risk of discovery, it was a steady hand and deliberate thinking that cut this precise duo of marks. Like the items 'placed in order or arranged' at Chapman's feet, and the piece of Eddowes' intestine 'placed between the body and the left arm', these cuts were made by 'design'.

No one would deny that Jack was into ritual. So what did these marks mean, to him or to anybody else? Predicated on Dr Brown's measurements, we can get an actual-size idea of how they looked.

Ring any bells? Probably not if you're writing an article for the *Ars Quatuor Coronatorum*, but they look like a pair of compasses to me. Let us hear it again from Bro Warren, recalling the most indelible adventure of his Masonic life. Among the stones of Solomon's Temple, he wrote, 'the next visitor will see … the Square and Compasses, as cut by our hand'.

'A Master Mason, in teaching apprentices,' writes Masonic historian Bro Dr J. Fort Newton, 'makes use of the Compasses and the Square.'[1] Over the next few pages I want to explore the proposition, to examine whether these curious symbols meant anything to Warren. (The compasses on Mitre Square. Ha ha.)

But a problem immediately presents itself, and it's the same problem that faced Jack. The scene of Eddowes' murder on the Square wasn't in Warren's manor, so if he's to enjoy the 'Funny Little Game', some ingenuity must be employed. The question was, how could Eddowes be connected with Stride, the duo becoming the single and simultaneous presentation of a 'Double Event' to the tortured and ridiculous Boss Cop?

As with Annie Chapman, Jack cut Eddowes' pockets open. As with Chapman, he was looking for all things metal. His hunt for metal was part of the 'Funny Little Game'. No novice Mason can decline this timeless ritual, and in Jack's Masonic nightmare, nor could any victim.

Every piece of metal in Eddowes' possession was removed, and strewn about her body. They included tin boxes, a tin matchbox, a small metal cigarette case, a knife, a metal teaspoon, a metal thimble 'laying off the finger', and several metal buttons 'found in the clotted blood after the body was removed'. The rules of the psychotic game also demanded body parts. Trophies. Eddowes' left kidney and uterus were extracted with rudimentary skill. These organs 'would have been of no use for any professional purpose', noted Dr Brown, excusing himself of any support for Baxter's 'Womb-Collector'.

When Jack had finished, he sliced off a piece of Eddowes' apron – 'about a half of it', according to testimony given at the inquest. These Victorian aprons were around nine feet square. So we're looking at a sizeable piece, something in the order of four or five square feet of cloth. The consensus amongst Ripperologists is that he used it to wipe blood and excrement from his knife and hands. But he could have done that just as well without cutting it off. I think he used it to wrap the kidney and uterus (the *Telegraph* described the purloined sheet of apron as 'wet with blood', suggesting more than a hand-wipe).

Although Eddowes had satisfied the signatory requirements of Jack's idea of fun, one thing was missing from the equation, and that was Warren. It was probably at this juncture that the metaphorical light went on. Rather than discarding the repugnant piece of cloth (wrapping body parts or not), the Ripper decided to convert this specific of City evidence into an intriguing 'Metropolitan clue'. It's my view that he carried this piece of apron out of one police jurisdiction and into another simply because he didn't want to entirely throw away the success of Eddowes on City Commissioner Smith.

For about fifteen minutes he walked east with his apron and his trophies, back into Warren's precinct of the Met. Why he didn't run into a tidal wave of coppers following the Stride murder isn't explained. Were there no patrols out hunting him? Apparently not. The police didn't seem to be bothered with him any more than he seemed bothered by them. Warren's claim that he had saturated Whitechapel with extra police requires explanation, and will later be exposed for the fairy tale it was. 'By the supineness and fatuous stupidity of the police,' jibed the Yorkshireman, 'one would have thought that for their own credit's sake the authorities would have organised such a system of espionage and patrol over that terror-ridden portion of the metropolis that an attempted repetition of such crimes would be instantly detected.'

Meanwhile, the 'lair' idea has taken a bit of a bashing. Jack wasn't looking for anywhere to hide, and he still had some way to walk. Had any copper cared to stop him, he might well have wondered what this man's business was with a nine-inch blade and bits and pieces of a woman's body. But no one was going to question Gentleman Jack, and he knew it.

And here's something of interest. After leaving the Eddowes crime scene, Jack vanished for the best part of forty-five minutes. During this time the kidney, and almost certainly the uterus as well, were transferred into a preservative – subsequently determined, for the kidney, to be spirits of wine (i.e. alcohol). Trophies pickled, he was left with the piece of bloody apron. Virtually every other assassin on earth would now be scurrying anxiously to conceal this tell-tale piece of evidence, to destroy it in any way he could.

But not Jack.

At about 2.30 a.m., doubtless spruced up, he emerged from his inspired choice of digs. He was looking for an appropriate surface on which to write his funny little Masonic teaser for Warren, and he found it in the entrance of some tenements in Goulston Street, Whitechapel. The wall was black, and so was the passage. He could stand off the street without being seen. It was in this doorway that he left his bloody clue and, having a stick of chalk about him, wrote on the wall above it:

The Juwes are
The men that
Will not
be blamed
for nothing.

About half an hour later a thirty-three-year-old constable called
Alfred Long was proceeding down Goulston Street. His beat that
evening had brought him past this doorway before, but he'd noticed
nothing unusual. Now he stopped and shone his light at the writing
on the wall.

I was on duty at Goulston Street on the morning of 30 Sept: at
about 2.55 a.m. I found a portion of apron covered in blood lying
in the passage of the doorway leading to Nos 108 to 119 Model
Dwellings at Goulston Street.

Above it on the wall was written in chalk 'The Juews [sic] are the
men that will not be blamed for nothing.' I at once called the P.C.
on the adjoining beat and then searched the staircases, but found
no traces of any persons or marks. I at once proceeded to the
station [Commercial Road] telling the P.C. to see that no one
entered or left the building in my absence. I arrived at the station
about 5 or 10 minutes past 3, and reported to the Inspector on duty
of finding the apron and the writing.

The Inspector at once proceeded to Goulston Street and
inspected the writing. From there we proceeded to Leman St
[police station] and the apron was handed by the Inspector to a
gentleman I have since learned is Dr Phillips. I then returned back
on duty at Goulston Street about 5.[2]

Police Constable Long obviously believed he'd found something of
importance, otherwise why post the guard and get the Inspector?
The Inspector obviously concurred, otherwise why at once proceed
with Long and his evidence to Whitechapel's most senior cop at
Leman Street? It was the first disastrous move of this notorious
night.

Other than for his description of the discovery of the piece of
apron and his rush to Leman Street, Long's account is unsound on
virtually every level. It had been tailored to harmonise with the

requirements of his superiors, most notably Warren, but also Thomas Arnold, the fifty-three-year-old Superintendent of H Division at Leman Street, who went into zombie-like mode to take charge of the proceedings.

The first hint of iffiness about Long's account is its date. His report is not that of a constable on duty in late September, but a curious retrospective written about five weeks later. It is curious too that Warren and Arnold should have created their retrospective accounts of the Goulston Street saga on precisely the same date, 6 November 1888. Even by the risible standards of the Metropolitan Police, this was unacceptable practice.

'An officer's duty requires that as soon as practicable after hearing any important statement he shall record it in writing,' wrote the chief of the CID at Scotland Yard, Robert Anderson, adding that should he find any officer in neglect of that duty, 'I should lose all confidence both in his judgement and his truthfulness'.[3] Despite the source, I couldn't have put it better. What PC Long concocted in November is in no way an accurate account of what happened on that September night. Such adventures in amnesia also dominate the nonsense cooked up by Superintendent Arnold. It seems that as far as Arnold was concerned, Long and his apron were meaningless. Both he and Long appear to have been smitten by lassitude, Long telling us that he remained at Leman Street as though neither he nor Arnold knew diddly-shit about the atrocity in Mitre Square.

With its customary precision, Ripperology supports this fiction. Here's what page 256 of its Ripper 'dictionary', *The Jack the Ripper A to Z*, has to say about Long's appearance at the Eddowes inquest: 'He was mildly criticised by a juror for not conducting a thorough search of the rooms in the building, but reasonably replied that he did not know of Eddowes' murder.'

Imagine, if you will, consulting a source of supposed reference, a dictionary of zoology by way of example, looking for 'dog': '*Dog* – A member of the cat family, such as ducks.'

I exaggerate the point only to make it. Never mind the editorial slant – 'reasonably replied' – this entry is so inaccurate it qualifies as fiction. PC Long knew perfectly well of Eddowes' murder in Mitre Square, and said so at her inquest: 'When I found the piece of apron I at once searched the staircases leading to the buildings. Having searched I at once proceeded to the station. Before proceeding there *I had heard of a murder having been committed, I had heard of the murder in Mitre Square.*'[4]

And so had Arnold. And so had Bro Dr Bagster Phillips. I love the way Phillips is presented here, as though he was just hanging around at the police station for the doughnuts. In fact he and Arnold had been busying themselves at Dutfield's Yard: 'The arrival of the Superintendent [Arnold] took place almost simultaneously with that of the Divisional Surgeon [Phillips].'[5] Soon after, Phillips was on his way to Mitre Square. 'Before we moved the body,' deposed Dr Gordon Brown at the inquest, 'Dr Phillips was sent for, as I wished him to see the wounds, he having been engaged in a similar case recently.'[6]

While Warren was still in bed, Acting Commissioner of City Police Major Sir Henry Smith was already on the scene. 'By the time the stretcher had arrived,' he recorded, 'and when we got the body to the mortuary, the first discovery we made was that about half the apron was missing. It had been severed by a clean cut.'[7]

This missing piece of apron instantly became the motor for frenzied City enquiries – find the other half, you might find the murderer. Bro Dr Phillips was in and out of all of this, involved well before PC Long rushed in with his bloody half of the apron. It was a *startling* piece of evidence, and given Long's admitted awareness of the Mitre Square murder, a potentially vital link between Eddowes and the writing on the wall. Yet Long's concoction thirty-six days later, on 6 November, makes no mention whatever of the significance of his find. The Mitre Square Eddowes/Goulston Street link had been quite forgotten.

Detective Halse of the City Police gave evidence that he too was at Goulston Street at precisely the time PC Long reported that he was there: 'I came through Goulston Street at 2.20 a.m.,' he said. And PC Long said: 'I passed the spot where the apron was about 2.20.' It therefore seems logical to suppose that Halse himself was the probable source of Long's information about the second murder. Detective Halse was in plainclothes, PC Long was not, and as the former was desperately looking for a murderer and a piece of apron, it is likely that he would have quizzed the uniform about anything he might have seen.

But when Long actually found the bloody piece of apron and pitched up with it at Leman Street police station forty-five minutes later, Superintendent Arnold immediately did absolutely nothing.

While City cops sweated their arses off in Whitechapel's streets, Arnold scratched his at the police station. He sent nobody to secure Goulston Street, and nobody to search the building. What he did was to telegraph Bro Charlie Warren at home, who couldn't get his socks on fast enough to get down to Goulston Street and destroy the evidence.

Chief of the City Police Detective Department, Inspector James McWilliam, also put out a telegraph: 'I wired Scotland Yard [at 3.45 a.m.].' Result: nil. Nothing. The City had more than half a dozen of their top detectives on the street; Scotland Yard sent nobody, showing no more interest than Arnold. If it wasn't a waste of ink, one might well ask what happened to the Met's senior detectives, such as Frederick Abberline, Walter Andrews and Henry Moore?

Meanwhile, PC Long had his feet up at Leman Street, with nothing to do. He says he stayed at the police station until he went back on duty at 5 a.m., but it is a challenge to believe it. Long says nothing in his statement about the arrival of three of Commissioner Smith's detectives, minutes after his own, and nothing of what importance they attached to his discovery.

They were City officers – DC Halse, DS Lawley and DS Hunt – hotfoot from Mitre Square, who had heard of the writing and the piece of apron found under it, and were aware of its vital importance, even if Superintendent Arnold was predisposed to ignore it.

At the inquest, where PC Long was put up as a tongue-tied patsy, Detective Halse had this to say: 'I came through Goulston Street at 2.20 a.m. and then went back to Mitre Square and accompanied Inspector Collard to the mortuary. I saw deceased stripped and saw a portion of the apron was missing. I went back with [Commissioner] Major Smith to Mitre Square where [we] heard that a piece of apron had been found at Goulston Street. I then went with Detective Hunt to Leman Street police station. I and Detective Hunt went on to Goulston Street where the spot was pointed out where the apron was found.'

Who did the pointing out? Neither the unnamed Met Inspector who had accompanied Long to Leman Street, nor the unnamed PC who was then on guard duty at Goulston Street was called at the inquest to give his version of events. I suggest that the most logical person to have pointed out where the apron was found would be the man who found it. And seeing that Long had nothing to do at Leman Street, I suggest that it was he who did the pointing. To contest what is a virtual certainty would also require an explanation of why neither Long nor Arnold made any mention of the arrival of the City detectives in their respective fabrications. Perhaps neither of them noticed Detectives Halse, Lawley or Hunt? Perhaps they were on the toilet, or brewing tea? Perhaps indeed it was some other anonymous person from the Tinkerbell Squad who took this phalanx of City detectives back to Goulston Street to point out where the apron was found? Perhaps the nameless Inspector, or a copper whistled up from the adjoining beat? But neither of these had found the bloody piece of cloth, and, like the professional investigator he was, Halse would have wanted to know *exactly* where such momentous evidence had been discovered. Was it to one side of the writing to which it referred, or the other? Or directly beneath it? Lacking any detective from the Met, Halse and his fellow City men would have wanted to know all and everything, including Long's first thoughts and immediate actions when he had discovered such a prize.

According to Halse, he saw some chalk writing on the black facia of the wall: 'I remained there and sent [a message to McWilliam] with a view to having it photographed.' City Inspector McWilliam takes up the narrative:

> I had been informed of the murder [of Eddowes] and arrived at the detective office at 3.45 after ascertaining from [Inspector] S.S. Izzard what steps had been taken in consequence of it. I wired to Scotland Yard informing the Metropolitan Police of the murder and went with D.C. Downes to Bishopsgate Station & from thence to Mitre Square. I there found Major Smith, Superintendent Foster, Inspector Collard & several Detective Officers. Lawley and Hunt informed me of finding the apron & the writing on the wall, the latter of which I ordered to be photographed and directed the officers to return at once and search the 'Model' Dwellings [108–119 Goulston Street] and lodging houses in the neighbourhood. I then went to the mortuary in Golden Lane, where the body had been taken by direction of Dr Gordon Brown and saw the piece of apron – which was found at Goulston Street – compared with a piece the deceased was wearing & it exactly corresponded.[8]

Still not a Metropolitan Police officer in sight, and we had better enjoy this description of a proper and professional City police investigation while we may. Bro Warren was on his way.

We are about to get into one of the most extraordinary mind-games ever played by two human beings. It's a game in which one side is predetermined to win, and the other must pretend not to lose. The rules of the 'Funny Little Game' were chosen by the dominant player, and were exclusively Freemasonic. It was a clever strategy by a clever psychopath. Freemasonry was an arena in which the killer was omnipotent and the System was most exposed. To protect itself, the System was obliged to protect him – and that's about the size of the 'mystery'.

What Long, Arnold and Warren were later to write of that September night was an outrage. The City Police were busting a gut to find the bastard, whereas Arnold was fretting over how he might dismiss the evidence that had been left by him.

On essay day, 6 November 1888, Arnold was to write: 'I was apprehensive that if the writing were left it would be the means of causing a riot.' (In which case, why hadn't he already ordered up a hundred police as a contingency plan?) As a complementary fiction, from Warren, we read: 'Having before me the report that if it [the writing] was left there the house was likely to be wrecked.'[9]

This threat of the demolition of numbers 108–119 Goulston Street had never occurred to any officer of the City Police, and is nowhere to be found in Arnold's November composition. So what 'report' is Warren referring to? Does anyone imagine that imminent riot and attendant calamity was the tenor of the wire City Inspector McWilliam had sent to Scotland Yard?

I don't think so. There had been two murders in the last two hours. Who was to say there wouldn't be a third? Why wasn't every available Metropolitan policeman in London on the street? Indeed, why wasn't Warren, like Commissioner Smith, already down there, having been telegraphed about the earlier discovery of Elizabeth Stride's body? Plus, if the writing on the wall was really so volatile, why had Arnold left it showing at all? Why dither for another hour and a half over something that could be covered up and guarded within two minutes?

If, as was subsequently claimed, the writing was nothing more than a bit of inflammatory scribble ('graffito'), why was it necessary for Warren to see it for himself before it was destroyed? If he needed to see it, he could have seen the City's intended photographs, so avoiding any problems with the local residents – who McWilliam's search was going to wake up anyway. So what was it that actually brought the treacherous buffoon scuttling out of his bed? Anyone of an enquiring mind might think there was a little more to it than anxiety about a possible riot in the deserted streets. That perhaps there was some arcane agenda, and that it was the true reason for the Bro Commissioner's nocturnal haste.

From the moment of Arnold's intercession, every imaginable effort was made to trash the importance of the writing on the wall. At first sight, Jack's 'schoolboy'[10] scrawl was enough to send PC Long running. An Inspector from Commercial Road ran with him. But subsequent to that, no Metropolitan policeman was allowed to comprehend the matter of it. Priceless evidence linking Catherine Eddowes to the writing was to be transformed and repackaged into something else.

Superintendent Arnold, a copper of thirty-five years' experience, put in a report of that night's proceedings as if he were some kind of social worker, engaged above all else to look out for the sensibilities of the Jews. I reproduce it in full.

H Division
6th November 1888

I beg to report that on the morning of 30th Sept last my attention was called to some writing on the wall of the entrance to some dwellings No 108 Goulston Street Whitechapel which consisted of the following words 'The Juews [sic] are the men that will not be blamed for nothing', and knowing that in consequence of a suspicion having fallen upon a Jew named 'John Pizer' alias 'Leather Apron' having committed a murder in Hanbury Street a short time previously a strong feeling existed against the Jews generally, and as the building upon which the writing was found was situated in the midst of a locality inhabited principally by that sect, I was apprehensive that if the writing were left it would be the means of causing a riot and therefore considered it desirable that it should be removed having in view the fact that it was in such a position that it would have been rubbed by the shoulders of persons passing in & out of the building. Had only a portion of the writing been removed the context would have remained. An Inspector was present by my directions with a sponge for the purpose of removing the writing when the Commissioner [Warren] arrived on the scene.

T. Arnold Supd.[11]

The word 'bullshit' doesn't rise to the occasion. You couldn't even call it tosh. This was a *doorway*, in the middle of the night. PC Long felt confident of securing it with a single policeman whom he had instructed 'to see that no one entered or left the building in my absence'. But where was everyone now? Apart from a solitary cop whistled up from his adjoining beat, not a man from the Met is ever reported as being on guard at Goulston Street.

Instead, in grotesque disproportion to the circumstance, the Jews were elevated to a status they had never previously enjoyed, and that would never come their way again. Hitherto, virtually every fantasy of police suspicion had fallen upon a Jew, and Jews were the focus of practically every false accusation and arrest. Yet that wasn't convenient here. The Jews were suddenly the Met's best mates; none more so than Mr John Pizer (a.k.a. 'Leather Apron'), a Jew, according to *Lloyd's Weekly Newspaper*, 'of unusually thick neck', a 'disgrace to their tribe',[12] who on this occasion Arnold was manipulating into a vulnerable alibi.

Never mind any suspicions over evidence of a 'Double Event' that are glaring at him; he's concerned, he says, about the suspicion that fell upon Pizer in 'consequence' of the murder at Hanbury Street. Poor thick-necked Pizer's Hebrew sensibilities have been transformed into a reason for destroying the most flagrant 'clue' Jack ever left. Yet the cops had hounded this innocent Yid through every casual ward and lodging house in Whitechapel, stirring up anti-Semitism as they went. 'The public are looking for a monster,' noted the weekly *Public Opinion*, *à propos* of Pizer, 'and in the legend of "Leather Apron" the Whitechapel part of them seem to be inventing a monster to look for.'[13] As will be discovered at Eddowes' inquest, it was a policeman, appropriately named Thick, who invented this toxic junk.

Arnold's highly selective hand-wringing for the Jews is bogus. 'A strong feeling existed against the Jews,' he laments. But this was as nothing compared to the strong feeling, amongst Jews and everyone else, that existed against the psychopath in their midst.

Arnold was a Superintendent of *detectives*, and the general idea is that he was hunting one of history's most infamous and dangerous criminals. Yet not once in his cowardly 'report' does he mention that the writing on the wall may well have been the work of that very man. Not once does he allude to the piece of apron, proved unequivocally to have been taken from Eddowes, and thus of inestimable importance to the writing above it. Not once does he refer to the City Police, and their efforts to preserve such evidence rather than, insanely, for it to be destroyed. And not once does he refer to that tiresome little sideline of cut throats and guts all over the pavement about a mile away.

So obscene and implausible is Arnold's explanation, you wouldn't want to tell it to a snake. What we're witnessing here is a breathtaking perversion of justice, bricklaying the cornerstones of the great 'mystery'. Like Bro Baxter and his non-existent 'Womb-Collector', the whole Goulston Street episode reeks of pusillanimous deceit. While the City had its officers on the street – Collard, Izzard, Downes, Foster, Marriot, Outram, Lawley, Halse, Hunt, McWilliam and Commissioner Smith himself – Scotland Yard sent no one, and had but one senior officer, John Reid, working the Stride murder in isolation at Dutfield's Yard.

The reason for this paucity of enthusiasm, of course, was that Scotland Yard didn't dare show any interest, because if it had it would have made the destruction of the writing on the wall all the more outrageous. You can't put a guard up around vital evidence and then destroy it. In other words, the more defensive initiative it took, the more impossible it would have been to justify Bro Warren's hooliganism. So it took none.

It was left to the City Police to search the model dwellings at Goulston Street, which Inspector McWilliam did at once. In spite of the frenetic activity of his men, the Met had to keep up the illusion that the writing on the wall was nothing more than a bit of anti-Semitic scribble. Arnold had to pretend it didn't matter much, and thereafter everyone else had to pretend the same. Hence the coordination of the triple fictions presented to posterity by PC Long, Warren and Arnold himself some five weeks later.

For his contribution to this corrupt policing, Arnold was given an immediate £25 pay rise, a reward that miffed the *East London Observer*. Commenting on the 'obloquy cast on our local police during the recent murders', it considered this 'rebuke from head-quarters' a somewhat unusual 'punishment'.[14]

SIR C. WARREN VIEWING HANDWRITING ON WALL

THE FUNNY LITTLE GAME

As has been mentioned, this dawn visit to the mysterious East was Warren's first appearance there in respect of these crimes. The previous murders of Nichols and Chapman had never brought him anywhere near the place, and neither did a pair of murdered women now. Now that he was here, he was indifferent to the ripped-up whores. The 'most pressing question' was what was written up on a wall in front of him, and once he'd confirmed what it was, he wanted it gone.

Contemporary photographs suggest that the streets of Whitechapel were replete with such inscriptions, and if any reflection of Victorian society, much of it would have been anti-Semitic. So what's the deal?

The answer is that the writing on the wall wasn't specifically anti-Semitic at all, and even if it was, it hardly required the attention of London's Commissioner of Metropolitan Police.

Would today's Commissioner fire up the Jag at four in the morning to expunge the words 'Fuck Islam' written on an East End wall? He might, in certain circumstances, want it secured, but with two cut throats on the slate, it wouldn't exactly be the place he visited first. Charles Warren was the man who brutally put down a riot of thousands in a public place as large as Trafalgar Square, yet we're required to believe that slumbering Jews and their phantom adversaries were the 'most pressing' of his concerns.

Now, this concept of spontaneous affray amongst a non-existent rabble had clearly never occurred to City Commissioner Smith. Although its location was outside his jurisdiction, he had the temerity to think that this writing was of high forensic value, and had organised for it to be photographed. After all, it was a very strange text, by now empirically associated with a very strange ritual murder in Mitre Square. Even if it was presently indecipherable, would not photographs of this writing be of great worth? What if there was a hidden message? Could this not evolve into the breakthrough 'clue' Scotland Yard insisted it was praying for?

Dream on, Smith. Warren wanted rid of it precisely because it *was* the breakthrough clue. By definition, it became one of the most remarkable clues in criminal history – one Commissioner of Police wanted at all costs to preserve it, while another Commissioner of Police wanted it gone. This astonishing counterpoint of opinion is the pivot point of 'the Ripper mystery'.

'I do not hesitate myself to say,' wrote Warren, 'that if the writing had been left, there would have been an onslaught upon the Jews, property would have been wrecked, and lives would probably have been lost.'[15]

Even the Victorians refused to buy into this crap, and when it leaked there was a furore. How can such drivel cut it for Ripperologists today? I want to laugh in its face, it's so ridiculous. If it had been remotely true, anyone with a shirt-cuff could have scrubbed the message out at once, and Warren could have stayed, more usefully, in bed. I doubt such a point was ever made to so distinguished a personage. Nevertheless, compromises were offered by the City Police. The only remote intimation of anti-Semitism was the word 'Juwes'. So how about erasing just that, and getting a picture of the rest? *Ergo*, a photograph of

The — are
The Men that
will not
be blamed
for nothing

'The — are the men that will not be blamed for nothing'? Good God! Warren couldn't permit stuff as volatile as that to remain on a public wall! As Arnold had pointed out, the writing was still there for anyone to see (and presumably an imaginative hoodlum might fill in the missing word, and riot).

All right then, said the exasperated City cops, how about erasing 'Juwes', hanging a blanket over the rest, and only taking it down momentarily when there was enough daylight for a photograph?

No deal. This building was a hive of snoring Israelites. They'd be abroad soon, and who would be able to stop them, or anyone else, from tearing off the blanket? Or, in Warren's own words, '[It] could not be covered up without danger of the covering being torn off at once.'[16]

I dislike the expression, but you couldn't make it up. It's an argument worthy of that half-wit detective played by Peter Sellers. But this wasn't an actor with a latex nose, it was Sir Charles Warren, Commissioner of Metropolitan Police.

What Warren lacked in argument, he made up for in rank. This was his manor, and the evidence had to go. So there it was. After thirty-five minutes of dissent, just after 5.30 a.m. the writing was washed off, the most senior policeman in the kingdom personally supervising the obliteration of the most revealing clue the Ripper had ever left. And to do that, of course, to wipe out the clear Masonic connotation, was precisely the reason Bro Warren had quit his bed for a scuttle down to the East End.

Warren, with his fantasy riot, was lying like a kid with jam around his mouth. It seemed to have escaped his attention that he controlled a police force almost half the size of the entire US Army. Admittedly, 13,000 policemen would have caused a bit of a crush around a doorway, but how about fifty, or even five? Not a mile away, in Mitre Square, Inspector Izzard and his constables had secured the entire area and shut it down. The square was about eighty feet by seventy-five, and with three entrances and three exits it was patently a tad more difficult to control than a doorway. 'The [City] Police and Detectives speedily mustered in force,' reported journalist and eyewitness Thomas Catling. 'Every avenue leading to Mitre Square was closely guarded.' You couldn't get in, and you couldn't get out.

By contrast, the criminal farce at Goulston Street wasn't even a crime scene. A single copper could have secured it, and indeed one had, replicating the circumstance at Dutfield's Yard, where PC Lamb had been obliged to take temporary and single-handed control of the landscape created by the murder of Elizabeth Stride. 'I put a constable at the gate and told him not to let anyone in or out,' deposed Lamb. 'When further assistance came a constable was put in charge of the front door.'

When Warren finally showed up at Dutfield's Yard, it was only to sniff around like a valet after the Ripper. The place was crawling with evidence requiring suppression. Anything that couldn't be immediately dismissed would be taken care of in the next few days. Courtesy of its Commissioner, the Metropolitan Police had just become amongst the most corrupt police services in the world.

But the betrayal had hardly begun.

In respect of 'Juwes', and setting a trend for future apologists (almost all of Ripperology), Warren figured out a slim fiction in his efforts to try to explicate the writing: 'The idiom does not appear to be written in English, French, or German, but it might possibly be that of an Irishman speaking a foreign language. It seems to be the idiom of Spain or Italy. The spelling of Jews is curious.'[17]

But not as curious as J-u-w-e-s. Anyway, you can take your pick. He's certainly not English, but he could be a Mick.

Warren's speculations remind me of nothing so much as Ebenezer Scrooge when presented with the reality of Marley's Ghost. 'You may be a bit of undigested beef,' he hazards, 'a blot of mustard, a crumb of cheese, a fragment of underdone potato.' Like Scrooge, Warren dared not acknowledge what was staring him in the face.

Attempts to explain away the writing on the wall have become the stimulus for some amusing invention. Anyone who thinks Warren's 'riot' was a trifle fanciful should stand by for the contribution of Ripperologist Mr Martin Fido:

> I postulate (quite speculatively) that a Gentile customer bought something that proved NBG, and the Jewish vendor refused to take it back. (The Wentworth Street old and cheap shoe market was on the street just outside the model dwellings, which were almost entirely occupied by Jews.) On taking back (say) a pair of unwearably uncomfortable shoes, the buyer is met with some bland refusal to accept responsibility ('Well, they fitted you this morning, my friend!'), and chalks up his angry anti-Semitic comment 'The Jews won't take responsibility for anything' on a nearby wall.[18]

And having made himself quite clear, he then throws his portion of Catherine Eddowes' bloody apron under it.

Citing imaginary shoes in preference to an established piece of apron isn't useful. Neither is it useful to attempt to change the quote. Such fantasy in preference to reality is also popular in Masonic quarters, whose explanations can often be juxtaposed with Ripperology without drawing breath.

Where the two become one and the same, we're presented with what I call 'Freemasology'. For a classic example of this, enter Bro Dennis Stocks, who quotes Mr Martin Fido – or is it the other way around? 'It is highly likely,' surmises Bro Stocks, 'that the writing was simply and hastily scrawled by a disgruntled customer who had less than satisfactory service from one of the numerous Jewish craftsmen in the area and wrote his frustrations on the wall that the Jews won't take responsibility for anything, especially, presumably bad workmanship.'[19]

It would require earth in place of a brain to buy into this. By proffering it, both Mr Fido and Bro Stocks are reducing the mental capacity of the City detectives to that of apes. Is that what they'd have us believe? That seasoned coppers living and working in East London didn't know the difference between evidence in a murder case and a bit of scribble about aching feet?

The City Police boundary went down the middle of Whitechapel, at what is now called Petticoat Lane. Was local knowledge so vastly different on opposite pavements – tight shoes at one side of the thoroughfare, and a murderer's calling card at the other? Smith isn't going to send for a camera, and Warren isn't going to get into a thirty-five-minute tizz, over a pair of fucking shoes.

I'm afraid there's a bloody great hole in the lifeboat, and I conclude that Mr Fido is either pulling our leg, or is bewitched by some arcane consideration he declines to share.

Warren's lunacy caused outrage that threatened to enmesh the entire Metropolitan Police. To try to diminish what he did is in fact to demean oneself. It isn't the City Police who are the monkeys. Plus, as is clear to anyone who bothers to know anything about it (excepting Mr Fido and Bro Stocks), the Ripper didn't write 'Jews'. He wrote 'Juwes'.

'It's a mystery,' writes Ripperologist Mr Paul Begg, 'why anyone ever thought that "Juwes" was a Masonic word.'[20]

If Mr Begg was here – and he'd sincerely be welcome – I'd like to ask him what his credentials are for broadcasting so flamboyant a certainty. 'Juwes,' he writes, 'is supposed to be the collective name for Jubela, Jubelo, and Jubelum … they featured in British Masonic rituals until 1814, but they were dropped during the major revision of the ritual between 1814 and 1816.'

N(o) t(hey) w(ere) n(ot), and Mr Begg is misinformed, reiterating almost word for word the misinformation put about by Bro McLeod. To accept it is to buy into a deception, fatal to any hope of understanding the writing on the wall. 'By 1888,' continues Mr Begg, again resonant of McLeod, 'it is doubtful if many British Masons would have even known their names.'

This pushes beyond the word 'fib'.

The names Jubela, Jubelo and Jubelum can in fact be found in any late-nineteenth-century Masonic encyclopedia. We need reach no further than for a volume authored by Warren's pal and fellow founder of the Quatuor Coronati, Bro Reverend A.F.A. Woodford. In 1878 Woodford edited *Kenning's Cyclopaedia of Freemasonry*, and here's what one of the epoch's foremost Masonic scholars has to say about the Three Jewish Assassins:

> JUBELA, JUBELO, JUBELUM: Words familiar to Masonic students, but about which little can now be said distinctly … in our opinion they are a play on words. (p.368)[21]

Thus, despite protestations of extinction in 1814, they were in reality 'words familiar to Masonic students' in the last quarter of the nineteenth century.

'They are a play on words,' writes Woodford, and they most graphically became one at Goulston Street. 'Juwes' is nothing more complex than an infantile sobriquet for Ju(bela), Ju(belo) and Ju(belum) – or if you want to make an 'in-house' Masonic joke of it, 'Juwes'.

But Mr Begg has no sympathy for such exotic sources as Woodford, and argues it away like Bro Warren. 'Juwes,' he insists, 'is not and has never been a Masonic word, nor has "Juwes" or any word approximating it ever appeared in British, Continental or American Masonic rituals.'[22] I(t) i(s) a M(ystery), etc., etc.

Mr Philip Sugden agrees with Mr Begg's 'mystery' angle, citing him as 'one of the most dependable students of the case'. I have to disagree. You can't have it both ways, demonstrate confusion and claim authority.

Of course 'Juwes' isn't a Masonic word. It isn't a word at all. But it is a *play on words*, like 'Krazy Kat'. 'Sponk' isn't a word either, but was anyone in the Metropolitan Police innocent of what it meant? With reference to HRH Queen Victoria, a correspondent signing himself 'Jack the Ripper' wrote 'I shot sponk up her arse.' Does anyone imagine he didn't know how to spell 'spunk'? The word is used like a toy, intentionally deformed to increase its potency, heightening an already adequate and shocking insult.

'Juwes' comes from the same brain; and incidentally, it wasn't written for the average sightseer who might happen to be taking a

constitutional around Whitechapel in the dead of night. It was written with a specific man in mind, a Masonic historian, and the very
man who got out of bed for it. His nickname was 'Jerusalem Warren',
and in my view he is part of the same funny pun.

Let us just remind ourselves of Warren's ineptitude in the matter
of weird words and arcane hieroglyphics in respect of Bro McLeod's
dismissal of his expertise. The following is part of a letter he wrote
to the PEF, dated 18 June 1875:

> I would call attention to the manner in which many modern Arabic
> words may differ from Hebrew or Aramaic, just as do modern
> Spanish words from the Latin. Thus we have in Latin and Spanish
> respectively:– Porcus, puerco; Bono, bueno; Bos, Beuy; Capillus,
> Capillulus, Cabelluelo, Cornu, cuerno; Ternpus, tiempo: And we
> have in Hebrew and Arabic:– Socho, Shuweikeh; Saphir, Sawafu,
> etc. Following on this track we obtain from Luweireh, Loreh;
> Dawaimeh, Dumeh; Suweimeh, Sumeh; Kawassimeh, Kassimeh;
> Hawara, Hara; etc. No doubt there are many known differences in
> European languages which may be found also to apply to Hebrew
> and Arabic. I have to suggest that a few simple rules on this subject
> might be arrived at which would aid the explorer in rapidly making
> a tentative examination of any Arabic word in order to test its like-
> ness to Hebrew or Canaanitish.[23]

I suggest that 'a few simple rules' on Jack the Ripper might also be
arrived at. Assistant Commissioner Robert Anderson offers handy
assistance in one of his many theological volumes. 'Take these
words, for instance,' he writes: '"The Lord Jehovah is my strength
and my song; He also is become my salvation." Now, to the believer,
as such, the question of the spelling or the etymology of the name
is of no more importance than that of the type in which it is printed
[or written on a wall in chalk]. The only practical question is
whether he has the conception *which the name is intended to call up*
[my emphasis].'[24]

Warren knew everything there was to know about the teasing
etymology of 'Juwes', Assassins and Ruffians. He knew the half-
dozen variations for the name of Hiram, including Chirum, Chiram
and Churani, in Samuel, Kings and Chronicles respectively. He
knew the name Jehovah, Ye'hovah or Iehuvah, and could read any

one of them in Hebrew. There was no question under heaven that Warren didn't understand the significance of the word 'Juwes', and to suggest otherwise presupposes intellectual challenge from a potato.

'Respectable historians,' opines Masonic scholar Bro Hamill, 'have always taken the "Juwes" inscription to be an expression of anti-semitism prevalent in the East End of London in the 1880s and 1890s.'[25]

How disrespectful is that? Does Bro Hamill really mean that anyone who has the temerity to question Freemasonry in respect of *Jack the bloody Ripper* is not respectable? Exactly who are these 'respectable historians'? And on whose terms does he define 'respectable'? Is Edward, Prince of Wales exempt from criticism over his multiple adulteries because he was a Freemason? Does Freemasonry make cheating inside a marriage respectable? Was Prince Albert Victor, the Duke of Clarence, respectable when risking life imprisonment for buggering about with that idiot Euston at a harem of Post Office boys? And what about the conniver who most ludicrously nominated him as Jack the Ripper's assistant, Worshipful Master Bro Thomas Stowell CBE. Oh dear, oh dear, how disrespectful was that?

Reality can be offensive, but springing to your feet and waving your rectitude about won't change it. All cults, all creeds, all religions have their murderers (King Solomon murdered his brother). I'm sorry if this history offends, but carving a woman from her genitals to her throat is not a 'respectable activity', and I regret to say that a Freemason is no more exempt from committing such a crime than is any other man.

Mr Sugden says, 'Only by shameless selection of evidence can the Masonic theory be invested with apparent credibility'[26] – whereas, to the contrary, I believe it is only by shameless manipulation that it can be dismissed. Mr Sugden and Bro Hamill are flogging a substantial untruth, and an Everest of evidence doesn't accommodate such shameless distortion.

As far as Masonry is concerned (and for that matter the gang-thinking of Ripperology), you can have as many suspects as you like: masturbators, womb-collectors, medical students, doctors, slaughtermen, Irishmen, sailors, cowboys, and no end of Jews. But what you can't have is the most egregious Israelites of them all. After the Clarence/Sickert inoculation, it isn't permitted to consider the

'Mystic Trio', infamous among Freemasons for their shouldered entrails and throats cut across.

Nothing is more important than this Masonic taunting of Bro Warren at Goulston Street. The mocking on the wall is the sum of the whole of Jack the Ripper, a key to his psyche – and, by the insanity of his reaction, Bro Sir Charles Warren's too.

Here's what Warren (and some other hand) put together as his 6 November report. I bother here only with the first couple of sentences: 'On the 30th September on hearing of the Berners [sic] Street murder after visiting Commercial Road station I arrived at Leman Street station shortly before 5 a.m. and ascertained from Superintendent Arnold all that was known relative to the two murders. The most pressing question at that moment was some writing on the wall at Goulston Street evidently written with the intention of inflaming the public mind against the Jews.'[27]

Now, I don't know about anyone else, but if my intention was to inflame the public against the Jews, I think I could have chosen somewhere more provoking than a pitch-black doorway in the middle of the night. Perhaps under a street lamp? Plus, where did this phantom inflamer get his piece of apron, a technicality Warren declines to address anywhere in his preposterous essay. Like Arnold, he doesn't mention it at all: 'The most pressing question at that moment was some writing on the wall at Goulston Street'.

This 'most pressing question' is most curiously expunged from Mr Sugden's version of Warren's report. He reproduces it as 'I ... went down to Goulston Street ... before going to the scene of the murder.'[28]

Why Mr Sugden should take it upon himself to censor Warren is of course his prerogative – he may write what he likes, as do I – so long as we both avoid 'shameless selection'. I don't know what his intentions are, but by fiddling about with this sentence, he defuses the urgency associated with the writing on the wall, which by Warren's own admission was 'the most pressing question'.

This 'most pressing question' becomes mind-boggling in context. Less than a mile away are two murdered women, and it's likely that the man who killed them isn't much further off. Is not *he* the most pressing question? What instruction did the Commissioner issue in respect of his apprehension? Where was the urgent call for his top detectives and ancillary support?

For a stupefied Freemason like Warren, a guardian of the 'Mystic Tie', the wall was indeed 'the most pressing question', which, with the subsequent assistance of Ripperology, he successfully managed to present as merely a bit of racist scribble.

But Warren knew rather different. Another Masonic historian and expert practitioner, an American scholar by the name of Albert Pike, wrote about Jubela, Jubelo and Jubelum some twenty years before anyone had heard of Goulston Street. His book, published in 1872, is called *Morals and Dogma*, and is a classic of Masonic erudition. In respect of the homicidal trio Jubela, Jubelo and Jubelum, he wrote: 'That in the name of each murderer are the two names of the good and evil Deities of the Hebrews, for Yu-Bel is but Yehi-bal or Yeho-bal, and that the three final syllables of the names, a, o, um (Life-giving, Life-preserving, Life-destroying), are represented by the mystic character, Y.'[29]

The mystic 'Y' is explained in simple terms by a contemporary Masonic academic, Dr B. Fisher, in whose book (as in *Morals and Dogma*) the Three Assassins Jubela, Jubelo and Jubelum are referred to in their original form, as Yubela, Yubelo and Yubelum, spelt with the mystic Hebrew 'Y'.[30] Albert Mackey's *Lexicon of Freemasonry* (1855) underlines the convention: 'In all these names the J is to be pronounced as in Y.'

Warren, of course, was hip to such occult minutiae, and so was Jack the Ripper. Three days after writing his funny little 'Juwes' message at Goulston Street, he posted a letter to Bro Warren, on the envelope of which he changed the 'J' in his trade-name to 'Y', creating 'Yack Ripper' (see opposite).

Thus we have Yubela, Yubelo, Yubelum and Yack. Postmarked 4 October 1888, this envelope is important because it reveals knowledge of the writing on the wall almost a week before the press got wind of it. The earliest significant mention of anything untoward at Goulston Street began to leak about 8 October – this, by way of example, from the *Pall Mall Gazette*:

A startling fact has just come to light. After killing Catherine Eddowes in Mitre Square, the murderer is now known to have walked to Goulston Street, where he threw away the piece of the deceased woman's apron on which he had wiped his hands and knife. Within a few feet of this spot he had written upon the wall,

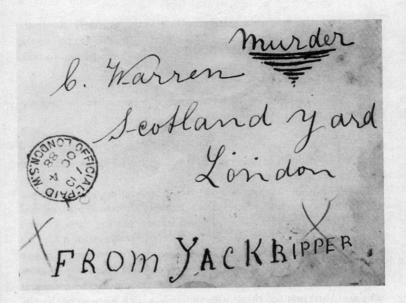

'The Jews shall not be blamed for nothing.' Most unfortunately one of the police officers gave orders for this writing to be immediately sponged out, probably with a view to stifling morbid curiosity it would have aroused.[31]

No mention of riot or the destruction of buildings, not even an eyebrow raised in the direction of anti-Semitic onslaught, just probable 'morbid curiosity', which in reality was about all the writing would have got. But the *Gazette* was in no doubt of the magnitude of the error of its obliteration: 'In doing so a very important link was destroyed, for had the writing been photographed a certain clue would be in the hands of the authorities.'[32]

Even with so little to go on, the *Gazette* was already well aware that 'a very important link' had been destroyed: 'Witnesses who saw the writing state that it was similar in character to the letters sent to the Central News and signed "Jack the Ripper". There is now every reason to believe that the writer of the letter and postcard (facsimiles are now to be seen outside every police station) is the actual murderer.'[33]

The infamous 'Dear Boss' letter and the publicity it inspired are the business of the next chapter. Suffice it to say that the police had received a letter and a postcard revelling in the murders, the latter describing the horror of Stride/Eddowes as a 'Double Event'. As the *Gazette* says, facsimiles of these communications were posted outside every police station:

> Any person recognising the handwriting is requested to communicate with the nearest police station.

'The police are very anxious,' affirmed the *Gazette*, 'that any citizen who can identify the handwriting should without delay communicate with the authorities.'[34]

Unfortunately, one of the only men who might recognise it was the very man who had destroyed a sample of it. Now, if anyone had come along in the dead of night and started tearing these posters from the front of police stations, he'd have probably found himself in the cells of one of them. Yet a transfixed Commissioner of Police did worse than that: he was actually covering up a murderer's tracks.

In concert with their pre-doomed posters, honest brokers at Scotland Yard printed thousands of flyers, which were to be distributed on 3 October. So here we have something rather singular in progress. 1) The Metropolitan Police approve the time and expense of publishing posters and thousands of door-to-door flyers. 2) Three days before these flyers are to be distributed, on 30 September, the Chief Officer of the Metropolitan Police wipes out the only evidence that might link these posters with London's most wanted criminal.

By 11 October the press had a handle on this, and it was taking shape into a full-blown scandal. Following a sparse but basically accurate summary, the *Gazette* posed a rhetorical question:

WHO ORDERED IT TO BE RUBBED OUT?

> ... who was the infatuated person who thus in defiance of protest insisted in rubbing it out? It was none other than Sir Charles Warren himself! The fact would have been brought out in the inquest if the City Coroner had not feared to seem as if he was holding up Sir Charles Warren to contempt.[35]

This concession was the least of the favours the coroner was poised to offer. Had contempt not been overridden by deference (and other arcane considerations), this Masonic aberration could have been nailed. But, as always, the System looked after its own.

Keeping Warren out of court, however, didn't keep him out of the newspapers, and the *Gazette* sent a reporter to try to get an interview at Scotland Yard. Predictably, its hopes were dashed. As PC Walter Dew and a variety of others record, the press was habitually 'kept at arm's length' from Warren, and couldn't get in to see the vainglorious oaf: 'The representative saw Sir Charles Warren's private secretary, who stated that, "Sir Charles Warren was in Goulston Street shortly after the murders, and if he had wished to make any communication to the press on the subject he would have done so then."'[36]

An editorial followed, in which the newspaper succinctly put its finger on it: 'Considering how promptly Sir Charles Warren contradicts any statement that can possibly be contradicted with any semblance of truth, his silence is equivalent of admission of the fact.'[37]

The fact is, Sir Charles Warren was up to his nostrils in lies that would soon overwhelm him. His tactic of silence persuaded no one. Even his City counterpart, Commissioner Smith, regarded Warren's anxiety for the Jews as bogus, describing it as nothing more than 'alleged'. And when, at seven o'clock on that infamous morning, Warren at last arrived for discussions with the City Police, Inspector McWilliam put aside conventions of rank and told him to his face that he had made a 'fatal mistake' – and fatal it proved to be. Warren's brainless priorities were to become responsible for the death of Mary Jane Kelly and the sickening destruction of an innocent little child called Johnnie Gill.

The *Pall Mall Gazette* was among many who had already had enough. Incidentally, there was not a lot of 'graffito' about in 1888. Like the rest of Fleet Street, the *Gazette* referred to the Ripper's message as

THE HANDWRITING ON THE WALL

The case against the Chief Commissioner is overwhelming. The evidence given at the inquest yesterday proves that in all human probability the murderer left behind him in Goulston Street an invaluable clue to his identity, the obliteration of which has supplied the last conclusive demonstration required for the utter unfitness of SIR CHARLES WARREN for the place which he holds.[38]

Warren should have been summarily dismissed and prosecuted for misfeasance, if not conspiracy. Six weeks later, when the Ripper had driven this worthless menace out of office, an unworthy Home Secretary, Henry Matthews, attempted to sell the idea that Warren had 'resigned' over a minor procedural misdemeanour (re a Home Office minute of 27 May 1879), 'by which officers attached to the Home Department were enjoined not to publish any work relating to the Department without the previous sanction of the Secretary of State'.

Warren had written some bland essay for *Murray's Magazine* – reading it is like a dose of Seconal – but it was the excuse Matthews grasped. According to this hopeless lickspittle, the 'rules' didn't allow such literary indiscretion, and the Commissioner would have to go.

Yet at Goulston Street, Warren broke every rule in the policeman's book. 'If SIR CHARLES WARREN,' charged the *Gazette*, 'had but read pages 248–9 of MR HOWARD VINCENT'S Police Code, he would have seen how flagrantly he was violating the first duty of a policeman in cases of murder.'

Vincent, MP for Sheffield Central and himself a prominent Freemason, had formed the CID in 1878, after a criminal scandal amongst Metropolitan cops, and following it, wrote his Police Code. Rule 18 summarises the whole, and in my view justifies the eternal condemnation of Bro Warren:

> 18: It must finally be remembered, in dealing with cases of murder, that any oversight, however trivial, any communication of information, any precipitancy, or any irregularity of procedure may be fatal to the end of justice … No irregularity will be countenanced … In cases of murder, everything must be done with the utmost celerity, every channel pursued to the exclusion of any individual theory, although every possible step must be taken to bring the murderer to justice, and to prevent his destroying the evidence of his own guilt.[39]

If Warren had gone through this ticking off with a pencil, he couldn't have violated the prescription more effectively. 'No irregularity will be countenanced', say the Rules; 'every channel pursued to the exclusion of any individual theory' – and this to include, presumably, moonshine scenarios in respect of riot against the Jews.[40]

Rubbish from the start, by now the 'anti-Semitic' angle had all but collapsed. Fairy tales of mayhem had been supplanted by genuine resentment from Jews themselves, their voices naturally attracting less attention than the official spin. When the spelling became public, certain hysterical policemen at Scotland Yard continued to insist that 'Juwes' was what it wasn't: 'The police authorities attach a great deal of importance to the spelling of the word "Jews" in the writing on the wall,' proclaimed an unnamed agency. 'The language of the Jews in the East End is a hybrid dialect, known as Yiddish, and their mode of spelling the word "Jews" would be "Juwes".'

In other words, the Jews were accusing themselves – the Ripper was a Yid, and only a Yiddish-speaking fiend could have written it. 'This is absolutely incorrect,' countered the *Star*, correctly. 'The Yiddish word for Jew is Yidden, the word "Yiddish" meaning, of course, the language of the Yiddens.'[41]

Even though it was all so confusing to Warren, at least one man at the Home Office could have confirmed it. According to his secretary Ruggles-Brise, Home Secretary Matthews spoke fluent Yiddish, and could have nailed this nonsense in its tracks. But that wasn't exactly in the Establishment's interest, so what the hell, maybe the Jews did call themselves 'Juwes'.[42]

'Much indignation,' continued the *Star*, 'is felt among the Jews at these repeated and unjustifiable attempts to fasten the responsibility for these dastardly crimes on them.'

'Juwes' was a word that had motivated Superintendent Arnold into an uncompromising regard for the safety of Jews, and now 'Juwes' was a word accusing them. But the clique at Scotland Yard had to fasten blame on someone – anyone but Bro Jack – and the Yids didn't seem to understand that, together with the Irish, they were the first-call scapegoats for diversionary prejudice. Far from being protected, their position was now entirely reversed, and we're back where we started, with the thick-necked tribe of 'Leather Apron'.

It was a Jew what done it! Or an Irishman talking foreign! Flouting every forensic protocol in the book, Warren not only didn't prevent the Ripper from 'destroying the evidence of his own guilt': he did it for him.

'Any irregularity may be fatal to the ends of justice,' wrote Vincent. But justice wasn't what Warren was about. The last thing anyone wanted was an arrest, God forbid. It would have put an entire (and clandestine) ruling elite in the dock – its morals, its monarchy – and would possibly have had the cataclysmic side-effect of extirpating Freemasonry from the judiciary, the police and the royal family for all time.

Justice? Forget it. Fuck who he killed, so long as the bastard doesn't interfere with their divine right to rule. The Ripper must and would go free. Justice didn't mean diddly-shit to a rotten little whore like Matthews – 'a pitiful creature', observed the *Star*, 'a poor and spiritless specimen of the race of smart adventurers who creep into politics by the back door'.[43]

It was the exit about to be used by Warren.

'The chaos and bitterness at Scotland Yard surpasses belief,' wrote the *Gazette*.[44] 'There is no confidence anywhere, but discontent everywhere, and this discontent is felt most keenly in the headquarters of the force – in Scotland Yard.' But

MR MATTHEWS is satisfied with SIR CHARLES WARREN. And SIR CHARLES WARREN is no doubt satisfied with MR MATTHEWS. What a Home Secretary! He is indeed a worthy counterpart to the Chief Commissioner, but he is alone in his satisfaction. The City Police are not the only constabulary whose chiefs are in a state of indignation over Scotland Yard. The Chief Constables of our great municipalities are looking on with amazement at the incredible folly which is being displayed at headquarters, and with shame and indignation … it is a black and burning disgrace for the government to allow such a state of things as we have brought to light to remain a single day without prompt and vigorous action.[45]

A black and burning disgrace it was. But what the hostile press didn't understand was that the 'crapulous decrepitude', as the *Chronicle* put it, was in fact organised crisis management.

I don't believe for a second that Warren went down to Goulston Street via Commercial Road police station, as he claimed. The siren call came from Leman Street, where sat the 'crapulous' Arnold. In my view the inclusion of Commercial Road is mere upholstery to distract attention from his 'most pressing question'. And as a matter of fact, I don't think he went to Leman Street either, but directly to the Freemasonic message on the wall.

Arnold wrote, 'An Inspector was present by my directions with a sponge for the purpose of removing the writing when the Commissioner [Warren] arrived on the scene.' And that's exactly where he did arrive, at a gallop, his brain sizzling like a putrescent egg.[46]

We'll perhaps never know the content of Arnold's never-seen telegraph to summon Warren, but you can bet the bank it had nothing to do with snoring Jews. Only a respectable historian or a hapless Freemason would believe that, and those who do are welcome to it. Every scintilla of evidence, however, points to a more arcane commission. It suggests that Arnold was under strict instructions not to interfere with – shall we say – possible 'Occult manifestations' until the past Grand Master of the world's only Lodge of Masonic Research had personally inspected them.

'If we had been called upon,' wrote the disparaging *Gazette*, 'to imagine what would afford the public an exact measure of SIR CHARLES WARREN's utter incapacity for the work he has in hand, we could not have conceived anything more cruelly conclusive than this.'[47] (And that includes Baxter's 'Womb-Collector'.)

It was at this instant of cruel conclusiveness at Goulston Street that 'the mystery of Jack the Ripper' was assured. There could be no turning back, no deviation from the lie, nor honour for the victimised fraternity that had to tell it. Freemasology is still rushing around with the sponge. 'There is no indication,' chirps Bro McLeod, 'that the Graffito had any connection with the murder, or that it was written by the Ripper.' Useful support comes as usual from Mr Sugden, who having censored Warren and laughably misrepresented Vincent's Code, now reminds us that 'Chief Inspector Swanson referred to the writing as "blurred" which suggests it might have been old.'[48]

In which case it's got nothing to do with murdered women, and couldn't possibly have caused a riot. You can't have it both ways – old when you're trying to disconnect it from the Ripper; fresh when you're trying to sell the 'riot'.

In reality, Swanson suggested no such thing as 'old'. If his words suggest anything at all, it is that he was, as usual, tampering with the record. Outside that, two certainties negate the fictions of Bro

Inspector Donald Swanson. 1) He never saw the writing. 2) Neither Warren nor Arnold (much less PC Long) says anything about its physical characteristics in their November essays. So what makes Swanson think it was 'blurred'?

What Arnold said is that 'it was in such a position that it would have been rubbed by the shoulders of persons passing in & out of the building'. 'Would have been rubbed' is different from 'blurred', thus the 'it could have been there for ages' idea (conveniently divorcing the writing from the apron) has no substance. Such cavalier inaccuracies can mean the difference between the detection of a murderer and a murderer getting off scot-free, as I'm sure Bro Inspector 'Shifty Nib' Swanson and his pusillanimous Boss knew well.

But what of that most excellent pie-baker, Bro McLeod? Appropriating Ripperology's burlesque jargon, he denies any connection between the writing and the Ripper. Mr Fido and his bunions would agree. But I do not, and neither did the chief of London's Criminal Investigation Department.

From the autumn of 1888 the CID was under the command of a virulent Christian, the already mentioned Robert Anderson.[49] Himself a master baker, Anderson was the last man you would want to trust with an autobiography, although twenty-two years later he was engaged in just such a publication, serialised in *Blackwood's Magazine*.

It's tiresome to judge the deficiencies in Anderson's record by what's in his memoir and what's kept out of it – the writing on the wall at Goulston Street being confined to the latter. Neglect of this notorious topic generated an irate response from at least one contemporary critic: 'He might have recalled – but did not – the crass stupidity of Scotland Yard men who wiped out from the wall of the labourers' buildings in Goulston Street, the only tangible piece of evidence ever obtained pointing to the identity of Jack the Ripper.'

This ruffled the old bigot's vanity, and more in self-defence than defence of Scotland Yard, Anderson produced a typically disingenuous response. 'I beg to assure you,' he wrote, 'that here you do an injustice, not only to me, but to the Criminal Investigation Department. The night on which the murder in question was committed I was on my way home from Paris, and great was my indignation when, next day, I heard of what you rightly call an act of "crass" stupidity. But the Scotland Yard men were in no way responsible for it – it was done by officers of the uniform force in the division, under the order of one of my colleagues.'[50]

Converting Warren into a nameless 'colleague', he blames the uniforms – blames anyone but the man responsible – but nevertheless confirms that it was Jack the Ripper who was responsible for the writing on the wall. Let us be in no doubt here. This isn't Mr Fido with his cobblers, but the opinion of the most exalted officer in London's CID, Robert Anderson KCB. He had reason enough to keep his trap shut in 1888.

If you could get a cigarette paper between Anderson's teeth, he was probably lying. Bewitched by his own self-righteousness, he didn't know the difference between lies and expediency. Mystery was expedient in the autumn of the Ripper, but now, in 1910, with his reputation under threat, he considered that sufficient autumns had gone by for the regurgitation of some truth. Blaming the uniforms, and still camouflaging Warren, he wrote: 'The exact words of the "mural inscription" *which the murderer chalked upon the wall*, were the Jews were not the men to be blamed for nothing' (my emphasis).[51]

Anderson's anti-Semitism is responsible for the mis-spelling of 'Juwes', but he is unequivocal that it was the Ripper who wrote the message. Stand by for the 'mystery' paramedics, eager to explain Anderson's statement away. Ripperologists Mr Melvin Harris and Mr Philip Sugden work themselves into rather a froth over it, and would have us believe that when Anderson says 'the "mural inscription" which the murderer chalked upon the wall', he actually means that he didn't chalk it, and that virtually every Victorian newspaper, plus the Commissioner of Police for the City of London, his detectives, and Assistant Commissioner of Metropolitan Police Robert Anderson himself, are mistaken. To qualify this adventure in casuistry, Mr Sugden seeks out minor inconsistencies in Anderson's recollections, and elevates them into 'glaring errors'.[52] These 'glaring errors' are then attached to the writing on the wall, and the confection assaulted as a package. Disqualification of trivialities apparently brings entitlement to repudiate the whole. Reminiscent of Chapman's farthings (to be considered in due course), such argument is of little merit. What Anderson is doing is confirming the established conviction of Detective Halse, Inspector McWilliam and Commissioner Smith. Were all of them similarly out to lunch? Mr Sugden's attempts to dismiss Anderson climax in one of the most extraordinary concoctions concerning 'prejudice' that I've ever read.

Because I – and everybody else who voiced an opinion – know perfectly bloody well that 'Yack' wrote that Masonic message on the wall, we are comically dismissed as 'Anderson partisans'. Sugden can't attack the evidence, so he attacks the person reading it. 'The committed Anderson partisan,' he heaves, 'may not be willing to internalise the implications of this or indeed any evidence that runs counter to his prejudice, but it is important, nevertheless, to set it down and source it here so that rational and fair-minded students may draw their own conclusions.'

'*Source it here*'? This isn't a source, it's Sugden's *opinion*. The *source* is Sir Robert Anderson, not an apologist in 1994 who disagrees. What in Christ's name is going on here? Why is it that every time there might be some light cast upon the 'mystery' it is stamped on, navigated, dismissed and feebly argued away?

The question, of course, is rhetorical.

The 'fair-minded students' Mr Sugden favours – like the 'respectable historians' of Bro Hamill – may well be willing to indulge this fanciful sophistry dismissing Anderson, but they cannot so easily dismiss a contemporary and rather more impartial source supporting him. This man wasn't a 'student' at all, but a senior detective at Scotland Yard by the name of Chief Inspector Henry Moore, a policeman who, like Anderson, was not kept short of inside news on the Ripper. Moore's statement corroborating Anderson is very relevant, because it precedes Anderson by a dozen years, and was kept secret for a further ninety.

I don't want to get into the Ripper correspondence quite yet, but in 1896, right out of the blue, Scotland Yard received another letter signed 'Jack the Ripper'. Whether it was genuine or not is immaterial to the question in hand, although the passage of time should not automatically condemn it as a hoax. A century later, the American serial killer Dennis Rader would wait almost twenty years before recommencing his taunting letters to the Kansas police.

Scotland Yard supposed it was a hoax. 'Considering the lapse of time,' wrote Chief Inspector Moore after careful comparison with previous correspondence, 'it would be interesting to know how the present writer was able to use the words – "The Jews are people that are blamed for nothing" – as it will be remembered that they are practically the same words that were written in chalk, undoubtedly by the murderer, on the wall at Goulston St. Whitechapel, on the night of September 30th 1888, after the murders of Mrs Stride and Mrs Eddowes.'[53]

'Undoubtedly [written] by the murderer', says Moore. Are those who disagree with Sugden now 'Inspector Moore partisans'? It must be remembered that Moore's statement was not for public consumption. He had no reason to dissemble: his report was to remain internal to Scotland Yard.

So, we have two very senior policemen of one point of view, and Bro McLeod, Mr Sugden and another Ripperologist called Harris of another. We also have the entire known opinion of the City Police, shared by an overwhelming majority of the contemporary press. Mr Sugden may care to review what he means by 'prejudice', and what reason his active imagination can divine for Inspector Moore making his statement up.

Earlier in this narrative I wrote that I didn't sit down wondering how I could have a go at Freemasonry. The same must be said for Ripperology. I had no idea the 'mystery' would be cowering behind two shields. Let me try to demonstrate the point. Sir Charles Warren, who had more to conceal than most, called the inestimably important writing on the wall at Goulston Street 'the writing on the wall at Goulston Street'. Every eye that looked upon it, every newspaper, whether friend or foe of the police, called it 'the writing on the wall at Goulston Street'. Ripperology calls it 'the Goulston Street graffito'. My question is, from whence comes this fanciful vocabulary? What is the point of amending what the Victorian police themselves called 'the writing on the wall' to rewrite it as scribble?

'Graffito' is a word that manipulates thinking. In contemporary use, 'graffito' is a pejorative loaded with connotation, like its plural form 'graffiti' – the trivial and worthless scribbling of louts. Such negative association is not useful when considering the writing on the wall at Goulston Street.

'Graffito', 'canonical', 'marginalia' – they are all prescriptions of Ripperology, all nonsense, and nothing whatever to do with Jack the Ripper. 'Canonical' means 'generally accepted', and is used to mean five victims, confining Jack's outrages to the East End of London. But who says he only murdered five, and who says they were restricted to the East End? Well, none other than that fount of dispassionate accuracy Sir Melville Macnaghten, for one. And Sir Melville and his associates had a harsh agenda, and much reason for isolating the Ripper show to a quintet of unfortunates in Whitechapel.[54]

The problem with this valueless lexicography – 'canonical' and its like – is that although meaningless, it is cute; it sounds as if it means something, and its nuisance is absorbed into a constricting vernacular. 'Marginalia' invests a note in the margin of Anderson's highly suspect autobiography (published in 1910) with more significance than the writing on a wall in Whitechapel (1888) that unequivocally was written by the murderer.

This message, for that's what it was, was – outside of Mary Jane Kelly and Johnnie Gill – probably the most meaningful piece of evidence the Ripper ever left. But because it doesn't conjugate with the questionable requirements of Ripperology, it's reduced to a bit of scrawl called 'graffito', and the enthusiasts fall for it, hook, line and Sugden.

With one or two notable exceptions (and they know who they are), I'm reticent about having Ripperology accompany me further into this enquiry, and look forward to being free of it once I move beyond the 'canonical' murders. I tire of its blindness, constipated thinking and phoney academia. I tire of its 'shameless manipulation'. Ripperology is like a gang of shagged-out seagulls in the wake of a phantom steamer. From time to time something might come over the side: 'Quick, boys! Dive! Dive! It might be a "marginalia", or even another Jew!' Squabbling and counter-squabbling ensue, squawking from those known for it, parsimonious smiles from those who know better, and the HMS *Canonical* ploughs on.

Meanwhile, in respect of Mr Sugden's invitation to 'source it here', he writes, 'fair-minded students may draw their own conclusions'. Well, I'm not a 'student', but here are mine. My conclusions are that Scotland Yard under Bro Sir Charles Warren was corrupt from its back door to the front, and, as the *Star* put it, 'rotten to the core'. That message on the wall is truly the $E=MC^2$ of Jack the Ripper. It's the paradox explaining why he was never caught, and why he so easily could have been. That he had the balls to write it, and then to mock it with the apron, is indicative of how he understood his own immunity.

No serial killer worth the name is going to leave homicidal garbage lying around a crime scene as Jack the Ripper did. He was tossing Freemasonry about like confetti. The whole mechanic of this got-up 'mystery' reeks of amateur dramatics, and that's precisely what it was: stage-managed theatricals construed as a 'lark' in the capsized psyche of a very unusual gentleman indeed. The Ripper was a 'recreational' killer in the literal sense of the word: a totally sane, highly intelligent psychopath whose sense of fun animated in some esoteric area of his thinking where humour and homicide collide.

The very *obviousness* of who they were looking for prevented the police from looking. The Machine had seized. It was moribund, paralysed with anxiety. To quote the brilliant journalist Simon Jenkins, 'the cynic's maxim that every organisation ends up being run by agents of its enemy' couldn't be more apposite. In respect of this terrible murderer, London now had no police force. It was in the hands of its enemy. The more outrageous he was, the more the police must cover him up. They were like Christians charged with preserving the anonymity of a Judas in their midst.

The dynamic of Warren's dilemma was soon to overwhelm him, and would palpably threaten the System itself. 'The question now turns on a matter of policy, as if fresh murders were committed the public at large might make such an outcry that it might affect the stability of the government,' were Warren's own words in his statement of 6 October 1888. He was echoing an editorial in the *Star* of a few days before, warning of the 'urgent need to bring light to Whitechapel before the district gave birth to a revolution that would "Smash the Empire", bringing about a republican regime'. Unknown to the public, the obverse of this argument (actually catching the murderer) was just as dangerous. Jack had something in common with the System, and the System had something in common with Jack. Both he and the Commissioner of the Metropolitan Police had sworn the same Masonic oath:

> The point of a pair of compasses is placed upon his left naked breast, and he himself holds it with his left hand, his right being laid upon the Gospel opened at Saint John.
>
> 'I [Charles Warren] of my own free will and accord, I promise before the Great Architect of the Universe and this right Worshipful Lodge, dedicated to St John, do hereby and herein most solemnly swear that I will always hale, conceal, and never reveal any of the secrets or mysteries of Freemasonry that shall be delivered to me now, or at any time hereafter, except it be to a true and lawful Brother, or in a just and lawful Lodge of Brothers and Fellows, him or them whom I shall find to be such, after just Trial and due Examination. I furthermore do swear that I will not write it, print it, cut it, paint it, stint it, mark it, stain and engrave it [and presumably photograph it] or cause it to be done, upon anything movable or immovable, under canopy of Heaven, whereby it may become *legible or intelligible* [my emphasis] or the least appearance of the character of a letter, whereby the secret Art may be unlawfully obtained. All this I swear [under the usual penalties of t.c.a. etc.] with a strong and steady resolution to perform the same without hesitation, mental reservation, or self evasion of mind in any way whatsoever.'[55]

In other words, wash off the wall. 'A Royal Arch Mason,' wrote Avery Allyn in 1831, 'would have felt consciously bound to conceal; having taken an oath, under penalty of death, to conceal the secrets of a Companion Royal Arch Mason, murder and treason not excepted.'

Welcome to the 'Funny Little Game'.

Mirth was what the Ripper was about. He liked jokes and anagrams and juvenile riddles, he loved the profanity and blasphemy of it all. Part of his thinking was like that of a vicious schoolboy mocking the grown-ups; and the greater society's affront, the greater his merriment. Solemn oaths sworn by the grown-ups were an amusement to the Ripper, like a fart in church. 'The Gospel of St John is especially important to Freemasons,' wrote the prolific early-nineteenth-century scholar of Freemasonry, the Reverend George Oliver, 'because it contains the fundamental principles of the order of which he was Grand Master and patron saint. And every Brother ought always to remember that he had laid his hand on that Gospel, and is thence bound never to withdraw his love from his Masonic Brothers and fellows, in compliance with the doctrines contained in that sacred book.'[56]

Bollocks. Ha ha.

Every outrage dragged Warren further out of his depth, and by implication the System of which he was a totem. The following, published in 1875, expresses a somewhat contradictory point of view to the Reverend Oliver's:

> Can you trust the fortunes of your country and the safety of your family to men, however honourable and high-minded they may be, who have committed themselves to the guidance of an authority unknown to themselves, who are confederated under the most fearful sanctions of a secret oath, and who are compelled to an inexorable silence, even though tenets should be revealed and orders transmitted from which their innermost soul recoils with unutterable loathing? Sick at heart, driven half-mad at the revelation of the hideous secret, they dare not go back; and oppressed with a deadening despair, they are forced to connive at deeds which they utterly abhor.

Although this sounds a bit like the penalties for the Victorian masturbator, I think it is a generally accurate representation of what was going on inside Warren's head. I think he was driven 'half mad', as well as driven from office, by Bro Jack the Ripper. The Masonic oath may now mean nothing more than an allegorical rendition of 'Cross my heart and hope to die,' but in the nineteenth century it ran the country. A Brother was required to keep all of a Brother's secrets, and in the case of the Royal Arch, 'murder and treason not excepted'.

By now the anger at Warren's subservience to the 'unspoken' had migrated. In both Europe and the United States the press was short on flattery. 'Great indignation,' reported the *New York Tribune*, 'had been expressed in England respecting the too apparent and official helplessness and ignorance of the elementary methods of detection … If a really clever officer was to go to work and discover the murderer, it is all but certain that he would for his pains receive a tough snub from headquarters for going outside the scope of his instructions. Herein lies the whole secret of the immunity from arrest of the Whitechapel Murderer.'[57]

It doesn't get any clearer than that. Nor, in my view, more accurate.

After Goulston Street there could be no turning back – the press would howl, for sure, but most of the public were in the dark, and the rest swallowing Fowler's Solution. Providing the nightmare could be confined to an East End slum, the executive had a shot at brazening it out. They had plenty of scapegoats and plenty of allies. They could blame the victims themselves, as both Warren and Anderson did. But also on-side was the class fascism of their time. For those who represented the debris of 'Victorian values' there were not only upmarket recommendations of genocide in the snootier London tourist guides, but useful letters like this, published in 'the world's premier newspaper', *The Times*:

Sir, – will you allow me to ask a question of your correspondents who want to disperse the vicious inhabitants of Dorset Street and Flower and Dean Street? There are no lower streets in London, and if they are driven out of these, to what streets are they to go? The horror and excitement caused by the murder of the four Whitechapel outcasts imply a universal belief that they had a right to life. If they had, then they had the further right to hire shelter from the bitterness of the English night. If they had no such right, then it was, on the whole, a good thing that they fell in with the unknown surgical genius. He at all events had made his contribution towards solving the 'problem of clearing the East End of its vicious inhabitants'. The typical 'Annie Chapman' will always find someone in London to let her have a 'doss' for a consideration. If she is systematically 'dispersed', two results will follow. She will carry her taint to streets hitherto untainted, and she herself will [illegible] in larger sums than before for the accommodation. The price of a doss will rise from 8 pence to 10 pence or a shilling, the extra pennies representing an insurance fund against prosecution and disturbance.[58]

Annie Chapman's life is valued at two pennies above the market rate, so all six victims added together to a shilling. By this computation the Ripper would have had to kill 120 women to cost a quid. This correspondent's address, 64 Eaton Place (just around the corner from Charles Warren), reveals more about him than his text. Here is a voice from one of the most salubrious areas of London; it's the voice of the class the System served to protect. The calamity of these atrocities is reduced to the impact they might have on Eaton Place and its environs, including Buckingham Palace, the Houses of Parliament and the Athenaeum. In short, these homeless scum have brought the hand of 'genius' upon themselves, and are better dead than spoiling the view around here.

Reality is turned on its head, and it is the victims who are the vicious. I think such heartlessness explains the government's shrewd assumption that, provided information could be carefully managed, the majority would buy into the 'mystery', and nobody else who mattered would give tuppence of a damn.

5

The Savages

Clench the fingers of the right hand, extend the
thumb, place it on the abdomen, and move it upwards
to the chin, as if ripping open the body with a knife.

Richardson's Monitor of Freemasonry (1860)

The 'Double Event', as the Stride/Eddowes murders were christened by their perpetrator, is not original to the 'Saucy Jacky' postcard he sent, but was a vulgar colloquialism of the age. It meant to
simultaneously suffer venereal disease of both the anus and the
genitals. Jack's choice of such a pleasantry may be trivial, but I don't
think it is. Although characteristic of a pun, I think it had a more
substantive meaning for the murderer, and I interpret the 'Double
Event' as both sobriquet and expression of disgust.[1]

The Ripper's choice of target was opportunistic, but not accidental. Self-evidently he was looking for a 'type', his selection of a victim
in life no less specific than the signature he wrote into their deaths.
This fabulously cruel man didn't rip the 'sex' out of East End whores
because he lacked the wit to kill elsewhere. He killed in Whitechapel
as part of his statement. He wanted 'sex' as low as it got. The furnace
of his rage was in his victim's womb, the 'filthiest part' of her being,
and he was disgusted with her for what his hatred would have him do.

Theories seeking to link these women to their killer (as in Clarence)
are as risible as the use Freemasonry attempts to make of them. The
victims were linked only in circumstance, and insomuch as they were
available. As far as this narrative is concerned, Catherine Eddowes'
life lasted about thirty-five minutes: from the time she left the police
lock-up to the time the Ripper killed her. Many accounts detail what's
known of her past, her lousy life and those in it, but none of that is of
much interest here. Eddowes' biography matters no more to me than

it did to the man who eviscerated her. On her drunken arrest earlier that evening she gave her name as 'Nothing', and that's just about it. She was just another bit of trash in the ugly East End rain.

A psychopath is at his most dangerous when he's having fun. Jack was having a lot of fun, playing off the angels and the ogres in his own homicidal fairy tale. Authority would feel the weight of his spite, and women the depths of his revenge. Angels don't fuck, and in the vernacular of his hatred, I believe that's how Jack saw women, as either mother-angels or whores. It's my view that he killed these women as surrogates, punishing them for the sexuality of another, and I believe one woman in particular was on his mind. She was a mother-angel who had proved herself lower than the filthiest whore. Until he got to her, and destroyed her, he owned her in Eddowes and the rest, cut out her mother-part for a trophy, like a huntsman with the head of a vanquished animal. He was 'walking with God', as the great detective Robert Ressler characterises the mindset of such a psyche, and what fault there was belonged to the victims.

'It wasn't fuckin' wrong,' claimed American serial killer Kenneth Bianchi. 'Why's it wrong to get rid of some cunts?'[2]

'Four more cunts to add to my little collection,' brags a letter signed 'Jack the Ripper' (dismissed with infantile pomp by Ripperology as a hoax).

Eddowes was a cunt, and the Ripper put his hands inside her and excoriated what he pulled out, literally *hated* her guts.

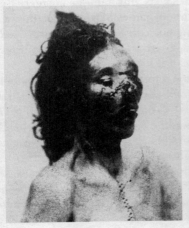

The question, then as now, is: who was he? Dozens of writers – some admirable, many not – have taken their shot. The list of candidates is phenomenal. If all the Rippers had been in the East End on the same night they'd have been elbowing into each other up the alleyways. There would have been about thirty Fiends out there at first fog. It's worth a glance at a few of the names. They were (and are) Kosminski, Ostrog, Druitt, Klosowski, Clarence, Pizer, Gull, Austin, Cutbush, Cream, Sickert, Isenchmid, and James Maybrick.

None of the above was remotely plausible as far as I was concerned. But when the name Maybrick turned up, I was interested. As I intended to set out in the Author's Note at the beginning of this book, but didn't, my curiosity about tackling a murder mystery kicked off with reading Raymond Chandler. In his memoir, published in 1962, the inimitable crime writer nominated the case of Florence Maybrick as one of classic forensic interest. Exploring it over about a dozen pages, he concludes that evidence of her guilt is cancelled out by evidence of her innocence, and that the resulting conundrum remains insoluble. What made the name Maybrick interesting to me was that it was not only already associated with an unresolved murder mystery but, many years after Chandler's death, with the mother mystery of them all.

This development, reprising the name Maybrick, came via a 'scrapbook' that emerged in Liverpool in 1992, provenance unexplained. Ludicrously misnamed as 'The Diary of Jack the Ripper',[3] it implicated James Maybrick as our famous purger. Beyond Chandler, I knew nothing about James Maybrick, or the mystery surrounding his wife either, but considering both were accused (albeit over a hundred years apart) of being famous murderers, I thought both were worth a closer look.

In 1880 James Maybrick was a forty-one-year-old Liverpool-based cotton broker who had met and wooed Florence Chandler, a seventeen-year-old Alabama beauty, on an Atlantic crossing. Their wedding the following year was the biggest mistake of her life. Eight years later, and now with two kids, Florence was about to take her seat in the front row of a nightmare.

It doesn't take long to dismiss James (or 'Jim', as he was nicknamed) as Jack. As a candidate for the Fiend, he suffers from two immediately apparent disqualifications. Firstly, in May 1889 he was supposed to have been murdered by Florence, who in gaslit tradition poisoned him with arsenic soaked out of flypapers. A bowl of such liquid was discovered at their Liverpool residence, and bingo – the System that framed her had both evidence and motive. Florence (who was having an affair with a younger man) was accused of disposing of her much older husband with periodic doses of her lethal soup. The problem with this scenario is that James Maybrick was a lifelong arsenic addict, or as Raymond Chandler put it, 'Why Doesn't an Arsenic Eater Know When He's Eating Arsenic?' If Florence had been attempting to cull him with his favourite hit, he'd have sought out her stash, quaffed the lot, and probably asked for more. The second and insurmountable problem for the fans of James is self-evident. Jack the Ripper was in the business of murdering women, not being murdered by one of them – particularly not by Florence, who in the scrapbook is apparently the focus of his homicidal rage.

Anyone who thinks this fifty-one-year-old arsenic-head was going to sprawl on his deathbed while some scatterbrained girl murders him with his drug of choice might not be best qualified to examine the complexities of the so-called 'Maybrick Mystery'. But 'the Liverpool Document' suggests just that. Its misleading christening by excited publishers as a 'diary' is something I don't want to get into.

As a matter of fact, I don't want to get into this document at all. Argument and counter-argument as to its authenticity is entirely counterproductive. Apparently various scientists, graphologists, ionising-ink experts, ultraviolet paper buffs, and even a clairvoyant have examined it. One proves it's genuine, another proves it isn't, and they're all wasting their time. Personally, I couldn't give a toss whether it's real, fake, or written in Sanskrit. This document and its association with the word 'mystery' means you've got to junk all the crap and start thinking sideways. There's an ancient Chinese adage: 'When a finger points at the moon, the imbecile looks at the finger.' Not that I'm accusing devotees of James Maybrick of imbecility, simply that they're up the right arsehole on the wrong elephant.

Only two things about this document are of any interest to me: 1) The name Maybrick (which the text doesn't actually mention); and 2) Its potent association with Freemasonry (which the text doesn't mention either).

James Maybrick's Freemasonry has been guarded as a precious ingredient of the 'mystery' for about 130 years, and as far as I'm aware is here made public for the first time. In a later chapter it will become clear why such effort has been lavished on keeping it a secret, and when you know it, you understand why.

James was a prominent Liverpool businessman, a provincial Mason of zeal and eminence, 'initiated into the mysteries and privileges of Freemasonry' on 28 September 1870, although he was clearly unaware of what kind of 'mystery' he was going to get. He remained an enthusiastic Freemason until the day of his murder in Liverpool in May 1889.[4]

It was almost certainly James who introduced his younger and equally zealous Freemasonic brother Michael to the Craft. He was initiated into the Athenaeum Lodge (1491), London, on 3 May 1876, at the age of thirty-five. Michael was a successful singer, songwriter and composer, a rising star heading for the glittering pinna-

minute examination of the body [Eddowes], Dr Gordon Brown
taking a pencil sketch of the exact position in which it was found.
This he most kindly showed to the representative of Lloyd's when subsequently explaining the frightful injuries inflicted upon the body of
the deceased.[8]

The emphasis is mine, banged in to demonstrate that Dr Gordon
Brown was not averse to showing confidential material to certain
friends in the press. The *Lloyd's* reporter was there with his notebook while the frightful injuries were 'explained', and equally present while the police composed their list, 'Tin Matchbox Empty' and
all. He was *the only reporter* allowed into the Golden Lane mortuary
that night, where he could have taken notes in respect of Dr Brown's
sketch, a copy of the police itinerary, or anything else from the
accommodating City Police physician. Indeed, there is first-hand
evidence that he did, that Dr Brown shared 'secrets' with this journalist – 'more than could be published', he wrote. We will come to
them by and by.

'At twenty minutes past five [a.m.],' records the *Lloyd's* reporter,
'we left the mortuary after the interview most kindly accorded by Dr
Gordon Brown.'[9] The journalist who conducted this exclusive inter-
view in the presence of Eddowes' corpse and effects was Bro Thomas
Catling, Worshipful Master of the Savage Lodge, habitué of the
Savage Club, and intimate of fellow member Bro Michael Maybrick.

The 'Savage' was a bohemian hangout for writers, artists, musicians and journalists. According to an official club memoir of the
time, 'There is no place in the world, perhaps, where more amusing
copy can be picked up than is to be had for the asking at the Savage
Club.'[10] Everyone in London was talking about Jack, and it's no
stretch to imagine what an informed 'Ripper insider' might be telling his fellow members in the smoking room of the Savage – and
Catling was known for his mouth. 'Mr Catling tells us of his astounding feats in nosing out copy,' continues the memoir, 'in obtaining
the earliest information in respect of murder … For obvious reasons
many of the good things are not for publication.' This was the
currency of smoking-room gossip, 'to be had for the asking' at the
club.[11]

Thus, from Catling's notebook to a dozen eager ears (including
those, I hazard, of Michael Maybrick), the unpublishable details of

Catling

Mitre Square were told. That a Liverpool cotton broker could have known about an empty tin matchbox in London's East End is, I'm afraid, no great mystery, but is in fact rather mundane. From Bro Catling to Bro Michael, and then passed just as easily to James. He was Michael's brother, and a frequent visitor to his London residence at Regent's Park. Had either written the so-called 'Diary', the mysterious 'inside information' becomes no mystery at all.

Does that not blow a rather sizeable hole in Harris's misplaced certainty that prior to 1987 there is no possible way that James Maybrick could have known about the matchbox? Either one of the Brothers Maybrick could comfortably have been aware of this information ninety-nine years before Mr Rumbelow rediscovered it. *Ergo,* the Liverpool 'scrapbook' purporting to have been written by Jack the Ripper can easily be associated with the name Maybrick, via Bro Thomas Catling.

Too abstruse for the Harris school? All right, let's knock Catling out of the equation and go directly to the source. I refer to none other than the man up to his elbows in Catherine Eddowes' guts, forty-five-year-old surgeon to the City Police and fellow of the 'Mystic Tie' since 1868, Bro Dr Frederick Gordon Brown.

Brown, with his gregarious tongue, would have been even more worth listening to than Catling – presupposing you had a particular interest in the case, and were inclined to ask. Like Catling, Dr Brown was a regular on the Maybrick circuit, sharing more than one enclave of rendezvous. He was a member of both the Savage Club and the Savage Club Lodge (2190), a pal of top London nobs and a familiar figure on the social scene.[12]

According to the weekly *The Freemason*, under the heading 'Grand Lodge Representatives' we learn that 'To represent another Grand Body near one's own is considered a very high honour.' Bro Dr Gordon Brown and Bro Michael Maybrick did precisely that at a Grand Soirée at the Holborn Restaurant, a favoured haunt of members of Orpheus Lodge. Maybrick was co-founder of Orpheus Lodge and Chapter (1706), which later in this book will get a chapter of its own. On the night in question, Saturday, 26 October 1889, 'Grand Lodge was represented by Bros Edwin Lott P.G.O., Doctor Gordon Brown G.S. and Michael Maybrick P.M.'

When the speeches started, it is recorded that 'In responding for the Grand Lodge Officers, Bro Maybrick remarked that the position he held as G.Org. [Grand Organist] reflected honour upon the Lodge, because he believed he owed his office to the fact of his being Past Master of the Lodge.' Bro Dr Gordon Brown 'made effective replies for the visitors who were strong in force'. 'The commendably short speeches,' continues *The Freemason*, 'were interrupted with music. Bro Maybrick sang the solos of the National Anthem.'[13]

Though the events of the evening took place in 1889, there is abundant evidence that Dr Brown and Michael Maybrick were well known to each other a good time before that. The initials 'GS' after Brown's name stand for Grand Steward. He was first elected in this capacity of service to Grand Lodge in 1887. The following year he took a breather, becoming PGS (Past Grand Steward), and we find him as such together with GO Michael Maybrick at a Grand Lodge celebration in that same year, its ensuing banquet presided over by none other than 'I thought they were girls' the Earl of Euston. 'A beautiful vocal and instrumental concert was given under the direction of Bro Sir Arthur Sullivan,' one of Maybrick's close melodious pals.

The Lord Mayor of London, Bro Sir Polydore de Keyser, was a prominent member of the exalted who were present. Among the newly elected Senior Grand Deacons was Bro Edmund Ashworth, a fellow member of James Maybrick's St George's Lodge of Harmony at Liverpool. Bro the Earl of Lathom was in the chair, supported by Bro Hugh Sandeman, thirty-third degree, Past Grand District Master of Bengal and member of Michael Maybrick's St George's Chapter (42), London.

The 'Mystic Tie' could not be more in evidence, and it returns us briefly to the Liverpool of James Maybrick. 'It is a truism,' announced *The Freemason* of 20 October 1888, 'to say that West Lancashire (wherein is Liverpool) is one of the strongholds of Freemasonry in this country.' A Past Master and very present member of James Maybrick's St George's Lodge of Harmony was Colonel Le Grande Starkie, an enormously wealthy landowner with 12,000 acres of Lancashire to prove it. Another member was Lord Skelmersdale, a.k.a. the above-mentioned Earl of Lathom, who like Starkie had a few fields out of town. Lathom was old money and a lot of it, and, second only to the Prince of Wales himself, the most important Freemason in England. At his seat at Ormskirk in 1888 he threw a week of parties celebrating a visit to the province by the Prime Minister Lord Salisbury and his wife, but under less festive circumstances his duties were usually confined to London.

Earl Lathom was Lord Chamberlain to Her Majesty the Queen, entrusted with the 'well being of her swans' and, on a more prosaic level, vetting guest lists for the Palace *soirées*. To this end he wore an enormous symbolic ceremonial key, a reminder that 'everyone the Queen receives must wear the white flower of a blameless life' – which makes one wonder how half her relatives got in. The picture opposite shows him in business at the Palace (he's the man in tights with the long beard), standing next to Edward's wife, the Princess of Wales, who was herself standing in for Queen Victoria. The Prince himself is to the right, under the chandelier, and to his right is the bald bulk of Prime Minister Lord Salisbury.

Concurrent with the ceremonial key and the organisation of the Masonic affairs of Lancashire, the Earl, among a select few, was also a member of a London Obligation, once again named in honour of St George. This was St George's Chapter (42), a confluence of well-heeled members of the Masonic hierarchy wherein we discover fellow member Bro Michael Maybrick. Thus, with membership of (32) in Liverpool and (42) in London, Lord Chamberlain to the

THE DRAWING-ROOM HELD BY H.R.H. THE PRINCESS OF WALES ON BEHALF OF THE QUEEN AT BUCKINGHAM PALACE, April 23, 1896.

Queen Bro the Earl of Lathom forms a distinctive link between the Masonic activities of Bros Michael and James Maybrick.

But you would never know it, unless you were prepared for a very protracted search indeed. As far as the records at Freemasons' Hall in London are concerned, James Maybrick wasn't even a Freemason. As will become clear, he has been quite spirited away. This presents a dilemma for the researcher, to which we can add the elusiveness of Chapter (42). Like Lord Euston's exclusive 'Encampment of the Cross of Christ', of which Michael was also a member, (42) is not to be found on Michael Maybrick's c.v. Indeed, there is a palpable absent-mindedness surrounding it.

Meanwhile, on 23 April 1888, St George's Chapter (42) presented an MWS Jewel (Most Wise Sovereign of a Rose Croix Chapter) to Bro Michael Maybrick 'for services rendered during the past year'.[14] His award was conferred by a galaxy of eminence, representing some of the most distinguished names in English Masonry. Only one need detain us.

Colonel Thomas Henry Shadwell Clerke, author of the quote at the beginning of Chapter 3, Grand Secretary of English Freemasons and liaison officer between Masonry and the Prince of Wales, was a close personal friend of Michael Maybrick.[15] Whenever Edward failed to show, which was just about always, it was Shadwell Clerke who made the apologies. 'As regards H.R.H.,' he was oft to say, 'the brethren must not fancy, because they do not see him at their meetings, that he is neglectful of the Craft.' He (Clerke) could assure them from personal knowledge that HRH 'took the greatest interest in all that concerned Masonry'. When their MWGM (Most Worshipful Grand Master) was in London, he (Clerke) 'was in constant attendance at Marlborough House, for all matters of importance were submitted to H.R.H.'. And further, if they couldn't have the fat man, 'The names of Lord Carnarvon and Lathom were well known, for these two Brethren exercised a watchful care over all that affected Freemasonry.'

In the matter of James Maybrick, more watchful eyes could hardly be imagined. But back to Bro Michael, who was no less eminent a Mason than Lathom and Clerke, serving, as they did, as an Officer of the Grand Lodge, a body constituting the zenith of Freemasonic authority in the land.

246

SUPREME GRAND CHAPTER OF ROYAL ARCH MASONS.

OFFICERS FOR THE YEAR 1891-92.

His Royal Highness The Prince of Wales, K.G.	Grand Z.*
The Right Hon. The Earl of Lathom	Pro Grand Z.*
The Right Hon. The Earl of Mount Edgcumbe	Grand H.*
The Right Hon. The Lord Leigh	Grand J.
Colonel Shadwell H. Clerke	Grand Scribe E.*
Sir John Braddick Monckton	Grand Scribe N.
Robert Grey	Pres. of Com. of Gen. Pur.
George Everett	Grand Treasurer.*
Frederick Adolphus Philbrick, Q.C.	Grand Registrar.*
Rev. Oliver James Grace	Prin. Grand Sojr.
John Aird, M.P.	1st Assist. Grand Sojr.
Hamon Le Strange	2nd Assist. Grand Sojr.
Edmond Kelly Bayley	Grand Sword Bearer.
Arthur J. R. Trendell, C.M.G.	1st G. Standard Bearer.
Thomas Hastings Miller	2nd G. Standard Bearer.
Richard Clowes	3rd G. Standard Bearer.
George J. McKay	4th G. Standard Bearer.
Frank Richardson (P. Assist. G. Sojr.)	Grand Dir. of Cers.
George Henri Bué	Dep. Grand Dir. of Cers.
Walter Hopekirk	1st Assist. G. Dir. of Cers.
Thomas Webb Whitmarsh	2nd Assist. G. Dir. of Cers.
Michael Maybrick	Grand Organist.
Alfred Albert Pendlebury	Assist. Grand Scribe E.
Henry Sadler	Grand Janitor.

I put Michael Maybrick into the picture not with the intention of impugning anyone around him, but to demonstrate just how much a part of the picture he was. Maybrick was no less a public celebrity than he was (in occult places) a celebrated Freemason, both facts that put him inside the inner social circles of London's greatest past-master of decadence, Edward, Prince of Wales.

Nothing encapsulates this more succinctly than his membership of the Savage. Maybrick joined on 5 July 1880, preceding His Royal Highness's initiation by a couple of years. By the time Maybrick walked through its portals at 6–7 Adelphi Terrace, the club had elevated itself into something of significance, opening its doors to 'practitioners of every branch of science, including the law, with the result that Music Hall Stars, political cartoonists and actor-managers rubbed shoulders with distinguished lawyers such as Bro Lord Justice Moulton, Bro Sir Richard Webster, Bro Sir Edward Clerke Q.C.' and many more who have made or will make themselves known to this narrative.

The most illustrious of them all, Edward, Prince of Wales, was invited to become a lifetime honorary member on the occasion of the club's twenty-fifth anniversary, in April 1882. He was further invited to nominate one or two pals as special guests, and selected a duo who wouldn't have spoiled Michael Maybrick's evening, because, at the risk of labouring it, Sir Arthur Sullivan and Sir Frederick Leighton were special friends of his too.

It's perhaps worth pointing out that, just as Michael Maybrick was one of Sullivan's closest friends, so too was Sir Charles Russell QC MP, making subsequent events at the High Court in Liverpool more than somewhat mind-blowing. (It was Russell who was to 'defend' Florence Maybrick against the charge of murdering her husband James.)

But I've run out of detour, and return to the Savage and its special gala night. It was what the Victorians liked to describe as 'a singular occasion', with actors, musicians, singers and wits all eager to do their dazzling thing. Among them was Wilhelm Ganz, a leading light in Masonic and musical circles, and long a friend of Michael Maybrick. By coincidence, Ganz lived a few doors down from Sir Charles Russell in Harley Street.

'The entertainment which followed the annual dinner, was simi-lar to that which occurs every Saturday evening,' wrote the man

THE PRINCE OF WALES AT THE SAVAGE CLUB.

from the *Illustrated London News*, 'and Mr Harry Furniss has happily depicted the best points of it in our engraving.'

Michael Maybrick is represented at the piano (middle row, second from right). His performance that evening was preceded by Mr George Grossmith's rendition of 'Itinerant Niggers', the fun of which must have contrasted agreeably with the pathos of Maybrick's 'The Midshipmite', his hit song from 1879.

Leighton, Sullivan, Russell and Maybrick were fellow Savages and fellow Masons. They were among the men 'in the know', as Rudyard Kipling put it, who between politics and Freemasonry and the law knew just about everything there was to know. Like His Royal Highness's plenipotentiary Bro Sir Francis Knollys, 'who saw everything, heard everything, and was consulted about everything for forty-two years', and who, above all, 'knew how to be silent', so did this confederacy of savages.[16]

In 1888 the Worshipful Master of the Savage Lodge was J. Somers Vine MP, installed in February of that year at Freemasons' Hall by Maybrick's fraternal pal Bro Colonel Thomas Shadwell Clerke, in the presence of a distinguished assembly that included the Earl of

Lathom. Almost exactly a year later the proceedings were replicated for the incoming Worshipful Master, Bro Thomas Catling. On the grand night of installation, Catling put all propriety aside and rose amidst the toasts to propose 'the election of an honorary member of the Savage Club Lodge, the Right Worshipful H.R.H., Prince Albert Victor, the Duke of Clarence'.

Clarence's membership was unanimously approved and applauded, but not every member had been able to attend. The future Commander of Her Majesty's Army, Bro Lord Wolseley, regretted that the pressure of official duties precluded his presence, a sentiment echoed by the Lord Chancellor, Bro Lord Halsbury. Further apologies were received from a Brother who wrote that he 'had been looking forward with great pleasure to the evening's entertainment, but was prevented by sudden indisposition', leaving one wondering just what Police Commissioner Sir Charles Warren was busy with.[17]

With Thomas Catling and Dr Gordon Brown (and possibly even Sir Charles Warren) as fraternal associates of Michael Maybrick, both (short of murdering her themselves) were as intimate as it got to the slaying of Catherine Eddowes. It becomes incredible to claim their supposed first publication in 1987 as a disqualification for the authenticity of the words 'Damn it, the tin box was empty' in the Liverpool Document.

It was in the course of my research into Michael Maybrick that I discovered that his brother James was a Freemason. This wasn't without interest, because I was certain Michael had murdered James, and framed James's wife Florence for the deed. I was also certain that the flagrancy of the Masonic 'clues' decorating the crime scenes in Whitechapel was grist to the enterprise, as indeed was his so-called 'diary'. In other words, they were the work of a crazy Mason, or someone trying to blame one. It wasn't just Florence who was to be framed. It was also Brother Jim. James was not only married to an American, but had spent years living in the United States. Hence the 'Americanisms' in the Ripper correspondence (of which more later). The clues Jack left were the servants of a unique criminal, and presented an intriguing scenario.

But with James Maybrick in ceremonial apron, the jigsaw began to shape up. The Ripper was flaunting Freemasonry, and James was

a murdered Freemason whose Masonry was suppressed by
Freemasons. You don't have to be Sherlock Holmes to find something of interest in that. As has been mentioned, James has been
considered by some as a Ripper candidate. Mr Paul Feldman wrote
a sizeable book about just such a possibility,[18] as did Mrs Shirley
Harrison. Between them these two authors share perhaps a decade
of research, yet neither of them, and subsequently no one plaguing
the internet for twenty years after, has ever discovered James
Maybrick's 'Masonic secret'.[19]

The obvious question is, why not? The equally obvious answer is
that certain parties had gone to quite astonishing lengths to cover
it up. In fact, as much effort has gone into exorcising James
Maybrick's Masonic career as has been applied to camouflaging the
Ripper's Masonic pantomime in the East End. They are opposite
ends of the same stick, each lopped off for precisely the same
reason. Jack's Masonic contribution was expunged by the police as
they pretended to investigate his crimes, while James's Masonic
secret was posthumously imposed by Freemasons themselves.

As far as publicly available records are concerned, James Maybrick
was not a Freemason. Freemasons' Hall in London had never heard
of him. 'Further to your enquiry we have checked our records for
the above name without success,' was their honest response – honest
because he'd been cleaned out a very long time ago. Such frustrations were ignored as I looked for another source, my researcher
Keith later mining a basement at a Liverpool library where we finally
got lucky. I now had an abundance of proof that the poor murdered
bastard was a Bro. Intense enquiry at last resulted in a letter from
Supreme Council (Royal Arch), together with a document. It
purports to suggest that James was indeed a Freemason, but only
briefly, between perfection (i.e. induction) on 24 January 1873 and
resignation in 1874.

Although it looks the part – i.e. it is Victorian – it took only
seconds to realise that this document was decidedly iffy. It's titled
'Return of Members of the *** *** *** Liverpool Chapter ***
Liverpool'.

Liverpool Chapter by the name and number of what? (Apparently
by the name and number of ****.) By now I knew rather a lot about
my subject, was familiar in fact with most of the long-forgotten
names that appeared with James on the Chapter's members' list.

Like him, many were cotton brokers, and one or two instantly stood out. Horace Seymour Alpass, by way of example, was listed as 'mort' (dead) in 1881, when in reality he was very much alive, expiring, according to his death certificate, on 31 August 1884. By contrast, James Gaskell, soundly dead on 26 April 1868, is here listed as paying his Masonic dues in November 1873. James Maybrick's 'resignation' is equally problematic. Reliance on this document would give the impression that he quit Masonry in 1874, when in fact at that date his Masonic career was poised to flourish.

Meanwhile, a fascinating paradox has presented itself. We now consider two candidates who were Freemasons – a half-witted homosexual son of the heir to the throne of England, and an arsenic-eating middle-aged cotton broker from Liverpool. Bro Clarence and Bro James share Masonry in common, but manifest vastly different provenances. It was a distinguished Freemason, the aforementioned Bro Thomas Stowell, who brought Clarence's name into the public domain as a bogus Ripper suspect, and it was Freemasonry that since 1889 had kept James Maybrick out of it. Upon Maybrick's demise the System was panicked into believing it had urgent reason for denying his Masonry, and simultaneously silencing his wife. When the time came, the Establishment closed

Michael Maybrick

ranks, abandoning James like a man with plague, denying his Masonry even if it meant hanging an innocent woman. The Crown got up phoney charges against Florence, and in a 'trial' as filthy and corrupt as any on God's earth, consigned her to life imprisonment. This is known as 'the Maybrick Mystery', an adjunct of mind-boggling wickedness sharing its taproot with 'the Mystery of Jack the Ripper'.

Both 'mysteries' were fabricated to protect the ruling elite, and Bro Michael Maybrick was the nucleus of both.

6

On the Square

Make the Moor thank me, love me, and reward me for
making him egregiously an ass.

Iago

Complementing 'Juwes', there was another funny little Masonic jest
for Charlie Warren about a mile away from Goulston Street. When
Catherine Eddowes was released from her lock-up at Bishopsgate
police station, she asked the duty officer what time it was. Just before
one o'clock, he replied – 'Too late for you to get another drink.'
Somewhat the worse for wear, she vanished out of the police station
with the stated intention of going home.

Eddowes lived at number 6 Fashion Street, an inappropriately
named Whitechapel slum directly east of Bishopsgate.[1]

By any assessment, the place of her death was not on her way home. Around some corner the most dangerous man in London was looking for just such a sweetheart, and in his company Eddowes walked away from Fashion Street and directly south. At any turn in this gloomy labyrinth he could have chosen to kill her. Instead he escorted her to a location of gaslight and multiple windows in which, if anything, he was actually more exposed.

In my view, her assassin took her to Mitre Square 'by design', as a requisite of his 'Funny Little Game'. Cutting compasses into her face up some anonymous back alley would not have conjured the symbolism he was after. What Jack wanted to leave as 'his fearful sign manual'[2] was the ubiquitous and most recognisable Masonic icon of them all, 'compasses on the square' (see opposite).

Eddowes was initiated into the 'Funny Little Game' with the full Jubelo – her throat cut across, entrails hauled out, and all metal removed. 'The intestines were drawn out to a large extent and placed over the right shoulder,' deposed Dr Gordon Brown at the inquest. 'A piece of about two feet was quite detached from the body and placed between the body and the left arm.'

CITY SOLICITOR: By 'placed', do you mean put there by design?
BROWN: Yes.

Yet we're enjoined to believe that the symbols carved into Eddowes' face are a meaningless afterthought. That you can 'design' with flopping intestines, but not with the point of a knife. That you can carry a piece of this woman's apron as a beacon for a message, and then write something above it of no discernible meaning or consequence, and that 'Juwes' and a Mason's Mark are indecipherable abstractions.

Two slayings that night meant two concurrent but quite separate coroners' courts. The City was an independent entity, responsible to the Corporation of London, and immune to interference from the Home Office and the Metropolitan Police. The Met couldn't manipulate and control this court as it was to manipulate and make preposterous the inquest into the death of Elizabeth Stride.

City Coroner S.F. Langham, a sixty-five-year-old blueblood behind rectitudinous pince-nez, had spent his entire professional life listening to stories of the dead. First appointed Deputy Coroner for Westminster in 1849, he moved to the City, where he was promoted to Boss Coroner in 1884. His official address was 'Coroner's Office, City Mortuary, Golden Lane',[3] and it was here on 4 October 1888 that the inquest into the murder of Catherine Eddowes began. Proceedings were watched by Inspector McWilliam and Assistant Commissioner Smith himself.

The attendance of such eminent spectators is perhaps indicative of the importance the City attached to the case, further underlined by the presence of its thirty-eight-year-old star solicitor. Henry Homewood Crawford was one of the smartest brains on the block. A polyglot, a musician and a talented amateur actor, in the words of a contemporary biography, 'He may fittingly be described as Attorney General of the City. He is legal advisor to the Right Hon the Lord Mayor, legal advisor to the Aldermen in their capacity as Justices to the City, and also to the Commissioner of Police. He is the City Public Prosecutor, and, apart from the recorder and Common Sergeant, is necessarily the active legal luminary in the Corporation.'[4] In short, 'the active legal luminary' was no dope. Co-author of *A Statement of the Origin, Constitution, Powers and Privileges of the Corporation of London*, he knew his City business, and was one day to become its Lord Mayor. Although he began by seeking Langham's consent to ask the occasional question, Crawford ended up asking almost all of them.

The proceedings at Golden Lane opened with the usual civilities, and a dispiriting traipse through those who had seen little – and most of them less than that. The coppers (and the nightwatchman) who had discovered Eddowes' still-warm body came in and read from their notebooks. The jury heard from Inspector Collard and City Architect Frederick Foster, who had made drawings of the crime scene and drawn up a plan. Without depriving the narrative of substance, all can be dispensed with until we get to the deposition of Dr Gordon Brown. Brown's contribution is replete with medical jargon, and is too long to reproduce in full here. I therefore use the version reported in *The Times*, supplementing the text from the original where necessary. 'Frederick Gordon Brown, 17 Finsbury Circus, Surgeon of City of London Police, being sworn saith':

> I was called shortly after 2 o'clock. I reached [the Square] about 18 minutes past 2 my attention was called to the body of the Deceased … The body was on its back – the head turned to the left shoulder – the arms by the side of the body as if they had fallen there, both palms upwards – the fingers slightly bent, a thimble was lying off the finger on the right side. The clothes were drawn up above the abdomen, the thighs were naked, left leg extended in line with the body. There was great disfigurement of the face. The throat was cut across

to the extent of 6 or 7 inches. The abdomen was all exposed. The intestines were drawn out to a large extent and placed over the right shoulder – they were smeared with some feculent matter. A piece of about two feet was quite detached from the body and placed between the body and the left arm, apparently by design.

Crawford's question *vis à vis* 'design' has been quoted on a previous page. Dr Brown's statement continued: '… The lobe *and auricle of the right ear* [my emphasis] were cut obliquely through; there was a quantity of clotted blood on the pavement, on the left side of the neck and upper part of the arm … The body was quite warm (no rigor mortis) and had only been there for a few minutes.' 'Before they removed the body', he 'suggested that Dr Phillips should be sent for, and that gentleman, who had seen some recent cases, came to the mortuary … Several buttons were found in the clotted blood after the body was removed … There was no blood on the front of the clothes. There were no traces of recent connection [i.e. no sponk]. When the body arrived at Golden Lane the clothes were taken off carefully from the body, a piece of the deceased's ear dropped from the clothing.'[5]

This will prove of significance. Dr Brown had noticed at the crime scene that 'the lobe and auricle of the right ear were cut obliquely through' (i.e. the whole ear), but only a part of the ear, the lobe, was discovered on arrival at the mortuary. Where the auricle went, whether it was retrieved or had been taken away by the murderer, is not disclosed.

Brown then goes on to describe a truly astonishing catalogue of injuries. The assassin had ripped through Eddowes as if he was on his way to somewhere else: 'The womb was cut through horizontally leaving a stump 3/4 of an inch, the rest of the womb had been taken away with some of the ligaments … the peritoneal lining [the internal surface of the abdomen] was cut through on the left side and the *left kidney taken out and removed.*' (My emphasis.)

Crawford asks if the stolen organs could be used for any professional purpose. Brown's answer was in the negative: 'I cannot assign any reason for these parts being taken away.' Crawford then asks: 'About how long do you think it would take to inflict all these wounds, and perpetrate such a deed?' The physician reckoned about five minutes, and confirmed his opinion that it was the work of one man only. He was then asked 'as a professional man' to account for the fact of no noise being heard by those in the immediate neighbourhood.

BROWN: The throat would be so instantaneously severed that I do not suppose there would be any time for the least sound being emitted.

CRAWFORD: Would you expect to find much blood on the person who inflicted the wounds?

No. He would not. But he could confirm that bloodspots on Eddowes' apron (which was produced) were recent.

Crawford asked: 'Have you formed any opinion as to the purpose for which the face was mutilated?' This is an interesting question. Crawford suggests that the face may have been mutilated for a purpose. The doctor had no opinion, thinking it was 'simply to disfigure the corpse'. He added that a sharp knife was used, 'not much force required'.

If anyone on the jury had any questions about those inverted 'V' marks on Eddowes' face, they were out of luck, because Coroner Langham here adjourned, reconvening the court one week hence.

The next few days gave Crawford time to reflect, perhaps even to dwell on the 'purpose' of the curious mutilations, and what they might mean in concert with the ritualistic mutilations of Annie Chapman. Crawford must have been as cynical as everyone else about the fabulous adventures of 'the American Womb-Collector', particularly when a doctor had just told him that the burgled organs would be useless for medical purposes.

So why would the coroner at Annie Chapman's inquest, Baxter, countenance such hogwash? Was it in any way connected with Warren's destruction of the writing on the wall? Was there some undisclosed reason for wanting it rubbed out? These were questions to ponder, albeit with answers which Crawford had already determined.

On Thursday, 11 October, *The Times* reported on the resumption of the inquest, claiming that a 'good deal of fresh evidence' was on the cards. 'Since the adjournment,' it continued, 'Shelton, the Coroner's Officer, has, with the assistance of City Police authorities, discovered several new witnesses.' These included a couple of (briefly suspected) male associates of Eddowes, and even her long-lost daughter. No one paid much attention to this crew, and neither do I. But there were some new witnesses of interest.

At about 1.30 a.m. on the night of Eddowes' murder, three gents left their club in Duke Street, and stepped out into the rain. The Imperial Club was an artisans' night out, exclusively Jewish, catering to the upper echelons of the working class. Two of the men walked slightly in advance of the third. They were Joseph Levy, a butcher, resident just south of Aldgate, and Henry Harris, a furniture dealer of Castle Street, Whitechapel.

Mr Harris wasn't called to give evidence at the inquest, because he said he saw nothing, and that his companions saw nothing either, 'just the back of the man'. But one of them clearly did see something. He was a forty-one-year-old commercial traveller in the cigarette trade, by the name of Joseph Lawende.

Lawende had already attracted press attention. On 9 October, two days before the resumption of the inquest, the *Evening News* had published a summary of what the public might expect in respect of this trio's exit from the Imperial Club: 'They noticed a couple – a man and woman – standing by the iron post of the small passage that leads to Mitre Square. They have no doubt themselves that this was the murdered woman and her murderer. And on the first blush of it the fact is borne out by the police having taken exclusive care of Mr Joseph Lawende, to a certain extent having sequestrated him and having imposed a pledge on him of secrecy. They are paying all his expenses, and 1 if not 2 detectives are taking him about.'

It's assumed by *The Jack the Ripper A to Z* that the City Police were protecting Lawende from the press. This may be so, but it's obvious that they were also protecting him from the Met. They didn't want anyone making – shall we say – unhelpful suggestions about what he may or may not have seen. This is corroborated by a Home Office minute later in the month. With quite startling hypocrisy, it states: 'The City Police are wholly at fault as regards detection of the murderer. They evidently want to tell us nothing.'[6]

If I were the City Police – most particularly over the farce at Goulston Street – I wouldn't want to tell the Home Office anything either. It's clear, in respect of wash-it-off-Warren, that the City Police were attempting to protect the integrity of their witness.

Two days later, Levy and Lawende were in court. But this time there was an adjustment in approach from the 'active legal luminary'. Crawford knew perfectly well why Warren had washed off that wall. He also knew about the article in the *Evening News*, and was about to prove it correct.

It had been pouring with rain on the night of the murders, and Joseph Levy told the court 'he thought the spot was very badly lighted', and that his 'suspicions were not aroused by the two persons': 'He noticed a man and a woman standing together at the corner of Church Passage, but he passed on without taking any further notice of them. He did not look at them. From what he saw, the man might have been three inches taller than the woman. He could not give a description of either of them … he did not take much notice.'

What are we to make of so vacuous a deposition? It was what novelists call a filthy night in a poorly lit alleyway. Levy had a brim-down glimpse of a man and a woman. 'From what he saw, the man might have been three inches taller'. Eddowes was a diminutive five feet, meaning her paramour 'might' have been five feet three inches. However, if he was a taller man, he 'might' have been leaning down to whisper sweet nothings in her ear. We cannot know, and certainly not from Levy, because 'He did not look at them.'

Peripheral estimates such as his are worthless. An on-site witness, Abraham Heshburg, who actually saw Elizabeth Stride as she lay dead at Dutfield's Yard, estimated her age as twenty-five to twenty-eight – she was forty-four, and Heshburg was about twenty years out.[7] Predicated on the enormous variations of physical description, we can assume that the Ripper was between five and six feet tall, and between thirty and fifty years old – like virtually half the male population of London. It is only when a description is *specific* that it begins to have some worth, and this perhaps explains why Levy was not under police escort.

We now come to the man who was.

JOSEPH LAWENDE 45 Norfolk Road, being sworn saith:– On the night of the 29th I was at the Imperial Club. Mr Joseph Levy and Mr Harry Harris were with me. It was raining. We left there to go out at half past one and we left the house about five minutes later. I walked a little further from the others. Standing in the corner of Church Passage in Duke Street, which leads into Mitre Square, I saw a woman. She was standing with her face towards a man. I only saw her back. She had her hand on his chest. The man was taller than she was. She had a black jacket and a black bonnet. I have seen the articles which it is stated belonged to her at the police station. My belief is they were the same clothes which I had seen upon the Deceased. She appeared to me short. The man had a cloth cap on with a cloth peak. I have given a description of the man to the police.

But he isn't giving it here, where only the man's hat is described. 'The man was taller than she was … She appeared to me short.' Did she appear short because the man was much taller than her? It's a question I would like to have asked, but Coroner Langham asked the question instead: 'Can you tell us what sort of man it was with whom she was speaking?'

Lawende had clearly been warned off, and again described the man's hat: 'He had on a cloth cap with a peak.' The jury had already heard that, and just in case anyone was looking for a little more description than a hat, Crawford interceded:

Unless the Jury wish it I have *a special reason* [my emphasis] why no further description on this man should be given now.

The City Police had been protecting Lawende, and now they shut him up. The jury 'assented to Mr Crawford's wish', although I don't imagine they realised it would be sustained for the next 130 years. Here was a witness who had information about the killer – height, age, whatever – under the 'exclusive care' of the City Police, who had imposed 'a pledge of secrecy'.

Crawford had just defended the pledge, adding veracity to the *Evening News* report. Here was a man who, at a minimum, had had a glimpse of Jack the Ripper, yet his description was suppressed, and remains a secret to this day.

Cue the fairy dust.

On page 247 of his book, Mr Philip Sugden makes a convoluted and unsuccessful effort to explain away the description Crawford wanted kept secret. He would like us to believe that it is no secret at all, but was brought into the open by the Metropolitan Police on 19 October 1888. He refers us to a description in the Met's own weekly newspaper, the *Police Gazette*. The *Gazette* was founded by Howard Vincent in 1884, and was brought into disrepute by Warren and his boys with the kind of casuistry proffered by Mr Sugden.

'Lawende saw the man too,' he writes energetically, 'but the official transcript of his inquest deposition records only that he was taller than the woman and wore a cloth cap with a cloth peak. Press versions of the testimony, however, add the detail that "the man looked rather rough and shabby", and reveal that the full description was suppressed at the request of Henry Crawford, the City Solicitor, who was attending the hearing on behalf of the [City] Police. Fortunately,' he enthuses, 'this deficiency in the record can be addressed from other sources. Lawende's description of the man was fully published in the *Police Gazette* of October 19th 1888.'[8]

To which I add the word 'Bollocks.'

Here is Mr Sugden's historic breakthrough, as published in the *Police Gazette* on 19 October 1888: '… a MAN, aged 30, height 5ft 7 or 8 in., complexion fair, moustache fair, medium build, dress, pepper and salt colour loose jacket, grey cloth cap with peak of same material, reddish neckerchief tied in a knot; appearance of a sailor'. This description of 19 October, grasped by Mr Sugden, was in fact published in *The Times* on 2 October, more than a week before Lawende gave his evidence, and more than two weeks before its appearance in the *Police Gazette*. It therefore can have *absolutely nothing whatever* to do with the description Crawford suppressed at the inquest.

This is what *The Times* printed on 2 October: '... the man was observed in a court in Duke Street, leading to Mitre Square, about 1.40 a.m. on Sunday. He is described as of shabby appearance. About 30 years of age and 5ft 9in in height, of fair complexion, having a small fair moustache, and wearing a red neckerchief and a cap with a peak.'

Apart from knocking a useful inch or two off the height and adding a bit of nautical gibberish, the *Police Gazette/Times* descriptions are as near as makes no difference, red neckerchief and all. Thus Mr Sugden's supposed revelation is no such thing, and certainly has nothing to do with the description Crawford suppressed.

I am aware of *The Times*'s description 130 years after it appeared. Are we to imagine that a man as sharp as Henry Crawford was ignorant of something published in *The Times* only nine days before? Crawford was a man of rare intellect, and it is simply ridiculous to imagine that he would try to suppress something that had recently been printed in 40,000 copies of the world's most prestigious newspaper. Crawford would have to be as foolish as Sugden to suggest it. And the *Evening News*, despite *The Times* piece a week before, was very well aware on 9 October that the City Police were keeping something secret.

Unless Mr Sugden thinks a 'pepper and salt'-coloured jacket glimpsed in darkness and rain is some kind of dramatic breakthrough, the *Police Gazette* has elucidated *absolutely nothing*. Sugden describes this grey jacket as 'a fortunate addition to the deficiency of the record'. I call it worthless twaddle. This belated confection in the *Police Gazette* doesn't explain Crawford's imposition of secrecy, and has no value. It is simply a cooked-up, out-of-date newspaper reprint, another dispatch from the Land of Make Believe. If this description had any validity to the Metropolitan Police on 2 October, why not print it in the *Police Gazette* on that day? Or the 5th? Or the 9th? Or the 12th? Or the 16th? Why wait for the issue of 19 October?

The real reason the Met regurgitated this unsourced 'description' was to coincide with an internal report Bro Inspector Donald Swanson had prepared on the same date. Destined for the Home Office, this concoction of 19 October makes reference to the man with the red neckerchief, and since they'd never bothered with him before, it would look most untoward it they didn't fabricate some interest now. Hence, seventeen days after his appearance in *The Times* 'the Seafaring Man' makes his debut in the *Police Gazette*, only to be dismissed on the very same day by Swanson himself. 'I understand from the City Police,' he wrote, 'that Mr Lewin [sic] one of the men who identified the clothes only of the murdered woman Eddowes, which is a serious drawback to the value of the description of the man' (which, incidentally, Lawende never publicly made).[9]

So despite a front page of the Met's house journal, even Swanson thinks he's got nothing on Jack, and only a description of Eddowes' clothes. Crawford would have had to have been some kind of full-blown half-wit to want to conceal that.

Bye bye, sailor.

The problem with Mr Sugden is that he is all wallpaper and no wall. I sincerely have no desire to isolate him for criticism, but at *every point of contention* he's there with his paste-pot and paper. It's so frequent (not only from him, but from Ripperology in general) that it reads like a kind of corporate hypnotism.

But this description of the man with the 'reddish' neckerchief raises some questions. To have been published on 2 October, it must have been known to *The Times* on the 1st. Where did it get the information? Harris said he saw nothing. Levy said he saw nothing either. He therefore didn't see a thirty-year-old, five-foot-nine-inch man with a fair moustache and a red neckerchief tied in a knot. Two of these three witnesses are thus dismissed as sources, and what Lawende saw was withheld ever after.

I think this nautical geezer with the red neckerchief is in the tradition of Metropolitan Police inventions (riots in Goulston Street, etc.), slipped by an unknown source to *The Times*. By this time the Met were under catastrophic pressure, and Warren was less than forty days from the exit. Swanson's 'report' from Scotland Yard was three parts panic, and the rest distortion to fit the fiction Warren was committed to tell. We will never know from whence the seafarer and his neckerchief came, any more than we can know what description Crawford suppressed.

But I don't like half-arsed 'mysteries', and though I might never be able to find out *what* Crawford withheld, I thought there was a better-than-odds-on chance of discovering *why* he withheld it. I got a red light about Crawford, and I think it was precisely the same red light he had about 'Juwes' and Jack.

If there really was a 'special reason' for stifling Lawende's description, why was it not later revealed? Was it, in the short term, an effort to keep it secret from the Met? After the shenanigans at Goulston Street, it's possible. Commissioner Smith never forgave Warren, calling his erasure of the writing on the wall 'an unpardonable error'. Maybe he was determined to keep the slippery bastard out. But I was persuaded that there was a more complex dynamic to be discovered.

Immediately following Levy/Lawende, PC Long was the next witness to be called – a patsy put up to try to divert attention from the duplicity of the men who didn't care to show themselves.

Long was the only representative of the Metropolitan Police to appear before the court. Neither Arnold nor Warren was called – the latter, according to the *Pall Mall Gazette*, because the court didn't want to hold him to contempt. But contempt over what? It wasn't yet widely known that London's Commissioner of Police had colluded to conceal the identity of London's most wanted killer. On 11 October the *Evening News* ran a report commenting on the court proceedings.

> The words 'The Jews are not the men who will be blamed for nothing,' were almost certainly written by the murderer, who left at the spot the bloody portion of the woman's apron as a sort of warranty of authenticity. On Police Constable Long's report consultation was held and the decision taken *to rub out the words* [emphasis in the original]. Detective Halse of the City Police protested. A brother officer had gone to make arrangements to have the words photographed, but the zeal of the Metropolitans could not rest. They fear a riot against the Jews and out the words must come. And the *only clue* [my emphasis] to the murderer was destroyed calmly and deliberately, on the authority of those in high places.

Attempts to navigate the Juwes/apron débâcle were still high on the agenda of Warren's hidden anti-detective work. On 3 October he had written to his City counterpart, Commissioner Colonel Sir James Frazer, attempting to solicit his blessing for a grab at the surreal. The 'riot' angle clearly lacked traction, so to accompany 'the Nautical Man' and 'the Womb-Collector' he conjured up the limpest suspect yet, 'the Goulston Street Hoaxer'.

In a rambling text, Warren asks Frazer 'If there is any proof that at the time the corpse was found the bib [sic] was found with the piece wanting that the piece was not lying about the yard [sic] at the time the corpse was found and taken to Goulston St by some of the lookers on as a hoax & that the piece found in Goulston St is without doubt, a portion of that which p'y was worn by the woman.'[10]

Never mind conflating Dutfield's Yard with Mitre Square, implicit in this letter is Warren's utter worthlessness as a common police-man, much less Commander in Chief of Scotland Yard.

Even though it was in ignorance of his letter to Frazer, the *Evening News* agreed. 'We cannot blame the inferior police,' it wrote (refer-encing one such constable, who now stood in front of Crawford), 'but the public have a right to know who gave the order to efface the murderer's traces. His proper place is not in the Criminal Enquiry department.'[11]

It was within Coroner Langham's powers to insist that both Warren and Dr Phillips attend his court, but he didn't insist, and they didn't attend, although Phillips was actually scheduled to appear, and his name is on the witness list.

Maybe he had a head cold on the day in question? But that can't be, because he was concurrently dissembling at the Elizabeth Stride inquest. Had he shown up, Crawford's line of questioning would of necessity have had to include the discovery of the apron, and a time-line *à propos* of it. Long handed the apron to Phillips at five or ten minutes past 3 a.m. By 3.30 at the latest it was in the possession of Dr Brown (and Thomas Catling) at the Golden Lane morgue.

3.30 a.m. is a time to remember.

Meanwhile, Crawford had nobody to question about the prove-nance of the portion of Mrs Eddowes' apron but the hapless Police Constable Alfred Long.

CRAWFORD: Had you been past that spot previous to your discovering the apron?
LONG: I passed it about 20 minutes past two o'clock.

And was it there then? No, it was not. Crawford had simply *listened* to the evidence from everybody else, but was actually *interrogating* PC Long.

> CRAWFORD: As to the writing on the wall, have you not put 'not' in the wrong place? Were not the words 'The Jews are not the men that will be blamed for nothing'?
> LONG: I believe the words were as I stated.
> CRAWFORD: How do you spell 'Jews'?
> LONG: J-E-W-S.
> CRAWFORD: Now, was it not on the wall J-U-W-E-S? Is it not possible you are wrong?
> LONG: It may be as to the spelling.
> CRAWFORD: Why did you not tell us that in the first place? Did you make an entry of the words at the time?
> LONG: Yes, in my pocket book.
> CRAWFORD: As to the place where the word 'not' was put? Is it possible you have put the 'not' in the wrong place?

According to *The Times*, 'Witness again read the words as before,' although we are not told what he read them from. Whatever it was, it wasn't satisfactory to the jury, its foreman making the point.

> FOREMAN: Where is the pocket book in which you made the entry of the writing?
> LONG: At Westminster.
> FOREMAN: Is it possible to get it at once?

Crawford then asked Langham to direct that the book be fetched, and Long was sent scuttling to Westminster to get it.

I don't imagine he'd forgotten his notebook by accident. A copper called to give information at an enquiry into a murder will have his book with him. But Long hadn't thought to bring it.

No such deficiency was attendant on City Detective Halse, who was next to face Crawford's questions. The solicitor covered the same ground as he had with Long, and everything was pretty much in sync until it came to the discovery of the writing on the wall.

> HALSE: At 20 minutes past two o'clock I passed over the spot where the piece of apron was found, but I did not notice anything then. I should not necessarily have seen the piece of apron, because it was in the hall.

Halse's deposition is in direct conflict with Warren's. In order to enhance the apron's incendiary credentials, Warren moved both it and the writing as near to the street as fiction would allow. In his 6 November concoction he wrote: 'The writing was on the jamb of the open archway or doorway visible to anybody in the street.' Except, apparently, at 2.20 a.m., when Long and Halse passed by. They stated respectively that the apron 'was lying in a passage leading to the staircases', and 'the writing was in the passage of the building itself'. It's noticeable that nowhere in this entire hearing is the name Warren mentioned, and of further note that henceforth Crawford spells the crucial word Jews as 'Juwes'.

> CRAWFORD: Did anyone suggest that it would be possible to take out the word 'Juwes' and leave the rest of the writing there?
> HALSE: I suggested that the top line might be rubbed out, and the Metropolitan Police suggested the word 'Juwes'.

It would seem that at least someone in the Met wanted to preserve the writing for the photographer – but he wasn't the same member of the Metropolitan Police who wanted it rubbed out.

> CRAWFORD: Read out the exact words you took in your book at the time.
> HALSE: 'The Juwes are not the men that will be blamed for nothing.'
> CRAWFORD: Did the writing have the appearance of being recently done?
> HALSE: Yes. It was written with white chalk on a black facia.

Not 'blurred', not 'rubbed', not 'old', as Mr Sugden might wish it. But here comes the killer question that Warren, and not a few of his apologists, might wish had never been asked.

> FOREMAN: Why was the writing really rubbed out?[12]

Bang goes the twaddle about 'riot' – this member of the jury simply didn't believe it. Not a ridiculous word of it. Why the writing was *really rubbed out* was precisely the point Crawford was trying to establish. Keeping his own counsel, the cautious solicitor allowed Detective Halse to answer the foreman's question.

HALSE: The Metropolitan Police said it might cause a riot and it was on their ground.

It isn't recorded whether the foreman thought he'd had a satisfactory answer, but to judge from the ensuing furore in the press, it would seem that he had not. Why this writing was *really rubbed out* has defined the life-blood of Bro Jack and the circus of smokescreens and moving mirrors ever since.

From the moment of its discovery there was an intense effort on the part of the Metropolitan Police to withhold, obfuscate, misrepresent, obscure and destroy any link between the writing on the wall and the butchery in Mitre Square. Nothing could be more important than this nexus, what the *Evening News* accurately described as 'a warrant of authenticity'.

Such a warrant should surely have been the starting point of the subsequent investigation. Instead, like Laurel and Hardy in bizarre harmony with Freemasonry, the intention of Ripperology has been not to explore it, but, like Warren, to get rid of it. The initiative of the City Police is marginalised in favour of supporting the lunacy of Warren and his preposterous 'riot'. The writing must be diminished into some kind of nonsensical 'graffito' that supposedly no one can understand. Well, Crawford understood it, and with the return of Constable Long, he was about to have his understanding confirmed.

The immediate question to be answered from Long's retrieved notebook was the entry he made at the time concerning discovery of the writing on the wall.

CRAWFORD: What is the entry?
LONG: The words are, 'The Jeuws are the men that will not be blamed for nothing.'

Contradicting Halse, he spells Jews 'J-E-U-W-S'. Not good enough for Crawford, who referred him to an inspector's report. Since this report was never written into the record, we don't know who this inspector was. Was it the inspector PC Long brought hurrying from Commercial Road, or was it another report from another inspector?

> CRAWFORD: Both here [in the notebook] and in your Inspector's report, the word 'Jews' is spelled correctly?
> LONG: Yes, but the Inspector remarked that the word was spelled 'J-U-W-E-S'.
> CRAWFORD: Why did you write 'Jews' then?
> LONG: I made the entry before the Inspector made the remark.
> CRAWFORD: Why did the Inspector write 'Jews'?

Long couldn't say; but Halse could, and Crawford chose the unequivocal spelling out of his more properly available notebook. It all would have been so much easier if the jury could have relied on photographic evidence. Be that as it may, the spelling confirmed in this court was 'J-U-W-E-S', and never mind what 'respectable historians' later tried to make of it.

Although the jury may not have understood why, it's incontestable that the particularity of this spelling was of considerable importance to Crawford, albeit without the remotest interest in ill-fitting footwear or the distractions of anti-Semitic rioting.

He wasn't investigating a potential riot, he was investigating an actual murder, and as was later pointed out, 'Crawford was trying to prove something, and not that the Ripper was bad at spelling.'[13]

So what was this urbane and highly competent solicitor up to? What could he see in the spelling of 'Juwes' that Bro Charlie Warren apparently could not? And what was the difference for Crawford between 'The Jews are not the men that will be blamed for nothing' and 'The Juwes are the men that will not be blamed for nothing'? Crawford was after accuracy because the two sentences mean starkly different things. The first may be interpreted as anti-Semitic, blaming a general race of men called Jews; the second narrows it down to a more specific group, blaming a particular type of man the Ripper elected to spell as 'Juwes'.

Ripperologist Mr Paul Begg makes a point that misses the point as he makes it: 'The erasure did not prevent the spelling of the word becoming known,' he writes. 'Moreover, even if the writing had been left, who – other than senior Masons – would have known the significance of the word, and would senior Masons have been any less anxious than Warren to keep the Masonic connection unrevealed?'[14]

No, they would not. Masons keep their mouths shut, so Mr Begg's point is irrelevant. I'm not sure if he's here acknowledging that only 'senior Masons would have known the significance of the word'. If he is, I am in agreement, because the Commissioner of London's police was a senior Mason.

But the conundrum – public or not – of 'Juwes' is not actually the point at issue. Of course its significance was apparent to anyone acquainted with Freemasonic ritual: examples of whom are Bro Jack the Ripper, Bro Sir Charles Warren, and City Solicitor Bro Henry Homewood Crawford.

Crawford knew what 'Juwes' meant, because he was a Mason, and what with the rest of it, he put it together just as fast as Warren had before he got out of bed. Crawford had confirmed what he already knew, and was now in the loop himself. A sentinel of the Establishment, and virulently conservative, he had taken the same oath as Warren, and was no less a subject of the Mystic Tie. Having done its business in Bro Baxter's court, the 'Mystic Miasma' now relocates its hypnotic vapours to Langham's.

Their effects are immediate, and as wondrous as anything achieved by any fairy godmother. Extraordinary as it is to behold, Crawford now begins a process of obfuscation himself, shifting his allegiance away from the jury and towards the Met. His tone respecting PC Long changes from accusatory to conciliatory; from now on Bro Crawford becomes no less defensive of the shenanigans at Goulston Street than Bro Sir Charles Warren himself.

> JUROR: It seems strange that a police constable should have found this piece of apron and then for no enquiries to have been made in the building? There is a clue up to that point and then it is altogether lost?

Switching the substance of the question away from the Met, Bro Crawford answers one about the City that was never asked:

CRAWFORD: I have evidence that the City Police did make a careful search in the tenement, but it was not until after the fact had come to their knowledge. But unfortunately it did not come to their knowledge until two hours after. I'm afraid that will not meet the point raised by you [the juror]. There is the delay that took place. The man who found the piece of apron is a member of the Metropolitan Police.

JUROR: It is the man belonging to the Metropolitan Police that I'm complaining of.

Ignoring this criticism of the Met, Crawford again deflects to the City Police, investing them with a totally phoney timeframe: 'Unfortunately,' he said, 'it did not come to their knowledge until two hours later.'

Not to put too fine a point on it, this is a lie. City Inspector McWilliam ordered photographs at 3.45 a.m., and 'directed the officers to return at once to the model dwellings'. But Crawford would now have the jury believe that two hours had elapsed, meaning the City Police didn't get to Goulston Street until 5.45 a.m., forty-five minutes after Warren had pitched up there.

Given what the jury had already heard, Crawford's explanation is untenable, and as the juror was well aware, a search of the building was technically nothing to do with the City. Goulston Street was in Warren's manor, and such a search was the responsibility of the Met. That they didn't search the building was the reason the juror thought the clue 'altogether lost'.

Indifferent to such trivialities, Crawford put a couple of already answered questions to Long before making the two-hour time leap himself. What time did Long leave Leman Street police station and return to the wall?

LONG: About five o'clock.
CRAWFORD: Had the writing been rubbed out then?
LONG: No, it was rubbed out in my presence at half past five.
CRAWFORD: Did you hear any one object to its being rubbed out?
LONG: No.

And Crawford lets him get away with it. He seems to have entirely forgotten the protest from City Detective Halse, amongst others, and the divisional friction over the preservation of this evidence that extended for half an hour (the half-hour Long says he was there). If Halse was still in court he must have thought Crawford had gone nuts – but then, he was unaware that this most excellent solicitor was subservient to a higher authority than a coroner's court.

Bro Crawford had all but come to the end of his questions, and Langham was about to pay the traditional valediction to some person or persons unknown.

Coroner Langham's closing speech is remarkable, paying not the slightest attention to any of the evidence his court had heard. In the spirit of Victorian orthodoxy, his summing-up ignored everything that didn't suit the predetermined outcome. Observing that 'the evidence had been of a most exhausting character', he totally disregarded it. 'It would be far better now,' said the rented mouth, 'to leave the matter in the hands of the police, to follow up with any clues they might obtain.'

Which brings us back to precisely where this charade started: with the Metropolitan Police. One can only blink at the peripheries of Wonderland at what 'clues' he had in mind. The verbiage he'd just ejaculated made no mention of a *single clue* the police already had. To summarise the summing-up: both 'suspects' (a couple of irrelevances who had formerly been associated with Eddowes, called Thomas Conway and John Kelly) had been eliminated, one of them proving to have been asleep at the time of the crime. It was also established that a day or two before her murder Eddowes had gone to Bermondsey, in South London, looking for her daughter. 'Something might turn on the fact that she did not see her,' announced the mouth, 'but the daughter had left the address there without mentioning any other address to which she was going' (Langham neglected to mention that this address was two years old, and that Eddowes hadn't seen her daughter since 1886).

While the jury absorbed the implications of these forensic exactitudes, Langham came to his point. 'There could be no doubt,' he intoned, 'that a vile murder had been committed.' And doubtless grateful for the mention of it, the jury was dismissed.

This most eminent pie-baker declined to remind them of any evidence that might apply itself to the identity of the murderer.

Where did he go during the missing forty-odd minutes between Mitre Square and Goulston Street? If the purpose of the severed apron was only to wipe his hands, why transport it over so great a distance? Was it really to try to blame the Jews (he could have blamed the Jews just as easily at Mitre Square), or for some other reason? Neither Jews nor riot appear to have had any relevance for Langham, and not an iota of comment is given on either. He declines even to consider the altercation over photographing the writing on the wall – as a matter of fact, he makes no mention of the writing at all. PC Long's round trip to Westminster passes unremarked, as does the confirmation of the much-contested spelling of 'Juwes'. The unanswered question over why the writing was 'really rubbed out' is of no concern, which probably explains why the piece of apron that came with it had entirely slipped Langham's mind. Although such evidence could have hanged the Ripper, both it and its relationship with the murderer had vanished into thin air. Langham had quite forgotten it, making no mention of the apron, nor of the events preceding or following its discovery. PC Long's beeline to Leman Street and his inexplicable languor on arrival there were no concern of this court.

Neither, apparently, were missing body parts. Was not Langham of a mind to remind the jury of them? Repudiating the comic gibberish regarding 'the Womb-Collector', Dr Gordon Brown determined that the stolen organs would have no professional utility. So for what reason were they taken? And what should be made of it if any of these organs (a kidney, for example) should be discovered, or in some way reappear?

A multitude of unanswered questions left the jury in a vacuum. What did 'Juwes' actually mean, and why was its precise spelling of such importance to Crawford? Why didn't the Metropolitan Police search the model dwellings at Goulston Street – and where indeed *were* the Met's senior detectives? Why were no photographs taken of the writing on the wall, why was it 'really rubbed out', and what kind of idiot could have demanded it? And lastly, who or what was Crawford concealing when he suppressed Joseph Lawende's description of Jack the Ripper?

It remained only for Langham to 'thank Mr Crawford' on the jury's behalf, 'and the police for the assistance they had rendered the enquiry'.

Gratitude extended well beyond Langham's little emporium. It was felt in the highest echelons of Scotland Yard, and in the apartment of a gentleman psychopath living in London NW.

The Ripper had made another convert, adjusting Crawford's integrity to the level required. Just as Coroner Wynne Baxter had been subject to its gravity over Annie Chapman, so now had Crawford with a jury of his own to deceive. We are heading into a phenomenon that will reiterate itself with escalating duplicity in proportion to Establishment panic. At Chapman's inquest, a Freemason suppressed evidence. At Goulston Street, a Freemason suppressed evidence. At Eddowes' inquest, a Freemason suppressed evidence, including a description of the murderer himself.

The Victorian authorities knew perfectly well that they were looking for a Freemason (or rather, that they were protecting one). But they didn't yet know who he was.

We shall never know what Joseph Lawende saw. Notwithstanding that, anyone scratching around Crawford and his 'secret' will discover some fascinating ancillary information.

If not quite in the exalted league of Sir Charles Warren, Bro Henry Homewood Crawford was nevertheless well situated in the Masonic hierarchy. Founder of the Guildhall Lodge (3116), Past Master in Grand Master's Lodge (No 1), and elevated into the Royal Arch in the same Chapter, in the spring of 1889 Crawford was appointed Grand Steward of the United Grand Lodge, and found himself among some distinguished company. It was a big day, followed by a big banquet, 'most beautifully served'. A report of the proceedings can be found in the *Freemason's Chronicle*:[15]

The festival, which is held, according to ancient custom, on the Wednesday next St. George's Day, was preceded by a meeting of Grand Lodge, to which *rulers* of the Craft only were admitted [my emphasis]. The minutes respecting the Prince of Wales as Grand Master at the last Grand Lodge having been confirmed, Sir Albert Woods [Garter] King-at-Arms, proclaimed His Royal Highness, according to ancient form. The mandate of Grand Master was then read, reappointing the Earl of Carnarvon Pro Grand Master, and the Earl of Lathom as Deputy Grand Master. The other officers were invested as follows:

Bro. Lord George Hamilton, M.P.	-	Senior Warden
Sir J. E. Gorst, M.P.	-	Junior Warden
The Hon. and Rev. Francis Byng	}	Chaplains
Rev. T. B. Spencer (Preston)	}	
Edward Terry	-	Treasurer
F. A. Philbrick, Q.C.	-	Registrar
Col. Shadwell Clerke	-	Secretary
Dr. Ernest Emil Wendt	-	Sec. for German Corres.
Sir Lionel Darell	-	} Senior Deacons
Sir Polydore de Keyser	-	}
Col. Addison Potter, C.B.	-	} Junior Deacons
Chas. Chester Cheston	-	}
Col. R. W. Edis	-	Supt. of Works
Sir A. W. Woods (Garter), C.B.	-	Director of Ceremonies
C. Belton	-	Deputy D.C.
G. H. Haydon	-	Assistant D.C.
Eugene Monteuuis	-	Sword Bearer
T. G. Bullen	-	} Standard Bearers
G. Taylor	-	}
M. Maybrick	-	Organist
A. A. Pendlebury	-	Assist. Secretary
T. W. Whitmarsh	-	} Pursuivants
D. D. Mercer	-	}
H. Sadler	-	Tyler

The following were appointed Grand Stewards for the year :—

Bros. Henry Homewood Crawford 1, Edward John Vivian Hussey 2, John Arthur Hughes 4, Arthur Ball 5, Philip Charles Novelli 6, Heby Pullman, 8, William Regester 14, Joseph Warren Zambra 21, Frederick Pinches 23, Reid Taylor 26, Frederick Burgess 29, Edward Wollaston Stanton 46, Sheriff Edward James Gray 58, Eliab Rogers 60, Frederic Charles Watts 91, Edward Humphreys 99, Marcus Sharpe 197, and Charles Percival Henty 259.

Henry Homewood Crawford was elected as a Grand Steward on the day my candidate was elected as Grand Organist. Once again, I make no sinister imputation towards members of this assembly who hadn't the remotest idea of the assassin in their midst. But this is a yet further example of how Michael Maybrick was embedded in the Brotherhood he despised and was betraying.

At this august event, the fraternal associate of James and Michael Maybrick, Bro the Earl of Lathom, was reappointed as Deputy Grand Master. One or two of the names represented become faces in the engraving opposite. Celebrating Her Majesty's fifty years of rule at her Jubilee in 1887, this montage displays the apogee of Masonic authority together with its indivisible association with the Crown. The woman in the picture wasn't a Freemason, but in regal *quid pro quo*, Freemasonry couldn't have existed without her. Her Majesty aside, at least three of these men are close associates, if not intimates, of Michael Maybrick: Woods, Lathom and Colonel Shadwell Clerke.

THE QUEEN & THE CRAFT

Ich Dien

THE EARL OF CARNARVON,
PRO GRAND MASTER.

H.R.H. THE PRINCE OF WALES,
M. W. GRAND MASTER.

THE EARL OF LATHOM,
DEPUTY GRAND MASTER.

ASCENDED THE THRONE JUNE 20TH 1837
TO COMMEMORATE THE JUBILEE 1887

H.M. THE QUEEN CHIEF PATRONESS R.M.I.G.
G. PATRON R.M.I.B.—V. PATRON R.M.B.I.

JUBILEE
1887.

BRO. THOS. FENN, PRES. BD GEN. PURP.

SIR ALBERT WOODS,
GRAND DIRECTOR CEREMONIES.

COL. SHADWELL CLERKE,
GRAND SECRETARY.

But let us stay with the list of revered 'rulers', not a few of whom were of no little importance in the Victorian hierarchy: Senior Warden Lord George Hamilton (First Lord of the Admiralty in Salisbury's Cabinet); Junior Warden Sir John Eldon Gorst, MP for Chatham (Under Secretary for India 1886–91, Financial Secretary to the Treasury 1891–92, and ofttimes a resident at Toynbee Hall, the 'university for the poor' in London's East End); Chaplain the Honourable and Reverend Francis Byng (Chaplain to Her Majesty Queen Victoria 1865–89); Senior Deacon Sir Polydore de Keyser (Crawford's boss and Lord Mayor of London during the Ripper crisis, serving until 9 November 1888); Superintendent of Works Colonel Robert Edis (a leading light in 'Mark Masonry', close to Edward, Prince of Wales, as he was to Michael Maybrick, commanding officer of the 20th Middlesex Rifles, 'the Artists Volunteers', whose Honorary Colonel was one of Prince Edward's closest personal friends, Sir Frederick Leighton, an unlikely overlord of a battalion we shall be hearing more of, and to which Captain Michael Maybrick belonged); Director of Ceremonies the ubiquitous Sir Albert Woods 'Garter' (and intimate of everyone worth the effort, with especial emphasis on the King to be). It was Woods who presided over Prince Edward's investiture as Grand Master of English Masons in 1875. Sir Albert and his Prince can be seen in an engraving of more topical interest. Published in tangential coincidence with the beginning of the Ripper terror, it appeared in the *Graphic*, 4 August 1888.

Sir Albert stands next to Prince Albert Victor, the Duke of Clarence, who himself stands next to one of his father's pals, the Earl of Lathom. The Prince of Wales wears the Holy Cloak; Sir John George stands at his side with sword raised in a tradition of fealty stretching back to the Crusades. And last but not least, we see Masonic historian and Commissioner of Metropolitan Police, Bro Sir Charles Warren.

Warren was well in favour with his future King, a house-guest at the country pile where Edward would guzzle, gamble, hunt, and fuck other people's wives. In January 1888 'The Prince and Princess of Wales were present at a special meet of the West Norfolk Hunt at Sandringham, the principal guests of their Royal Highnesses taking part in the sport.' The occasion was Clarence's twenty-fourth birthday, and 'Bro Sir Charles Warren arrived at Sandringham on a visit

Bishop of St. Albans   Sir Albert Woods   Prince Albert Victor   Earl of Latham   Duke of Teck   The Prince of Wales   Sir Charles Warren   Viscount Templeton

INSTALLATION OF THE PRINCE OF WALES AS GRAND PRIOR OF THE HOSPITAL OF THE ORDER OF ST. JOHN OF JERUSALEM IN ENGLAND

that same day'.[16] Broadening the legal side of life, Edward's intimates further included Lord Brampton, 'the clever, witty, and eccentric judge' better known as Sir Henry Hawkins (who had put Ernest Parke in prison), and the corpulent Sir Charles Russell, who, as already noted, was to become a star performer in the so-called 'Maybrick Mystery'.

All were members of a self-regulating occult matrix in which everyone knew everyone, and everyone knew in which direction the bowing was done. 'In every age monarchs themselves have been promoters of the Art; in return Freemasons have always shown an unshakable devotion to the Crown and its legal government.'[17] Fealty was the name of the game, and somewhere inside it was a psychopathic bomb that could have shafted the lot of them.

Jack the Ripper had the guile of Satan, and would bring catastrophe to any who had a mind to challenge him. He was the embodiment of corruption, and corrupted whatever came into his sphere. Fear was his power, far beyond Whitechapel. It was an idiosyncratic fear with implications right to the top.

Was Warren – or anyone else – going to put the ruling elite at risk for a handful of whores? Endless falsehoods answer the question, endless nonsense underlines it. In order to protect themselves the Establishment would do anything in their power to brazen out any criticism, fix any court, and tell any lie.

Warren wasn't an evil man, far from it, but presented with so unique an evil he became its supplicant. I have to admit to a momentary sympathy for Charlie – a man of his age – when faced with the momentous dilemma on that wall at Goulston Street. Never mind Commissioner Smith's City Police photographs, the pictures below were etched into the very essence of Warren's being.

Bro the Prince of Wales, and his brother the Duke of Connaught

Warren had less than forty days to survive as Commissioner of the Metropolitan Police, and he devoted every one of them to breaking the law. Motivated by misplaced loyalty and authoritarian hubris, a coterie of senior officers at Scotland Yard conspired to create and coordinate an environment that couldn't have been more favourable to the psychopath in their midst.

'The Whitechapel Murderer is certainly a marvelous being,' wrote the *New York Tribune*. 'He is not only able to carry out his bloody work without molestation, but may even have it in his power to overturn a government.'[18]

Jack had a 'Funny Little Game', and survival was the name of Warren's, articulated most succinctly by the Birkett Committee some sixty years later. 'The detection and suppression of crime,' it opined, 'is essential to good government in any society, but not so fundamental as the security of the state itself.'[19]

Audi, Vide, Tace.

7

The Ink-Stained
Hack

Where law ends, there tyranny begins.

William Pitt, 1770

The function of the Establishment was (and is) the preservation of the Establishment. The Official Secrets Act was presented to Parliament in 1888 by Salisbury's legal butler, Bro Sir Richard Webster. Made law in 1889, it has ever after been abused and become a bolt-hole for scoundrels.[1]

Concurrent with the Ripper scandal, literally on a day-to-day basis, the Salisbury government was engineering a 'foul conspiracy' (not my words, but those of the Lord Chief Justice Lord Coleridge in 1889) to destroy the Irish Nationalist leader Charles Parnell. Chief of the CID Sir Robert Anderson was the helmsman of this particular conspiracy, which is why the record has scant reference to him in respect of the Whitechapel Fiend. Anderson could lie like a back-alley slut, and was up to his dandruff in a clandestine duplicity. At the zenith of both his and Warren's criminal activity (the autumn of 1888) he is supposed to have 'gone on holiday' to the Continent, when in reality he was secretly manipulating and conspiring with both press and Parliament in what it was hoped would be a death blow to Parnell and his dream of an independent Ireland.

Documents in respect of Anderson's covert activities were originally classified under the 'hundred-year rule'. But when the hundred years was up, they were reclassified to keep them secret in perpetuity. They are an 'official secret'. So even today, in the twenty-first century, British citizens are not allowed to know what nineteenth-century policemen were up to.[2]

In respect of Jack the Ripper, the Metropolitan Police (MEPO) files are not working documents of an investigation, but largely heavily-weeded scraps of dubious concoction. They are not a record, but a 'story' as the System wanted it told, and it was Chief Inspector Donald Swanson who was chosen to tell it.

After the ritualistic murder of Annie Chapman on 8 September 1888, Charles Warren took two strategic decisions relating to the Metropolitan Police's investigation. The first was a suffocating ban to prevent any information getting out; and the second, draconian control of all information within. Other than as a conduit for mis-information – the search for 'lairs', promoting the idea of a 'Jew', etc. – the press was to be kept at the end of a very long arm. 'Under pain of dismissal,' recorded a contemporary pressman, 'the detectives refused information, even to accredited representatives of the London papers.'[3]

At Scotland Yard, things were no different. By a process later known as 'compartmentalisation', information was to be channelled upwards, as the exclusive property of an elite. On 15 September, exactly one week after Chapman's death, Warren wrote, or more likely dictated, a memo (pomposity requiring a few self-congratulatory words before he got to his point). 'I am convinced,' he mused, 'that the Whitechapel Murder case is one that can be successfully grappled with if it is systematically taken in hand. I go so far as to say that I could myself unravel the mystery provided I could spare the time and give individual attention to it.'[4]

Well, bravo to you, you self-serving idiot, and a pity it is you found time at five o'clock in the morning to apply individual attention to a wall.

'I feel therefore,' he continued, 'the utmost importance to be attached to putting the whole Central Office work in this case in the hands of one man who will have nothing else to concern himself with.'

That man was a forty-year-old Scot, the aforementioned Swanson, 'who must be acquainted with *every detail* [Warren's emphasis]. I look upon him for the time being as the eyes and ears of the Commissioner in this particular case.' Acquisition of Warren's blighted organs wasn't the end of it. 'He must have a room to himself, and every paper, every document, every report, every tele-gram must pass through his hands. He must be consulted on every subject,' insists the memo. 'I would not send any directions anywhere on the subject of the murder without consulting him. I give him the whole responsibility … *All the papers* [Warren's emphasis] in Central Office on the subject of the murder must be kept in his room. I must have this matter put on a proper footing, everything depends on a careful compliance with these directions.'[5]

Certainly the subterfuge Warren was initiating depended on compliance, and a paragraph added in his own hand is indicative of his determination to hammer the instruction home: 'Every document, *letter received* [my emphasis] or telegram on the subject should go to his room before being directed when necessary. This is to avoid the possibility of documents being delayed or action retarded.'

Underneath are the initials of those in the loop: 'A.C.B.', Assistant Commissioner Alexander Carmichael Bruce, acknowledged the directive on the day it was written, as did 'A.F.W.', Chief Constable Adolphus Frederick Williamson, who noted, 'seen 15/9/88'.[6]

Swanson's mandate covers everything: every docket, document, plan and telegram, every 'letter received'. For the time being, I want to confine interest to the receipt of just one such letter.

On 29 September 1888, the Central News Agency forwarded a letter it had received to Scotland Yard. It was marked for the attention of Chief Constable Williamson, who as signatory to Warren's instructions was duty bound to pass it on to Swanson post-haste. Because both of them were in the same building, this shouldn't have taken more than a minute or two.

Swanson was now looking at what is probably the most notorious document in this whole hideous pantomime. Known subsequently as the 'Dear Boss' letter, and considered to be the first outing of the Beast's *nom de plume*, it is signed, 'yours truly Jack the Ripper'.

25 Sept 1888

Dear Boss

I keep on hearing the police have caught me but they wont fix me just yet. I have laughed when they look so clever and talk about being on the *right* track. That joke about Leather Apron gave me real fits. I am down on whores and shant quit ripping them till I do get buckled. Grand work the last job was. I gave the lady no time to squeal. How can they catch me now. I love my work and want to start again. You will soon hear of me with my funny little games. I saved some of the proper *red* stuff in a ginger beer bottle over the last job to write with but it went thick like glue and I can't use it.

Red ink is fit enough I hope <u>ha ha</u>. The next job I do I shall clip the ladys ears off and send to the police officers just for jolly wouldn't you. Keep this letter back till I do a bit more work, then give it out straight. My knife's so nice and sharp I want to get to work right away if I get a chance. Good luck.

yours truly
Jack the Ripper
Don't mind me giving the trade name.

Written at a right-angle below the main text and as an apparent afterthought:

Wasnt good enough to post this before I got all the red ink off my hands curse it. No luck yet. They say I'm a doctor now <u>ha ha</u>

Bro Donald Swanson (Lodge of St Peter's 284)[7] was an apt choice as Warren's 'eyes and ears'. It was his responsibility 'to avoid the possibility of documents being delayed or action retarded'. Under such an uncompromising stricture, knowledge of 'Dear Boss' and the letter itself must have gone directly to Warren. We know he was in London, and Scotland Yard wasn't a corner shop. If Superintendent Arnold can wake Warren in the middle of the night to inform him of some writing on a wall, it shouldn't have been a difficult task for Swanson to inform his boss of the arrival of a letter in the middle of the day. Broad daylight, no telegraph or telephone required (although the boss had both). Chances are it was only a stroll into the next-door office.

The ramifications of this are startling. We are talking about 29 September, the daylight before the night of the 'Double Event'. By any balance of probability, it means that Warren would have known about 'Dear Boss' when he scurried out of bed that night to wash off that wall. Indeed, I'd bet my low card it was the reason he did it. Following hard on his heels came a poster campaign that must rank amongst the most ridiculous in history.

The Metropolitan Police reproduced the letter and a subsequent postcard, and slapped posters up all over East London. The universal petition that 'Any person recognising the handwriting is requested to communicate with the nearest police station' was rendered a tad academic, since the only person who might have recognised it was the Commissioner of Police, and he'd just washed it off.

This novel reaction to evidence has been examined in a previous chapter. Without wishing to re-tread the cobbles at Goulston Street, and irrespective of the forever lost handwriting, I want to explore how 'Dear Boss' might otherwise relate to the writing on the wall. Take a look at this. It's a letter from an intelligent citizen, published in the *Daily News* on 2 October 1888, and I think it gets close to identifying the problem.

> Sir – As the track of the Whitechapel monster or monsters becomes more and more thickly besprinkled with the blood, and bestrewn with the mutilated remains of successive victims, there is something almost paralysing in the ghastly sameness with which the newspaper reports wind up:– 'No clue to the identity of the murderer has yet been found'; 'No circumstance speedily tending to the discovery of the criminal has yet been observed'; and, 'It is understood that, although not the remotest clue has been discovered, the police have a theory,' and so on ad nauseam … Now, Sir, is this not a matter of grave complaint against our detective system? It is easy to say that without something to work upon the police cannot be expected to smell the murderer out. Most emphatically I maintain that it is the duty of the detective to discover and pursue for himself clues suggested by such trifling indications as would escape the attention of the casual or the unskilled observer. We retain a large and expensive body of men, and we have the right to demand at their hands things which, except to specialists and experts, may rightly be called impossible. Sir Charles Warren, pious disciplinarian and enthusiastic soldier that he is, must feel deeply his responsibility for all this …
>
> T.B.R.

That he did, but it wasn't a responsibility as understood by this correspondent. T.B.R. perceptively identifies the 'spin' and reality of what was actually going on – *NOTHING* – but he doesn't understand that Warren wasn't interested in detection, but in the strategy of its avoidance. He was an iron filing at the mercy of a magnet, subject to a dynamic of which the public could have no inkling, and he would tell any porky, promote any falsehood, and rush to any location to facilitate the subterfuge. Bro Warren couldn't catch Jack the Ripper: he was *precisely the reason he was never caught*.

Mr Paul Begg informs us that 'the Masonic Conspiracy', as he calls it, 'has now been thoroughly discredited'.[8] My response to this assertion is, by whom? Certainly not by Ripperology, or indeed by the Freemasons, whose protestations implode like a line of perished balloons. The single 'thoroughly discredited' contrivance is the bullshit put about by a Freemason in the first place, implicating the Duke of Clarence. Ripperologists who dismiss the chalked-up message do so with a superficial understanding of British Masonic ritual. Although wildly incorrect, Mr Begg at least concedes that 'In the United States however, the names Jubela, Jubelo, and Jubelum, were and are used.'[9]

Well, that's a start, and in terms of detection it may have been of interest to correspondents like T.B.R. The Victorian police may well have demonstrated what the *Evening News* described as 'the nous of tailors' dummies',[10] but even they were able to identify and draw attention to 'Americanisms' in 'Dear Boss'. They could hardly do otherwise. The newspapers were doing it for them. 'Boss, Fix me, Shant Quit and Right Away, are American forms of expression. The writer is probably an American,' concluded the *Daily Telegraph*, which, with quite extraordinary accuracy, continued, 'or an Englishman, who has mixed with "our cousins" on the other side of the Atlantic.'[11]

If Mr Begg can acknowledge the murderous trio of J.J.J. as familiar names in nineteenth-century American Freemasonry (just as they were, according to Bro Woodford, in English), and the police themselves are able to recognise American slang in 'Dear Boss', what's the problem with considering an American Freemason, or someone pretending to be one, as 'yours truly Jack the Ripper'? 'Just for jolly', Mr Begg? Just as part of 'no clue too small', as that inimitable investigative force Sir Robert Anderson so fastidiously put it?

We had an American Gatherer of Wombs; what's wrong with an American Ripper? Or is that a forensic leap too far? It certainly was for Charlie Warren and his boys, who were leaping in the opposite direction. Warren and his minions speedily denounced 'Dear Boss' as a hoax, and predictably the hypnotised herd went along with him.

Ripperologist Mr Melvin Harris is not only an expert, but according to his own dust-wrapper 'one of the world's top experts', and Mr

Harris tells us 'Dear Boss' is a fake. It's the work of a juvenile 'ink-stained hack', he decrees, and let's hear no more about it. 'While the press fished around for copy,' says Melvin, 'an immature and irresponsible journalist decided to manufacture some of his own in the form of a mocking letter supposed to be penned by the killer himself. It was dated 25th September but not posted until the 27th, and not sent to the police or any specific paper but to the Central News Agency in Fleet St.'[12]

Irresponsible this creation certainly was, but it suggests more talent in the department of clairvoyance than journalism. Harris knows it now, and 'yours truly' knew it then, but who at the time knew that the next murder was imminent. 'Keep this letter back,' he instructs, 'till I do a bit more work.' And it's clear that he himself kept the letter back – it's dated 25 September, but was withheld until the 27th. It's not difficult to suppose that he was trying to coordinate its arrival for maximum impact on Saturday the 29th.

The concept that this letter is a 'hoax' begins to evaporate with the reality of its premise. By way of comparison, let us say an anti-terrorist officer sits at Scotland Yard, and circuitously a letter arrives threatening to blow up a plane. That night, not one, but two aeroplanes are blown to pieces.

Is the letter a hoax? Or is the officer who tosses it in the trash – let's say Inspector Melvin Harris – making an assumption that is beyond his intellectual capacity? There are many men and women whom I revere for their cognitive expertise, but Melvin isn't one.

'Hoax' comes from 'hocus pocus', a world of Tinkerbell, conjurers and that most mesmerising of ingredients, 'mystery'. It is the vernacular of deception, as in a magician's trick. But where is the deception in a pair of cut-throats? Was that the work of a journalist, or a psychopath? Both the letter and the writing on the wall had the intention of mocking the police, and 'Dear Boss' came first. Unless Mr Harris believes the killer was influenced by a letter he couldn't have seen (short of writing it himself), how could an 'ink-stained hack' predict not only the timing, but also the tone of a murderer? Or does he think it was an immature and irresponsible journalist who cut off and brought a piece of Catherine Eddowes' apron to Goulston Street?

This history is choke-fed with the kind of mind-numbing vaudeville propagated by men like Harris. It is endless and everywhere, erupting down the years like an anaesthetising virus. 'Who christened the phantom killer with the terrible sobriquet of Jack the Ripper?' asks R. Thurston Hopkins, a long-dead forefather of the Harris school. 'That is a small mystery in itself,' he says. 'At the time the police bag bulged with hundreds of anonymous letters from all kinds of cranks and half-witted persons who sought to criticise or hoax the officers engaged in following up the murders.'[13]

To acquiesce in the face of such damned silliness is not only to compromise reality, but also to miss the most important credential of the 'Dear Boss' letter.

And that is that it was the first.[14]

'Dear Boss' was *not* one of hundreds plucked from a bulging post-bag. It was a one-off. At the time of its receipt it was *unique*. Within twenty-four hours, two women lost their lives in Whitechapel; can even the most ardent apologist persist with the asinine certainty of 'hoax'?

'Sir,' wrote a correspondent to the *Daily Telegraph* on 5 October 1888,

> Permit me to suggest in reference to the tragedies that are presently occupying the mind of everyone:–

> 1) That the idea that the letters attributed to the murderer could have been a 'practical joke' or 'hoax' is quite untenable. It is inconceivable that any human being, even the most degraded, could joke on such a subject. Rather, the more degraded the class, the more sympathy there would be with the unfortunate women. Whereas, these letters breathe the very spirit of such a murderer.

> 2) It is unlikely that the man's dress or exterior is at all in keeping with his crimes. Probably he is well dressed, and his entire appearance is such as to totally disarm suspicion, otherwise women would not trust themselves in his company in the way that they seem to do.

In my view this contemporary opinion is worth more than five hundred Melvin Harrises. Later in the narrative I shall confirm the provenance of much of Jack's correspondence. Meanwhile, let it be said, the Central News Agency made no attempt to exploit this letter. It was forwarded directly to the police, who clearly considered it genuine enough to slap it up all over East London. Why Warren was forced into its publication is a matter I'll presently explore, and we can use Mr Harris's world-class expertise as a stepping stone.

As Melvin is not best-known for his original thinking, I wanted to find out from where he had purloined his opinion. This didn't waste much of my morning. His 'ink-stained hack' surfaced from the inkwell of Sir Melville Macnaghten, the man who gave us a lead on Kosminski, a.k.a. 'the Whitechapel Wanker'. 'In this ghastly production,' Sir Melville wrote of 'Dear Boss' in 1914, 'I have always thought I could discern the stained forefinger of a journalist.'

But Macnaghten wasn't yet at Scotland Yard at the time of the murders, so he can't be Harris's source. We therefore descend the autobiographical ladder from 1914 to 1910, where no less a figure than Sir Robert Anderson waits with support for Melville and Melvin. 'The "Dear Boss" letter,' writes Anderson, 'now preserved in the Police Museum at New Scotland Yard, 'is the creation of an enterprising young journalist.'[15]

So, in other words, the very outfit that put the posters up (Scotland Yard) declares that 'Dear Boss' is false? By definition, they then are also hoaxers? It's something to get your mind around. But wait a minute, the barmy pulpiteer isn't yet spent: 'Having regard to the interest attached to this case, I am almost tempted to disclose the identity of the murderer and of the pressman who wrote the letter above referred to.'[16]

The identity of the murderer? Holy Christ, that's a statement from the chief of London's CID. Not only could he have arrested some 'ink-stained hack', he could also have arrested Jack the Ripper! What was the problem, Bob?

'The only person who ever got a good view of the murderer unhesitatingly identified the suspect the instant he was confronted with him; but he refused to give evidence against him.'

What a rotter. I bet he was a Hebrew.

'In stating that he was a Polish Jew, I am merely stating a definitely ascertained fact.'[17]

I don't know where to attack this horseshit first. Let us not forget who's writing it. This was the head of the Criminal Investigation Department at Scotland Yard, writing of 1888. Allow me to give a brief reprise. Anderson says he knew the writing on the wall was *genuine*, 'chalked up by the murderer', but colluded at its public suppression. And he says he knew 'Dear Boss' was *fake*, yet connived at its promotion, plastering posters on what may well have been the same bloody wall.

This endless contradictory junk is pawed over by Ripperologists in their tireless quest for answers that do not involve police duplicity, when such answers there are none. Macnaghten and Anderson are doormen at the house of mirrors, touts selling tickets for the 'Mystery Show'. There was no 'Irresponsible Journalist', no 'Ink-Stained Hack', just as there was no 'Womb-Collector', 'Goulston Street Hoaxer' or 'Nautical Man'. Irresponsibility was the prerogative of the Metropolitan Police. At the time 'Dear Boss' went up on posters, somebody at Scotland Yard clearly considered it genuine enough to publish. This is where historical reality must impinge on even the misplaced certainties of Melvin Harris. There's no way a man saturated in this affair, like Inspector Moore, is going to spend half an afternoon comparing the text with the inventions of some ink-stained idiot whose identity is supposedly already known to Robert Anderson. Mr Harris is trying to pull out a rabbit without a hat. His empiricisms are in fact confections culled from the memoirs of a pair of easily discredited liars.

The police knew 'Dear Boss' was about as genuine as it got, but as the unarrestable purger proceeded with his rampage, certain hallmarks of his correspondence had become very un-OK. It was therefore decided, almost simultaneously with the publication of 'Dear Boss', that all letters from Jack, both the fake and the real, were to be surreptitiously tainted with the word 'hoax'. A process of transparent but enduring spin kicked in, men like Macnaghten retrospectively mopping up spilt milk just as Charlie Warren did at the wall.

The trashing of evidence was by now endemic, posing the question, why put the 'Dear Boss' posters up in the first place?

We come to the nub of Warren's dilemma, and yet again it was Jack calling the shots. Early in the morning of 1 October, the Central News Agency received another communication. Subsequently known as 'Saucy Jacky', it was a postcard signed 'Jack the Ripper':

> I was not codding dear old boss when I gave you the tip, you'll hear about saucy Jacky's work tomorrow double event this time number one squealed a bit couldn't finish straight off. had no time to get ears for police thanks for keeping the last letter back till i get to work again – Jack the Ripper.

Receipt of this card coincided with the first public appearance of 'Dear Boss', its *text only* reproduced early that same morning in the *Daily Post*. Hoax or not, it was assumed by press and public alike that the letter and the postcard were the work of the same pen. Later that day the evening papers printed the *text only* of both, the reaction to them summarised by the *Evening News*:

> It is not necessarily assumed that this has been the work of the murderer. The idea that naturally occurs being that the whole thing is a practical joke. At the same time the writing of the previous letter immediately before the commission of the murders of yesterday was so singular a coincidence that it does not seem unreasonable to suppose that the cool, calculating villain who is responsible for the crimes has chosen to make the post a medium through which to convey to the press his grimly diabolical humour.

In my view this is a very reasonable supposition, which a variety of apologists have been trying to navigate ever since. If you want to ascribe the entire Ripper correspondence to hoaxers, it is first necessary to discredit the most important letter of them all. Experts like Melvin Harris have applied themselves to the task with muscular zeal, and where Harris flunks it, Mr Philip Sugden picks it up. Both deny that 'Dear Boss' has any connection with the murderer, and both deny any reason to assume one, since the threat to Eddowes' ears wasn't carried out.

'The next job I do,' forewarned the letter, 'I shall clip the lady's ears off and send to the police officers just for jolly.'

'The threat was not carried out,' counters Mr Sugden. 'Claims made on behalf of the Jack the Ripper letter and postcard are easily refuted.'[18]

I think they may be a little more difficult to refute than he imagines. Obviously, had there been an assault on Eddowes' ears, it would massively up the ante in favour of the genuineness of 'Dear Boss'. In fact, it would then be foolish to claim the letter was a hoax. For how could any hoaxer predict the intentions of an unknown psychopath with such astonishing specificity? If ears, or an ear, had been cut off, only the murderer could have written 'Dear Boss'.

'Unfortunately for the argument,' writes Mr Sugden, 'the medical records tell a different story. Dr Gordon Brown, examining

Kate's body in Mitre Square, did discover that the lobe of her right ear had been severed. But one detached earlobe does not constitute evidence of any attempt to remove both ears and, given the extensive mutilation of Kate's face and head, can hardly be deemed as significant.'[19]

Mr Sugden may pursue any argument he pleases, but he might want to check out Gordon Brown's medical report with a little more precision. Reading from his notes at the inquest, Dr Brown said, 'The lobe *and auricle* of the right ear were cut obliquely through.'[20]

Auricle: The external ear, or that part of the ear that is prominent from the head.

The definition comes from *Webster's Dictionary*, 1888. Thus, according to Dr Gordon Brown, the Ripper had amputated Mrs Eddowes' right ear in its entirety. This included the lobe. We have a mortuary sketch that clearly shows her right ear as missing, and it is a reality confirmed in various postmortem photographs. Where this 'auricle' went is not accounted for.

THE MITRE SQUARE VICTIM

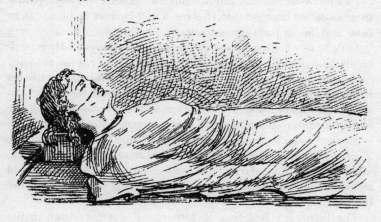

Brown's original drawing shows a dark slash in place of the amputated ear, its absence confirmed by the photograph of Eddowes in her coffin, where instead of an auricle there is a black hole. This is hardly the trivial distraction of an accidentally severed lobe.

Contrary to Mr Sugden, I think this amputated ear may well constitute evidence of an intention to amputate the other. But as stated in
'Saucy Jacky', maybe the murderer didn't have the time or the security to harvest both.

Meanwhile, congratulations to our immature and irresponsible
'ink-stained hack'. He must have been some hot scribe, with a facility of insight little short of the supernatural. Hitherto, the object of
his fantasy had not mutilated the head or face of any previous victim,
knife activity being kept to the torso. But now, in perfect synchronicity with his homicidal muse, both the 'ink-stained hack' and Jack the
Ripper move on to new territory, one threatening ears, and the
other actually cutting one off. It is to be hoped that this ink-stained
journalist with a talent to access the future had a triumphant career,
beyond the ersatz blather of Mr Melvin Harris and Mr Philip Sugden.

Ever eager to get into line behind the 'authorities', Ripperology
took up the task of misinformation, the following being a contribution from *The A to Z*: 'Since the "Dear Boss" letter was published in
the morning papers on October 1st, when the "Saucy Jacky" card
was posted, the latter might easily have been an imaginative hoax by
another hand.'

I want to evaluate this 'might easily'. To explore it, I will separate
these so-called hoaxers into Hoaxer A and Hoaxer B, being 'Dear
Boss' and 'Saucy Jacky' respectively.

Let's have a look at that word 'easily' in relation to Hoaxer B.
Firstly, how does he know whether the Ripper has cut off two ears,
one ear, or none? Dr Brown's report on the missing ear was not yet
in the public domain. Thus either Hoaxer B must have access to
inside information (like the Maybricks with their matchbox), or he
is the murderer. But conjecture over ears pales into insignificance
compared with the next hurdle Hoaxer B must surmount. *The A to
Z* correctly states that 'Dear Boss' was published on 1 October, in the
same dawn as 'Saucy Jacky', but neglects to mention a problem of
some circumstance for Hoaxer B, and that is the matter of the
handwriting.

The printed, *typeset* text of 'Dear Boss' was published in the
Morning Post of 1 October, but not in facsimile of the handwriting it
was written in. As far as Hoaxer B could know, 'Dear Boss' might
have been written in capitals, slanting forwards, slanting backwards,
in copperplate or ignorant scrawl.

For access to the physical appearance of the handwriting, Hoaxer B would have had to wait for another three days before the facsimile posters went up. If Hoaxer A and Hoaxer B were not one and the same, Hoaxer B must have been rushing around London like the proverbial blue-arsed fly. Not only would he have to be certain of his ears, contradicting 'Dear Boss' and championing a negative, he would also have had somehow to discover the printworks where the Met were preparing to set up the facsimiles for their as yet unprinted posters. And it is here that, like the 'ink-stained hack', his talents truly bloom. By some photo-telepathic gift, as yet unexplained, Hoaxer B was able to reproduce the handwriting of Hoaxer A's 'Dear Boss' as accurately as if it had come in on a fax.

Former CID officer and handwriting specialist Douglas Blackburn approaches the analysis of such enigmas as 'Dear Boss' and 'Saucy Jacky' on the premise of something he calls 'the law of probabilities'. 'It is asking too much,' he writes, 'to expect one to believe that there should be two different persons, probably strangers, who possess the same peculiarities of penmanship.'[21]

It is 'asking too much' for anyone to believe it. So, by way of experiment, I ask the authors of *The A to Z* to look at the text of this page, and at four in the morning, on any windy corner of choice, to reproduce a single line of it in *my* handwriting, or anything that even vaguely approximates it.

'Might easily' has become 'frankly ridiculous'.

By mid-morning on 1 October 1888, two newspapers, the *Evening News* and the *Star*, had run the text – but not the facsimile – of the Ripper correspondence. 'A postcard bearing the stamp London E October 1, was received this morning,' reported the *Evening News*. 'The address and subject matter being written in red and undoubtedly by the same person from whom the sensational letter already published was received Thursday last.'

It's interesting to note that both the *Evening News* and the *Star* acknowledge the Central News Agency as their source, and not the Metropolitan Police. There appears to have been no consultation with the police on whether the letters should be published, and pressure of time suggests that no authority was sought. It seems 'Saucy Jacky' was too hot a news item to risk a tangle with red tape, and in deference to commercial interests, it went out immediately. By ten that morning the cat was out of the bag.

That same day, the original 'Dear Boss' came into the hands of Commissioner Henry Smith of the City Police, *The Times* commenting, 'No doubt is entertained that the writer of both communications, who ever he may be, is the same person.'

That didn't do a lot for *The A to Z*, and I can guarantee it didn't do a lot for Warren. Twenty-four hours earlier he'd ruffled not a few feathers in the City, Smith being particularly sour after Warren's failure to protect the writing on the wall.

Irritability among the City Police was great, as was the antipathy of the press (although Fleet Street was as yet ignorant of the farce at Goulston Street). Any more dismissal of evidence, or potential evidence, and Smith might have gone bananas. If Warren had tried to trash these letters (as his mendacious pals were later to do), a dangerous public row might have erupted between the City and the Met. Warren could hardly rub out one lot of handwriting and just as casually dismiss another. He didn't obliterate the writing on the wall in order for it to become public – he wanted it to stay a secret, so as to avoid precisely the furore it caused when it got out.

I therefore suspect Smith of being a more likely reason the posters were stuck up than any pressing desire from Warren. Maybe posters would draw the sting of denying Smith his photographs. Plus, there were tactical advantages. First, it would make the press and the public think the police were actually doing something – which, apart from covering up, they were not. And second, a poster campaign would hopefully distract attention from Scotland Yard's flagrant ineptitude.

Week one of October 1888 must have been amongst the worst of Charles Warren's life. It wasn't Saucy Jacky doing the rushing about, but rather the reverse. Jack was out of control, and it was Dear Old Boss who had to run in the night. He must have been traumatised with apprehension, gone to work expecting to find a body hanging over the telegraph wires or a head in his desk drawer. Certainly, as will be explored, on 4 October a headless piss-take was discovered in the vaults of his new building at New Scotland Yard. Oh my God, did they ever struggle to navigate that one. Everywhere Warren looked was murder, and with it came the inevitable condemnation. The people were 'bitterly angry', and the press reflected it. 'In the

East End of London these two latest atrocities have caused a reign of terror,' bawled the *Evening Post*.

> Feelings of hopelessness, horror, and despair spread through the crowded populations on Sunday evening. Thousands of people are thronging the scenes of the murders, and people are angrily crying out against Mr Matthews, the Home Secretary, and against the futility of the work of the police. They are indignantly discussing amongst themselves what they consider the proven ineptitude of the police. They point out that it is only after the murders are committed that the police come into play at all; that they are never at the right spot at the right moment; and that what ever their preparations and organisation may be, there stands the indisputable fact that nothing is accomplished.[22]

A day later, on 2 October, the Whitechapel Board of Works sent a stringent letter to Warren demanding an increase in the number of police in Whitechapel: 'This Board regards with horror and alarm the several atrocious murders recently perpetrated within the district and its vicinity and calls upon Sir Charles Warren so to regulate and strengthen the police force in the neighbourhood as to guard against any repetition of such atrocities.'[23]

Caught in the headlights, Warren sought an exit by blaming everyone but himself. He replied the following day, rejecting demands for more coppers while reproaching Jack's victims for their lack of entrails. 'I have to point out,' he wrote, 'that the carrying out of your proposals cannot possibly do more than guard or take precautions against repetition of such atrocities so long as the victims actually, but unwittingly, connive at their own destruction.'[24]

In other words, Catherine Eddowes was complicit in the loss of her ear, kidney and womb. She shouldn't have been walking around flaunting such stuff at a murderer. Fury was the response, and it's difficult to select from the cacophony of outraged newspapers. 'Warren must know,' spat a Socialist rag called *Justice*, 'that a vast majority of East End prostitutes are compelled to earn the 3 or 4 pence for their bed before they can obtain a night's lodging.'

If he knew, he didn't care any more than did his neighbour at number 64 Eaton Place. Turning the argument on its head, Warren marginalises the Ripper and again focuses on the victims as the problem. 'I have to request and call upon your Board,' he lathers, 'to do all in your power to dissuade the unfortunate women about Whitechapel from going into lonely places in the dark with any persons. The unfortunate victims appear to take the murderer to some retired spot and place themselves in such a position that they can be slaughtered without a sound being heard; *the murder therefore takes place without any clue to the criminal being left*' (my emphasis).[25]

The Boss Cop has just contradicted any notion of assessing clues, and actually dismisses the utility of having a detective force at all. His forensic capability is reduced to overhearing a scream. That's what he says. If no one shouts, or no one screams, no clue to the criminal is left.

Even by Warren's standards this must rank as one of the biggest pieces of shit ever to have come out of Scotland Yard. He says he wants a scream, but unless he's more stupid than despicable he must know he's never going to get one. All postmortem evidence (for example, that given by Dr Brown) suggests that Jack silenced his victims in an instant, so it can't be imagined how this clown in a hat thought anyone could yell with their head half off.

'You will agree with me,' wrote Warren (which nobody in Whitechapel did), 'that it is not desirable that I should enter into particulars as to what the police are doing in the matter. It is most important that our proceedings should not be published, and the very fact that you may be unaware of what the detective department is doing is only the stronger proof that it is doing its work with secrecy and efficiency.'[26]

Almost a hundred years later, Commissioner of the Metropolitan Police Sir Robert Mark was rejecting such junk in the columns of the *Observer*. 'Detectives at the Yard,' he wrote, 'sheltered behind "a fictional police detective mystique" made all the easier by denial of proper facilities for the press.'[27]

Plus ça change. This nonsense didn't cut it with Mark in the late twentieth century any more than it did with Fleet Street in 1888. 'Warren's letter,' determined the *Star*, 'is pitiful to read. We are asked to believe that because we hear nothing of discoveries by detectives, that only shows the detectives are especially active and energetic, and we are told for the thousandth time that the Metropolitan Police are hopelessly handicapped in dealing with a situation like this for want of reserves to draw on in an emergency.'

The *Star* had put its finger on it. On the one hand Warren was bemoaning the lack of police, and on the other bolstering them with dishonest claims of covert activity. We now come to this missive's greatest contradiction and most vital deceit: 'A large force of police have been drafted into the Whitechapel District.'[28] The 'saturation' of the East End with an influx of cops is a favourite amongst the Fowler's drinkers, swallowed whole and broadcast in all the popular books. Bearing Superintendent Thomas Arnold in mind, hear this from a leading Ripperologist: 'Clearly the streets of Whitechapel and Spitalfields at this time were saturated with the dedicated men of the Metropolitan Police.'[29]

Clearly they were not. With a 'dropsical eye' on the Socialist mob, Victoria herself was nagging Scotland Yard. She feared 'that the detective department is not as efficient as it might be'.[30] You can say that again. And she did, the royal anxieties summoning new fiction out of Robert Anderson. 'In reply to the Secretary of State's enquiry,' he wrote, 'I have the honour to report that since the 8th September, the date of the Hanbury Street murder [Chapman], extra police precautions have been taken in the districts of the murders.'

'Extra police precautions' is not the same thing as 'extra police'. It just sounds like it. Everything Anderson writes sounds the part, including the figures he gives for November: 'The Division has been augmented by 1 Sergeant and 42 Constables, in addition to which 70 Constables have been supplied nightly from other divisions to fill the vacancies caused by men being supplied in plain clothes as above, and to patrol the Division; giving a total of 8 Sergeants and 112 Constables for night duty.'

I have no doubt that cosmetic displays for the press were occasionally organised, rather as a municipal toilet might be freshly painted for a visiting royal, but there is not a scrap of evidence – *none whatsoever* – in the record to substantiate Anderson's claims of a radical augmentation of Whitechapel's police.

Whitechapel belonged to Jack and his 'Funny Little Game', and some sections of the press were beginning to understand this, in both its overt and covert manifestations. After the dispatch of the next cunt in the Genius's collection, *Reynold's News* published an article that was as devastating as it was perceptive:

We have been assured that specially trained officers, both in uniform and plain clothes, are daily and nightly on the watch against another crime ... Well, another was provided ... and because the murderer – quite naturally, of course – from the point of view of the *game* [my emphasis] between him and authority, escaped once more ... Must he oblige the police by committing the murder under their noses? They have exhibited an incapacity that amounts to imbecility, and whether it is the outcome of divided counsels in high quarters, or sheer incompetence, the result is the same.

For 'divided counsels in high quarters', read 'Masonic paranoia'. By December Charles Warren had been replaced as Metropolitan Police Commissioner by James Monro, and we shall shortly be in a position to compare the window-dressing put up by the former with the reality of more police on Whitechapel's streets under the latter.

In the meantime, camouflage of the royal-toilet variety continued. 'The most extraordinary precautions were taken,' enthused the *Daily Chronicle* on 8 October. 'Large bodies of plainclothes men were drafted by Sir Charles Warren into the Whitechapel District from other parts of London.' These were presumably members of the same large body of men who were so secret that nobody had ever seen them.

By contrast, Smith had his men on the City streets in unmistakable uniform. 'The City Police,' continued the *Chronicle*, 'far from being outdone in their exertions to ensure the protection of the public, more than doubled their patrols, so that almost every nook and cranny of the various beats came under police supervision every 5 minutes.' Meanwhile, needless to add, Warren's undercover contingent sustained their remarkable invisibility. *Punch* magazine suffered from no delusions about the number of police on the street, and neither did the citizens of Whitechapel.

The caption reads:

FIRST MEMBER OF 'CRIMINAL CLASS': 'FINE BODY O'MEN,
   THE PER-LEECE!'
SECOND DITTO: 'UNCOMMON FINE! – IT'S LUCKY FOR HUS
   AS THERE'S SECH A BLOOMIN' FEW ON 'EM!!!'

PUNCH, OR THE LONDON CHARIVARI.—October 13, 1888.

WHITECHAPEL, 1888.

First Member of "Criminal Class." "FINE BODY O' MEN, THE PER-LEECE!"
Second Ditto. "UNCOMMON FINE!—IT'S LUCKY FOR HUS AS THERE'S SECH A BLOOMIN' FEW ON 'EM!!!"

"I have to observe that the Metropolitan Police have not large reserves doing nothing and ready to meet emergencies; but every man has his duty assigned to him, and I can only strengthen the Whitechapel district by drawing men from duty in other parts of the Metropolis."—Sir Charles Warren's Statement. "There is one Policeman to every seven hundred persons."—Vide Recent Statistics.

On the day this cartoon was published, 13 October, the *East London Observer* reported a 'Great Meeting at Spitalfields', being a congregation of the irate who turned up to hear speeches from local worthies and dignitaries 'condemning the police' and demanding 'better police protection'.

'The incompetency of the Metropolitan Police Force,' declared Mr J. Hall, to unanimous agreement, 'had never been better exemplified than when three murders were allowed to take place *without any steps being taken to increase that force* [my emphasis]; or when, after all these terrible crimes had been committed, they still refuse to offer a reward.'[31] Clearly no one in the hall had read the *Chronicle*, because not a voice was raised to the contrary. Where exactly were the extra police? These people lived and worked in the killing zone, and they well knew that the joke in *Punch* better represented their circumstances than anything coming out of treacherous Charlie. The local police were themselves appalled, insisted Mr Hall, 'so disgusted with the manner in which they were tyrannised over, that he veritably believed that they were not at all disinclined for a strike against Warren and the Home Secretary'.

Interspersed with cheers or cries of 'Shame!', speaker after speaker condemned the 'demoralisation and corruption of the Metropolitan Police Force'.[32] We can but pity the honest cop on the street. His adversary was not only the most dangerous criminal in England, but also potential nemesis of the traumatised rabble in Whitehall, terrified that he might be caught.

'We have had enough of Mr Home Secretary Matthews,' declared the *Telegraph* with corrosive sincerity, 'who knows nothing, has heard nothing, and does not intend to do anything. It is clear the detective department at Scotland Yard is in an utterly hopeless and worthless condition: that were there a capable director of CID [rather than Anderson] the scandalous exhibition of stupidity revealed in the East End inquests and the immunity enjoyed by criminals committing murder after murder, would not have angered and disgusted the public feeling as undoubtedly it has done.' The paper demanded a clean sweep of red tape.

Red tape and spin were all Warren had. Two days after the perversion of Masonic ceremony had put an end to the life of Annie Chapman, the *Echo* became the designated vehicle for official propaganda: 'the hundred and fifty police who, it is asserted, have been drafted down into this neighbourhood'.[33] The only word of substance here is 'asserted', because these additional coppers were a figment of the imagination. Nothing had happened except an exchange of correspondence between Charlie and the Home Office. In one flight of fancy, Warren claimed that he was about to write to the Secretary of State asking for three hundred additional men – six hundred boots on a worthless scrap of paper.[34]

Amidst all the outrage and anguish, letters to *The Times* and waste-of-ink petitions to government, a moustached face had come to the fore. He was a forty-nine-year-old builder and decorator living off the Mile End Road, by the name of George Lusk.

At their wits' end with Warren, Lusk and a bunch of local tradesmen had formed a Vigilance Committee. If the cops couldn't catch the bastard, they would try, and night after night they congregated to patrol the streets. At the same time, as Chairman of the Committee, Lusk wrote to whoever he thought might listen – which

was basically nobody: at a meeting of the Committee it was announced that 'a third letter sent to the Home Secretary remained unanswered'. Despairing at the official indifference, they pledged to press on, adjourning their meeting with a vote of thanks 'passed by acclamation, to the City Commissioners of Police'.

It is praise for Smith and condemnation for Warren that tells the tale of public feeling in the streets. They could *see* Smith's police, but could only read about Warren's. While preparing its own fore-doomed letter, there was exasperation on the part of the Board of Works over Warren's practice of importing in replacement men from different divisions. A contribution from the Reverend Dan Greatorex of Whitechapel exemplified the point. 'He regretted,' he said, 'the frequent change of police divisions which was now the custom. If a neighbourhood was to be properly guarded, the constable should be permanently in charge of it, and know by sight almost every person in it. The new system made this impossible and was breaking down.'[35]

The *Star* agreed, and stuck it to Charlie. He had wrecked the police force, 'disorganised it utterly, and thinking he had a genius for stamping out dangerous social tendencies [after suppressing the disorder at Trafalgar Square], let the rank crop of crime and misery grow untouched and uncared for'.

Warren's system meant that units of police came and went, but it doesn't mean that the number of constables was increased. On the day of the Board of Works meeting, Anderson authorised thirty-seven H Division coppers to wear civilian clothes. Thus, instead of thirty-seven helmets, there were thirty-seven bowler hats. These fellows were the mainstay of Warren's 'stronger proof' that the detective department was 'doing its work with secrecy and efficiency'. I'm sure they were doing their tyrannised best, but a change of hat turns no one into a detective, any more than it increases the aggregate number of police on the streets.

On 22 October Arnold wrote to Warren summarising the realities of the H Division picture. Reacting to the tradesmen's petition, he begged to report: 'It is impossible to at all times keep a constable on each Beat as owing to the number of men absent from duty from sickness, leave, attending the Police Court, or sessions [at night?] or employed on special duties, which are necessary, but for which no provision has been made.'

No mention of the phantom three hundred. The division has men missing, 'for which no provision has been made'.[36] Arnold makes it clear he can't even cover the regular beats with so much as a single constable. Even if he had been able to do so, many commentators had identified 'beats' as the essence of the policing problem. 'They go on Beats it takes them more than half an hour to cover,' noted the *Bradford Observer*. 'Beats of a night policeman should not be of uniform length. At present a criminal who knows his district can usually tell to a nicety, after an officer has passed a given spot, how long it will take to bring him to the same spot again.'[37]

If some provincial hack knew this, then so did Jack the Ripper. In our day it's possible to access at least some information that was kept well hidden from the recalcitrant mob in EC2. We can actually see what the police numbers were on a day-to-day basis. Such information is contained in 'Police Orders', published at Scotland Yard for each twenty-four-hour period and signed off by senior officers – Warren, Anderson, Carmichael Bruce, etc.

Beginning prior to the death of Chapman on 1 September 1888, and throughout the following two months, there isn't a single reference either to the murderer or to any increase in the number of police. Not one. The week-ending figures for uniformed police in Whitechapel in H Division are as follows:

1 September
Sergeants – (1st class) 19; (2nd class) 5; (3rd class) 13
Constables – (1st class) 220; (2nd class) 105; (3rd class) 143
8 September [Chapman murder]
Sergeants – (1st class) 19; (2nd class) 5; (3rd class) 13
Constables – (1st class) 219; (2nd class) 106; (3rd class) 144
16 September
Sergeants – (1st class) 19; (2nd class) 5; (3rd class) 13
Constables – (1st class) 219; (2nd class) 106; (3rd class) 145

Thus, a week after Chapman's murder there were an additional *two* police officers working H Division Whitechapel, compared to the week before it.

22 September
Sergeants – (1st class) 19; (2nd class) 5; (3rd class) 13
Constables – (1st class) 219; (2nd class) 105; (3rd class) 145
29 September [Stride/Eddowes murder]
Sergeants – (1st class) 19; (2nd class) 5; (3rd class) 13
Constables – (1st class) 219; (2nd class) 104; (3rd class) 146
6 October
Sergeants – (1st class) 19; (2nd class) 5; (3rd class) 13
Constables – (1st class) 218; (2nd class) 105; (3rd class) 146
13 October
Sergeants – (1st class) 19; (2nd class) 5; (3rd class) 13
Constables – (1st class) 218; (2nd class) 106; (3rd class) 147
20 October
Sergeants – (1st class) 19; (2nd class) 5; (3rd class) 13
Constables – (1st class) 219; (2nd class) 106; (3rd class) 146
28 October
Sergeants – (1st class) 19; (2nd class) 5; (3rd class) 12
Constables – (1st class) 219; (2nd class) 106; (3rd class) 146

It can be seen that there was only a negligible variation in the number of police officers on the streets of Whitechapel throughout these crucial weeks. The pre-Chapman figures are almost identical to those following the Double Event (in fact, there was one constable less). In his letter of 22 October, Arnold had recommended an additional twenty-five men: 'ten for Leman Street & ten for

Commercial Street', and the remainder to 'Arbour Square which immediately joins Whitechapel and where the beats are somewhat long'. His request was at last granted, five days before Bro Jack finished Bro Charlie off on 9 November.

4 November
Sergeants – (1st class) 19; (2nd class) 5; (3rd class) 14
Constables – (1st class) 221; (2nd class) 110; (3rd class) 181[38]

The murderer, aware of this belated increase, abandoned the streets in favour of homicidal fun indoors. 'The celerity with which the Ripper accomplished his purpose,' wrote the *New York Herald*, 'might be accepted as evidence that he was waiting for such an order, and that at the moment it was given he was aware of the circumstance.' Mary Kelly was cut to bits in her own room on the following Saturday.

These extra coppers had come into the frame literally days before the authorities would decide it was all over. As Macnaghten insists in his silly memoir, the Ripper had 'drowned himself in the Thames' on or about 10 November 1888, and his reign of terror was done. *Ha ha.*

I don't want to get into the 'Ripper suicide' here, nor his subsequent slaying of Alice McKenzie et al. I mention McKenzie only to illustrate the difference between Warren's paper police and the helmets his successor actually put on the street.

James Monro had been reinstated as Commissioner for eight months when Jack hit McKenzie on 17 July 1889. Immediately, on the same day, Monro made a request to the Home Office for more police, enabling us to contrast the utility of a relatively honest cop with the wretched little trickster preceding him. There was no fanfare in the press, but with accountable bureaucracy we can follow a logical and simple paper trail. On 17 July 1889 Monro's letter is recorded in the Home Office 'Confidential Entry Book', confirmed by Police Order indexes, and two days later, on 19 July, printed in 'Police Orders' themselves.[39] H Division was immediately augmented by the additional policemen Warren could never find: one divisional inspector, five sergeants and fifty constables. Six months after McKenzie's death, Whitechapel was still being patrolled by an extra 150 police officers. Despite Charlie's publicity stunts (bloodhounds in Hyde Park, for example), and for all his support by the conservative press, there is not a single reference following the Double Event to any augmentation of officer numbers that can be officially confirmed. Warren's instructions are as invisible as his phoney police.

Public disgust at this pest's ineptitude, and at the Warren/ Matthews alliance, meant that it was the people themselves who were forced to take the initiative. As early as September 1888 they were demanding government-funded rewards for information leading to the apprehension of the killer. This proved as contentious as the hordes of transparent constables. Within twenty-four hours of the Stride/Eddowes calamity, the City authorities had posted a reward of £500, with the full backing of its Commissioner of Police. It took Warren and pals six days to announce that there would be no reward at all.

Incredulity and anger greeted the news. At a Board of Works meeting on 6 October, Mr Maurice Abrahams spoke for all. 'Why,' he asked, 'should the head of one department stand out against the whole of the metropolis in this matter? Ninety-nine men out of a hundred were in favour of a reward being offered, and surely all the sense and all the intellect of this country was not centred in one man?'

Certainly not the intellect, but the survival of a degenerate System was centred on one man – Warren was merely its exposed figurehead. This was about 'Victorian values', about the maintenance of a vice-like grip on the honeypot. Behind the scenes all the usual obfuscatory processes were proceeding apace. From the first it was obvious that neither the Met nor Matthews wanted anything to do with any financial inducements that might have contributed to catching this prick. Never mind what the City did – they had no control over the City – the last thing the Met needed was any extra prying eyes on the streets.

George Lusk and his men were the only totally committed boots on the block. 'The exertions of the Committee have been redoubled,' reported *Lloyd's Weekly* on 16 September, 'some of the members in couples now perambulating the streets from midnight to dawn.' When Lusk wasn't perambulating, he was continuing to canvass for a reward. His Committee wrote to Her Majesty, who was probably too busy auditing her possessions to reply.[40] But he kept on writing to the newspapers, and by extraordinary coincidence a letter from Lusk and his associate Joseph Aarons was published in the *Morning Post* on 1 October, directly underneath the text of the first appearance of the 'Dear Boss' letter. I think it more than likely that Jack took almost as much satisfaction in Lusk's contribution as he did in his own. I also think it likely that it was here that he became aware of the fun he might have with the name George Lusk.

Victoria's insouciance reflected the official trend. Despite his endless approaches, the authorities didn't want to engage with Lusk. The record is full of his supplications, mirrored with the dismissive responses from the Home Office. No, they didn't want to go to his meeting. No, they didn't want to cough up funds. 'NO GOVERNMENT REWARD', confirmed *Lloyd's*, publishing both Lusk's letter to the Home Secretary and the weasel's reply. Mr E. Leigh-Pemberton of the Home Office dutifully did the deed:

> I am directed by the Secretary of State to acknowledge receipt of your letter of the 16th inst., with reference to the question of an offer of a reward, and I am to inform you that had the Secretary of State considered the case a proper one for the offer of a reward he would at once have offered one on behalf of the government, but that the practice of offering rewards for the discovery of criminals was discontinued some years ago because experience showed that such offers of reward tended to produce more harm than good.[41]

So bugger off.

On the publication of Leigh-Pemberton's letter, wrote *Lloyd's*, 'a tremendous storm of indignation was roused in the breasts of the public, and fierce denunciation of the Home Office authorities was heard at every house and at every street corner. Meetings were held at over forty places for the one purpose of denouncing the letter, which was described by one speaker as "the lamest piece of official-ism ever issued from a government office".'

It was also a lie. Rewards for the apprehension of criminals were in fact issued by the Home Office whenever it took Matthews' fancy; Leigh-Pemberton's sneaky reference to their discontinuance 'some years ago' was nothing but another waft in the orchestrated smoke-screen. Rewards were in fact issued all the time. For example, we find this entry from the 'Secret Council Minutes' at Bradford a little over twelve months before (I'm interested in Bradford for reasons that will introduce themselves):

> Saturday 6 August 1887. *Murder Case*. Wrote to Home Secretary [Matthews] as to reward.
> Saturday 13 August 1887. *Murder Case*. Letter from Home Secretary [Matthews] offering £100 reward.

One hundred pounds, or even fifty, would have done George Lusk very nicely. His local MP, Samuel Montagu, had personally offered £100, which the Home Office had duly refused. He had also offered to print posters at his own expense, which it also refused. This miffed Montagu, because shortly before, according to the *East London Observer*, 'In a case of a man who was shot, the police put up notices offering a reward that was privately offered.' Now, at the Ripper's convenience, it was against Home Office policy.

Curious, ain't it? Matthews doesn't mind slipping a hundred quid Bradford's way to ease their homicidal woes, but won't approve a penny to try to catch this sack of shit. Was there something so different about these two murderers? The camouflage of fake precedent behind which Warren/Matthews were hiding was set out by Warren in a letter to the Home Office that it would then parrot back to Lusk. 'The practice of offering rewards was discontinued some time ago,' he wrote, 'because experience showed that in their general effect such offers produced more harm than good, and there is a special risk that the offer of a reward might hinder rather than promote the ends of justice.'

There was also a 'special risk' of an innocent woman having her guts ripped out. When Warren writes of promoting 'the ends of justice', he doesn't say which end he meant. The supposed cessation of rewards was in fact nothing to do with the citizenry, but had been introduced in 1884 in an attempt to stamp out police corruption. What the then Home Secretary Sir William Harcourt and the then Assistant Commissioner James Monro had done in 1884 was intended to bust up an iniquity that was fertilising villainy inside the Met, and it was inside the Met – self-evidently not in the City – that such rewards had been terminated. Many innocent Victorians must have languished in jail to supplement the incomes of Her Majesty's Metropolitan Police.[42]

In ignorance of, or indifferent to, the domestic issues of Scotland Yard, George Lusk continued to batter at the Home Office. On 7 October he wrote to Matthews: 'It is my duty to humbly point out that the present series of murders is absolutely unique in the annals of crime, that the cunning, astuteness and determination of the murderer has hitherto been, and may possibly still continue to be, more than a match for Scotland Yard and the Old Jewry [City Police] combined and that all ordinary means of detection have failed. This being so I venture most respectfully to call your attention to the fact that the only means left untried for the detection of the murderer has been the offer of a government reward.'[43]

Matthews was a lawyer, and Lusk was not, and he should have taken more care of his words. In his final paragraph he went on to make an error of the kind upon which lawyers thrive, suggesting 'a government proclamation of a really substantial reward with the extension of a free pardon to any person not the actual assassin'.[44]

Matthews ignored the 'reward' and jumped on the 'pardon'. Home Office minutes reveal that after consultation with Warren and Anderson, he decided that a 'pardon' would be just dandy, pulling a fast one that would ease their ignoble confederacy off Jack's hook. In a memo that followed the meeting we can see the actual process of twisting Lusk's words. 'Say to Mr Lusk,' it advises, 'that the expedience of granting a ~~reward~~ [deleted] pardon to persons not actually concerned in the commission of the murders and not implicated in the terrible guilt of contriving or abetting them, has been more than once under the consideration of the Secretary of State.'[45] That same day, Warren endorsed the scam. 'In reply to your immediate letter just received,' he wrote to Matthews, 'on the subject of Mr Lusk's proposal as to a pardon to accomplices in the Whitechapel Murders ...'

Mr Lusk proposed no such thing. His specific demand for a reward in respect of a killer *who exists* has been transformed into a pardon for a nebulous accomplice *who almost certainly does not.* The Home Office itself had concluded as early as 10 September, 'It is generally agreed that the Whitechapel Murderer *has no accomplices* [my emphasis] who could betray him.'[46] In other words, it was prepared to offer a 'pardon' based on a proposition of an accomplice *who it knew didn't exist.* Warren and his treacherous little legal chum in Whitehall were all too aware that the Ripper was a one-man band,

and it was also the general view of informed opinion inside and outside the Met. Police surgeon Dr Gordon Brown reiterated it during his questioning at Catherine Eddowes' inquest. 'Are you equally of opinion,' he was asked, 'that the act would be that of one man, one person only?' 'I think so,' replied Brown. 'I see no reason for any other opinion.' And even in his ludicrous summing-up, neither did Coroner Langham: 'The medical evidence conclusively demonstrated that only one person could be implicated.' Such a conclusion was later repeated by the man who shovelled a good deal of Jack's next victim, Mary Jane Kelly, into a bucket. 'There is no evidence he had an accomplice,' wrote police surgeon Dr Thomas Bond. The 'Murderer's Accomplice' had no more credibility than the 'Ink-Stained Hack', but was promoted with equal vigour.

Ignoring everything but Warren and Matthews' own predetermination, the offer of a pardon for this non-existent creature was made official, but only inasmuch as he may have had a hand in the murder of Mary Jane Kelly. 'The offer of a pardon was confined to the one murder,' pronounced Matthews on 12 November, three days after Kelly's death – and never mind the other victims. Basking in his own duplicity, Matthews had managed to write off the whole series. There would be no reward, no pardon (except in respect of Kelly); and soon after, there would be no possibility whatsoever of catching the son of a bitch, because, subsequent to Kelly, the Ripper himself was to be designated as dead and floating about in the Thames.

Thus, for fans of Macnaghten's memoir, the pardon offer was somewhat short-lived, existing only between Kelly's murder on 9 November 1888 and Jack's 'death' on 10 November 1888. We note a Home Office comment appended, with remarkable synchronicity, to Matthews' statement, wherein Kelly is absurdly nominated as 'the last of the series of East End murders'. 'This step,' continues the memo, 'was taken on 10th November 1888, after consultations with the cabinet.'

So there we have it. No reward and a worthless pardon, Mary Kelly designated as the last of the victims, and Jack's only true accomplices lounging at Downing Street and Scotland Yard.

'Mr Matthews has neither courage nor opinions,' wrote the *Star* on 13 November, 'but only the base instinct of self-preservation.' It was ever thus. What we're looking at here is a catastrophic failure inside the executive, 'filings' moving with the magnet, matched in my lifetime only by Tony Blair's nefarious decision to join in with the American oil grab in Iraq. 'The illegal we do immediately,' quipped Henry Kissinger. 'The unconstitutional takes a little longer.'

Ha ha.

Blair was afraid to admit that his nation's foreign policy belonged to a foreign nation, just as Warren and his culpable mob were afraid to admit that their investigation of Jack the Ripper belonged to Freemasonry. But with customary nous, the residents of Whitechapel knew the truth in their bones, knew very well that the authorities were lying. Once again it was Ernest Parke's newspaper, the *Star*, that gave insight into the anger fermenting in London's East End: 'We have heard the wildest stories as to the reason which popular opinion in Whitechapel assigns for Mr Matthews' obstinate refusal to offer a reward. It is believed by people who pass amongst their neighbours as sensible folk that the government do not want the murderer convicted, that they are interested in concealing his identity.'[47]

This was erroneously dismissed even by the paper that printed it, but just like the multitudes who marched in London's streets in opposition to war over the nonsense of WMD, so the people of Whitechapel intuitively knew the score with J.T.R. They thought they were being lied to, and they were right.

Warren's investigative endeavour was a melody from the Land of Make-Believe. Provided Jack could be kept isolated in the East End, nobody in the ranks of the Establishment gave much of a toss. Salisbury's constituency was the public at large, and for them the unfathomable romance of 'mystery' was spun, the Met representing itself as a beleaguered outfit doing its best, when in fact it was a corrupted burlesque that couldn't have done worse.

> I am the terror of the town,
> My fame spreads far and near.
> Six women have I now cut down
> While live the rest in fear.
> About a dozen yards or so
> From the policeman on his round
> A murder I commit, and Lo!
> The Murderer can't be found.
> With Fiendish grin, I watch the crowd

That hurries to the spot:
And in its midst, I laugh aloud
To think they find me not …
Next were I to stop and cry,
'Hi, policeman, I am he!'
I wonder will he make reply,
'I'll wait, sir, till you flee.'
Do what I will, with all the skill
By which my crime's attested,
Right under their nose,
As I tread on their toes,
I cannot get arrested …

'All hope of discovering Mrs Chapman's murderer must now be abandoned,' jibed the *Tatler.* 'The Police have got a clue!' In fact the police were *drowning* in clues their revolting mentor was only too pleased to provide. Chapman had had her throat cut across, her abdomen ripped open, and her intestines 'placed' over her left shoulder. A ring or rings were 'wrenched from her fingers',[48] and 'two farthings polished brightly' were found at her feet. 'The law about any metallic substance,' wrote Bro historian A.F.A. Woodford in 1878, 'is so well known to Freemasons, even to the Entered Apprentice, that we need not dilate upon it here. Money and any metallic substance are equally forbidden, symbolically, as we shall remember for two reasons.'[49]

I referred earlier to the controversy over the farthings as 'trivial', but they couldn't be more important. It is apparent that Bro Jack was both punishing his victims and initiating them into his funny little Masonic hell; and coins, particularly coins that shone like brass, become intriguing props in the frolic. In conjunction with Chapman's symbolic mutilations, the presence of farthings would represent a clue of extreme significance. In this context they become no more trivial than spent cartridge cases after a death from gunshot. They are the cherry on the ritual cake.

Q: Why were you deprived of all metal?
A: Because money is an emblem of vice.

Look out – Mr Sugden's back, and he definitely doesn't like the farthings. He's convinced himself that these coins are the product of a journalist's imagination, and that the 'myth' of the farthings has somehow cross-infected one of the senior policemen working the case. But it wasn't just the *Telegraph* that reported the farthings at Chapman's crime scene. At the inquest of another victim, Alice McKenzie, the local head of Whitechapel's CID, Inspector John Reid (nine months later and now with his guard down), was questioned at the coroner's court.

> FOREMAN: In previous cases was any similar coin found as that which you picked up in this instance? [A farthing was found under McKenzie's body]
> INSPECTOR REID: In the Hanbury Street case [Chapman] two farthings were found.

Mr Sugden doesn't like this at all, and with Gradgrindian authority he tells us the policeman is wrong. There is little to argue with over the ritualistic injuries, nor the totemic positioning of items at Chapman's feet, so he makes a song and dance over something he says wasn't even there. He finds no favour with farthings for reasons that are diametrically opposed to mine. Predictably, he defers to the Warren school of detection, all but commiserating for lack of that vital scream. 'In the light of these [investigative] disappointments,' he writes, 'Chief Inspector Swanson's remark that the Chapman investigation "did not supply the police with the slightest clue to the murderer" is perhaps understandable.'[50]

Is it?

I think it's laughable. How can any modern writer promote this drivel, much less agree with it? In preparation of his argument over Inspector Reid, Mr Sugden says of the disputed farthings, 'It isn't in the files' – as though this could support anything more than the fatuousness of his point. What Mr Sugden doesn't tell his readers is that there is nothing in these 'files' about anything much at all. Those available at the National Archive are titled 'Unimportant Series', and of these, eighteen folios are marked as 'Destroyed'. What's left are the dregs of anything that isn't listed as 'Missing'. What the 'Important Series' of Ripper files consisted of no one can say, because no one, including Mr Sugden, has ever seen them.

Neither he nor I know what was included in the destroyed files, so we must move our thinking sideways a little.

Farthings were most certainly discovered at Chapman's crime scene (put there by the Ripper), but before we arrive at why, it's necessary to test Mr Sugden's protestations over why they were not. Let it be said at the outset, I don't need to prove the existence of these farthings. It is already established, two primary contemporary sources confirming it (Inspector Reid and the *Telegraph*). Independent of one another, and about a year apart, the consistency of their accounts is potent, and just about as good as it gets. The onus therefore is on Mr Sugden to corroborate his 'myth', and prove they were wrong.

On page 109 of his book he introduces us to his counter-farthing campaign. He tells us reporters converged on 29 Hanbury Street (its back yard being Chapman's crime scene). Among them was a man by the name of Oswald Allen, who concocted a press report describing Chapman's rings as having been wrenched from her finger and 'placed carefully at the victim's feet'.

Anyone who knows anything about Hanbury Street (including Mr Sugden and myself) knows this is incorrect. There were no rings at Chapman's feet. But Oswald has nicely set Mr Sugden's scene. He has established a foundation of inaccuracy as some kind of bookend by which we're supposed to measure the rest of Sugden's argument: i.e., Oswald Allen was wrong, *ergo*, so were Reid and the *Telegraph*. In other words, he's pre-positioned his 'myth', and now goes on to try to associate it with fact, apparently hoping that the dismissal of one somehow proves the non-existence of the other.

But this isn't an argument about rings. It's an argument about *coins*. To associate the questionable with something under question is a tactic I'm suspicious of. It is my sincere wish not to misrepresent Sugden, therefore I quote him in full.

> Reporters converged on 29 Hanbury Street like angry hornets on the morning of the murder. One of the earliest on the scene was Oswald Allen of the *Pall Mall Gazette*, and his report which appeared on the streets later in the day carried the assertion that Annie's rings had been wrenched from her finger and placed at her feet. On the following Monday the *Daily Telegraph* printed another fable: 'There were also found two farthings polished brightly, and,

according to some, these coins had been passed off as half-sover-
eigns upon the deceased by her murderer.' The farthings quickly
passed into legend. Even two policemen later gave them credence.
In 1889 Inspector Reid told a different murder inquiry that two
farthings had been found on or about the body of Annie Chapman,
and in 1910 Major Henry Smith alleged in his memoirs that two
polished farthings had been discovered in her pocket. Neither
man, however, had personally investigated the Hanbury Street
case. Reid had been on leave at the time, and Smith, as Chief
Superintendent of the City of London force, had no responsibility
for policing Spitalfields. In succeeding years the rings and farthings
became an obligatory part of the collection of items found at the
feet of Annie's corpse.[51]

And now the reality.

The *Telegraph* says *nothing* about rings, and *nothing* about feet, and
therefore has *nothing* to do with any conflicting statements made by
Oswald Allen. The association between him and the *Telegraph* is
made only by Mr Sugden, so that he can package the two together
and dismiss them as one. Moreover, Commissioner Henry Smith
says *nothing* about farthings being discovered in Annie Chapman's
pocket. What he writes in his memoir (page 148) is this: 'After the
second crime I sent word to Sir Charles Warren that I had discovered a man very likely to be the man wanted. He certainly had all
the qualifications requisite. He had been a medical student; he had
been in a lunatic asylum; he spent all his time with women of loose
character, whom he bilked by giving them polished farthings instead
of sovereigns, two of these farthings having been found in the
pocket of the murdered woman.'[52]

Nowhere does Smith mention Chapman. He refers to 'the second
crime', which, as Mr Sugden must know, was Polly Nichols. I'm
afraid that yet again Phil is indulging in a little 'shameless selection'.
In his own book (page ix) he nominates Annie Chapman as the
fourth of Jack's victims.

He must also know that Chapman's pockets were entirely cut
open so their contents could be purloined, and that *nothing*, including farthings, was found in what was left of them. And neither did
Inspector Reid say that farthings were found 'on or about the body
of Annie Chapman'. What he said was: 'In another case of this kind

– the Hanbury Street murder – two similar farthings were found.'[53] The word 'on' is an invention.

Mr Sugden seems a tad over-eager for his readers to believe that metal was left *in situ* on Chapman's ritually murdered body when it was not. What he's up to is, of course, his business. I leave 'fair-minded students' to 'draw their own conclusions'. In the matter of farthings he's made no case, merely taken a rather convoluted route to agree with himself. Plus, if a week at the seaside disqualifies Reid as a witness, I hate to think what the passage of a century does for Mr Sugden. His wishful thinking makes a lousy argument worse. For to dump Reid also means abandoning one of Ripperology's darlings, the man responsible for wielding Bro Warren's famous sponge.

Chief of H Division Whitechapel, Superintendent Thomas Arnold was also away on leave, from 2 to 28 September 1888.[54] So what faith can we put in all his fabulous excuses for washing off a wall? 'In consequence of a suspicion having fallen upon a Jew named "John Pizer",' he wrote, '… I was apprehensive that if the writing were left it would be the means of causing a riot.'

How could he know that? Arnold didn't 'personally investigate' the case, and was away on leave throughout the Pizer saga. According to Mr Sugden's hypothesis, as he wasn't there he couldn't have known anything about it. Thus all that infantile fibbing over riot and concern for Jews goes out the window, and none of the Pizer/riot rubbish can have any credibility.

While I agree 100 per cent with that, I don't imagine Mr Sugden will. But you can't have it both ways – one man's holiday bringing ignorance, and another's bringing comprehensive insight. Of course Arnold knew about Pizer, just as Reid knew about the farthings, and Robert Anderson, who was also away, knew about all of it. How? Because all were senior policemen, and someone had told them. They had access to a constant traffic of information, and until it was weeded into virtual transparency, there was something called 'evidence' in the files.

The *Telegraph* report remains sound, as does the testimony given by Reid. There were farthings on the ground at Chapman's crime scene, and considering the overt Freemasonic piss-take it was, it would be surprising if there were not. Reid had been inadvertently indiscreet, but he had good reason for lowering the threshold over

McKenzie, and when we arrive at her murder on 17 July 1889, it will be readily apparent why.

As we approach the end of the chapter, this may be as good a place as any to see the back of Pizer and his Jewish sensibilities. He was one of the witnesses called at the Chapman inquest, and he had a good day. It was clear to him, if to no one else, that the police had fitted him up. 'I wish to vindicate my character to the world at large,' he said. 'I have called you in your own interests,' replied Coroner Baxter, 'partly with the object of giving you the opportunity of doing so.'

Pizer went on not only to exonerate himself of being 'the Womb-Collector', but also to successfully reject all of the police accusations, including even his damning sobriquet. From the outset he protested that 'Leather Apron' was an invention of the Metropolitan Police, and that he had no idea he was called by such a name until Sergeant Thick had baptised him on arrest. Investigations by the press substantiated this, family and neighbours denying that Pizer had ever been known to them as 'Leather Apron'. Thick had tailored Pizer to fit the crime, a fabrication the accused could barely comprehend: 'Sergeant Thick who arrested me has known me for eighteen years.'[55]

'Well, well,' rejoined Baxter with shrewd dismissal. 'I do not think it necessary for you to say more.'

Any more wouldn't have been useful. Holiday or no holiday, everything Arnold said about Pizer is proved to be nonsense.

Almost from the beginning it became apparent to me that I wasn't investigating a mystery, but *why* it was a mystery, and why, ludicrously, it remains so to this day. It became clear that Ripperology was the wholesaler of the mystique, and that to investigate Jack I'd constantly be running into gangs of revisionist paramedics.

The A to Z claims that contemporary criticism of the police was the result of 'swamping the district with uniformed patrols, who the press claimed were a serious nuisance'. I am unaware of the press to which this refers. Certainly the police were seriously criticised in an eruption of public rage, but it was hardly for 'swamping the district with uniformed patrols'. To present this as a consensus is absurd; to proffer it as any kind of excuse is reprehensible.

Virtually every contemporary criticism of the police was for the lack of them – be it from the Board of Works, the Whitechapel

traders, Lusk's Vigilance Committee or the student vigilantes operating out of Toynbee Hall. Why does anyone imagine the vigilante
committees formed themselves? It was because of a *lack of police*, as
is confirmed in the columns of almost every publication that had an
opinion to give. Yet *The A to Z* sweeps all this aside and finds differently, elevating a bunch of non sequiturs into some kind of exem-
plary acquittal. An ape at the zoo could have made a better fist of it
than Warren, and yet, 'contrary to popular belief', minces *The A to
Z*, 'the police investigation was professional and competent'.[56]

Tell it to the ghosts.

I do not care for corporate thinking, and therefore I do not like
Ripperology. It seems to me to be a feeble thing, afraid of itself,
forever looking over its shoulder in case one of its 'experts' like Mr
Melvin Harris disagrees with something it says. In my view, few have
done more to pollute this material than Ripperologists such as Mr
Harris and many like him, who routinely underestimate the intelligence of their readers as parallel with their own. I don't know if
Mr Philip Sugden is hypnotised by this material, or is seeking to
hypnotise others: a police inspector draws attention to some
farthings and provokes an indignant diatribe of denial; a coroner
proposes a risible camouflage effervescent with lies ('the Womb-
Collector'), and Mr Sugden obligingly asks how much truth there
may be in it?

For what it's worth, I've been a professional writer for the best
part of forty years. I've researched widely, from the Manhattan
Project to the Khmer Rouge, but until confronted with Ripperology
I had never laboured through such an expulsion of syncopated crap
masquerading as history in all my life. It knows all the 'facts', does
Ripperology – knows the name of Elizabeth Stride's home town in
Sweden and the number of teeth in her upper jaw – but in respect
of context, it hasn't got a fucking clue. It seems to think the
nineteenth-century governing classes (and their police force) were
some kind of gold standard of propriety, and as a consequence the
corporate effort (with one or two exceptions) is a ludicrous rehash
of Victorian propaganda.

Coroner Bro Baxter gave a revealing demonstration of just how
artificial this 'mystery' really was. It's populated by a cast of walk-on
conveniences, including 'Leather Apron' (a good all-rounder, both
as bogus suspect and then as alibi for the destruction of evidence).

And we mustn't forget the 'reward' that became a 'pardon' for the 'accomplice' who didn't exist.

Ripperology is somehow blind to it all, comic absurdities accepted as though they'd never appeared. It is a 'mystery' that was made up as it went along, characters being invented to fit the twists and turns of the limelit melodrama. Ripperology gawps in the stalls, starry-eyed at each new scene change and baffled by the special effects. It cannot, or will not, see the wires that make the mirrors move, or the bellows that fart out puffs of smoke. Instead, it gasps in the darkness of marvels – 'Look! Look! It's the Ink-Stained Journalist! I tell a lie, it's the Insane Medical Student! Ha ha. But look! Who comes there? A suspicious-looking cove if ever I've seen one. Why, it's the dear old cobbler who sold the tight shoes! It's a wonderful show!! Who wrote it? Why, a man called Swanson, and he's got lots and lots to come!! You should see the tricks he pulls before your very eyes! And you'll never see how it's done! There are Jews and Irishmen and mastur-bating dwarfs, Malays from ships in the Port o' London, and cowboys even from the American Wild West!! All will pass before you! All will dazzle!!! There's even a comedian singing a topical hit called "Vincent's Code". But you'll never *see* the star of the Great Masonic Mystery Show, because he might fuck it all up, and he must forever remain a "Mystery".'

In a previous chapter we saw how the police denied and destroyed their best ever evidence at Goulston Street. In the next, we will see how they denied and destroyed their best ever witness.

8

The Double Event:
Part Two

Whoever fights monsters should see to it that in the
process he does not become a monster.

Friedrich Nietzsche, *Thus Spake Zarasthustra*

Of all the atrocities committed by Jack the Ripper, it is paradoxically
his least successful that is the most revealing.

By that I don't necessarily mean revealing of his identity, but
rather of those struggling to conceal it. The tomfoolery masquerading as investigation into the murder of Elizabeth Stride is character-
ised by its brainlessness and breadth of deception, what the *East
London Observer* recorded as 'demoralisation and corruption inside
the Metropolitan Police'.[1] The *East London Advertiser* was more
specific. 'It is clear,' it wrote, 'that there is no detective force in the
proper sense of the word in London at all.'[2] In reality, it was worse
than that. The Met was no longer a police force, but as a result of
the efforts of certain senior officers had actually become a force for
non-detection.

Ditto the coroners' courts. Bro Wynne Baxter was back in the
chair for Elizabeth Stride, and having all but shot his bolt with 'the
Womb-Collector', he wasn't going to make the same mistake again.
Brothels have doubtless been managed with more propriety than
Baxter brought to these proceedings. His enquiries into the destruction of Mrs Stride were a mere formality on the road to a predetermined outcome.

Stride, it will be remembered, was done to death at a place called
Dutfield's Yard, Berner Street, just off the Commercial Road. The
Reverend Samuel Barnett of Toynbee Hall had been campaigning
without success for more lighting there. 'It is a dim, miserable looking place,' reported the *Globe*. 'Nowhere is the niggardly expendi-

THEY ALL LOVE JACK

ture of gas more apparent than just before the court where the crime was committed.' Almost all the adjacent premises were rented to small businesses – cigarette-makers, hatters, that kind of thing. Until Jack turned up there wasn't much to distinguish Berner Street from the rest of the brickwork, except that a young Jew called Israel Lipski had snuffed his landlady (or was at least accused of having done so) in a nearby tenement a little over a year before.

Dutfield's Yard was about halfway up the street, behind a set of wooden gates bearing the inscription HINDLEY TACK MANUFACTURE & A. DUTFIELD VAN AND CART BUILDER. To the right of the yard and forming part of its wall was a house patronised almost exclusively by immigrant Jews. It was the home of an establishment called the International Workingmen's Educational Club, and if you were a hard-up Socialist from east of the Rhine, this was probably the place for you. There were classes and discussions, Marx was a god, and songs were sung past the small hours in a variety of mother tongues.

But the singing stopped abruptly that night, and by dawn the gates to the yard were secured and 'jealously guarded' by policemen. Important footsteps were on their way. Having done his best to wipe out all evidence at Goulston Street, Warren arrived here at about 7 a.m. to continue tidying up. Yet again, there was evidence to be destroyed. According to Walter Dew, then a twenty-six-year-old constable, but destined, as Chief Inspector, to become one of Scotland Yard's most famous icons: 'In the little Berner Street Court, quite close to where the body was found, detectives searching every inch of the ground came upon a number of grape skins and stones.'[3]

Once again we're looking at a lead that could have caught the Ripper. Predictably it was suppressed by the Met, and it doesn't fare any better today. Ripperology dismisses Walter Dew's recollection of grape-skins with the same enthusiasm with which Mr Sugden denies Inspector Reid's memory of farthings. Inevitably, of course, grape-skins will prove to have been found at Stride's crime scene. Meanwhile, it was grape-skins and stones that freaked Warren, and for the same occult reason as the message that he washed off the wall. Dutfield's Yard was literally splattered with what any honourable cop would have preserved as significant evidence, but being the cop he was, Warren allowed these grape-skins and stones to be washed down the drain.

Quite an achievement for a Commissioner of Police: he'd laundered two sources of evidence in a single night. The evidence of grapes would henceforth be hurried into the house of mirrors, and purged by the corrupt process of turning the most obvious of clues into the stuff of incomprehensible 'mystery'.

To get a handle on just how debased this Masonic fandango had become, we need to take another look at the 'Double Event', from the other side of that September night.

It's just before 1 a.m. on Sunday, 30 September 1888. Commissioner Warren is still tucked up, the streets of Whitechapel are all but silent, sinister here and there in the intermittent gaslight, but predominantly black with rain. A coster turns into Berner Street, his cart hauled by an exhausted pony. It's been a long day, and a long journey home from Westow Hill Market at Crystal Palace. The coster is a twenty-six-year-old part-time dealer in trinkets and cheap jewellery, a Russian Jew called Louis Diemschutz. He lived at, and was also steward of, the International Workingmen's Club, where his wife was presently in the downstairs kitchen making tea. Neither she nor anybody else around Dutfield's Yard had been aware of anything untoward that night. The usual crew had been in, chewing the usual fat – capital, exploitation, trade unions – and now they'd set the world to rights, they were all upstairs for the music.

Diemschutz must have heard the singing as he turned into the gates, which were open as usual, but now he was startled by a jolt as his pony refused the darkness. Something was spooking it, and no way was it going in there. 'I couldn't make out what was the matter,' said Diemschutz, 'so bent my head to see if there was anything to frighten him.'

Two minutes later Mrs Diemschutz was hysterical at the door, and the yard was full of people. 'We struck a match and saw blood running from the gate and all the way down to the side door of the club.' Stride's throat had been so deeply cut it had almost taken her head off. Her bonnet had fallen to one side, and inside it, 'apparently with the object of making the article fit closer to the head, was a folded copy of *The Star* newspaper'.[4] Such was the sad and ignominious end of Elizabeth Stride.

The witnesses stared in shock, and some of them need names. A club member called Maurice Eagle didn't want to look at the body – 'the sight of blood upset me' – so he looked for a policeman instead. Despite the 'saturation' he was out of luck: no officer was to be found. A Pole by the name of Isaac Kosebrodski takes up the story. 'I went to look for a policeman at the request of Diemschutz,' he told the *Evening News*, 'but could not find one.' Instead he ran into Eagle, who was still batting about the streets, and at last they discovered a pair of helmets in Commercial Road. One was dispatched for a doctor while Eagle ran on to Leman Street police station 'and called out an Inspector'. Back at Dutfield's Yard, Police Constable Lamb was the first uniform to pitch up. 'On arrival of that officer,' reported the *Telegraph*, 'he perceived that the woman was lying on her left side, and was clutching some grapes in her right hand and sweetmeats in her left.'[5] Superintendent Arnold arrived shortly after, together with Drs Blackwell and Phillips. 'While the doctor was examining the body,' recalled Kosebrodski, 'I noticed that she had some grapes in her right hand and sweets in her left.'[6]

It cannot go unnoticed that we now have confirmation of Walter Dew's recollection of 'grape skins' from two sources who were actually there, Isaac Kosebrodski and PC Henry Lamb, who independently of each other report grapes clutched in Stride's right hand. Virtually every London newspaper published on the morning of 1 October carries a report of grapes being discovered at Dutfield's Yard. By way of corroboration of Dew, Lamb and Kosebrodski, let's hear from Mrs Fanny Mortimer, resident of 36 Berner Street, 'four doors down from the tragedy':

I was standing at the door of my house nearby, the whole time between half past twelve and one o'clock this [Sunday] morning, and did not notice anything unusual. I had just gone in doors and was preparing to go to bed, when I heard a commotion outside, and immediately ran out, thinking there was another row in the Socialists' Club close by. I went to see what was the matter, and was informed that another dreadful murder had been committed in the yard adjoining the clubhouse, and on going inside I saw the body of a woman huddled up just inside the gates with her throat cut from ear to ear. The body was lying slightly on one side, with the legs a little drawn up as if in pain, the clothes being slightly disarranged, so that the legs were partly visible. The woman appeared to be respectable, judging by her clothes, and in her hand were found a bunch of grapes and some sweets.[7]

Could these be the same grapes seen by Lamb and Kosebrodski, their 'skins and stones' specifically referred to by Walter Dew? I pose the question only to those who seek to deny their existence, and move on to the next and most important witness, the man who actually discovered Stride's still-bleeding body.

Louis Diemschutz had no reason to fabricate anything, much less any opportunity to concoct and coordinate so abstruse a fantasy as grapes to go with the shock of discovering a murdered woman with her throat cut. You'd have to be maladjusted or even mad to do it, and that was far from the impression Diemschutz gave to the press. 'He is a Russian Jew but speaks English perfectly,' wrote the *Evening News*. 'He is a man with more intelligence than is usually to be found amongst men of his class, and in every way he is a credit to the neighbourhood in which he resides. This may not seem to be a compliment,' it continued, 'but we mean it as such, for our informant is, so far as we are able to judge, an honest, truth-speaking man, on whose evidence we feel that we are able to rely.'[8]

Such credence was given to Diemschutz's statement that the *Evening News* published it under what is known as a kicker headline:

'GRAPES IN HER HAND'
… In her right hand were tightly clasped some grapes, and in her left hand, she held a number of sweetmeats …

THE FIFTH VICTIM OF THE WHITECHAPEL FIEND.

Even the contemporary sketch on the previous page includes grapes clutched in Stride's right hand. So stand by for the obligatory debriefing.

'It is unlikely,' writes Sugden, 'that grapes were found at the crime scene.'[9] That's what he says, and apart from Inspector Walter Dew, Police Constable Henry Lamb, Mrs Fanny Mortimer, Mr Isaac Kosebrodski, Mr Louis Diemschutz, the *Morning Advertiser*, the *Evening Standard*, the *Evening News*, the *Daily News*, the *Globe*, the *Telegraph* and *The Times*, it's hard to imagine why anyone might disagree.

As my detective friend at the LAPD was wont to articulate, 'Give me a fucken break.' We have five on-site witnesses confirming the grapes, and Mrs Rosenfield and Miss Eva Hartstein reported seeing 'grape stalks' at the very same location, bringing the number of attributable sightings to seven. Yet we are required to believe that these grapes were some kind of collective hallucination. Mr Sugden classifies them as a myth on a par with the troublesome farthings.

In reality, it wasn't in the police's interests for these grapes to exist, and by the time of Bro Wynne Baxter's coroner's court, they didn't. Like the writing on the wall, they had been made to vanish. No way was anyone lying about the murder and the crime scene of Elizabeth Stride, or the grapes that went with it, except the Met and its fully compliant surgeon, Bro Dr Bagster Phillips.

In this malign world of smoke and mirrors it's refreshing to confront a certainty. Either Louis Diemschutz and everyone else who was in Dutfield's Yard is lying, or Bro Bagster Phillips is lying. There can be no middle ground. Phillips's version of events must wait for Baxter's courtroom. But before moving in that general direction, I want to take a last look at what Diemschutz is reported to have said. There are a variety of sources, and I select this from the *Evening News*: 'Her hands were tightly clenched and when the Doctor opened them I saw that she had been holding sweetmeats in one hand and grapes in the other.'

Now, it seems to me that there are two words here that contribute enormously to the credibility of this statement. They are 'tightly' and 'clenched'. By choosing them, Diemschutz was describing something he couldn't possibly have either fabricated or known about, because it is a symptom of a rare condition, understood in 1888 only by those very well versed in forensics.

It's called 'cadaveric spasm', and I travel forward half a century to find a description of the phenomenon by one of England's most formidable forensic scientists, Professor Sir Keith Simpson. 'This is an uncommon event,' he wrote, 'consisting of a violent spasm of the muscles at the moment of death. The change most frequently involves the hand, which may remain gripping a weapon, clothing or grass, etc., affording evidence assisting in the reconstruction of events immediately preceding death from violence.'[10]

No photographs seem to have been taken at Stride's crime scene, and certainly not of her hands. But Simpson's description is accom-

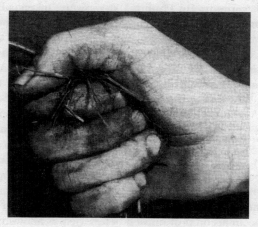

panied by a picture of a woman's hand in cadaveric spasm, tightly clenched just as Diemschutz described.

An earlier assessment of cadaveric spasm is to be found in Dr William R. Smith's *The Principles of Forensic Medicine*, published in 1895.[11] Describing sudden and violent death, Smith writes of the murdered person 'clutching the object he held a moment before'. 'This fact is of great importance from a medico-legal point of view,' he continues. But not, apparently, at Dutfield's Yard – because, like Philip Sugden, Dr Phillips was blind to the presence of the grapes.

Phillips was among a contingent of physicians called by the coroner, and it was principally he and Dr William Blackwell who made the first on-site inspection of Stride's injuries. There had been no facial or any other evident mutilation, and it seemed almost certain that the arrival of Diemschutz had disturbed her killer: Mrs

Mortimer was one among many who suspected that the Ripper 'must have made his escape immediately under cover of the cart'.

By now the International Club members were enjoying a distinctly hostile attitude from the police. About thirty people were still on the premises, and the whole lot of them were suddenly under suspicion. The gates to the yard were locked and closely guarded, and no person was 'allowed egress'. There were jibes in the press about the slamming of stable doors.

On the arrival of Superintendent Thomas Arnold from Leman Street, which took place almost simultaneously with that of the Divisional Surgeon Dr Phillips, 'steps were taken to ascertain whether the members of the club were in any way connected with the murder'. Arnold's concern for the sensibilities of the Jewish community was curiously absent here. Despite his comic lamentations over possible blame for the tribe of 'Leather Apron', he demonstrably had no problem stirring up anti-Semitic friction at Dutfield's Yard. 'After the body had been removed to St George's mortuary,' reported the *Chronicle*, 'the detectives entered the club and made careful examination of the inmates. The names and addresses of all the men present were taken, and a vigorous search of persons and premises was instituted, much to the annoyance of the members. Their pockets were searched, their hands and clothes particularly scrutinised, and some of them allege they were made to take off their boots. All knives had to be produced, and each man had to give an account of himself before he was allowed to depart. Some of the members say that the detectives treated them badly, swearing at them and shouting, "You're no foreigners, or else where's your knives?"'[12]

It's worth mentioning that it was a common prejudice amongst the ruling classes that only Jonnie Foreigner carried a dastardly knife. As the *Illustrated London News* succinctly put it, 'Can there be anything more un-English?'[13] Meanwhile, an Englishman who carried the sharpest knife in the business was busy with it about a mile away. After three hours of pissing away precious time, Arnold's boys were coming to the end of their enquiries at Dutfield's Yard. 'It was five o'clock before the police finished their investigations,' and it had been an entirely predictable waste of time. If PC Long and Dr Phillips knew of Eddowes' murder by 3 a.m. at the latest, then so did Superintendent Arnold.[14] Thus, if he'd scratched his nuts and screwed up his eyes real tight, he must have realised that Jack the Ripper *could not possibly* be one of the men at Dutfield's Yard.

What the cops were actually up to here was ignoring the Ripper in favour of indulging in a bit of anti-Semitic spite. The International Workingmen's Club had been under constant police surveillance throughout 1888, attracting multiple entries in the 'Crime Department's Special Branch' ledger.[15] The targets were primarily those who put the wind up the nobs – Jews and the Irish – and here was a heaven-sent opportunity to get in there and hassle them. My assessment isn't idle, but is based on a verbatim account given by one of Special Branch's most senior officers. In respect of that night at the club, Met Inspector Patrick McIntyre wrote: 'Concerts and dancing took place here on Saturday nights ... at the very moment when these people were indulging in festivity in an upstairs room, the "Ripper" was cruelly murdering an unfortunate in the courtway adjoining. It is worth noting that *no kind of suspicion fell upon the Anarchists in this connection; no one believed for a moment* that the anonymous stabber was one of their confraternity [my emphasis].'[16]

And yet it was 5 a.m. before they were allowed to go about their business. The waste of time is notable, because it was at 5 a.m. that Warren arrived at the wall in Goulston Street. Let us remind ourselves of his anxieties for the well-being of Leather Apron and his ilk: 'The most pressing question at the moment was some writing on the wall evidently written with the intention of inflaming the public mind against the Jews ... if the writing had been left, there would have been an onslaught upon the Jews' etc., etc.

It's a matter of record that a crowd had already assembled in Berner Street: 'The fact that another murder had been committed soon became known,' reported the *Daily News*, 'and long before daybreak the usually quiet thoroughfare was the scene of great excitement.'[17]

Never mind the 'onslaught' and the 'wrecking of property'; amongst this 'great excitement' there is no report of anything hostile beyond the odd non-recorded fart. Scores of people had arrived in Berner Street – 'immense numbers', according to the *Daily News* – yet there was not a rioter in sight. Surely someone could have popped over to Goulston Street and had a word in Charlie's ear? Told the Boss Cop not to fret, there were already hundreds of people on the streets, and not a hint of a squabble anywhere?

Warren was all but having an epileptic fit over a bit of writing in a passageway. If he really believed the Ripper (or anyone) was attempting to inflame the public mind against the Jews, how about a dead body outside a Jewish club? By the logic invoked at Goulston Street, suspicion must fall massively upon these Jews. So what provision had Bro Sir Charles Warren made to protect them from anti-Semitic riot at Berner Street?

Answer: none.

Despite the predictions of mayhem, there had been a profound switch in attitude. If anything, the police were actually exacerbating whatever anti-Semitic sentiment might have been abroad. Warren claimed he was fearful of exciting it, while at Dutfield's Yard the boys in blue were all but provoking it.

Anyone who believes Warren's riot bullshit would probably have difficulty with the plots of Enid Blyton. This wasn't a bit of chalk on a wall, it was a yard full of Jews with a murdered body in the middle of them. Did Arnold not think that pushing Jews about, locking them in with accompanying insults and demands to see knives, might not stimulate public animosity towards the denizens of this club, if not appear to be an outright intimation of guilt? Might not such provocative behaviour from a bunch of policemen precipitate the very riot they all claimed to be in fear of? This senseless alienation of potential witnesses at the club underscores the tosh put about to camouflage the reality behind Warren's rapid adieu to his mattress.

The intrepid minders in Jack's wake were only partially successful with the writing on the wall, but they did rather better with the grapes at Dutfield's Yard. Even Ripperologists Mr Stewart Evans and Mr Don Rumbelow refer to 'the Legend of the Grapes'.[18] Over most Ripper matters I have a good deal of time for these gents, but in respect of the grapes they get themselves into a rather intriguing tangle.

Despite the universal ridicule for Coroner Baxter at the Chapman inquest, he had managed to reinstall himself for the inquest into Stride. And it's from this farrago that Evans/Rumbelow source their idea of 'the Legend of the Grapes'.

Let us have a brief recap of contemporary opinion of Bro Baxter and his court. A 'Comic Coroner', wrote the *Truth*, 'should be retired summarily and quickly'. 'Altogether preposterous', said the

Observer.[19] 'A scandalous exhibition of stupidity', from the *Telegraph*. And lastly the *Lancet*, commenting on Baxter's half-witted inventions, which 'may probably lead to a diversion from the real track of the murderer' – which was precisely what the System wanted, and the reason he wasn't fired.

It is upon this utterly discredited individual that Mr Evans and Mr Rumbelow rely. He is a scoundrel. Unless there is a persuasive explanation for why seven independent eyewitnesses are lying, which includes an explanation for Stride's cadaveric spasm, then the grapes and grape-skins at Dutfield's Yard were no 'legend'. These accounts come from people who were actually there, people whose eyes bore witness. So what is it about this affirmation of the presence of the grapes that Mr Evans and Mr Rumbelow construe as 'legend'? Fortunately, they themselves answer the question. 'They did not exist,' they write, 'as may be seen from the inquest evidence.'[20]

We have arrived at the nub of it. Mr Evans and Mr Rumbelow believe there were no grapes at Dutfield's Yard because there were no grapes in Bro Baxter's court. Oh dear, oh dear ...

No grapes out of Baxter apparently proves that there were no grapes in Stride's hand. Thus the man dismissed by the *Lancet* and the *British Medical Journal* as a dangerous menace is here made credible beyond doubt, while everyone else apart from this discredited Freemason is indulging in some inexplicable 'legend'? Oh dear, oh dear ...

Donald 'Shifty Nib' Swanson was Warren's 'eyes and ears', but he wasn't the only eyes and ears about. Warren himself was the eyes and ears of a higher authority, whose reach extended into every function of state. On the afternoon of 1 October 1888, the eyes and ears belonged to a Masonic coroner called Bro Wynne Baxter. His court was all about arriving at a foregone conclusion, in this case 'murder by a person or persons unknown'. Predetermining the outcome of judicial proceedings was nothing special. Although that opinion might be seen as outrageous, it is not mine, but that of Assistant Commissioner of Metropolitan Police James Monro.

Monro approached the problem of controlling the court by controlling the man in charge of it, i.e. the coroner. *À propos* of the ruse in question, I've edited Monro's account only to avoid particularities and superfluous names:

> The coroner was seen and the importance of the case explained to him. I took great care that the representatives of the press were duly informed that an inquest would be held, and the result was that on the appointed day the coroner's room was filled with what one of the papers described as a singularly respectable audience. As a matter of fact, half of the audience consisted of detectives, the other half newspaper reporters. The police who were present thoroughly trusted that I had some definite objective in view, although they did not understand what it was. The next day all the papers commented in a bewildered fashion upon the inquest and what it meant. Of course they did not know what it meant.[21]

This comment from an Assistant Commissioner of Police demonstrates the underhand control men of bad faith could exercise over such proceedings. A court as compromised as Baxter's could be made to arrive at any conclusion desired.

It requires no significant imagination to understand the suppression of the grapes. Where had they come from? How had they arrived in Stride's hand? Had Stride been discovered with a bicycle pump shoved down her throat, it might well have behoved investigators to begin their enquiries at the nearest source of such pumps. Two doors down from Dutfield's Yard was a little grocer's shop. It was open for business that night, and – would you believe? – selling grapes.

Acknowledgement of grapes and their debris would have demanded the examination of a witness who, to put it mildly, would have been as important as he was unwelcome. Berner Street was as black as your hat, and lousy with rain. But there was a better than even chance that the fruit-seller might actually have seen Elizabeth Stride with the man who murdered her.

Denial of the grapes was therefore paramount to Warren and his deceitful crew. If Monro could have a word in a coroner's ear, then so too could Charlie Warren (although of course the 'word' was already out). With the word in mind, and with Inspector Reid of H Division watching on behalf of the CID, Wynne Baxter opened his enquiries into the murder of Elizabeth Stride at the Vestry Hall, Cable Street, St George in the East.

Baxter began as he meant to continue, establishing the parameters within which he intended to remain. Several 'witnesses' were called on that opening day, the first demonstrating where Baxter was at. He was a printer named William West who worked at premises adjoining the International Workingmen's Club. A radical Yiddish-language newspaper was published out of them called *Der Arbeter Fraint* (The Worker's Friend).

Anyone of a cynical disposition might not consider West an ideal witness. He was nowhere near Dutfield's Yard at the time of the murder, and was probably asleep. Declining to be sworn, he affirmed who he was, following this with a description of the club and the printing works in relation to the crime scene. 'On the left side of the yard is a house,' he said, 'which is divided into three tenements, and occupied, I believe, by that number of families. At the end is a store or workshop belonging to Messrs Hindley & Co., sack manufacturers. I do not know if a way out exists there. The club premises and the printing office occupy the entire length of the yard on the right side.'

West recalled that the compositors had finished work at two in the afternoon that Saturday and gone home, leaving only the editor in the building. His name was Philip Krantz, and he was to remain there until the discovery of the body.

'On Saturday last,' continued West, 'I was in the printing office during the day and the club during the evening. From nine to half past ten at night I was away seeing an English friend home, but I was in the club again until a quarter past midnight. A discussion was proceeding in the lecture room, which has three windows overlooking the courtyard. From 90 to 100 persons attended the discussion which terminated soon after half past eleven, when the bulk of the members left using the street door, the most convenient exit. From 20 to 30 members remained, some staying in the lecture room and the others going downstairs. Of those upstairs a few continued the discussion while the rest were singing.'

BAXTER: How do you know that you finally left at a quarter past twelve o'clock?
WEST: Because of the time that I reached my lodgings.

West lived at 2 William Street, Cannon Street Road, five minutes' walk from Dutfield's Yard. He left the club forty-five minutes before the murder, and was almost certainly in bed at the time of it.

According to testimony subsequently given by Inspector Reid, there were twenty-eight people detained in the yard that night, and Baxter took evidence from not one of them. Instead, he elected to open proceedings with the recollections of a man who was at home a dozen streets away. Would it not have been more productive to have taken evidence from Philip Krantz, the editor of the newspaper, who was actually still present at Berner Street? But Krantz wasn't heard from for another five days, his appearance wedged in at the very end of the penultimate hearing, and so fleeting as to be ridiculous. He was asked nothing of substance. The few seconds he got were contrived towards diversion, rather than to anything he might actually have seen.

> BAXTER: Supposing a woman had screamed, would you have
>   heard it?

Baxter must have known that the nature of the violence inflicted upon Stride would have made a scream impossible. He had been told this repeatedly by the doctors. No one needed to know what Krantz didn't hear. The jury needed to know what he had seen. Of a mind to avoid such a delicate topic, Baxter came up with a question that must surely go down as a classic: 'Did you look to see if anybody was about – anybody who might have committed the murder?'

What do you mean? Apart from the geezer with the canine fangs and bloody knife? Funny you should mention that …

It seems incredible that anyone could be beguiled by this malarkey. Krantz was asked *nothing* about the body, *nothing* about the yard, in fact *nothing* about anything.

We now return to Dutfield's Yard for the exit of William West. Before leaving the club, he 'had occasion to go to the printing office to put some literature there'. There was no light in the yard, he said, 'no lamps in Berner Street that could light it'. When he arrived at the office, Krantz was still in there, reading. Voices could be heard from the club, 'but there was not much noise on a Saturday night'. West walked back across the yard towards the gates. Nothing unusual attracted his attention. 'I'm rather short-sighted,' he said. And with that, Baxter's debut witness vanished into the myopic rain.

Having heard the full account of the man who was a quarter of a mile away, let us brace ourselves for testimony of the next witness up. It will be remembered that it was Mr Maurice Eagle who scurried off in search of the elusive policemen. 'I and others went off to find the officers,' he testified, 'so I had no opportunity of seeing the body.'

Thus, of Baxter's first two witnesses, one wasn't there, and the other didn't look at the body. So far, so good, for anyone in denial over grapes. But with West and Eagle out of the picture, Baxter was facing difficulties. At least seven other people had seen the grapes. His selection of further witnesses was therefore somewhat circumscribed. According to the *Evening News* of that very day, 'The next person on whose information we may look forward to getting a clue to the perpetrator of these outrageous crimes is Mr Isaac M. Kosebrodski.'[22]

It could have printed the name in neon, but Baxter was apparently in perfect ignorance of it. It hardly needs to be restated that Kosebrodski was one of the first witnesses into the yard that night. In a statement to the press, he had said, 'While the doctor was examining the body, I noticed that she had some grapes in her right hand.'[23] Needless to say, Kosebrodski was not called to give evidence at any of the Stride hearings.

We therefore move on to Mrs Fanny Mortimer, who had corroborated Kosebrodski's account with the following: 'The woman appeared to be respectable, etc., etc., and in her hand were found a bunch of grapes and some sweets.'[24] Needless to say, Mrs Mortimer was not required to give evidence at any of Stride's hearings either.

It's presumably upon this basis that Mr Evans and Mr Rumbelow conclude that there were no grapes or grape remains at Dutfield's Yard. I think such a judgement is untenable. Witnesses who had seen grapes were dealt with by the same means that would be deployed energetically at the Mary Kelly inquest some weeks hence. Mouths were kept shut by ignoring them. Such a strategy served the System well, albeit with an occasional unavoidable intrusion.

Because it was he who had discovered Stride's body, it would have been problematic not to call Louis Diemschutz, so on that first day he was put up. Everything he had told the press about grapes, hands and cadaveric spasm had now entirely escaped his mind. 'As soon as the police came,' reported *The Times*, 'witness went into the club and remained there.' Thus, from being the best of witnesses, Diemschutz had become no witness at all.

BAXTER: Did you notice the hands?
DIEMSCHUTZ: I did not notice what position her hands were in.

Twelve hours earlier he'd told the *Evening News*: 'her hands were tightly clenched, and when they were opened by the doctor, I saw immediately that one had been holding sweetmeats and the other grapes'. Does anyone imagine that Diemschutz (and six others) was making that up? Or, bearing in mind what Monro had written about police interference with coroners' courts, might one imagine that Baxter and the police were causing it to be suppressed?

If the cops had told Diemschutz they had very good reason for withholding any mention of grapes, he would naturally have accepted that, just as the jury at Catherine Eddowes' inquest accepted Crawford's instruction to Joseph Lawende to withhold his description of a suspect. Plus, Diemschutz had reason enough to be 'really afraid of the consequences' if he defied the police. By March of the following year, both he and his pal Kosebrodski would be in jail for precisely that.[25]

Diemschutz's amnesia was terminated by an adjournment. PC Henry Lamb was the first witness up that afternoon. He described his arrival at Berner Street, where he had blown his whistle: 'I turned my light on and found it was a woman.' He put a hand on her face, and felt it slightly warm. 'I then felt the wrist but could not feel the pulse.'

BAXTER: Did you do anything else to the body?
PC LAMB: I did not, and would not allow anyone to get near the body.

He estimated that there were about twenty or thirty people in the yard. By now one or two more uniforms had arrived. 'I put a constable at the gate,' said Lamb, 'and told him not to let anyone in or out.' Despite what he'd told the *Telegraph*, he made no mention of grapes, Baxter cueing him with an opportunity not to: 'Did you examine her hands?' Lamb replied: 'I did not. But I saw that her right arm was across her breast, and her left arm was lying under her.'

These dead hands will shortly start dancing around like an Italian describing a car crash. They will be open, closed, hidden, exposed, each new witness proffering a new untruth to try to make them fit the required point of view.

The duplicity over Stride's hands escalated with the arrival of the medical contingent. Edward Johnson, assistant to Drs Kay and Blackwell, was first on the scene. He made a cursory examination of Stride and her injuries, insisting that no one had disturbed the body, but adding that he undid her dress to see if her chest was warm. He said he 'found that it was all warm with the exception of the hands which were quite cold'. Baxter asked: 'Did you look at the hands?' To which Johnson replied: 'No. I saw the left hand was lying away from the body, and the arm was bent.'

We're already into a major contradiction, and this between witnesses who were but minutes apart. PC Lamb said 'her left arm was lying under her', while Johnson said 'the left hand was lying away from the body, and the arm was bent'. These are not idle witnesses. One was a medical assistant to a pair of police surgeons, the other a police constable. Both are under oath. They can't both be right. A page or two must pass before the disharmony over the hands compounds into the usual burlesque.

Meanwhile, with his colleague posted at the gates, Lamb was making a search of the yard and knocking up residents. He went on to describe how he had searched water-closets, dustbins and a dung-heap, finally looking through the windows of Messrs Hindley, whose doors were locked. 'When I returned from there, Doctor Phillips and Chief Inspector West had arrived.' That just about wraps it for Lamb. Before dismissing him, Baxter asked a question that was to become meaningful. It referred to the constable's regular beat earlier that night: 'Did you see anything suspicious?' Lamb replied: 'No, I saw lots of squabbles and rows such as one sees on Saturday nights.'

Such altercations were clearly common on Whitechapel's streets. They will evolve into a point worth remembering.

By now it had become almost a maxim of my research to go after whatever the authorities tried to dismiss. Nowhere was the hush-up more obvious than in the matter of the grapes. Baxter would habitually ask a witness to consider the victim's hands, providing an opportunity for abstract denial. 'Did you see the hands?' became obligatory, prompting Diemschutz, Lamb and Johnson to say that they had not. Under any circumstances this seems implausible,

Lamb having felt for a pulse, and Johnson feeling both hands to see if they were warm. This constant proof of a negative is most noticeable, and in view of what was to develop, nobody should be surprised.

Baxter's court had been convened within thirty-six hours of the murder and its attendant coverage in the following morning's newspapers. It was likely that many of the jurors were unacquainted with the press reports. This would have been useful à propos clenched hands and grapes. Such a consideration may well have been material to the urgency with which the inquest was held.

It was haste without precedent. Two days had elapsed before a jury assembled for Annie Chapman, three for Mary Anne Nichols, and the City inquest into the murder of Catherine Eddowes wouldn't kick off for another five days. How the Met had time to sort out the witnesses is baffling. But I would argue that the intention was to avoid calling them. In my view they had only one to worry about, and he, Louis Diemschutz, was successfully dispensed with on the opening morning. Baxter must have been signing warrants before he had got out of bed. This isn't as absurd as it sounds. Inspector Reid, who had been awake all night, was sitting in court on behalf of the Metropolitan Police. It was he who at 4.30 a.m. had taken time out from the enquiries at Dutfield's Yard to go personally to Baxter's residence and inform him of the murder. The Comic Coroner would thus have had a first-hand account of whatever evidence had been discovered, or was considered pertinent for him to suppress.

Back in court, Drs Phillips and Blackwell came and went on consecutive days, contradicting themselves and each other with a frequency too tedious to get into. Both, however, confirmed the discovery of some cachous. 'The left arm was extended,' said Phillips, 'and there was a packet of cachous in the left hand. A number of these were in the gutter. I took them from her hand and handed them to Doctor Blackwell.' The presence of these sweets substantiates the descriptions given to the press by Kosebrodski, Mortimer, Diemschutz et al. We're halfway there, although neither physician trespassed into a description of Stride's right hand. But that right hand wasn't going to go away, and neither was the reality of the grapes. On 6 October the *Daily Telegraph* published a letter that was to be the harbinger of unwished-for problems:

In reading your report on Monday of the murder in Whitechapel I notice that the unfortunate woman, when seen by Constable Lamb 252 H Division, was clutching some grapes in her right hand and sweets in her left. Is it not probable that the murderer bought the grapes for his victim? Supposing that to be so, is it not also probable that the grapes were purchased only a few minutes before the murder and in the immediate neighbourhood? I would suggest a strict enquiry among the vendors of fruit in that locality.

This was everything Baxter & Co. didn't want to hear. Mr Webb of Bedford House, Bognor, had hit a barely hidden nail right on its obvious head. Of course it was probable that the murderer had bought the grapes for his victim, and of course it was probable that the grapes had been purchased in the immediate neighbourhood. Written on 4 October, Webb's letter could (and certainly would) have been ignored, had it not been for a startling revelation published that same day. The very man the police were desperate to avoid had decided to speak up.

On 4 October the *Evening News* published 'MATTHEW PACKER'S STORY', describing it as an 'INTERVIEW WITH THE MAN WHO SPOKE TO THE MURDERER' and claiming it was at his fruit shop in Berner Street that Jack had 'BOUGHT THE GRAPES FOUND BESIDE THE MURDERED WOMAN'. A symphony of flatulence must have echoed around Scotland Yard. Mr Packer's intercession was to become the catalyst for one of the most extraordinary escalations of misfeasance to engulf Warren's tenure. A vigorous programme of damage limitation was initiated, Vincent's Code torn up like shit-paper. At all costs this fruit-seller had to be shut up.

Meanwhile, his intervention had an immediate effect on Baxter's ongoing enquiries. Having ignored all the press reports of grapes, our serpentine coroner was now anxious to put up questions about them. On 5 October, the day after Packer's sensation, Dr Bagster Phillips was recalled. On this occasion proceedings were watched for the first time by Superintendent Arnold for the Met.

Baxter cut to the chase. They needed to deal with the matter of the grapes as quickly as they had done with Diemschutz. The most notable absence, of course, was Packer himself. Here was a fruit-seller who lived two doors from Dutfield's Yard. If true, his evidence was of incalculable importance. Why was his story not immediately put to the test of a jury? If he was lying, he could be ignominiously dismissed. If he was lying maliciously, he could be put into prison. But he wasn't called.

Instead, Phillips told the court that subsequent to his last examination of Stride's body, he had returned to the mortuary and made a more careful examination of the roof of the victim's mouth. 'I could not find any injury or absence of anything from the mouth.' What was he talking about? Her teeth or her tongue? Having set the scene, he went on to deal with Packer in the same vein. 'I have also carefully examined the handkerchiefs,' he said, 'and have not found any blood on them. I believe the stains on the larger one were fruit stains. I am convinced that the deceased had not swallowed either skin or seed of a grape within many hours of her death.'

A sigh of relief must have gone up in certain quarters. Grapes had officially been denied. But Phillips was flirting at the very hem of perjury. Notice how the cunning bastard phrases it: 'I am convinced that the deceased had not swallowed *either skin or seed* of a grape within many hours of her death.'

So the fuck what? No pith or peel wouldn't mean that she hadn't eaten an orange. No shells wouldn't mean that she hadn't eaten eggs. What about the *flesh* of a grape? Phillips found no evidence of seeds or skins because *Stride had spat them out.* Rather than dismissing the grapes, he's inadvertently corroborating Inspector Walter Dew. 'Detectives searching every inch of the ground,' wrote Dew, 'came upon a number of grape skins and stones.'[26] Choosing a more appropriate word than 'seeds', he called them 'stones', because that's what they were like: like baubles of grit, which together with the skins Stride spat out before wiping her lips on the handkerchief. Was Baxter not even slightly curious about the origin of these 'fruit stains', and what sort of fruit had caused them?

Drip by poisonous drip, we shall establish that grapes were indeed clutched fast in Stride's right hand – unless, of course, Inspector Dew, like PC Lamb, Diemschutz, Kosebrodski, Mortimer and now Packer, was indulging in some inexplicable deceit. Were they all lying? Or was someone else? It was the reality of these grapes sold by Packer that was to send the authorities scurrying like rodents with an aversion to the light. Within hours it would cause Bro Baxter to shut down his lousy little court. Pending the slammed door, a bit of diversionary nonsense over Stride's right hand was put up for the punters: 'Have you formed any opinion how the right hand of the deceased was covered with blood?' 'No,' said Phillips – but wait for the fairy – 'that is a mystery.' That word, beloved of Warren's boys and Ripperology alike, was inevitable. It was transparently no 'mystery' at all, and Bro Dr Bagster Phillips transparently knew it.

Mr Johnson was the assistant at the postmortem conducted by Phillips and Blackwell. Why was he not recalled to clear the 'mystery' up? He, Lamb and Diemschutz had made it clear that Stride's right arm was across her breast. He undid her dress to 'see if the chest was warm'. He couldn't have unbuttoned it if there was a dead arm lying across it. 'I did not move the head at all, and left it exactly as I had found it,' he said. But he had obviously moved the arm. According to Blackwell, blood was 'trodden about' – in Diemschutz's estimate, 'quite two quarts on the ground'. Four pints is a lot of blood, and I suggest that when Stride's right hand went down onto the ground, blood would have saturated the back of it. When Johnson had finished, he picked up the arm with its now bloodstained hand, and put it back where he had found it. But Johnson wasn't recalled, and the 'mystery' was sustained.

It is apparent that different questions were tailored to different days, as were different questions to different witnesses. Baxter wanted one lot to deny they'd seen the hand, and the other to see only what the Metropolitan Police required them to have seen. Error was therefore frequent. It was an ungainly question from Baxter that put Phillips back on the spot: 'Does the presence of cachous in her hand show that it was done suddenly, or would it simply be a muscular grasp?'

Come again?

A 'muscular grasp' is precisely how Sir Keith Simpson character-ised cadaveric spasm, and is consistent with a variety of statements in the newspapers, including that of Diemschutz. But no such description had been given in this court (Blackwell had said the hand was open), so where did Baxter get it? Was it part of the particulars Reid had made available in the middle of the night, emerging here as a bit of a *faux pas*? Whatever its provenance, Phillips responded with obfuscation: 'I cannot say.' Anyone on the jury with an IQ into double figures must by now have been confused. Were the hands open, or in a 'muscular grasp'? If Phillips didn't know, who did? Anybody hoping for clarification was to be disappointed shortly after, when Dr Blackwell was recalled. 'I have little to say,' declared the doc, 'except to confirm Doctor Phillips' statement,' adding, 'I removed the cachous from the left hand which was nearly open.'

That can't be true, because he was already holding them. Phillips had stated, under oath: 'I took them [the cachous] from her hand and handed them to Doctor Blackwell.' They can't both have taken the cachous from Stride's left hand and handed them to each other. If Phillips took them, how could he be in ignorance of the hand's appearance? Was it open, or clenched? But never mind the details; Baxter certainly didn't.

'The packet had been lodged between the thumb and fourth finger,' lied Blackwell, 'and had almost become hidden. That accounted for it not having been seen by several of those around.' It accounted for no such thing. Plenty of people had seen the cachous – Diemschutz, Kosebrodski, Mortimer, and who knows how many of the other thirty who were never called as witnesses. Dr Phillips had said that a number of them were spilled 'in the gutter'. Clearly, the visibility of the cachous was not the problem. The problem was trying to pretend that nobody had seen the grapes.

Blackwell wasn't as seasoned a performer as Phillips, who had piggybacked out of a previous inquest on Baxter's fantasy Frankenstein with his bag of wombs. No such exit presented itself here, and attempting to square the circle of an open hand and a muscular grasp, Blackwell proposed a compromise that included both. Abandoning his previous deposition, he said, 'I believe the hand relaxed after the injuries were inflicted, as death would arise from fainting owing to the rapid loss of blood.'

At last we get a concession to the clenched hands. For a hand to 'relax' after death, Blackwell is accepting that it was in some way stressed before it. Clenching hands is precisely the point, and we're back with cadaveric spasm – which, incidentally, is a permanent phenomenon, immune to fainting, and triggered only by sudden death itself.

Were Baxter an honest agent he would have stood these conflicting physicians down pending a comprehensive re-evaluation. Certain witnesses would have to be recalled, and depositions taken from those hitherto excluded. But Baxter wasn't an honest agent.

He was a deluded little footnote who considered it his occult duty to keep these witnesses out.

Baxter had become a figure of fun after Chapman. After Stride he should have been laughed into obscurity. By stealth and selection the wretched pantomime wore on. In came Clerk to the Swedish Church Sven Olsson, to confirm Stride's nationality and age. She was born near Gothenburg, and she was forty-five (sic). Sven was followed by a worthless effort called William Marshall. He'd seen Stride in Berner Street talking to a man wearing a hat, 'something like a sailor would wear'. He was a standard short-arse, about five foot six, wearing a 'small black coat and dark trousers'. This was heady stuff.

> BAXTER: Are you quite sure this is the woman?
> MARSHALL: Yes, I am. I did not take much notice of them. I was standing by my door, and what attracted my attention first was her standing there some time, and he was kissing her. I heard the man say to the deceased, 'You would say anything but your prayers.'

The shortcomings in Marshall's evidence render it all but irrelevant. He says there was no lamp nearby, and he couldn't see the face of the man – so how could he be so sure of the face of the woman? On 1 October, reporting the mob accruing in Berner Street, the *Globe* wrote: 'The rough crowd who met there last night could barely see one another's faces.'

Marshall's certainty must be assessed in the context of the testimony given by Stride's own sister, Mrs Mary Malcolm, who had spoken at a previous session. She was Baxter's kind of witness – miles away and fast asleep at the time of the murder – but Mary had had a 'premonition'.

> BAXTER: Did you not have some special presentiment about your sister?
> MARY MALCOLM: About 1.20 a.m. on Sunday morning I was lying on my bed when I felt a kind of pressure on my breast, and then I felt 3 kisses on my cheek. I also heard the kisses, and they were quite distinct.

THE REMARKABLE DREAM OF THE SISTER OF ELIZABETH STRIDE - AT THE ACTUAL HOUR OF THE CRIME.

Could this be the breakthrough they were all waiting for? Like Marshall, she'd been to the mortuary to identify the murdered woman. 'When I first saw the body I did not at first recognise it, as I only saw it by gas-light' – which was a better look than Marshall got. On the following day she returned, stating, 'but the next day I recognised it'.

No she did not. Not that Baxter gave a toss, but she wasn't even Stride's sister. It was left to the Central News Agency to sort it out. 'It will be remembered,' it reported, 'that Mrs Mary Malcolm swore positively that the deceased was her sister, Elizabeth Watts, who she had last seen on Thursday preceding the murder. The Central News caused enquiries to be made, and as the result has succeeded in finding Elizabeth Watts alive and well in the person of Mrs Stokes, the hard-working, respectable wife of a bricklayer living in Tottenham.'

The fact that this woman got into the court while the fruit-seller Matthew Packer was kept out of it tells us all we need to know about Baxter's 'inquest'. Mary Malcolm was a nut, 'a gin-soaked virago' according to one press report, whose 'transparent objective was to turn the catastrophe to account somehow'.[27]

"SISTERS —"
A RECOGNITION IN THE MORTUARY.

James Brown was next up. He also claimed to have seen Stride talking to a man, about an hour later than Marshall. Baxter was now scraping the barrel – this pair weren't even in Berner Street. 'I saw a man and woman standing by the wall in Fairclough Street. As I passed them I heard the woman say, "No, not tonight, some other night."'

Such a fastidious selection of her clientèle must have been rare for an impoverished prostitute struggling to find coin for her doss. Whores don't flirt, they fuck for money. It makes one wonder what she was doing on the streets at all. But then, this wasn't the right street, and it probably wasn't the right woman either. Be that as it may, Brown's testimony allowed the police to once again hammer home the notion of the Ripper being vertically impaired. This one was five feet seven inches tall.

The next time Brown made an association between this uniden-tified couple and the murder was also aural. By now he was sitting in his room in Fairclough Street eating his supper. 'When I heard screams of "Police" and "Murder" I opened the window but could not see anyone and the screams ceased.' Brown's evidence was heard with barely a murmur. It was utterly worthless.

We come now to the penultimate witness, hauled up in an attempt to short-circuit Packer. Police Constable William Smith made deposition on 5 October, the day after the fruit-seller's newspaper revelations. Smith's contribution is so patently fabricated that I'm going to reproduce virtually every word of it as it appeared in *The Times*.

> Police Constable William Smith, 425 H, said that on Saturday night his beat went past Berner Street. It was an ill-lit geography of alleyways and streets, finally grinding back to the starting point in Commercial Street and took him between 25 minutes and half an hour. 'I was last in Berner St at about half past 12 or 12.35. At 1 o'clock I went to Berner Street on my ordinary round. I saw a crowd of people outside the gates of No. 40. I did not hear any cries of 'police'.
>
> When I got there I saw Constables 12 H [Collins] and 252 H [Lamb]. I then saw the deceased, and, looking at her, found she was dead. I then went to the station for an ambulance. Dr Blackwell's assistant came just as I was going away.

BAXTER: When you were in Berner Street the previous time did you see any one?

PC SMITH: Yes, a man and a woman.

BAXTER: Was the latter anything like the deceased?

PC SMITH: Yes, I saw her face. I have seen the deceased in the mortuary, and feel certain it is the same person.

BAXTER: Did you see the man who was talking to her?

PC SMITH: Yes; I noticed he had a newspaper parcel in his hand. It was about 18 in. in length and 6 in. or 8 in. in width. He was about 5ft 7in. as far as I could say. He had on a hard felt deerstalker hat of dark colour and dark clothes. I did not see much of the face of the man except that he had no whiskers.

BAXTER: Can you form any idea as to his age?

PC SMITH: About 28 years. He was of respectable appearance. I noticed the woman had a flower in her jacket.

A brief exchange ensued over the direction Smith had taken out of Berner Street. And then Baxter asked about the weather: 'When did it last rain before 1 o'clock?' Smith replied: 'To the best of my recollection it rained very little after 11 o'clock.'

Baxter's question about the rain isn't as random as it might seem. It is in fact important in respect of discrediting Matthew Packer's statement to the *Evening News*. 'It will be remembered,' the *News* had written on 4 October, quite independently of Packer, 'that the night was very wet, and Packer naturally noticed the peculiarity of the couple standing so long in the rain. He observed to his wife, "What fools those people are to be standing in the rain like that."'

The time in question was around half past twelve, just about the time PC Smith said he turned into Berner Street. Was it raining or not? If you want to discredit Packer, it wasn't. If you want to believe Packer, it was. It's a tough call to be sure of the weather on a lousy Sunday 130 years ago. But at one o'clock half a mile away it was pissing down. According to Lawende, it was the rain that delayed him and his pals at the Imperial Club. His evidence is supported by the *Daily Telegraph*, which reported of Stride: 'Her dress, *which was saturated with rain* [my emphasis], was of a common black material.'[28]

Even if Packer had invented the rain, he could hardly have extended his fiction into the columns of the *Telegraph*. Either Packer, Lawende and the *Telegraph* are right, or Constable Smith is. In reality, he was saying what he'd been told to say. But he was about to drop a clanger. The foreman of the jury asked, 'Was the man or the woman acting in a suspicious manner?'

'No,' replied Smith.

'Do you see many prostitutes hanging about in Berner St?'

Again he answered in the negative: 'No, very few.'

INSPECTOR REID: Did you see these people more than once?

PC SMITH: No. When I saw the deceased lying on the ground I recognised her at once and made a report of what I had seen.

I beg your pardon? He saw Stride talking to a man, and thirty minutes later he saw her again with her throat cut. And he 'made a report'?

This was inadvertent dynamite, and Baxter instantly moved in to defuse it. Dismissing Smith without another word, he recalled another previously interrogated irrelevance by the name of Michael Kidney. Kidney had lived with Stride for about three years, and had complained in his earlier deposition of going to Leman Street 'for a detective to act on my information, but I could not get one'.

But never mind that. Baxter had whipped out a hymn book. 'Have you ever seen this hymn book before?' Yeah, sure he had, he recognised it as belonging to Stride – and so the fuck what? Recognition of a hymn book had no relevance whatsoever.

If Baxter had held up Wycliffe's first-ever English Bible it would have had no relevance either. What was vitally relevant is that PC Smith had claimed to have recognised Stride on the deck in Dutfield's Yard, and Baxter was trying to hide it.

'I recognised her at once,' he said. The woman he'd seen less than thirty minutes before with the 'respectable' man was now very dead. The man, therefore, could be nothing other than a prime suspect, if not her actual killer. And yet Smith raised no alarm. He says he 'made a report'. To whom did he make it, and when? Did he drop it into the nearest postbox?

Why was not Arnold immediately informed? Instead of wasting time harassing Jews, why wasn't every copper in Whitechapel out looking for the man in the deerstalker hat? Was anyone at Dutfield's Yard standing under such a hat? PC Smith could have saved everyone a lot of time and trouble. For here was a copper popping into a crime scene who might just have seen Jack the Ripper. And yet he's struck speechless, says nothing to nobody, not to 12 H Collins, not even to 252 H Lamb. Instead, before any doctor has arrived, this turnip in a helmet singularly diagnoses death, and waddles off into the darkness to 'make a report'.

I don't believe a word of it. This wasn't a random drunk in an alley; for all the world, as everyone at the scene must have been aware, it was another Ripper hit. Nobody needed a report, and nobody needed an ambulance. What PC Lamb urgently needed, right here, right now, was help. It's why he blew his bloody whistle. He had a yard full of people – twenty or thirty, he said – at this point (based on police activity) all potential suspects, and a crowd was already beginning to assemble in the street. Lamb was all alone. 'When further assistance came,' he said, 'a constable was put in charge of the front door.'

Why was not PC Smith commandeered? This was *his beat, his murdered body, his responsibility,* and everyone was running around in circles looking for police. Again, I don't believe a word of it. The yarn Smith had been put up to tell is as risible as it is crude. Not a single witness mentions seeing Smith at Dutfield's Yard. The only time he is mentioned is when he couldn't be found. 'When I was fetched,' said Lamb, 'I was going in the direction of Berner Street. Constable Smith is on the Berner Street beat.' But it wasn't Smith who ran with Lamb. It was a copper on fixed-point duty at the end of Grove Street. Nobody saw Smith anywhere. Somehow he remained as elusive as his invention in the hat.

Smith was shut up by Baxter because his accidental evidence presented an instant dilemma. First, to say that he had told any senior officer he had seen a 'respectable' man with Stride would reveal the search of the Workingmen's Club to be the sham it was. Second, both PC Smith and the fruit-seller claimed to have seen Stride with a man at precisely the same time. How can one of these men have credibility, while the other does not? To invest his suspect with credibility would have meant comparable credibility for Matthew Packer. Packer and his grapes would enter the picture, and this was something the System was lying its arse off to prevent.

Inspector Reid came on next to tell everybody what they already knew. He was to be the last witness anybody would be hearing from for rather a long time. Naturally enough, he made no mention of the 'respectable man', whose appearance in Berner Street had become as ghost-like as Smith's. Reid talked the talk without interruption: 'A thorough search was made of the yard, but no trace could be found of any person likely to have committed the deed.' This isn't so surprising, because at that time he was in Mitre Square cutting out one of Catherine Eddowes' kidneys. 'A description was taken of the body and circulated round the surrounding stations by wire.' All very admirable, but they weren't looking for a dead body, they were looking for the man who had made it so. At what point did Reid become aware of the 'respectable man' in the deerstalker hat? He doesn't say. Smith was evidently still keeping it to himself. 'About 4.30 the body was removed to the mortuary.' At last, after a wait of three and a half hours, Smith got the chance to proffer his ambulance.

By definition, Reid, Arnold and West must have been in ignorance of Smith's 'suspect' at the time of their search, otherwise they would have known it was doomed to futility. How could any of the people locked up at Dutfield's Yard have murdered Eddowes? If they were in there, they were innocent.

This seemed beyond the intellectual capacity of the police, and most especially Smith. Apart from a bit of descriptive ephemera referencing business at the morgue, Reid had just about wrapped it up for the cops: 'Since then the police had made a house to house enquiry into the immediate neighbourhood, with the result that we have been able to produce the witnesses that have appeared before you.'

To wit: five people who'd seen nothing; two doctors who were selectively blind; one inebriate who'd had a 'vision'; one copper with a mouthful of twaddle; and one genuine witness who had discovered the body, Louis Diemschutz, who had been shut up.

'At this stage,' reported *The Times*, 'the enquiry was adjourned to Tuesday week.'

Such a hiatus was to prove nothing like long enough.

Rotten to the Core

Repetition does not transform a lie into the truth.

Franklin D. Roosevelt

The Metropolitan Police were anxious to persuade the public that the Ripper was a tall dwarf. On 19 October 1888 the front page of their weekly, the *Police Gazette*, featured a description of various Rippers sought. At the shorter end he was five feet five, and at the upper five feet eight. They of course knew that these descriptions were bullshit, because they knew Bro Crawford had successfully withheld a key description at Catherine Eddowes' inquest. Whatever Joseph Lawende had seen was still a secret.

APPREHENSIONS SOUGHT.

MURDER.

METROPOLITAN POLICE DISTRICT.

1.—

The woodcut sketches, purporting to resemble the persons last seen with the murdered women, which have appeared in the "Daily Telegraph," were not authorised by Police. The following are the descriptions of the persons seen :—

At 12.35 a.m., 30th September, with Elizabeth Stride, found murdered at 1 a.m., same date, in Berner-street—A MAN, age 28, height 5 ft. 8 in., complexion dark, small dark moustache ; dress, black diagonal coat, hard felt hat, collar and tie ; respectable appearance. Carried a parcel wrapped up in newspaper.

At 12.45 a.m., 30th, with same woman, jp. Berner-street —A MAN, age about 30, height 5 ft. 5 in., complexion fair, hair dark, small brown moustache, full face, broad shoulders ; dress, dark jacket and trousers, black cap with peak.

At 1.35 a.m. 30th September, with Catherine Eddows, in Church-passage, leading to Mitre-square, where she was found murdered at 1.45 a.m., same date—A MAN, age 30, height 5 ft. 7 or 8 in., complexion fair, moustache fair, medium build ; dress, pepper-and-salt colour loose jacket, grey cloth cap with peak of same material, reddish neckerchief tied in knot ; appearance of a sailor.

Information to be forwarded to the Metropolitan Police Office, Great Scotland-yard, London, S.W.

The disclaimer in the first line, referring to woodcut sketches, is a reference to some illustrations published in the *Telegraph*, based on the description Matthew Packer gave the paper of the man who'd bought the grapes. They will be investigated later in this chapter.

But the rest first.

Description one is PC Smith's version of the man he saw in Berner Street, and of whom he 'made a report' after nipping into the crime scene. Here he is minus his deerstalker, although he's acquired a small moustache and a collar and tie.

Description two is a stir-fry of Marshall and Brown as given in Wynne Baxter's court, and is as worthless now as it was then. Brown saw a man and a woman in Fairclough Street, and while chewing his dinner in that same street he opened his window and heard shouts.

Description three is a worthless amalgamation of Levy and Harris, the latter not called to give evidence, both of whom claimed to have seen two people, and is all that can be salvaged without revealing Lawende's description, which was withheld from the jury.

The readers of this rubbish are invited to look out for a man between five feet five and five feet eight inches tall, aged twenty-eight to thirty, with a small dark/fair moustache, of respectable or seafaring appearance, carrying a parcel wrapped in newspaper, with a red neckerchief tied in a knot and not wearing a deerstalker hat. Anyone seeing such a man should immediately contact Scotland Yard. Anyone who'd seen anything different was unwelcome. Apart from Lawende, one man who had was the fruit-seller Matthew Packer, and his emergence well put the wind up Warren and his boys.

If the house-to-house search was the reality Inspector Reid claimed, the police could not fail to have been aware of the little grocery shop two doors down from Dutfield's Yard. The *Evening News* was certainly aware of it, and on Thursday, 4 October it ran Packer's story.

> We are enabled to present our readers this morning with the most startling information that has yet been made public in relation to the Whitechapel murderer, and the first real clue that has been obtained to his identity. There are no suppositions or probabilities in the story we have to tell; we put forward nothing but simple facts, each substantiated by the evidence of a credible witness. What they

go to establish is that the perpetrator of the Berner Street crime was seen and spoken to whilst in the company of his victim, within forty minutes of the commission of the crime, and only passed from the sight of the witness TEN MINUTES BEFORE THE MURDER and within ten yards of the scene of the awful deed.

The *Evening News* prefaced Packer's story with a description of how it came by it. It was sourced, it says, from two private detectives, 'Messrs Grand and J.H. Batchelor, of 238, Strand': 'When they began their quest, almost the first place at which they sought evidence was at 44 Berner Street, the residence of Matthew Packer. His shop is an insignificant place, with a half-window in front, of the sort common in the locality, and most of his dealings are carried on through the lower part of the window case, in which his fruit is exposed for sale.'

Before looking at what Packer is said to have told Grand and Batchelor, it's as well to look at what the newspaper itself made of its source. On the day before publication, Wednesday, 3 October, the *Evening News* sent its own 'Special Commissioner' to Whitechapel to hear the story from Packer and his wife.

WHERE THE MURDERER BOUGHT THE GRAPES
INTERVIEW WITH THE MAN WHO TALKED WITH HIM

Last evening was far advanced when I walked into the greengrocer's little shop where the murdered woman was 'treated' to some grapes, late on Saturday night, by the inhuman monster who shortly afterwards shed her blood. The shop is kept by a quiet and intelligent fruiterer and his wife. They are both a little past their prime and are known as respectable and hardworking people. Their unpretending premises are situated just two doors down from the scene of the murder, and the presumption of any kind of ordinary intelligence would be that it was the very first place at which the detectives and the police would have made their enquiries. *They did nothing of the sort*, as the man's simple straightforward narrative will show.

The 'Special Commissioner' took a seat and asked Packer to tell him everything he knew about the events of Saturday night last. 'Well, that's soon told,' was his answer.

'I had been out with my barrow most of the day, but hadn't done much business; and as the night came on wet, I went home and took the place of the missus in the shop here.'

THE MURDERER AT THE WINDOW

'Some time between half past eleven and twelve a man and woman came up Berner Street from the direction of Ellen Street, and stopped outside my window looking at the fruit. The man was about 30 to 35 years of age, medium height, and with a rather dark complexion.'

It's hardly worth pointing out that everyone who bought from 'the lower part of the window case' at Packer's shop would be stooping, and reduced to 'medium height'. But let me not get in the way of his account.

'He wore a black coat and a black soft hat. I am certain he wasn't what I should call a working man or anything like us folks that live around here.'

And what about the woman? 'She was dressed in dark clothes, looked like a middle-aged woman, and carried a white flower in her hand. I saw that as plain as anything could be, and I am sure I would know the woman again.'

Batchelor and Grand now come back into the picture, clearly conducting a test on behalf of their unknown 'clients' that could have stopped Packer in his tracks: 'I was taken today to see the dead body of a woman in the Golden Lane Mortuary (she was Mrs Eddowes in the City Morgue), but I can swear that it wasn't the woman that stood at my shop window, on Saturday night.'

Thus, the subterfuge of trying to confuse Packer had failed.

THE SOUND OF THE ASSASSIN'S VOICE

'Well, they hadn't stood there for more than a minute when the man stepped a bit forward, and said, "I say, old man, how do you sell your grapes?"

'I answered, "Sixpence a pound the black 'uns, sir; and four-pence a pound the white 'uns." Then he turned to the woman and said, "Which will you have, my dear, black or white? You shall have whichever you like best."

'The woman said, "Oh, then I'll have the black 'uns, cos they look the nicest."

'"Give us half a pound of the black ones then," said the man. I put the grapes in a paper bag and handed them to him.

'He spoke like an educated man,' said Packer, 'but he had a loud, sharp sort of voice, and a quick commanding way with him.'

THE MURDERER LAYING HIS PLANS

'They stood near the gateway leading to the club for a minute or two,' said Packer, 'then they crossed the road and stood right opposite.' For how long? 'More than half an hour, I should say; so long that I said to my missus, "Why them people must be a couple a' fools, to stand out there in the rain, when they might just as well have had shelter!"'

They were still standing there when Packer and his wife went to bed, he couldn't say exactly when, 'but it must have been past midnight', he said, 'for the public houses were shut up'.

'Well, Mr Packer,' said the 'Special Commissioner', 'I suppose the police came at once to ask you and your wife what you know about the affair, as soon as the body was discovered?'

'The Police,' replied Packer. 'NO. THEY HAVEN'T ASKED ME A WORD ABOUT IT YET!!!'

I doubt the exclamation marks or the capitals were Packer's – rather this was a journalist pushing his scoop.

Both the Metropolitan Police and subsequently Ripperology have dismissed Packer's account, regarding the grapes as fantasy – 'the Fable of the Grapes', etc. – the same hallucination suffered by those who weren't called to give evidence at Elizabeth Stride's inquest.

But some took Packer at his word. The first copper who did was Inspector Henry Moore, the forty-year-old son of a cop in the Criminal Investigation Department at Scotland Yard. Moore was sitting in his office on the morning of 4 October when a copy of the *Evening News* landed on his desk. Considering Reid's claim to have knocked on every door in Berner Street, it must have come as quite a surprise. Who was this potentially vital witness called Packer? Having never heard of the fruit-seller or his grapes, Moore concluded that the police must somehow have missed him. It must

THEY ALL LOVE JACK

surely have been startling to Moore to read of the reporter's raw incomprehension at Packer's response to his questions.

'I'm afraid you don't quite understand my question, Mr Packer,' wrote the *Evening News*'s 'Special Commissioner'. 'Do you seriously mean to say that no Detective or policeman came to enquire whether you had sold grapes to anyone that night? Now please be very careful in your answer, for this may prove a serious business for the London Police.'

A serious business indeed. Moore, being an honest copper, must have been stunned as he read Packer's answer. 'I've only got one answer,' he said, 'because it is the truth.'

'EXCEPT A GENTLEMAN WHO IS A PRIVATE DETECTIVE, NO POLICEMAN OR DETECTIVE HAS EVER ASKED ME A SINGLE QUESTION, NOR COME NEAR MY SHOP TO FIND OUT IF I KNEW ANYTHING ABOUT THE GRAPES THE MURDERED WOMAN HAD BEEN EATING BEFORE HER THROAT WAS CUT!!!'

Moore was understandably shocked. 'I beg to report,' he wrote posthaste to his superiors, 'that as soon as the above [the *Evening News* article] came to my notice I at once directed Police Sergeant White H, to see Mr Packer, and take him to the mortuary with a view to the identification of the woman Elizabeth Stride, who it is stated was with the man who purchased grapes at his shop on the night of the 29th inst.'[1]

So far, so good. It looked as if Packer's interview in the press was going to pay off. Meantime, in comes Sergeant White to receive instructions. Clearly neither he nor Moore was yet in the anti-detection loop. Their induction into the Swanson school of policing would take place in the next few hours.

Later that afternoon, having liaised with Swanson, Sergeant White would claim to have already interviewed Matthew Packer four days previously, on 30 September, recording the encounter in a 'special book' supplied for the enquiry. On that occasion Packer had supposedly given him the brush-off, categorically stating that he had neither heard nor seen anything.

Now, this is curious. If it were true that White had already taken a statement from the fruit-seller, why didn't he say anything about it when the *Evening News* was spread out on Inspector Moore's desk? White would have had to have been a vegetable not to acquaint his superior with the statement he had already taken. If such a statement existed, there would have been uproar on either side of the desk – White furious that he'd been cuckolded by a newspaper, and Moore furious that Packer had maliciously tried to make a fool of the police.

But White said nothing. He said nothing because he hadn't interviewed Packer. I give as much credibility to White's 'special book' as Moore did – none – because he wasn't shown it. Neither he nor White made reference to it, because it didn't yet exist. In the tradition of PC Smith at Berner Street, a retrospective 'report' was cooked up later that day. When it finally emerged at about four o'clock that same afternoon, its phoney account was unequivocal:

I in company of P.C. Dolden, Criminal Investigation Dept., made enquiries at every house in Berner Street, Commercial Road on 30th, with a view to obtain information respecting the murder. Any information that I could obtain I noted in a book supplied to me for the purpose. About 9 a.m. I called at 44 Berner Street, and saw Matthew Packer, Fruiterer in a small way of business. I asked him what time he closed his shop on the previous night. He replied, half past twelve.

He closed at 12.30, he said, because 'in consequence of the rain it was no good for me to keep open'.

I asked him if he saw anything of a man or woman going into Dutfield's Yard, or anyone standing about the street about the time he was closing his shop? He replied, 'No, I saw no one standing about neither did I see anyone go up the yard. I never heard anything suspicious or heard the slightest noise, and knew nothing about the murder until I heard of it in the morning.'[2]

If any of this was remotely true, why wasn't Inspector Moore immediately informed of it? There could have been scant point in dispatching White to Packer's shop, and there inviting him to identify a dead body that he'd already insisted he'd never seen alive. Instead of sending White to escort Packer to the morgue, why was he not instructed to threaten the old bastard with prosecution? Either White or Matthew Packer was lying.[3]

As the *Evening News* had succinctly put it to Packer: 'please be very careful in your answer, for this may prove a serious business for the London Police'. Serious it was. If the lies were coming from Packer, he could have gone to prison. There were stringent laws against malicious defamation of Her Majesty's Police:

> All acts which are calculated to interfere with the course of justice, are misdemeanours at the common law, punishable with imprisonment ... this may be by *preventing or persuading a witness from giving evidence* ... or by wilfully producing false evidence, or by *publishing information that may prejudicially affect the minds of the juror* [my emphasis] ... any combination which has for its object the perversion of true justice, is a criminal conspiracy and indictable as such.[4]

Packer's revelations were published when Baxter's court was in full swing. He had broken every law in the book. Either Packer was guilty of 'criminal conspiracy', or this statute applied to the entire hierarchy of Scotland Yard. According to Justice Fitzjames Stephen, 'preventing or persuading a witness from giving evidence is a criminal conspiracy'. By all that is empiric, either Scotland Yard or this East End grocer was perverting the course of justice.

Remaining mute about his 'special book', Sergeant White dutifully trotted off that morning to Berner Street, and saying no more to Packer than he had said to Moore, dutifully trotted back. 'The Police Sergeant returned at noon,' wrote Moore, 'and acquainted me as in report attached (No 52983); in consequence of which Telegram No. 1 was forwarded to Chief Inspector Swanson and the Police Sergeant sent to Central Office to fully explain the facts.' We don't know what White told Swanson at Central Office, or what Swanson had to say about Packer's 'original statement' as recorded in his 'special book', but I hazard that it was nothing at all. Because the 'special book' was one of Swanson's many retrospective inventions, and until the intercession of the *Evening News*, the police had avoided Matthew Packer like the plague.

What followed that afternoon would barely have made it into a two-reel Keystone Kops. What the record presents us with is an absurdity. 'On the 4th inst,' wrote White, 'I was directed by Inspector

Moore to make further enquiries and if necessary to see Packer and take him to the mortuary.' 'If necessary'? That was the substance of the order? And what further enquiries? Moore wasn't aware there had been any enquiries into Packer at all. But then, this was only the most important murder investigation in the entire history of the Metropolitan Police.

White says he went to Berner Street, where Mrs Packer informed him that two detectives had taken her husband to the mortuary. On his way there himself, White ran into Packer and an unidentified man. Where had Packer been? 'This Detective asked me to go and see if I could identify the woman.' And did he? 'Yes, I believe she bought some grapes at my shop about 12 o'clock on Saturday.'

How could any honest copper swallow this, when only four days before he said he'd heard the opposite? Why didn't White tear into the old bastard, threaten him with defamation of the police? That he didn't answers the question. Sergeant White could say nothing about the grocer's devastating revelations in the *Evening News*, because there was no previous statement.

He now goes about writing one:

> Shortly after, they were joined by another man. I asked the man what they were doing with Packer and they both said they were detectives. I asked for their authority. One of the men produced a card from his pocket book, but would not allow me to touch it. They then said they were Private Detectives. They then induced Packer to go away with them. From enquiry I have made there is no doubt that these are the two men referred to in an attached newspaper cutting, who examined the drain at Dutfield's yard on the 2nd inst.

The implausible so infects this report that it's difficult to know where to begin. Sergeant White is an officer of the Metropolitan Police, with the Queen's initials on his helmet. In circumstances that are already extraordinary, he has been instructed by his superior to go down to Whitechapel and escort Matthew Packer to the morgue. In this he has singularly failed.

Imagine, if you will, that you are such a police officer, engaged in perhaps the most incendiary enquiries of your lifetime, and that you are now re-engaging a man who previously told you he saw nothing, but who now says he saw everything, and moreover fills a page of a newspaper with it. Would you not caution him? Would you say nothing at all? Would you meekly defer all authority invested in you as a police officer to a pair of characters you had never seen before, and who refused even to properly identify themselves? Would you allow these two anonymous coves to usurp your witness, neglecting your orders in favour of a pair of strangers, staring gormlessly while they walk off with him?

It is untenable, and by the end of the next sentence it becomes utterly incredible. These two men were not kosher private detectives: one of them was in fact a habitual criminal, currently being sought by the Metropolitan Police. But we're in such a wonderland it hardly matters. Swanson was to claim that these 'detectives' were working for Mr Lusk's Vigilance Committee in association with the press. This was to prove demonstrably untrue.

Not many weeks before his encounter with Messrs Batchelor and Grand, Sergeant White had actually arrested a man for 'representing himself as a detective'. White didn't trust the man's demeanour, and ran him in. This phoney detective, by the name of Louis Hahn, was found to have a book in his possession, 'containing addresses, Sir Charles Warren's among them'.[5] We can be sure Mr Grand had Warren's and Anderson's addresses too.

Mr Charles Le Grande, alias Charles Grandy, Colnette Grandy, Charles Grant, Charles Granby, Christian Nelson, Briscony and Neilson, of Danish birth, was a thirty-five-year-old professional criminal, presently on the run from the police.

Le Grande's enormous catalogue of offences is too time-consuming to get into here. But it kicked off in 1877 with eight years' penal servitude, and would evolve by 1891 to twenty years in prison for various outrages including attempted murder of a policeman. This was one bad actor.

On the morning of 4 October, having relinquished his witness to Mr Le Grande, Sergeant White returned to Scotland Yard to put in his noon report. Later that afternoon he was back in Packer's shop, his purpose unknown – perhaps he had gone down there to discuss the price of seasonal fruits? Clearly no official instruction had been given 'to bring the grocer in', because at about 4 p.m. Batchelor and Le Grande turned up in a cab. White stood next to the cabbages while the wanted criminal and his sidekick 'induced Packer to enter the cab, stating they would take him to Scotland Yard to see Warren'.

This they certainly did. But as they gallop off, we might want to consider one or two questions. Why was no legitimate police officer sent to collect Packer? Why delegate the task to an arsonist, thief, bomb-maker and foreign scoundrel? We know Le Grande had no difficulty getting into Scotland Yard, but it is surely a wonder that he ever got out of it. From where did these two idiots obtain their authority? Lusk's outfit couldn't have given it, and neither could the press. The only authority that could empower such a villain as Le Grande was a policeman senior to Sergeant White himself. We're looking at an authority who could leapfrog the System, which in this case wasn't difficult, because it *was* the System. Here was a lowly fruit-seller, complaining that he never so much as had a copper knock at his door, now whisked away by a criminal to Scotland Yard to see the most senior policeman in England.

A decidedly sinister circumstance was in progress, but as yet it had hardly begun. As the much-maligned Stephen Knight remarked, 'Something peculiar was going on.' What authority did Batchelor and Le Grande have for carrying out an investigation of Packer independently of the CID? How did they hope to get into the presence of Warren? In other words, by what official chicanery was this jailbird Le Grande involved?

The London Post Office Directory has no listing for any 'Le Grande' in 1887 or 1888. It is not until 1889 that we find an entry, under 'Enquiry Offices', for 'Grande Charles & Co., 238 Strand,

London W.C.'. By the time this directory was published, Le Grande was back in prison, clocking up two years' hard for blackmail. Whoever had hired him was working ex-directory.

Who could be craven and corrupt enough to get into business with this reprobate? 'Shifty Nib' Swanson claimed that Batchelor and Le Grande were 'acting conjointly with the Vigilance Committee and the Press, who upon searching a drain in the yard found a grape-stem which was amongst other matter swept from the yard after its examination by police & then called upon Mr Packer whom they took to the mortuary where he identified the body of Elizabeth Stride as that of the woman'.

Swanson couldn't look at a bottle of ink without fishing it for lies. Firstly, the Vigilance Committee. George Lusk was justifiably perceived as amongst the most zealous enemies of the criminal in their midst. No man could have done more to try to have him stopped. He called assemblies, instigated patrols, and was the author of innumerable letters to the powers in charge. In desperation, on behalf of the people of Whitechapel, Lusk had even petitioned Her Majesty the Queen. The ensuing cold shoulder, like that received from Home Secretary Matthews, may have been suitably regal, but was still a matter of Her Majesty's regret.[6]

Nobody was listening to Lusk. As a habitual fact, he sought maximum publicity for his cause, and by that alone he is exonerated from any involvement with Batchelor and Le Grande. Lusk put his money where his mouth was. If he was paying these goons, why the silence here? Nothing would have pleased him more than to have got a foot into Warren's door, but regrettably his supposed employees had neglected to include him.

George Lusk was one of London's best. Despite the constant brush-offs, he remained indefatigable. He may have been an average man, but he was of above-average integrity. It's true the Vigilance Committee hired private detectives, but no way was a man like Lusk going to rent a man like Le Grande. 'Only those who are physically and morally equal to the task' was the criterion of the Committee. Le Grande was a moral degenerate who would spend more of his life in custody than out of it. Nobody knocking at the door of Scotland Yard would be stupid enough to arrive with a liability like him. Warren would have used Le Grande's record to discredit both Packer and Lusk.

But the vigilant Mr Lusk was nowhere to be seen, and was never told about his imaginary link with the two 'private detectives'. Apart from the ink-stained fingers of Swanson, whose fictions would remain secret for another hundred years, there isn't a scintilla of evidence to connect the Vigilance Committee with Batchelor and Le Grande, any more than there is with any newspaper.

In fact, rather the opposite. On 3 October the *Morning Advertiser* had reported a special meeting of the Committee held the previous evening. 'An intimation at this stage reached the meeting that some private detectives wished to be engaged in the case on behalf of the Vigilance Committee, but Mr Reeves and Mr Aarons announced they already had three detectives at work and the services of these gentlemen were therefore declined.'

The identity of these gentlemen isn't hard to divine. On 5 October the *Daily Telegraph* published a lengthy report on the Committee and an update on its progress. There wasn't a great deal to celebrate. 'Suspicions, surmises' was just about the substance of it, with no mention of any excursions to Scotland Yard.

The explosive intercession of Matthew Packer came between 2 and 5 October. At no time on, before or after 4 October did the Vigilance Committee acknowledge any association whatsoever with Packer, Batchelor, Le Grande, grapes, a grape-stem, or the drains at Dutfield's Yard. Nor did it claim any association with any newspaper, just as no newspaper claimed any association with it. Had such a union existed, the *Evening News*, of all journals, could hardly have been unaware of it – it would be bragging about it – because via their 'conjoined efforts', according to Swanson, it was supposed to be the *News* and the Vigilance Committee that had hired Batchelor and Le Grande.

It's all the usual Swanson rubbish. No way did anyone associated with the press get anywhere near Warren. Examples of his virulent antipathy towards the newspapers are legion. A Home Office memo demonstrates the point: 'Sir Charles came to see me both yesterday & today about the Whitechapel murders.' The Boss apparently had things under control, 'but he remarked to me very strongly, upon the great hindrance which is caused to the efforts of the police, by the activity of agents of the Press Association & newspapers. These "touts" follow the detectives wherever they go in search of clues, and then having interviewed persons with whom the police have had conversation and from whom enquiries have been made, compile the paragraphs which fill the papers.'[7]

Which brings us back to Batchelor and Le Grande. Swanson tells us they were working with the Vigilance Committee and the press, precisely the breed Scotland Yard had locked out. Blackmail and bomb-making aside, were these two not classic examples of 'touts'? And yet these 'pressmen', as Swanson called them, were able to breeze through the sacred portals of Scotland Yard? I don't think so.

So who were these two 'private detectives' actually working for? According to Sergeant White, they were the men 'who examined the drain at Dutfield's yard', and according to Swanson they 'found a grape-stem'. Who could have had authorised access to this 'zealously guarded'[8] crime scene, and what was their interest in grapes well before Packer had made himself known to the *Evening News*? Of one thing we can be certain: these two slippery bastards were not working for any newspaper, but for someone of more circumspect authority.

At the hub of the rot was Robert Anderson. Later down the line we'll arrive at this sordid 'Christian's' sub-life. His predecessor and associate in the burgeoning secret police, Sir Edward Jenkinson, said of Anderson's appointment in 1888: 'If it were known what sort of man he is, there would be a howl all over London.' Anderson was corrupt and a creature of the gutter, spending most of his career floundering in its trash. Touts, narks, spies and hoodlums like Le Grande were right up his street. But exposure of the Pulpiteer and his crooked menagerie must wait.

Warren's anti-press bleat was written ten days before the 'Double Event'. From the beginning there was police reticence to share information, but after Annie Chapman, resistance to Fleet Street became endemic. A rolling catalogue of press grievances makes the point. 'On pain of dismissal', officers were instructed not to talk to representatives of the press. The order in action was ubiquitous. 1 October, the *Daily Chronicle*, re Dutfield's Yard (where Batchelor and Le Grande poked about at their leisure): 'Police have taken great precautions up to the present to exclude all representatives of the press.' 3 October, the *Echo*: 'Of course no information as to what has transpired is offered by any of the officers, who – as evidenced by their attitude towards the press – very zealously obey the stringent orders they have to "give nothing to reporters".'

Except for Batchelor and Le Grande?

I leave it to Robert Anderson to vanquish the silly lies of Swanson in respect of Batchelor and Le Grande being pressmen: 'The activity of the police has been to a considerable extent wasted through the exigencies of sensational journalism, and the action of unprincipled persons, who, from various motives have endeavoured to mislead us.'[9]

Meanwhile, a pair of unprincipled persons, together with a person in the vegetable trade, were tramping up the stairs of Scotland Yard. Sir Howard Vincent would not have been impressed.

But this wasn't about policing – it was about something of an entirely different complexion. It was about the System protecting itself from an enemy within by protecting the enemy. Packer had seen Jack the Ripper, and it brought the System to the brink of panic. The man they didn't dare put in front of a jury was instead ushered into the presence of the world's most compromised policeman. Here was a humble grocer holding his hat, facing the power of the Victorian state with a medal on its tit. Downstairs (if not actually in the room), a dangerous criminal was perhaps looking at himself on a wanted poster, and this is beginning to feel like something out of Kafka.

It isn't clear who was in the room. The 'pressmen' said they were taking Packer to see Warren, so he was either there or he wasn't, according to your point of view. His second-in-command was most certainly present, a lawyer and Assistant Commissioner by the name of Alexander Carmichael Bruce.

There is no indication that Packer had made any previous statement, or that the police were aware of one. White's 'special book'[10] was as elusive as he was. But at last the Met had an opportunity of getting a *signed document* confirming what this witness had or hadn't seen. An honest cop would have countenanced nothing less. But this old grocer was in the presence of the bewitched. Under the embossed seal of Metropolitan Police stationery, Carmichael Bruce scribbled some barely legible notes. No time. No place. Just a name.

Matthew Packer
Keeps a small shop in Berner St. has a few grapes in window, black & white. On Sat night about 11 p.m. a young man from 25–30 – about 5.7. with long black coat buttoned up – soft felt hat, kind of Yankee hat rather broad shoulders – rather quick in speaking, rough voice. I sold him ½ pound black grapes 3d. A woman came up with him from Back Church end (the lower end of street) She was dressed in black frock & jacket, fur round bottom of jacket a black crepe bonnet, she was playing with a flower like a geranium white outside and red inside. I identify the woman at the St George's Mortuary as the one I saw that night – They passed by as though they were going to Com-Road, but – instead of going up they crossed to the other side of the road to the Board School, & were there for about ½ hour till I shd. say 11.30. talking to one another. I then shut up my shutters. Before they passed over opposite to my shop, they waited near to the club for a few minutes apparently listening to the music. I saw no more of them after I shut up my shutters. I put the man down as a young clerk, He had a frock coat on – no gloves. He was about 1½ inch or 2 or 3 inches – a little higher than she was.

ACB 4.10.88.

This confection debases the paper it was written on. It's doubtful Packer ever saw it. He certainly didn't sign it. Without his signature it was worthless, as everyone in that room well knew. But this rubbish was soon on its way to Swanson, where that shifty little ink-monger would make much of it. I will get into the 'statements' attributed to Packer when they become the focus of Swanson's fictions. However, a couple of points demand attention now.

Bruce's sheet of paper concedes that Packer saw a man with Elizabeth Stride, and sold him grapes. It is the *timing* of the event that the Met is so anxious to change. Had it really been 11.30 when he shut up shop, nobody would have given a toss about Packer. 11.30 was ninety minutes before the murder, and grapes or no grapes, Stride could easily have met another man before her death. 11.30 dismisses Packer as irrelevant. 12.30 is a whole different ball-game.

If he sold grapes to the man around midnight, Packer's suspect becomes dynamic. It in fact meshes with the evidence given by Police Constable Smith. Both say they saw Stride with a man at about 12.30 a.m. It is therefore simply incredible to put up Smith at Baxter's court while simultaneously gagging Packer.

If Packer was lying, like Mrs Mary Malcolm, let his lies be put before a jury. What aberrant species of policeman could have a problem with that? Look no further than Bro Sir Charles Warren. It's the grapes clutched in Stride's right hand that he cannot concede. The grapes, confirmed by a galaxy of similarly suppressed witnesses, could have caught the Whitechapel Fiend.

Carmichael Bruce writes that Packer's man had a 'rough voice'. East End labourers have rough voices – a 'rough voice' belongs to a man like Bill Sikes. In the only 'statement' we can reliably attribute to Packer (the one that appeared in the *Evening News* on 4 October) he said, 'He spoke like an educated man, but he had a loud, sharp sort of voice, and a quick and commanding way with him.'

Bruce puts the suspect's height at about five feet seven inches, then amends it to 'about 1½ inch or 2 or 3 inches – a little higher than she was'. Elizabeth Stride was five feet two inches. By Carmichael Bruce's calculation, the suspect could only have been five feet five. At one and a half inches taller than Stride, he would have been five feet three and a half inches.

We have arrived at the reason Mr Packer's so-called 'statement' at Scotland Yard remains unsigned. In Sergeant White's 'statement' of the same day, claimed as the second he took from the fruit-seller, Packer put the time at which the man and woman came to his shop at 12.30, reiterating what he had told the *Evening News*. This 12.30 was subsequently amended in the margin of Carmichael Bruce's 'statement' to 11.30, and initialled 'A.C.B.'. Carmichael Bruce had thus dumped an hour, and kept Packer in ignorance of the chicanery – hence no signature. This falsified 'statement' must be borne in mind when Swanson dismisses Packer as an elderly man who kept changing his story. In reality, and most scandalously, it was the Assistant Commissioner of Police who was making the changes.

In his impending overview of 19 October (a document held in reverence by certain Ripperologists), Swanson summarises Packer's misbegotten relationship with the Met. He naturally makes no mention of the visit to Scotland Yard, or the names of the men who took him there. To open the doors of this place to 'representatives of the press' was to contradict everything Swanson had written and the police had enforced.

It had been a busy week for Batchelor and Le Grande. On 2 October they had taken Packer to the morgue in Golden Lane and shown him the body of Catherine Eddowes, pretending it was that of Elizabeth Stride. Who had instigated this test? Why were others who had identified Stride not put through the same procedure – morons like Mary Malcolm, for example? Packer came through with flying colours; it was Batchelor and Le Grande who failed. But if Packer had botched it, wouldn't it have been a wonderful spoiler to leak to the press? Somebody was already at it before the ink was dry on Carmichael Bruce's unsigned 'statement': the *Star* was putting the boot into Packer on that same afternoon: 'The police most emphatically deny the truth of the story that has been published as to the discovery of the shopkeeper who had talked with the murderer and his Berner Street victim, and sold them grapes, and had seen them at the entrance of the fatal alley for ten minutes before the deed was done. The fact is that the alleged informant contradicts himself, and there is no evidence that there were any grapes in the possession of the woman.'[11]

Who told the *Star* Packer was contradicting himself? How did it know what was said in the hallowed confines of Carmichael Bruce's office? How can the police 'most emphatically deny' grapes when the Assistant Commissioner has just initialled a 'statement' confirming them? It is only the timing that is in dispute. If the coppers didn't like evidence as published in the *Evening News*, let them put Packer before a jury. After all, it was a 'criminal conspiracy' to prevent a witness from giving evidence. Instead, Warren preferred to try to discredit this turbulent witness via the very medium he excoriated.

It's noticeable that Messrs Batchelor and Le Grande evaporate as quickly as they appeared. It seems that after the Sergeant White fiasco, their anonymous employer had no further use of them. They fall off the map. Le Grande's role would only become public when he was back behind bars in 1889.

But never mind Batchelor and Le Grande. As usual, the guardians of the grail are falling over themselves to denigrate Packer – 'the Legend of the Grapes' – and get some mirrors up around the Met. The A-Team are so anxious to fall into line with Swanson that they facilitate invention for him. The worthless 'statement' taken by Carmichael Bruce is given a bit of a leg-up. Here's what Mr Stewart Evans and Mr Don Rumbelow have to say about Packer's ride to see the Boss Cop at Scotland Yard: 'It seems the three did go to Scotland Yard, but they would not have been seen by the Chief Commissioner, who does not deal with the public at that level. It is likely that Packer saw a detective inspector, probably Moore, and a signed witness statement would have been obtained by him. The statement has not survived.'[12]

This nonsense is setting up a false prospectus and attempting to confirm it by drawing our attention to its non-existence. If Packer saw Moore, how come Moore signed his 'statement' 'A.C.B.'? Alexander Carmichael Bruce is unequivocally established as being in the loop as a signatory to Warren's 'eyes and ears' document referencing Bro Donald Swanson. Does anyone imagine the Metropolitan Police would allow themselves to drown in the impending onslaught of press humiliation if they had a *signed statement* from Matthew Packer? Enough bogus 'statements' are ascribed to Packer without inventing another one that 'hasn't survived'.

'If further doubt needed to be cast on the whole Packer episode,' continue Rumbelow and Evans, 'we need look no further than one of the two private detectives involved.'[13] A list of Le Grande's extensive career in crime follows, rounding off with his last appearance in court before that frightener and servant of his age, Mr Justice Hawkins. The fearsome Hawkins slammed him up, and *shut him up*, by sentencing Le Grande to twenty years.

For reasons beyond any construction that I can understand, Mr Evans and Mr Rumbelow manipulate this tariff into further denigration of Packer. I'm afraid I can't follow the logic. Does the fact that Le Grande is a criminal make Packer a liar? If the Kray twins arrive uninvited at Mr Evans' and Mr Rumbelow's respective front doors, are the two Ripperologists thereby converted into East End hooligans? Give me a break. Le Grande's criminality has no bearing *whatsoever* on Matthew Packer's character, and to suggest that it has is mischievous. I think it is infinitely more credible to locate the root of this deceit amongst the 'clueless' men in blue, who, as the *Star* quaintly put it, 'were infected with the miracle of lying'. Evans and Rumbelow know nothing of this lying, but conclude their corporate forensics with: 'Packer's change of mind was no doubt influenced by a reward being offered by the Whitechapel Vigilance Committee, and the changes he made to his story were no doubt made in the hope of collecting this reward.'

Once again we have an excrescence that disgraces the page. Moreover, it conveniently leaves out the far greater reward advertised by the City of London. It isn't possible to slander the dead, but with this, Evans/Rumbelow come close. It seems that anything can be said, and anyone defamed, if the end game is to hide Warren. I don't know where they sourced this caprice, but it's probably from that most reliable of students, Mr Philip Sugden. He had a tilt at smearing Packer with something suspiciously similar. 'Why *should* Packer seek to deceive the police?' he asks with righteous burlesque.[14]

Mr Sugden is entitled to pose any question he likes, but such enquiry cannot be isolated to Matthew Packer. If Packer sought to deceive the police, a tribe of others were also in on the act. Rather, the question is, why did Diemschutz, Kosebrodski, Mrs Mortimer, PC Lamb and Chief Inspector Walter Dew seek to deceive the police? All, at one point or another, corroborate Packer. Why *should* Wynne Baxter have kept their evidence of grapes out of his court? Why *should* thirty other witnesses at Dutfield's Yard be kept out, while a mad dipso-hag like Mrs Malcolm is invited in? Why *should* Baxter allow witnesses like her while denying Matthew Packer? Why *should* Packer have been taken clandestinely to Scotland Yard to have a 'statement' altered behind his back by Carmichael Bruce? Why did Sergeant White wilt in the presence of a scoundrel like Le Grande, and what happened to his 'special book'? These adjuncts – if he's in good faith – are all part of Mr Sugden's question. Why *should* Mr Sugden ignore them?

As I say, his question is his prerogative, and he goes on to answer it. 'It's possible,' he muses, 'that the fantasy was designed to enhance this modest grocer's status amongst his neighbours by providing him with the key role in the drama.'[15]

Is there the *remotest glimmer of evidence* that Packer bragged to his neighbours about the thrill of it all? Well, perhaps not. To compensate for the deficiency, Mr Sugden ventilates another theory. 'A much more likely explanation,' he flutes, 'will be found in the sudden escalation in the scale of the reward money prompted by the double murder. On the night of the 1st and 2nd of October,' he continues, 'lured by the rewards, amateur sleuths appeared in force on the streets of the East End.' And the next day the *Star* spoke of others 'who turn in descriptions on the chance of coming near enough the mark to claim a portion of the reward if the man should be caught, just as one buys a ticket for the lottery'. Packer apparently to the fore, waving a cucumber. He's already told the *Evening News* what he saw *gratis*, so why try to associate him with sleuths on the make? But let me not impede Mr Sugden in his creative flow. 'This prescient columnist [in the *Star*] seems to have hit the nail on the head, for by then there seems little doubt that Packer had joined the gold rush.'[16]

I think it's desirable not to get too intoxicated with one's own invective, just as it's as well to pay a little attention to fact. Where does this 'little doubt that Packer had joined the gold rush' come from? What microdot of evidence does Mr Sugden have for this moonshine? Where is the *remotest sniff* that Packer was trying to wring a buck out of Jack the Ripper? Did he go to Scotland Yard of his own volition? Did he ask for coin when he got there? With cops like Carmichael Bruce eager to hear him, Packer was in a better position to cut a deal with the authorities than any other man in Whitechapel. He was holding a bit of an ace. He could have shunned the Met (which had no reward on offer), hailed a cab and gone straight to the City for a word with Commissioner Smith.

Did he go to the City seeking £500? Did he go to the Vigilance Committee? Did he so much as ask anybody for the price of a halfpenny stamp? Did he? Is there really 'little doubt that Packer had joined the gold rush'? It is the usual obfuscatory twaddle. Why *should* Mr Sugden seek to deceive his readers?

4 October 1888 was a tough day at Met HQ. On that day Fleet Street had published facsimiles of the 'Dear Boss' letter and the 'Saucy Jacky' postcard. Jack was having the time of his life, and the

press was becoming more hostile by the day. Only four days in, and this was already shaping as a catastrophic month. The happy assassin was on Bro Warren's case, and every day brought more to hide. PC Long was presently in court trying to hide the dissent over the destruction of the writing on the wall. Bro Crawford was in court hiding Lawende's description, and Bros Phillips and Baxter were in another court trying to hide the grapes.

Packer aside, there was also the troubling little matter of the body of half a woman discovered two days earlier in the foundations of Warren's offices-to-be at New Scotland Yard, and the frantic efforts to keep this archaeologically-inspired atrocity separate from the hits in Whitechapel. Jack was grinning and the Commissioner was scurrying, stunned by another victim in his own back yard, henceforth to be known as 'the Scotland Yard mystery'.

On 5 October Warren received a letter from the Home Office. Matthews could be no less aware of the fruit-seller than anyone else. The already hyper-stressed Home Secretary basically wanted to know what the fuck was going on. Warren didn't reply to the letter.

A day later, Packer was back in the newspapers. The *Daily Telegraph* published a sketch of the man who supposedly bought the grapes. This was everything Warren didn't need. Many such portraits had already appeared in various publications without a murmur from Scotland Yard, this pair by way of illustration:

SKETCH OF SUPPOSED MURDERER

THE MAN SEEN HAUNTING HOUSE OF MR LUSK

ANOTHER SKETCH OF SUPPOSED MURDERER

THE MAN SEEN WITH LAST TWO VICTIMS.

On the left is an all-purpose Yiddish Ripper, 'eyes small and glistening, lips usually parted in a grin which is not only reassuring, but excessively repellent'. On the right is the 'seafaring man', with a red neckerchief and tufted anus. Nobody at Scotland Yard gave a toss for this rubbish, but Packer propositioned something rather different, and by their reaction we know it ramped up anxiety amongst the Boss Cops.

SKETCH PORTRAITS OF THE SUPPOSED MURDERER.

The *Telegraph* can tell its own story: 'The above sketches are presented not, of course, as authentic portraits, but a likeness which an important witness has identified as that of the man who was seen talking to the murdered woman in Berner Street and its vicinity until within a quarter of an hour of the time she was killed last Sunday morning.'[17] A quick roll-call of Baxter's witnesses follows – William Marshall, James Brown, PC Smith – before the *Telegraph* arrives at the only eyes of real merit: 'The evidence of another witness has yet to be taken, and this man seems to have had a better opportunity of observing the appearance of the stranger than any other individual, for it was at his shop that the grapes which the other witnesses saw near the body were bought.'[18]

The 'other witnesses' were of course those (like most newspapers) who were infected with 'the Legend of the Grapes', and who were also kept out of Wynne Baxter's court. 'This witness, Matthew

Packer,' continues the *Telegraph*, 'has furnished information to the Scotland Yard authorities, and it was considered so important that he was examined in the presence of Sir Charles Warren himself. He has also identified the body of Elizabeth Stride as that of the woman who accompanied the man who came to his shop, not long before midnight on Saturday. In accordance with the general description furnished to the police by Packer and others, a number of sketches were prepared, portraying men of different nationalities, ages, and ranks of life.'[19]

The two drawings published in the *Telegraph* are the *only* sketches that were approved by Packer. The 'general description' published in the same newspaper is a compilation of the descriptions given by PC Smith and others at Baxter's court. It is of the twenty-eight-year-old, five-foot-seven-inch man. Anything said in front of Baxter we can assume to be as bent as the evidence given by Dr Phillips and Mrs Malcolm. Either way, none of it can be attributed to Packer. His contribution in the *Telegraph* is without quotation marks, and is in fact lifted directly from the *Evening News*; it is *not* his description, but that of the now vanished police touts, Messrs Batchelor and Le Grande.

The police weren't reticent to use Fleet Street when it suited (for example, the leak to the *Star*). They could have got rid of Packer by prosecuting him for 'publishing information that may prejudicially affect the minds of the juror', or at a minimum, humiliated him by releasing his 'signed statement' to the press. The problem was, they didn't have a signed statement.

Even Scotland Yard's most ardent apologists must recognise that there was an overwhelming obligation for Packer to appear at Baxter's court. But instead of testing his evidence, these stultified accessories to Jack the Ripper tried to ride it out behind locked doors. It wasn't only the *Telegraph* that was banging to get in. On 6 October the *East London Advertiser* delivered a whammy. 'It is a matter of common knowledge,' it wrote, 'that some grapes were found in one hand of the murdered woman, so that the finding of a fragment of this grape-stalk, though important as binding the links of the evidence closer together, was scarcely necessary to establish the fact that the victim had been eating the fruit immediately before her death.'[20]

This isn't Ripperology kissing Warren's arse a hundred years later, it is a newspaper published in Whitechapel six days after Stride's murder. It was 'common knowledge' that Stride was clutching grapes – everyone knew it, except the police and subsequently Ripperology. Here was a man who 'had a better opportunity of observing the appearance of the stranger than any other individual'. Be this true or false, if there was a coroner's court, they had to call the fruit-seller; they couldn't continue the hearings without him. So they didn't continue the hearings.

Baxter had galloped through witnesses on 1, 2, 3 and 5 October. Proceedings were then postponed for almost three weeks, to give the police a chance to further discredit Packer. They went about it with purpose. On Monday, 8 October, a breathtakingly ridiculous article appeared in the *Manchester Guardian*. It seems likely that a provincial newspaper was chosen because nothing published in London would disgrace itself with such trash. It's absurd enough to have come directly from Swanson, and it probably did. Under a sub-headline of 'Police Precautions', it kicks off with the usual spin: 'Large bodies of plain-clothes men were drafted by Sir Charles Warren into the Whitechapel district from other parts of London, and these, together with detectives, were so numerous that in the more deserted thoroughfares almost every man met with was a police officer.'

Official Police Orders for 29 September naturally repudiate this crap. In reality, the number of constables was reduced by two, and the number from CID remained exactly as it was a week before. But never mind that, the article had barely touched upon its motive: 'Supplementing the energy displayed by the police, hundreds of people living in the back streets sat up all night, whilst dozens of sturdy householders paid occasional visits to yards and other secluded spots in their immediate vicinity.'

The *Guardian* is all sympathy for the difficulties of the police, and goes on to render examples of the kind of 'absurdities' they were having to cope with. The purpose of the piece becomes clearer by the line. It is to establish an environment of 'absurdities', and to include Matthew Packer among them: 'As a specimen of the vast amount of absurd "information" which is imparted to the police, and through which they have to wade, a man called at Commercial Street Police Station, stating that he had a clue. Upon inquiry, it was ascertained that he knew a man who cut a baby to pieces twenty years ago, and afterwards escaped to America, it being his impression that the baby mutilator might have returned and committed the recent horrible mutilations.'

Having set the scene with 'the baby mutilator', the text shifts without pausing for breath to Matthew Packer: 'In that case [that of the baby mutilator] he said he could give a description. A sketch portrait of a man has been made *by the Scotland Yard authorities* [my emphasis] answering as nearly as possible to the description given by Matthew Packer, 44 Berner Street, and that of two other witnesses, who assert they saw the man, and actually conversed with him prior to committal of the murder.'

Invoking a phantom of twenty years before (1868), 'the baby mutilator' is here conjoined with Packer, and a specimen of 'absurd information' is now made whole. It's so crude a monkey could see through it. So stupid it could only have come from the police.

In the first place, the Scotland Yard sketch had *nothing whatever* to do with the sketch published in the *Telegraph*. It was the *Telegraph* sketch, *approved by Packer*, that panicked them. Secondly, the two witnesses 'who assert they saw the man, and actually conversed with him' are nothing less than scandalous bullshit; but the spinners haven't finished with it. 'Packer keeps a fruit shop next door to the yard adjoining The Working Man's Educational Club,' continues the *Guardian*,

> and indignantly protests that two grape stalks were found near the body of Elizabeth Stride by a woman living up the yard. He seems positive that the grapes were sold by him to the man who murdered Stride. Traces of the sketch made of the supposed murderer have been sent to all those who are likely to identify him, amongst them being Packer, who contemptuously states that it bears no resemblance whatever to the man he said he endeavoured to describe. If a man was found who answered to the description of the sketch in every detail, he could not possibly swear he had seen such a man. The man he saw was about thirty years of age, whereas the portrait was that of a mere boy without any expression whatever, and from what he could judge, practically useless for identification.[21]

Clearly, we're looking here at two different sketches: 1) The sketch approved by Packer which was printed in the *Daily Telegraph*; 2) A sketch of an expressionless boy, published Christ knows where, but apparently created by the Scotland Yard authorities. This is remarkably reminiscent of the scam at the morgue, where the now evaporated Batchelor and Le Grande attempted to spike Packer by presenting Eddowes as Stride. He didn't buy that, and he doesn't buy this. Packer endorsed the sketch in the *Telegraph*, but contemptuously rejected that of Scotland Yard's 'mere boy'.

Only those seeking to deceive could have instigated such duplicitous garbage, and only those seeking to deceive could invest it with credibility. Ripperologist Mr Paul Begg seizes upon it without inhibition, enhancing it with a bit of judicious pruning. Neglecting to include the bogus sketch of the boy, he creates an outrageous sentence that suggests Packer is rejecting the sketches he approved in the *Telegraph*.

'On October 6th,' he writes, 'the *Daily Telegraph* published a sketch of the man seen by Packer, but, despite the assurances of the newspaper that it had been "unhesitatingly selected" by Packer, Packer himself is elsewhere reported to have stated with some contempt that it "bore no resemblance whatever to the man".'[22]

Correct. It didn't, because it was a '*boy*'. What glass eyes are in business here? They are those shared by Evans, Rumbelow, Sugden et al. Anyone with even nursery skills can see that Packer was not referring to the sketches in the *Telegraph*, but contemptuously rejecting police sketches of a child.

On 10 October the *Evening News* was congratulating itself: 'On Thursday last the *Evening News* was the first and only paper to give to the world important evidence of Matthew Packer which has supplied the police with valuable material to work with.'

They were working on it all right, but not in the way the *News* might have imagined. The intention was not to investigate Packer's evidence, but to destroy his credibility. Of all newspapers, you would have thought the *News* might have got a handle on where this was heading. On the same day, on the same page, it ran a piece on the Met which was somewhat less than complimentary.

According to their own account – but very reluctantly supplied – the police are scouring the highways and byways of the metropolis for the Whitechapel murderer. At the risk of casting one more stone at these wonderful myrmidons of Sir Charles Warren, one might ask with Cowper,

> How much a dunce that's sent to roam
> Excels a dunce that stays at home.

'The police are like Polly Eccles's neighbours,' sneered the *Evening News*, 'who, according to that damsel, could not think because they had not been brought up to it.'

I'm not familiar with Polly Eccles's neighbours, but I know what 'myrmidon' means in this context. It means a hired ruffian, a base servant, and in pejorative terms, a policeman. It sounds to me as if the *Evening News* had rumbled Batchelor and Le Grande. Despite Bro Swanson's insistence that they were 'conjoined with the press' (most obviously with this newspaper), they were now and forever more noticeable by their absence. Far from claiming credit for any detectives it had hired, the *Evening News*, in concert with every other newspaper in London, ignored them, and never again would their forensic exploits disturb the inkwells of Fleet Street.[23]

Meanwhile, Warren was looking at another letter from the Home Office. On 13 October the Permanent Under Secretary of State, Sir Godfrey Lushington, wrote pressing for a reply to the unanswered letter of 5 October. Home Secretary Matthews wanted a 'report', and something urgent needed cooking up. Who could be better suited to the task than Warren's 'eyes and ears', Chief Inspector Bro Donald Swanson. On 19 October Swanson released his 'overview'. It's a classic piece of chicanery, bloated with dishonesty.

Swanson says that Packer made 'different statements', and it is a point that would subsequently be hammered to death by Ripperologists. One of their sort, a Mr Dave Yost, refers to 'an interesting aspect of the many Packer statements', when in reality the most interesting aspect is that Packer made no official statement at all.

We have six 'statements' to consider.

1) Sergeant White's 'statement', recorded in his 'special book'. This document has never been seen. It exists solely on Sergeant White's word, claimed to represent an interview with Packer on 30 September, but emerging only as a retrospective written up on the afternoon of 4 October. Since the 4th was a bad badge day for White, on which he relinquished his authority to a career criminal, we are entitled to consider any action he took (including keeping this 'statement' secret from Moore) as a bit on the iffy side. Why would White have taken so comprehensive a 'statement' from a man who'd seen nothing? Packer *so* saw

nothing, he gives the times when he didn't see it. Scotland Yard never used this elusive 'statement' to prove Packer a liar, and it almost certainly didn't exist. *Unsigned.*

2) Sergeant White's second Packer 'statement' of 4 October. This was not taken at Packer's shop, or in the street where White's authority was usurped by Le Grande. It was written at an unknown place, and never seen by Packer. Its timings were subsequently altered by Alexander Carmichael Bruce. *Unsigned.*

3) A.C.B.'s 'statement' itself. Not a statement at all, but a page or two of barely legible notes that may or may not have been written up in Packer's presence. *Unsigned.*

4) Batchelor and Le Grande's 'statement' published in the *Evening News* on 4 October. Attributed to Packer, it is almost word-for-word identical with the 'statement' penned by A.C.B. Both claim the suspect as five feet seven inches, with a 'rough voice and a quick way of talking'. *Unsigned.*

5) Packer's interview with the 'Special Commissioner' of the *Evening News*. This is as near to a 'statement' as we get, and the only description that can reliably be attributed to Packer. Conflicting with the two previous 'statements', Mr Packer does not describe the suspect's voice as 'rough', but 'educated'. Neither does he stipulate any precise height: 'The man was about 30 to 35 years of age, medium height, and with a rather dark complexion.' Packer sold his fruit 'through the lower part of the window case', which as I've previously suggested, would render almost everybody medium height. 'It was a dark night,' wrote the *News*, 'and the only light was afforded by an oil-lamp which Packer had burning outside his window.' Considering the circumstances, coupled with the fact that he could have no idea he was talking to a murderer, it is remarkable how comprehensive the fruit-seller's recollections were. *Unsigned.*

6) Packer's 'statement' published in the *Telegraph* of 6 October, together with the sketches of the suspect which he approved. Artwork apart, the text is a direct lift from the *Evening News*, claimed as such by that newspaper. It is a reiteration of the 'statement' given by Batchelor/Le Grande (rough voice, five feet seven, etc.). Its source makes it equally suspect. *Unsigned.*

Thus, *no statement* from Packer exists. There are plagiarised accounts from outside sources, but nothing given under oath, and nothing that could survive one. It wasn't Packer giving different statements, it was others giving different 'statements' for him. Under the Common Law of England, the evidence of a witness is not admissible unless he has been sworn to tell the truth. Under the Evidence Act of 1843, 'No person should be excluded from giving evidence [and] it is also an offence to attempt in any way to keep witnesses away.'

Packer showed no disinclination to give evidence. It was Scotland Yard that was keeping him out, and Scotland Yard that was breaking the law. Forefather of Ripperology, Inspector Donald 'Shifty-Nib' Swanson, was busily at it. It was Swanson's job to get rid of Packer, and it was he who kicked off the tradition of deceit: 'It was not until after publication in the newspapers of a description of a man seen by PC Smith,' lied Swanson, 'that Mr Packer gave the foregoing particulars.'[24]

Nice try, Shifty. The only problem is that Packer said it first. His interview in the *Evening News* was given on 3 October, and published on the 4th. PC Smith said nothing until 5 October, and it was published in newspapers on the 6th.

How could Packer base his interview on what Smith hadn't yet said? Short of being a soothsayer, he could have no way of coordinating with anything PC Smith might say two days later.

Mr Sugden has spotted Swanson's cunning, and goes about puffing the usual smokescreen. 'Inevitably,' he writes, 'one suspects that this rejuvenation of Packer's man had something to do with the release of PC Smith's description, for the Constable's account was circulated in the press from October 1st.'[25]

NO IT WAS NOT.

An unsourced description was published in *The Times* – the very same one previously used by Mr Sugden when trying to explain away Bro Crawford's 'secret', now reconstituted by Mr Sugden to try to explain away Matthew Packer.

First time around this twaddle was proffered *vis à vis* Eddowes/Lawende in Mitre Square, a *City beat*, and absolutely *nothing whatever* to do with Stride/PC Smith in Berner Street, a *Met beat*, in Bro Warren's Metropolitan Police district. Was PC Smith in Mitre Square that night? No, he was not. So where does PC Smith give a description of a man in Berner Street that Packer was able to copy?

For elucidation, we return to Mr Sugden. Page 225 of his book refers us to note 8. Note 8 is at the rear of the tome, on page 502. 'For release of Smith's account to the press,' it says, 'see ch. 10. n. 26.' Whereupon, having seen it and being none the wiser, we are escorted to page 212, where note 26 is discovered. This note orbits us yet again to the back of the book, where page 501 rewards us with the following:

> For early release of PC Smith's account of going to press, see reports of Chief Inspector Swanson, 19th October 1888, HO/144/221/A49301C/8a, DN, DT and *Star*, 1st October 1888.

In other words, the source corroborating Swanson is Swanson. Why not simply say so? Why take us around the houses to arrive back at the 19 October Swanson fiction, which is where we started? Why *should* Mr Sugden seek to deceive his readers? Halfway through this silly hike (on page 212) we read: 'Only a version of PC Smith's description was then in circulation.' It's become a 'version'. And it is this (Mitre Square) 'version' that Shifty, and now Mr Sugden, would have us believe is the source of Packer's specific descriptions of suspect, time and place, which he gave to the *Evening News* fully two days before PC Smith got anywhere near a newspaper. All the endnotes in the British Library will not disguise the fact that Packer articulated his 'version' *before* PC Smith gave his concoction two days later in Bro Baxter's court.

Swanson proffers straws which Sugden drowns with. Packer says it was raining; PC Smith was told to say it wasn't. And of course Ripperology agrees. Mr Paul Begg has this:

> Packer had told Sergeant White that he had not done any business because of the heavy rain and that he had closed his shop early, but the rain began about 9 p.m. and had stopped about 11 p.m. If Packer shut up shop because of the rain, then he must have closed before 11 p.m., and in fact Packer said that the man and woman had stood in the rain for over half an hour, putting the sale of the grapes at least as early as 10.30 p.m. The rain is important in another respect, because Dr Blackwell said Stride's clothes were not wet from the rain, so, if Packer sold grapes to anyone who stood in the rain, it was not Elizabeth Stride.[26]

Mr Begg is so agog to prove Packer a liar that he buggers himself with his own contradictions. Literally three pages earlier (page 143) in his same book he quotes two men, J. Best and John Gardner, who were 'entering the Brick Layers Arms in Settles St'. 'At eleven p.m. as they went into the pub,' he writes, 'a woman who they felt certain was Stride was leaving with a man. It was *raining very fast* and they did not appear willing to go out.'[27] (Begg's words, my emphasis.)

So at 11 p.m. it was pissing down in Settles Street, while a hundred yards away in Berner Street it was dry as a bone?

'The rain stopped at about 11 p.m.' is Mr Begg's requirement, and you can believe it if you will. Although the *Telegraph* reported Stride's dress as 'saturated', Dr Blackwell couldn't see the rain, for the same reason he couldn't see the grapes.

Official weather reports for that night, located at the London Meteorological Library, blow Blackwell (and Begg) away in favour of Packer: 'Sudden heavy rain at 9.05 p.m. lasting till after midnight.' 'It was a wet night,' wrote Walter Dew. 'The rain beat mercilessly on the windows.' A mile away in Mitre Square, it was still raining hard enough at 1.30 a.m. to detain Lawende and pals at the Imperial Club.

Apparently, together with Best, Gardner, Dew, Harris, Levy and Lawende, Packer was also hallucinating the same wet night. It was probably a species of the same disturbing mass hallucination that persuaded a variety of witnesses to think they'd seen grapes.

In *King Lear*, Shakespeare writes: 'Get thee glass eyes, and like a scurvy politician, seem to see the things thou dost not.' In Ripperology, the instruction is reversed: 'Get thee glass eyes, and seem not to see what's staring you in the face.'

What is it with this weird little confederacy, peopled by 'students' of dubious provenance, quoting each other, organically defensive, bereft of the vaguest cognitive insight, who, like the Victorian police and Freemasonry, are all about preservation of the so-called 'mystery of Jack the Ripper'? What could possibly link them all?

Extant correspondence between Scotland Yard and the Home Office makes it clear that the latter weren't easily buying into Swanson's yarns. Indeed, his final paragraph on Packer was to ensnare the Met in no end of lies. 'Packer, who is an elderly man,' wrote Swanson, 'has unfortunately made different statements so that apart from the fact of the hour at which he saw the woman (and she was seen afterwards by the PC and Schwartz as stated) any statement he made would be rendered almost valueless as evidence.'

'Schwartz'? Who the hell is 'Schwartz'? It's a name nobody had remotely bothered with before 19 October – not the police, not in Baxter's court, nowhere. So who is Swanson talking about?

'Schwartz' is from the same casting couch as the Insane Medical Student and the American Womb-Collector, and is an example of the bone-marrow rottenness then permeating Scotland Yard. What 'Schwartz' turns out to be is an outlandish solution to an intractable problem. Despite Mr Sugden's fun with his notes, Swanson was aware that he couldn't easily get around the reality of Packer's interview.

On 4 October the press had been expecting, if not demanding, Packer's appearance in the coroner's court. On 13 October the *East London Advertiser* reprinted the sketches approved by Packer, reiterating the obvious. In terms of witnesses, Packer was the only show in town. Any day now, the coroner would be obliged to reconvene. Time wasn't on Swanson's side. He needed somebody between Packer and Stride, to deflect attention away from the fruit-seller and become a new focus for the Home Office. He needed what you might call a 'wedge', and sniffing around the press, he found what he was looking for in the *Star* of 1 October.

On the preceding evening, 30 September, a well-dressed foreigner with the 'appearance of being in the theatrical line' had walked into Leman Street police station. He spoke no English, but brought a friend to interpret. On the day in question, the man and his wife had been in process of moving from Berner Street to new lodgings a couple of streets away. A name and address were evidently given, 'but the police have not disclosed them'. This didn't deter the *Star*, whose reporter found him in Backchurch Lane.[28]

According to the unnamed Hungarian, at about a quarter to one in the morning of 30 September he had been on his way home to his new lodgings via Berner Street. Turning into it from Commercial Road, 'he noticed some distance in front of him a man walking as if partially intoxicated. He walked on behind him, and, presently, he noticed a woman standing in the entrance to an alleyway where the body was afterwards found. The half-tipsy man halted and spoke to her. The Hungarian saw him put his hand on her shoulder and push her back into the passage, but feeling rather timid of getting mixed up in quarrels, he crossed to the other side of the street.' He hadn't gone a few yards before he heard the sounds of a quarrel, and looking back,

A SECOND MAN CAME OUT

of the doorway of the public house a few doors off, and shouting out some sort of warning to the man who was with the woman, rushed forward as if to attack the intruder. The Hungarian states positively that he saw a knife in the second man's hand, but he waited to see no more. He fled incontinently [sic] to his new lodgings.[29]

Notwithstanding the state of his underwear, the Hungarian was able to offer a description: 'About 30, rather stoutly built and wearing a brown moustache. The man who came at him with a knife he also describes. He says he was taller than the other but not so stout, and that his moustache was red.'

'The police,' continues the *Star*, 'have arrested one man answering to the description the Hungarian furnished. This prisoner has not been charged, but is held for enquiries to be made.' By the following day these had been made, and together with some other innocent nonentity with a moustache, 'both were discharged during the day'.

Before these fruitless detentions were even made, the *Evening Post* had accurately summed up the Hungarian's evidence: 'The idea of a quarrel having preceded the murder is generally discredited.'[30] Too right it was, because in terms of Jack the Ripper, such a scenario is risible. We don't know which of these persons the Ripper is meant to have been, but Jack did not hunt drunk, and the last thing you would have seen in his hand was a knife. People tend to run away from knives, as did this unnamed foreigner, and tipping off his victims wasn't Jack's style.

What the Hungarian had seen (and almost certainly not in Berner Street) was no more than a typical Whitechapel fracas. 'I saw lots of squabbles and rows,' deposed PC Lamb, 'such as one sees on Saturday nights.' The inebriate waddling in front of this supposed witness could not have looked less like the world's number-one murderer, and no newspaper believed he was.

By now the unnamed foreigner had been comprehensively dismissed by the police and the press. He was over. He was wrapping cod and chips. That should have been the end of him, and it would have been had it not been for Swanson's desperate efforts to dispose of Matthew Packer.

Far from disappearing, the Hungarian was about to get a Christian name. This anonymous bit-part player was to be elevated into a star. From the management that gave you 'the Nautical Man', would you now please put your hands together and give salutations to 'Israel Schwartz', the witness who never was.

With 'Israel Schwartz', Shifty Nib scaled new heights, abandoning any notion of reality to his muse. A yard of compromised ink was squandered on the Hungarian's story, characters fleshed out, and there is even a bit of colourful dialogue. Our police dramatist re-conjures the scene to a place that couldn't have been Dutfield's Yard, and it is here that the previously drunken, but now sober, suspect stops and speaks to the woman.

'The man tried to pull the woman into the street,' pens Swanson, 'but he turned her round and threw her down on the footway: & the woman screamed 3 times, but not very loudly.'[31]

It had to be a 'little scream' to explain why it wasn't heard by Mrs Mortimer, or anyone in the club. Swanson now becomes positively inspired. 'On crossing to the opposite side of the street he saw a second man lighting his pipe. The man who threw the woman down called out apparently to the man on the opposite side of the road, "Lipski", & then Schwartz walked away, but finding he was followed by the second man, he ran as far as the railway arch but the man did not follow so far.'[32]

At this juncture there's a marginal note: '(The use of "Lipski" increases my belief that the murderer was a Jew)'.

Schwartz cannot say whether the two men were together or known to each other. Upon being taken to the mortuary Schwartz identi- fied the body of Stride as that of the woman he had seen & he thus describes the first man who threw the woman down: – age about 30 ht 5ft 5in comp, fair hair, dark small brown moustache, full face, broad shouldered, dress, dark jacket & trousers, black cap with peak; had nothing in his hands.[33]

Swanson's task was to confuse. If anything of this rotten little copper's invention had value, which it doesn't, 'Israel Schwartz' would indeed be a formidable witness. 'Schwartz' was claimed to have been on the scene later than Matthew Packer and PC Smith (whose creature in a deerstalker is also wiped out), and he had seen Stride assaulted fifteen minutes before she was murdered. Although 'the knife' has evaporated in Shifty's account, she was thrown brutally to the ground, and she screamed. 'Schwartz' apparently enhanced his veracity with a positive identification of Stride at the morgue. If the whole of it wasn't a preposterous fantasy, such a witness might justifiably put Packer in the shade, perhaps explain- ing why he was kept out of court in favour of 'Schwartz'.

The only problem with this hypothesis is that 'Israel Schwartz' was no more called to give evidence than was Packer.

Swanson cobbled up this bullshit on 19 October, four days before Baxter reconvened his brothel on the 23rd. Given the dynamic of his evidence, 'Schwartz' would naturally be first witness up. Should have been, but wasn't. Having served his diversionary purpose he disappeared, morphing back into a distraction that had long been rejected by the police and the press alike. As early as 7 October, the *Sunday People* had reported that Swanson's flight of fancy was in fact 'a man and his wife quarrelling', and 'no notice had been taken of it'. The Hungarian may well have seen a row, but not where he thought he had. There was no 'railway arch' anywhere near Berner Street – 'Schwartz' would have had to run the length of it, turned into Ellen Street, then Phillip Street, and finally Pinchin Street, before finding one. Nobody else in Berner Street that night saw any sign of a woman in jeopardy or anyone running away from the scene. Nobody saw the drunken man, or the knife man, or the second man lighting his pipe. And nobody heard anybody shout 'Lipski.'

The Met knew all about 'Israel Schwartz' on 1 October. Why then put out false statements, attributed to the still-secret description of Lawende, while ignoring the 'statement' of this unique witness? Why does it take until 19 October for Swanson to become interested in the man with the red moustache?

Ripperology rushes in with the mirrors. Among popular excuses for 'Schwartz's' failure to show at Baxter's court are 'translation problems'. But if 'Schwartz's' story couldn't be translated, from where did Swanson get his statement? 'I questioned Schwartz very closely' is recorded from Inspector Abberline. And it wouldn't have been difficult – the Victorian courts were a common haunt for translators. Not three weeks earlier, the *East London Observer* reported: 'On the application of Chief Inspector Abberline of Scotland Yard, Mr Saunders [a ferociously anti-Semitic magistrate] again remanded the accused. He also allowed Abberline to interview the accused, with the Interpreter, Mr Savage.' Where was Mr Savage now? As Bro Baxter had said himself – before his topical induction into the Mystic Tie – 'I've never heard of evidence being withheld from a Coroner's Court.' Now he was hearing of it wholesale. Failing Mr Savage (and three other interpreters listed in Swanson's private notebook) there was always Mr Karamelli, who the previous year had been the interpreter in another famous East End case; which brings us back to 'Lipski'.

I don't want to veer too far from 'Schwartz', but the politics of the Lipski case are not without relevance. I refer to 'Schwartz' in quotes because there's no hard evidence that that was even his name. I think a bit of subliminal creep may have been at work in Shifty's creative process. Mix Israel Lipski with endemic anti-Semitism, and you're not far off a Christian name for 'Israel Schwartz'. Be that as it may, the two Israels were of similar circumstances and age, poor as mice and ignorant of English. Lipski rented rooms from a Mrs Miriam Angel in Batty Street, where he tried to set up a business in the attic making walking sticks. Part of the process required nitric acid. Lipski went out and bought some, hiring a pair of local ne'er-do-wells to assist him. On 28 June 1887, the day these two men came to her house, Mrs Angel was done to death by being forced to swallow nitric acid. Lipski, suffering the effects of a similar draft, was discovered unconscious under her bed. A cashbox was involved, and one of the ne'er-do-wells had scuttled off prompt to Birmingham.

The policeman who was later to hound and give a name to 'Leather Apron' was put in charge of the case. Detective Sergeant Thick arrested Lipski, and he was put up for trial in front of Mr Justice Fitzjames Stephen. It was an inauspicious choice for the Jew. Fitzjames Stephen (who would later try Florence Maybrick) was losing his marbles, and ignoring evidence favourable to Lipski, he fixated on the word 'bed', convincing himself that this was a crime motivated by lust. The accused, he reasoned, had seen Mrs Angel through a window and, using his acid as a threatening inducement, had barged in demanding sex. After ravishing her, he supposedly drank the acid himself in a fit of guilt.

Lipski was sentenced to death. But because of glaring deficiencies in the indictment, public opinion shifted in the Jew's favour, and the case raised unwonted debate. W.T. Stead in the *Pall Mall Gazette* was predictably among the first in Fleet Street to champion the convicted man's innocence. Careers were suddenly on the line. Home Secretary Matthews and Justice Fitzjames Stephen were passing anxious hours on the eve of the execution – to hang or not to hang, that was the question – when, to the relief of all concerned, Lipski unexpectedly 'confessed'. Next day the bell at Newgate Prison tolled, and the almost certainly innocent Lipski met his God.

The corks came out in Whitehall, and Matthews kept his job. In his excellent account of the case, *The Trials of Israel Lipski* (1984), Martin Friedland writes: 'It seems likely that Lipski's confession saved Matthews' political career.' Never mind the Jew with the broken neck, there was general congratulation amongst the Establishment that Matthews had delivered a knockout blow to Stead and his *Pall Mall Gazette*, which had relentlessly mocked the System in its defence of the accused. Now it was Stead's turn for the pillory, and the authorities revelled in it. Matthews' star rose, and he was to remain Home Secretary for the next five years, managing to navigate a little upset or two with the Whitechapel Fiend, and finally berthing in the House of Lords as a useless Lord Llandaff.

'A later Under Secretary of State, Sir Edward Troup,' writes Friedland, 'certainly thought Lipski's confession saved Matthews. A storm of protest was raised, which would almost certainly have driven him from office had not Lipski on the eve of his execution confessed to the murder. Moreover, it is possible that if Matthews, the only Catholic in the Cabinet, had resigned, the government would have fallen and Home Rule for Ireland would have been introduced. Incredible as it may seem, then, the confession of a poor immigrant Jew, who could not even speak English, may have been a factor in the future of the United Kingdom, having repercussions even today in the troubles of Northern Ireland.'[34]

This is the dispassionate opinion of a professor of law.

If Friedland thinks an innocuous Jew like Lipski could have had this impact, becoming a factor in the future of Britain itself, imagine, if you will, the impact a Freemasonic monster might have had on the ruling elite. The exposure of my candidate would have had catastrophic consequences all the way up to the Crown. Lipski wasn't in the same league.

19 October 1888 was a trying day at the Yard. To coincide with Swanson's overview of that day, the Met formally put an end to Packer in the *Police Gazette*: 'The woodcut sketches, purporting to resemble the persons last seen with the murdered woman, which have appeared in the *Daily Telegraph*, were not authorised by the police.' Descriptions of 'approved Rippers' followed. They were the twenty-eight-year-old five-foot-five-inch concoction, and the Nautical Man with the red handkerchief tied in a knot.

A composite figure was stalking the East End. He was an inky-fingered, seafaring, short-arsed Israelite without a deerstalker (and you couldn't miss him, because he'd be hobbling due to his uncomfortable boots). The introduction of 'Schwartz' as a wedge to rid it of Packer was to cause the Met more problems than might have been imagined, and any day now Anderson and Warren would be caught telling some serious lies.

On 23 October Baxter at last reconvened his worthless inquest. The Bro's summing-up must represent a milestone in judicial duplicity. About a third of it was apportioned to sorting out the problem of Mrs Mary Malcolm, whose perplexing input was written off as a 'comedy of errors'. 'The first difficulty that presented itself,' opined Baxter, 'was the identification of the deceased. It has since been clearly proved that she [Mary Malcolm] was mistaken, notwithstanding the visions which were simultaneously vouchsafed at the hour of her [Stride's] death to her husband.'

Baxter yabbered on in a miasma of half-truth, no truth, and junk. Despite considerable press interest, Matthew Packer was never mentioned. There were no grapes, no grape-stalks, not even a fruit-stained handkerchief. So anxious was the stooge to avoid mention-ing the fruit-seller, he actually moved Stride from the crime scene, relocating her a hundred yards away from the International Club to the other end of Berner Street.

'At 12.30 p.m.,' he warbled (confusing p.m. with a.m.), 'the constable on the beat [Smith] saw the deceased in Berner Street standing on the pavement a few yards from Commercial Street' (confusing Commercial Street with Commercial Road).

Such flagrant disregard for established fact was no problem for Bro Baxter. He had a jury to deceive. The bewitched coroner went on to compare the wardrobe of PC Smith's man with those of Brown's man and Marshall's man – and of course this went nowhere. A variety of hats were on offer, including a cheeky little nautical number with a peak 'like a sailor's'.

Irrespective of the ink lavished on him by Swanson, the man supposedly seen by 'Israel Schwartz' didn't get a look-in, any more than 'Schwartz' himself. The Hungarian and his 'statement' were gone like dust on the October wind. Is this not most curious? 'Schwartz' is either an important witness, or he is not. If he isn't important, why was his suspect featured in the *Police Gazette* only four days before? And why was he still there, on the front cover of the issue on the very day of this court? You can't have it both ways, and truth tolerates neither. The only place 'Israel Schwartz' survived was in Swanson's deceit. Like 'the Ink-Stained Journalist' and the soon-to-be-premiered 'Insane Medical Student', 'Schwartz' was a distraction, and far from functioning as a witness, he was soon to become a nuisance.

On and on waffled Baxter, finally noting the similarity between 'this case and the mysteries which had recently occurred in the neighbourhood'. Poised to wrap it up, he now thanked the cops: he was 'bound to acknowledge', he said, 'the great attention which Inspector Reid and the police had given to the case'.

Establishment gratitude wasn't limited to Baxter. Within weeks, Inspector Reid, Sergeant White and PC Dolden (who was suppos-edly present for Packer's first 'statement') were all 'recommended for reward' by Robert Anderson.[35] It couldn't have got more rotten, and with her death formulaically attributed to a 'person or persons unknown', the inquest into the murder of Elizabeth Stride was over.

Jack had won another hand, and with cause the press reflected public outrage: 'The "Bitter Cry" of London is only now beginning to be heard. The Police have become a laughing-stock. People taunt them in the street as they pass.'[36] By now Warren's destruction of the evidence on the wall at Goulston Street was a scandal in flood. His renegade loyalties were leaching dangerously into government. 'The Home Secretary goes on in his own blundering stupid way,' scoffed the *Telegraph*. 'What do the police do with all the clues?' demanded the *Yorkshireman*. 'The Whitechapel murders have furnished them with clues enough to hang a whole community.'[37] On top of it all was Matthew Packer. Nobody but a zoo animal could have been unaware of the fruit-seller.

On the very day Baxter wound up his court, Anderson wrote to the Home Office. Now the verdict was in and the heat was off, he decided to risk sending in Swanson's 'overview'.

Whoever had the disagreeable task of reading this gibberish isn't known, but it was probably the Permanent Under Secretary of State, Sir Godfrey Lushington. Well aware of Packer, he must have been completely baffled by the introduction of this hitherto-never-mentioned gentleman called 'Schwartz'. If it were true that he'd identified Stride at the morgue, and had seen her ten minutes before the deed that put her there, he was God's own witness.

But it wasn't true, and within days Warren and Anderson would be obliged to wriggle on Swanson's hook.

Packer wasn't the only vital witness kept out of Bro Baxter's court. At about 12.45 a.m. on 30 September Mrs Fanny Mortimer had been out on her doorstep for about half an hour.[38] She didn't see a man with a knife or a red moustache, or a woman lightly screaming as she was thrown to the ground, but she did notice a man walking briskly past a few minutes before 1 a.m. He had a black bag, and considering this suspicious, she later reported him to the police. His name was Leon Goldstein, and Swanson attempted to navigate his existence with dialogue worthy of Tweedledum. 'At about 1 a.m. 30th,' he writes, 'Leon Goldstein of 27 Christian Street Commercial Road, called at Leman Street & stated that he was the man who passed down Berner Street, with a black bag at that hour.' In other words, Goldstein called at Leman Street police station and reported himself walking down Berner Street at the very moment he was doing it. For no apparent reason. He just popped into Leman Street to report himself before Mrs Mortimer had reported him.

That's what Swanson writes. What it actually means is that Goldstein was walking down Berner Street at about 1 a.m. on 30 September, and a day later, on 1 October, he called at Leman Street police station to identify himself as the individual Mrs Mortimer had seen walking briskly with the black bag.[39]

So why doesn't Shifty say so? The answer is because Leon Goldstein in Berner Street at 1 a.m. on 30 September screws 'Israel Schwartz'. A Home Office note in the margin asks an edifying question: 'Who saw this man go down Berner Street?' It's a question in want of any known answer, because it blows 'Schwartz' right out of the water. Neither Mortimer nor Goldstein saw anything of any fracas, any Hungarian running away from it, or heard anyone shout 'Lipski.' Swanson was trapped in a classic liar's dilemma. On the one hand he must talk 'Schwartz' up as a surrogate for Packer, while at the same time back-pedalling in case anyone asked why 'Schwartz' didn't appear in court. The struggle to present such a contradiction reduces Swanson's prose to a peculiar species of pidgin English: 'At the same time account must be taken of the fact that the throat only of the victim was cut in this instance which measured by time, considering meeting (if with a man other than Schwartz saw) the time for agreement & the murderous action would I think be a question of so many minutes, five at least, ten at most, so that I respectfully submit it is not clearly proved that the man Schwartz saw is the murderer.'[40]

Meaning that even Swanson is dismissing 'Schwartz'. He says 'it is not clearly proved', when it is only he who is trying to prove it. 'This rather confused', says a note in the margin, and you might consider that an understatement. It's a musical chairs of nonsense, and would have been proved so if legitimate witnesses hadn't been suppressed.

Elizabeth Stride went willingly into that yard, at ease with her well-spoken paramour, beguiled by a treat of grapes. This 'Schwartz' rubbish would barely persuade an intelligent child, and would need lies piled on lies to sustain it. The first came out of that notable reptile Anderson a few days later.

Under pressure of Home Office correspondence he wrote: 'With ref. to yr letter &c. I have to state that the opinion arrived at in this Dept. upon the *evidence of Schwartz at the inquest of Eliz. Stride's case* is that the name Lipski which he alleges was used by a man whom he saw assaulting the woman in Berner Street on the night of the murder, was not addressed to the supposed accomplice but to Schwartz himself.'[41] It's my emphasis, and this is the Chief of London's Criminal Investigation Department. It hardly merits repetition, but 'Schwartz' *did not appear at Stride's inquest*, and Anderson is lying through his teeth.

'Schwartz's evidence was in the highest degree material,' dribbles *The A to Z*. 'It would be a serious offence for the police to withhold an important witness from the coroner, and Wynne Baxter was not a coroner who would let any defalcation of duty pass lightly.'[42]

Ha ha. So why did they withhold it?

Their answer is in Pecksniffian tradition. Avoiding the only point at issue, which is *Anderson's lying in respect of his claimed appearance of 'Schwartz' at the Stride inquest*, they press their fingertips together and come up smiling with this: 'So there remains the possibility that Dr Robert Anderson's passing remark [sic] in the exchange of memos over the cry of "Lipski" was accurate and not a slip of the pen: that he meant what he said when he wrote, "the evidence given by Schwartz at the inquest in the Elizabeth Stride case", and he was not misremembering.'[43]

Not misremembering? What the fuck are they talking about? Robert Anderson *is lying about 'Israel Schwartz'*. Hammers of condemnation fell upon Matthew Packer for so much as (correctly) suggesting that it was raining, but when Anderson is disgorging lies, it becomes subsumed as a 'passing remark'. We're in the world of make-believe and 'slipping pens'. Well, the pen kept slipping when, a day later, Bro Warren heaved up the same lie. 'With reference to your letter of the 29th ulto,' he wrote, 'I have to acquaint you, for information of the Secretary of State, that the opinion arrived at upon *the evidence given by Schwartz at the inquest in the Elizabeth Stride case* [my emphasis] is blah blah and furthermore blah blah ...'[44]

Why *should* London's Commissioner of Metropolitan Police seek to deceive the Home Office? If this charade were not toxic with deceit, if 'Schwartz' were remotely the witness Shifty had claimed him to be, then it is beyond credibility that he wasn't called to any one of the five sessions of the inquest.

Two men – Matthew Packer and Joseph Lawende – had seen Jack the Ripper, and both were shut up. The public were helpless, but not brain dead, and everyone knew Baxter's court was a farce. 'We need not go beyond the Coroner's inquest for illustrations of stupidity,' was the damning verdict of *Lloyd's*, and the statement of a sister paper merits repetition: 'It is a matter of common knowledge that grapes were found in one hand of the murdered woman.'[45]

Packer had seen the Ripper, and Warren knew it. He took a fatal decision on behalf of his epoch that has long passed utility. Nothing could more endorse the importance of the sketches approved by Matthew Packer than the effort put into discrediting them.

Jack the Ripper wasn't a Martian, or some other kind of extra-terrestrial being. He wasn't a criminal genius. He was a psychopath shielded by servants of the Victorian state. Had Warren really wanted to nail this miscreation, he could have done so in short order. There would have been no red neckerchiefs or half-witted clairvoyants, no washing off of walls and the rest of the fantastic tosh. Witnesses would have had their evidence heard and properly tested, whether it concerned grapes or anything else. Above all, the fruit-seller would have been allowed to tell his story, the sketches of the man he had seen would have been admitted, and perhaps – just perhaps – the press, the public and London's police would have been looking for the right man.

There is nothing so patient as truth. It was Freemasonry's adopted saint, St John, who said 'The truth will set you free.' Masonry could rid itself of this hideous millstone, and the good news is, there would be no blame attached to it. The culprit was the age. Contemporary Masonry is no more responsible for the sins of the nineteenth century than today's generals are culpable for the idiot decisions of generals in the First World War. The Prime Minister at that time, Lloyd George, famously said, 'If people really knew [the truth], the war would be stopped tomorrow. But of course they don't know and can't know.' Ditto Jack the Ripper. We are in the twenty-first century. It's time for the dark soul of this fabricated 'mystery' to be consigned to history and be gone.

10

'They All Love Jack'

> If you're hanging on to a rising balloon, you're
> presented with a difficult decision. Let go before it's
> too late? Or hang on and keep getting higher? Posing
> the question, how long can you keep a grip on the
> rope?
>
> Danny the dealer

Michael Maybrick called his singing 'the shouting businefs', and it
was a trade at which he excelled. By the late 1880s he was at the
zenith of his career and the high end of London's elite. 'Of course
no one could mistake Mr Maybrick,' enthused the *Tatler* magazine,
'or Mr Lawrence Kellie.'[1]

The *Tatler* was at the Royal Institute covering another plunge into the jewels, lies and perfume, the kind of *soirée* Michael Maybrick invariably enjoyed in the company of a younger man. Kellie was a looker, a bit of a throb on the concert circuit himself, although with nothing like the fame of his date. At the time of the sighting Kellie was twenty-four, and Maybrick, like the ladies he charmed, of an unaudited age. 'He possesses the muscle and brawn of an ideal Life Guardsman,' beamed a society rag, 'and his passion for every form of outdoor pursuit has enabled him to retain the full vigour of youth much longer than the rest of his contemporaries.' He looked thirty-five, shrugging off a dozen years with ease.[2]

Not a minute from the bash at the Institute was Maybrick's local in Regent Street. The Café Royal was about as close to Paris as London got. Its tabletops were marble, and the champagne endless. If you could afford the vintages you could come in here and listen to Oscar Wilde creasing them all with his epithets. It was all too too utterly divine. 'One sat there night after night,' recalled Jimmy Glover, 'together with every sort of art, genius, and talent, all came to this, at that time, the only real "*intime*" café in London.' A musician of note himself, Glover was a habitué of the Royal. 'I have played dominos with Michael Maybrick,' he wrote, 'who composed a hundred great songs as Stephen Adams,' and who was among the most famous men in the room.[3]

A magazine called the *New Era* described the Maybrick/Adams phenomenon: 'It will not have been forgotten that Mr Maybrick displayed early talent for composition, but it was not until 1876 that it was reserved for "Stephen Adams" to produce a ballad that is probably the most successful ever written.'

'Nancy Lee' was a sensation without precedent. It sold like Harry Potter, and put a fortune into the Maybrick/Adams bank account. 'No song has ever gained such enormous popularity,' said the *New Era*. 'Everyone was singing it, humming it, or whistling it in the street, dinned into every ear, morning noon and night. Mr Maybrick has much to answer for,' it continued in mock admonishment, 'in having given forth this inspiration to the world, for it seems to have fallen like a spell on every individual capable of making musical sounds.'[4]

It certainly fell like a spell on the singing stars of the day, and Maybrick was suddenly up there with them. It may seem hard to believe, but he was as famous as Wilde, or his lifelong pal Sir Arthur Sullivan, whose music his far outsold. No one I know had ever heard of Michael Maybrick/Stephen Adams, and until I became enmeshed in his story, neither had I. But then, I'd never heard of Signor Foli either, nor Trebelli, Sims Reeves, Edward Lloyd or Charles Santley, all of whom were blazing stars in the last quarter of Victoria's reign.

Charles Santley was Michael Maybrick's hero. It was by one of those freaks of history that their lives were destined to entwine. Both were born in the great seaport of Liverpool, and almost in the same street. The Orpheus gene was in their bloodlines, and both were probably listening to music before they could talk. Santley's father was a talented amateur who took singing lessons from Maybrick's uncle (another Michael), and thus before birth they shared an inter-family association.[5]

Born in 1834, seven years before Maybrick, as a child Santley learned violin and piano, but his talent for singing was greater than his ability at the two instruments put together, and by the age of fifteen he was elected a performing member of the Liverpool Philharmonic Society. Maybrick's gifts were scarcely less precocious. When he was fourteen one of his neophyte compositions was played at the Covent Garden Opera House in London. He won a prize for 'harmonious invention',[6] and followed Santley into an association with their fellow Liverpudlian W.T. Best, a virtuoso performer and composer on the church organ. Maybrick's affinity for the great bulldozer of an instrument was immediate, and he was blasting on the keyboards of St George's church when he wasn't singing solos in its choir.

Meanwhile, Santley had taken his talent to Italy, where he trained under Geatano Nava, a singing teacher of international repute who in just a few years was to get another young aspirant from Liverpool. Maybrick had gone to study composition under Hans Richter at Leipzig, where to the astonishment of everyone, including apparently himself, a fine baritone voice was discovered. This put him back in Santley's footsteps. At the age of twenty-one he too went to Milan, to perfect his entry into the shouting business under Nava.

By the late 1860s, and back on home turf, Santley was already a star. Together with Sims Reeves his name got the capital letters, while Michael Maybrick climbed the bills in their wake. In June 1870, after an inauspicious spell with Carl Rosa's opera company, Maybrick was united with Santley at a major concert at St James's Hall in London. Conducted in part by Santley's friend and mentor Wilhelm Ganz (soon to become an intimate of Maybrick), it was a farewell tribute to a wilted diva whose name no longer matters.

Habitually on the same bill over the ensuing concert seasons, Maybrick and Santley consolidated their friendship, sharing the same midnight carriages and sometimes the same digs. 'I dined with Maybrick and Santley at their comfortable old fashioned hostelry at Edgbaston,' recalled Walter McFarren, 'and had a jolly good afternoon and evening with them.'[7]

This was in about 1872, by which time Maybrick was already writing the ballads that were to bring him international fame. He'd formed a partnership with a Bristol-born lawyer and lyricist by the name of Frederick Weatherly, and together they'd already enjoyed a couple of inconsequential hits. Maybrick sang them both, but farmed them out with more success to an established concert regular called Edward Lloyd. 'The Warrior Bold' became the catalyst for another lasting association, and Lloyd also sang Maybrick's next two efforts, 'True Blue' and 'True to the Last', conglomerates of patriotism and vapid sentiment that were lapped up by Victorian audiences.

Maybrick was now in with the in-crowd, sharing the cream provided by a ravenous market. Nowhere was this more evident than at St James's Hall, Piccadilly, where a music publisher and promoter by the name of John Boosey invented a new kind of concert.

Boosey represented or published the music of a galaxy of stars. Arthur Sullivan was one, and Michael Maybrick another. Almost everyone with a name, or a name to make, appeared at the St James's concerts – the 'pops', as they were known – and for a decade or more the profits were stratospheric: 'They were the days when the ship of the publishers sailed forth with cargoes of sheet music and returned to harbour with much weight in gold.' Maybrick was becoming rich, the golden boy at Boosey's offices just up the road at 295 Regent Street.

By the middle of the 1880s, two sets of partners dominated the musical money machine. The first, of course, with their Savoy operas, was W.S. Gilbert and Arthur Sullivan, who with Nanki-Poo and the rest of it owned London's West End. The other pair of names were 'Stephen Adams' (Michael Maybrick) and Frederick Weatherly. The *Musical World* had this: 'A setting of Mr F.C. Weatherly's words by Stephen Adams was received by the audience with acclamations. Author and composer have worked together with reciprocal intents that remind us of the combined efforts of Sir Arthur Sullivan and Mr Gilbert.'[8]

Maybrick was at the top of his game, hit after hit streaming from his pen. Between 1880 and 1890 he and Weatherly released almost fifty songs, some sung by Maybrick, most by Lloyd, and many outselling even 'Nancy Lee'. At the end of the decade a journalist from the *World* interviewed the prolific songwriter in his bachelor apartments at Clarence Gate, Regent's Park. By now Maybrick was an officer in the 'Artists Rifles', an eccentric adjunct of Her Majesty's armed forces that we'll arrive at in a page or two.

CELEBRITIES AT HOME

'Pleasant melodies must have pleasant surroundings' was a favourite axiom of 'Stephen Adams' long before he set all England singing such familiar airs as 'Nancy Lee', 'The Midshipmite' and 'They All Love Jack'. The chimes of a clock have scarcely died away before you turn into a sunny room, where the stalwart lieutenant of the 'Artists' is hard at work before a table littered with quill pens and almost as many boxes of cigars and cigarettes. As he talks to you of the last Easter (Artists) manoeuvres or of the next meeting of the Grand Lodge (for 'Stephen Adams' has risen to the Masonic rank of Grand Organist), he runs his hands involuntarily over the keys, but the stirring chorus you listen to is not that of the 'Entered Apprentice', but the potential lineal successor of 'They All Love Jack'.[9]

It's hardly necessary to comment on that last little inadvertent beauty, but I interrupt to point out that the honour of Masonic Grand Organist was bestowed on Maybrick in 1889. A year or two previously the accolade belonged to Sir Arthur Sullivan, and before him to Wilhelm Ganz.

When 'Stephen Adams' is not working, he is either drilling at Somerset House, imbibing ozone at his Isle of Wight cottage, rowing on the Thames, riding over Highgate Hill, or enjoying the conviviality of the Arts Club. Michael Maybrick puts his whole strength and soul into everything he does. He regards his exercise out of doors and the social evenings he spends at one or other of his clubs as the most welcome preparation for his labours at home.[10]

The quality that most strikes me about this article is the overbearing 'maleness' of it all – male clubs, male Masonry, male army, and a lungful of bracing masculine air on the Isle of Wight. In the whole text there isn't the remotest sense of the feminine. It's all oars, horses, cigars and 'Artists Volunteers', Maybrick's entire social orbit being amongst those who sweat. I get the impression that no woman has ever been in this apartment, except perhaps to clean it. The Earl of Euston liked an arse, in an amateur sort of way, and all the indications are of something similar here.

'One item of family mythology which interests me,' writes Mr Derek Strahan (whose wife is apparently a great-niece to Maybrick), 'concerns the relationship between Michael and his librettist, Fred Weatherly, which was always thought by the family to have been a close personal one, in other words, gay.'[11]

Such a proposition tends to focus my take on the above-mentioned Mr Lawrence Kellie. His family home was on the coast at Shanklin, near Maybrick's cottage on the Isle of Wight. I took a look at a contemporary Who's Who to see if the two shared any interests. Kellie, recreations: Yachting, Cycling and Tennis. Maybrick, recreations: Yachting, Cycling and Cricket. I don't actually know if Maybrick was homosexual, but predicated on that infallible adage, 'If it walks like a duck, etc.,' he was probably a bit of a ducky.

In 1886 he joined the army, the 20th Middlesex (Artists) Rifles, known as the 'Artists Volunteers'. This wasn't exactly the bully-beef end of the military – most of its members would have been just as at home at the Café Royal as in the officers' mess, and were certainly there more frequently. The Artists was an elite corps of some of the most impressive artistic and musical talents alive. England's greatest living painter, Sir Frederick Leighton, was Honorary Colonel, and his subordinates a confederation of celebrity.

Many of the painters had names that remain world-famous: Millais, Frith, Alma-Tadema, and a National Gallery of others, including Dickens's illustrators Luke Fildes and Marcus Stone. Sir Henry Irving was but one of the many theatrical stars. 'Among musicians,' says the official history, 'Sir Arthur Sullivan and Michael Maybrick (then one of our Captains and better known as Stephen Adams), the whole forming a most wonderful collection of eminent men.' Virtually without exception, they were Freemasons. 'There had always been a strong esprit de corps in the Artists,' wrote J. Bromfield, in demobbed reminiscence, 'and a species of Freemasonry, analogous to the spirit among the old boys of our public schools.'[12]

The Artists had originally met at the Argyle Rooms, Piccadilly, then moved to one of Maybrick's clubs, the Arts in Hanover Square, which in 1884 he listed as his London address. A few records miraculously survive. According to the muster roll, Maybrick joined the battalion on 6 February 1886, declaring his profession as 'Musician'. His age is recorded as forty (which was incorrect – he was forty-five), his chest measurement as forty-one inches, and his height as six feet and one half inches in his socks.[13]

Extrapolating from these statistics and his description in the *Musical World*, we get a picture of a powerful and athletic man, forty-seven years old at the time of the murders, but retaining 'the full vigour of youth', and 'braced with air' from the Isle of Wight.

Maybrick's commanding officer was an architect and fellow Freemason of high distinction, Colonel Robert W. Edis, and it was his task (after a brief occupancy at Fitzroy Square) to seek finances for more permanent headquarters for the Artists. 'The first thing our Colonel did,' says the official history, 'was to form a strong committee of soldiers (including Bro General Wolseley) and artists of every kind.'

Edis and his committee were successful, and the new headquarters were formally opened by the Prince of Wales and his wife Princess Alexandra on 25 March 1889. It was a 'splendid success', with Maybrick second on the bill, shouting Gilbert and Sullivan's 'Sentry Song' from *Iolanthe*. At the end of it all the Prince got to his feet and gave them the pleasure of a few words. It must have been a particularly gratifying earful to Maybrick, who had put the show together, and whose name appears on the cover of the programme.

20th Middlesex (Artists') R.V.

Honorary Colonel, SIR FREDERIC LEIGHTON, Bart., P.R.A.
Colonel ROBERT W. EDIS, F.S.A., Commanding.

MATINÉE

On the occasion of the OPENING OF THE NEW HEAD-QUARTERS,

BY THEIR ROYAL HIGHNESSES

The Prince & Princess of Wales,

MARCH 25TH, 1889.

Conductor—Captain W. H. THOMAS, *Artists' R.V.*

The ENTERTAINMENT arranged by Mr. MAYBRICK (Lieut. Artists' R.V.)

HEAD-QUARTERS,
DUKE'S ROAD, EUSTON ROAD. W.

Sharing the credit is Captain W.H. Thomas, who with Maybrick was Musical Director of the Artists B Company. In civilian mode Thomas was a prominent conductor and benefactor who taught music at St Jude's University Campus, Toynbee Hall, less than a minute's walk from the infamous wall at Goulston Street.

As an inhabitant of this superior world, Michael Maybrick seems a most unlikely candidate for Jack the Ripper. 'A very handsome man', according to his publisher John Boosey, he was talented, intelligent, successful and rich – not exactly the qualities one immediately associates with a serial killer. In fact, he was just about the last man in London you'd finger as the Ripper. Murder is ugly. When the assassin remains a 'mystery' we see only his debris, the blood and the fatal misery, the hideousness of the victim in death. Murder shocks, and in the case of the Ripper it utterly degrades. Sexual ugliness is its trademark.

We don't associate violent homicide with a handsome face. In our revulsion we automatically associate it with the face of the dead. There was actually a law in the Middle Ages: if two people were suspected of a crime but only one could be guilty, they would hang the uglier one.[14] In this book I have consciously avoided descriptions of the East End. Those dripping alleys, flickering gaslights and the rest of it tend to subliminally describe the murderer, and it's just around the corner from this kind of stuff that we get the obligatory 'lair'. The Ripper almost certainly arrived in Whitechapel by the underground railway.[15]

The 1970s American serial killer Ted Bundy is in the same category of psychopath. Robert Ressler describes Bundy, 'the most celebrated killer of his time', as a serial murderer 'at the other end of the scale': 'Perhaps because he was so photogenic and articulate that many people concluded he could not have committed the crimes ... a handsome, intelligent young man who seemed to some people to have considerable sex appeal, a student at law, respected, a former Mr Nice Guy.'[16]

'Ted's path was straight-upward,' wrote his friend the journalist Anne Rule, 'excelling at everything he put his hand to, superbly educated, socially adept.' He was an ideal citizen. He even drew a commendation from the Seattle Police Department when he ran down a purse-snatcher and returned the stolen bag to its owner. In the summer of 1970, it was Ted Bundy who saved a three-and-a-half-year-old toddler from drowning in Green Lake in Seattle's North End. No one had seen the child wander away from her parents – no one but Ted – and he dashed into the water to save the youngster.'[17]

But saving a youngster wasn't the reason the state of Florida put Ted Bundy to death in January 1989. 'Far from being the Rudolph Valentino of the serial-killer world,' writes Ressler, 'Ted Bundy was a brutal, sadistic, perverted man. By his verbal skills Bundy would habitually lure girls and young women into positions of vulnerability, then bludgeon them with a short crowbar ... He'd kill them by strangulation ... mutilate and dismember them, sometimes committing necrophilic acts, for instance ejaculating into the mouth of a disembodied head ... This man was an animal ... [it is] estimated by the FBI that he murdered between thirty-five and sixty women in different states.'[18]

All this with a handsome, intelligent face. The horrendous Bundy and the Whitechapel nightmare have not a little in common. Ted was charming, and I suspect Jack was too. They shared the gift of the gab, able to put their marks at ease, most notably, in Jack's case, in the dialogue preceding the attacks on Elizabeth Stride and Catherine Eddowes. I believe these unfortunate women were on the alert for a police-inspired cliché, 'a short man with a rough voice', when what they got was six feet of charm from a well-spoken, educated West End gent, military tones and all – 'a loud, sharp sort of voice, and a quick commanding way with him', as Matthew Packer put it. Both Bundy and Jack strangled their victims, indulging in postmortem mutilation, orientated around their respective perversions. And most important of all, both appeared to be, and indeed were, completely sane.

There is another derivation of the term 'Double Event' that may well have appealed to my candidate. It comes from the concert stage, and means two performances on a given night.

MR. and Mrs. GERMAN REED'S ENTERTAIN-MENT.—Managers, Messrs. Alfred Reed and Corney Grain. TO-NIGHT, at 8. Miss Fanny Holland, Miss Marion Wardroper; Mr. Corney Grain, Mr. North Home, and Mr. Alfred Reed.—St. George's-hall, Langham-place. No commission for booking stalls. United Telephone No. 3,840.

FAIRLY PUZZLED, TO-NIGHT, at 8. Written by Oliver Brand, music by Hamilton Clarke. Last Representations. Morning Performances Tuesday, Thursday, and Saturday, at 3. Evenings, Monday, Wednesday, and Friday, at 8.

A LITTLE DINNER, TO-NIGHT, at 9.15. A Musical Sketch, by Mr. Corney Grain. Last Representations. Morning Performances every Tuesday, Thursday, and Saturday, at 3. Evenings, Monday, Wednesday, and Friday, at 8.

A DOUBLE EVENT, TO-NIGHT, at 9.45. By Arthur Law and Alfred Reed. Music by Corney Grain. Last Representations. Morning Performances, Tuesday, Thursday, and Saturday, at 3. Evenings, Monday, Wednesday, and Friday, at 8.

WEDNESDAY, June 18, entire change of programme.—Revival of NOBODY'S FAULT. Written by Arthur Law, music by Hamilton Clarke. First time of a New Musical Sketch, entitled SHOWS OF THE SEASON, by Mr. Corney Grain, and a New Second Part, entitled A TERRIBLE FRIGHT, by Arthur Law, music by Corney Grain.

I don't know if this is the source of the Ripper's pun, but I don't think it can be discounted either. I think Maybrick – 'that charming singer and composer', as the artist Tennyson Cole remembered him[19] – was very like Bundy, an engaging veneer camouflaging what I believe was a mortal disease of the ego. Jack suffered from no undue modesty in this department. It was ego that countenanced the risks he took at his crime scenes and the correspondence with which he taunted the police. He fuelled his narcissism through the destruction of his victims. He owned them, and took parts of them away, like a hunter. He was the apogee of homicidal vanity. In our search for a plausible candidate, it seems to me that we're looking for an *ego* – a man like Bundy who believed he was cleverer than all the rest of them put together, a man who felt he was, in Ressler's phrase, 'walking with God'.

Michael Maybrick had an ego the size of a house. We have an indication of it in the recollections of Florence Aunspaugh, the daughter of one of his brother James's closest friends: 'Michael had the idea, especially after he wrote "The Holy City", that he was floating on the celestial plains and did not belong to earth. He thought he should be classed with Shakespeare, Byron, Milton and Tennyson.' The family joke, from his younger brother Edwin, was that 'he had already engaged a tomb in Westminster Abbey'.[20]

If not walking with God, he was certainly strolling in that direction. It wasn't only Scotland Yard that was trying to shut Matthew Packer up. The sketches based on his description of the Ripper appeared in the *Telegraph* on 6 October, and postmarked that same date, someone signing himself 'Jack the Ripper' mailed him a warning.

6 Oct 1888

You though yourself very clever I reckon when you informed the police But you made a mistake, if you though I dident see you Now I know you know me and I see your little game, and I mean to finish you and send your ears to your wife if you show this to the police or help them if you do I will finish you. It no use your trying to get out of my way Because I have you when you dont expect it and I keep my word as you soon see and rip you up   Yours truly

Jack the Ripper

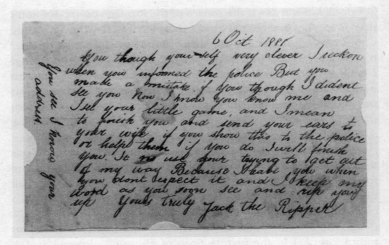

Letters from Jack were almost always proactive (he described what he was going to do), but this one was decidedly reactive. 'Now I know you know me', he wrote, and I suggest this could only have been written in response to a genuine recognition of himself.

On the left is the man Packer claims he saw, the man who bought the grapes; and on the right is my candidate, Michael Maybrick.

It would seem that two people in London became alarmed by the publication of this sketch. One was Warren, and the other Jack the Ripper. Rage, and perhaps even panic, may have been the catalyst for the immediate dispatch of a threat to Packer, anxiety possibly causing this uncharacteristic postal indiscretion. The letter was mailed in the London NW district, which included Clarence Gate, Regent's Park, where Michael Maybrick lived.

Written vertically down the side of the letter are the words 'You see I know your address.' I don't think Packer would have been in any hurry to get his grapes out. He took the letter to the police, who dismissed it as they had dismissed Packer himself. It was a 'hoax' they said, which in my view was unlikely. Why would a hoaxer ignore the press descriptions and instead conclude that a fruit-seller, rejected by the police, had come up with a description that produced a sketch that looked like Jack?

Although we have the Met's file number confirming the postal district, the envelope is missing (either by accident or design). Was the letter therefore addressed to Packer? In certain quarters of Ripperology I've seen attempts to ascribe the recipient of this threat as 'Schwartz'.

This is nothing if not ridiculous. On 6 October the name 'Schwartz' was still an unconstituted fantasy in Shifty's inkwell. So who is the 'hoaxer' going to address his envelope to? 'You see I know your address.' The Hungarian's address was never given to the press,[21] while Packer's at 44 Berner Street was. Plus, Packer did not claim to have seen a woman thrown to the ground, or a knife-wielding man with a red moustache – who didn't exist until Swanson invented him on 19 October 1888.

The writer was looking at a sketch in the paper, and also demonstrating a remarkable similarity of signature with the author of 'Dear Boss'.

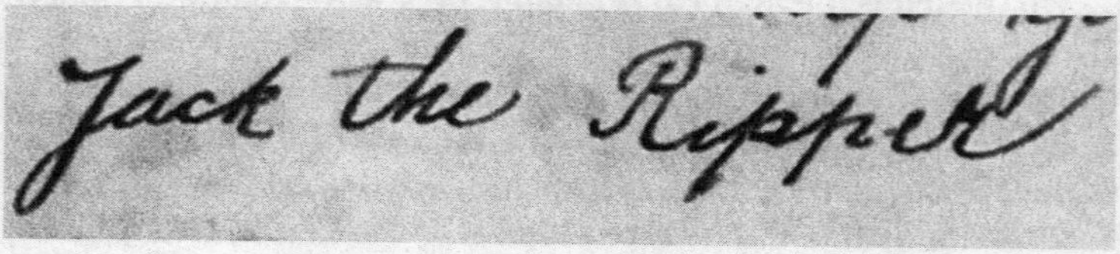

The 'Packer' letter

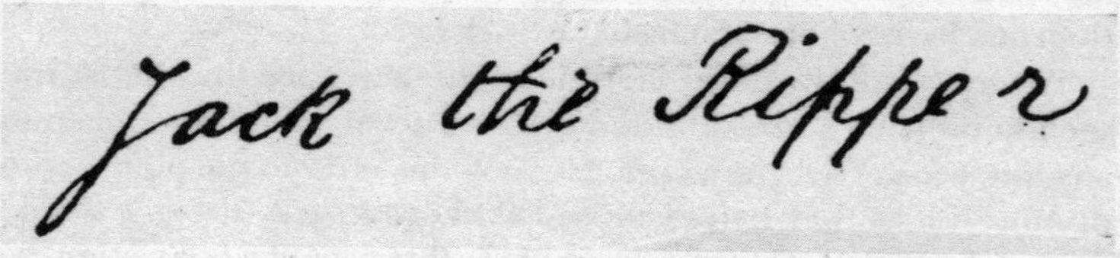

'Dear Boss'

Packer was Jack's target, and future letters refer to him again. On 8 November (the day before the murder of Mary Jane Kelly), Warren got this:

> Old Packer the man I bought the grapes off saw me the other night but was too frightened to say anything to the police he must have been a fool when there is such a reward offered never mind the reward will not be given.

Even the Ripper knows Packer hasn't sought reward. It's only in the febrile imaginings of Ripperology that he has. Moreover, it's curious that despite all the official dismissal of the fruit-seller and his grapes, this so-called 'hoaxer' does not dismiss them. It's Scotland Yard that takes another shot at it: 'It is earnestly desired by the police that the newspapers will refrain from publishing any portraits or descriptions of the supposed perpetrators of the Whitechapel murders. The purely imaginary portraits which have hitherto been published have had the effect of depriving the police of all assistance from the public, whose scrutiny was directed towards a single object, the lineaments of a man who did not exist.'[22]

In reality, it wasn't Packer and his portraits that alienated the public, it was the Metropolitan Police. The people were sick past indifference of the chicanery, sick of the lies, and sick of being misled. The Ripper didn't have to shut Packer up, the coppers were doing it for him. Warren and his occult chums were now accessories to murder, before, during and after the fact.

Just over a week after the receipt of the disturbing threat to Packer, another postal nightmare was in progress. Shortly after one o'clock on the afternoon of Monday, 15 October a 'tall man' walked into a leather dealer's shop in Jubilee Street, Whitechapel. Miss Emily Marsh was minding the shop in her father's absence when 'a stranger dressed in clerical costume entered, and referring to the reward bill in the window, asked for the address of Mr Lusk, described therein as the President of the Vigilance Committee'.[23]

Miss Marsh suggested the cleric should visit the Treasurer of the Vigilantes, a Mr Aarons, who lived only thirty yards away. But the iffy vicar didn't want any truck with Aarons; he wanted Lusk. With escalating suspicion, Miss Marsh found a newspaper in which Mr Lusk's address was given as Alderny Road, although there was no street number. She offered the stranger the paper so he could read it for himself, but his preference was for her to 'read it out' while he copied it into a pocketbook.

Despite his religious costume, or perhaps because of it, by the time the man left the shop his demeanour had so alarmed Miss Marsh that she sent her shop boy after him to see 'that all was right'. Young John Cormac followed him out, coincidentally running into his employer, Mr Marsh, who happened to be coming along on the pavement outside. Thus three witnesses – Emily Marsh, John Cormac and Mr Marsh – were able to give a full description of the man, which was published in the *Telegraph* on 20 October: 'The stranger is described as a man of some forty-five years of age, fully six feet in height and slimly built. He wore a soft felt black hat, drawn over his forehead ... His face was of a sallow type, and he had a dark beard and moustache. The man spoke with what was taken to be an Irish accent.'

I think we're looking at Joseph Lawende's withheld description. Packer's portrait looked like Michael Maybrick, and this one sounds like him. Glancing back over Maybrick's army record, he's described as forty-five years of age, and fully six feet in height. He also wore a black moustache, and (if it wasn't fake) could easily have put on a bit of precautionary 'dark beard' post-Packer.

Here was a broad-daylight description from three alert and respectable witnesses of an unusual man, considered suspicious by Miss Marsh to the point of alarm. You might have thought the police would have shown a bit of interest – maybe sent Sergeant White round with his 'special book'. After all, it suddenly looked as if Warren's speculations were on the money. Here was a highly suspicious 'Irishman', precisely the nationality of the man he'd proposed as the author of the writing on the wall. For a cop on a murder hunt, he could hardly have it better. However, there's nothing in the record about this sinister Mick, nor any statement from Mr Marsh, Emily, or John Cormac.

Now this is a curious circumstance, because the next evening Mr George Lusk got a parcel through the post containing half a human kidney. What was doubly curious was that the address on the box it came in lacked any street number, suggesting a potent symbiosis between the iffy vicar and the information about the address that Emily Marsh was unable to give. Moreover, the letter accompanying the body part claimed that the writer had fried the other half and eaten it, and that it was 'very nise'.

By no means a usual note. Given the fact that they were hunting a homicidal joker who'd just hacked a woman to bits and burgled her left kidney, it's perhaps no wonder that the Met dismissed it as a hoax. The kidney could have belonged to a dog, they mused. But it didn't.

Mr Sugden gives a logically presented assessment of the Lusk kidney. His premise is: 'If the kidney really was Kate's [Catherine Eddowes'], the accompanying letter *was written by her murderer*.' I couldn't agree more, but I would add: 'If the accompanying letter was written by her murderer, *suspect one* becomes the man who asked for Lusk's address in Marsh's shop.'

Lusk got his kidney on the evening of Tuesday, 16 October,[24] and we can only imagine the moment. It arrived in a box about three and a half inches square. It was cut laterally, a stub of renal artery still hanging off, and there was the accompanying letter.

From Hell

Mr Lusk
Sor
I send you half the Kidne I took from one woman prasarved it for you tother piece I fried and ate it was very nise I may send you the bloody knif that took it out if you only wate a whil longer
   Signed

Catch me when you can
Mishter Lusk

Before approaching the text, there's plenty to consider. Let's assume the absurd – that the tall man in Marsh's shop and the man who sent this kidney and the letter are independent actors. Of one, we have a comprehensive description: a six-foot, forty-five-year-old vicar with an 'Irish accent'. The other is unknown, but had to procure a human kidney. According to police propaganda, he's an 'Insane Medical Student' with a nasty sense of fun.

Fans of the medical student run into immediate problems. How could he know the nationality of the 'Tall Vicar'? The vicar had an 'Irish accent', and so does the Lusk letter. It has 'Sor' for 'Sir'. Even *The A to Z* says of it, 'The authors note that "Sor" and "Mishter" are two normal nineteenth-century transcriptions indicating a stage Irish accent.'

The kidney and its accompanying letter were received on 16 October, but the suspicious 'Irish Vicar' remained unreported until the *Telegraph* picked it up four days later, on the 20th. Nobody had yet read the word 'Irish' in connection with this latest communication. So the medical student is not only insane, he's a clairvoyant of startling talent.

It was the *arrival* of the Lusk kidney that initiated the Marsh press interview, Miss Marsh concluding that perhaps the kidney and 'the Tall Man' were connected, a deduction far beyond the intellectual capabilities of anyone at Scotland Yard.

You'd have thought the police would have been all over Marsh's shop. How real was the beard? How real was the accent? Are you certain you didn't give this man the street number?

We've either run into the most incredible coincidence of two unconnected actors pretending to be Irish, or a confirmation that 'the Vicar' and 'the Medical Student' are one and the same.

Experts have been at work on this letter, and have determined that it was written by a 'semi-literate person' with a particular pen; and from this I determine that they are experts at bugger-all. Nobody writes 'Sor', even if their mother was a leprechaun. Americans say 'erbs' for 'herbs', but they don't spell it like that. Irrespective of their dialect, they write 'herbs', from Alaska to Tennessee. A Texan may say 'Surr', but he writes it as 'Sir', just as does an Irishman cutting peat in Donegal.

This letter screeches theatre: the rage is real, the presentation as phoney as it gets. The question here is not its literacy, but why Lusk? These 'hoaxers' were primarily targeting Charlie Warren, so why send a masterwork (the kidney) – proof, if you like – to a painter and decorator in the East End? I think the answer lies in precisely what happened next.

Lusk was angry with the authorities. They didn't want to know about his reward or his Vigilance Committee – he was no more getting through than Jack himself. What both of them needed was some limelight, and when Lusk got it, he did exactly what the Ripper wanted him to do.

Had the kidney gone to Warren, it would have disappeared, like Eddowes' ear, into the bafflement. Jack didn't want to get caught, but by Christ he wanted the fame. This kidney is asking, what else do you need to know me by?

Lusk first informed Joseph Aarons of the kidney at a meeting of the Vigilance Committee. Aarons is reported as saying that Lusk was in a state of considerable excitement. He thought Aarons might laugh, and apparently he did, but Lusk said, 'It's no laughing matter to me.' The question everyone must have been asking was exactly the question Scotland Yard would go out of its way to avoid. Was this body part anything to do with Catherine Eddowes?

It wasn't long before the members of the Committee were on their way to a local doctor's surgery. Dr Wilas was out, but his assistant F.S. Reed took a look, and accurately stated that the kidney was human, and had been preserved in spirits of wine. For specialist confirmation Reed carted it off, submitting it to Dr Thomas Horrocks Openshaw, surgeon and curator of the Pathological Museum at the London Hospital on the Whitechapel Road.

According to Openshaw (via Aarons), the organ was a portion of human kidney, a 'ginny kidney' – that is to say, one that belonged to a person who drank heavily. He was further of the opinion that it was the organ of a woman of about forty-five years of age (again, spot on) and had been taken from the body within the last three weeks.

Although this information proved to be utterly accurate, Openshaw later denied ever saying it, reducing his prognosis to little more than that the kidney was a left-hander, and was dead. But his denial can't compete with his original statement, given on 19 October, because it got into the press before the denial, which came the following day. If Aarons had made it up, he was an augur of phenomenal precision, because his fib was to be corroborated by one of England's leading kidney specialists, and an autopsy report nobody could possibly have seen.

Of Catherine Eddowes, Dr Gordon Brown had written that her abdominal lining was 'cut through on the left side, and the left kidney carefully taken out and removed. The left renal artery was cut through.' It's important to remember how Brown describes this artery: 'cut through', and not cut out, meaning that a portion of it must have been left in the body. Dr Brown then turned his attention to the remaining kidney: 'Right kidney pale, bloodless, with slight congestion at the base of the pyramids.'

This description probably means little more to you than it did to me. But a practising surgeon with an interest in Whitechapel matters, Mr Nick Warren, has confirmed that these symptoms unquestionably point to what used to be called 'Bright's Disease' (chronic glomerulonephritis) – a pathological condition known colloquially in Victorian medicine as 'ginny kidney'.[25]

Why Openshaw would repudiate something he'd publicly said only twenty-four hours before is a question. I was reminded of another doctor, Bro Bagster Phillips at the Chapman inquest. I wondered if in Openshaw we were seeing a replication of those occult 'interests of justice' that never saw justice done. Had someone had a word in Openshaw's ear? I have no idea. What I do know is that, like Dr Bagster Phillips and Dr Gordon Brown, Dr Horrocks Openshaw was a Freemason, and that none of the 'mystery' surrounding this kidney can reasonably be looked at without bearing that in mind.[26]

Next stop in the kidney's journey was Leman Street police station, where it came into the possession of one of the most experienced detectives in London. Detective Inspector Frederick Abberline's reaction is indicative of where he thought this organ was at. Viewing the kidney as potentially important, he immediately forwarded it to the City of London Police. By handing it to Commissioner Smith, Abberline was explicitly connecting the kidney with the murder of Catherine Eddowes. He would be the first and last man in the Metropolitan Police to do so.

Following consultation, Smith had no reservations about what he was looking at. 'The renal artery is about three inches long,' he wrote; 'two inches remained in the corpse, one inch attached to the kidney.' Moreover, 'the kidney left in the corpse was in an advanced stage of Bright's Disease; the kidney sent to me was in exactly similar state'. As far as Smith was concerned, this was Catherine Eddowes' missing left kidney, and he went about the business of confirming it. 'I made the kidney over to the police surgeon,' he writes, 'instructing him to consult with the most eminent men in the profession and send a report without delay.'[27]

Dr Gordon Brown was once again in charge and as instructed he consulted with the man. He was Mr Henry Sutton, a senior surgeon, also of the London Hospital, and according to Smith 'one of the greatest authorities living on the kidney and its disease'. Sutton agreed with Brown's autopsy and the original assessment of Openshaw, adding, 'He would pledge his reputation that the kidney submitted to them had been put in spirits within a few hours of its removal from the body.'[28]

If this is correct, it substantially ups the ante in favour of the kidney coming from Eddowes. 'The body of anyone done to death by violence,' wrote Smith, 'is not taken to the dissecting room, but must await an inquest, never held before the following day at the soonest.' This was electric stuff for Commissioner Smith, Sutton's conclusions 'effectively disposing of all hoaxes in connection with it'.

A very different point of view was brewing up in another part of town, and the City & Met were once again in conflict. The last thing Warren wanted was for the kidney to belong to Eddowes, because if it did, Scotland Yard would be forced to take cognisance of 'the Tall Man' in Mr Marsh's shop. It was one thing to try to manipulate the press after Goulston Street, but in this instance the *Telegraph* had got there first: 'The suspicious circumstance of the tall, clerical-looking individual who called at the shop of Miss Emily Marsh, 218 Jubilee St Mile End Road, has not been properly accounted for.'[29]

Too late for Scotland Yard to do anything about that except keep its head down and pray the newspapers dropped it. The Yard had maintained an absolute silence in respect of this 'Tall Man'. Warren was going to have to concoct a bit of shifty paperwork to cover himself, and we discover it slipped into a report addressed to the Home Office on 6 November 1888. A majority of this document is the usual disingenuous casuistry, attempting to resurrect 'Leather Apron' and his Hebrew vulnerability, here repackaged as one of Warren's humanitarian motives for washing off the wall. But it is the Lusk kidney that attracts the important agricultural. Bro Swanson writes: 'On 18 October, Mr Lusk brought a parcel which had been addressed to him to Leman Street. The parcel contained what appeared to be a portion of a kidney. He received it on 15 October.'[30]

And it is at that date we skid to a halt. Lusk *did not* receive the kidney on 15 October, but the following evening of 16 October. Shifty is shifting dates. By pulling the date forward a day, Scotland Yard has effectively, and officially, written out the possibility of 'the Tall Man' having anything to do with the kidney. If it had arrived on 15 October, the tall Irish cleric couldn't have posted it.

Apologists, and there are many, might argue that this was an Anderson-like 'slip of the pen', but the tone of careful deceit in the rest of this document argues the opposite. The Yard, as always, are completely baffled. They've got a murdered woman with no kidney, and a kidney that might have been sent by her murderer. Faced with so insuperable a 'mystery', they chuck in the towel, can't make head nor tail of it. 'The result of combined medical opinion', opined Shifty, 'is it is the kidney of a human adult, not charged with fluid, as it would have been in the case of a body handed over for purposes of dissection in a hospital, but rather as it would be in a case where it was taken from a body so destined. In other words similar kidneys might and could be obtained from any dead person upon whom a postmortem had been made from any cause by students or a dissecting room porter.'[31]

Or, come to think of it, it might have come from a murdered woman. Wasn't there some sort of dead person out there with a cut throat and her kidney missing? Did not the fact that Lusk's kidney was 'not charged with fluid' virtually guarantee that it had not come from a dissecting room?

Far from bothering themselves with such baffling trivialities, the police instead added a deranged 'Hospital Porter' to their cast list. This was useful. Did they interview all hospital porters, as they attempted to track down the 'Insane Medical Student' and the rest of their ludicrous non-starters? Even a drudge at the Home Office had written in the margin of Swanson's document: 'Was any such postmortem made within a week in the E., or E.C. districts?'

Scotland Yard had resorted to these phantom walk-ons so often that a London correspondent of the *New York Herald* decided to investigate. Under the strapline 'The Medical Student is Knocked on the Head', he reported his findings, gleaned at one or two hospitals and their attendant medical schools.

'The Anatomy Act is one of the most stringent there is,' said a source at one school. 'Besides, the bodies are injected with preserving fluid, and everyone could detect the presence of arsenic. There is a gentleman in charge of the room from the time it opens until it closes. No one can pass in or out without his knowledge. And so strict are the rules that even if a part is left in an untidy state, the Demonstrator at once brings it to the Warden's notice. The laws regarding the dissection of bodies are exceedingly strict. There is an Inspector of Anatomy, who is responsible to the Home Secretary for every body obtained.'

Given the clamour generated by these murders and the subsequent arrival of the kidney, had any hospital declared a kidney missing? I don't think so. I don't think so because the Met would've flung themselves upon it like heaven-sent vindication.

But let us suppose our hoaxer had managed to swipe a kidney, as Swanson suggests. Unlikely, but not impossible. It only becomes impossible when you factor in the rest of the hoaxer's dilemma. Obtaining a kidney is the least of it. He's got to procure a kidney with credentials.

Nobody had mentioned that Catherine Eddowes was suffering from any disease, let alone specified it, until Dr Openshaw examined the kidney on 18 October. Yet here is our 'hoaxer' consigning his kidney to the post on 15 October. Not only did he manage to steal a diseased kidney, but he got the specific malady right, pre-empting Openshaw and Sutton by a minimum of three days. Forget uraemia, forget cancer – he wanted one with glomerulonephritis. This hoaxing medical student was apparently able to diagnose the pathological condition of a murdered body he'd never seen, accurately corroborating a police autopsy that was indisputably unavailable to him.

According to Commissioner Smith, 'two inches [of the renal artery] remained in the corpse, one inch attached to the kidney'.[32] His description is confirmed by an account in the *Telegraph* on 20 October: 'Only a small portion of the renal artery adheres to the kidney, while in the case of the Mitre Square victim a large portion of this artery adhered to the body.' Full marks again to the 'hoaxer' and his attention to detail. With more artery in the body than attached to the kidney, he's even managed to get his respective measurements right.

Prepare for entry into the house of mirrors.

Following the above report in the *Telegraph*, a reporter from *The Times* called on Dr Gordon Brown that same night. 'So far as I could form an opinion,' said Brown, 'I do not see any substantial reason why this portion of kidney should not be the portion of the one taken from the murdered woman.' In the same interview he says, 'The probability is slight of it being a portion of the murdered woman.' Put another way, it is likely to be Eddowes' kidney, but it is also likely not to be.[33]

These contradictions constitute the beginning and end of Brown's interview with *The Times*. The Bro doc is therefore either inexplicably confused, or suffering a dose of Bagster Phillips's disease. More confusing is what Brown has to say about the renal artery. Contradicting Smith, he says, 'as has been stated, there is no portion of the renal artery adhering to it'.

Stated by whom? Only a dozen hours before, the *Telegraph* had stated precisely the opposite. Who had 'unstated' it? Whoever this anonymous intermediary was, Brown confirmed their unstatement that there was no renal artery, 'it having been trimmed up, so, consequently, there could be no correspondence established between the portion of the body from which it was cut'.

Commissioner Smith was therefore hallucinating? He was, after all, prone to such 'turns', foolishly imagining, for example, that some writing on a wall was 'evidence' rather than criticism of a lousy bootmaker, ha ha. What does Brown mean by there being no 'correspondence' between the Lusk and Eddowes kidney? What about the left and right kidneys suffering from the same malady? 'It is symmetrical, both organs being alike involved.'[34] Bright's Disease isn't mentioned, and is apparently no longer of consequence. Mirroring Bro Openshaw, Bro Brown is now coy about the presence of kidney disease as established in his own autopsy.

What we have here is two *doctors* telling the truth, and two *Freemasons* lying. Either they or City Commissioner Smith are manipulating reality. But let us return to another Freemason, Bro Swanson, and his bucketful of Victorian whitewash: 'The postmarks on the parcel are so indistinct that it cannot be said whether the parcel was posted in the E. or E.C. districts, and there is no envelope with the letter, and the City Police are therefore unable to prosecute any enquiries upon it.'[35]

I beg your pardon? What's an envelope got to do with it? Did not the kidney come to Lusk in a package, and was not this package addressed in handwriting exactly as any envelope would have been? So what relevance has a non-existent envelope?

In his report of 27 October, Inspector McWilliam of the City Police had correctly written that Lusk received the kidney on 16 October, and that 'every effort is being made to trace the sender',[36] a statement converted by Swanson into 'the City Police are therefore unable to prosecute any enquiries'.

The problem with many of these MEPO reports is that they are the literary equivalent of jet-lag, glazed eyes being inadequate to deal with this volume of deceit. This *package* is infinitely more valuable than Swanson's smokescreen around a non-existent envelope.

Being too large for a normal postbox, the size of the package had already restricted it to a small number of post offices. How was it wrapped and secured – with glue, string, sealing wax? Did the way it was packed suggest intelligence, or the efforts of an oaf? Was the handwriting on the box the same as the barmy scrawl inside, or was it more considered, to help it through the mails? Swanson refers to 'postmarks', although there could only have been one. There were eight choices in London in 1888:

Postal Regulations.

There are eight Postal Districts in London and the Suburbs, viz.:—

Eastern Central,	. . . .	E.C.
Eastern,	. . . .	E.
Western,	. . . .	W.
Western Central,	. . . .	W.C.
Northern,	. . . .	N.
North-Western,	. . . .	N.W.
South-Eastern,	. . . .	S.E.
South-Western,	. . . .	S.W.

The addition of the proper District initials to the address of a letter, frequently hastens its delivery.

In the E.C. District, there are twelve *deliveries* daily; within the *town limits* of the other Districts (viz., about three miles from the General Post-Office), there are eleven deliveries. The first is made about 8 or 8.30 A.M.; the last, from 9 to 10 P.M.

There were twelve deliveries daily in the EC district, a fact that would have been of extreme importance to any honest detective. Had the time of posting been shortly after the enquiries made by 'the Tall Man' in Marsh's shop, it would have put a noose around his neck. But that's why the 'postmarks', in the plural, were 'indistinct'.

On 22 October a letter from a postal worker was published in the *Evening News*:

I would beg to offer a few suggestions with regard to tracing the origin of the revolting package stated to have been received by parcels post to Mr Lusk. It may not generally be known, but if the box in question was sent by parcels post, it must have been handed in at a post office by someone, and the printed label of that office would be affixed thereto. The necessary postage in stamps would most probably be attached by the sender, it being against the regulations for the poster to do so himself. Doubtless, if application were made to the Secretary of the General Post Office, he would furnish the police authorities with the time of handing in.

I'm afraid this would require a policeman with a brain bigger than a pea. But even he could ask if the package had been handed in by a tall man dressed as a vicar. With or without a distinct postmark, ink comparisons could have been made with stamp pads at various post offices. Out of the question, of course. Like the writing on the wall, the Lusk package had got the Swanson 'smudge', and was therefore beyond baffling. Any detective, any schoolboy, could have isolated this package to a specific area and time of posting. But the E and EC district was obviously a little too close for 'Tall Man' comfort.

On 19 October the *Telegraph* and the *Star* were the first to publish the abbreviated text of the letter, captioned 'From Hell', that had accompanied Lusk's receipt of the kidney: 'Enclosed in the box with it was a letter worded in revolting terms, the writer stating that he had eaten "tother piece", and threatened to send Mr Lusk the "knif that took it if you only wate a whil longer". The letter was dated "From Hell", E.4 and signed "Catch me when you can."'

That's it for the quotes. There was no mention of the spelling of the word 'kidney'. However, on the same day, someone from the pool of 'hoaxers' wrote, 'I wonder how Mr Lusk liked the half of a kidne I sent him Last Monday [15 October].' Thus, even the Ripper confirms Swanson was manipulating the date of postage.

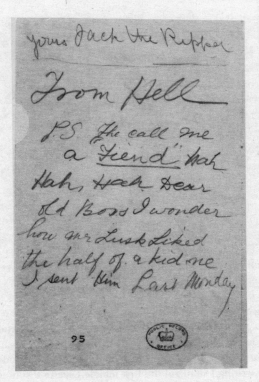

95

How did the 'hoaxer' know that kidney was spelt 'kidne' in the Lusk letter? He couldn't have got it from the newspapers, which had published 'a limited amount of information', excluding the word. And 'kidne' is obviously by intention: the writer makes no other spelling mistake, not even with the more difficult word 'fiend'. Like the 'hoaxer' who knew about Catherine Eddowes' Bright's Disease, and the 'hoaxer' who knew about the stage Irishman, this 'hoaxer' knew about the joker's spelling of 'kidne'.

The letter was discovered shoved into a letterbox in West Ham, dated, like the *Telegraph* article, 19 October. Once again it originated 'From Hell', its author displayed multifarious skills as a penman, and it featured, like many Ripper letters, a vignette of crossed bones.

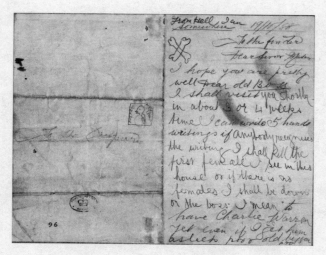

From Hell I am
Somewhere

19/10/88

[drawing of crossed bones]

To the finder

I hope you are pretty well Dear old Boss I shall visit you shortly in about 3 or 4 weeks time I can write 5 handwritings if anybody recognises the writing I shall kill the first female I see in this house or if there is no females I shall be down on the boss. I mean to have Charlie Warren yet even if I get him asleep poor old beggar ...

On the day before, the coppers had made a house-to-house search 'in the neighbourhoods of Hanbury Street, Commercial Street, Dorset Street, Goulston Street, etc.', but, not unnaturally, 'not the slightest clue to the murderer has been obtained'. The *Star* even refers to police looking 'under beds',[37] and I can't resist propositioning a bit of dialogue:

POLICEMAN: Cor blimey O'Reilly, Sarge!
SERGEANT: What is it, Hampton?
POLICEMAN: Why, here he is, sir! Under the bed! Next to the bleedin' po!
SERGEANT: Love a duck! It's the *Fiend*!

At every house and tenement the Met's men visited, they left 'a copy of the subjoined Police Notice: TO THE OCCUPIER'.

POLICE NOTICE.

TO THE OCCUPIER.

On the mornings of Friday, 31st August, Saturday 8th, and Sunday, 30th September, 1888, Women were murdered in or near Whitechapel, supposed by some one residing in the immediate neighbourhood. Should you know of any person to whom suspicion is attached, you are earnestly requested to communicate at once with the nearest Police Station.

Metropolitan Police Office,
30th September, 1888.

Printed by M°Corquodale & Co. Limited, "The Armoury," Southwark.

This was a reissue of a handbill first put about on 3 October. It inspired the envelope in which the Ripper sent his latest letter 'From Hell'. Written in pencil with a crude drawing of a stamp, it was addressed 'To the Occupier', immediately establishing itself as another sneer at the police. But, irrespective of its author's amusement at mimicking their toy-town endeavours, it is 'kidne' that makes the letter important, representing a habitual goading of the Commissioner, and using the same terms to express it.

'I mean to have Charlie Warren' is an expression that crops up all over the correspondence, as does the nasty little trademark of the crossed bones – both were common amongst 'hoaxers', although neither was made public for another hundred years.

We can now either use common sense, or refer the matter to Tinkerbell. The Lusk letter and the West Ham letter must have been written by the same man who sent the kidney. The alternative to this is independent hoaxers deciding to spell 'kidne' in the same way, just as independent hoaxers decided to bring an Irish tone into the proceedings.

By coincidence, on the day of writing this I acquired a new book. It's called *The News from Whitechapel*. Although exclusively concerned with the coverage of the Ripper case by the *Telegraph*, it takes a distinctly conservative point of view, and doesn't trouble its pages with the *Telegraph*'s reportage of the 'Tall Irish Cleric' in Mr Marsh`s shop. In respect of initial newspaper reports of the Lusk kidney, one of its authors, a Mr DiGrazia, is dismissive. 'All of these reports,' he says, 'can be traced back to the imaginations or misreporting of four people – Dr Openshaw, F.S. Reed, Joseph Aarons or an anonymous reporter.' We're back in a wonderland of mass hallucination.[38]

Leaving Commissioner Smith, Inspector McWilliam, Dr Sutton, Detective Inspector Abberline and Lusk out of it, he continues: 'There is no need to take them seriously, particularly as Openshaw himself (and later Dr Gordon Brown) would emphatically deny the extravagant gilding of Lusk's package as being more than just half of a common human kidney.'

A 'common human kidney'? Of the sort we commonly receive through the post, does he mean? Or the sort we commonly keep in our bodies? Mr DiGrazia is still peering under beds.

Lusk sought police protection 'for some days' after receipt of the kidney. Whether he got it or not I don't know, but requesting guards is a curious reaction to a hallucination. In later years Bro Lusk affected to laugh the whole thing off as 'a practical joke', but the laughter rings hollow, and I believe there was a more esoteric explanation for his change of mind. I believe this same occult explanation may also be applied to the vacillations of his fellow Masons, Bros Drs Openshaw and Brown, who similarly repudiated their original, and in my view accurate, conclusions.

It was to Bro Dr Openshaw that the Ripper, or the procurer of the common human kidney, now turned his attention. On 29 October Openshaw received a letter, presumably delivered to the same department of the London Hospital in which he had examined the Lusk kidney. It read:

> Old boss you was rite it was
> the left kidny i was goin to
> hopperate agin close to your
> ospital just as I was goin
> to drop my nife along of
> er bloomin throte them
> cusses of coppers spoilt
> the game but i guess i wil
> be on the job soon and will

> send you another bit of
> innerds Jack the Ripper
> O have you seen the devle
> with his mikerscope and scalpul
> a lookin at a Kidney
> with a slide cocked up

As far as I'm concerned, both this and the letter sent to Lusk are transparent amateur-dramatic absurdities from the same brain. The experts went after both texts, wasting everyone's time with discussion of phonetic minutiae and paragraph after paragraph of worthless oral forensics. By way of example:

> The consonant 'S' and the combination 'St' are pronounced by East London speakers exactly as by standard English RP [i.e. received pronunciation] ones. Where East London differs markedly from RP is in what it does with the 't', finally and in some medial positions as before 'le' or 'en' and intervocally. The interruption of the air-flow, breath, is by the East Londoner made not by bringing the tongue into contact with the alveolar ridge, but by constricting the glottis to form a glottal stop, in place of the RP lateral or nasal placing, as in 'kettle' or 'kitten'.[39]

To spare us the rest of it, I'll get to his point. After a torrent of bile/file/mile/pile/rile and tile, the writer concludes, correctly, that nise/knif/kidny and Mishter are bullshit, and judges 'the apparent illiteracy of this letter to be feigned'.

I couldn't agree more, although from the opposite corner. Handwriting expert Mr Thomas Mann isn't having it. The conclusion at the end of his audit is that 'the author of the Lusk letter is a semi-literate person'. The script is 'a product of finger movement rather than forearm or whole arm movement', he writes, 'a method of writing that permits only slight lateral freedom and is a characteristic of the semi-literate'. And just in case you don't buy that, 'Numerous ink blots attest to someone little concerned with legibility and clarity and relatively unskilled in the use of his writing instrument' (an expert's way of describing a pen).[40]

You can choose which expert you like. In my view one's right and one's wrong, but not for the reasons given by either.

Swanson bemoans the lack of an envelope, as a lame excuse for not proceeding with an investigation into the Lusk kidney. In other words, the police would have investigated had they had an envelope. Here we have one. Didn't anyone investigate it?

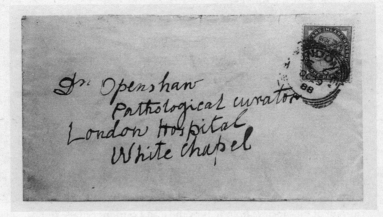

What's the point of getting into an intellectual tizz over 'kidne' when the fucker can spell 'Pathological curator'? The address is written without error. And why? Because the sender wants it to get through the postal system, and therefore makes no purposeful mistakes. He doesn't want it intercepted by the police.

If the creator of the Openshaw letter can manage 'Hospital' on the envelope, what's all this 'ospital' nonsense in the text? In my view this envelope demolishes the contrived fatuity of the letter it encloses. It exposes the writing as utterly bogus, 'whole arm movement' and all. No ink smears or spelling mistakes on the envelope – those mystifying ingredients are saved for inside. How can it be that comparatively arcane words are spelled accurately on the envelope, while the letter is replete with errors in simple words like 'goin' and 'agin'?

It is tempting to dismiss this text solely because of its asinine attempt at disguise (suggesting that it was the work of an idiot). But it wasn't written by an idiot at all. It was written with a man in mind who had American connections, hence the use of 'I guess'.

I imagine the apologists would say the writer copied Openshaw's address from a newspaper. I would respond, why then can he not copy the word 'kidney'? But to speculate over spelling errors and ink blots is to make an idiot of one's time. The writer is urbane enough not only to be aware of an uncommon bit of verse, but also sophisticated enough to adapt it.

> O have you seen the devle
> with his mikerscope and scalpul
> a lookin at a Kidney
> with a slide cocked up …

We have a correct spelling of 'kidney' here (he's having such fun he's forgotten it's 'kidne'). This manipulated rhyme is an almost direct rip-off of a Cornish folk tale published in 1871:

> Here's to the devil
> with his wooden pick and shovel
> digging tin by the bushel
> with his tail cock'd up …

But the Ripper's facility for lyrical adaption isn't what interests me. I would expect as much from a successful composer of songs. It is the line 'O have you seen the devle' that abstracts itself from the page. I'd seen this before. Indeed, the same question was pasted onto a card and mailed from the NW district of London on 10 October, nineteen days before Openshaw received his letter.

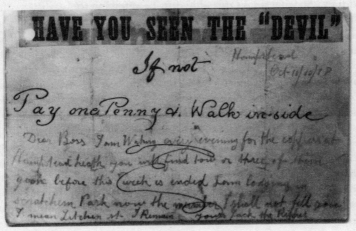

Full marks yet again to our 'Hoaxing Medical Student'. He got his Irish tone right, his left kidney right, his Bright's Disease right – all before the event – and now he reaches back into the parapsychological void to get his source for 'have you seen the devil' right. He's a soothsayer, sharing an extraordinary telepathy with other hoaxers possessed of clairvoyant skills that will continue to amaze in the next chapter.

HAVE YOU SEEN THE "DEVIL"
If not
Pay one Penny & Walk in-side

If the empirical has got anything to do with it, this text blows the 'hoaxers' angle right out of the water, and serves to include the Openshaw letter in the body of Ripper correspondence. Had the card been sent *after* the Openshaw verse, it would of course be easy for the intrepid Ripperologists to dismiss it as based on something the sender read in a newspaper. But reality has it the other way around. And this postcard was never published in the press, or anywhere else. Thus, to consider these two 'Have You Seen the Devil[s]' in isolation from each other is absurd. Irrespective of handwriting, they come out of the same brain. There is a single train of thought here, and if there isn't, let's hear how two separate 'hoaxers' came up with the same startlingly esoteric quote. It's hardly as common as 'a common human kidney'. So what might this little ditty be referring to?

Well, I think it came from 'close to your Ospital' – in fact, almost from the opposite side of the street. I think it came from a flyer advertising a waxworks.

'There can be no doubt that a waxworks museum did flourish opposite the London Hospital,' write Michael Howell and Peter Ford in their history of Joseph Merrick, 'the Elephant Man', 'for in September 1888, in the midst of the Whitechapel Murders committed by Jack the Ripper, a correspondent who called himself John Law was writing in the columns of the *Pall Mall Gazette.* "There is at present almost opposite the London Hospital a ghastly display of the unfortunate women murdered. An old man exhibits these things, and while he points them out you will be tightly wedged in between a number of boys and girls, while a smell of death rises in your nostrils."'[41]

It was in this place, formerly the premises of an undertaker, that the eminent surgeon Sir Frederick Treves had discovered that saddest of God's creatures, 'the Elephant Man'. Further confirmation of this revolting entertainment at 123 Whitechapel Road is given by Montagu Williams QC, who in 1892 published a memoir called *Round London*: 'The undertaker had for his successor an East End showman. This was ringing the changes with a vengeance. Mutes had given way to masqueraders; tights and spangles had taken the place of crepe; and, as it subsequently appeared, the solemn realities of death had been succeeded by a coarse burlesque of murder.'

'I paid my penny and entered.'

Williams gives the last line a new paragraph, and because of its importance, so do I. It's the same entrance fee requested by the Whitechapel Fiend. 'Pay one Penny & Walk inside'. 'In the body of the room was a waxwork exhibition, and some of its features were revolting in the extreme. The first of the Whitechapel murders were fresh in the memory of the public, and the proprietor of the exhibition was turning the circumstance to commercial account.'[42]

I think it was while admiring these effigies of his handiwork that Jack procured his printed 'Have You Seen the "Devil"'. Or perhaps it came from a local newspaper or a flyer given away in the street, which he subsequently cut out and pasted onto his letter.

Both the Openshaw letter and the 'Penny' invitation sneer at the coppers in the same mocking way. Their artificial illiteracy is identical. If they're the work of the same man – and by any criteria it's impossible for them not to be – then so is the apparently different handwriting. 'I can write in 5 different hands', boasts the second 'From Hell' letter.

And I for one believe him.

11

On Her
Majesty's Service

Test everything. Retain what is good.

St Paul

My candidate was famous, and left a lot of shadows. Even so, this narrative was more difficult than anything I've ever attempted. Every day when I sit down to write I face a gang of hostile ghosts – Victorian coppers and Victorian Freemasons – demanding that the truth belongs to them. Ripperologists don't have this problem, because they're friends of one and ignore the other. Like Bro Charlie, Ripperology is dedicated to the non-detection of J.T.R.

Nowhere is this more apparent than in its dismissal of the Ripper correspondence. In the expert opinion of these boys the letters are all bogus, the product of a variety of hoaxers attempting to impede the saint-like efforts of the Metropolitan Police.

This is Ripperology at its worst (or best, depending on your point of view). None of its multiple candidates can survive acknowledgement of these letters: they go down like flies. Hence the happy acquiescence to the nonsense put about by the Victorian police. For the police to have acknowledged this correspondence as genuine, as much of it is, would have meant that the kingdom's most repugnant Freemason would have been caught. His erstwhile chums in high places knew this as well in 1888 as I do today.

Deconstruction of these texts wasn't what you might call easy. Written primarily between the autumn of 1888 and the summer of 1889, there are many of them, and most look like the exertions of madmen. Mailed from all over the country, often from places hundreds of miles apart, there's no apparent consistency to them, not in paper, pens or inks. They might be in blue, black or red ink, or a combination of all three. Some are crafted in painstaking copperplate, many are in barely intelligible scrawl. It is my contention that virtually every one of them was written by the same hand.

This chapter, then, is about trying to prove that a substantial number of these so-called 'hoaxes' were in fact penned by the Ripper, and pursuant to that, attempting to associate them with my candidate, Michael Maybrick.

By myopic convention we are invited to assess these letters in precisely the wrong way. In other words, to look at how they look, rather than at how their author was thinking. I don't think Jack was necessarily anxious to disguise his handwriting, but simply manipulated it for a laugh. The grin in the ink is one incontrovertible consistency of the letters, and with that as my compass, I ignored the visuals and went after the 'voice'.

It is habitual to psychopaths to believe they're cleverer than everyone else, and usually they are of high intelligence. Before we get into Jack, take a look at these. They were both penned by the same psycho, a particularly unsavoury piece of work called Peter Kürten, who conducted a 'reign of terror' in Düsseldorf, Germany, in the interwar years. Like Jack, he killed women and children, and like Jack (who incidentally was his role model) he enjoyed bragging about it.[1]

Kürten's 'normal' handwriting is above, and on the following page in homicidal mood.

'The mass-murderer, Kürten,' writes the psychoanalyst Theodor Reik, 'always listened attentively to conversations about the murders [and] followed the investigations with feverish interest. He described his mental state while doing so as one of apprehensive excitement; and he also had a distinct feeling of superiority because he knew better.'[2] (He'd have been all ears at the Savage Club.)

Unlike Scotland Yard, which for private reasons couldn't catch anything more fascinating than a cold, the German police finally nailed the Düsseldorf Monster through his handwriting. Anyone can see the graphological similarities between Kürten and Jack, and anyone who thinks the Ripper correspondence is the corporate work of a compromised IQ may well be in possession of something similar. Artfulness reeks from its locutions – the exasperating repetitions and the preposterous handwriting are not in default of literary ability, but are prime ingredients of the writer's malice. Like some precocious kid with a whistle, he knows exactly how to annoy, pulling the wings off the same fly again and again – and more often than not the fly is Charlie Warren.

What a dance I'm leading all these fools in London. Why I'm passing them by the dozens against Scotland Yd way & don't i laugh & say damn fools, you work them too hard, poor fellows.

> The police, alias po-lice, think themselves devilish clever I
> suppose, they'll never catch me at this rate you donkeys, you double
> faced asses.[3]

The Commissioner of the most powerful police force on earth is
treated like a twat. A majority of the letters to Sir Charles Warren are
consistent in their pitying animosity, calling him a 'friend' while
berating him as an imbecile. It is the voice of a spiteful child, a brat-
man who hated authority almost as much as he hated women. The
first he mercilessly vilified, and the second he slaughtered.

Authority figures are an obsessive target: the Prime Minister is an
'old jew', the monarch an 'old bitch' and the Commissioner of
Metropolitan Police an 'old pig'. He took joy in pressing the
castrated old stooge's buttons, trashing everything he held precious:
his religion, his Masonry, his sovereign – 'four more to do then I'll
kill the bloody old queen'. A construct of anti-Warren venom permeates these letters, a train of thought as clear as the writing on the
wall. Warren's past is the Ripper's present, his homicidal muse, as
would be sensationally realised in the so-called 'Scotland Yard Trunk
mystery'. We're back in 'Bible Land' for this one, so personal to
Warren that it would attract more lies than Goulston Street.

'Very numerous and searching enquiries have been made', wrote
Warren on 25 October 1888, explaining to his worthless little pal of
a Home Secretary that 'these have had no tangible results so far as
regards the Whitechapel Murders, but information has been
obtained which will no doubt be useful in future in detecting cases
of crime'.[4]

So it all turned out rather well, then? This letter was written about
a fortnight before a significant amount of Mary Kelly was carried
away in a bucket, and little more than three weeks after Catherine
Eddowes was robbed of her kidney and womb. But at least it'll help
them catch a few pickpockets? This is a scandalous statement to
have come from a Commissioner of Police, and scandalous for a
Home Secretary to blithely accept.

Warren should have been fired on the spot, and under any other
circumstances it's likely he would have been. But these weren't like
any other circumstances, and this wasn't like any other murder
inquiry. Jack had them by the nuts, and they were rushing around
in a frenzy to hide the Masonry while simultaneously concocting the

'mystery'. To have a hope in hell of selling it required lying on a monumental scale, so of course the Ripper correspondence had to be converted into 'hoax'.

By the middle of October 1888 a handful of letters had mystically been transmuted into thousands. As myth would have it, the Met was 'swamped' by the crazed inventions of evil hoaxers seeking to undermine and confuse. Ripperology was to endorse this fantasy with enthusiasm. In sympathy with the Victorian police, later 'experts' designated these letters as a loony sideshow, and a relentless burden on Scotland Yard that could safely be dismissed. After all, how could anyone cope with, let alone isolate anything genuine from, this avalanche of postal deceit?

In reality, there wasn't much avalanche, but an awful lot of deceit. There were no letters 'in their thousands', to the Metropolitan Police or anyone else. 'It is said,' wrote Warren's biographer and grandson, Bro Watkin Williams, 'that Scotland Yard received about 1,200 letters daily.'[5]

Said by whom?

As far as I can determine, said by no one but Watkin Williams himself. From where did he source this information? Who said the Met got twelve hundred letters a day? Or even ten?

It certainly wasn't said by his grandfather, Sir Charles Warren, who was the target of most of them. On 10 October 1888, at the height of the supposed deluge, Warren put in an official report to the Home Office. 'We have received scores of hoaxing letters,' he wrote.[6] A 'score' is twenty, and 'scores', in the common understanding of the word, is less than one hundred. Warren did not say 'We've received thousands of hoaxing letters,' or even hundreds, but 'scores'.

Three score? Four score?

Let us again go for the common understanding, based if you like on the Biblical dose of life expectancy – 'three score years and ten', in other words about seventy. Let us reasonably conclude, then, that by 10 October 1888 Scotland Yard had received about seventy so-called 'hoax' letters. By the time he sneaked out of the nightmare about a month later, Warren had written (in the very article that was supposed to have caused his resignation), 'It may be mentioned that among the several hundred letters received from correspondents of all classes lately about the Whitechapel Murders ...'[7]

Here the Commissioner is confirming 'several hundred' as the total number of letters received throughout his disastrous tenure, an estimate confirmed by his successor, Sir Melville Macnaghten, who many months later wrote of inheriting a postbag that 'bulged large with hundreds of anonymous communications on the subject of the East End tragedies'.[8]

Both Macnaghten and Warren agree that this correspondence was at maximum 'hundreds', or 'several hundred'. So why did Bro Watkin Williams invent *tens of thousands* of non-existent letters? By his own computation, October 1888 alone would have produced about 36,000.

It's only necessary to open his *Life of General Sir Charles Warren* at any page you like for the answer: he's trying to save his grandfather's face. If the police were 'drowning in letters', it's easier to excuse their treacherous inability to select the key correspondence that would facilitate arrest of the homicidal maggot. But with only two or three hundred to examine, such a subterfuge falls to bits. Hence thousands upon tens of thousands of make-believe letters are conjured into a bewildering torrent, with not a clue among them.

It should be noted that a majority of the hundreds of letters had nothing to do with 'hoaxers', but were sent to Scotland Yard by concerned members of the public, writing in with suggestions and offers of assistance. They were thanked by Warren for their efforts: 'He has been quite unable to respond in a great number of instances,' peeped *The Times* on 18 October, 'and he trusts that the writers will accept this acknowledgement in lieu of individual replies. They may be assured that their letters have received every consideration.'

When the Victorian police declared all the Ripper letters a 'hoax', Ripperology jumped on it like free money. It was a birthday present for the 'experts', and it gave a leg-up to every daft candidate in the book. If you didn't have to worry about the letters, you didn't have to worry about much at all.

Try fitting Kosminski to an Edinburgh postmark, or Michael Ostrog to Liverpool or Leeds. Forget it – the lights go out. These letters were dispatched from all over the country, and even if only one in ten was genuine, that knocked out practically every candidate on offer. So Ripperologists relished dumping the letters, and simply adored the word 'hoax'. 'Hoax' gave potential credibility to their man, and it was magnificently official – a MEPO, no less. Lips could be pursed together, and the field was wide open. Lord Randolph Churchill? Why not? Lewis Carroll? Mark that man!!! Denial of the letters meant that any concocted idiocy could stand for nomination, and if they got lucky, it might even get the nod from Melvin Harris.

Let us navigate this Victorian propaganda and look at these letters as if we're intelligent coppers of today. Seemingly at random, they were coming from all over the kingdom, with hardly a city that didn't have a 'Ripper wannabe'.

Let's start by asking an obvious question. When did these letters 'flood in' from the provinces? *October 1888.* When did the killings in Whitechapel abate? *October 1888.* After the Double Event of 30 September, there were no murders in the following month. Might that not mean that the individual who had been killing women in London couldn't do it because he was mainly out of town? I'll get into the geography presently. For the moment I want to stay with the philosophy, to consider myself an open-minded cop with no occult preconditioning.

So here we are, squatting in Scotland Yard with seventy-odd letters. Apart from the recurring name 'Jack the Ripper', are these letters conceivably linked? In most the handwriting looks very different, no question about that. But maybe their author had a talent for disguising it? Maybe it gave him pleasure? It's worth a moment to quote an example of just such a man (also a psychopathic killer) who had just such a talent. He could change his handwriting, or copy the handwriting of others, at will, and was described by authorities at Scotland Yard as 'the greatest forger they had ever known. John George Haigh could write whole letters in the hand of a dozen or more people … at a second's notice he could switch from one style to another. A forgery of fifteen pages was described by experts at Scotland Yard as "a masterpiece".'9

The 'mystery' who was Jack the Ripper may well have been possessed of a comparable talent, so the question I posed myself was: could the letters, at least many of them, have a similar chameleon-like provenance, and be the work of one man?

Ripper mail was arriving from as far apart as Aberdeen in the north and Penzance in the extreme south-west. We're looking at different paper, different pens, and different ink. If they were mailed by the same man, how could this possibly be? What is it that might take a man to such disparate places at opposite ends of the land?

I think the first thing we might want to look at is a profession. What might be his *métier*? In our day we might consider an aeroplane pilot, or a truck driver. But this is Victorian England, with no planes and no trucks. If he were to travel these huge distances, it would have to be by railway. So what might cause him to do this? What job, if job it were, would take him to all these apparently unconnected locations – from Folkestone to Bristol to Glasgow, and many places in between? Pass me today's newspaper.

UK AND IRELAND DECEMBER TOUR 2015

3RD - DUBLIN, OLYMPIA THEATRE

4TH - BIRMINGHAM, THE INSTITUTE

5TH - BOURNEMOUTH, O2 ACADEMY

7TH - CAMBRIDGE, CORN EXCHANGE

8TH - BRISTOL, O2 ACADEMY

9TH - GLASGOW, O2 ABC

11TH - MANCHESTER, ALBERT HALL

12TH - LEEDS, O2 ACADEMY

14TH - LONDON, BRIXTON O2 ACADEMY

These are the tour dates of a contemporary artist whose name is without relevance to this book. Pressure of dates means a fair amount of tramping about – Dublin, Bristol, Glasgow … But what of the Ripper's day? What kind of mileage could a Victorian concert singer expect to put in?

Miss Ada Crossley was just such a singer. In an interview with *Cassell's Saturday Journal* she spoke of the stresses of a performer's life:

Of course the amount of travelling that one is called upon to do is trying. Here is what I did in one ordinary week this year. I had two vacant dates – Wednesday, October 31st and Thursday, November 1st – and being in the North of England I returned to London with the intention of enjoying a little rest. Now, on these two days, Miss

Clara Butt had arranged to appear at Derby and Nottingham, but having fallen ill she asked me to take her place, and I consented, at absolutely a moment's notice. No sooner was I out of one train than I had to dash into another. Well, on the Friday I left Nottingham and sang that same afternoon at St James's Hall. The next afternoon I fulfilled an engagement at the Queen's Hall at three, and an hour later I was speeding on my way to Manchester, where I sang the same evening. But this was not all. At the conclusion of the concert I drove to an hotel, got into my travelling dress, and took the midnight train for London, arriving at six o'clock. I thus covered nine hundred miles in four days.[10]

Ada may have missed some sleep, but she was no exception. For the successful artiste such distances were *de rigueur*. 'He was always travelling,' wrote C.E. Hallé of his father, the conductor Sir Charles Hallé. 'Many and many a time he would travel, say, from Manchester to Edinburgh, conduct a rehearsal in the afternoon, and a concert in the evening, and return to Manchester that same night, reaching home at four or five o'clock the next morning.'[11]

Vast distances went with the music. I shall come to Michael Maybrick's migrations in due course, but for the moment I include an itinerary of one-nighters by someone enjoying a very similar career to his.

MR. DURWARD LELY
AS NANKI-POO IN "THE MIKADO"

[Photo by Barraud]

Although, as the composer of the songs he sang, Maybrick was very much wealthier, he and Mr Durward Lely shared much in common. Both were figures of urban celebrity, fellow members of the Savage Club, and both intimates of Sir Arthur Sullivan, Lely frequently singing a leading role in his blisteringly tiresome Savoy operas. In 1892 the *Musical Herald* published a list of Lely's dates. It's only by chance that this record has survived, but because of the similarities of their lifestyles it could equally apply to Charles Santley, or Sims Reeves, or Michael Maybrick.

According to this correspondent, 'the distance travelled is astounding'. Apart from Lely's opera commitments, 'he fills up the vacant evenings with concert engagements elsewhere'.

By any measure it's a punishing schedule – Liverpool, London, Leeds, and back to London. Had Lely been of the inclination, he could have posted as many perplexing letters from far-flung locations as he liked. Without the singer, the geography seems insane, the letters arbitrary. But one-night stands make the link – and that, I believe, is how Jack the Ripper posted his.

Mr. Durward Lely.

A 'CORRESPONDENT writes:—" A short time since Mr. Durward Lely was in Sheffield, and showed me his diary of engagements. It was so interesting that I copied it down to send you for insertion in the *Musical Herald* as a compliment to a singer who is never backward in championing Tonic Sol-fa. Many people imagine that a professional singer has nothing to do but walk on to a platform, sing, and pocket the fee with no further trouble. But the distances travelled in this list are astounding. Altogether it shows 101 engagements in four months:—Aug. 10-17, Patti's Castle ; 18, London (Carl Rosa) ; 24-26, Blackpool ; 27, Swansea ; 28, Patti ; 29, Blackpool ; 31, Sept. 2 & 4, Liverpool ; 7, 9, 11, Birmingham ; 12, Covent Garden ; 14, Derby ; 15, Covent Garden ; 16, Derby ; 17, Covent Garden ; 18, Derby ; 19, Glasgow ; 21, Northampton ; 22, Covent Garden ; 23, Northampton ; 24, London Promenade Concerts ; 25, Manchester ; 26, Drury Lane ;

Jack couldn't kill in London in October 1888, because he was constantly in and out of it. It's noticeable that Lely's tour dates (September to December 1888) all but synchronise with the dates of the Ripper's provincial correspondence. The postmarks of the letters frequently put the Ripper and Lely in permutations of the same towns – Edinburgh, Liverpool, Bolton, Bradford, Derby, Leeds and Dublin, to name but a few. Wherever Lely crooned a quickie (although on a different date, of course), someone signing himself 'Jack the Ripper' would invariably post a single letter.

It is also noticeable that having mailed a single letter from a particular town, the Ripper 'hoaxer' always packs it in. So, far from suggesting the work of independent 'hoaxers', I believe this ghost itinerary points to the work of one man, dashing from city to city, following a similar concert circuit to that of Mr Durward Lely.

I think the Ripper (like Michael Maybrick) was touring the provinces in the autumn of 1888, and because he was obsessive and very much enjoyed murdering, he took advantage of his engagements to keep the fun alive. Miss the fun and you miss the Fiend. So I'm looking for puns, syllogisms, acronyms and metaphors, all the juvenile word-play that kept him amused. But above all I'm looking for evidence supporting the hypothesis of a solitary Beast on the road.

A link presents itself immediately, and it is one of many characteristics these 'regional hoaxers' share. The 'hoaxers' don't claim to live in the town they're writing from, but are always passing through, generally disparaging the place they're in and looking forward to the next. Thus we have a phalanx of disgruntled Rippers travelling through the country seeking urban content. Birmingham sucks? How about Bolton, Burnley or Liverpool? But there's no peace for the wicked: wherever 'they' go, dissatisfaction is inevitable. By way of example is this dispatch from the Midlands, postmarked 4 October 1888:

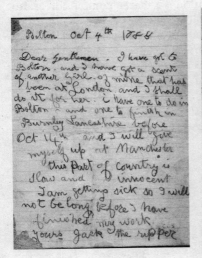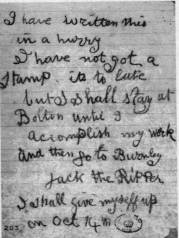

Dear Gentlemen – I have got to Bolton, and have got a scent of another Girl of mine that has been at London and I shall do it for her. i have one to do in Bolton – and one to finish in Burnley Lancashire before Oct 14th and I will give myself up at Manchester this part of country is slow and innocent I am getting sick so I will not be long before I have finished my work

    Yours Jack the Ripper

    I have written this in a hurry I have not got a stamp, its to late but I shall stay at Bolton until I accomplish my work and then go to Burnley

Jack the Ripper

Another move is effected overnight. 5 October: 'Have arrived here [Bradford] after a pleasant journey.' 8 October: 'I am as you see by this note amongst the slogging town of Brum [Birmingham].' 10 October: 'I am in Lester [sic] for a holiday.' On the same day comes another from Edinburgh, then London on the 12th and Colchester on the 13th. Leeds and Bristol via Portsmouth and London, and then it's 'Off to Brum today, post this on me way,' which he did, on 19 October.

If these correspondents are independent 'hoaxers', how come they're all doing the same thing? How can it be that all of them are incessantly travelling? This migration is a shared compulsion as the 'team' move through the provinces, managing by some curious unspoken intercourse to participate in synchronised thinking.

All of them are on the road, but that's just the beginning of it. These 'hoaxers' share more than just telepathic intelligence, they also pool technique. Apart from 'Dear Boss', no facsimile of an envelope was ever made public. Yet out there in the sticks our supposedly independent 'hoaxers' share an identical joke on their envelopes. Many of them were working simultaneously for the Queen.

'On Her Majesty's Service'

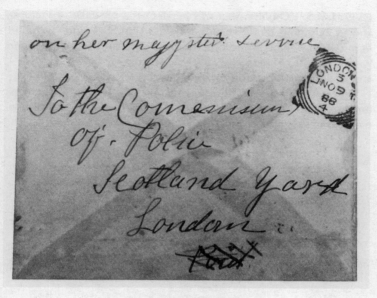

'on her magystes service'

'O.H.M.S.'

'O.H.M.S.' (On Her Majesty's Service) is a piss-take of Victoria, and an egregious theme. Examples of 'O.H.M.S.', written in full or as initials, are to be found on envelopes of 12 and 18 October and 9, 10, 12 and 13 November 1888, reappearing on 18 February 1889, and again, after an almost two-year gap, on 6 December 1890.

Unless these 'hoaxers' were sharing notes on the road, or perhaps meeting at some unknown 'hoaxers' HQ', by what species of telepathy were they able to indulge in the same joke?

'O.H.M.S.'

'On Her Majesties Service'

'O.H.M.S'

'On her Majestys Service'

'on her majesterys service'

The last example illustrated is the most interesting of them all. 'On her majestys service' is dated 24 September 1888, and therefore precedes 'Dear Boss' by about three days. It set a precedent for future Ripper correspondence before anyone had even seen the infamous name.

Jack was to repeat 'O.H.M.S.' in a variety of guises, busting the variations of penmanship wide open. How could anyone possibly copy the theme of this unpublished and totally unacknowledged envelope? It establishes a consistency of thinking, and you don't have to think too hard to understand why Warren chose to ignore it.

You can fake the handwriting, but not the pissy little intellect. It advertises itself. A glance at the archive of these so-called 'hoaxes' reveals another notable characteristic: an antipathy towards paying for stamps. Of the surviving envelopes, barely one is pre-paid, the rest almost all require postage to be coughed up by the recipient, i.e. Warren and the Metropolitan Police.

There's a childish spitefulness about this – like the police in China, who apparently send an invoice for the price of the bullet to relatives of the loved one they have just shot. Jack would have enjoyed the joke, and in similar spirit occasionally created his own postal service. But even then he only volunteered half: 'J.R. Postage 1d'. But a twopenny insult to the cops.

It's worth mentioning that Michael Maybrick didn't like stamps either. In a letter to his friend and publisher John Boosey he wrote, 'You talk of stamps!!! what are <u>they</u> for???'

Whether Maybrick's dislike of stamps is significant or not, it's true to say that, excepting postcards, stamps were rarely used by anyone signing himself 'Jack the Ripper'.

The Victorians created a magnificent railway network. You could get anywhere, and usually fast: in 1888 the fastest train in the world plied between Edinburgh and London (Euston). Posting an identically dated letter from either city (and stops in between) was perfectly feasible for any traveller in J.T.R.'s day.[12]

The first 'Limited Mail Train' steamed out of London for Scotland in 1859. By 1885 special mail trains were running on the London and North Western Railway and the Caledonian Railway between London and Aberdeen, and a similar system operated on the Great Western Railway between London (Paddington) and Penzance. One of the innovations of this service was the provision of a 'late fee box', enabling mail to be posted while a train was at a station. Thus, while changing trains at any one of the major junctions, you could pop your missive into 'the letter box on the side of the carriage, kept open while the train is standing in a station'.[13] In his travels throughout the provinces, a smart-arse like the Whitechapel Murderer may well have availed himself of this facility. By this means each letter became a phoney alibi for the next – 'post this on me way'.[14]

Because Aberdeen was a mail terminus, it was there that letters would pick up their postmarks, and I suspected that most of the Scottish Ripper correspondence would be sourced to that city. In fact, apart from Glasgow and a 'McRipper clump' around Galashiels, all the Scottish letters originate in Aberdeen.

In two letters, dated 3 October and 1 November 1888, the same correspondent, 'J. Gordon', apparently writes from two different addresses in Aberdeen: 9 Bridge Street and 52 Leadside Road respectively.

Both letters have a pharmacological theme, accusing 'medical men' of being responsible for the Ripper's crimes. But what makes the 1 November letter interesting is its reference to Matthew Packer: 'Please allow me to suggest Sir that you may depend on the Whitechapel Murderer attempting to kill the only person who can identify him, namely the fruitsellers.'

A London correspondent signing himself 'Jack the Ripper' was of the same view. But the police were not, and they had made a big deal of publicly dismissing Packer. Yet this 'Scotsman', living four hundred miles away in two different houses, remains unconvinced.

None of these provincial 'hoaxers' ever puts a foot wrong. While they're on the road they are somehow miraculously aware that their hero is similarly indisposed, because no 'hoaxer' is ever caught out, and the postmarks on their letters are always dates on which the Ripper did not kill.

On occasion Jack would send a telegram. Not a few rags of the day criticised post office clerks for accepting a transmission signed 'Jack the Ripper', although you've got to wonder, what they were supposed to do about it? Personally, I would've avoided attempting a citizen's arrest, and would have been only too pleased to send the bloody thing as instructed. But things weren't actually that straightforward. Henry Labouchère described the way one of the telegrams was dispatched with his customary guile: 'This telegram was not handed in at a post office in the usual way, but stamped and deposited in a letter box, whence it was taken in the ordinary course when the box was cleared to the nearest telegraph office and dispatched. Now it is not everyone even among the educated classes who is aware that a telegram can be sent in this manner. To my mind, this is one more indication that the Whitechapel assassin is more likely to belong to the "classes" than the "masses".'[15]

I give attention to this revealing opinion not only for its allusion to an educated man, but because we're about to see a further use of sophisticated and cunning postal conjuring tricks, particularly in respect of transatlantic mail services out of Liverpool.

The trick by which Jack sent a letter to the London cops via Philadelphia is one of his cuter efforts. Letters were arriving from all over the country, and right in the middle of them comes a Jack the Ripper letter mailed from the USA. One man can't be in two countries at once, which is handy if you're trying to push the idea of 'hoax'.

There were several letters 'posted in America'. First up is this apparently baffling taunt 'from Philadelphia'. Designated simply 'Philadelphia Docket No 1157', it has no date and no surviving envelope, but its journey from the United States is certain. It was received by the Metropolitan Police in London towards the end of October 1888.

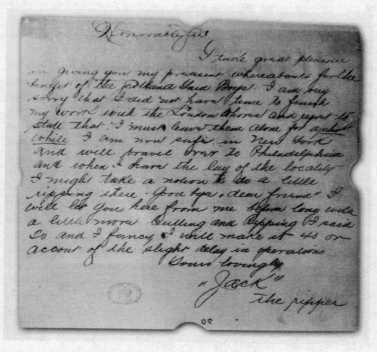

It's not by accident that this is one of the very few Ripper letters without a date. It's undated, because the sender didn't know when it would arrive.

Honorably Sir

I take great pleasure in giving you my preasent whereabouts for the benifit of the Scotland Yard Boys. I am very sorry that I did not have time to finish my work with the London Whores and regret to state that I must leave them alone for a short while I am now safe in New York and will travel over to Philadelphia and when I have the lay of the locality I might take a notion to do a little ripping there. Good bye "dear friend" I will let you here from me before long with a little more Culling and Ripping I said so and I fancy I will make it 40 on account of the slight delay in operations

Yours lovingly
"Jack"
the ripper

To take this letter at face value would mean that 'Jack' the Ripper had gone to America, and there are certain plausible reasons for imagining he had. The writer seems well informed of Jack's intentions, citing a 'slight delay in operations', which in October 1888 was indeed the case. There were no murders while Michael Maybrick was on provincial tour, or rather when Jack was in Philadelphia. 'I am very sorry that I did not have time to finish my work with the London Whores,' he writes, 'and regret to state that I must leave them alone for a short while'.

How can there be two Jacks writing simultaneously from either side of the Atlantic? The answer is that one of them wasn't. Jack didn't go to New York, but a letter written by Jack the Ripper did. This tricky little wheeze 'from Philadelphia' was in fact posted out of Liverpool, possibly about 10 October, giving it time to get to New York, get some provenance, and return directly to London. How was this done? Well, rather as mail was bounced around England on the railways.

In 1888 the fastest transatlantic liner would make Liverpool to New York in under a week. There were a variety of companies to choose from, Cunard and White Star being the most famous. 'On many of these ships sea post-offices are established, where mails are sorted in transit and made ready for delivery at the completion of the voyage.'[16]

The picture overleaf shows one such sorting office in action. Speed was of the essence, and on a ship's arrival in New York a

special tender pulled alongside, and the mails were on their way long before the passengers disembarked. The tender with its canvas mail-chute is shown opposite, 'so that as soon as it is landed it may be scattered at once to its various destinations without going to a district office to be sorted'.

Jack the Ripper would have had no difficulty in introducing his letter into the system at Liverpool. All that was necessary was to board a ship and post it in a sea-mail box.

In those days, of course, citizens didn't have to conduct their lives in a state of relentless obstruction and paranoia. There were no body checks, no X-rays, and no passport control. A gentleman could come and go aboard these great ocean liners as he pleased, and this was especially true in the case of Michael Maybrick, who may well have known some of the captains. His brother James certainly did: Captain P.J. Irving of the White Star Line was a personal friend, and left his ship the *Republic* to dine with the Maybricks at their Liverpool home a week before James's murder.

'Jack' may well have shaken Captain Irving's hand on a crisp October morning as the *Republic* prepared to sail. Just happened to

be at the docks, perhaps, and thought he'd pop aboard and wish Irving good day. And if not his ship, then one of many others, availing himself of the postbox as he left.

I want to examine the provenance of another 'American' letter out of Liverpool. It's addressed to the Lord Mayor of London, and has important connotations in respect of the destruction of Florence Maybrick, to be explored in a later chapter.

Its author dates it 20 July 1889, three days after the murder of Alice McKenzie and ten days before the commencement of proceedings against Florence for murdering her husband James. The letter purports to originate from Washington, DC, but transparently does not. Even the date blows it. The author writes the date as '20/7/'89', putting the day before the month, as all Englishmen do; whereas if he were really the American he pretends to be, he would have written 7/20/89, following the convention of putting the month first, as all Americans do (9/11, by way of example).

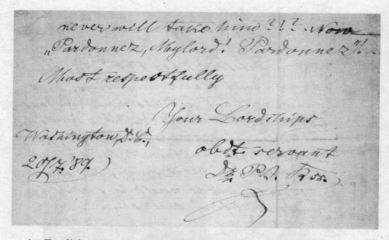

An Englishman wrote this date, and I can illustrate the point with the envelope, which fortunately survives:

The month of course precedes the day on the New York harbour stamps: 7/20/89. The letter's claim of origin in Washington is phoney: once again it was bounced out of New York. Like the Philadelphia letter, this one travelled from the Liverpool docks, copped a stamp from a maritime sorter, and immediately began its journey home.

The crossed '7' in his date tells us something else about this English correspondent. He was educated, and had almost certainly lived in Continental Europe. The bar on the '7' was doubtless a slip of the mental nib after he had written the French word '*pardonnez*'.

> My Lord!
>
> <u>Important</u>
>
> Pardon the liberty to address your Lordship about that horrid bestial brute of a murderer of those poor lost Girls at <u>Whitechapel</u> – "Jack the Ripper"! … That reprobate must be taken away from the good City of London and its formerly so good police, the best of the world, as I have read often, and I get – perhaps – a logical idea (thought) to it … it may – at first – look peculiar (or strange) perhaps ridiculous –: Who can assert Your Lordship, that '<u>Jack the Ripper</u>' don't walk along in the dress of a woman …

And so it rambles on, *ad infinitum*, before finally arriving at the shared obsession of many of Jack's letters, that a man of 'high muscular power should dress himself as a woman'.

Whether from 'Washington' in the US or Leeds in the UK, trans-vestism is a common signature of the letters. But from wherever they were mailed, most dispatches resonate with spite for authority, and particularly the buffoon at Scotland Yard. Warren is the addressee of no fewer than twenty-seven of the surviving letters. Allowing for occult weeding and loss over the years, we can assume that he received about twice that number, perhaps fifty or sixty; in other words, about 71,942 fewer than those invented by Bro Watkin Williams.

Michael Maybrick himself had many styles of handwriting, and used many different pens – his table was 'littered with quill pens', noted the *New Era* article. And he was prone to some unusual affectations of style.

Early in my research I travelled to the Isle of Wight, and was fortu-nate to acquire a copy of the postcard overleaf. At the time I had no idea how rare examples of Maybrick's correspondence would prove to be. Anyway, something about the handwriting in the address to Maybrick's niece Doris in Liverpool focused my attention, and it won't take the reader a moment to realise what it was. When you spot it, you're looking at my first abstruse but possible link between Michael Maybrick and Jack.

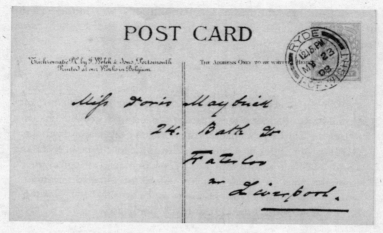

It is of course 'Mifs' for 'Miss', spelled with the long or medial 's', as in 'Bofs' for 'Boss' in many of Jack the Ripper's letters. 'Dear Bofs' is at the head of a letter addressed to Warren at Scotland Yard on 10 November 1888, the day after the murder of Mary Jane Kelly. Scrawled in thick blue pencil and purporting to have been sent 'From Hell', it is largely illegible, and characteristically has no stamp.

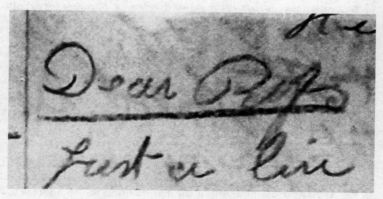

According to the Department of Manuscripts at the Victoria and Albert Museum, the use of an 'f' for 's' was obsolete by the beginning of the nineteenth century, 'discarded in favour of the ordinary S and seldom seen after 1800 except as an affectation'.[17]

This is interesting, because 'an affectation' is an ego thing, a kind of written vanity. I went after it, and the V&A was right. By the late nineteenth century the long 's' was regarded as effete, but was not entirely extinct, its use confined to the sort of gentleman who considered himself of particular merit. Abraham Lincoln's son Robert, who would serve as ambassador to London from 1889 to 1893, used it, as did the Queen's Lord Chief Justice, Lord Coleridge. It was a grandiloquent statement of *self*. Amongst the riff-raff it was non-existent. It was certainly never used by the barely literate, any more than it would have been common to a chimpanzee writing home.

I was intrigued by 'Bofs', because this 'f' for 's' turns up all over the Ripper correspondence. We get 'clafs' for class and 'pafs' for pass from Jack, and most notably 'businefs' for 'business' from Michael Maybrick.

I didn't believe for a second that 'Dear Bofs' was the work of a ham-fisted oaf. Rather, it was an obvious and artful contrivance.

Here's another example, received by the City Police about a week before Eddowes' pillaged kidney was so dramatically to reappear. Once again it has all the hallmarks of a venomous piss-take. It spells 'can't' as 'cunt', and, in a sort of cod Scottish vernacular, 'house' as 'hoos' (like the stage-Irish 'sor' for 'sir').

… from mi youar frend … Wat if [is] a frend too mi … der if [is] agrat sicret … inded after i left … My self a tropi … Ring and of a tropi …

It seemed to me that this unsigned contribution was referring to Eddowes' kidney and Chapman's similarly missing rings. Either way, it demonstrates an artifice that betrays the calligraphy. No struggling illiterate is going to use a median 's' with handwriting that looks like a louse crawling in ink.

Irrespective of 'f' for 's', Maybrick indulged further idiosyncrasies, often under- and overlining capitals in his text. We see it on the postcard to his niece, over the 'W' in 'Waterloo', and it's well demonstrated in the many contracts signed between himself and his publisher John Boosey.

Two peculiarities are of note in one such contract: the under- and overlining of the capital 'H' in 'Hero', and the affectation of a spur on the capital 'S'.

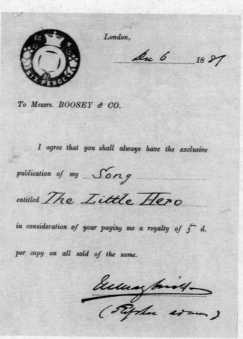

London,

Dec 6 18 87

To Messrs. BOOSEY & CO.

I agree that you shall always have the exclusive

publication of my Song

entitled The Little Hero

in consideration of your paying me a royalty of 5 *d.*

per copy on all sold of the same.

Both signed Maybrick (Stephen Adams), here's another, with a capital 'L' under- and overlined, and spurs on two capital 'S's:

I agree that you shall always have the exclusive

publication of my Song

entitled "Sprung a Leak"

in consideration of your paying me a royalty of 5 d.

per copy on all sold of the same

Compare these with a letter from the Ripper dated 8 October 1888 – again featuring spurs on the 'S':

Identical affectations appear on a postcard addressed to Major (in fact Superintendent) Foster of the City Police:

We have an under- and overlined capital 'M' in 'Major', and every capital 'S' in the text is decorated with a spur:

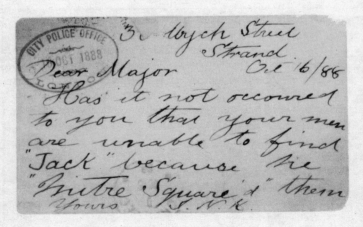

October 16 1888

Dear Major

Has it not occoured to you that your men are unable to find "Jack"
because he "Mitre Square'd" them

    Yours J. N. K.

The letter was mailed on 16 October, to coincide with Lusk's receipt
of the kidney. 'Mitre Square'd' is a transparent reference to
Freemasonry.[18] According to this correspondent, it wasn't only
Eddowes who got the Masonic treatment, it was all Jack's victims,
inculcating a collective blindness in the Met, and the reason its men
were unable to find Jack. In other words, it's Masonry that's hiding
him. I think this text supports the proposition that Eddowes was
intentionally cajoled into Mitre Square to play by the rules of the
'Funny Little Game'.

    The inverted 'V V' marks cut in her face were not in the public
domain for another hundred years, and outside the authorities
there is no way that anyone but her assassin could have known about
them – no one, that is, except an 'accomplice' of the Ripper by the
name of M. Baynard. Jack had obviously told him about the compass
joke 'on the square', because he includes it here as a mocking
gesture at the bottom left-hand corner.

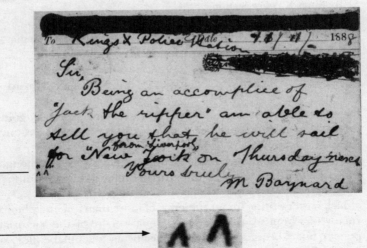

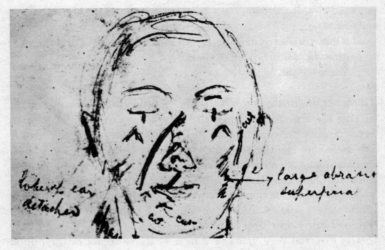

Curious that Ripperology doesn't leap to its feet at this as it does over 'Tin Matchbox Empty'. If nobody could have known about the tin matchbox prior to 1987, how does M. Baynard know about the inverted 'V V' in 1888?

11/11/1888

To: Kings X Police Station
Sir,
    Being an accomplice of "Jack the ripper" am able to tell you that
he will sail from Liverpool, for "New York" on Thursday next
                              Yours truly
                                            M Baynard

'New York' is in inverted commas because he isn't actually going there, although another letter quite possibly is. We shall be returning to M. Baynard in due course.

These letters are not about the handwriting, but a train of thought with a spiteful grin and a lot of pens. To understand their author's thinking, it's necessary to understand his targets.

Jack wasn't writing for an audience of more than a century hence (many of whom would affect a myopia worthy of the Victorian police), but to be understood then, specifically to taunt, bewilder or personally sting the hamstrung comedians pretending to hunt him.

Virtually everything he wrote was intended to ridicule the 'authorities', most especially senior policemen, to whom he referred as 'po-lice' in a caveman's hand, and then as 'po-lice' as a copperplate man, on 15 and 23 October respectively.

In best Neanderthal style, the following letter is in fact a sophisticated lampoon:

> November 5/88
> London
>
> Sir
>
> From the shoe black at. 11. o.clock this morning I saw A man go in to mr Barclay & son he had A bag in his hand and it snap open and I saw to feet and A head of A human Person he had A large knife in his pockit. at the corner of farringdon st and fleet Lane yours truly
>
> andy-handy

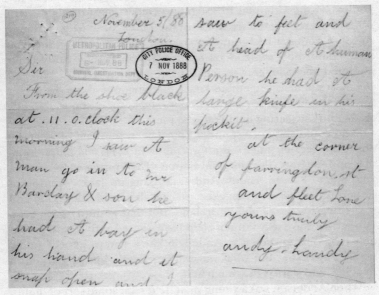

This apparently meaningless hoax came through the letterbox at Scotland Yard on 6 November 1888. At a glance it looks like the work of a half-wit. But I'm not looking at the writing. I'm looking at the thinking. As with Warren and his wall, this letter demonstrates an inside knowledge of its target's past, and is infinitely more cunning than its handwriting. What we have here is a joke within a joke. A couple of weeks before this letter was mailed, *Punch* aimed a jibe at the CID and its founder, Howard Vincent. His outfit (under Anderson) was such a waste of time, the magazine printed his name backwards.

No. 1.—Of what use was VINCENT HOWARD in the Detective Department?
No. 2.—Of what use is he anywhere?
. *A prize will be given for a moderately satisfactory solution of either of the above conundrums.*

Jack despised religion, and enjoyed belittling the religion of others, Charles Warren in particular, but in this case it's Warren's pious sidekick Anderson who gets the sacrilegious taunt. Of immediate note is the signature. The writer didn't sign himself 'andy-handy' by accident. He meant it to mean something, and in the context of the Criminal Investigation Department it might seem obvious. Reversing the name (as in the *Punch* joke) we get 'Handy Andy', a fictional Irish buffoon starring eponymously in a comic novel published in 1858 by Samuel Lover. Handy Andy is an all-round idiot who gets into all sorts of scrapes: 'A fellow who had the most singularly ingenious knack of doing everything the wrong way. So the nickname the neighbours stuck upon him was Handy Andy, and the jeering jingle pleased them.'[19]

Who could this correspondent have been thinking of when he chose the 'jeering jingle'? Born in Dublin in 1841, and unquestionably an Irish idiot, the chief of London's CID springs to mind. As a role model I think 'Handy Andy' was bang on Jack's opinion of Robert Anderson, an evangelical twerp with a head full of God and a loathing for the people of Ireland. But that wouldn't have been enough for the Saucy Purger. He'd have wanted a sting in it, preferably religious, to stick it to Anderson like a stamp. I knew 'Andy' meant Anderson, but what was the key to the insult? I couldn't imagine, and started to scratch at it.

When Anderson was a young man he'd seen some sort of 'light', and considered a career in the cloth. 'It's astonishing when I think of the number of people who have been saved,' wrote the Lord's young salesman. Proffering salvation, he tramped about Sligo with another religious fanatic, preaching the sort of stuff you're better advised to keep to yourself.

Anderson's God was embraced by the Irish like a finger down the throat. 'The evangelists were treated to a crusade of abuse and ridicule,' observed the missionary's son and biographer, 'one newspaper accusing them of preaching for filthy lucre' – and of getting their tainted funds from London.

Anderson's back-up on the stump was a pea-eyed oddity called George Trench, whose lucubrations were so welcome that the Micks stabbed his horse to death under him.[20]

When Trench had had enough he left for home, writes Anderson Junior. 'Some doggerel verses in a newspaper, described the quarrel which led the "Trencher" to desert his pal, "Handy Andy".'[21]

Anderson had acquired a nickname, and herein was Jack's joke. 'Handy Andy' was about as insulting as the Irish could get, and it would do just as well for the Ripper. Resurrecting and reversing the 'jeering jingle' to make it even more foolish appealed to Jack's sense of fun, reminding the chief of London's CID that he was, and remained, a public laughing stock.

Anderson

Trench

But Anderson was not in the league of the Masonic zombie running the show. Let's kick this off with a recurring Warren theme. 'Next one I cop I'll send you the toes and earols for your supper,' says Jack, and continuing this cannibalistic motif, we shift into an area where Warren himself becomes the dinner.

7. 11. 88.

Dear Boss

I am writing you this while I am in bed with a sore throat but as soon as it is better I will set to work again on the 13th of this month, and I think that my next job will be to polish you off and as I am a member of the force I can soon settle accounts with you, I will tear your liver out before you are dead and show it to you. And I will have your kidneys out also and frie them with pepper and salt and send them to Lord Salisbury as it is just the sort of thing that will suit that old Jew and I will cut of your toes and slice off your behind and make macaroni soup of them and I will hide your body in the houses of parliament so you grey headed old pig say your prayers before I am ready ...

'Frie' is the usual nonsense, while the more difficult words 'parliament' and 'macaroni' are spelled correctly. The text comes with some artwork: 'this is your portrait.'

Ten days later a similarly inspired wag sent a portrait of himself:

'Heres my photo Im considered
a very handsome Gentleman'

These triangular little bodies in profile, with legs at opposite corners and an identical rearward tilt, are unquestionably drawn by the same hand. Neither was ever published, so the first could not have influenced the second. They look like the work of a ten-year-old – 'Charlie and Jack', stars of the Ripper Show, one having a bad time and the other the time of his life. Their creator is certainly having fun with the calligraphy. The handwriting in the first letter, with the drawing of Warren (7 November), is crude but conventional. That in the second, with the self-portrait (16 November), is more informal, accelerating from the quasi-literate into a full freaked-out, Kürten-like explosive mess.

Predicated on the drawings, it is *absolutely certain* that these letters were written by the same man. Thus, different handwriting does not mean a different author.

Permutations of artifice rage in Jack's correspondence, hallmarks of a singular breeding-place of thought. The letters are not one-offs from a reservoir of oafs stationed throughout the land, but an interconnected narrative, no less relevant to understanding the psyche of the Ripper than the links between the murders themselves.

The joker who sent in the portrait of Warren writes only about Warren, while in identical vein, the same man who sent in a 'photo' of himself writes only about himself, and has one or two interesting things to say:

> I live in George St, very comfortably. I'm 30 years old, tall and dark
> ... if you can't find me you're a lot of fools
> Yours Truly Joe the cats meat man
> Look out old Charlie Warren
> Heres my photo Im considered a very handsome Gentleman

The writer locates himself not in Whitechapel, but in one of the more salubrious areas of London's West End. George Street runs parallel to Regent Street, connecting Conduit Street to Hanover Square – where in 1884 Michael Maybrick claimed residence at the Arts Club. Maybrick's niece Amy Maine's judgement of her uncle as 'exceptionally handsome'[22] was shared by his music publisher John Boosey, whose offices were about a minute's walk away, at 295 Regent Street.[23]

To get traction on these letters I needed something that connected the Ripper to this area. At the same time I was looking for something to connect the Ripper to Warren, some hidden link they may have shared. It was simple enough in terms of my candidate – both he and Warren, for example, could be found at the Savage Club, and both were members of the United Services Club. But I needed something more specific, and therefore by definition more difficult. I was looking for a letter that could be related to Warren and just as easily to Michael Maybrick. In other words, a letter with the Ripper as pig-in-the-middle.

Superficially, Warren and Maybrick had much in common. Both were top-end gents of the Establishment, both liked uniforms, Warren in the togs of the Royal Engineers, Maybrick the Artists Volunteers. Both were generals – Warren for real, Maybrick as an adopted nickname: he called himself 'Blucher', after the famous Prussian general who saved Wellington's reputation at the Battle of

Waterloo. The great Blücher was an ardent Freemason, as were Warren and Maybrick. But perhaps most curious of all, both the policeman and the musician owed their fame to Jerusalem: Warren for digging under it, and Maybrick for his hit composition about it, 'The Holy City'.

The novelist and fellow founder of the Quatuor Coronati, Walter Besant, put it down for Charlie: 'It is certain that nothing will ever be done in the future to compare with what was done by Warren. Whatever else may be done, his name will always be associated with the Holy City which he first recovered.'

Ditto for Maybrick. The sheet music for 'The Holy City' made it the best-selling song of the entire nineteenth century.[24]

To judge by Jack's surviving letters, the weeders had burnt the midnight oil. I believe the 'Yack the Ripper' envelope referred to earlier survived because they didn't understand it. No civil servant is going to sit there scratching it over an anonymous 'hoaxer's' use of the word 'Yack'. This one crept through with its Freemasonry intact. But I was looking for something else.

I was looking for a letter that expressed some sort of specific association between Warren and Maybrick. The Ripper had to have made mistakes, and the weeders censoring in his wake had to have missed more than just 'Yack'. In fact they missed much more. But Conduit Street was one of the first links I found.

London W

Dear Boss

Back again & up to the old tricks. Would you like to catch me? I guess you would well look here – I leave my diggings – close to Conduit St to night at about 10.30 watch Conduit St & close round there – Ha-Har I dare you 4 more lives four more cunts to add to my little collection & I shall rest content

Do what you will you will never trap

Jack the Ripper

Watch P.C. 60 C. light moustache shaven clean rather stout he can tell you almost as much as I can

G.F.S. [crossed through]
F place. R. St. W.

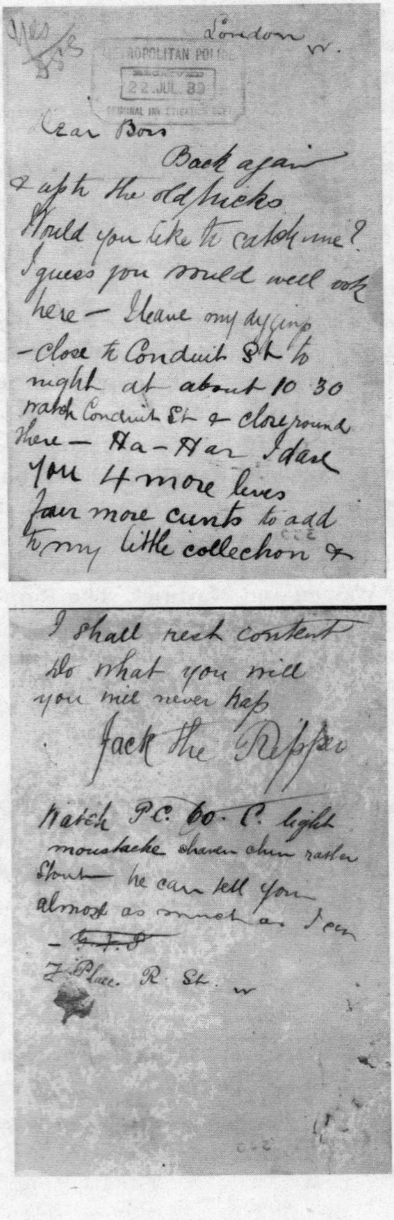

London W.

METROPOLITAN POLICE
RECEIVED
22 JUL 89
CRIMINAL INVESTIGATION DEPT.

Dear Boss

Back again & up to the old tricks Would you like to catch me? I guess you would well look here — I have my digging — close to Conduit St to night at about 10 30 watch Conduit St & close round there — Ha — Ha — I have you 4 more lives four more cunts to add to my little collection &

I shall rest content Do what you will you will never hap

Jack the Ripper

Watch P.C. 60. C. light moustache shaven chin rather stout — he can tell you almost as much as I can — J.T.R.
Z. Place. R. St. W

At the time of the murders, the Post Office listed 28,000 streets in London; and out of all those, the Ripper chose to draw attention to Conduit Street.

A more dramatic opposite to Whitechapel you couldn't get. Conduit Street links Bond Street with Regent Street, right at the heart of London's West End. Piccadilly is to the south, and within two minutes you can be drinking champagne at the Café Royal.

Jack's interest in Conduit Street became my interest. Why would a man signing himself 'Jack the Ripper' shift his thinking so purposefully away from the East End?

The geography is intriguing. Eight months after the 'tall and dark … very handsome Gentleman' had nominated George Street as his place of residence, this correspondent had put himself in precisely the same area. We had one Ripper that lived in George Street, and another who was apparently to be seen that night in a street running into it. What was the story here?

Arts Club   George Street   Conduit Street

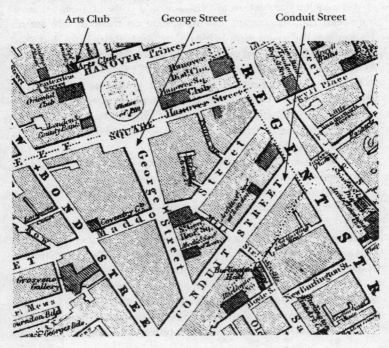

This Conduit Street letter was received by the Met about a week after the murder of Alice McKenzie in Castle Alley, Whitechapel, on the night of 17 July 1889. Warren had slung his hook the previous December. Although he was no longer Boss Cop, Jack had continued writing to him. 'Back again & up to the old tricks' is a reference to the apparent lull in activity since the atrocity of Mary Kelly on the morning of 9 November 1888, which had finally forced Warren to resign. As far as the public were conditioned to believe, Kelly was last of the series, 'investigation' replaced by 'mystery', and flogged off as such by Ripperology to this day. We will come to Kelly by and by. Meanwhile, let us try to unravel this 'R(egent) St(reet) W(est)'.

As is well established, Warren, like Anderson, was an Evangelical Christian, which I imagine would have put a smirk on the Purger's chops. The departed Boss was a Bible-driven Masonic archaeologist, so it was no great leap in thinking to wonder if 'diggings' could be anything to do with his archaeological activities under Solomon's Temple in the Holy City.

Were such a connection to exist, it would consolidate my reasoning about the obliteration of the writing on the wall. Solomon's Temple was the inspiration behind that (and all the lying that went with it). Was Yack joking over something similar in Conduit Street? And if so, where did it fit in the 'Funny Little Game'?

I could see two possible reasons for Jack's use of the word 'diggings'. Could it be a pun on 'digs', where the Ripper might have a residential connection? Or did it refer to an archaeological investigation – 'diggings' – where the connection might be Bro Warren's? It turned out to be both.

At 9 Conduit Street was the Society of Biblical Archaeology. Post Office records reveal that its Secretary was a Mr W.H. Rylands. Did that name mean anything to me? It most certainly did. He was Bro William Harry Rylands, First Senior Warden and founder member of Warren's Quatuor Coronati Lodge of Masonic Research. In terms of seniority, he was second only to Warren himself (see opposite).

Warren was Number 1 on the exalted list, and Rylands Number 2; thus 9 Conduit Street had become an interesting address.

As Secretary of the Society of Biblical Archaeology and past Grand Steward of Quatuor Coronati, Rylands kept a foot in both camps. Others were similarly disposed: William Simpson, Number 9 in Quatuor Coronati and its Worshipful Master, was Honorary Librarian

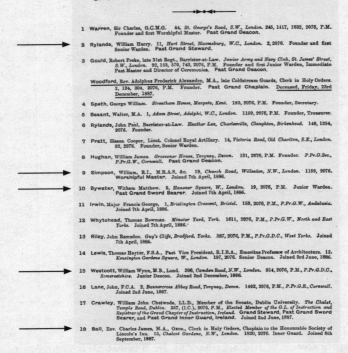

Members of the Lodge in the Order of their Seniority.

1 Warren, Sir Charles, G.C.M.G. 44, *St. George's Road, S.W., London.* 245, 1417, 1832, 2076, P.M. Founder and first Worshipful Master. Past Grand Deacon.

2 Rylands, William Harry. 11, *Hart Street, Bloomsbury, W.C., London.* 2, 2076. Founder and first Senior Warden. Past Grand Steward.

3 Gould, Robert Freke, late 31st Regt., Barrister-at-Law. *Junior Army and Navy Club, St. James' Street, S.W., London.* 92, 153, 570, 743, 2076, P.M. Founder and first Junior Warden, Immediate Past Master and Director of Ceremonies. Past Grand Deacon.

Woodford, Rev. Adolphus Frederick Alexander, M.A., late Coldstream Guards, Clerk in Holy Orders. 2, 124, 304, 2076, P.M. Founder. Past Grand Chaplain. Deceased, Friday, 23rd December, 1887.

4 Speth, George William. *Streatham House, Margate, Kent.* 183, 2076, P.M. Founder, Secretary.

5 Besant, Walter, M.A. 1, *Adam Street, Adelphi, W.C., London.* 1159, 2076, P.M. Founder, Treasurer.

6 Rylands, John Paul, Barrister-at-Law. *Heather Lea, Charlesville, Claughton, Birkenhead.* 148, 1354, 2076. Founder.

7 Pratt, Sisson Cooper, Lieut. Colonel Royal Artillery. 14, *Victoria Road, Old Charlton, S.E., London.* 92, 2076. Founder, Senior Warden.

8 Hughan, William James. *Grosvenor House, Torquay, Devon.* 131, 2076, P.M. Founder. P.Pr.G.Sec., P.Pr.G.W., *Cornwall.* Past Grand Deacon.

9 Simpson, William, R.I., M.R.A.S., &c. 19, *Church Road, Willesden, N.W., London.* 1159, 2076. Worshipful Master. Joined 7th April, 1886.

10 Bywater, Witham Matthew. 5, *Hanover Square, W., London.* 19, 2076, P.M. Junior Warden. Past Grand Sword Bearer. Joined 7th April, 1886.

11 Irwin, Major Francis George. 1, *Brislington Crescent, Bristol.* 153, 2076, P.M., P.Pr.G.W., *Andalusia.* Joined 7th April, 1886.

12 Whytehead, Thomas Bowman. *Minster Yard, York.* 1611, 2076, P.M., P.Pr.G.W., *North and East Yorks.* Joined 7th April, 1886.

13 Riley, John Ramsden. *Guy's Cliffe, Bradford, Yorks.* 387, 2076, P.M., P.Pr.G.D.C., *West Yorks.* Joined 7th April, 1886.

14 Lewis, Thomas Hayter, F.S.A., Past Vice President, R.I.B.A., Emeritus Professor of Architecture. 12, *Kensington Gardens Square, W., London.* 197, 2076. Senior Deacon. Joined 3rd June, 1886.

15 Westcott, William Wynn, M.B., Lond. 396, *Camden Road, N.W., London.* 814, 2076, P.M., P.Pr.G.D.C., *Somersetshire.* Junior Deacon. Joined 2nd December, 1886.

16 Lane, John, F.C.A. 2, *Bannercross Abbey Road, Torquay, Devon.* 1402, 2076, P.M., P.Pr.G.R., *Cornwall.* Joined 2nd June, 1887.

17 Crawley, William John Chetwode, LL.D., Member of the Senate, Dublin University. *The Chalet, Temple Road, Dublin.* 357, (I.C.), 2076, P.M. Elected Member of the G.L. of Instruction and Registrar of the Grand Chapter of Instruction, Ireland. Grand Steward, Past Grand Sword Bearer, and Past Grand Inner Guard, Ireland. Joined 2nd June, 1887.

18 Ball, Rev. Charles James, M.A., Oxon., Clerk in Holy Orders, Chaplain to the Honourable Society of Lincoln's Inn. 15, *Chalcot Gardens, N.W., London.* 1820, 2076. Inner Guard. Joined 8th September, 1887.

of the Biblical Archaeologists, and the Reverend Charles Ball, Number 18 in the Quatuor Coronati, was a council member (see overleaf).

Lifting the lid on the SBA revealed not only the Masonic link between Warren and Conduit Street, but some interesting ancillary names. We're at the nucleus of the British Establishment. Bro Lord Halsbury is an egregious example. This most accommodating of government lawyers was also Grand Warden of English Freemasons. Not a few of the names in evidence have, or are about to have, an unwitting place in Jack's narrative, not least Bro William Wynn Westcott, to whom Jack would dedicate a murdered child. There is also Bro Witham Matthew Bywater, Number 10 in the Quatuor Coronati, who had the distinction of being Grand Sword Bearer in Michael Maybrick's Orpheus Chapter.

Bywater and Rylands were as close to Warren as they proved close to my candidate. Rylands was not only a leading member of Warren's

COUNCIL, 1888-9.

President

P. LE PAGE RENOUF.

Vice-Presidents

Rev. Frederick Charles Cook, M.A., Canon of Exeter.
Lord Halsbury, The Lord High Chancellor.
. The Right Hon. W. E. Gladstone, M.P., D.C.L., &c.
The Right Hon. Sir A. H. Layard, G.C.B., &c.
The Right Rev. J. B. Lightfoot, D.D., &c., Bishop of Durham.
Walter Morrison, M.P.
Sir Charles T. Newton, K.C.B., D.C.L., &c., &c.
Sir Charles Nicholson, Bart., D.C.L., M.D., &c., &c.
Rev. George Rawlinson, D.D., Canon of Canterbury.
Sir Henry C. Rawlinson, K.C.B., D.C.L., F.R.S., &c.
Very Rev. Robert Payne Smith, Dean of Canterbury.

Council

Rev. Charles James Ball.	Prof. A. Macalister, M.D.
Rev. Canon Beechey, M.A.	Rev. James Marshall.
E. A. Wallis Budge, M.A.	F. D. Mocatta, F.S.A.
Arthur Cates.	Alexander Peckover, F.S.A.
Thomas Christy, F.L.S.	J. Pollard.
Rev. R. Gwynne.	F. G. Hilton Price, F.S.A.
Charles Harrison, F.S.A.	E. Towry Whyte, M.A.
Rev. Albert Löwy.	Rev. W. Wright, D.D.

Honorary Treasurer—Bernard T. Bosanquet.

Secretary—W. Harry Rylands, F.S.A.

Honorary Secretary for Foreign Correspondence—Rev. R. Gwynne, M.A.

Honorary Librarian—William Simpson, F.R.G.S.

Quatuor Coronati and Secretary to the Biblical Archaeologists, but also an officer of the Supreme Chapter of Royal Arch Masons, a covenant whose Grand Organist was Michael Maybrick.

I determined that my criteria for the link between Warren and Maybrick had to be non-negotiable. I wasn't simply looking for an affiliation between a pair of Freemasons, but something more definitive, putting both Maybrick *and* the Ripper in Conduit Street.

This isn't *me* choosing a street. It's supposed to be a 'hoaxer'. And out of all the streets in London, he's hit on one with potent associations to Warren. That's about a 28,000-to-one shot. If this could be dismissed as coincidence, I'd like to up the odds a little.

'Watch Conduit St & close round there,' taunts Jack. I looked where he suggested, at Conduit Street, and found my candidate.

As I've indicated, archive material *vis à vis* Michael Maybrick is very rare. There is no collection of Maybrick/Adams, as there is for every one of his equally famous contemporaries. After much research I was in possession of but one Michael Maybrick letter, and it turned out to be the lucky one. The address at which it was written is given as 9 Conduit Street, meaning its author sharing the same front door with Rylands' outfit. 'Digs' and 'diggings' had coalesced, and I had my Warren/Ripper/Maybrick connection.

It's from this letter that I discovered Maybrick's epithet for singing as 'the shouting business' – or rather 'businefs': the entire text is written with the median 'f' for 's'.

I don't know at exactly what date Michael Maybrick was in residence at 9 Conduit Street, or what he was doing in the same building as the Society of Biblical Archaeology. Maybe he kept rooms there – a rehearsal room, or a West End *pied-à-terre*? What's incontestable is that Conduit Street was as clearly in the picture to Maybrick as it was to Jack the Ripper.

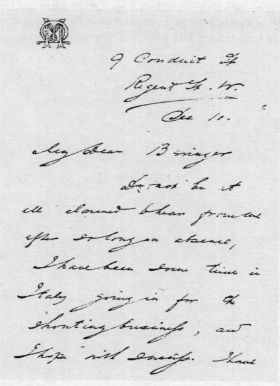

The letter is addressed to 'My dear Berringer', and is too long to reproduce in full. Dated Dec[ember] 10, it's unfortunately without a year, although the typeface of the colophon – an 'M' along with a round-topped 'M' – is typical of the 1880s, and virtually identical with a round-topped 'M' of 1889 as used by the Artists Volunteers.

The Ripper had described himself as a 'tall, handsome man', with an undisclosed association to Conduit Street. Michael Maybrick was a tall, handsome man, with an address in Conduit Street. In one of his letters the state-protected maggot brags, 'It'll be a clever man who catches me.' I think you overestimate yourself, Jack. You and the laughable guardians of your anonymity seem as transparent to me as any shop window in Regent Street, London, West.

But let us stay with the Biblical theme – which, with Warren as its muse, the Ripper certainly did. Warren's Biblical digging gives a natural segue back into his archaeological exploits in the Holy Land (the Land of Moab, to be precise), and an embarrassing event there that would have tickled Jack pink.

12

The Mouth of
the Maggot

For murder, though it have no tongue, will speak with
most miraculous organ.

Hamlet

The Land of the Moabites has classic unsavoury Old Testament origins: 'And it came to pass, God destroyed the cities of the plain.' (I can't help wondering whether this destruction wasn't as a result of earthquakes releasing storms of flammable, religious-looking petroleum gas, 3,500 years before oil companies got in on the act.) Mix such flaming erudition with lightning and simple minds, and you've got a decent amount of 'wrath'. Ditto a supply of gas to 'the Burning Bush'.

Anyway, fearful of the fiery skies and quakes, the righteous citizen Lot had gone up into the mountains suffering the fear. When he got to the new location he lived in a cave with his two daughters, neither of whom had a husband. Both were worried about the preservation of their race. 'There is not a man in the earth to come in unto us,' the elder of them said. Therefore they devised a plan to get their dad rat-arsed on wine and take it in turns to fuck him. 'Behold, I lay yesternight with my father,' said the elder. 'Let us make him drink wine this night also; and thou go in and lie with him that we may preserve the seed of our father.' The younger one went in that night and got on with it, and 'Thus were both the daughters of Lot with child by their father and the first born bore a son and called his name Moab.'

About 3,500 years later, in August 1868, a Frenchman called Frederick Augustus Klein was in the area. Klein was a reverend attached to the Anglican Mission in Jerusalem. He was on his way up the eastern side of the Dead Sea, and stopped for rest one night in a town called Dhiban. A friendly-looking Arab pitched up and asked him if he wanted to see something no white man had ever seen before. Had the Arab been wearing a mackintosh, Klein might well have declined. However, he followed him into some ruins, where a large basalt slab was located. 'This stone,' recorded Klein, 'was lying amongst the ruins of Dhiban, perfectly free and exposed to view, the inscription uppermost.' Miraculously, the stone was in perfect condition. It was the inscription, of course, that was of interest, written in a very ancient script which, according to his guide, nobody had ever been able to decipher.

Mr Klein had just discovered the 'Moabite Stone'.[1]

Various European legations operated out of Jerusalem, and Klein went through the doors of one. A pro-German citizen of Strasbourg, he laid the news of his discovery on the German archaeological equivalent of Charles Warren, a Freemason called Dr Heinrich Petermann. He was the very same man who had risked it with Warren in the bowels of Solomon's Temple, consecrating the unique Masonic lodge, 'Warren's Lodge', under the place where the three Assassins had murdered Hiram Abiff. Petermann immediately went about the business of securing the stone for his national museum. All this was conducted in utter secrecy, a bunch of Nubian thugs being hired by Petermann to guard his new treasure.

By the time Warren got whisper of it all the ingredients for a bitter controversy were in place. Facilitated by Sir George Grove and the Palestine Exploration Fund in London, Warren managed to bungle up an environment wherein the precious artefact was destroyed.

The Arabs would have sold the stone to anyone who wanted it for fifty cents, but by now the French also had wind of it. All this colonial interest aroused Muslim suspicion, and they started to get defensive. Warren went out to Dhiban one night, and there was a punch-up on the shore of the Dead Sea – 'Blows were exchanged,' says his biographer.

Make no mistake, it was the Germans' stone. Petermann had actually secured its purchase and permission to transport it out of the country. That didn't stop the British and the French from wanting it, or at least an impression of it, for their own national museums. It all got bitter, as everybody wanted a part of somebody else's history. In obliging mood, the sons of Lot freaked out and smashed the thing to bits, resulting in plenty of shattered pieces to go around.

This was bad enough. Back in London, Sir George Grove made it worse. On 8 February 1869 he published a letter in *The Times*, claiming that Warren 'has made a discovery that promises to be of great importance'. In fact Warren had discovered nothing, but by his interference he had had quite a lot to do with the stone's demise. This was of little consequence to Grove, who ploughed on with his eulogy: 'A few months ago, Captain Warren heard of a stone in the old country of Moab. The stone was then whole, but on finding that the Franks [Europeans] were enquiring for it, the Arabs broke it up into several fragments, which they hid in the granaries of their neighbouring villages.'[2]

Sir George's letter went off like a bit of a bomb in Jerusalem, and Warren was transformed overnight into an international pariah. 'It threw a completely false and discreditable light on Warren's actions,' lathered Watkin Williams. As far as his grandson was concerned, Warren was a Victorian giant, bestriding an inviolate plinth. Where there was fault it was always somebody else's – in this case Grove's: 'By claiming him as the discoverer it put him wrong with Klein, it put him wrong with the Germans generally leaving them to infer that he had meddled in their affairs, it proclaimed to the British public that his enquiries had caused the destruction of the Stone, and that he had allowed the greater part of his discovery to pass into the hands of another nation.'[3]

All this was true, of course. With customary cack-handedness Warren had botched it. The French managed to get the stone, restore it, translate it, and shove it up in the Louvre. Petermann's rage, shared by his countrymen (who, as history would have it, were presently engaged in a war with the French, and besieging Paris), was described by Williams as 'irritation in German quarters'. 'When I saw [Grove's] letter,' wrote Warren with some honour, 'I saw but one course before me. I wrote home and resigned my connection with the Palestine Exploration Fund.'[4]

It was all very sore indeed. But there was another element here that didn't get into the pages of Watkin Williams's book. Ever shy of his hero's Freemasonry, he neglected to mention the personal hurt this affair brought upon Warren. The fraternal bond between himself and Petermann was now smashed as surely as the stone itself. Grove had driven a wedge into the event of a lifetime, and it must have cut Warren to the quick.

'Warren's Lodge', with its carved compasses and whatnot, together with the catastrophe of the 'Moabite Stone' were among the Commissioner's most indelible memories, and were also to become an irresistible inspiration for Jack. Just as 'Juwes' had its source in the gloom of Warren's past, so too would a funny little joke over 'Moab'.

When Warren wasn't digging, he was writing about digging. Before his summary disassociation from the PEF (happily later repaired) he had contributed a variety of papers for publication. The Fund produced quarterly statements, in which Captain Warren's expertise was generously in evidence. In a table of 'Conversion of Hebrew Sounds into Amharic' (1876), we find his explication of '3' (or something similar beyond the capacity of my typewriter): 'where pronounced hard in Hebrew it seems to have become Qaf in Arabic, which is vulgarly pronounced as a hard "G" – instance – Gedoroth – Katrah'.[5]

This from a man who couldn't work out 'Juwes' on an East End wall. Warren's overriding passion, of course, was buried in the subterranean mysteries of Solomon's Temple. It was the myth or reality of Hiram that had driven his shovel in those perilous foundations. What was the truth of it all? Then, as now, Freemasons looked for substance in the Hiram Abiff tradition.

At Shadwell Clerke's consecration of the Quatuor Coronati on 8 November 1886, Bro Hayter Lewis read a paper, 'On an Early Version of the Hiramic Legend', a theme taken up by Warren himself at the formal inauguration on 3 March 1887: 'My object this evening is to call attention to the orientation of Temples, with special reference to the Temple of Solomon and the Master Mason's Lodge.'

An erudite dissertation followed, Biblical sources welded into Warren's antediluvian perceptions of Masonry. He thought it was as old as the hills – at any rate, not much their junior. 'With all mankind the Deity first abode in Heaven,' he said, and the closest you could get to it was the mountaintops where sacrifices were made. 'But as the worship of the heathen gradually degenerated', the people began to look upon these high places 'as the occasional haunts of the Gods'. It was primitive man who kept God at high altitudes, and it was Solomon who was to change all that. In a dream 'God promised him the gift of wisdom', and he came to realise that the hitherto stratospheric omnipotence could handle business just as easily at ground level. The rising of the sun in the east, and its setting in the west, could be represented by symbol in the artifice of a great building. 'Behold the Glory of the God of Israel came from the way of the East.' *Ergo*, Solomon's Temple and the subsequent orientation of every Masonic lodge thereafter. 'The key to the whole subject,' declaimed Warren, 'may be found in the book of Ezekiel.'[6]

Ezekiel is a name to be remembered. The Ripper was to use the Book of Ezekiel as a virtual workshop manual in orchestration of the destruction he visited upon Mary Kelly. No prophet in the Bible is of more interest to Freemasonry than Ezekiel; or, by the time we get to Kelly, of more interest to me.

Meanwhile, Warren continued to argue his case, quoting again from the Book of Solomon: 'Then spake Solomon. The Lord said he would dwell in thick darkness. I have *surely built thee an house* [my emphasis] to dwell in, a settled place for Thee to abide in forever. And Solomon stood before the altar of the Lord in the presence of all the congregation of Israel, and spread forth his hands towards heaven and said, Behold [the House of the Lord].'[7]

Inevitably, Warren moved on to this temple's architect and builder, Hiram Abiff: 'I have come to the conclusion that our legends are of an ancient date and have a substantial basis … I put forward as a solution that modern Masonry is a combination of the mysteries of the Hebrews, the Phoenicians, and the Egyptians, that it thus forms the chief of the triads running so remarkably through all Masonic Lore.'[8]

By the late nineteenth century, however, Masonry's claims to antiquity began to look a bit shaky, its rituals and icons suggesting a more recent provenance. Not a lot stands sure against any objective enquiry, and this includes Hiram Abiff.

Perhaps Hiram was an eighteenth-century fabrication, ripped off from the Old Testament? Bro G.W. Speth, one of the founders of the Quatuor Coronati and Number 4 in its hierarchy, addressed just such a question in *Builders' Rites and Ceremonies: The Folk Lore of Masonry*. His book doesn't do a lot for the mystique of Hiram. It 'not only shows the origin of the present day custom of burying coins under foundation stones, but also gives numerous instances both of "foundation sacrifices" and "completion sacrifices"'. These architectural horrors were based on 'the old idea that stability of an edifice would be best secured *by sacrificially immuring within it, the body of an artificer'*.

Examples of this practice are to be found in the Bible. In Kings 1.16.34, a deluded God-fearer called Hiel the Bethelite buries his firstborn in the foundations of an important building as an amulet to fortune. Not quite confident of the efficacy of this sacrifice, Hiel similarly inters his younger son, Segub, under the city gates. Most hideously, it seems these kids were buried alive. I don't know if Bro Speth had first-hand knowledge of uncovering these Old Testament horrors, but Warren unquestionably did. Such 'foundation sacrifices' were to be discovered all over the forgotten lands of Moab and Midian.

'The widespread custom of "foundation sacrifice" survives in Palestine,' wrote Biblical historian Stanley Crook in 1908, 'when popular opinion required that blood shall be shed at the inauguration of every important new building.' Blood was still gushing at the close of the nineteenth century, although by 1898 (for a jetty at Haifa) it was from a sheep instead of a child.[9]

The children of Solomon's time were not so lucky, particularly as the King was more or less preoccupied with real estate. He built not only at Jerusalem, but at Megiddo, Hazor and Gezer (Kings 9.15). On the site of his great administrative building at Gezer, 'a gruesome discovery was made'. Secreted in the foundations was the skeleton of a young girl – or at least the upper portion of it, for she had been sawn in half. She was estimated to have been about sixteen years old at time of death. Near the mouth of the cistern in which she was discovered were 'the decapitated heads of two girls'. Unfortunately we have no picture of this sacrificial site, but a PEF photograph of another young female skeleton found at another dig gives the gist of it. This one was disinterred with her head intact, and replicating the other, had been ritually sawn in half (see opposite).[10]

Bearing this unfortunate creature in mind, we now shift attention through thirty-five centuries to Charles Warren's new police headquarters on Victoria Embankment. Retaining the name 'Scotland Yard' from its former location, this sprawling edifice was still under construction.

Cue the 'Fiend' and 'Friend' of the Commissioner. What a wheeze it would be to stick one down, in the style of a Moab sacrifice, in the foundations of Charlie's new building, ha ha. Forty-eight hours after

the 'Double Event' and its short-lived message on the wall, a labourer working in the rubble-filled vaults of New Scotland Yard discovered a curious parcel secured with strings. He thought it was discarded bacon, but investigation proved it to be the headless and armless torso of a young woman who had been sawn in half.

This archaeologically inspired piss-take would henceforth be known as 'the Whitehall mystery', or 'the Scotland Yard Trunk mystery'. I'm not going to get into a protracted analysis of its 'investigation', because there wasn't one. Jack's outing into the bowels of New Scotland Yard was a shade too close to the Commissioner's knuckle, and every effort was made to disassociate this outrage from the Ripper. The Met was characteristically 'without a clue'. 'The police never imagined there was any connection with the Whitechapel Murders,' chimes *The A to Z*, 'despite press speculation.'

To dismiss the link with J.T.R. as no more than 'press speculation' is to dismiss the Scotland Yard trunk in its entirety. We have nothing but the press. Jack's ersatz sacrifice certainly can't be examined from Metropolitan Police files, because there aren't any. Not a scrap of contemporaneous paper is to be found: no statements, no interviews, no nothing. This is a crime as audacious as anything Alfred Hitchcock might have dreamed up, literally in the guts of the Commissioner's emerging new headquarters, yet it is without a history?

The nearest we get to archive material is three meagre sheets (MEP05/271) summarising the atrocity as though it were a myth rather than a Ripper reality. Since these pages are dated October 1936, forty-eight years after the event, I imagine even the most acquiescent of 'students' might find them a bit late in the day. This lack of material reveals more than it tries to hide. Although the Met couldn't wash away 'the Scotland Yard Trunk mystery', it was just as hysterically motivated to try to cover it up.

The new police building had been a while in coming. The riverside site had originally been intended for a grand opera house, but the scheme ran into financial difficulties. The backers couldn't afford a roof, and what had been built was demolished. In 1885 the land was acquired by the Receiver of the Metropolitan Police, who went about the business of commissioning a new police headquarters.

A cartoon in *Punch* (1886) tells the dispiriting tale. The state had little use for opera singers, and preferring policemen to Rossini, one of the latter was kicked out in lieu of Warren and his unsteady gang.[11]

AUGUST 14, 1886.] PUNCH, OR THE LONDON CHARIVARI. 75

LAW v. MUSIC.
The site once intended for the New Opera House, on the Victoria Embankment, is to be utilised for the Central Metropolitan Police Offices.—*Daily Paper*.
Policeman X. "WHAT ARE YOU A-DOING A-LOITERING 'ERE? THE PUBLIC DON'T WANT YER, AND I WANT THIS 'ERE GROUND MYSELF! SO COME, MOVE ON!"

Designed by Norman Shaw, one of the leading architects of his age, New Scotland Yard was, according to the *Echo*, 'at the very centre of our civilised community'. Not a stone's throw from the Home Office, 'it is beneath the very shadow of the House of Commons itself'. 'They are the buildings,' waxed the *Echo*, 'which are intended as the new Metropolitan Police Headquarters, the future of our whole protective system!'[12]

The construction of New Scotland Yard was half complete. Scaffolding was up, and nascent stairways disappeared into the gloom of its foundations. Like a medieval dungeon they were a labyrinth of hazard and places where daylight never came. On 2 October 1888, together with his mate, a carpenter called Frederick Wildbore was early into the vaults. For the previous three weeks Wildbore had been working here from Monday to Saturday, hiding his tools overnight in a maze of recesses destined to become cells. In one of them he rediscovered something he'd been aware of in the darkness the day before, but had ignored. A light was struck, and the men found themselves looking at some kind of parcel. About two feet by three feet, wrapped in cloth and bound with strings, it had no smell, nor any attraction, and neither was inclined to touch it. Later that day Wildbore mentioned the find to his foreman, William Brown, who ordered the item to be brought into the light for examination.

SHOCKING DISCOVERY IN WESTMINSTER.

Wildbore returned to the vaults in the company of a bricklayer by the name of George Budden. 'I struck a light,' said Budden, 'and saw the top bare, and the rest wrapped up in some old cloth.' Thinking little of it, he dragged it over a makeshift bridge into a part of the vault where there was daylight. 'A lot of old strings of different sorts were tied up all round it several times across each way.' Budden cut the strings, and to everyone's shock they found themselves looking at the headless upper half of a woman's body. 'I was not alone when the parcel was opened,' he said. 'There were present the Foreman Bricklayer [William Brown] and Wildbore.'[13]

The coppers arrived in short order from nearby King Street, and the Divisional Surgeon was sent for. Whatever was said was said, and down they all went to the recess, where Detective Hawkins (A Division) made a preliminary inspection of the scene. The torso appeared to have been wrapped in some kind of dress material, another piece of which was discovered in the recess. The area where the parcel had been placed was seething with maggots.[14]

By now Dr Thomas Bond had arrived. A Fellow of the Royal College of Surgeons, and Surgeon to the Met since 1867, it was he who was to prepare a report for Robert Anderson, determining that the Whitechapel murders were all the work of the same hand, and that their perpetrator 'must have been a man of physical strength and of great coolness and daring'.

Such qualities were palpably in evidence here. The torso weighed fifty pounds, and how Jack had managed to transport it in unremitting darkness was everyone's puzzle. 'Not only would the risk of detection be very great,' surmised *The Times*, 'but he would also stand a good chance of breaking his neck.' Such peril was corroborated by the workmen. Gaining access to the vault meant crossing a trench on a plank. 'It was so dark, even in daytime,' said Wildbore, 'and people who didn't know the place wouldn't have found their way there.'[15]

Joined by Detective Wren and Inspector Marshall, Dr Bond made a brief examination of the torso before looking about the recess where it had been discovered. 'The wall was stained black at the place where the parcel had rested against it,' he said. 'I thought the body must have been there *several days* [my emphasis] from the state of the wall.'[16]

That evening the coroner's officer delivered the torso to the mortuary at Millbank Street, where Bond made preparations for a postmortem the following day. As it was already in advanced putrefaction, he stored it overnight in spirits of wine.

He wasn't the first to try to preserve it. Although the postmortem was to be conducted in the strictest secrecy, a part of the secret was already out. On 3 October the *Evening News* revealed that the torso had previously been pickled in some strong disinfectant, and correctly considered this a significant lead: 'For weeks he must have kept the body concealed near either his office or apartment, waiting for favourable opportunities to make away with the body piecemeal.'

Implicit in the *News*'s coverage was an understanding that the victim had been butchered at an earlier date, and then preserved at the assassin's discretion until he considered it opportune to transport his mocking handiwork to New Scotland Yard. He chose a time that couldn't have been more embarrassing for Warren. Two days had passed since the outrages of Catherine Eddowes and Elizabeth Stride, and here was another one, mutilated beyond belief and dumped like an insult, under his nose.

'The remains, it is almost certain, were hidden in the building sometime between Saturday evening and Tuesday morning,' determined the *Evening News*. It was a considered assessment, as was its caveat: 'There is now no doubt that a terrible murder has been committed, as from the way in which the body has been treated it is impossible that it could have been spirited away from a dissecting room after having answered the purpose of lawful operation, and a more sickening spectacle than the remains present can hardly be imagined.'

Bond got into it early the following morning. By 8 a.m. on 3 October, he and his assistant Charles Hibbert had begun the mouthwatering process of trying to work out exactly what it was they were looking at. For two hours the doors were locked and the press kept on the other side. Bond was to withhold the details of his findings in deference to the Home Office 'for their guidance at the inquest', scheduled four days hence, under Westminster coroner John Troutbeck. Why civil servants should be offering a physician 'guidance' isn't stated, but more official interference was brewing, and it was to the Home Office that Bond and his notes would go.[17]

Press exclusion naturally didn't quell press interest, and the scraps the papers assembled over the next few days were to prove remarkably accurate. 'The head and neck have been severed at the juncture of the caryical and spinal vertebrae,' reported the *Evening News*, 'the arms have been disarticulated at the shoulder joints, while not only are the legs missing, but the pelvis has been *sawn clean through* [my emphasis], exposing all the viscera, and it is believed the organ referred to in the Chapman case [the womb] is also missing.'

Indeed it was. But in compensation for the missing womb, something else had turned up, or rather found its way into Jack's scenario. About three weeks before, on 11 September, a workman called Frederick Moore had noticed something curious on the mudbank of the Thames, which ran adjacent to his timberyard. A ladder was procured, and a few minutes later he was on his way back up it, carrying a human arm. The limb quickly found itself in the possession of a policeman, who wrapped it in newspaper before transporting it to his station at Gerard Row.[18]

The Divisional Surgeon was called, a Dr Neville of nearby Pimlico Road, who had little difficulty in identifying the arm as that of a 'well-formed, tall, and well nourished young woman, probably about 25 years of age'. In his view the victim was recently dead, and the arm had been in the water 'two or three days'.

Who was she? Where was the rest of her, and had she been murdered? As soon as the medical examination was concluded, a Police Inspector had the arm removed to the mortuary, where it was preserved awaiting the orders of the aforementioned coroner, John Troutbeck. It was considered unlikely that any inquest would be held, but no one really knew, and the police went about the business of trawling the river for more body parts. After one day the project was abandoned, without success.

In the meantime, a familiar theory was on the road: the arm might have been 'thrown onto the river bank by a medical student with a view to create a scare'. In response to this claptrap a representative of the Central News Agency ignored Scotland Yard and visited one of the leading London hospitals. He was assured that 'the arm could not possibly have been removed by a student from any hospital dissecting room. Students are allowed to dissect only in the room set apart for the purpose.'[19] This tallied with Dr Neville's judgement. Although some surgical skill was evident, 'the handiwork was scarcely good enough for a person acquainted with the principles of anatomy'.

The following day, a journalist from the *Star* interviewed Neville.

'Were there any rings on the hands [sic] Doctor?'

'No, and no sign of rings being worn that I could see.'

'Was there anything to indicate whether the arm was that of a woman of refinement or the reverse?'

'Well, I should say not a refined woman, for the nails were dirty.'

'That might be due to immersion in the dirty water of the river?'

'Certainly; but I also observed that the nails were not neatly trimmed as a lady's generally are.'

Neville dismissed any possibility that it might be a man's arm: 'No doubt that of a young woman; under thirty years of age, I should say, judging from the freshness of the skin and the tension of the muscles and sinews.'

The arm had been tied near its shoulder end with a piece of cord, like a tourniquet. Neville had no explanation for this, 'unless it was to prevent blood flowing from the limb while it was being conveyed to the water'.

'Could this limb possibly have come from some dissecting room?'

'I do not think so for a moment. If it had, there would have been on it some evidence of the dissection.'

No such sign was evident here. 'Moreover,' said Neville, 'no dissecting room authorities would allow the removal of a limb.'

'Then this discovery could not be due to some medical student's hoax?'

'I consider the matter of that explanation an impossible one. The limb must have been severed with a large sharp knife, whereas a dissecting knife is a small one.'

Irrespective of such informed opinion, the coppers were not going to abandon their 'Insane Medical Student'. Loss of such an actor would compound the difficulty of selling Catherine Eddowes' travelling kidney as a 'hoax'. So what did Neville think the explanation was? 'It certainly suggests to me that it was murder.'

The newspapers were in no doubt of it, and three weeks later Neville's assumption had evolved into a certainty.

Back at Millbank mortuary, Dr Bond and his assistant Mr Hibbert had barely got the torso out of its preservative before Bond reportedly exclaimed, 'I have an arm that will fit that.'

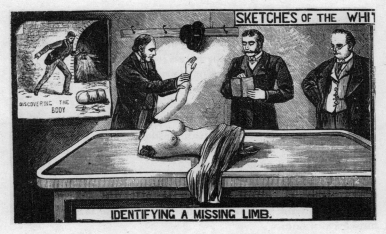

SKETCHES OF THE WHI[T

DISCOVERING THE BODY

IDENTIFYING A MISSING LIMB.

It's more likely that the perception was Hibbert's – he had previously examined the arm on 16 September. Now it was rejoined with the Scotland Yard trunk, and its fit was found to be impeccable. The body had cautiously begun to reveal something of itself, and thus some insight into whoever had killed her.

If Dr Neville had been right on 11 September that the arm was recently dead, and that it had been in the water two or three days, then the victim had been killed on or about 8 September – the same day as Annie Chapman.

Despite police efforts to disassociate this murder from the Whitechapel series, the date remains of resonance. If this unidentified woman *wasn't* killed by the Ripper, then the police were obliged to accept that two independent killers with identical intent were abroad in the metropolis, and that these two different killers had murdered two different women on what was probably the same day. Moreover, both were of an identical mindset, making off with their victims' wombs, and both electing to make a drama of their handiwork.

It was (and is) suggested that the assassin hauled his fifty pounds of putrescent flesh into the dangerous environs of New Scotland Yard in order to hide it. My perception of his reasoning is precisely to the contrary. I think he hauled it into the Met's headquarters because that's where he wanted it found. He'd used a saw to cut his victim in half, cut off her head, and carve through the bones of her arms. From there on he had demonstrated absolute control over the body parts: the head, legs and left arm were still missing, but he had flagged up his crime – the right arm in the river. Had he wished, of course, he could easily have slung the torso in after it. But he was thinking of Charlie. He was thinking of Charlie when he carried his segment of bloody apron to Goulston Street, thinking of Charlie when he cut compasses in Eddowes' face on the square; and it was the same preposterous copper who brought him here. Jack was soon to make his motive in the vaults transparent, but even at this juncture the world's most wilfully blind policeman must have known what was up.

We've seen Jack's interpretation of Jubela and Jubelo at the crime scenes of Chapman and Eddowes. But what of Jubelum, the last to suffer Solomon's vengeance? 'It is my order that you be taken without the walls of the Temple, and there have your body severed in two, and divided to the north and south.'

Although Charles Warren was one of the world's leading Masonic historians, we are enjoined to believe that not the remotest shadow of Solomon's penalties crossed his mind. 'No clue in the hands of the police,' dribbled Home Secretary Henry Matthews, 'however apparently unpromising, should be neglected.'[20]

The sawn-in-half body at New Scotland Yard, delivered as a possible jocular take on a 'foundation sacrifice', looked very promising indeed. It was right out of Warren's past, out of Masonry, out of the Land of Moab – and Warren utterly neglected it. As a matter of fact, he made a point of going nowhere near it. Such insouciance (i.e. Establishment panic) 'fanned the fire of rage and indignation', wrote the *New York Herald*, 'with which the blundering blindness of the London police is viewed in the great metropolis'.[21]

While Warren was fully engaged with the details of covering Jack's tracks, the ungrateful psychopath was still having fun with body parts. Two more arms were to appear. The first had been found on Friday, 28 September, about a mile down the river in the grounds of the Blind School at Lambeth. It was quickly dismissed as having 'nothing whatever' to do with the torso at Scotland Yard. 'An examination [by a medical expert],' reported *The Times*, 'shows that whereas the arms have been wrenched from the sockets of the body on the Embankment, the bones at the St George's Mortuary consist of a complete arm and include the shoulder blade. Moreover, the arm found in the Thames at Pimlico was freshly amputated, but the arm in question must have been detached from the female trunk to which it belonged some very considerable time ago. Lastly, the bones constitute the left arm, and as the arm found in the Thames was also a left arm, they must belong to different bodies.'

This was apparently what Ripperologist Mr DiGrazia might call a 'common arm', or 'garden arm', of the sort that occasionally turns up in flowerbeds. 'The police [it goes without saying] attach no importance to the Southwark [Lambeth Blind School] discovery.'

With this *The Times* has contradicted everything, including itself, and sounds like Swanson's parrot. In his preliminary examination, Dr Hibbert categorically stated that the Pimlico arm was the *right* arm, and thus does not dismiss the arm in question here. And even if the Lambeth arm didn't fit the Scotland Yard trunk, might not another arm suggest another murder? The police eagerly 'attach no importance' to it, but was it not once attached to a woman's body? Furthermore, no doctor had said that the arms from the torso had been 'wrenched from their sockets'. According to Hibbert, they were first cut into with a very sharp knife and then disarticulated through the joint, with a saw being used after that.

But why trouble with forensic niceties when Bro Swanson's emergency service is on permanent call-out? 'The Lambeth arm,' concluded *The Times*, 'is stated to have been the subject of dissection [i.e. sourced at a hospital], and is supposed to have been placed where it was found as a hoax.' We might recall what Dr Neville said not two weeks before about 'hoaxes' pulled by medical students: 'I consider the matter of that explanation an impossible one.' Impossible is the word. The London medical schools didn't open their doors to students for the autumn semester until 1 October.[22]

But even so, 'the Student Arm-Collector' had been up to his rotten little tricks again, in Peckham.

Given the circumstances, one might imagine the cops could have caught this mad little medic, even if they couldn't catch the Ripper. One might imagine that the hospital authorities would by now be especially alert to missing arms. But the indefatigable 'Medical Student' managed to smuggle another arm out, which he deposited (after boiling it) in an East London street – timed, it would seem, to coincide with the resumption of Troutbeck's second inquest into the Scotland Yard trunk.

Be they left or be they right, these Peckham bones were those of a woman's arm. 'There was a supposition in the locality that the discovery might have some connection with the discoveries at Whitehall and Pimlico,' penned *The Times* in hushed acquiescence, 'but this is not encouraged by the authorities.' You can bet your Bobby's helmet it wasn't. So what – we wait breathlessly – might these bones have been? The authorities 'appear to hold the belief that the present "find" is due to a senseless freak on the part of a medical student'.

Keep swallowing that Fowler's Solution.

I just mentioned, somewhat prematurely, Troutbeck's second inquest, and now I begin with the first. It was convened at the Sessions House, Westminster, on the morning of Monday, 8 October, Detective Inspector Marshall watching for the police. Frederick Wildbore, who found the torso, was naturally first witness up. Reiterating his story, he described the hazards of the vaults, and how he was *more than certain* the body wasn't there before 28 September: 'I know for a fact it wasn't there last Friday because we had occasion to do something at that very spot.'[23]

George Budden, who brought the bundle out, told the same story, underlining the vault's inhospitality: 'It is a very dark place, always as dark as the darkest night in the day.'

Detective Hawkins, the first copper on the scene, had no argument with that. 'The vault where it was said the body was lain was very dark, and the recess was across a trench [via a plank] which was also in the dark. I looked further along the recess where it had been and saw a piece of more dress material. The wall was very black and the place full of maggots.'[24]

Troutbeck heard next from the foreman of the works, William Brown, who deposed: 'The works on the Embankment are shut off by a hoarding, 8 feet or 9 feet high, and there are three entrances with gates, two on Cannon Row and one on the Embankment.' Although there was no nightwatchman, all these gates were locked at night except one, which was secured by a latch and string, admitting only those who knew how to pull it. 'The approach to the vault from Cannon Row,' said Brown, 'was first by planks and steps, and planks again.' He confirmed that his men had frequently been active in the vaults during the week before the discovery.

So we're looking at an eight- or nine-foot fence, fifty pounds of dead flesh, and a place of hazard and absolute darkness. How the perpetrator got his burden there was unknown. But *when* he did it was irrefutably established. It had to have been after the works were closed on the night of Saturday, 29 September. This fact was finally nailed by a labourer called Ernest Hedge. He was in the vaults, he said, at five o'clock that afternoon, and was the last to leave the site. They were shutting down until Monday, and he had gone to fetch a hammer. Striking a light, he crossed the trench and had a last look around. 'The vault led to nowhere,' said Hedge, 'and there was no parcel there then.'[25]

This unequivocal evidence, establishing that there had been no torso in the vaults before Saturday, 29 September, was to have dramatic repercussions. Although Wildbore and his mates were certain about what they had seen – or rather not seen – the scenario was about to cop a bit of a bombshell. At the second inquest, some two weeks later, the authorities would try to deny the men's deposition, insisting that all five had been blind to the body in the vault. Wildbore's statement that 'the body could not have been where it was found above two or three days' was to be elasticised by the authorities into a comfortable six weeks.

It was quite the reverse of the shenanigans at Berner Street. There, those who had *seen the grapes* couldn't possibly have seen them, while here, those who had *not seen the torso* couldn't possibly have missed it. In other words, at both locations the conviction of on-site witnesses was to be subsumed within the requirements of an official cover-up.

As yet in ignorance of what he'd be obliged to say at the second inquest, Dr Bond was next to take the oath. His evidence constituted an emerging impression of the victim. 'The trunk was that of a woman of considerable stature, and well nourished.' It was seventeen inches long, twenty-eight inches at the waist, with a thirty-six-inch bust. He assumed she must have been about five feet eight, and maybe twenty-four or twenty-five years old. Details of her butchery came next. 'The lower part of the body and pelvis had been removed (about an inch and a half below the navel) and the fourth lumbar vertebra had been sawn through in the same way as the removal of the head.' Decomposition was advanced.[26]

The absence of the lower organs, including the womb, made it impossible to determine whether or not she had ever borne children. Neither could he say whether wounds to the neck were the cause of death. 'There was nothing to suggest that it was sudden,' said Bond. But internal examination revealed that the heart was pale and totally drained of blood, with no blood-staining of any other organ. This suggested death was not by suffocation or drowning, but most likely from blood loss, 'proving to my mind, that she died of haemorrhage'.[27]

She bled to death, but her arm didn't? This possibly explains the tourniquet around it, designed to keep blood in the limb while the rest of her body was drained.

'The date of death,' continued Bond, 'as far as we could judge, would have been six weeks or two months before the discovery, and the decomposition occurred in the air and not in water.' He found no other wounds on the torso, but over it 'were clearly defined marks, where the strings had been tightly tied'. 'The body appeared to have been wrapped up in a very skilful manner, and was absolutely full of maggots.'[28]

Certain of these conclusions were soon to resonate:

1) The date of the victim's death.
2) The absence of blood in the body.
3) Its infestation with maggots.

Bond had just about done, and was poised to hand over to Dr Hibbert for his findings on the arm. But at Troutbeck's intercession he concluded with a résumé: 'She was not a stout woman, but she was a fully developed one. There was no abnormal excess of fat, but the body was that of a thoroughly well nourished plump woman.' In his view, as he'd indicated, 'the hand was certainly not that of a woman used to manual labour'. Raising issues of class, this was a point of interest to Troutbeck. 'Would the hand be that of a refined woman [i.e. not a whore]?'[29]

It was left to Hibbert to complete the reply. He confirmed that it was a right arm, and summarily quashed any hopes that its discovery might be the result of a jape by a medical student. 'For a surgical motive the cut would have been made to leave the skin outside,' but in this case the arm 'had been separated from the trunk at the shoulder joint and then the bone was sawn through'. Although the amputation could have served no anatomical purpose, he acknowledged that it had been made with a certain amateur skill. The arm was severed, he said, 'by a person who knew where the joints were, and then cut them pretty regularly'. Did this apply to both arms? Hibbert answered in the affirmative.

Intelligence rather than anatomical expertise had guided the knife. Unlike the torso, the limb was charged with blood, and 'when the string was loosened it was found there was a great deal of blood in the arm'. The skin appeared very thin and corrugated from immersion in the water, but in comparison to the body was not much decomposed. There were no scars or bruises. A few dark hairs under the arm matched hairs on the torso, and gave an indication of hair colour: she was a brunette. Hibbert's testimony was of particular interest in terms of forming a picture of the victim. Assessing her as a few years younger than Dr Bond would have it, he estimated her age as twenty. 'The hand itself was long, well shaped, and carefully kept, and the nails were small and well shaped.'[30]

Unless she'd had a manicure at the morgue, this was curious. Dr Neville had described the nails as 'not neatly trimmed as a lady's generally are'. But this of course preceded the discovery of the torso. Bearing in mind that no postmortem was anticipated for the arm, it's easy to suppose that Neville's view was formulated in the expectation of the cops dismissing the limb, as they were to do with the Lambeth arm, and the Peckham arm. But now it couldn't be ignored, and no way was its owner a skivvy. This hand hadn't shoved a scrubbing brush or heaved coal. If its owner worked, it was probably in the service of a lady, assuming she wasn't a lady herself.

À propos of that, Inspector Marshall was next up, with some pertinent information. It was revealed that the torso was wrapped in a dress that, if not worn by her at the time of her death, had very probably belonged to the victim. But he didn't bother to give the jury any measurements, so we cannot be sure. 'It is a broche satin cloth,' he said, 'of Bradford manufacture, but an old pattern, probably of 3 years ago.' There was nothing special about it – it probably cost sixpence ha'penny a yard. He went on to describe his visits to the vault immediately after the discovery of the torso, and later with two other officers: 'I made a thorough search about the vaults in the immediate vicinity. I examined the ground and found a piece of newspaper [produced]. I also found a piece of string, which seems to be a piece of sash-cord and Mr Hibbert handed me two pieces of material which he said had come from the body. With regard to the piece of paper, I have made enquiry, and find it is a piece of the *Echo*, dated the 24th August 1888. Mr Hibbert also handed me a number of small pieces of paper which he said were found on the body, and I find they are pieces of *The Daily Chronicle*.'[31]

Marshall went on to contradict everyone who had given an opinion on the matter of access to the site. 'It is easy, I think, to get over the hoarding in Cannon Row, but there are no indications of anyone having done so.' As to the length of time the torso had been in the vault, he deferred to the builders, and especially Hedge. 'I should think,' he said, 'the body had been where it was found for days, from the stain on the wall. But the witness who has been examined declares most positively that it was not there on Saturday, as he was on the very spot.' Troutbeck recalled Hedge, and he reconfirmed this: 'I looked into the very corner with a light for the hammer. *I am quite sure the parcel could not have been there without my seeing it* [my emphasis].'[32]

This was to become a point of supreme importance, and to present a dilemma for the court. 'The fact that everyone is of opinion that no stranger could have put the parcel in such an out of the way corner,' said the *Post*, 'considerably narrows the scope of the enquiry, and on Monday week other workmen will be called who will prove that the parcel was not in the vault on the Saturday before the Monday it was found.'

With everyone certain the torso wasn't there until after the works closed on Saturday, 29 September, Troutbeck adjourned for two weeks.

The press was in no doubt that this was another Ripper outrage. 'There are upon the body found in the cellars exactly the same proofs of a purpose as have been afforded by two, at least, of the cases in Whitechapel' (as was obvious to everyone but the Metropolitan Police), wrote the *Scotsman*. 'The first of the series of the murders and mutilations was committed on August 7th, the second August 31st. Put these facts by the side of the statement of the medical men that the woman whose mutilated body has been found on the Thames Embankment was murdered in early August, and it becomes impossible to doubt that the same person was responsible for all the bloodshed.'[33]

It was a 'PERFECT CARNIVAL OF BLOOD IN THE WORLD'S METROPOLIS', headlined the *New York Times*. 'It is an extremely strange state of affairs altogether – THE POLICE APPARENTLY

PARALYSED.' This was certainly true of the mesmerised dupe at their head. A hysterical Freemason was working mirrors out of Scotland Yard, and straight coppers didn't have a chance. 'Careful inquiries', together with 'a thorough search of the enclosed ground', were reported. But Jack had another trick up his sleeve, and such painstaking subterranean efforts were soon to manifest themselves as an embarrassing sham.

'Of course,' moaned the *Daily Echo*, 'no information as to what has transpired is afforded by any of the officers, who – as evidenced by their attitude to the Press in the East End during the past few days – very zealously obey the stringent orders they have to "give nothing to reporters". Their object is to ascertain whether any other portions of the mutilated body have been hidden away, either beneath the heaps of debris lying about on all sides, or in the long corridor-like vaults beneath the buildings.'[34]

The police put up the usual appearance of going about their investigations, claiming to have scoured every inch of ground and even draining an abandoned well. Marshall was specifically looking for the victim's head. But even without it, he must by now have had a reasonable understanding of who she was.

Give or take a year or two, she was about twenty, an imposing young woman, voluptuous even, and tall by the standards of the day. She had dark brown hair, and took care of her appearance: there were no working-girl scars on the arm, and it was a well-manicured hand. Certainly she was no malnourished unfortunate from London's East End. The common material of her dress indicated that she looked like a lady rather than actually being one. It was a pretty safe bet that she was a girl in service. She had been dismembered indoors, and her torso most probably stored (in a vat or a barrel of disinfectant) in the same place. Were this the case, she was less likely to have been employed as a lady's maid than as some sort of domestic in the house of the man who killed her. No way was Jack crazy enough to haul fifty pounds of murdered flesh too far, and the locations at which the body parts were found suggested that she might well have lived in the area of their discovery – at Pimlico, on the north side of the Thames, or maybe Battersea, just over the bridge. It wasn't too wild a guess, therefore, to picture a tall, rather refined girl, in domestic service, perhaps to a gentleman, in residence near the river.

Somebody out there thought they recognised her.

Lilly Vass was eighteen years old when she vanished in July 1888. With only the clothes she stood in she had left her home in Chelsea, and had never been heard of since. On 7 October, motivated by reports of 'dreadful things' in the newspapers, her mother went (again) to the police, and shortly after found herself in the mortuary at Millbank. Understandably, she was 'quite unequal to the ordeal of making an inspection', but nevertheless was able to give details of her missing child. Lilly seemed to fit the bill. About five feet six inches tall, she was 'fairly stout, with fine arms, and of dark complexion'. Mrs Vass said that her daughter had been in service with a lady at Sealcott Road, Wandsworth Common (adjacent to Battersea), and had left home on 19 July, 'ostensibly to go back to her situation'. But Lilly had lied: 'Although I have always found her a truthful girl, I am bound to say that she had deceived me in one respect.' She had in fact left her situation in Wandsworth, 'although she had told me she had not'. For some reason Lilly had quit, and had apparently elected to keep her new whereabouts a secret.[35]

'She was not a girl devoid of sense,' said her mother. 'I think that if she were alive she would write, even if she did not wish me to know where she was.' Mrs Vass was convinced her daughter had been abducted, and it was therefore possibly her employer who didn't want anyone to know where she was. This mystery person may have been a new 'mistress', but more likely it was a 'master', and her murderer. The reason she lied may well have been so as not to upset her mother with any intimation of immorality. Did this explain why she had left home without packing any clothes? Had she been promised a new wardrobe? She had told her mother 'that she thought she was going to travel [with her employer] to the Isle of Wight'.[36]

Now, the Isle of Wight has no less interest to me than does Conduit Street. Ten thousand places in England would mean nothing compared to this frequent haunt of my candidate, where he sailed his yacht and 'took in the bracing air'. It seems that Lilly's new employer had promised to take her on a ferry, but had actually had something rather different in mind. Two days after Mrs Vass went to the police, a letter was received at Leman Street police station in Whitechapel. 'I am going to do another job right under the very nose of damned old Charlie Warren,' it warned. We can confidently assume that the first job was already under Warren's nose at New Scotland Yard.

Lilly Vass barely made the London press – the above is sourced from provincial newspapers. Journalists in the capital showed a curious lack of interest, but not less than did the police, who quietly dropped any further investigation. The geography was too dangerous. Although the British press willingly sold the 'Fiend in his Lair' routine, they kept well away from the West End. Only one Dr Forbes Winslow broached the possibility of an upmarket assassin. In a letter to *The Times* he expressed his 'confident belief that the murderer is not of the class to which "Leather Apron" belongs, but is of the upper-classes of society'. This went down like a rock, and Winslow was virtually in a minority of one.[37]

Not so in the United States. With no predisposition to protect certain class interests, the American newspapers took a more inquisitive view. Interviewed by the *New York Herald* in early October, a physician called Dr Alan Hamilton demonstrated a remarkably modern understanding of the serial killer. In response to a question about the Ripper's state of mind (and he had no doubt that the Scotland Yard trunk was Jack's work) Hamilton replied, 'Oh, he is probably reading the newspaper accounts of the murders and enjoying it, going all over the crimes again in his imagination.' And fantasy would 'demand more reality': 'The more he gives way to his passion, the more pleasure it is likely to give him.' Referencing similar 'monomaniacs', he thought it was very likely that the culprit was 'an intensely refined, over-educated man, who had degenerated into a condition of ultra-sensuality'. Capping this assessment, he added, 'I should not be at all surprised to hear that he is a man living in an aristocratic part of the city.'[38]

Such conclusions, however, could be given no credence by the Metropolitan Police. If Jack was operating outside the East End, they were going to have to start investigating outside the East End – and that would be a whole different ball-game. Victorian gentlemen would not be so ready to call Jack a 'genius' if his target became Kensington ladies. With West End wives and daughters on the slab, they might demand more than the pathetic sideshow from the police thus far. Warren's arse was already on the line. Society might panic, the idiot might be fired, and a real policeman brought in. Disaster would ensue. Any honest broker wouldn't need more than a wet weekend to sort this nonsense out, and Salisbury's government would fall. It was an inflammatory time for Jack to up the ante.

On 5 October the Central News Agency received another letter. Following 'Dear Boss' and 'Saucy Jacky', it was designated as the murderer's third. This extraordinary communication could, and should, have busted Jack the Ripper. Instead, by selectively quoting from it, the police turned it into another writ of deceit.

On 8 October, under the headline 'ANOTHER COMMUNICATION KEPT SECRET', the *Evening News* published a version of it: 'A third communication has been received from the writer of the original "Jack the Ripper" letter and postcard, which acting upon official advice, it has been deemed prudent to withhold for the present. It may be stated, however, that although the miscreant avows his intention of committing further crimes shortly, it is only against prostitutes that his threats are directed, his desire being to respect and protect honest women.'

Could any trick the Met pulled ever approach the obscenity of this? Suddenly everyone is prepared to give the Purger's mail a bit of credibility. Suddenly everyone is supposed to see the socially responsible side of Jack. Far from belittling this letter as the work of a 'hoaxer', now everyone wants to take him at his word – not a bad chap, really, bit of a gent even: he doesn't kill anyone but fourpenny whores, and then only in Whitechapel. You can rest easy in your West End beds. So utterly ridiculous is this deception a sloth could see through it. By trying to invest the murderer with some sort of 'moral code', the authorities are attempting to dissuade the public from believing he's moved up West.

Laughably, like the Victorian police (and in deference to the 'canonical'), Ripperology is also obliged to try to dismiss the Scotland Yard trunk. It invalidates all their favourite candidates. This wasn't Kosminski carrying half a woman who weighed almost as much as he did out of the East End. The letter could not have been written by Kosminski either, a certifiable moron who probably had difficulty spelling his own name. Nor was it penned by that hilarious non-starter Michael Ostrog, who existed only as some sort of disturbance in the mind of Sir Melville Macnaghten.

How does this letter square with that mincing junk out of *The A to Z* in respect of the torso? If 'the police never imagined there was any connection with the Whitechapel Murders', what were they doing withholding a letter signed 'Jack the Ripper' that made an unequivocal reference to it? Clearly a connection *had* been made, and when we come to the full text of this letter it will be understood why. It was 'deemed prudent to withhold [it] for the present', wrote the *Evening News*. But like Joseph Lawende's description of the man in Mitre Square, it was withheld forever.

This is *the only letter from the Ripper that the Metropolitan Police wanted everyone to believe was genuine*. 'Hoax' had gone onto temporary hold. It is little wonder that Scotland Yard withheld the accurate text. It went into Warren like an arrow. This wasn't a policeman attempting to protect the public, it was a Freemason attempting to protect Masonry – at least, the upper echelons of its ruling elite. I shall have more to say of this letter by and by (including the manipulation of its text), but for the moment, this is how it is presented in the archives.

The handwriting below isn't the Ripper's, but belongs to a journalist at the Central News Agency called Thomas J. Bulling. Why he copied the original rather than sending it to Scotland Yard is supposedly unknown. 'It is odd,' writes Ripperologist Mr Stewart Evans, 'that Bulling chose to transcribe this letter instead of sending it.' In my view it is less 'odd' than obvious.

It is a document that screeches of interference. By copying it, you could make it say whatever you like. At this juncture, what the police most definitely would have liked was for Jack himself to deny responsibility for the Scotland Yard trunk, and that's exactly what this dodgy bit of conjuring purports to do. 'I swear I did not kill the female whose body was found at Whitehall.' I do not believe Jack the Ripper wrote that. I think it was written at the behest of Donald Swanson. Before we get into it, let's have a look at Bulling's text.

THE CENTRAL NEWS LIMITED

5 New Bridge Street
London Oct 5 1888

Dear Mr Williamson

At 5 minutes to 9 o'clock tonight we received the following letter the envelope of which I enclose by which you will see it is in the same handwriting as the previous communications

"5 October 1888

Dear Friend

In the name of God hear me I swear I did not kill the female whose body was found at Whitehall. If she was an honest woman I will hunt down and destroy her murderer. If she was a whore god will bless the hand that slew her, for the women of Moab and Midian shall die and their blood shall mingle with the dust. I never harm any others or the Divine power that protects and helps me in my grand work would quit forever. Do as I do and the light of glory shall shine upon you. I must get to work tomorrow treble event this time yes yes three must be ripped, will send you a bit of face by post I promise this dear old Boss. The police now reckon my work a practical joke, well well Jacky's a very <u>practical</u> joker ha ha ha Keep this back till three are wiped out and you can show the cold meat

Yours truly
Jack the Ripper"

Yours truly
T J Bulling

431

At the top of his letter Bulling says he encloses the envelope, 'by which you will see it is in the same handwriting as the previous communications'. Thanks for that, and I'm quite sure they could see it. But why then could they not see the letter? It can't be lost, or it couldn't be copied. Jack swears he's got nothing to do with the Scotland Yard murder, but who's accusing him? Certainly not the police. They're doing everything they can to disassociate him from it, and this, of course, is part of their effort. No other Ripper letter was transcribed, so what's the deal with this one? Why did the police not demand the document itself? Warren and his team of barcodes had just stuck posters up all over East London reproducing the first two communications – 'Any person recognising the handwriting is requested to communicate with the nearest police station.' So why so coy about Jack's latest bleat of triumph?

The answer, of course, is because the text had been manipulated to satisfy police requirements, and leaked in part to the press, which explains why the original has never been seen. Its author (or rather, the pen that translated him) is anxious to disassociate himself from the Whitehall torso, offering even to do the detective work for them: 'I will hunt down and destroy her murderer'.

Well, thank you for the sentiment, Jack, but anyone of an enquiring mind might imagine this is more an expression of police paranoia than anything as absurd as the Ripper's code of ethics. This was a man who was to cut out Mary Kelly's cunt, and I think we're justified in treating any declarations of his 'honour' with all due caution. I also think we're entitled to treat this transparently prompted fakery out of Bulling with the greatest contempt. It reeks of the sidewinding chicanery of Swanson, who invented his own history and knew nothing of Warren's. So anxious were the 'eyes and ears' to camouflage this West End outing, they overlooked the very element that gives it away.

Just as Jack chose Conduit Street out of 28,000 streets in London, so here he chooses 'Moab' out of 3,237 names in the Bible. Bro Swanson was too hypnotised to realise it, but both had intimate connections with his boss. The words 'Moab' and 'Midian' do not appear by accident. They are not the average patter of a murderer, and most particularly not in the context of this torso secreted in the style of a sawn-in-half Moabite 'foundation sacrifice' at New Scotland Yard.

It was all part of the 'Funny Little Game', coordinated to embarrass 'the biggest fool in London'. Putting aside the rueful episode of the Moabite Stone, Warren's sojourn in the lands of Moab and Midian was amongst the most uncomfortable memories of his life. It was there he put a murderer to death; it was there he indulged his passion for 'Biblical diggings', turning up foundations where sawn-in-half girls were not entirely uncommon. Just as a chill of sickening nostalgia was in wait on an East End wall, so too in the foundations of his own new buildings was this homicidal/Biblical joke from his past.

The Ripper was on Warren's case, and Warren was playing by the Ripper's rules. Get into Warren's history and that's where the Ripper was, persecuting him with Masonic esoterica and cod Biblical vernacular that could have been lifted right out of the Old Testament. Jack will 'bless the hand that slew her', and 'their blood shall mingle with the dust'. It is not I, but the Metropolitan Police, that gave this letter its credibility, 'Do as I do and the light of glory shall shine upon you.' Ha ha …

This text, with its Americanism 'quit forever', is as revealing of the Ripper as it is of Warren himself. His tormentor was holding up a mirror, and if Bro Charlie had had the balls, he could have seen the Ripper's face. He dared not look. He couldn't sponge this one away, so he stayed away from Scotland Yard, hoping to gull the public into believing that an entirely different killer was abroad in the metropolis. (No one bought into it but the authors of *The A to Z*.)

Two weeks later Jack wrote again, and this missive too was withheld. But without Bulling's accommodation in calligraphics, it presented a more credible scenario. No denials here: the Ripper was claiming the torso as his own work. 'One of the two women I told you about was a Chelsea girl [almost certainly Lilly Vass] and the other a Battersea girl. I had to overcome great difficulties in bringing the bodies [sic] where I hid them. I am now in Battersea.'[39]

Was there another body in the foundations of New Scotland Yard? It is quite possible. As will soon become apparent, the police had barely troubled to search the place. Covering up for a criminal had assumed more importance than his crimes, and on every conceivable level Warren was inhibiting the process of detection.

Warren was indeed a 'Masonic stooge', rushing around like a headless chicken. He was constantly in denial. 'Juwes' had to be denied, grapes had to be denied, Packer's man with the 'educated voice' and the sketches that went with him had to be denied, and the torso screeching provenance was denied along with them.

It wasn't always thus. Paradoxically, it was in the lands of Moab that (the then Captain) Warren had shown the wherewithal of a policeman. In 1882 a team of his archaeological associates, led by Professor Edward Palmer and Lieutenant William Gill of the Palestine Exploration Fund, had been slaughtered by Bedouins. Warren got up a posse that tracked down and captured the perpetrators, 'avenging' their crime by 'promptly executing the murderers'.[40] But he dared show no such vengeful initiative in 1888.

Without it yet having been revealed who had done it, the scandalous mopping-up at Goulston Street was beginning to leak, and on 8 October the *Evening News* headlined the 'STUPIDITY OF A POLICE OFFICER'. Two days later the truth was out, and condemnation avalanched on the 'worthless' Commissioner: 'It is clear the Detective Department at Scotland Yard is in an utterly worthless and hopeless condition. That were there a capable Director of Criminal Investigation, the scandalous exhibition of stupidity and ineptitude revealed in the East End inquests, and immunity enjoyed by criminals, murder after murder, would not have angered and disgusted public feeling as it has undoubtedly done.' Telling it like it was from the *Telegraph*. And where was this incapable Director of Criminal Investigation, 'Andy Handy'? Why, he was ordering another *café au lait* up the nearest *rue* in Paris.

W.T. Stead of the *Pall Mall Gazette* didn't have a lot of time for the preposterous encumbrance either: 'The Chief official who is responsible for the detection of the murderer is as invisible to Londoners as the murderer himself. You may seek Dr Anderson at Scotland Yard, you may look for him in Whitehall Place, but you will not find him.' And why, at the height of the most febrile crisis in the history of British criminal investigation, was that? Because Robert Anderson was 'taking a pleasant holiday in Switzerland'. (In reality he was in Paris on behalf of Salisbury's government, colluding with *The Times* in the expectation of destroying Charles Parnell.*)

Meanwhile the warped house of cards was in imminent danger of collapse. Warren was drowning. His inclination must have been to run, and on 10 October 1888, that's exactly what he did.

---

* See Appendix I, 'The Parnell Frame-Up', page 761.

Less than a week before, Henry Matthews had written to his private secretary, Sir Evelyn Ruggles-Brise, recommending that it 'is essential that some visible evidence of effort – of ingenuity – of vigorous & intelligent exertion should be on record'. Without it, continued Matthews, 'Sir C.W. will not save himself'. What was needed was a bit of high-profile spin, 'some visible evidence of effort', and just such an asinine diversion took place four days later. Thirteen thousand coppers had 'not a shadow of a clue', so Warren decided to hand the case over to animals. He threatened to buy a puppy, train it up and have it ready for next March (a prospect that must have filled the Purger with dread). In the meantime he hired a couple of bloodhounds, whose names I've withheld to protect the innocent.[41]

Future plans involved tracking the Fiend from a crime scene to his 'lair', and to that end a test was organised wherein Charlie would assume the role of Jack, and the dogs would sniff along as a pair of manhunters. Considering that Warren himself had declared the Ripper 'left no clue', we can only wonder what it was they were expected to follow. Presumably they were supposed to smell something, but as even Dr Bagster Phillips had pointed out, they were more likely to want to smell the victim than the murderer. That didn't deter Warren, who'd probably offered the hounds a whiff of his strap.

To ensure that the exercise was representative, he selected an area with the closest topographical similarity he could find to Whitechapel, i.e. Hyde Park. Three hundred and eighty-eight resplendent acres of boating lake and flowerbeds up the road from Kensington Palace was just the ticket. The dogs were probably told that Rotten Row (rue du Roi, where fashionable people made their promenade) was a bit like Buck's Row, EC; and with your nose on the deck, what's the difference?

Anyway, at 7 a.m. on 10 October, off they all took, the Commissioner sporting a pair of knickerbockers in ingenious replication of the outfit in which the Fiend was known to commute through East London. The hounds gave desultory chase, and Warren was last seen rushing up the Serpentine and vanishing around the back of the tea rooms. Everyone had a good laugh, apart from the authorities. Doggerel from the journalist George Sims gave a flavour of the pantomime.

The brow of Sir Charles it was gloomy and sad,
He was slapped by the Tory and kicked by the Rad;
The populace clamoured without in the yard
For Matthews, Home Sec, to be feathered and tarred;
'Do something – do something!' Lord Salisbury cried,
'We've done all we can!' worried Warren replied:
'We keep on arresting as fast as we can,
And hope soon or late we shall get the right man.'
Then, goaded by taunts to the depths of despair,
The poor First Commissioner tore at his hair,
And fell upon Matthews' breast with a sob.
But the Whitechapel vampire was still on the job!
At last when the city was maddened with fears,
And the force had dissolved into impotent tears,
They brought him of bloodhounds the best to be
found,
And the 'tecs' and the dogs sought the murderer's
ground;
Then the bow-wows were loosened with noses to earth,
They trotted away mid the bystanders' mirth.
The bloodhounds ran north and the bloodhounds ran
south,
While Matthews looked on with a wide-open mouth.
'Good heavens!' he cried, 'Are you dotty, Sir
Charles?
Is it possible you, with your stern common sense,
Believe in this melodramatic pretence?'

Warren had nothing to offer but 'melodramatic pretence'. The hysteria in government must have been incredible, featuring inter-departmental hallucinations of the headlines 'RIPPER CAUGHT – PROMINENT FREEMASON – THE YARD HAD COVERED HIM UP'.

Nobody in their right mind was interested in arresting that, any more than they had been inspired to imprison regal buggers abusing boys at Cleveland Street. The machine's job was to keep this scandal up East, and providing nobody panicked, between manipulation and bluster they believed they could get away with this, brazen a way through; and, as history is my witness, they did.

But it wasn't going to be easy, because Jack had a surprise for them in the vaults. While Warren twiddled time away in humiliating make-believe, proposing to buy a puppy for fifteen quid and train it, another dog was already on the case.

SMOKER, THE DOG DETECTIVE.

The dog's name was 'Smoker'. It belonged to a journalist called Jasper Waring, and within two minutes they were to expose the 'meticulous search' of the new police buildings as a charade.[42]

'The police have had another discovery forced upon them,' mocked the *Evening News*. 'A gentleman who had great faith in the scenting powers of his Spitzbergen Terrier offered its services to the police at Westminster, but the offer was declined without thanks.' Ignoring the 'tailor's dummies', Waring obtained consent from the works contractor at New Scotland Yard, a Mr Grover. 'The dog was placed in the dark vaulted recesses where the body was found,' continued the *News*, 'and the animal at once made it apparent that it had the scent of something underground. The earth was removed, and at a little more than half a foot depth, the dog seized something, which turned out to be a human leg. The police eventually made themselves useful, by wrapping the leg carefully in brown paper and taking it to the mortuary.' The *News* added as an acid codicil: 'Anybody is at liberty to make his own comment.'[43]

I don't know what these comments might have been, but I suspect they may have been influenced by the now universal public disgust felt for Warren's police force. If its entranced Commissioner hoped to draw attention away from New Scotland Yard by hauling his silly arse around Hyde Park, he had most singularly failed. I imagine the public were asking why he didn't take his bloodhounds into the foundations of his own building – Warren didn't visit the vaults until 19 October – and further, why the Metropolitan Police had consistently deceived the public it purported to serve.[44]

'The police would make a thorough search [and] this would occupy some considerable time' (the *Echo*, 3 October). 'The grounds where the remains were found were yesterday subject to rigid examination' (*The Times*, 4 October). 'The police are searching in all directions for the missing portions of the body' (*Lloyd's*, 7 October) – but not, apparently, even six inches into the dirt underneath the spot where the torso was found.

'Smoker' had tossed a potentially disastrous spanner in the works. Dr Bond was on his way, and when he got there he pronounced the leg to be human, and estimated that it 'had been buried at least six weeks'.

Oh dear. Did this ever put the police in Shit Street. Detective Dog had changed everything. Reality was swept aside, and suddenly the authorities were obliged to insist that the torso had been there all the time, because if the workmen were right, and the body hadn't been there when the leg was buried, it meant that Jack had visited the vaults at New Scotland Yard *twice*.

'The statement of the workmen,' wrote *The Times*, 'that the body found a fortnight ago had only been in place from the Saturday until the Tuesday, is a matter of the greatest difficulty to those who have investigation of the mystery.'[45] We might reasonably consider this an understatement. Jack must have been there once, on or about 24 August, to bury the leg, and again on or about 29 September, to secrete the torso. Bond couldn't yet say whether the leg belonged to the body, but that was irrelevant to the matter of public deception.

This wasn't some East End nut trying to hide a body, but a psychopath with a plan; and the plan looked as if it had something to do with Charlie Warren. Jack had tossed the arm in the river, and had he wished, he could just as easily have tossed the leg in too. But he didn't wish anything of the sort, and instead on two separate occasions suffered the enormous hassle of bringing his body parts to New Scotland Yard.

A 'lack of clues' simply wouldn't do to explain it, because this *was* a clue, and by Jack's oath on the 'women of Moab and Midian', let no one try to pretend the police didn't understand it. It was they who took the letter seriously, they who selectively leaked from it, and they who ultimately withheld it. The choice of Warren's new building wasn't trivial – it was clearly targeted. And if such a reality became public, some very uncomfortable questions might get asked.

Various newspapers were already speculating along these lines: 'Perhaps this "fiendish assassin" was taunting Warren?'[46] Oh dear, oh dear, that was at the very nub of it. At all costs the workmen had to be proved wrong – made to see what they hadn't seen. And if they wouldn't see it, then the authorities had other means at their disposal.

John Troutbeck reconvened his coroner's court on the morning of Monday, 22 October. The ground for his proceedings was prepared. Since the discovery of the leg the press had been the conduit for diversionary tosh, such as this from *The Times*, on 19 October:

The opinion is confirmed that the body must have lain there more than the days declared by the men. It is to be remembered that when it was discovered it was not by the smell, for that was altogether unnoticed, and it is easy to account for the non-observance of any smell by the workmen when it is brought to mind that in such places deserted and starved animals frequently crawl to die, and moreover, in the excavations of old foundations like those about Westminster there are frequently cesspools which are all taken as a matter of course. A board leaning across the angle in the wall in which the body was found would have effectively concealed the parcel altogether, and it would not now have been brought to light but for the fact that some lost clothes were thought to have been discovered by accidental survey of the dark recess. Thus the men may have given honest testimony, to the best of their belief, in saying that the parcel was not there on the last Friday and Saturday in September, the fact being that they had not observed it, and anyone who has seen the place can bear testimony that it would be easy to overlook anything hidden in that darkest recess of a dark vault.

In a later chapter we will explore the depths of criminal collusion between Sir Robert Anderson and *The Times* newspaper. Meanwhile, such villainous crap is indicative of the crisis the Establishment acknowledged itself to be in. *The Times* had proposed a bunch of worthless deceptions in order that it might argue the irrelevant. Every specious reason to discredit the workmen is here enshrined. Acknowledging that the parcel wasn't discovered by its stench, it posits that the men couldn't have smelt it anyway, because the foundations were apparently awash with decaying animals. This smoke-screen of human and animal smells is utterly fallacious, because anyone who ever got near the torso – Wildbore (who found it), Budden (who hauled it out) and Brown (who ordered it opened) – said it had no smell at all. Having put up a camouflage in respect of the stench, *The Times* moved on to try to camouflage the torso itself. A non-existent and never previously mentioned 'board' is brought into the equation, and this board 'would have effectively concealed the parcel altogether'. Forget the retrieval of tools (Wildbore's kit and Hedge's hammer), the discovery was now predicated on 'the fact that some lost clothes were thought to have been discovered by accidental survey of the dark recess'. 'Lost clothes' are now substituted for the habitual concealment of tools at that very spot in the foundations where workmen had been busy for the last three weeks. Nothing was 'accidental' about the discovery of the torso, but never mind what Wildbore and Hedge had said at the previous hearing. 'It would be easy,' concluded *The Times*, 'to over-look anything hidden in that darkest recess of a dark vault.'

In other words, stand by for another nobbled inquest.

'Inspector Marshall, who has the character of not leaving a clue untouched' (except for a leg), sat in again on behalf of the Met. By now the jury were familiar with the story, but perhaps not with the way it was about to be retold. What the authorities required was a repudiation of the evidence given by the workmen at the previous session. Any idea of a dual visit by the murderer was most unwelcome, and Troutbeck's task therefore was to unite the torso and the leg in a single delivery. Bogus 'witnesses' were put up to try to effect this, stuffing the benches to fabricate a dynamic. At failing theatrical presentations this is known as 'papering the house'.

Nothing new was brought to the proceedings. What is of interest is what was left out.

The only familiar face to be called belonged to the foreman of the works, William Brown. He told the court he'd been in the vaults on Friday, 28 September. 'He did not examine the recesses,' he said. 'The body might have been there without him seeing it.' To wit, he is a non-witness. He didn't go into the recess, so what was the point of asking him what was in it? Moreover, Brown didn't come into the picture until 2 October, when the torso was discovered by somebody else, so who gives a toss what he didn't see on 28 September?

If Brown's evidence was worthless, what are we to make of the next waste of breath? Mr George Errant, Clerk of the Works, stated that he was 'on the works' on Saturday, 29 September, but said nothing about going into the vaults. Errant had seen less than nothing – and this isn't surprising, since he was a pen-pusher in the office upstairs.

The 'papering' continued with a carpenter's labourer called Lawrence, who had at least been into the vault, but, startlingly, had seen nothing either, because 'the place was *so* completely dark'. Another labourer, Alfred Young, 'gave similar evidence', as did Mr Franklin, who like Brown had been down in the vaults on Friday, 28 September, 'but did not absolutely look upon the corner where the body was found'.

Thus five 'witnesses' were able to say what they hadn't seen. Astute members of the jury might have noticed that (excepting Brown) none of these men had been called at the previous inquest, and none who had given evidence then were recalled now. Where, for example, was Frederick Wildbore, the man who had actually found the body, who had struck a light in the recess and had stated unequivocally, 'I know for a fact it wasn't there last Friday because we had occasion to do something at that very spot.' Would not a reiteration of his evidence have cleared the matter up? Indeed it would, and it was precisely for that reason that Wildbore wasn't called.

Nor did Troutbeck call George Budden, the man who had hauled the bundle out. Eyewitness accounts from those who'd first encountered the body would have been most unuseful, and would have kyboshed the forensic swindle coming up from Dr Bond.

It was a revelation to me, genuinely astonishing, how these coroners' courts were bent into compliance with the desired outcome, how the *certainties* of original witnesses were subverted to the corrupt requirements of a predetermined verdict. Under no circumstances could anyone be allowed to believe that Jack had made multiple visits to New Scotland Yard.

Having explored nothing of 29 September, much less 2 October, Troutbeck deftly consigned the discovery of the torso onto a back burner, shifting the focus forward to 16 October and the underground detective work of 'Smoker'. His owner, Mr Jasper Waring, and Waring's associate Mr Angle, related how they had gone into the foundations with the dog, but now adjusted its disinterment of the leg to the opposite side of the recess. It had also plunged to a greater depth, and had confusingly become an arm: 'The arm [sic] was found some 12 inches down' – whereas the leg, according to Waring, was 'at the depth of only 4 or 5 inches when the stones were removed'. It was this barely hidden limb that, despite his 'exhaustive search',[47] had been missed by Marshall.

Such raw incompetence was of no interest to Troutbeck, who in Wynne Baxter mode had one last difficulty to navigate before the lads from the Yard were home and dry. This was Ernest Hedge, saved to the last, when his evidence could be put up in direct contradiction with the 'expert evidence' that would follow. Hedge was adamant about his visit to the vault on the 29th, though he now had a slightly different story to tell. 'With respect to Saturday 29th,' recorded *The Times*, 'when he went into the vault, he said to look for a hammer, he now said he saw the tools deposited on the opposite side to where the body lay. He struck a light to look into the recess, and the parcel was not there then.' Nor could it have been, because when the torso arrived later that night it was deposited in the recess opposite. By its usual casuistry, *The Times* says this was 'where the body lay'.

Dr Bond was the next witness, and was in no doubt of it. But, temporarily ignoring the issue of the torso, he opened his deposition with a statement on the leg:

> I went into the recess of the vault where the body was found, and found there a human leg partially buried. It was uncovered but had not been removed from the place where it was found. I examined the earth which had covered it, and I found that this gave unmistakable evidence of having covered the leg for several weeks – that

the leg had been there for several weeks. Decomposition had taken place there, and it was not decomposed when placed there. The upper part of the leg was in a good state of preservation, but the foot had decomposed, and the skin and the nails had peeled off. We found that the leg had been divided at the knee joint by free incisions, and very cleverly articulated without injury to the cartilages.

He had no doubt that the leg belonged to the body and the arm. At last he came to the point at issue if a dual visit to the vaults was to be denied: 'I took the opportunity, I may say, while in the vault, to examine the spot where the body was found,' and in direct contradiction to what he had said before, he now claimed that there was no argument about it, the builders were wrong: 'The body must have lain there for weeks, and it had decomposed there.'

'You think it had decomposed in that spot?'

'Yes,' insisted Bond. 'The decomposition was of a character of a body only partially exposed to the air. The brickwork against which it leant was deeply covered with the decomposed fluid of the human body turned black, and it could not have been done in a day or two. The stain is not superficial, but the brickwork is quite saturated. I should think it must have been there quite six weeks when found – from August.'

At the previous hearing Bond had said, 'I thought the body must have been there several days from the state of the wall,' although he couldn't be sure. Now he was certain it had been there for several weeks, rotting away for half the summer.

Troutbeck let him get away with it, but Bond was lying. Established facts militate against his revised point of view. Dr Neville had said the Pimlico arm was from a recently dead body (about 8 September), and Dr Hibbert was broadly in agreement: 'It wasn't much decomposed.' Unless the perpetrator had murdered the arm at a different time to murdering the torso, Dr Bond's assessment is impossible. The body couldn't have been in the vaults since August, when the arm was still living in September.

Bond didn't work in the vaults, but Wildbore and Hedge, who did, were positive that the torso had not been there prior to 29 September. Both were eyewitnesses, so that's two against one – and 2,000 against one if you include the maggots.

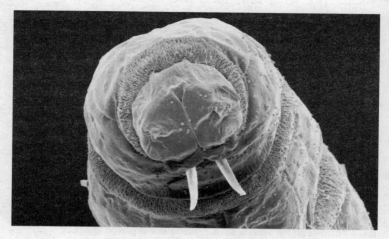

I do not believe for a moment that Dr Bond was innocent of the significance of the maggots. By the nineteenth century it was well understood that their presence in a corpse could be used to determine the time of death. It is in fact an ancient science, used in cases of homicide for the best part of seven hundred years. In our day it is known as 'forensic entomology', and one of its leading practitioners, Dr Mark Benecke, has a philosophy that couldn't be more appropriate to the New Scotland Yard trunk: 'Maggots don't lie.'

Let us navigate that servile little creep Troutbeck, and return again to the previous hearing. Bond had said the body was 'absolutely full of maggots'. This statement, out of the physician's own mouth, bears witness to the certainty of the workmen, and whether he was aware of it or not, it proves that Bond was wrong.

'Flies typically lay eggs on a corpse – which it can detect at a very great distance – minutes after death, and the eggs take a few hours to a day to hatch into maggots. Maggots have a life-cycle that can be used to date the material they feed and breed on.'[48] The maggots most usually encountered on lifeless flesh can be sourced to three different types of fly:

1) The common bluebottle. Eggs are laid on fresh rather than putrefied flesh. The maximum number by a single female is 2,000, in groups of about 150. The eggs hatch at between eight and fourteen hours, depending on temperature. At a further

eight to fourteen hours the first skin is shed and a larval instar emerges. The second instar emerges after two or three days, and the third stage within seven to eight days, and remains feeding for a further five days. When fully grown the maggot leaves the body and travels some distance, where it buries itself in soil and pupates. Twelve days completes the cycle.

2) The greenbottle, entirely similar to the above.

3) The common housefly. The female lays about 150 eggs which hatch in between eight to fourteen hours, the first larval stage lasting thirty-six hours. Second instar, one or two days, third instar three or four days, depending on conditions (temperature, etc.). The pupal stage (buried in the earth) generally seven days.[49]

Bond said the body was 'full of maggots' (second instars), and this is consistent with the workmen's timeframe of two to three days. The temperature in London on 29 September 1888 was 61° Fahrenheit. On 2 October it was 42°.[50] The relatively cool environment may have slowed the larval development by a day or two, but it is quite impossible for the torso to have been full of maggots and also *in situ* for six or more weeks. If the body had been there in August it would have been infested within twenty-four hours. The maggots would have pupated and been long gone, leaving nothing but a filthy mess of bones.

Let no one imagine it was the dress that protected the body from insect attack, because at the first inquest George Budden had stated, without dissent, that it was 'open at the top'.

Why would Jack interfere with his own expertly tied parcel? I suggest it was to initiate the very chain of events over which Bond and this court were now obliged to dissemble. He wanted his handiwork discovered, and that's why he exposed it. 'Maggots don't lie.'[51] They leave that to the Victorian police.

The Ripper was destroying women, but he was also destroying Charles Warren. He was targeting authority as represented by its most senior policeman, and its most senior policeman knew it. He could make himself look ridiculous with as many bloodhounds as he liked, but he could never catch the Ripper. They were in a kind of homicidal stalemate – Jack as trapped in his own obsession as Warren was trapped in the results of it.

The great American forensic psychiatrist Dr James Brussel, who in the 1960s busted into the thinking of Albert DeSalvo (known as the Boston Strangler), was a master at understanding this mindset: 'The motivations behind the acts of a madman possess their own logic. The [psychopathic] murderer does not act wholly irrationally. There *is* a method to his madness; there is a logic, a rationale, hidden behind what he does and how he does it, however wildly bizarre and completely without reason it appears to be. The challenge to the psychiatrist/criminologist is to find that logic … seeking out the hidden mathematics of the disturbed mind.'[52]

DeSalvo didn't escalate the sexual humiliation, or the grotesque 'pretty bows'[53] he tied about his victims' necks, by accident, and neither by accident did Jack the Ripper elaborate his crime scenes with flagrant Masonic symbolism. You would have to be blind as a bloody bat, a Freemason, a Ripperologist, or all three, not to consider the 'hidden mathematics' here.

Jack was in Charlie's face, and the maggots make it impossible for him not to have visited New Scotland Yard twice. He buried the leg at some time in August, before murdering Lilly Vass (if she it was) and tossing her arm into the river about 8 September, but preserving her torso in disinfectant until he judged the time right to inflict maximum embarrassment on Warren, delivering it as a 'Moab' pisstake to the vault over the weekend of the 29th, to coincide with the 'Double Event'.

If the leg was buried in August, before the arm's owner was murdered, they couldn't belong to the same body. It would seem the Ripper sourced different corpses to make his deposits at New Scotland Yard. In a letter dated 23 October, he was happy to clear the matter up: 'The leg you found at Whitehall does not belong to the trunk you found there.' This probably explains what he meant by 'a Chelsea girl' and 'a Battersea girl'.

We now return inexorably to Troutbeck's court for the dénouement. It was another classic nonsense, challenging nothing of the tradition established by the likes of Wynne Baxter.

Troutbeck's dismissal of evidence (otherwise known as the summing-up) was predictably curt. He rehearsed nothing of the dates, the discrepancies in the evidence, or the difficulties the assassin would have had accessing the vaults. How Jack had scaled a nine-foot hoarding with his body parts was of no interest, nor did

Troutbeck wish to explore to whom those body parts might have belonged. 'There was no evidence, of the identity or of the cause of death,' he said.[54]

Apparently he had paid no attention when Dr Bond had stated that death had most likely been caused by 'haemorrhage'. But even if he'd missed it in court, he could have read it in the newspapers. 'Death,' reported *The Times* on 10 October, 'is defined as having been one which drained the body of blood.'

Now this is most pertinent, and anyone actually interested in apprehending this monster might have been grateful to have it as part of the official record. It was an abstruse diagnosis that would reiterate itself in the corpse of another of Jack's victims, dubbed 'the Pinchin Street Torso', and also more importantly some eight weeks hence at Bradford, where the Ripper would murder a child, Johnnie Gill, draining his body of blood.

Steering well clear of this kind of thing, Troutbeck had almost finished. 'The medical evidence,' he said, 'was that the body had been cut up after death, and that no mortal wounds had been discovered.'[55] So what have we got? 'The jury had before them the surmise that no one would mutilate a body except for the purpose of concealing an identity, which, once established, might lead to the detection of a terrible murder, but beyond that fact, they could not go except by supposition.'

It was hardly necessary to establish the identity of the victim to conclude that this was a terrible murder. But did not this wretched little coroner wonder who might have had some part in it? Apparently nothing was further from his mind. 'He left it,' wrote *The Times*, 'to the jury to say whether they would return a verdict of "Found Dead" or "Wilful murder against some person unknown".'[56]

She was most certainly 'found dead'. There could hardly be any conjecture over that. But the fact that she was found dead about a mile away from where her arm was found dead must surely have precluded Troutbeck's proposed choice of verdicts. Found dead by what means? Was it a suicide? Did the torso decapitate itself before throwing its arm in the river and sawing itself in half? 'Found dead' is nothing beyond a statement of the obvious. Troutbeck may as well have offered the jury 'found downstairs'.

But 'wilful murder' was a little sensitive in these troubled days, and might have associated this West End atrocity with the East End

Purger. You were definitely 'found dead' if Jack hit you in Whitechapel (but let no one imagine this was a Ripper hit).

The last word the public were ever to hear of the Scotland Yard trunk comes again from *The Times*. 'The jury,' it wrote, 'after a brief consultation, found a verdict of "Found Dead", and were then discharged, the police being left, the Coroner said, with the charge of solving the mystery.'[57]

This didn't look at all promising.

13

A Gentleman's Lair

Two nations between whom there is no intercourse
and no sympathy; who are as ignorant of each other's
habits, thoughts and feelings as if they were dwellers in
different zones, or inhabitants of different planets.

Disraeli

Toynbee Hall was established by the Reverend Samuel Barnett and
his wife Henrietta in 1884. At the very hub of Whitechapel, it was
conceived as a university for the poor, flourishing, in principle,
upon the benevolence of the compassionate rich. 'An East End
colonisation by the well to do' is how one contemporary magazine
described it. It was a kind of intellectual Oxfam, 'a crusade by
members of old universities amid the evils and shadows of one of

the most populous quarters of London'. Given the environment, it was an extraordinary campus, an outpost of the other Victorian world.

Barnett and his wife fought ignorance like a bitter enemy. Believing the Church had 'overslept', they planned a cultural uplift of their Whitechapel flock, 'under the aegis of an intellectual and artistic elite'. As Toynbee Hall grew, dozens of the most famous names in London paid their cab fares to teach, entertain, and often stay at Commercial Street in the heart of the East End.[1]

There were lectures, societies, and clubs across the spectrum. If you didn't like football you could row on the Thames with the 'Argonauts'. 'The work of the Entertainment Committee,' wrote Henrietta, 'reflects the many sided activities of which Toynbee Hall is the centre. Teachers, East End Club Members, University Extension Students, Working Men, Politicians, Men and Women of Science, Street Orderly Boys, Policemen, Railway Porters, Clergy and Philanthropists, have met in its rooms, friendships have been made, pleasure has been given [and] bonds of sympathy between many representing separate spheres of life have been strengthened.'[2]

'It is reassuring to know,' recorded the popular magazine *Varieties* in 1888, 'that there has long been a stream of West End people, who have come to visit regularly amongst the East Enders, and that it has included some well-known illustrious names.' Nowhere was this more focused than in the arts. The 'Elizabethan Literary Society' had on its committee some of the greatest writers of the day – Robert Browning, Edmund Gosse, Andrew Lang, Algernon Swinburne and many others.

In the visual arts the names were perhaps more impressive still. Samuel Barnett's dream of a picture gallery was made a reality by the generosity of the Bohemian elite, and artists of every rank loaned canvases and gave their time and money. Some illustrious names hung on the walls. Many are familiar to this narrative, and read like a roster of Michael Maybrick's intimates from the Arts Club and the Artists Volunteers. Frederick Leighton, William Holman Hunt, Lawrence Alma-Tadema and John Everett Millais were represented in pictures, and often in person.

'Among our hosts,' wrote Henrietta, 'were those whose professions afforded abundant interest, and evenings with Lady Battersea, Lord and Lady Brassy and Sir Frederick Leighton, are among treasured memories to many people who have climbed out of the degradation of Whitechapel into a purer environment.'[3]

Henrietta's fond reference to Leighton isn't surprising. Throughout 1888, the Honorary Colonel of the Aritsts Volunteers and his creative muster were ensconced at Toynbee Hall on a variety of levels. They brought their pictures and their music, and, as will become apparent, even their military expertise.

Music was always high on the agenda, the Hall's professional contingent performing in club rooms as 'opulent as any in Pall Mall'. In summer months there were open-air concerts 'in the lighted quadrangle of St George's Yard'. 'At all parties we had music,' wrote Henrietta, 'sometimes really fine renderings: Miss Fanny Davies, by way of example, was among those who made "joyful noise" in Whitechapel.'[4] Miss Davies was an exceptional young pianist, who by notable coincidence was to lease Michael Maybrick's new house in St John's Wood when he took off suddenly for the Isle of Wight.

Fanny Davies

Some of London's greatest concert stars came here to play or sing, and if they tarried too late past the chimes there were always the guest rooms, and handsomely appointed they were. If you couldn't sleep and fancied a walk, well, you were hardly out of step with an institution that, as *Varieties* reported, 'slumbered neither day or night'. 'Every Saturday was a musical evening,' it wrote, just as on occasion it was a night of savage murder.

'Toynbee Hall was at the heart of the terrorised area,' records an official history. 'One of the victims had been found within a few yards of the rear of the settlement. The panic was amazing. In August [1888] a Vigilante Association was formed at St Jude's [Barnett's church at Toynbee Hall] and the streets were patrolled by members of the Association, which included both residents and working men. The most important discovery,' continues the history, 'was the deficiency of the police.' Remarking on the utter 'inadequacy of policing', the author concludes of the Vigilantes: 'they were, in fact, doing the work which should have been done by the police', who were clearly 'swamping' elsewhere.[5]

Barnett and his wife were beyond exasperation. 'Into deaf ears,' wrote Henrietta, 'was loudly shouted the tale of the crimes of Jack the Ripper,' and particularly when the bastard put one down outside their own back door.[6]

Martha Tabram was the first in the series, murdered on a tenement stairway backing onto Toynbee Hall in the early hours of 7

452

August 1888. Like those to follow, she was a middle-aged drudge and part-time whore who liked gin and often needed pennies for a bed. Her life was snuffed out by multiple stab wounds, amounting to what today's professionals call overkill.

No official autopsy report exists for Tabram, and newspaper coverage was scant. It seems she was silenced by strangulation before the attack with a weapon began. According to the examining physician, more than one weapon was used: 'The wounds generally might have been inflicted with a knife,' deposed police surgeon Dr T.R. Killeen, 'but such an instrument could not have inflicted one of the wounds which went through the chest bone.' He thought this was caused by some kind of dagger. I think it was caused by a bayonet. There was much blood between the legs, which were positioned open, with the clothes pulled up. It seems very probable this area was the focus of her assassin's rage.

In such a crime, the victim is the only witness you're going to get. Tabram was the first of Jack's outings, and (excepting Lilly Vass) one of only two he killed under a roof. The supposed last of the Whitechapel series, Mary Kelly, was also murdered off-street.

In both cases I imagine the choice of location was deliberate, but for reasons that are entirely opposite. Kelly was obviously killed inside because by experience Jack had become cautious of the streets, but on this, his experimental debut, it was inexperience of the streets that dictated the relative safety of an inside location.

This seemed to me a point of importance. Jack was no homicidal Einstein, and I thought his initial clumsiness – two weapons and all – might well shed some light on his place of residence. Everyone's got to start somewhere, even a sadistic murderer, and Tabram was right at the beginning of Jack's learning curve.

Two of the world's greatest detectives, the Americans Robert Ressler and Robert Keppel,[7] have written extensively of the dilemma I, in my amateur way, was trying to unravel. I had a map on the wall, and got my first Whitechapel fix with cotton and pins. My 'X' was around the upper end of Commercial Street. Then I got lucky with another American, this time an anonymous journalist on the *New York Herald*. On 19 July 1889, two days after the slaying of Alice McKenzie a spit from Toynbee Hall, the *Herald* ran an overview by its London correspondent that reads like something ahead of its time.

The murderer, it is reasonable to suppose, was keen enough to realise that owing to the great excitement that prevailed and the vigilance instituted after [Tabram's] murder – which was one of the most atrocious of the lot – it would be extremely hazardous to attempt another in that immediate vicinity.

He is a marvellously bold and daring man, as his crimes attest, but he is evidently possessed of caution. [After Tabram] he went a mile or more to the eastward, in Buck's Row, to kill his next victim [Nichols]. This happened on 31 August, only three weeks after Tabram. Next he came back and mutilated his third victim [Chapman] as far westward as numbers (1) and (2) and only a few blocks to the northward. Three weeks later he jumped to about the same distance south or south-east of the centre and did the next murder the same night [Stride]. The short interval necessitated hurrying, and he went a few blocks to the westward to Mitre Square and slew number (5) [Eddowes]. Five weeks later number (6) [Kelly] was butchered only a short distance from the centre of the locality. And now number (7) [McKenzie] has her throat cut scarcely more than a stone's throw from where number (1) suffered in like manner.

Jack the Ripper had returned to the centre of his field of operations, around which, it is apparent, he has been hovering all the time when in murderous moods. He had been bent all along in killing his victims in that limited district of four or five blocks square. He has digressed north, east, south and west in order to puzzle the police, and very likely for reasons of personal safety.

And furthermore, 'He lives now or has lived in this crime centre, or at all events he has been a frequenter of it.'[8]

For a nineteenth-century newspaper this is classy thinking, vivid with perception that was apparently beyond the permitted or intellectual capacity of the Metropolitan Police.

1) Martha Tabram – St George's Yard
2) Mary Anne Nichols – Buck's Row
3) Annie Chapman – 29 Hanbury Street
4) Elizabeth Stride – Dutfield's Yard, Berner Street
5) Catherine Eddowes – Mitre Square (City)
6) Mary Jane Kelly – Miller's Court, Dorset Street
7) Alice McKenzie – Castle Alley

8) Lydia Hart(?) – Pinchin Street
9) Writing on the wall – Goulston Street

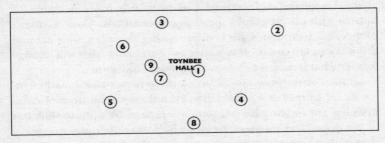

We can't actually go to Tabram's crime scene at George Yard Buildings; it's long since demolished. But this reporter from the *Herald* did: 'As I stood in George Yard, looking up at the balcony where the poor woman was found with strips of her remains tied round her neck [sic], I turned and saw lights gleaming in a large building separated from the court by a high fence. On enquiry I found it was a large hall where a much talked-about black and white art exhibition was being held. It seemed incredible that an institution reflecting the light and genius of the nineteenth century could actually exist and be filled with cultivated men and women with its windows looking down into the very purlieus of London.'

SUNDAY AFTERNOON IN THE WHITECHAPEL PICTURE GALLEY.

He was looking at Toynbee Hall.

Just over a hundred years later, in 1994, a professor of psychology at the University of Liverpool had justifiably made a name for himself with his geographic profiling of criminals: 'David Canter's pioneering techniques are revolutionising the way police act and think about criminals.' It is a species of thinking 'that will change forever what it means to follow a criminal's footsteps'.

Canter converts criminals into a kind of personalised mathematics. Be he a rapist or a serial killer, even the most cautious of criminals has got to hang his hat somewhere, and he's got to walk out of his door. The moment he does he's unconsciously making a map, putting down a personalised geography that Professor Canter is able to read. A metropolis becomes an area, and areas become streets. Computers (as yet) are never better than the brain they serve, and Mr Canter is not short-changed in this department. By a process of sophisticated deduction, he's able to find where 'X' marks the spot.

Canter has looked at a likely geographic profile of the Ripper. 'There is,' he determines,

the real possibility that Jack came into the area because of the opportunities available to carry out his mission. But the distribution of the crimes – around a small area, together with their timing, also offers the possibility that he had a base in the area.

If we assume that Jack did have a base in the area circumscribed by the crimes, then various forms of analysis are open to us to see if we can find its location. One approach, for example, is to assume that the crimes describe a region of activity spreading out from the base. On this assumption the base would be in the middle of a notional circle, but human activity is rarely so symmetrical, and I have found in many studies that the centre of the circle is not the closest estimate of the offender's home, although the home is frequently not far from the geometric centre. In the case of the Whitechapel Murders this would put the residence somewhere a little north of where Commercial Street meets Whitechapel Road.[9]

Professor Canter has put his 'X' within yards of Toynbee Hall. His conclusion startled me, because I had a dozen or more reasons for believing Jack was operating out of that very place. I came to the same 'X' spot, but from an entirely different geography of reasoning.

Jack's Conduit Street letter, referencing 'four more cunts to add to my little collection', contained an enclosure. It was a small card. Its top is partially destroyed, but it's a ticket to a 'Song Service' at the 'Polytechnic' – the Young Men's Christian Institute at 309 Regent Street, putting it literally next to John Boosey's offices. Written in pencil on the back of the card is 'Jack Ripper is in town JR'.

Anyone who cares to can read in a subliminal homosexuality here, and I'm one who does. It was 'cunts' Jack hated, and cunts he killed. The concert at the Young Men's Christian Institute was for 'Young Men Only'. It's quite impossible of course to know if Michael Maybrick was at that performance, but from the point of view of maintaining his anonymity this card proved to be a foolish move. Jack didn't enclose it by accident – he scrawled his name on its verso. Did something in his psyche oblige him to advertise his presence at this place? In my view it was because his ego was bigger than his secret, and it became a side door that will lead us right back into Toynbee Hall.

The Young Men's Christian Institute was a kind of poor boys' university. Although orientated towards industry, it also offered a variety of apprenticeships. If you were a youth of ambition you could hasten along and learn yourself a trade. You could go to classes in bootmaking, book-keeping, and even beekeeping. One course in bootmaking, beginning in October 1888, cost five shillings. We know all about it because for some reason somebody mailed a flyer about bootmaking at the Polytechnic to the City of London Police.

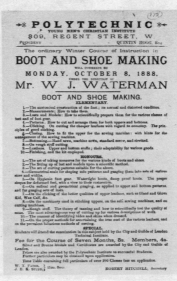

The making of boots was incidental to my interest. What interested me was why this supposedly independent correspondent should choose to focus attention on the same institution singled out by Jack.

The Polytechnic was founded by a remarkable Victorian called Quintin Hogg. His family's wealth put him through Eton, and it was there that he fell under a 'deep religious influence' that was to order the rest of his life. At eighteen he left school and headed to London with the intention of entering business. But it was the metropolis itself that was to become his vocation. 'Stirred to his depths by the sight of poverty and misery', he determined to do something about it. Thereafter his time was divided between his father's house in Carlton Gardens and the children of London's slums.[10]

These kids, the 'street Arabs', were the inspiration behind *Oliver Twist*, a detested underclass of infant criminals who knew nothing but brutality and fed out of the gutter like dogs. Hogg's efforts to help them were initially met with derision and hostility. Never daunted, he built them a school where bare feet got shoes and thieving hands learned a trade. 'Mr Hogg had already laid down the lines on which his work has since been carried out.' A quarter of a century later these principles were realised in the polytechnic he built at 309 Regent Street, then the largest of its kind in the world.

I ran into a lot of names while researching Hogg and his institute, and one of them was someone I didn't even know I was looking for. But it turned up repeatedly, and was a name I remembered from somewhere: 'the Reverend Richard Whittington'. Cut from the same Christian cloth as Hogg, Whittington was a mathematical master at the Merchant Taylors' School. In the latter half of the nineteenth century he had attempted to organise a version of what Hogg had now so magnificently achieved: 'to establish in every city parish, as part of the church organisation, evening classes for young men, where the ordinary subjects of commercial education should be very cheaply taught'.[11] Whittington 'gave ungrudgingly all his scanty leisure to teaching and administering at the evening classes'. But the reason Richard Whittington interested me was that in the City of London Ripper archive there is a letter signed 'Richard Whittington the Second'.

Whittington was a famous teacher of underprivileged boys. Was 'Richard Whittington the Second' similarly engaged? Did he have some sort of association with poor boys, and consider himself a teacher? 'The motivations behind the acts of a madman possess their own logic,' wrote Dr James Brussel, when describing 'the hidden mathematics of the disturbed mind'.[12]

So what was the 'mathematics' here? Here is the full text of the letter.

Leeds Sundy Januy 27th 1889

To the Chief Constable
City of London
(Sir) I posted a letter in Leeds about 13th November 1888 wrote in red ink Directed it to the Chief Constable City of London would you be so kind by Return of Post if you received that same letter

Yours truely
Richard Whittington the Second

I can confirm that they did. It's also in the City of London archives, posted from Leeds and dated 13 November 1888.

'Whittington' could not have sent his second letter if he hadn't written the first. Neither was ever published, and he must therefore be the same man. His first (unsigned text) from Leeds itself refers to a postcard mailed from Folkestone two days before.

FROM Jack sheridan the ripper

Folkestone
Nov 11 1888

Dear Boss
I am getting on the move Lively baint i made a good Job last time
getting better Each time a good joke i played on them three Laides
one Died two frighened Next time a woman and her daughter ta ta
Dear Boss

This card, with its reversion to silly handwriting, was mailed from
Folkestone, a seaside town in Kent, approximately 250 miles south
of Leeds. According to Whittington's first letter from Leeds (13
November), 'The Man that wrote the letter from folkstone Is the
Man that Committed The last 3 murders and that Man is William
Onion'.

Setting 'William Onion' aside, the Folkestone card could only
have been written by the Leeds correspondent, and following the
hidden mathematics, there is therefore a definitive connection
between 'Whittington' in Leeds and 'Jack the Ripper' in Folkestone.

Whittington and the Ripper are one and the same.

If Miss Ada Crossley could travel nine hundred miles in four days,
my candidate could easily do less than a third of that in two. My
suspicion was that he had a singing engagement at a theatre in
Folkestone (that was perhaps concurrently performing a play by
Sheridan), and then jumped a train for another gig in Leeds; just
like blue-arsed Ada.

The name 'Whittington' was intriguing because, like 'Andy
Handy', it referred to someone who actually exists. 'Richard
Whittington the Second' is not the kind of name your average
'hoaxer' would cook up. It meant something in the hidden mathematics. The genuine Richard Whittington was a socially motivated
Christian who taught disadvantaged boys. I presumed his anonymous surrogate might somehow be up to the same thing.

I won't trouble the text with the mountain of hours it took to get
to the obvious, but the solution brought me right back into 'the
heart of the terrorised area'.

Michael Maybrick's fellow soldier and musical associate in the
Artists Volunteers, Captain W. Henry Thomas, taught singing at
Toynbee Hall in an assembly called 'the Whittington Club'. Named

after a living Christian icon, the Whittington Club enjoyed a royal inauguration in February 1885. It was on his first official outing after coming of age (and doubtless his last ever visit to the East End) that Prince Albert Victor, the Duke of Clarence, did the honours. A scribe from *The Freemason* was *in situ* to record the regal verbals: 'the few hearty and encouraging words he addressed to the lads on that occasion showed what an affectionate feeling he entertained for the welfare of his fellow creatures'.[13]

The Reverend Barnett was also present, contributing a few words of his own, the irony of which must have been entirely lost on the royal dullard. Barnett said he had chosen to speak 'because he had lived through the growth of the Institution from a refuge to the culmination that day of the Whittington Club'. 'In their satisfaction,' he continued, 'it seemed to him that they should not forget that the existence of such institutions suggested profound dissatisfaction. In a country where a leisured class had to kill time as an employment, it was a shame that hundreds of boys should grow up neglected, untrained, and wild' in a kingdom 'overburdened with wealth'.[14]

It isn't recorded whether Albert Victor said 'Hear, hear,' but let us stay with Captain W. Henry Thomas. The first issue of the *Toynbee Record*, dated October 1888, has this: 'The singing classes are taught by Mr W. Henry Thomas, the well known conductor of popular ballad concerts.'[15] It was Thomas who would conduct the concert directed by Maybrick at the Artists' Royal Gala six months hence, the pair representing the musical elite of the regiment, their names invariably found on the same programme, frequently linked together (see opposite).

Thomas taught the lads to sing at the Whittington, and I don't doubt that he would have been delighted to have such assistance as he could get. He and Maybrick were masters of the Athenaeum Lodge,[16] fellow members of the Arts Club, and had a further association via the Guildhall School of Music, where Thomas lectured and Maybrick sponsored an annual 'Ballad Prize'. An invitation to assist at the Whittington from a close friend and fellow Artist may well have appealed, and I think that's where 'Richard Whittington the Second' acquired his new name.

The Whittington attracted a variety of West End notables. Another young talent, destined for fame and in later years a knighthood, was

20th Middlesex "Artists'" Rifle Volunteers.

HEAD QUARTERS, DUKES ROAD, EUSTON ROAD, W.C.

Honorary Colonel	- - -	SIR FREDERIC LEIGHTON, Bart., P.R.A.
Colonel Commanding	- -	ROBERT W. EDIS, F.S.A.

B (Musical) Company—Captain W. HENRY THOMAS.

20th Middlesex (Artists') Rifle Volunteer Corps.

Staff Officers.

HON. COLONEL—SIR FREDERIC LEIGHTON, BART, P.R.A.
LIEUT.-COLONEL COMMANDING—ROBERT W. EDIS (Hon. Col.), F.S.A.
MAJORS—LACY W. RIDGE (Hon. Lieut.-Col.) AND W. W. BRCE .
ADJUTANT—CAPTAIN H. GORE-BROWNE (King's Royal Rifle Corps).
QUARTERMASTER—CAPTAIN ARTHUR WIGG.
SURGEONS—WALTER PEARCE, M.D., AND J. CAGNEY, M.D.

A COMPANY (Painters). Capt. W. L. Duffield. Lieut. A. C. Pine. " G. Dodd.	D COMPANY (Comb. Univ.). Capt. A. J. Davidson. Lieut. J. B. Mercer. " T. A. Martin.	G COMPANY (Comb. Univ. & Medical). Capt. F. A. Lucas (Hon. Maj.) Lieut. J. A. Carpenter. " W. G. Weiss.
B COMPANY (Musicians). Capt. W. H. Thomas. Lieut. M. Maybrick.	E COMPANY (Architects). Capt. T. Brock, A.R.A. Lieut. R. Wilkie H. Edis. " F. G. Cowand.	
C COMPANY (Architects). Capt. W. L. Spiers (Hon. Maj.) Lieut. A. S. Haynes. " F. L. Pearson.	F COMPANY (Painters). Capt. Walter C. Horsley. Lieut. C. E. Fripp. " G. L. Wood.	H COMPANY (Painters). Capt. R. A. Todd. Lieut. H. A. R. May. " C. L. Pott.

William Rothenstein, who taught drawing to boys at the club. 'To become a worker in Whitechapel seemed an adventure,' he recalled. 'The East End was a part of London remote and of ill repute, which needed missionaries, it appeared, and it flattered my esteem to be one of these.'[17]

At the Whittington boys received instruction in an assortment of classes, including drawing, singing and military drill. Rothenstein was invited to join the 'Whittington Cadet Corps' as an officer. 'I fancied myself in a uniform with a sword,' he wrote, but ultimately declined, leaving the military stuff to a career soldier from the Artists Volunteers.

Lord (then the Honourable) Paul Methuen was an aristocrat and a professional soldier who would climb to the very top of the military tree. He was a personal friend of Colonel Robert Edis (acting commander of the Artists Volunteers), and had himself commanded the regiment in field exercises.

Methuen   Edis

The Artists' biographer H.R.A. May records:

Col Edis seemed to be acquainted with a vast number of distinguished people of every rank and profession, from Royalty downwards. I can also well recollect the evenings 'at home' given by Sir
Robert [Edis] at which all the notables in Art, Literature and Drama
might be met. Some very fine smoking concerts were arranged at
which some of the best talent in London gave their services, including Lionel Brough, Brandon Thomas, Michael Maybrick, and many
others. During his period of command many notable persons
visited us, not only the Prince of Wales, but the Duke of Cambridge,
Lord Roberts, Lord Wolseley, and Lord Methuen.[18]

The Honourable Lord Methuen was in charge of the lads' military
training at the Whittington Club, and was singled out for special
mention in the *Toynbee Record* of November 1888: 'Col the
Honourable Paul Methuen has greatly helped in reorganisation and
giving new life to the Corps.'

Officers of the Artists Rifles in 1878: Lieutenant Colonel Sir Frederick
Leighton, the commanding officer, is seated in the centre. 'They All Love
Jack', the Regimental March, was composed by Captain Michael Maybrick.

From Sir Frederick Leighton down, the Artists Rifles Volunteers
were all over Toynbee Hall. Not only were some of Michael
Maybrick's most intimate friends, including Thomas, Methuen and
Leighton, at Toynbee, but so were legions of boys and everything
he liked to go with them – uniforms and music – like a Junior
Artists V. A squad of disciplined youth in army togs sounds irresist-
ibly Maybrick to me. There was bayonet training and classes in
music drill. To join friends and fellow toffs doing Christian good
– just like Richard Whittington – may not have been entirely disagreeable to a psychopathic Freemason of the Bundy/Maybrick ilk.
After all, he could come and go whenever it suited, and if midnight
struck, there were always comfortable rooms 'for those staying at
odd times'.

Had Rothenstein, Methuen, or indeed W. Henry Thomas, been
Jack the Ripper, they would have enjoyed a most agreeable cover at
the Whittington Club while proffering their respective skills.

I want to take a brief look at a couple more letters before exploring
the murder of Martha Tabram at Toynbee's back door.

The first, dated 3 October 1888, comes out of a Midlands city, Stoke-on-Trent, and is addressed to the Lord Mayor of London.

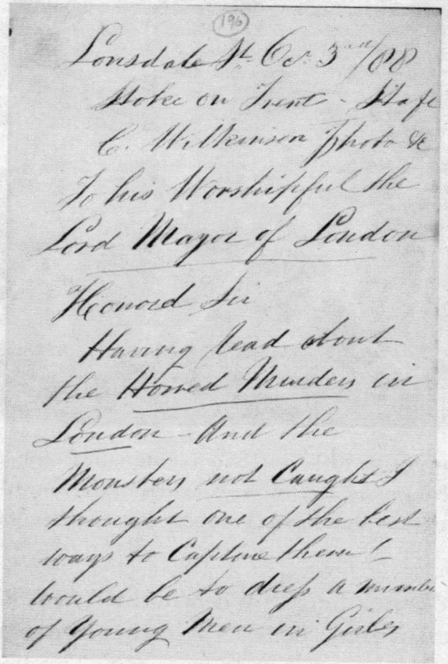

Oct 3rd 1888

Honord Sir

Having heard about the <u>Horrid Murders</u> in <u>London</u> – And the Monsters <u>not caught</u> I thought one of the best ways to capture them! would be to drefs a number of Young Men in Girls clothes.

The suggestion of drefsing men in female attire is a perverse signature that reiterates itself throughout the Ripper correspondence: 'Pafs when the man is in female attire' (1 October); 'Dress some of your smart detectives in women's clothes' (2 October). A letter dated 7 October 1888 and signed 'Homo Sum' will suffice for many more:

... I will suggest a mode by which it is possible the wretch who has committed these recent murders in London may be entrapped and brought to justice. As he seeks for his victims amongst women of the

class termed 'unfortunate', I suggest that strong but relatively slight
constables should be arraigned in women's clothes or as to resemble women …

Transvestism is featured in the City letters, just as the joys of murder
are in the Met's. But more egregious is the continuing religious
theme. We had an Irishman playing 'vicar' in Mr Marsh's shop, a
reverend in Leeds who signed himself 'Richard Whittington the
Second', and we have yet another reverend here. The 3 October
letter from Stoke-on-Trent is signed by a theologian of similar standing to Richard Whittington.

Charles Wilkinson was a star of the Victorian pulpit. Born in
Ireland in 1823, he rose through a variety of dioceses to become
Honorary Chaplain to Queen Victoria, and later served the religious needs of her son Edward, Prince of Wales. Whittington and
Wilkinson were evangelical icons conjoined in the same brain. Both
are another jibe at the detested god of the Establishment, and both
have an abstruse connection to Toynbee Hall.

The letter is signed 'Chas Wilkinson – Artist V'.

How dangerous can ego get? Replete with its instructors from the
Artists Volunteers, the Whittington Club was a thirty-second walk
from Leman Street police station (where that Vidocq of British
detectives, Superintendent Thomas Arnold, was brewing tea).

Not that Jack gave a toss for such trivialities as Bro Warren's
'Po-lice'. Just as he teased with the men of God, he even teased with
his own name, linking all three in a snickering intimation of Toynbee
Hall.

A letter out of Scotland, constituting one of what I call the
'McRipper clump', arrived from the environs of Edinburgh in early
October 1888. It crops up with two others (one of extreme impor-

tance) posted from the same area within forty-eight hours of each other.

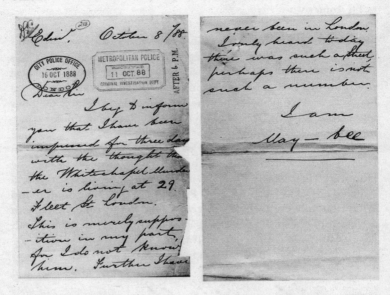

Once again we're looking at ego 'mathematics'. The letter's signature, 'May – bee', didn't happen by accident, any more than 'Artist V' – it meant something to the person who wrote it. Whichever way you look at it, its first half represents the first syllable of my candidate's name, and the curious spelling of its second half represents the last syllable of the place I was investigating.

May – brick
Toyn – bee
'May – bee'

Michael Maybrick, his 'Artist V' and 'Richard Whittington the Second' reek out of Toynbee Hall like homicidal DNA. At most it was a few minutes' walk from every crime scene, and only seconds from two of them. Even the most constipated of intellects would have to concede that Toynbee Hall would make a most inspired 'lair' for a visiting gentleman psychopath. Above suspicion, you could snuff at will and hasten back – a wash and brush-up and pickle your kidney – and with chalk in your pocket and 'Juwes' on your mind, stick on a hat and take a stroll at your ease up Goulston Street.

Nobody was looking into Toynbee Hall. It was people in there who were doing the looking out – pillars of the Establishment like Bro Sir Frederick Leighton and Bro Michael Maybrick.

Leighton   Maybrick

À propos of that, I can't help thinking of Robert Ressler's psychopathic ambulance driver, who contrived to take responsibility for picking up the bodies of those he had murdered.[19] I think Yack also immersed himself in the drama of his victims. 'I was in the crowd at Berner Street,' claims an October scrawl.

'If the police have a series of five homicides,' writes Ressler, 'that demonstrate the same MO, we advise looking most closely at the earliest one, for it will most likely have "gone down" closest to the place where the killer lived or worked or hung out … Often that first crime is not thoroughly planned, but succeeding ones will display greater forethought.'[20]

Had I been a detective in 1888, with or without cognisance of these letters, I'd have taken Toynbee Hall to pieces. I would have been particularly interested because the first Ripper hit happened so close to its premises. The crime scene actually shares a name with Toynbee Hall (George Yard Buildings), abutting St George's Yard, where in summer months cadets from the Whittington played their open-air concerts.

It is unlikely that Henry Thomas's lads were playing in the quadrangle over the first weekend of August 1888. The sky was leaden, and at around 50° Fahrenheit the temperature was unseasonably cool for the time of year. At about 2.30 a.m. in the dregs of that Monday, a Bank Holiday, J.T.R. was within the shadows of Toynbee Hall. He had a knife in his pocket, and possibly a bayonet. He may or may not have killed before. But tonight there was no option. The rage and expectation were of such intensity he wouldn't know whether what he felt was excitement or anguish.

One woman was in his thoughts. If fault there was, it was hers. She was a cunt, and he hated cunts. He was going to put one down.[21]

At about 3.30 a.m. a cab driver by the name of Albert Crow was returning home to George Yard Buildings. According to testimony at the inquest, 'As he was passing the first floor landing he saw a body on the ground. He took no notice as he was used to seeing people lying about there. He did not know whether the person was alive or dead.'

Tabram was an alcoholic who had been drinking heavily that night. She was last seen alive with a soldier almost three hours before. It's possible that for want of a bed, and anaesthetised from the booze, she crashed out in St George's Yard; it is also possible that it was there that her killer discovered her, and opportunistically attacked her in her sleep. But that is unlikely, because like Elizabeth Stride her hands were clenched when she was found.[22] More likely she ran into her client in the alley backing onto Toynbee Hall.

No official documentation of Tabram's injuries survives, but we can be confident that she was silenced by strangulation before her assailant got busy with the knife. A single penetrative wound to the heart would have caused instant death. However, police surgeon Dr T.R. Killeen believed all the wounds were inflicted while she was alive. This means her killer must have strangled her after she was dead, an absurd proposition. We know Jack was a novice, but he was not a half-wit.

I don't know the effect (nor the order in which they were delivered) of a precise thirty-nine stab wounds divided between the liver (five), stomach (six), left lung (five), right lung (two) and heart (one), but following strangulation, I find it hard to believe she was alive for all or any of them.

Killeen had accounted for nineteen stabs out of thirty-nine. That leaves twenty wounds in some unidentified place. Swanson compiled a characteristically vague retrospective the same month. He confirmed that the surgeon had found 'thirty nine wounds on the body, and neck, and private part with a knife or dagger'. (Doubtless a Toynbee Hall bayonet.)

On 11 August the *East London Observer* quoted Killeen as saying, 'The lower portion of the body was penetrated in one place, the wound being 3 inches in length and one in depth.' I think he was being economical with the truth. Why be so specific over nineteen stab wounds and so insouciant over the other twenty? There was much blood under Tabram, and palpably as much coyness over its source in the coroner's court. 'There was scarcely anyone present except the authorities and those connected with the case,' reported the *East London Observer*, 'the public being conspicuous by their absence.'

We shall never know what the court actually heard, but it seems suspiciously likely that Tabram's genitals were the focus of the Ripper's assault. 'The circumstances of this awful tragedy are surrounded with the deepest mystery.'[23]

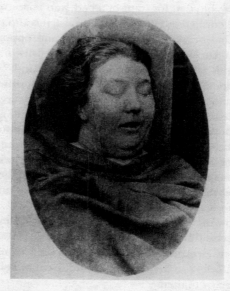

If Martha Tabram was the first of Jack's victims, Alice McKenzie was the last – at least the last in Whitechapel of interest to this narrative. McKenzie was a thirty-seven-year-old part-time whore with syphilis. At some time after midnight on the morning of 17 July 1889 she had her throat cut across in Castle Alley, an archetypal Ripper haunt running parallel to Goulston Street. Like his first hit at St George's Yard it was close to home, less than a minute away from Toynbee Hall.

According to *The Times*, 'This alley, which is entered by a passage not more than a yard in width, is entirely shut off from view of the main road, and would hardly be observed by the ordinary passer by.' Various houses and commercial properties backed into the darkness. Although the area was densely populated (Jews and dosshouses), nobody went up Castle Alley after dark unless they had to, really had to, and under such circumstances 'people generally enter from the Spitalfields end, especially at night on account of the dark and lonely nature of the alley, as well as the evil reputation it has always borne among the respectable portion of the inhabitants. The vans and other vehicles which crowd the thoroughfare,' continued *The Times*, 'notwithstanding the fact that the alley is lighted with three lamps, afford ample cover and secrecy for crime and violence.'

At about 12.45 a.m., McKenzie and her assassin walked up this thoroughfare in the intermittent rain. 'The exact spot where the body of the unfortunate woman was found was between two wagons, fastened together with a chain. Right against the wagons was a street lamp, and it was against this that the body of the murdered woman was discovered (at 12.50 a.m.) by a police officer.'

McKenzie's throat had been cut but minutes before. As with Elizabeth Stride, it would seem her killer had been disturbed. Her clothes were hauled up and her legs were wide apart, but only desultory mutilation had been performed. Even so, it 'bore a striking resemblance to the atrocities which so shocked and sickened London during the latter part of last year'.

Eight months had elapsed since the butchery of Mary Kelly. For this reason, and others of a more sinister genesis, the police didn't want to believe that McKenzie was part of the Ripper series, and had convinced themselves, and tried to convince everyone else, that the destruction of Kelly was the last of the outrages. The Fiend's apparent termination of his homicidal activity seemed inexplicable, and itself became an ingredient of the 'mystery'. Why had he stopped? A 'monomaniac' doesn't just toss in the towel and buy a newsagent's shop in Bournemouth. He goes on killing until something prevents him. So what happened?

The general consensus, to this day, is that either 1) he was incarcerated in a nut-house, or possibly in prison for some other crime; or 2) he was a short-arsed seafarer currently in foreign parts; or 3) he was dead.

The latter was the favourite. Melville Macnaghten, and not a few police chiefs after him, put it about that this multiple murderer and sadist of infinite rapacity had somehow given himself a dose of the creeps after Kelly and drowned himself. 'The probability,' wrote Macnaghten, 'is that his brain gave way altogether and he committed suicide, otherwise the murders would not have ceased.'[24]

They didn't. Jack went right on killing. He had killed Mary Kelly on 8 November 1888. Johnnie Gill would follow on 27 December

1888; James Maybrick on 11 May 1889; Alice McKenzie on 17 July 1889; the so-called 'Pinchin Street Torso' (Lydia Hart?) on 8 September 1889; Frances Coles on 14 February 1891; and likely many more.

The Ripper hadn't stopped killing at all. What had stopped was the police associating him with his crimes. Meanwhile, a conveniently screwed-up nonentity called Montague J. Druitt had stuffed his pockets with rocks and jumped in the big river. They pulled his corpse out of the Thames on the last day of December 1888, and were happy to conclude that this innocent stiff, with nothing to do with Jack the Ripper, was Jack the Ripper.

Druitt's suicide as a solution was handed down at Scotland Yard like a family tradition. Because of Macnaghten's 'memoranda' – a document revered by Ripperology, but as transparently bogus as Anderson's Continental holiday – Druitt became one of the prime suspects, sharing the honour with Ostrog, Kosminski, et al.

Macnaghten knew that the lot of them put together were rubbish on a dynamic scale. Druitt and Kosminski were passing straws converted into a life-raft, and the police clambered aboard and started lying. Even Abberline confirmed Druitt as a nonsense: 'absolutely nothing to incriminate him', he said.[25]

From Martha Tabram on, every action was made subservient to the evolving deceit known in the trade as the 'mystery'. A headless torso at Scotland Yard? 'The Whitehall mystery'. Body parts in the Thames? 'The Thames mystery'. A hideously murdered and mutilated child in Bradford? 'The Bradford mystery'.

Murder by 'person or persons unknown' was of course the predetermined dénouement. The investigation of Alice McKenzie's murder needn't detain us long. It was of the usual hopelessness, with the usual 'fruitless arrests'. It wasn't until after the inquest that anything of substance developed. Following his acrimonious dismissal as coroner preceding the Kelly cover-up, Bro Wynne Baxter was back, and Divisional Police Surgeon Bro Dr Bagster Phillips was giving his medical evidence.

Having described another extremely cut throat, the slippery physician moved on to McKenzie's wounds. 'There were several,' reported *The Times*, 'and those were most of them superficial cuts to the lower part of the body.'[26]

Although no one paid them any particular interest, these 'super-ficial cuts' were of *extreme* importance. *The Times* bothers no more with them, so we turn to the *Pall Mall Gazette*: 'Seven inches below the right nipple, in a line continuous with it, commenced an exter-nal wound. It was seven inches long and deepest in the middle part. It only divided the skin and not any muscular structure, and there-fore did not injure any internal cavity. There were scored wounds towards the navel, and seven more running downwards from the middle of the wound.'

I become interested when anyone seeks to withhold evidence, and especially alert when it's Bro Dr Phillips, the very same who had done his utmost to navigate the details of Chapman's injuries. On this occasion he got luckier with Bro Baxter: 'Dr Phillips sought and obtained permission to withhold certain facts that have come to his knowledge on the course of his examination of the body. What those facts are it is idle to conjecture.'

Another month was to pass before anyone found out what these 'facts' were, and by then they had lost all significance. I don't doubt this was the reason they were withheld. The inquest was formally postponed until Wednesday, 14 August 1889.

Just over two weeks before it reconvened, the Whitechapel Murderer mailed one of the most important and revealing letters he ever wrote. It is undated, but has the receipt stamp of the City Police, 30 July 1889, and contained an enclosure:

He surely is if you're a Freemason. 'The House of the Lord' is Solomon's Temple, as delineated below on the title page of this Masonic history, and articulated by Charles Warren himself at his Quatuor Coronati lecture: '*I have surely built thee an house*'.[27]

THE
HISTORY OF FREEMASONRY;
FROM THE
BUILDING OF THE HOUSE OF THE LORD,
AND ITS
PROGRESS THROUGHOUT THE CIVILIZED WORLD,
DOWN TO THE PRESENT TIME.

THE ONLY HISTORY OF ANCIENT CRAFT MASONRY EVER PUBLISHED, EXCEPT
A SKETCH OF FORTY-EIGHT PAGES BY DOCTOR ANDERSON IN 1723.

The letter accompanying the enclosure is of such importance it is astonishing that it has survived. I can only imagine it was because the Met had persuaded themselves of their own delusion that Jack had drowned himself, and that this belief had somehow infected the City Police.

a Startling echo
mat – 11ch – 12vs

Sir
Will you cause these Labels to be put up in the place were the woman was found dead in Whitechapel 17 inst and it shall fulfil that that the Lord hath designed it to do

they are to be put up at midnight –
for the Lord will look upon them.
Thus saith the Holy Ghost
my hand Slew them
my finger stabed them
my nails cut them in pieces.

Nahum 1 – 2 – 3

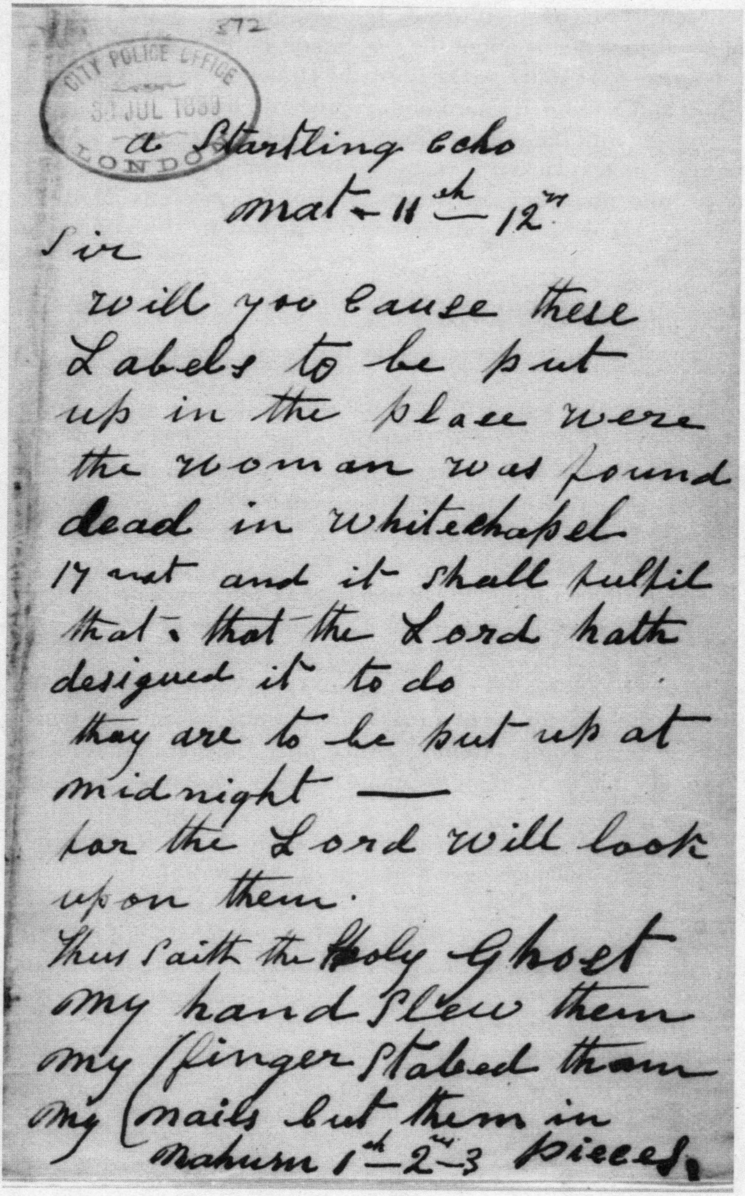

572

CITY POLICE OFFICE
31 JUL 1889
LONDON

A Startling Echo

Mat = 11th 12th

Sir

will you cause these
Labels to be put
up in the place were
the woman was found
dead in Whitechapel
17 inst and it shall fulfil
that: that the Lord hath
designed it to do
they are to be put up at
midnight —
for the Lord will look
upon them.
Thus saith the Holy Ghost
my hand slew them
my (finger stabed them
my (nails cut them in
Nahum 1st 2nd 3 pieces.

Sir Melville Macnaghten wrote, 'I do not think there was anything of a religious mania about the real Simon Pure,'[28] and apart from references to St Matthew, the Lord, the House of the Lord, the Holy Ghost and Nahum, it's hard not to agree with him.

Starting with the religious mania, I'm going to take this letter to pieces. The text kicks off (via St Matthew) with a Biblical reference to St John the Baptist, a patron saint of Freemasonry. Matthew, chapter 11, verse 12, references the Baptist in the context of violence:

> And from the days of John the Baptist until now the Kingdom of Heaven suffereth violence, and the violent take it by force.

Both John the Baptist and John the Evangelist are icons in Freemasonry, celebrated on their respective days of 24 June and 27 December. It is at St John that the Bible is opened for the initiate to take his Masonic oath. The Ripper's second Biblical quote, Nahum 1 verses 2 and 3, comes from one of the last books of the Old Testament: 'God is jealous, and the LORD revengeth, the LORD revengeth and is furious; the LORD will take vengeance on his adversaries, and he reserveth *wrath* for his enemies. The LORD is slow to anger, and great in power, and will not at all acquit the wicked.'

What wickedness was in Jack's mind? Certainly not his own, but I believe the wickedness of an adulterous woman. 'And the LORD hath given a commandment concerning thee,' fulminates the Prophet, 'that no more of thy name be sown. I will make thy grave, for thou art vile.'

Nahum is a waltz through vengeance and death. If you were a psychopath you might get a fix out of this junk. In his seminal Masonic work *Morals and Dogma* (1871), Albert Pike cautions justice tempered by mercy in the department of revenge, 'but if it be not in human nature not to take revenge by way of punishment, let the Mason truly consider that in doing so he is God's agent'.[29]

Jack was an agent of God.

This letter is radioactive with Freemasonry, and doesn't remotely disguise it. But it is its knowledge of the injuries inflicted on Alice McKenzie that makes it astonishing:

> my hand Slew them
> my finger stabed them
> my nails cut them in pieces

This reference to fingernails is key to the murder of McKenzie. It was the evidence Dr Bagster Phillips had successfully withheld. No information about cutting with fingernails was made public until Wednesday, 14 August 1889,[30] yet the writer knows about it, and brags about it, *more than two weeks earlier*, on 30 July, sixteen days before the resumption of Bro Baxter's court.

On 15 August the *Manchester Weekly Times* reported the proceedings. Bro Dr Phillips was the first to give evidence.

> Witness continuing, said there were some marks about the external abdomen which he *did not mention* [my emphasis] on the last occasion. They were five in number, but with the exception of one were on the left side of the abdomen. The largest one was the lowest. The small one was the exceptional one mentioned, which was typical of a finger-nail mark. They were coloured, and were caused, in his opinion, by the finger-nails and thumb-nail of a hand. He on subsequent examination assured himself of the correctness of his observations. The marks were caused after the throat was cut. They were caused by a broad hand.

At the first inquest Phillips had led the newspapers to believe that these 'wounds' were caused by incompetent use of a knife. On 18 July the *Telegraph* reported: 'They were only skin deep and did not divide the muscular structure beneath. They were scored and numbered 14 in all. It would seem from these facts that a less skilful hand was directing the knife than heretofore, or else the weapon itself was of a less formidable character.'

Nothing about fingernails, so even the most vigilant of hoaxers would have been out of luck. Phillips had clearly created the impression that these were superficial wounds inflicted by some bungling assassin with a blunt knife. By his manipulation of the evidence he was disassociating the murder of Alice McKenzie from the Ripper. At his second appearance he was actually perverting the course of justice, choosing mollifying words and contradicting the evidence in his own autopsy report.

In this withheld document of 17 July 1889, McKenzie had been cut so deeply with fingernails that Phillips listed the injuries under two different headings. Describing one of these 'mutilations' (his word) under 'Scoring and Wounds of the Abdomen', he wrote of it 'ending in a subcutaneous dissection of perhaps 3 or 4 inches'. 'The abdominal cavity was not opened,' he writes, but the lacerations were deep enough (incredibly) even to be considered in such a context.

These unique injuries were in fact a hyper-sadistic assault using the fingers as weapons. Phillips's suppressed report confirms that the murderer's nails were dug as viciously into his victim's corpse as he could get them. 'My nails cut them in pieces,' wrote Jack. No hoaxer on earth could have known this, and the author of the 30 July letter is Alice McKenzie's killer.

To cut your victim's flesh with fingernails may be common practice for the sadist, but to make a written point of it struck me as unusual. This signature obviously had some significance for the murderer. At a glance (as in the 'Women of Moab'), his reference to the wounds reads like a further citation from the Bible, and that's the first place I looked. A standard concordance lists eight references to nails, most of the variety that fastened Jesus to the Roman equivalent of the electric chair. Not the nails I was looking for, but it had to come from somewhere, and naturally my thinking didn't exclude what I knew about Michael Maybrick.

He and the lyricist Frederick Weatherly had composed many religious (sacred) songs, and Maybrick was a ringer for this kind of quasi-religious doggerel. In 1888 Maybrick published four new titles, and in 1889 three others, which later prompted music critic Maurice Disher to remark that they 'trembled on the brink of blasphemy'. Christian and Masonic themes coalesce in many of these compositions – 'The Star of Bethlehem', by way of example, and later 'The Holy City', inspired by St John's supposed 'Revelation'. From the late 1880s, Maybrick was in 'religious mode'.

In an interview given to the *Isle of Wight Observer* shortly before his death, Maybrick said, 'I am fond of reading, and my favourite authors are the great poets.'[31] I think one of them was Richard Crashaw, a seventeenth-century metaphysical genius who was big on fingernails, and right up Maybrick's street.[32] The curious metaphor of nails as knives surfaces in a poem called 'Sancta Maria Dolorum', or 'The Mother of the Sorrows'. It's a disturbing howl of mother-hood and grief. Every line is an anguish, and every line is death, including the phrase I was looking for: 'His nails write swords in her' appears in the third stanza.

> O costly intercourse of death's, and worse –
> Divided loves. While son and mother
> Discourse alternate wounds to one another,
> Quick deaths that grow.
> And gather, as they come and go.
> His nails write swords in her ...

'The Mother of the Sorrows' reads like an archetypical Maybrick/Weatherly lyric, their 'Sacred Songs' frequently ripping off poets like Spenser or Crashaw. Out went the rollicking mariners, and in came the angels, Christian morbidity developing into Maybrick's trademark: 'In the shade of death's sad tree' (Crashaw); 'As the shadow of a cross arose' (Weatherly). (Indeed, the line 'O costly intercourse of death ...' also appears in the so-called 'Diary of Jack the Ripper'.)

But, irrespective of its muse, we have a letter written by Alice McKenzie's murderer. It doesn't disguise its Masonry and elements of the co-Masonic sect known as Rosicrucianism. In some distinguished quarters they were considered one and the same: Charles Warren's pal and founder member of the Quatuor Coronati, William Wynn Westcott, argued that Masonry had evolved from Rosicrucianism. Alice McKenzie's murderer asks for his labels, 'SURELY THE LORD IS IN THIS HOUSE', to be put up at the crime scene: 'They are to be put up at midnight – for the Lord will look upon them. Thus saith the Holy Ghost.'

Midnight is magic and central to Rosicrucian doctrine, a sacred hour for the disciples, for 'Each night at Midnight there is a Service in the Temple' where the Brethren meet. It's here things fuse into the eclectic, as they did in the Ripper's head. 'The House of the Lord' is purely Masonic and belongs to the Holy Royal Arch. Masonic historian Bro W.L. Wilmshurst tells us that Psalm 122 represents a microcosm of 'all that is implied in the symbolic spectacle that greets the eyes of a Royal Arch Mason at the supreme moment of his restoration to light':

> I was glad when they said unto me
> Let us go up into the House of the Lord
> Our feet shall stand within thy gates
> O Jerusalem.

'He sees how he has "gone up",' writes Wilmshurst. 'Out of the Babylon of his old complex and distorted nature and upon the ruins, he has built for himself an ethereal body of glory, a "House of the Lord".'[33] The House of the Lord is built upon a city (the one Warren spent years excavating), 'and in this "city" the blessed condition, which mystically is called "Jerusalem", otherwise known as "The Holy City" … The antithesis of this "Heavenly City" is the confused Babylon City of this world, of which it is written to all captives therein, 'Come out of her, My People, that ye be not partakers of her sins and that ye receive not of her plagues' (Revelation 18).

The Book of Revelation insinuates itself into this history like a virus. This isn't necessarily to criticise the traditions of Freemasonry, any more than it is to criticise those of the Christian Church. The Ripper drew liberally from both, and returned his malignancy wholesale. It's no accident that Maybrick chose the title of his most enduring song, 'The Holy City', from the Book of Revelation, nor that the same thinking chose St John's 'Whore of Babylon' (the Catholic Florence Maybrick) to cut down.

Masons and Rosicrucians may have bickered about the genesis of their sects, but they shared a burning antipathy to 'the Scarlet Whore of Catholicism', Babylon in Revelations – representing Rome. In the case of the Rosicrucians, they called the Pope 'Antichrist, a blasphemer against Christ': 'They execrate him, and look forward to the time *when he shall be torn to pieces with nails.*' (Their emphasis.)

Slashing Alice McKenzie with fingernails was an impulse of thinking that doesn't explain itself any more than a lightning bolt unravels the complexities of a storm. Huge forces motivate both. McKenzie's abdominal lacerations were a flash of inspiration in the Freemasonic nightmare, just as were the inverted 'V' marks on Catherine Eddowes' face.

Doc Bagster Phillips was a Freemason with well-established credentials in judicial obfuscation. Why *would* any police surgeon withhold evidence about the Beast's fingernails, only to release it a month later in mealy-mouthed, deodorised waffle that by then had lost all public interest and significance?

Here's his forked tongue in action at the first inquest:

> BAXTER: Are the injuries to the *abdomen* similar to those that you
> have seen in other cases?
> DR PHILLIPS: No Sir. I may volunteer the statement that the
> injuries to the *throat* are not similar to those in other cases.

This is like asking a man the size of his *hat*, and being told the size of his *shoes*. He was avoiding one question and manipulating the other. Another opinion was sought on McKenzie, and the following day her body was re-examined by another surgeon, the ubiquitous Dr Bond. Phillips accompanied Bond to the mortuary, and Bond reported that Phillips informed him that 'the wounds in the throat had been so disturbed that any examination I might make unassisted would convey no definite information as to the nature of the injuries'.

This was unacceptable to Bond. Furthermore, he wrote, 'Dr Phillips stated that before the parts were disturbed, the cuts which I saw extending downwards really were in a direction upwards.' The two doctors were already in radical disagreement. Bruises suggesting the mechanics of the homicide to Phillips were rejected by Bond: 'I saw no sufficient reason to entertain this opinion.' And because 'the wounds on the abdomen could have nothing to do with the cause of death', Bond was convinced he was looking at another example of sexual/sadistic postmortem ritual. 'On the right side of the abdomen,' he wrote, 'extending from the chest to below the level of the umbilicus, there was a jagged incision made up of several cuts which extended through the skin and subcutaneous fat.' And more importantly, 'there was also a small stab of one-eighth of an inch deep and a quarter of an inch long on the mons veneris'.

A finger as a surrogate prick, ejaculating hate:

> my finger stabed them
> my nails cut them in pieces

It must not be forgotten that the McKenzie letter was received fifteen days *before* Bond revealed evidence of this wound, unequivocally proving that the writer was aware of something so extraordinarily specific as a 'stab' upon McKenzie's vagina with a fingernail. In respect of these wounds Bond wrote, 'the murderer must have raised the clothes with his left hand and inflicted the injuries with his right'. There was absolutely no doubt in his mind that this was another Ripper hit: 'I see in this murder evidence of similar design to the Whitechapel Murders, viz: sudden onslaught on the prostrate woman, the throat skilfully and resolutely cut, with subsequent mutilation. Each mutilation indicating sexual thoughts and a desire to mutilate the abdomen and sexual regions. I am of the opinion that the murder was committed by the same person who committed the former series of Whitechapel Murders.'[34]

This was bad news for Phillips and the boys, and Bond's conclusions were therefore not made public. He refers to 'mutilation', a word of somewhat less discretion than the 'marks' selected for dissemination by Bro Phillips. Bond had blown the gaff, and Phillips was now obliged to include fingernails in his evidence – or, I hazard, Dr Bond might have wanted to know why he had not. Bro Phillips must thus dissemble, once again perverting the course of justice.

'There were some marks on the abdomen which he didn't mention before,' he admitted at the 14 August inquest. The vicious stab to McKenzie's vagina was presented as: 'The small one was exceptional, which was typical of a finger-nail mark.' Nothing specified, and nothing in context. The average punter reading this would think McKenzie had a flea bite. It's no wonder the press thought these mutilations were the marks of an amateur's blade. Misinformation was Phillips's intention. At all costs he had to try to dismiss any relationship between this atrocity and the series preceding it. To tell the truth was to tell the world that Jack the Ripper was still alive, well, and active.

Dr Bond was not a Freemason, and nor was Charles Warren's replacement as Met Commissioner James Monro. Both were convinced the Ripper was responsible for the death in Castle Alley. Unless there were two Freemasons cutting throats in Whitechapel, then the Ripper killed Alice McKenzie.

By ignoring the murder of Johnnie Gill at Bradford in December 1888, the police had created an eight-month gap between the slaying of Mary Kelly and that of Alice McKenzie. The hiatus is utterly artificial, but nevertheless did its job, giving substance to fantasies of 'incarceration' (Anderson) and 'suicide' (for liars like Macnaghten).

Without Bro Dr Phillips, Macnaghten is a dead duck. If the Ripper killed McKenzie (which would require explaining away the 30 July letter if he didn't) then Messrs Druitt, Kosminski and Ostrog are bullshit, and his famous 'memoranda' nothing more than the paper to wrap it up in.

1) *Kosminski*: A non-starter from day one. According to Macnaghten himself, Kosminski was 'removed to a lunatic asylum about March 1889', so he couldn't have killed McKenzie (McKenzie is marginalised by Freemasologists for precisely this reason). Plus, Phillips said of McKenzie's mutilations, 'They were caused by a broad hand,' and as we've heard from Bond, 'The murderer must have been a man of physical strength.' *Ergo*, we've got a powerful man with big hands. Kosminski was a five-foot squirt with hands the size of a child's. Goodbye.

2) *Michael Ostrog*: It is proved the McKenzie letter could have been written by nobody but her murderer. Only a Masonic assassin could have written it. If Ostrog was a Freemason and Macnaghten knew it, he should have included that fact in his 'memoranda', and given it a little credibility. If he wasn't a Freemason, then he wasn't Jack the Ripper, but simply a half-witted con artist whose timely disappearance in 1888 facilitated the kind of candidacy you could have found from any name on a toilet wall. In respect of Ostrog, Mr Paul Begg writes of recent evidence suggesting that he was probably imprisoned in France: 'This discovery has naturally shed doubt upon the real value of the "Macnaghten Memorandum".' He adds: 'Why should someone [Ostrog] whose whereabouts were unknown, who therefore wasn't even known to be in London, let alone Whitechapel, be listed among the top three suspects?' A very good question. 'Sadly,' continues Mr Begg, 'the answer is that we don't know and it seems futile to guess.' No guessing is necessary. Macnaghten made it up.

3) *Montague Druitt*: Druitt was dead and buried, and therefore would have had difficulty murdering Alice McKenzie.

The 'Macnaghten Memoranda', Bro 'Swanson's Marginalia' and the rest of the twaddle are a waste of ink, best left to 'respectable historians'. Insemination of these fictions has perverted research for over fifty years, and coupled with Bro Stowell's garbage about the Duke of Clarence, almost destroyed it.

'Patrolled by policemen, who cannot see, hear or think', was the judgement of the *New York Herald* in respect of events in Whitechapel.[35] This was echoed by the *New York Tribune*. Jack was murdering 'without fear of interference from the London police', who were 'blind, stupid, blundering, and of impregnable apathy'.[36]

None of the players in this ugly saga did what they did – whether washing evidence off a wall, or nominating Kosminski – *by accident*. Their deafness to the pleas of Henrietta Barnett and their blindness to the psychopath laughing in their face wasn't *by accident*. Warren, Anderson, Macnaghten and a host of others enmeshed themselves in this enduring corruption known as 'the mystery of Jack the Ripper', to avoid the telling of it.

I've a certain sympathy for those who performed the bit parts, but little for the major players. They were wretches, in a wretched deceit, unworthy of the mercy of the years. We are on the shore of a great scandal, and a greater tragedy, and have barely set our sail.

14

'Orpheus'

One man's wickedness may easily become all men's
curse.

Publilius Syrus, 100 BC

The unluckiest day of Florence Chandler's life was the day of her
introduction to James Maybrick. It happened in March 1880, aboard
the SS *Baltic* out of New York heading for his home town of
Liverpool. She was seventeen and he was forty-one. During the 150
hours of this benighted voyage they became inseparable; it was what
the mags call a 'lightning romance'. Florence was pretty and bright
and educated; plus, there was no shortage of money. She wore
French dresses and her expensive shoes clattered delightfully on the
iron stairways. First-class deck-chairs looked back at America, a
charming Englishman escorted her into one of them, and this is
what she told him.

She was born in Mobile, Alabama, of the Southern aristocracy,
and was a frequent visitor to Europe, having been at school for a
while in Germany. She and her mother, with whom she was travelling, were on their way to Paris, where her elder brother Halbrook
was studying medicine. Her mother was a Baroness, the title coming
from her third, now defunct, marriage to a Prussian cavalry officer,
Baron Adolph von Roques. Her first husband, William Chandler, a
banker and Florie's dad, had died before Florie was born, and there
was obviously a 'daddy' thing in her attraction to the charming and
dependable-looking Maybrick.

Here's what he told her. One of five surviving brothers, he was
born on 24 October 1838. His father was a printer of undistin-
guished origin – but don't let that put you off. Shipping slaves out
of Africa and tobacco and cotton back home had made Liverpool

one of the richest cities on earth, and James was riding the tide. He was a cotton broker, dividing his time between his company's head offices in Tithebarn Street and its American branch in Norfolk, Virginia. Although he probably exaggerated his wealth to Florence, he was successful, becoming director of the Norfolk Cotton Exchange in 1881.

He would have told her about his famous musical brother Michael, climbing the bills with Charles Santley and about to overtake him as a star. He probably also told her about his other brothers – Thomas, in business in Manchester, and handsome young Edwin, also in the cotton business, who was later to become Florie's lover. Meanwhile there was flattery for the Baroness and her command of languages, ditto for her daughter's radiant blonde hair. They drank champagne in the opulence of the *Baltic*'s saloon, watched the moon rise over the Atlantic – and Christ, was a nightmare assembling.

This is what he didn't tell her. He didn't tell her that he was a 'seducer, an adulterer, and a debauchee'. Plus, he had a serious drug problem. At some time in the 1870s he'd contracted malaria, and arsenic had been prescribed for the fever. Maybrick continued to self-prescribe it for the rest of his life.

I don't know what the buzz is from this deadly toxin, but its use wasn't entirely uncommon amongst certain gents in the nineteenth century. In controlled doses it was credited as a kind of predecessor of Viagra, and if that was true Maybrick must have had a permanent hard-on, because his consumption was enormous. 'He used constantly to come to me for medications,' deposed his local pharmacist, 'usually for liquor arsenicles [which] he would sometimes take as often as five times a day.'[1] There were one or two other little details of his life that James doubtless withheld, not least of which was that he may already have been married – at least, he had fathered five kids with a woman called Sarah Ann Robertson. A Bible belonging to her was recently discovered with a dedication from James: 'To my Darling Piggy, from her Affectionate Husband J.M.'[2] Whether they were actually married or not is unknown, but when she died in 1927 she evidently thought she was: her death certificate refers to 'Sarah Ann Maybrick, otherwise Robertson'.[3]

Obviously in starry-eyed innocence of the arsenic and the adultery, Florence had apparently consented to become Mrs Maybrick by the time the *Baltic* docked at Liverpool.

The couple married in St James Church, Piccadilly, London, on 21 July 1881. Michael was James's best man, and he most decidedly didn't like the look of his brother's bride. Years later, in a house as sick as Maybrick himself, a tearful Florence would confide in one of the few friends she had, Mrs Humphreys, the Maybricks' cook. 'This is all through Michael Maybrick,' she said, claiming that 'he had always had a spite against her since her marriage'.[4] That was something of an understatement. Michael hated her, as his actions in the latter part of this narrative will prove. Perhaps she attracted him in some way, and he hated her for that?

After the wedding there was a quick honeymoon in Bournemouth before the pair returned to America. For the next few years they would commute between Virginia and Liverpool, where they finally settled in 1884. Early in 1888 they moved to a grand house opposite Liverpool Cricket Club in the upmarket suburb of Aigburth. It was an impressive residence called Battlecrease House, with a complement of servants, and peacocks strutting in its five or six acres. By now the Maybricks had two children, Gladys and James, nicknamed 'Bobo', who their parents doted on.

It might have looked the perfect picture of Victorian family bliss. But it wasn't. James's business wasn't going well, and what with her Parisian frocks and classy lifestyle, Florence was living beyond her husband's means. Uncomfortable elements of his past were also seeping through. Adultery was back on the agenda, possibly with Sarah Robertson, or maybe another woman, but either way, Florence had become aware of it, and the couple slept in separate rooms.[5]

A generation younger than her husband, Florie also took lovers. She fell in love with one of his associates at the Cotton Exchange, a handsome young bachelor called Alfred Brierley; and when she wasn't kissing him she was kissing Edwin, James's younger brother. Florence was a sexual butterfly, and James an arsenic-ridden old moth out of money. By mid-1888 she had run up some atrocious debts behind his back – silk dresses, handmade boots – and was becoming frightened of a knock on the door. She was borrowing money from wherever she could, including loan sharks in London and her brother-in-law Michael. 'She has come to me time and again for money,' he was to say, 'and she always got it.'[6] She borrowed £100 from Michael, although this would be carefully manipulated at her 'trial' to become a loan from an acquaintance called Matilda Briggs. But Mrs Briggs was of no inclination to lend Florence so much as a handkerchief to blow her nose in, and perjured the best part of her arse off in the witness box.

Michael lent Florence the money, but deeply resented it. He hated her, with her expensive airs and graces and indiscreet sexual favours, selling it like a lady when she was worth no more than wreckage you could fuck in Whitechapel for fourpence.

That's what I think he thought, and that's what I think Jack the Ripper thought too. The man who chose Whitechapel as the focus for his revenge bore a similar resentment over £100 loaned and never repaid. 'I suppose you would like to know why I am killing so many women?' posits Jack in a letter dated 23 October 1888. Together with all the usual hints and teases, he converts Florence Elizabeth Maybrick into 'three women', and her American identity is hinted at by a reference to 'San Francisco'.

> … the answer is simply this. When I was in San Francisco in July 1888, I lent three women from London about 100 pounds sterling to pay some debts they had got into, promising to pay me back in a

months time, and seeing that they had a ladylike look I lent the money. Well, when the month passed by I asked for my money, but I found that they had sneaked off to London. I swore that i would have my revenge, the revenge was this. That I would go to London and kill as many women as possible. I've killed 9 as yet. you've not found all the corpses yet. Ha. Ha. I've told Sir C. Warren that in a letter of 22nd inst [unknown]. In the last woman I killed I cut out the kidneys and eat them. you'll find the body in one of the sewers in the East End. The [leg] you found at Whitehall does not belong to the trunk you found there. The police alias po-lice, think them-selves devilish clever I suppose. they'ill never catch me at this rate you donkeys, you double faced asses, you had better take the blood hounds away or I will kill them. I'm on the scent of those women who swindled me so basely, living like well to do ladies on the money they sneaked from me, never mind that, I'll have em yet, afore I'm done, damn em. To tell you the truth you ought to be obliged to me for killing such a deuced lot of virmin, why they are ten times worse than men.

He signs himself from the London suburb where Lilly Vass had apparently gone into service before her supposed trip to the Isle of Wight:

> I remain etc
> Jack the Ripper
> alias
> H.J.C. Battersea

I think this text is about as near to a confession of motive as we're ever going to get. Knowing what this aberrant brain had in store for Florence, it's dispiriting to read. Money owed, and these 'three women', gnaw into Jack's disease. 'Three women done me wrong in Whitechapel,' declares another letter:

> I will cut
> out There
> Abdomen I dare say you
> Know what
> That means

I am Jack the Ripper
Whitechapel
Three women done me
wrong in Whitechapel
so I will kill every
woman there.
because of them

'The mind has mountains', wrote the poet Gerard Manley Hopkins, and we're poised to move into the psychopathic heights of Michael Maybrick's thinking. Every facet of these terrible crimes, from the butchery in the East End streets to the murder of James Maybrick in an exclusive Liverpool suburb, was carefully planned by the same remarkable mind. Michael was possessed of a catastrophic ego of limitless wickedness, and must have considered himself one of the smartest bastards alive, a genius no doubt, especially as the extermination of his brother was but a stepping stone to his dream target, the little whore, 'the mother of abominations', as she's described in Masonry's oracle, the Book of Revelation.

Jack's generosity with his Masonic clues was no accident. It was stage-managed, and it was this flagrant debris that panicked the executive and sustained the Ripper's immunity. It was reasonably assumed that anyone who left such incriminating junk in his wake must have been mad, and thus Charles Warren et al. took the view that the Ripper was an insane Freemason, and the psychopath's intention was precisely that.

James Maybrick was an active Freemason until the day of his death on 11 May 1889. As an immutable fact, his Freemasonry is the most important element to understand before anybody can hope to get traction on 'the mystery of Jack the Ripper'. Hence James Maybrick's posthumous Masonic wipe-out. His association with Freemasonry has been as comprehensively and vigorously stripped from his being as has Freemasonry from the Ripper himself. The monumental falsehood that neither was a Freemason is propagated by the wheezing outfit I call 'Freemasology', and it keeps up its mirrors around this single nefarious root.

Ripper correspondence abounds with references to Liverpool and the USA, Americanisms appearing frequently: 'quit', 'buckled', 'side-walk', 'so long'. The first letter – or at least one of the first –

known as 'Dear Boss', is redolent of an American or someone with American connections, and many people at the time, including Arthur Conan Doyle, thought the assassin might be a Yank. Michael Maybrick was laying what's known in screenwriting as 'pipe'. The intention is to bury elements in a narrative that will come together as an inevitable outcome when they are eventually revealed. In terms of fiction, Alfred Hitchcock was a master. In terms of fact, so was Jack the Ripper. He was laying pipe to point a plausible finger of accusation at the man and woman he'd elected to destroy.

From a Scotland Yard perspective of 1888 (had there been a Commissioner of Integrity), a thumbnail sketch of the Ripper would have indicated a powerful and intelligent man, subject to intermittent homicidal mania. A Freemason, or a man who knew a lot about Freemasonry. A man who killed only at weekends, and therefore possibly commuted to London to do it. Moreover, a man who might be an American, or who at least had connections to the USA.

Enter, unbeknown to himself, arsenic addict and serial adulterer James Maybrick, a Freemason belonging to a London lodge whose Saturday meetings required him to travel from Liverpool to London at weekends. A man who had lived in America and was married to an American, and who had continuing business affairs in that country.

Michael Maybrick framed his brother James as Jack, offed him with a hotshot of poison, then framed Florence for the murder. I do not doubt that at the time of the outrage Michael's ruse was believed, and the authorities willingly bought into the revelations that his fucked-up brother James was Jack. James's credentials were persuasive, and their informant was a gentleman of impeccable honour.

How devastating it must have been for the broken-hearted Michael. How hard he must have fought against it, exploring every avenue to prove himself wrong. But the 'facts' were no alibi to James, and in matters of such gravity, ties of blood must take second place to duty, and duty required the tip-off.

P.S. Florence Maybrick knows all. ha ha

By this means, with the cunning of Satan, Michael assured his own immunity and brought the executive gratefully on side.

When we get to the criminal atrocity known in the vernacular as 'the trial of Florence Maybrick', it will become evident just how deeply the authorities were implicated. Michael would exploit them all – government, Freemasonry, police – and all would readily acquiesce in deference to their own survival.

James Maybrick's Freemasonry has successfully been kept a secret for 130 years. Tracing his Masonic records took more time than it gives me pleasure to remember. It was an endless toil, and there are no surprises in that. If you wanted to cover up the Ripper you would most certainly have to cover up James.

Although the staff of the library at Freemasons' Hall in London were as accommodating as ever, as far as they were concerned James Maybrick was definitely not a Mason: 'Further to your enquiry, we have checked our records for the above name without success.'

No one was lying – they just didn't know.

But secrets in one attic aren't necessarily secret in another. On my travels through the archives I came across a bit of doggerel by Henry Wadsworth Longfellow. It tells the tale of long winter afternoons beyond the cobwebs of forgotten archives:

> No action, whether foul or fair,
> Is ever done, but it leaves somewhere
> A record, written by fingers ghostly,
> As a blessing or a curse, and mostly
> In the greater weakness or greater strength
> Of the acts which follow it, till at length
> The wrongs of ages are addressed,
> And the justice of God made manifest.[7]

I know little about God, but James Maybrick was a prominent Freemason in Liverpool, as well as a respected businessman. Like the rest of the elite of the city – its Members of Parliament, its worthies and mayors – he was a member of at least three lodges: the St George's Lodge of Harmony (35), the Liverpool Chapter (19), and another Royal Arch chapter, Jerusalem (32).

The earliest reference I found to him having taken the oath is dated 31 December 1869, and thereafter he remained in distinguished Freemasonic company until the day of his death.

Cataloguing James's Masonic history would mean a clog of documents, and I've banished most of them. But below, by way of example, is an entry from the annual register of St George's Lodge of Harmony, dated 24 January 1877. I include it because it's midway through James Maybrick's occult career, and is signed by him as newly elected Lodge Secretary: 'The W.M. [Worshipful Master] then nominated the following Brethren as officers for the ensuing year [James Maybrick is fourth on the roster], who were invested with their collars.'

Ten years later, on 26 October 1887, James is recorded as a 'Visitor' to the same lodge. Evidently he must have resigned from it. But the important point here is that he would not have been allowed, even as an ex-member, to visit St George's more than once.

Disqualification to visit.	152. No Brother who has ceased to be a subscribing member of a Lodge shall be permitted to visit any one Lodge more than once until he again become a subscribing member of some Lodge.

The rules are clear, and sanction only one such entry, but as the documents attest, James had also visited St George's Lodge of Harmony in the previous year, on 27 October 1886. There is no way he could have done so without being a proven member of another Freemasonic lodge, and it is this lodge that is the bedrock of the big secret.

In this chapter I want to develop the argument that before murdering him on 11 May 1889, Michael Maybrick 'set up' his brother James as the mad, Freemasonic Whitechapel Fiend.

Nobody but a madman would have so promiscuously decorated his crime scenes as Jack. He either *was* a madman, or he had reasons for pretending to be one. Nobody would dispute that his primary motive was a hatred of women, and whores in particular; even the hierarchy of one of the state's most corrupt institutions could acknowledge that. But the Metropolitan Police were wilfully blind to anything beyond it. The Ripper was 'unique', said Sir Charles Warren. The Ripper was 'unique', said Sir Robert Anderson. The Ripper was 'unique', said Dr Bagster Phillips. And all three of them said, 'He never left a clue.'

The glaring signature he left in his wake must have somehow conspired to baffle all of them, and in their wake Freemasology has spent the passing decades nourishing the 'mystery'. Book after book investigates the anonymous monster, differing in choice of culprit, but unanimously agreeing that no matter who the Ripper was, there is hysterical and overwhelming evidence to prove a negative. And that is that Jack the Ripper wasn't a Freemason. Ha ha.

The clues Jack left, the Americanisms, the weekend dates on which he chose to murder, the falsification of documents that would later emerge at Florence Maybrick's 'trial', and most especially the glaring onslaught of Masonic symbolism at his crime scenes, were not by accident, but as Dr Gordon Brown said, 'by design'; and they would serve Michael Maybrick well when the time came to point the finger of 'reluctant accusation' at James.

Coming from Michael, distraught as he was but honourable as he was, James was a ringer for Jack. Moving in the society he did, it wouldn't have been too much of a challenge for Michael to float a whisper that possibly, just possibly, it was his brother who hated his harlot wife enough to kill whores as her surrogate. After all, James was a junkie, much as it pained Michael to say it, already half insane with his addiction and about as stable as a snake when intoxicated. To dose himself as he did was in itself a species of madness, and it was well known that arsenic was a sexual stimulant, fuel for the homicidal furnace.

Smashed on poison and hatred, James might well tip into periods of transient lunacy, visiting his passion for revenge on the metaphorical equivalent of his wife. In these storms of monomania his desire for retribution would own him, he would become both judge and jury, his own little Solomon, 'Yack the Ripper', sequestrating his victim's metal and dishing out penalties according to the grotesque perversions of an insane Freemason.

Thus was brother Jim converted into Bro Jack.

Until the death of Alice McKenzie, or more accurately, until the death of James Maybrick, all the Ripper's victims were killed either side of or over weekends. Martha Tabram was murdered on Monday, 6 August (a Bank Holiday weekend); Mary Ann Nichols on Friday, 31 August, Annie Chapman on Saturday, 8 September, Catherine Eddowes and Elizabeth Stride on Sunday, 30 September, and Mary Jane Kelly, on Friday, 9 November, all in 1888.

To be the Whitechapel Fiend, James would have had to travel down from Liverpool to London at the weekends, and would have needed a reason to do so. It's the same reason that denies his Freemasonry, burying it with a posthumous imposition of secrecy.

The son of the god Apollo, Orpheus was a kind of antediluvian Elvis, blowing the Ancient Greeks away with his lyre. He was said to play with such magic that wild animals would come to listen, and even the trees bowed to him. He is no less revered in Freemasonry. 'Orpheus' (1706) was also the name of one of Michael Maybrick's more prominent London lodges.

The archive of 'Orpheus' is not stored at Freemasons' Hall, but under the aegis of the lodge itself. For well over a year I attempted to access these records, and was out of luck for every week of it. At first I was told the documents had been 'checked by the secretary', and that 'there was little in them about Michael Maybrick' – which isn't surprising, because three months later I was informed that 'all of the Orpheus documents had gone missing'. It was therefore beyond my imagination to know what the secretary had 'checked'

– but forget it, I was not going to get to look at them. It was a disappointment, but kosher. These were private papers, and I had to accept the right of the lodge to impose whatever sanctions it wished. But that didn't mean I couldn't research the Orpheus Lodge (1706).

Its history was written in 1977 by its then Grand Master, Bro T.G.E. Sheddon. A copy of his book was presented to the library at Freemasons' Hall, and together with a meagre dossier and one or two random bits and pieces, that was it for 1706. I've no reason to believe that Bro Sheddon was anything other than an honourable man, writing from the archive he could access. But this says something about the archive, because his work is shot through with staggering inaccuracies. Orpheus was essentially a musicians' lodge, its founders being among the outstanding talent of the day. Michael Maybrick was one of them, and it was he, together with about half a dozen others, who successfully petitioned for its constitution, a warrant approving it being issued by the Grand Lodge on 11 June 1877.

Its founding first officers included Bros William Alexander Barrett, Frederic Davison, William Hayman Cummings and Michael Maybrick. Orpheus was consecrated that same year by the Provincial Grand Master of the Isle of Wight, Bro Hyde Pullen, assisted by the Gentleman Usher to HM Queen Victoria, Captain N.G. Phillips. At the top of the Masonic tree, Phillips was Sovereign Grand Commander of the Ancient and Accepted Rite, and had been a member of the Supreme Council of Freemasons since 1864. Orpheus's inaugural event was followed by a celebration at Freemasons' Hall on Saturday, 18 August 1877, and a tradition was thus established. As the opening lines of Sheddon's history record:

Orpheus has always been a Saturday Lodge. In the fifty years covered by this history three hundred and forty meetings were held, three hundred and twenty seven of them on Saturdays, a truly emphatic indication of preference maintained to this day, for not in the last twenty years has any meeting been held on any other day.[8]

To visit Orpheus, and indeed to be Jack the Ripper, meant you had to be in London over a weekend. I had been pestering the library for months over the lack of material on Orpheus and had got nothing but Sheddon (which by then I had a copy of anyway), when suddenly a new document turned up. It was a photocopy of the original Orpheus Petition, and I assumed it must have been a concession from the Lodge Secretary. I think it was sent in good faith, but there was something immediately iffy about it. It would be easy to look at this piece of paper and see nothing but its age. And that would be precisely the wrong way to look at it.

PETITION FOR A NEW LODGE.

(See Book of Constitutions, page 126, Edition 1873.)

TO THE MOST WORSHIPFUL GRAND MASTER OF
THE UNITED FRATERNITY OF ANCIENT FREE
AND ACCEPTED MASONS OF ENGLAND:

" WE, the undersigned, being regular registered Masons of the Lodges mentioned against our respective names, having the prosperity of the Craft at heart, are anxious to exert our best endeavours to promote and diffuse the genuine principles of the Art; and, for the conveniency of our respective dwellings and other good reasons, we are desirous of forming a new Lodge, to be named *The Orpheus Lodge.*

" In consequence of this desire, we pray for a Warrant of Constitution, empowering us to meet as a regular Lodge, at *Freemason's Hall* on the *last Saturday* in *February, March, April, May, June, July, November and December* and there to discharge the duties of Masonry, in a constitutional manner, according to the forms of the Order and the laws of the Grand Lodge; and we have nominated and do recommend Brother *William Alexander Barrett* to be the first MASTER, Brother *Henry Gadsby —* to be the first SENIOR WARDEN, and Brother *James Shirley Hodson* to be the first JUNIOR WARDEN, of the said Lodge.

" The prayer of this Petition being granted, we promise strict obedience to the commands of the Grand Master and the laws and regulations of the Grand Lodge."

(See over for Signatures of Petitioners.)

It's obviously Victorian, and looks the part, but plays it like a ham. It purports to show that Orpheus Lodge absolutely didn't meet on any Saturday during the crucial killer months of August, September, October, and the first three weeks of November. In other words, should anyone consider any association between Orpheus and the East End murders, here was the antidote.

The petition purports to establish that Orpheus Lodge absolutely didn't meet on any Saturday during those crucial killer months. That's what it says, and it's transparently false. 'The meetings were adjusted,' writes Sheddon; 'they were originally the last Saturdays in October.' In a few words he contradicts the phoney petition, which 'originally' called for no meetings in October at all. Bro Sheddon was doubtless sincere, but careless in his research and gulled by bogus documents. A glance at *The Freemason* of 20 October 1888 (page 612) trashes both Sheddon and the petition. Orpheus meetings habitually took place on the last Saturday of October, in this instance, Saturday, 27 October 1888.

SATURDAY, OCTOBER 27.
CRAFT LODGES.
Audit Committee Boys' School, at 4.
1293, Burdett, Mitre Hotel, Hampton Court.
1297, West Kent, Crystal Palace, Sydenham.
1541, Alexandra Palace, Imperial Hotel, Holborn Viaduct.
→ 1706, Orpheus, Holborn Restaurant.
1777, Royal Hanover, Town Hall, Twickenham.
ROYAL ARCH CHAPTER.
1329, Sphinx, Surrey Masonic Hall, Camberwell.

The problem with this petition, and much like it, is its crudity – it leaps at you like some junk politician on TV. The actual dates for meetings of Orpheus Lodge were August, September, October, November, and through to the following April. *The Freemason* for 5 May 1888 has this: 'Orpheus Lodge (1706). The last meeting of the season was held on Saturday 28th April, after which the Brethren enjoyed the usual musical treat offered by this lodge.' There were no meetings in May, June or July.

This wished-for autumn hiatus simply didn't exist, and in serial contradiction of himself, Bro Sheddon's history is replete with Orpheus assemblies in August, September, October and November: 'The Lodge library contains a bound volume of such programmes covering every meeting from October 1880 to April 1890' (page 14); 'His death was announced to the Lodge in October' (page 25); 'Hodson duly ascended the Master's Chair on 25th of October' (page 41). Orpheus was in fact at its most active during the months the petition denies. The question, of course, is, why would anyone attempt to pretend anything different?

Was James Maybrick a member of Orpheus? With no access to the lodge archive it seemed impossible to prove either way. But in this caper you've got to keep stepping back, and I started to explore other London lodges. There were so many that I restricted the search to those associated with Michael Maybrick.

Frederic Davison was a fellow founder of Orpheus and a very eminent Mason. He was to prove the worth of Longfellow's words, 'No action, whether foul or fair, is ever done, but it leaves somewhere a record.' On 21 October 2001 I received a reply to a letter, via the library at Freemasons' Hall, from the aforementioned Secretary of Orpheus. 'With regard to James Maybrick the Secretary has confirmed that he was definitely not a member of Orpheus Lodge.'[9] It doesn't get any clearer than that; but I was asking a question to which I already knew the answer. Either the Lodge Secretary was wilfully concealing the truth (and I imagine nobody could blame him for that), or his records had been weeded like a municipal flowerbed. Because a member of Orpheus Lodge James Maybrick most definitely was.

Attention to security is paramount in Freemasonry. It is virtually impossible to get into a working lodge or chapter without comprehensively proving your right to be there. 'No Brother may be admitted to a Lodge unless he is personally known to, and vouched for by one of the brethren present, or unless he be well vouched for after due examination.' 'The Grand Master has no more right to pass the Tyled door of a Lodge without permission than has a superior officer to pass the guard without giving the password.' 'No Companion no matter how exalted in rank, should ever be permitted to enter without first being reported.'[10]

You didn't just waddle in.

These strictures are ubiquitous and applicable to all Masonic assemblies. It's a merciless rule, number 15 in the Constitutions, applied vigorously and without exception: 'You promise that no visitor shall be received into your Lodge without due examination, and producing proper vouchers of his being initiated into a regular Lodge.'[11]

And yet, according to the Secretary of Orpheus, all the above was waived on the night of 6 June 1878, when James Maybrick decided to pop into the Westminster and Keystone Lodge.

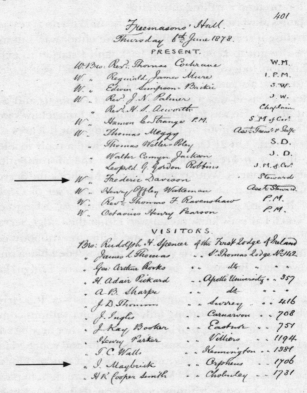

Among the 'Visitors' to the Westminster and Keystone that night was 'J. Maybrick. Orpheus 1706'. If James 'was definitely not a member of Orpheus Lodge', he must have somehow faked his way in, and it apparently bothered no one. Were that true, he would have made Masonic history. There is no way James Maybrick could have put a foot through the door of the Westminster and Keystone Lodge, and no way he could have been signed in as a member of Orpheus (1706), without producing his credentials.

The letter from the Secretary of Orpheus Lodge is utterly unsound. The documentation from the Westminster and Keystone speaks for itself. It's in the archives of that very lodge, and no amount of bluster can change it. James Maybrick's presence is corroborated in a pamphlet published years later, in 1907, by the W and K.

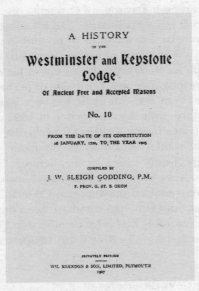

A HISTORY
OF THE
Westminster and Keystone Lodge
Of Ancient Free and Accepted Masons

No. 10

FROM THE DATE OF ITS CONSTITUTION
28 JANUARY, 1722, TO THE YEAR 1905

COMPILED BY
J. W. SLEIGH GODDING, P.M.
P. PROV. G. ST. B. OXON

PRIVATELY PRINTED
WM. BRENDON & SON, LIMITED, PLYMOUTH
1907

Wherein is an alphabetical list of its visitors:

Macaulay, T. Babington	St. Patrick's Lodge, Queensland	279 I.C.
Macbean, Captain		47 I.C.
Mackenzie, George	Mount Moriah Lodge	34
Macsorley, Rev. T. T., G.C. Ireland, 1867		
Mallam, B.	London Lodge, S.W.	108
Mannel	Amity Lodge	171
Maquay, Charles	St. George and Corner Stone Lodge	5
Marshall, John	La Tolerance	538
Mason, J. Oliver	Leigh Lodge of Rifle Volunteers	887
Matthews, J. D.	Canonbury Lodge	657
Matthews, P., P.Prov.G.W. Essex, 1858	Enoch Lodge	11
Maybrick, J.	Orpheus Lodge	1706
McIntyre, Æneas J., Q.C., G.Reg. 1862		
Mead, Frederick	Ionic Lodge	227
Mercier, Charles	Humphrey Chetham Lodge	645

It's not at all surprising that James should have visited Westminster and Keystone. His own Past Grand Master at Liverpool (St George's 32) and Chamberlain to Her Majesty Queen Victoria, the Earl of Lathom, was a member, as was its Worshipful Master, Colonel Le Grande Starkie, a man of vast estates and like the Earl a Freemason of considerable clout. Colonel Edis of the Artists Volunteers was also a member, and Frederic Davison (of Orpheus) one of its founders.

James Maybrick was a Freemason, and it's subsequent interference with documents that attempts to pretend he wasn't. I don't seek to impugn the integrity of anyone currently at Freemasons' Hall. The conspiracy to airbrush James out of his own history was cooked up a very long time ago. Curiously, or perhaps significantly, about a hundred years later his name was once again to become a focus of conjecture, with the emergence in 1992 of the so-called 'diary' linking James to the Ripper. Of particular interest to this narrative is that similar sensitivity to his name was occupying unknown 'fingers ghostly' over a century before.

My correspondence with the library was blowing holes in the camouflage. 'I've contacted the Supreme Council,' wrote the ever diligent librarian, 'and although they have been unable to give me any information regarding his Lodge membership, they've given me details of his membership of a Rose Croix Chapter.'

James Maybrick
Liverpool Rose Croix Chapter No 19
Perfected on the 24th January 1873
Profession: Broker
Address: Normanston, Christchurch Road, Claughton, Cheshire
Resigned: 1874

Apparently the only document they could dig up associating James Maybrick with Freemasonry was his 'resignation' from it? Even with every benefit of the doubt, this was ridiculous. If anyone at Supreme Council had wanted to check James out they needed to look no further than their own yearbooks. If he'd resigned in 1874, how is it that he's listed as an eighteenth-degree Freemason in 1888?

I've no wish to score points over those long since dead, or those who, for all I know, are in good faith. But James Maybrick did not resign from Freemasonry in 1874. On 21 December of that year the

Rules and Regulations

FOR THE

GOVERNMENT OF THE DEGREES FROM THE
4° TO 32° INCLUSIVE,

UNDER THE

SUPREME COUNCIL 33°

OF THE

Ancient and Accepted Rite

FOR

ENGLAND AND WALES, AND THE DEPENDENCIES
OF THE BRITISH CROWN,

TOGETHER WITH

A LIST OF MEMBERS.

Corrected to June 30, 1888.

OFFICE OF THE SECRETARY GENERAL,
33, GOLDEN SQUARE, LONDON, W.

---

156   LIST OF MEMBERS.

45 Martin, R. Diddulph 18	Maude, Col. C. O., *fa.S.C* 11
Martin, Richard Ryan 13	22 Maude, Rev. Samuel 11
Martin, Tom P. 13	22 Maughan, Rev. Henry Mac- 9
Martin, Rev. W. Willasey,	donald, *M.A.* 11
M.A. .... (n) 30	Maule, Augustus Henry ..11
1 Martyn, Rev. Chas. Jam.,	Maultin, Mathew John... 18
M.A. 18	Maund, J. O., late *R.H.A.* 9
Marwood, Arthur Octavius 18	91 Maunsell, Daniel Charles..11
23 Marwood, Thomas........ 30	40 Mavrojani, Spyridion Alex.11
23 Marwood, Thos. Nelthorpe 18	30 Maxwell, George 11
5 Masefield, William....... 18	40 Maxwell, Frederick David 18
Mason, Charles Edward.... 18	Maxwell, Hamilton 11
Mason, Charles Letch 18	Maxwell, John 11
39 Mason, Rev. Henry James 18	Maxwell, Lt.-Col. R.J.*9th*11
1 Mason, Henry Trood...... 18	May, John Jeffrey........11
Mason, James Cattley 13	Maybour, William.......11
Mason, James E. 30	42 Maybrick, James 11
29 Mason, John 18	2 Maye, William Bennett ..11
Mason, Joseph 18	55 Mayer, Joseph Briggs...11
Mason, Robert Henry 18	Mayfield, John 11
Mason, Thomas 18	Maynard, Wm. E. Maxwell 11
61 Mason, William........... 30	Maytham, Wm. Cornelius 18
27 Massey, Ambrose Shero ..18	10 McBride, C. Arthur Julius 11
10 Massie, Edward John 18	92 McCall, John Henry 11
76 Masson, David Parkes 18	McCarogher, Rev. John O.11
Massy, Kyre Henry Chas. ..18	McCarthy, Chas. Desmond 9
100 Massy, Sarg.-Maj. George 18	78 McClure, Will. Geo., *M.B.*11
Massy, H. Ingoldsby, 56th 18	McConnachy, John 11
100 Massy, Capt. Harry Stanley,	83 McConnell, William 18
19th Bengal Lancers.... 18	90 McCorkell, Gilmour, *fa.C.S.* 9
45 Masterman, William 18	McCormack, M.P.C., *M.D.*11
Mate, William 18	McCullagh, Major J. R.*,* 9
Mather, John Lawrence .. 18	*R.E.* 11
Mather, Maj.Gen.B.H.,*R.E.* 31	88 McCullough, William, *J.P.*11
Mathew, Thos. P. Ogden .. 30	100 McDougal, John, Srgt.-Maj. 9
Mathews, Col.Felix Anthony 18	8th Hussars 11
70 Mathias, Charles 18	97 McDowall, Andrew 11
101 Matier, Charles Fitzgerald 32	McFarlane, Ronald, 9th L.11
Matson, John Melville ... 18	29 McGovern, Thomas 11
62 Matterson, Geo. Octavius..18	55 McGowan, David Hugh ..11
Matterson, Robert Timothy 18	McGowan, Percy S. 11
Matthews, Rev. E. Walter 18	McGregor, David 11
1 Matthews, James Forrester 18	McGregor, Duncan 11
Mattison, Sylvester 18	McKay, Donald 11
	52 McKay, George John 11

Jerusalem Chapter (19) was 'attached to Lodge (32)', and like all of its other members, James remained with it. As a matter of fact, together with a future Mayor of Liverpool, Sir James Pool, he was elected as a 'Companion' of the new amalgamation.

The document kindly furnished to me by the Supreme Council states unequivocally that James had 'resigned' from an unnamed lodge in 1874. But once again, like the Orpheus petition, it is faked. There's no slip of the pen about this – it's a counterfeit, whose purpose was to deceive. It purports to be a register of members, listing their names and annual subscriptions.

Return of Members of the (?) Liverpool Chapter (?)
Alpass Horace Seymour – dues paid until 1881 – 'Mort'
Gaskill James – dues paid until 1873
Maybrick James – dues paid until 1874 – 'Resigned'

It took me less than a minute to recognise this as a fabrication, and less than twenty-four hours to confirm it. Among the thirty names listed, two jumped off the page. I'd seen one of them before, in the archives of the Liverpool Cotton Brokers Association.

I remembered James Gaskill because of a quote that came with him. He was 'an expert in the judgement of Surats, a knowledge which very few Brokers possessed until the American Civil War brought the despised fibre into general use'.[12] I had never heard of surats, and looked it up in a dictionary. It's a kind of substitute cotton. That's how I remembered James Gaskill.

That afternoon my researcher Keith pulled two death certificates from the Family Record Office. James Gaskill, who according to this document was still paying his Masonic dues in the spring of 1873, had been dead five years, croaking on 26 April 1868. Another on the list, Horace Seymour Alpass, described as having died ('Mort') in 1881, was in reality alive and well, and Grand Master of Liverpool Chapter (19), until he went tits up on 21 August 1884.

So we have one living man who was dead (Gaskill), one dead man who was living (Alpass), and another man who had 'resigned' but hadn't. James Maybrick's first entry into Supreme Council records is dated October 1874, the very year he was supposed to have left it. Whoever the hoaxer behind this document was, he gets ten out of ten for the copperplate, but zero for the research.

Disinterring James Maybrick's Freemasonic career sometimes felt like carving Lincoln's face out of a mountainside. The difficulty is indicative of how comprehensively these records were hidden. Once again, I imply no malfeasance to any of the present custodians – they didn't fake this document. It was produced late in 1888 or early in 1889, probably the latter, a conclusion that will become clear as Michael closes in on James. What was already clear is that some entity had a reason to disabuse history of the idea that James was a Mason at the time of the Ripper.

The records of Masonic lodges are called Tyler's books, and it is in these that the business of the lodge (such as resignations) is recorded. I had requested photocopies of these records in an earlier letter, and subsequent to the hoax resignation document had requested them again: 'The document you sent me is clearly of some age, but despite that it is unreliable and cannot be considered as primary research. Might I therefore ask a little more of your time and generosity to allow me copies of the *original* documents I requested.'[13]

It was at this juncture that it all started to get a bit choppy. I'd misguidedly thought the fail-safe tactic for denying any suggestion of a Masonic–Ripper connection was reserved for the Duke of Clarence. I'd expressed no interest in him, and none in Jack either. But never mind that, I'd got answers to questions I had never asked:

> I have myself looked slightly into this matter since you wrote and found that Mike Barratt has confessed on two occasions to forging the diaries, that the writing on the will of Maybrick is considered genuine and different from that of the diaries, and that, the use of the name of the Post House pub was anachronistic. Also it seems to be generally accepted that Florence Maybrick did not poison her husband. It therefore seems that you are pursuing a matter that has already been discredited.[14]

I beg your pardon? At first I thought he'd lost his glasses and written back to the wrong bloke. I was indeed pursuing a matter that had been discredited, and that was this fake resignation document. Other than that, I didn't know what he was talking about. I had no interest in Mike Barratt and what he may or may not have forged.[15] My specific interest was in the forgery in front of me, and was nothing to do with a pub or any person called Barratt.

This response was one of the few things that got me relatively miffed. Anyone who's 'looked slightly into this matter' is welcome to their own point of view. If you don't want to help, don't help. I'm used to that, that's your prerogative. But don't anyone give me history lessons in bullshit. I'm not interested in 'general acceptance', or other people's conclusions on what may or may not have been 'discredited'. If I were, I'd believe it was Bro Warren's Jewish sensibilities that washed off that wall, and bollocks about boots. I'd believe that the pathetic suicide in the Thames was Jack the Ripper, and that the inveterate liar Sir Robert Anderson was telling the truth. But I don't believe it. None of it. If I did, I wouldn't be writing this book. Of course Florence Maybrick didn't poison her husband. Of course James Maybrick wasn't the Ripper. Of course the 'diary' is a forgery. Of course its handwriting doesn't look like James Maybrick's, and of course its creation has nothing whatsoever to do with an idiot called Mike Barratt. Barratt didn't write the 'diary', and I wouldn't write about it either unless I was 100 per cent certain of its provenance. In the winter/spring of 1888–89 there were a variety of crooked pens forging documents in respect of James Maybrick, and in that context the 'diary' becomes an irrelevance.

Let us therefore leave the squawking to those who excel at it, and remain with the empiric. Notwithstanding the 'diary', there are three fabricated documents relevant to James Maybrick. We're presented with the fake Orpheus petition and an official denial that he was ever a member of that lodge. Supplementing this is a bogus document of 'resignation' underpinned by ancillary documentation that translates as a resignation from Masonry itself. These hoaxes are as contemporaneous as they are Freemasonic, and it is in that contiguity that the murder of James Maybrick and the subsequent framing of his wife pushes at the boundaries of credulity.

The 'Maybrick Mystery', is the substance of the last part of this narrative, wherein every institutionalised deceit characterising the scandal of the Ripper ascends to its apogee in a corruption called the trial of Florence Maybrick.

Meanwhile, a psychopath was still in the business of laying his pipe. There would be more letters 'from America', and many more with a focus on a madman living in Liverpool. On 9 October 1888 the *Liverpool Echo* had published a letter from a Ripper in Dublin, miffed at a Ripper in Liverpool, who in a letter to that same newspaper claimed himself as the genuine item. His complaint was published in the *Echo* on 10 October:

A LIVERPOOL FANATIC

The subjoined communication was addressed to the *Liverpool Echo* office yesterday on an ordinary postcard:–

Stafford Street

Dear Sir, – I beg to state that the letters published in yours of yesterday are lies. It is somebody gulling the public. I am the Whitechapel purger. On 13th, at 3 p.m., will be on Stage, as am going to New York. But will have some business before I go – Yours truly,

Jack the Ripper
DIEGO LAURENZ
(Genuine)

The intention to plant Jack as a 'Liverpool maniac' can be judged by the strapline 'A LIVERPOOL FANATIC', the city's premier newspaper subscribing to the amateur-dramatic horseshit that its correspondent is a Mad Liverpool Resident.

On the same afternoon that letter was published, Wednesday, 10 October, Jack underpinned his literary efforts by turning up in person (the Marsh family had had a similar visitation to their shop in Whitechapel from an Irish cleric). Published under the title 'A STRANGE LIVERPOOL STORY', it was reported by the *Bradford Telegraph* on 12 October. The gist of it concerns a young lady who was walking along Shiel Road, Liverpool, when she was abruptly stopped by an elderly woman, 'who in an agitated and excited manner urged her most earnestly not to go into the park. She explained that a few minutes previously she had been resting on one of the seats in the park when she was accosted by a respectable looking man, dressed in a black coat, light trousers and a soft felt hat, who enquired if she knew if there were any loose women about the neighbourhood, and immediately afterwards he produced a knife with a long thin blade, and stated that he intended to kill as many women in Liverpool as in London, adding that he would send the ears of the first victim to the Editor of a Liverpool newspaper.'

As can be imagined, this somewhat freaked the old duck, and she made off, 'trembling violently' as she related her story. It was taken seriously, the *Telegraph* reporting that a 'Detective from the Criminal Investigation Department at London has journeyed to Liverpool to investigate the movements of a suspicious character'.[16]

Thus on one day, 10 October 1888, we have a Liverpool fanatic in the paper and a Liverpool fanatic in the park, both going to some lengths in their claim to be Jack the Ripper. It was reasonable to assume that there was a lunatic in the city, and it is this assumption the authorities were invited to make. 'Diego' is the Spanish equivalent of the English 'James'. San Diego (St James) is the patron saint of Spain. Diego Laurenz, alias James the Ripper, was in Liverpool.

But more important, let's look at the name in context. We have a Liverpool Fanatic, and a Jack the Ripper ('Genuine') whose Christian name is James. Plus we have a correspondent in Scotland signing himself 'May – bee'. *Ergo*, with minimal extrapolation, we have a possible Jack the Ripper in Liverpool, called James May(bee). Now, it's my contention that James May(brick) was being set up as part of the Funny Little Game. All that would be required to finger him was for some unimpeachable individual to come along and make sense of the 'pipe'. I believe this informant was Michael Maybrick, stage-managing his Masonic brother.

To investigate this proposition further, we must return to another letter out of Scotland (one of what I call the 'McRipper clump'), dated the same day as 'May – bee', and posted one day before DIEGO LAURENZ.

'May – bee' was posted in Edinburgh, and the following letter is postmarked 'Galashiels', a town on the concert circuit about thirty miles to the south. It's dated (implausibly) 8 October 1888, but it wasn't received in London until 11 October.

> 8/10/88
> Galayshiels
>
> Dear Boss
> I have to thank you and my Brother in trade, Jack the Ripper for your kindness in letting me away out of Whitechapel I am on my road to the tweed factories. I will let the Innerleithen Constable or Police men know when I am about to start my nice Little game. I have got my Knife replenished so it will answer both for Ladies and Gents Other 5 Tweed ones and I have won my wager
> I am yours
> Truly
> <u>The Ripper</u>

This text is a specific illustration of the point I make. The ego is at it, and he can't help himself. There is a Jack the Ripper, 'my brother in trade', and the signatory himself, simply 'The Ripper'. This is perhaps the only letter we have referring to them as two different people, the former buried in a pun that is easy to deconstruct. James Maybrick is the 'brother in trade'.

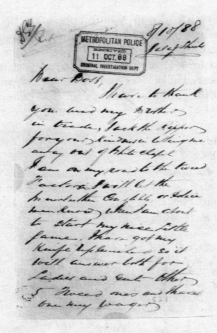

And on the reverse, it is signed 'The Ripper'.

Here is Florence Aunspaugh actually using almost the same words in a letter as 'The Ripper' uses in his: 'These English cotton brokers literally despised Michael. He spoke of the English Cotton Broker as, "Traded People".'

Michael Maybrick was an insufferable snob, up there in his psychopathic ether. He looked down from above on those around him, and especially the little people like Brother James.

I want a last look at another letter before moving on to the Masonically inspired atrocity of Mary Kelly. It's a Neanderthal scribble which provides another example of Bro James Maybrick as 'Jack'.

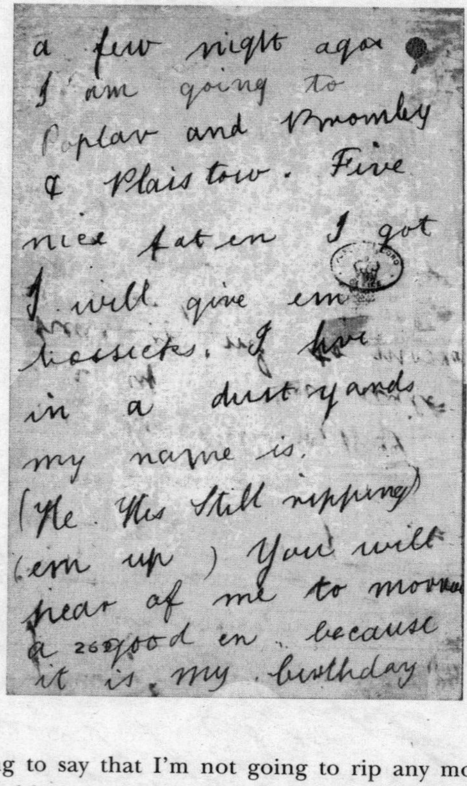

269 ⟶

Dear Boss

I am going to say that I'm not going to rip any more up in Whitechapel but one and that is one who was kicking up a row outside a public house in Commercial Road a few night ago I am going to Poplar and Bromley & Plaistow. Five nice fat un I got I will give em [illegible] I live in a dust yards my name is (He Yes still ripping em up) You will hear of me to morrow a good un because it is my birthday.

Written in red ink with no date, this letter is of interest for two reasons. Firstly because its author says he's going to Poplar, Bromley and Plaistow; and second because he says that the following day is his birthday. I'm looking for towns, and for any birthday that might be of significance. Originally filed by the police as Number 269, the letter following in the sequence, Number 270, has a date of receipt of 24 October 1888.

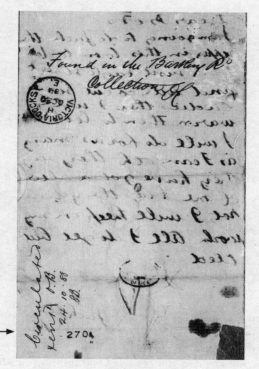

270 ⟶

If 270 was received on 24 October, it's reasonable to assume that 269 was received on or about 23 October, the day before the birthday 'tomorrow'. 24 October 1888 was James Maybrick's fiftieth birthday. Before anyone starts telling me 269/270 is an irrelevant coincidence, let's see if we can harden it up.

In 269 the Ripper says he's going to Bromley, and as far as my candidate is concerned, that's exactly where he went. Bromley is an unlikely night out for Jack the Ripper. It was a bucolic middle-class conurbation in Kent, about a dozen miles south-east of London, and hardly a place for the Whitechapel Fiend. Yet Jack was in town at this time, and we have another letter confirming it. It's addressed to 'Inspector Reilly, Bromley Police Station'. No date, and as usual there's no stamp. There's no postmark either, meaning it was almost certainly delivered to the police station by hand.

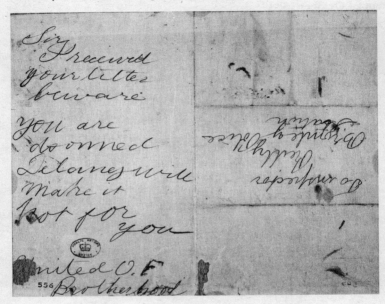

Sir
I received your letter beware you are doomed Delaney will make it hot for you

 United U.F. Brotherhood

 If you will give me 100 pounds I will inform you where the Whitechapel Murderer is hiding But if you don't choose then he will start work on some of the hores of Bromley

         Jack the Ripper

We don't know why Jack the Ripper would chose to relocate to Bromley, but we do know why Michael Maybrick got on a train and travelled there in that last week of October 1888.

The Musical World.

DRILL HALL BROMLEY, KENT.

MESSRS. F. LEWIS THOMAS' and W. C. HANNS' Third Annual Grand Evening Concert, Tuesday next. October 30. Artists: Miss Joyce, Miss Eleanor Rees, Mr. Edward Lloyd, Mr. Bertram, H. Salter, and Mr. Maybrick. Solo Violoncello: Mr. Wm. C. Hann. Solo Pianoforte: Mr. F. Lewis Thomas. Tickets of Strong & Sons and Collins, Bromley; and of Moody, Chislehurst Station.

I think it's of note that, like the 'my brother in trade' letter, Jack's Bromley letter switches in and out of the first and third person, reiterating his obsession with the sum of £100 as it does so: 'If you will give *me* 100 pounds I will inform you where the Whitechapel Murderer is hiding But if you don't … then he will start work on some of the hores of Bromley.'

Thus we have a Jack the Ripper and Michael Maybrick in Bromley, one to hand-deliver his letter, and the other to sing a song: 'Mr Maybrick gave a very spirited rendering of Mendelssohn's "I'm a Roamer",' reported the *Musical World* – and under the circumstances he could hardly have made a more appropriate choice. Throughout the autumn of 1888 Michael Maybrick was almost perpetually on the road, or rather the rails, clocking up thousands of miles on his provincial dates. Jack was similarly on the move, keeping the thrill alive with his letters. On 8 November Maybrick was singing at a Conservative Club in Surrey, and by 9 November both he and Jack were back in London.

15

'The Ezekiel Hit'

The key to the whole subject may be found in the
Book of Ezekiel.

Charles Warren, November 1886

The police investigation and subsequent coroner's court inquiry into the murder of Mary Jane Kelly were utterly corrupt. Evidence was withheld or distorted, destruction of files wholesale, and lying the norm. Kelly's Metropolitan Police file contains not much more than you'd expect the police to accrue from an average road accident. But secrecy itself is revealing, and in Kelly's case the less there is, the more there is to uncover.

Mary Jane Kelly was a twenty-four-year-old Catholic who differed from Jack's previous hits on two notable counts. Although by circumstance a part-time slut, she was younger and prettier than the rest, and unlike other victims she was butchered indoors, in her own little room just off Dorset Street, in Whitechapel. We don't know much about her, and we don't actually need to. She ran into the Ripper early in the morning of Friday, 9 November 1888. I think the date had significance for Jack. Firstly, because it was the day of the Lord Mayor's Parade and Banquet at Mansion House, where London's elite, including Prime Minister Salisbury and Sir Charles Warren himself, would dine. To upstage this mob of distinguished grown-ups sounds like a perfect Ripper day to me. Secondly, 9 November was the birthday of the world's most eminent Freemason, no less than its Grand Master, HRH Edward, Prince of Wales. Anticipating the murder of Johnnie Gill in Bradford, the Ripper promised 'Charlie, Dear Charlie' a 'Christmas Box' – so why not a birthday present for England's future King, 'the pot-bellied pig', according to Jack, 'whose tool he would cut off'. Further references to personages royal were made in a letter dated the day before Mary Kelly's murder – timed, I believe, not only to screw the Prince's birthday, but to coincide with and fuck up the Commissioner's night out.

Whitechapel
8/11/88

Dear Boss
I am still knocking about down Whitechapel I mean to put to Death all the dirty old ores because I have caught the pox and cannot piss I have not done any murders lately but you will find one done before long. I shall send you the kidney and cunt so that you can see where my prick has been up I am in one of the lodging houses in Osborn street but you will have a job to catch me I shoudent advise any coppers to catch hold of me because I shall do the same to him as I have done to others. Old packer the man I bought the grapes off saw me the other night but was to frighten to say anything to the police. he must have been a fool when there is such a reward offered never mind the reward will not be given. You will hear from me a little later on that I have done another murder. But not just yet. Dear Boss if I see you about I shall cut your throat. The Old Queen is none other but one of those old ores I have Been up her arse and shot sponk up her

I remain Dear
old Boss
Jack the ripper

To dismiss this letter as a 'hoax' is to understand just about nothing of the Whitechapel Murderer. It was written no more than twenty-four hours before, as he put it in his letter of 19 October, he cut Kelly's 'prat right out',[1] mutilating her so severely that the doctors at first could barely tell what sex she was.

This letter is truly shocking, its offensive power in no way diminished to this day. Its text is a dynamic of hate, a gloating pornography of violence towards women and denigration of the power of Warren. Everything about him is comprehensively trashed. His monarch, who knighted him, is herself deconstructed into an old whore with sperm up her backside – 'sponk', he calls it, and didn't it make him laugh?

The choice of icon is indicative of the duality of the killer's thinking, his targets Warren and Women, authority and sex. Victoria is the 'Mother of the Nation', but also a woman, and therefore a whore. He brags of sodomising the Queen and cutting out the 'kidney and cunt' of his next victim, associating Victoria and Mary Kelly as one, then spits his hooligan venom at Warren, 'so that you can see where my prick has been up'. It is the rage of a repugnant child.

On the night of Thursday, 8 November Mary Kelly had been drinking heavily. At about 2 a.m. she was seen in the company of a gentleman whose description was later supplied by a witness called George Hutchinson. He lived just around the corner from Kelly in Commercial Street, and was unemployed. His 'statement' is worthless, but necessary to explore the chicanery of the police.

According to Hutchinson he met Kelly in the street at about 2 a.m. She asked if he could lend her sixpence, and getting a negative, walked off saying, 'I must go and find some money.' On her way towards Thrawl Street a man coming in the opposite direction tapped her on the shoulder and said something, and 'they both burst out laughing'. The man then placed his right hand around her shoulders. He 'also had a small parcel in his left hand, with a kind of strap round it'. Hutchinson stood against the lamp of the Queen's Head public house and watched them as they passed. 'The man hung down his head with his hat over his eyes. I stooped down and looked him in the face. He looked at me real stern'[2] – and who wouldn't, with a stranger stooping down to peer at you for no apparent reason at two o'clock in the morning?

Attached to Hutchinson's statement was an addendum of creative writing courtesy of the Metropolitan Police.

Description, age about 34 or 35, height 5 foot 6, complexion pale. Dark eyes and eyelashes. Slight moustache curled up at each end and dark hair. Very surly looking. Dress, long dark coat, collar and cuffs trimmed astrakan and a dark jacket under, light waistcoat, dark trousers, dark felt hat turned down in the middle, button boots and gaiters with white buttons, wore a very thick gold chain with linen collar, black tie with horse shoe pin, respectable appearance, walked very sharp, Jewish appearance. Can be identified.

For a dismal night with intermittent drizzle and barely a street lamp, Hutchinson has done well. The only things missing are the inside-leg measurement and the suspect's probable blood group.

Except he wasn't a suspect, he was simply a pick-up for a girl in need of money, which puts a question mark after Hutchinson's inordinate interest in Kelly and her prospective bedfellow.

> They both went into Dorset Street. I followed them. They both stood at the corner of the court for about 3 minutes. He said something to her. She said alright my dear come along you will be comfortable. He then placed his arm on her shoulder and [she] gave him a kiss. She said she had lost her handkerchief, he then pulled his handkerchief a red one and gave it to her. They both went up the Court together. I then went to the court to see if I could see them but I could not. I stood there for about three quarters of an hour to see if they came out. They did not so I went away.[3]

Twelve hours later Kelly's room was full of doctors and cops, and we're supposed to believe that Hutchinson was somehow indifferent to it? The police said he gave his statement three days later, on 12 November – and I get a red light. It's only necessary to glance at the contemporary press to know that Whitechapel was incensed after Kelly's murder. Crowds 'hooted' Commissioner Smith (mistaking him for Warren) at the Lord Mayor's Parade.[4] Every mouth in Whitechapel was talking about Kelly, yet for three days Hutchinson stays silent? He had stood staring up Miller's Court for forty-five minutes, demonstrating a meticulous interest in Kelly before her death, yet is apparently insouciant after it? I simply don't believe it. What I do believe is that Hutchinson went to the police earlier, but they dismissed his statement because like everyone else in the locality they knew Kelly had been seen alive at about 8.30 the following morning.

Hutchinson had not seen Kelly with her killer, but the police wanted the public to believe he had. They needed a distraction from the illegality of their coroner's court, and a mirror in front of the crime scene. Don't look in there, Ladies and Gents, look out for the neckless Israelite. Compare Hutchinson's statement with that of Matthew Packer. The cops went out of their way to crush the fruit-seller and the drawings he confirmed, but avidly promoted Hutchinson's concoction, right down to the buttons on the spats.

'The very exactitude of his description,' wrote the *Graphic*, 'engenders a feeling of scepticism. The witness admits that at the time he saw him he did not suspect the person of being the Whitechapel Assassin; yet at two o'clock in the morning, in a badly lighted thoroughfare he observed more than most of us would observe in broad daylight.'[5]

George Hutchinson is another diversion in the tradition of 'Israel Schwartz', a 'witness' initially dismissed by the police, then wheeled out and championed when it became expedient.

The man Hutchinson saw, with the obligatory red handkerchief, may well have been a punter, but he was long gone before daybreak, and had absolutely nothing to do with Jack the Ripper.

'Dorset Street,' thumbnailed a reporter, 'consists of a nest of courts, most of the houses of which are let off in furnished rooms. Miller's Court, Dorset St, runs westward out of Commercial Street, within a hundred yards of Toynbee Hall.'[6]

The alarm came at 10.45 that same morning of 9 November. Kelly was late with her rent, and a servant of her landlord, Thomas Bowyer, was dispatched to collect it. He got no answer at the door, and turned his attention to the nearest window, a pane of which was broken. Mr Bowyer was able to push a curtain aside, and saw 'two lumps of flesh lying on the table'.

The cops arrived at about eleven. In the ensuing hours almost every Metropolitan policeman named in this book turned up, including Sir Charles Warren.[7] According to subsequent disinformation, Warren had resigned the previous day, 8 November, because of some ill-advised forays into journalism. Irrespective of that, he was telegraphed, and the first officer on the scene, Inspector Walter Beck, sent word for Inspectors Reid and Abberline.

A variety of uniforms and plain-clothes were quickly outside 29 Dorset Street. The *Telegraph* takes up the tale: 'Meanwhile the street was as far as possible closed to traffic, a cordon of constables being drawn across each end and the police took possession of Miller's Court, refusing access to all comers in the expectation blood-hounds would be used.'[8] (Please remember the impossibility of shutting off a humble doorway at Goulston Street.) 'Acting upon orders, the detectives and inspectors declined to furnish any information of what had occurred, and refused permission to the press to inspect the place.'[9]

This refusal was extended to the police themselves by Dr Bagster Phillips. Having shoved his head through the window, he concluded that 'the mutilated corpse lying on the bed was not in any need of immediate attention', and therefore instructed Abberline 'not to force the door', but to wait for the dogs.

Why a medical doctor should be giving a senior policeman instructions at a crime scene isn't readily clear. What is clear is that Bro Phillips was pulling a fast one. Whatever he was waiting for, it wasn't for dogs. We know this because not a month before, someone of some importance had determined that doggies were entirely useless in such an environment. That eminent opinion had come from Bro Dr Bagster Phillips. 'I gave my opinion that the operation would be useless,' he said at Annie Chapman's inquest. 'I think the blood of the murdered woman would be more likely to be traced than the murderer.'[10]

For the next two hours they all hung around pretending to wait for the bloodhounds. Apparently nobody had bothered to tell anybody in H Division, including senior detectives Abberline and Reid, what everybody else could read in the newspapers. On 11 October, the owner of the animals that had rushed up the Serpentine after Warren wrote to the editor of *The Times*: 'Sir, there is one statement in your otherwise excellent account of the trials of Bloodhounds in Hyde Park, which I shall be glad to be allowed to correct. My Hounds have not been purchased by Sir Charles Warren for use of the police.'[11]

No dogs. But in terms of detection, something equally useless turned up. Robert Anderson arrived in a cab 'at ten minutes to two o'clock, and he remained some time', every minute of it unquestionably devoted to working out how none of this evidence could ever become part of a murder investigation.[12]

By now of course the door had been forced. But it wasn't until Warren's laundryman, Thomas Arnold, pitched up at 1.30 with the startling news of no bloodhounds that entry was effected. 'A most horrifying spectacle was presented to the officer's gaze,' broadcast the *Telegraph*, 'exceeding in ghastliness anything which the imagination can picture. The body of the woman was stretched on the bed, fearfully mutilated. Nose and ears had been cut off, and, although there had been no dismemberment [incorrect] the flesh had been stripped off, leaving the skeleton. The nature of the other injuries were of a character to indicate that they had been perpetrated by the author of the antecedent crimes in the same district; and it is believed once more there are portions of the organs missing.'

An American newspaper got a whiff of some 'writing on the wall' of the room, and there is evidence of this in blood, but since Arnold was inexplicably absent at the inquest, we'll never know if his sponge had been busy in there. At the 'inquest', the following was just about all Phillips said:

> On the door being opened the table I found close to the left hand side of the bedstead and the bedstead was close up against the wooden partition, the mutilated remains of a female were lying two thirds over towards the edge of the bedstead, nearest to the door of entry she had only her linen garment on her, and from my subsequent examination I am sure the body had been removed subsequent to the injury which caused her death from that side of the bedstead which was nearest to the wooden partition, the large quantity of blood under the bedstead, and saturated condition of the paliasse, pillow, sheet, and that top corner nearest the partition leads me to the conclusion that the severance of the right carotid artery which was the immediate cause of her death was inflicted while the deceased was lying at the right side of the bedstead and her head and neck in the top right hand corner.

There are about 160 words here, and maybe a dozen of them refer to the actual corpse. Phillips didn't want to talk about the nature of Kelly's injuries, or what may have caused them. As a matter of fact he'd written to the coroner, Dr Roderick MacDonald, asking if his presence in court would be required.[13] After the débâcle of 'the Womb-Collector', he obviously didn't fancy it. The coroner replied that 'he thought it would be well that Phillips should attend, but need not go into details'. And he didn't, and that was about it from the medical contingent. Although four other physicians worked the room, Drs Bond, Brown, Duke and Gabe, none was put upon to give any evidence at the 'inquest'.

But surely there was more to it than that? Half Kelly's guts went out the door like meat. Were any organs missing? What was the supposed weapon and the presumed time of death?

MacDonald didn't want to know, and we're left to investigate these questions for ourselves. Meanwhile, bring on Abberline, who announced himself as 'in charge of this case', which makes one wonder why he waited for Arnold and took orders from Dr Phillips. Abberline was the last of the 'witnesses' to speak:

> I have heard the doctor's evidence and confirm what he says. I have taken an inventory [never produced] of what was in the room, there had been a large fire so large as to melt the spout off the kettle I have since gone through the ashes in the grate and found nothing of consequence except that articles of a woman's clothing had been burnt which I presume was for the purpose of light as there was only one piece of candle in the room.

Kelly didn't boil her kettle by setting fire to her clothes. There must have been coal. It wasn't until the following day that Abberline sieved the ashes, so probably the fire had still been burning, or at least the ashes were still hot – a report in the *Standard* quotes the police as saying the room was 'quite warm'. Abberline doesn't mention that Kelly's clothes were neatly folded at the side of the bed, or that he found anything curious in clothing being burnt 'for the purpose of light'[14] when there was half a candle available, or why anyone seeking light would slam a kettle on top of it? Various witnesses insist that they saw Kelly alive at 8.30 a.m. on 9 November. If she was killed that morning, no candle or fire would have been necessary, because the room would have been in daylight. In my view, that's why Jack didn't light the candle. We might therefore look at alternative explanations for a blaze 'so large as to melt the spout off the kettle'. Abberline wasn't a fool, and this melted kettle wasn't the result of some previous blaze; he knew what he was looking at, and was specific about it. So why the enormous fire? It wasn't until Warren and his Masonic scholarship arrived at a quarter to two that anyone knew what the furnace was for.[15] Sir Charles was able to read the runes of what had gone down in this charnel house as if it was written in a book.

It was.

Needless to say, Warren wasn't called to give evidence at the inquest. However, reported the *Yorkshire Post*, 'The Commissioner remained on the spot until the completion of the post mortem examination at a quarter to four, and then returned to Scotland Yard taking Dr Bond with him.'[16] The rest of the witness statements, from Kelly's landlord and neighbours, subsequently heard before a bent coroner, were primarily judicial padding, recorded so the court could look as if it was investigating something. Deposition from Kelly's ex-common-law husband confirmed that she was into booze and was a part-time hooker, had a father in Caernarvon, and blah blah. A woman called Prater said she was woken by her cat at about 3 a.m., heard a cry of 'Oh murder,' and went back to sleep.[17] Such hollers in the night were apparently common in Miller's Court. Her evidence sums up the relevance of most of the other witnesses: all had 'heard' something rather than 'seen' anything.

The exception was the 'Deputy of the Commercial Lodging House', Mrs Caroline Maxwell, who lived directly opposite Miller's Court at 14 Dorset Street. 'I have known the murdered woman well for the past six months,' she said. 'Yesterday morning [9 November] as nearly as possible about half past eight o'clock, I saw Mary Jane standing outside in the court. I said, "what brings you out so early?" and she answered, "I feel very queer; I cannot sleep; I have the horrors of drink upon me."' Having doubtless been drinking all night while intermittently fucking the man with the spats, she had a crucifying hangover. Maxwell suggested a glass of ale. 'I already did,' said Kelly, 'and I brought it up.' Maxwell further stated that she went to Bishopsgate and on her return saw Kelly again, 'talking to a short stout man at the top of the court'. Asked how she could so accurately fix the time, Maxwell said, 'Because I went to the milk shop, and had not been there for a long time, and she [Kelly] was wearing a woollen crossover that I had not seen her wear for some considerable time.' 'On enquiries being made at the milk shop, her statement was found to be correct, and the cross-over was also found in Kelly's room.' The *Times* report continues with reference to another witness 'whose name is known', and who has 'informed the police that she was positive that she saw Kelly between half past eight o'clock and a quarter to nine on Friday morning'.[18]

This second sighting was substantiated by yet a third. A tailor named Maurice Lewis says he was gambling (pitch and toss) in Miller's Court when he saw Kelly 'return and leave with a jug of milk', precisely corroborating Mrs Maxwell.[19]

That's three independent witnesses positive about the same time, and two with the same milk. Had Lewis, or the unnamed witness, been called to the coroner's court, George Hutchinson's suspect would have been exposed as worthless, spat buttons and all. Dr Phillips originally believed that Kelly had been dead for about eight hours, then extended it to twelve.[20] Modern forensics reduces this considerably, determining the time of Kelly's death in synchronicity with the witnesses.[21]

The logistics were something like this: Kelly left home about 8.30, shared her inebriated woes with Mrs Maxwell, bought some milk and returned to her hovel. She then went out again to the nearest pub, the Britannia, for another hair of the dog, heading home after nine, where she ran into J.T.R.

'I promised Kelly 2/6 [two shillings and sixpence] to have a fuck,' gloats a Ripper letter received by the police on 12 November; 'she gave a little scream but I act quickly by putting a chop in neck.'[22]

You don't chop with a knife, you chop with a chopper. Given the total news blackout, nobody but Kelly's murderer could have known this. There is no doubt that Jack turned up that morning with some kind of hatchet.

Crime-scene photographs indicate that 'Kelly's left femur has been split longitudinally from the hip downwards, exposing the marrow cavity. The outer part of the bone [cortex] stands out in clear relief. Now such an injury – the cleaving of the long bone in a healthy young adult – can only be inflicted with a weapon such as a hatchet. It is impossible with a knife, no matter how robust.' This assessment comes not from Dr Phillips, but from a surgeon 120 years later. 'The existence of the split thigh bone is unequivocal evidence a hatchet was used.'[23]

He killed her and killed her, attacking every quarter of her being except her eyes. Maybe there was something about her 'watching' what he did to her that gave him pleasure? Certainly the outstanding feature of this butchery was revenge. Few humans had ever broadcast their hatred like this. The 'cunt' had done it to him, and now he was doing it to 'her'. He perchance teased her in death with sweet names, made love to her with his hate. He hacked off her leg and cut out her heart, taking it for a deserved trophy. He may have kissed her missing lips, the lips he owned, savouring her bloody skull, masturbating, as he said he did, before bidding his whore-bitch carcass adieu.[24]

The consensus amongst Ripperologists is that Mary Kelly was the last of the victims; she had to be, in order to sustain the invention of the 'canonical'. Summing up her murder, Colin Wilson wrote, 'Jack the Ripper left Miller's Court and walked out of history.'

That comes nicely off the page, but he didn't. He walked out into Dorset Street. Not a few minutes later, 'a gentleman engaged in business, stated he was walking through Mitre Square at about ten minutes past ten on Friday morning, when a tall well dressed man, carrying a parcel under his arm, and rushing along in a very excited manner, ran into him. The man's face was covered with blood splashes, and his collar and shirt were also blood stained. The gentleman did not know at the time anything of the murder.'[25]

Whoever this 'gentleman engaged in business' was, he was another possibly vital witness ignored by MacDonald's court. An acrimonious air of deceit hung over it. At this point I may as well interrupt with a piece from *The Times*. Like everybody on the jury, the press were conned.

The jury had no questions to ask at this stage, and it was understood that more detailed evidence of the medical examination would be given at a further hearing. An adjournment for a few minutes then took place, and on return of the jury the Coroner said, 'It has come to my ears that somebody has been making a statement to some of the jury as to their right and duty of being here. Has anyone during the interval spoken to the jury, saying that they should not be here today?' Some jurymen replied in the negative. The Coroner: 'Then I must have been misinformed. I should have taken good care that he would have had a quiet life for the rest of the week if anybody had interfered with my jury.'

Anybody except himself, who was also interfering with the course of justice. In his statement, MacDonald pretended that his enquiries were going on 'for the rest of the week', when in fact they were not. His 'inquest' was bent from the start, and by the end palpably illegal. We have Mr Tom Cullen to thank for digging up the statute. As he points out, since the thirteenth century the fundamentals of a coroner's court have been carefully set down in English law. The court must not only determine the cause of death, the nature and number of injuries, including their 'breadth and deepness', but in the case of homicide, 'with what weapon, and in what part of the body the wound or hurt is'.[26] In other words, unless the jury knew what weapons did the deed and how often they did it, they cannot possibly deliver an acceptable verdict – *verdictum*, true speech. 'All these things must be enrolled in the roll of the Coroner,' writes Cullen, something MacDonald knew like thirst, '*yet he deliberately chose to suppress this evidence* [his emphasis]. What were the police trying to hide?'[27]

'The injuries inflicted upon the seventh victim, Mary Janet Kelly,' wrote J. Hall Richardson in 1889, 'have not been placed on public record. One result was to put into circulation a number of statements which may or may not have been in accordance with the truth, but which were misleading because not authorized. "Crowner's quest law" unmistakably sets out the necessity of recording the nature of *all* the wounds, the description of the weapon by which they were produced, and the circumstances under which they were inflicted, so that the action of Dr MacDonald in the Dorset Street case cannot be taken as a safe precedent.'[28]

MacDonald was too busy bullying to trouble himself with such niceties. Screw the rules, and screw the jury; and he was in immediate conflict with both. From the beginning the jury of Shoreditch men smelt a rat, and it was him. MacDonald had been sneaked in, and a subsequent row over jurisdiction was resolved with the police having their way. But the jury did not like it.

Stephen Knight gives a good account of the MacDonald/Met confederation, and I'm pleased to acknowledge dipping into it. 'The murder had taken place in Baxter's territory, the Whitechapel district,' he writes, 'but the inquest was finally held at Shoreditch Town Hall. This was an unprecedented deviation, and inspired one juror to take the new coroner to task.' He said: 'I do not see why we should have the inquest thrown upon our shoulders when the murder did not happen in our district, but Whitechapel.'

This was a reality contested by no one except the coroner's officer. 'It did not happen in Whitechapel,' said Mr Hammond. It apparently only 'appeared' to happen in Whitechapel, and thus the H Division police including Abberline, Arnold and Beck, were at 29 Dorset Street in error. Hammond's point was as foolish as the location of the hearing itself, purposely chosen to keep dissenting voices out. 'The room in which the inquest was held was exceptionally small, and very few of the general public were admitted.'[29] Among those excluded were two of the witnesses who'd seen Kelly alive on 9 November, and indeed the man who'd seen her the night before. Where was Hutchinson and his 'man in spats'?

> MACDONALD: Do you think we do not know what we're doing here? The jury are summoned in the ordinary way, and they have no business to object. If they persist in their objection I shall know how to deal with them. Does any juror persist in objecting?
>
> JUROR (objecting): We are summoned for the Shoreditch District. This affair happened in Spitalfields.
>
> MACDONALD (lying): It happened within *my* district.
>
> JUROR # 2: This is not my district. I come from Whitechapel, and Mr Baxter is my coroner.
>
> MACDONALD: I am not going to discuss the subject with the jurymen at all. If any juryman says he distinctly objects, let him say so. I may tell the jurymen that jurisdiction lies where the body lies, not where it is found.

'There are definite signs the coroner was on the side of the police,' writes Ripperologist Mr Stewart Evans – raising the question, whose 'side' were the police on? Unequivocally we must conclude it was that of a psychopath. The police were the opponents of the people, and the bullying of the jury was a manifestation of it.

Where was Arnold? Where was Anderson? The Assistant Commissioner seemed permanently beset by difficulties with the truth, but here he wasn't even asked to lie. MacDonald's inquiry was a whitewash, a flagrant contempt of the people and of the law he was entrusted to administer on their behalf. He led everyone to believe there would be further hearings, and via such duplicity managed to wrap this up that same day. 'There is other evidence which I do not propose to call,' he lickspittled, 'for if we at once make public every facet brought forward in connection with this terrible murder, the ends of justice will be retarded.'

Where have we heard that before? Almost word for word it is what Bro Phillips said when trying to sneak his way around truth of the ritualistic carve-up suffered by Annie Chapman. What 'ends of justice'? When was justice ever done?

'MacDonald not only broke the law in suppressing evidence,' writes Stephen Knight, 'but was under instruction to do so, for no government action was taken to correct the situation, despite indignant leaders in the national newspapers, like that of the *Daily Telegraph*.'

> It is in the power of the Attorney General to apply to the High Court of Justice to hold a new inquest, if he is satisfied that there has been irregularity of proceedings, or insufficiency of enquiry. This course is improbable as it is stated that Doctor Phillips, the Divisional Surgeon of Police, with whom the Coroner consulted in private, had had a commission from the Home Office for some time and does not consider himself a 'free agent',[30] but it is pointed out that by hurriedly closing the inquest the opportunity has been lost of putting on record statements made on oath and where the memory of witnesses is fresh. It is not improbable that a long interval may elapse before a prisoner is charged at a police court.

'A long interval'. How about forever? The *Telegraph* makes good sense, but had a rather romantic view of the Attorney General. Bro Sir Richard Webster was unlikely to get into a tizz over 'irregularity of proceedings' or 'insufficiency of enquiry', because he was presently up to his chops in the government-inspired conspiracy to destroy Charles Parnell. Webster was *in situ* to look after the legal needs of Viscount Salisbury, not to wet-nurse silly fantasies of upholding the law.

It will be remembered that it was this same Attorney General who manipulated proceedings in the matter of Cleveland Street, telling the House of Commons, 'No good is done by reporting cases of this description [i.e. buggery, perjury, perversion of the course of justice], and it is generally to the credit of the reporters of the press, that they almost invariably refrain from reporting them.'[31]

This phenomenon was about to be dramatically demonstrated in Fleet Street, silencing every newspaper including the *Telegraph*. Once again, Mr Knight sums up well: 'In normal circumstances, the Home Office would have been eager for justice to have been done. But with Jack the Ripper they were not.'[32]

Which, under the circumstances, might be considered a classic example of putting it mildly. If every law in the land could be bent as and when required, then a little sportive butchery by one of their own amongst the animal class presented few problems. At Miller's Court the lousy fairy tales came to an abrupt end. There would be no more 'Leather Aprons', no more 'Insane Medical Students', 'Womb-Collectors' or diminutive 'Nautical Men'. There would be no more Jack the Ripper.

'The most extraordinary thing,' writes Mr Paul Begg, 'is that whilst one would have expected the murder of Mary Kelly, by far the most horrendous of the series, to have sparked the press and public into another outburst of outrage and panic and sensationalism, the reverse was the case. Press interest poured away like bathwater when the plug is pulled out.'[33] And Patricia Cornwell writes, 'Immediately the press fell silent. It was as if the Ripper case was closed.'[34]

It was. Ha ha.

Another voice was silenced after Kelly, and it belonged to Mr George Lusk. Here was a man who had organised a Vigilance Committee, called public meetings, caused posters to be put up, and spent weeks shouting himself hoarse. He had predicted that the murders would continue, and they had. His worst fears and warnings had proved absolutely correct with this, the worst outrage of them all. A young woman had been *hacked to meat*; he had been vindicated. Now at last they must listen – and naturally Mr Lusk had nothing whatsoever to say. *Silence.* The man who had written letters to the Queen was at a sudden loss for words; like the press, the loudest voice in Whitechapel fell mute.

Now, this outburst of indifference doesn't play. The question has to be, is there anything of significance in Lusk's inexplicable speechlessness? I can answer the question with another. What is it that Bro Lusk, Bro Warren, and dear old Bro Jack had in common? As a matter of fact, what did a majority of the British ruling elite (including Attorney General Bro Richard Webster and the future King of England) have in common with the Whitechapel Thriller? We might now take an educated guess as to why Bro Lusk, Doric Lodge (993), and the press were silent after Kelly. Freemasonry was endemic in the police, in the judiciary and in Fleet Street. It filtered from on high down to the lesser ranks as and when required, just as 'stupidity' was imposed on honest policemen from above. Masonry was the motor-drive of Yack the Ripper, and Freemasonry covered it up, in the police, the judiciary, the coroners' courts and the press.

Not so the American newspapers, which suffered no such strictures, and didn't give a damn for the Brits and their Establishment shenanigans. 'It takes an event like this to show the London Press and London Police at their very worst,' was the view of the *New York Times*. Picking up where Fleet Street left off, the American papers published news the British weren't allowed to read.

Carefully nurtured propaganda (requiring the public to distance themselves from blood-guzzling Israelites) wasn't replicated in the American press – in fact, entirely the opposite. 'He is probably a monster of superior intelligence,' wrote the *New York Tribune* after Kelly, 'in all other respects sleek and sane.'[35] 'He seems to have an almost supernatural ability to disappear and leave no trace of himself behind,' wrote the same newspaper, dismissing the make-believe 'lair' and suggesting how Jack might do it: 'By taking a cab or the underground railway, he could break the trail and in a short time, place miles between him and his pursuers.'[36]

Three cheers for the obvious. The 'trail' referred to is that supposed to have been followed by Warren and his cancelled dogs. The bloodhound tactic didn't go down well with the US press, which universally identified it as the bullshit it was. 'The idea of using Bloodhounds as trackers in the heart of a densely populated district was so preposterous that it is amazing,' came another open-mouth from the *Tribune*, which added, 'The only type of Bloodhound that could hunt down the Fiend is one that is apparently unknown in London – a real detective.'[37] The condemnation from the American press was ubiquitous and harsh. Only one thing was certain: Jack the Ripper could go on murdering 'without fear of any interference on behalf of the London Police'.[38]

Despite Sir Melville Macnaghten's later efforts, the American consensus was that the Ripper was a religious nut, but not insane. A discussion held in New York City by the Society of Medical Jurisprudence and State Medicine was reported in the *New York Times*. 'These slaughters,' said one of the participating physicians, 'are wholly within the lines of the habitual conduct of barbarous ancestors, indulged in for the pleasurable sensation of witnesses' tortures. Cruel mutilations are not therefore, inconsistent with average soundness of mind. The Whitechapel murderer is behind the times. He is an anachronism, but not necessarily to be accorded the charity of considering himself insane.'[39]

To précis the American press, we've got a sleek, highly intelligent 'religious' fanatic who possibly takes the underground.[40] He seems to possess almost supernatural powers of evaporation, but these are assisted by the police's blundering stupidity, their only efficiency devoted to keeping the press away and thus maintaining public ignorance.[41]

But American journalists didn't have Bro Sir Richard Webster on their necks, and did better than their British counterparts. Out of the morass of police criticism, I pick one last astonishing quote. It comes again from the *New York Tribune*, and was published eight months after Kelly, when Jack had triggered yet another scandalous cover-up with his bestial fingernails in Castle Alley. Ignoring pitiful lackeys like Bro Dr Bagster Phillips, this long-dead journalist sat down to think. 'Who', he asked, and 'what' was this 'mystery' all about? He then went on to hit the nail right on its hideous head, suggesting the murders might have something to do with the Prophet Ezekiel.[42]

Bingo. He had just busted right into Bro Jack's thinking.

Our American scribe isn't the only one to associate Jack with the abominable Prophet. Preceding him by six months, and moving on from his 'assassin' or 'firm of assassins', Bro George R. Sims graced his column with this: 'This theory, which for purposes of reference may be called "the Ezekiel theory", is probably as near the mark as any of the "guesses at truth" which have been so plentiful of late. A new murder is confidently anticipated by the Vigilance Committee for this (Saturday) night, and extraordinary precautions have been taken to prevent the man who has taken the Book of Ezekiel too literally walking off again.'[43]

Ezekiel was what Bro Dr Bagster Phillips's visit to the Home Office was all about. Phillips wasn't a 'free agent', but an agent of the 'Mystic Tie'. Even Mr Philip Sugden agrees that 'from Phillips, above all others, we might have expected an authentic report about the condition of the body [of Kelly], but he tells us almost nothing. Certainly he spoke at the inquest three days later. On this occasion however, he deliberately suppressed the details of Mary's injuries.'[44]

And what were the details you would have liked him to reveal, Phil? Is it the geography of an atrocity according to the instructions of Masonry's Boss icon, the Prophet Ezekiel? Suppression was the name of the game, including the theft of Kelly's heart. This had been promised in a 'hoax' letter eight days before: 'I am going, to commit three more murders, two women and a child, and I shall take away their hearts.' He took Mary Kelly's heart, and he would prop Johnnie Gill's under his chin. But of course for the Victorian police and Ripperology, this letter was of no consequence.

Preceding Kelly's murder, there was a notable adjustment in several of Jack's letters. He converted the usual mocking 'Ha ha' into a double 'Ah Ah'. Below are a couple of examples, the first in a letter of 30 October, and the second 4 November.

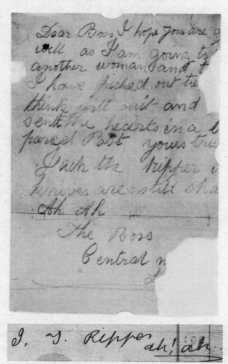

Nothing happens by accident. What was in his head?

'It is to be remembered that the Prophet Ezekiel,' wrote our perceptive American journalist, 'is referring to the wanton lives of the sisters Ahola and Aholiba.' And so was the Ripper. Jack's thinking begins at Ezekiel 23. The nasty old maniac is incandescent with rage towards all whores/women in general, but specifically towards two sisters, [Ah]ola and [Ah]oliba, a couple of the racy little sluts Ezekiel and Jack abhor. The Freemasonic Seal of the Grand Lodge of England begins to tell the tale. And what it's talking about is Ezekiel. On the left we see the compasses on the square, and on the right, done up in armorial disguise, the four elements of Ezekiel's second vision, to wit the Lion, the Ox, the Man and the Eagle. Underneath, usefully, is the Grand Motto of Freemasonry: 'Hear, See, Say Nothing'.

The Arms of The
United Grand Lodge of England.

This narrative has neither the desire nor the intent to push its understanding of Freemasonry beyond the calamity of Jack the Ripper. The Ripper, and not I, is the enemy of Freemasonry. I have no aspiration either to condemn or support Masonry; beyond an understanding of the corruption of its rituals by this most terrible of murderers. I am therefore like a man who has learned of Christianity with Judas Iscariot as his guide. Michael Maybrick *hated*

Freemasonry no less than he hated the women he killed.

It's an unhappy reality that this remarkable nineteenth-century American journalist never knew how close he got. Ezekiel and St John are written all over Mary Kelly's crime scene – if not on the walls, then into her body – no less than hatred was written into Jane Caputi's disgusting example of misogyny in Vietnam.

> The five books of Moses, the Prophecy of Ezekiel and the Apocalypse of St John are the three Kabbalistic keys of the Biblical edifice … The New Temple, the plan of which is given to exact Kabbalistic measures, is the type of labours of primitive Masonry. St John in his Apocalypse reproduces the same images and the same numbers, and reconstructs the Edenic world ideally in the New Jerusalem.[45]

In other words, the Temple of Solomon and the murder place of Hiram Abiff, its great structure predetermined in one of Ezekiel's visions and written up in Chapter 40 of his raving-mad prophecies.

30
PAST MASTERS DEGREE.

In this mid-Victorian representation we see all the usual symbols, including compasses on the square, superimposed on a Bible opened at Ezekiel 40. It is this Old Testament howl that raises the Prophet's star amongst Freemasons.

He's equally forthcoming in another department of more local interest, and that is his prurient fixation with the sexuality of young women, whom he enthusiastically converts into whores. Some of the language is frankly pornographic: '23.20: For she doted upon her paramours, whose flesh is as the flesh of asses, and whose issue is like the issue of horses …'

This is about a young woman making love, and the amount of sperm involved ('sponk' to the Ripper). Theologians might argue to the contrary, insisting that these vile outpourings must be read as a metaphor, and in this sense the theologians are right. Ezekiel and St John are virulent with symbol. But that is a facet of enquiry that needn't trouble us here, because the Ripper took them literally; it was all part of the Funny Little Game. And just in case anyone missed the Masonic message over Eddowes, it was made up for in his mutilations of Kelly, where he compensated for any shortcomings by literally 'going by the book', following instructions found in Ezekiel, 22 to 62:

23.25: And I will set my jealousy against thee, they shall deal furiously with thee: they shall take away thy nose and thine ears. 23.36: The Lord said moreover unto me: son of man, wilt thou judge Aholah and Aholibah? yea, declare unto them their abominations. 23.37: They have committed adultery and blood is in their hands.

Ezekiel's hatred of the adulteresses is transformed, by homicidal alchemy, into hatred for the adulteress Florence Maybrick. As a surrogate whore, Kelly must have her breasts cut off – 'plucked off', as Ezekiel quaintly puts it. Today this disturbing caveman would almost certainly be sectioned under various provisions of the Mental Health Act.

Ezekiel wasn't the only inspiration at Miller's Court. Further encouragement was supplied by that other sacred text of Freemasonry, St John's apocalyptic Book of Revelation. According to the nineteenth-century American historian of Freemasonry Albert Pike, the prophecies of Ezekiel and the Apocalypse of St John are beyond the grasp of most: 'St John did not write to be understood by the multitude.'[46] In this he was entirely successful, but I would add a caveat: most of Ezekiel and St John aren't worth understanding. Moreover, I prefer theological historian Solomon Reinach's critique of the Apocalypse: 'Among the absurdities and astrological speculations with which this book is filled, there are certain sublime passages which have become classics in all literature, but as a whole it is a work of hatred and frenzy.' Like Ezekiel, Revelation is a loony-tune, a howl from the suburbs of hell. Its author conjures a veritable rush-hour of demons and mystic has-beens, babbling of their capacity to do ill. The recurring highlight of this shocking scream is the visitation of punishment upon the WHORE and instructions for the subsequent carve-up.

It is said that the Book of Revelation was 'Writ with the Quill of an Angel's wing, by a Divine Inspiration',[47] its feathers represented in the illustration of the Past Master's Degree. Others might call this a tall story. Reinach thinks it's the work of a forger in third-century Cairo, and nothing to do with St John at all.[48] Either way, the Apocalypse exists in all its horror. In the head of a psychopath one could barely imagine a more dangerous endorsement. It is axiomatic that when the religious matches come out there are always more witches than wizards, the madmen become prophets, and the women Satan's Whores.

Albert Pike conflates Ezekiel and the Book of Revelation, and so did Jack. Theologians have burnt the oil trying to deconstruct these texts, but as far as the Ripper is concerned they needn't have troubled, because he took both by rote. He wasn't in the business of interpreting symbols in the entirely legitimate exercise of Masonic ritual; he was in the business of taking the Freemasonic piss. The whore in Revelation is symbolic of Papal Rome; the whore in Jack's book was Florence Maybrick. These texts are of course anodyne in the rituals of Masonry, but mix this pantomime of misogyny in the furnace of a psychopathic brain, and you don't get a benevolent assembly of Freemasonic Brethren, you get the Whitechapel Murderer.

We can look at the photograph overleaf as if it's a monstrosity from some long-forgotten sideshow, a waxwork or a work of fantasy. But it isn't, and it's horrifying. This was a young woman, poor as dirt, but she had a life, it belonged to her, and the infinite sadism of this most horrendous of murderers has left her like this forever.

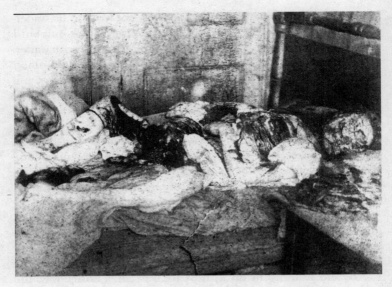

And the woman was arrayed, full of abominations and filthiness of her fornication. And upon her was a name written, MYSTERY, THE MOTHER OF HARLOTS AND ABOMINATIONS OF THE EARTH. And the 10 horns which thou sawest upon the Beast, these shall hate the Whore, and shall make her desolate and naked, and shall eat her flesh, and burn her with fire.[49]

In this minimally pruned passage from Revelation we get the lot: nakedness, cannibalism, and burning of flesh. But the Beast had barely begun to fulfil his Biblical obligations – detailed instructions to be found at Ezekiel, 23.29:

And they shall deal with thee hatefully, and shall take away all thy labour, and shall leave thee naked and bare: and the nakedness of thy whoredom shall be discovered, both thy lewdness and thy whoredom.

Now that the woman is in pieces, her breasts and face cut off, what did this vile augury decree should next be done with her?

22.20: As they gather silver and brass, and iron, and lead, and tin, into the midst of the furnace to blow the fire upon it, to melt it, so will I gather you in mine anger and my fury, and I will leave you there and melt you.

All very well, but how is the Beast to do it? He has flesh, but no furnace. He is alone in a filthy hovel in Miller's Court.

24: Set on a pot, set it on, and also pour water into it: Gather the pieces thereof into it, even every good piece, the thigh, and the shoulder, fill it with choice bones, and burn also the bones under it, and make it boil well, and let them seethe the bones of it therein ... to put whose scum is therein, and whose scum has not gone out of it! Bring it out piece by piece; let no lot fall upon it. For her blood is in the midst of her ... I will even make the pile for fire great. Heap on wood, kindle the fire, consume the flesh ... and let the bones be burned. Then set it empty upon the coals thereof, that the brass of it may be hot, and may burn, and that the filthiness of it may be molten in it, that the scum of it may be consumed. She hath wearied herself with lies, and her great scum went not forth out of her: her scum shall be in the fire. In thy filthiness is lewdness: because I have purged thee, and thou wast not purged, thou shall not be purged from thy filthiness any more till I have caused my fury to rest upon thee.

And something to that effect is what I believe Abberline and Dr Phillips found in the grate. Coal and bones and pieces of burnt flesh. I don't know if Kelly's kettle was brass or tin, but it's water that moderates during boiling, and it was the deliberate lack of it that caused the spout to melt. 'Set it *empty* upon the coals thereof,' says the Prophet, 'that the brass of it may be hot, and may burn, and that the filthiness of it may be molten in it.' Abberline testified that 'there had been a large fire, so large as to melt the spout off the kettle'.

'It has been ascertained that a very big fire must have been kept burning all Friday morning in the room in which Kelly was found,' wrote the *Evening Standard* on 12 November, 'as a kettle on the fire was very much burned, the spout having entirely disappeared. The police thought it likely that the murderer had burned something before leaving the room after the crime, and accordingly the ashes and other matter in the grate were carefully preserved. Yesterday afternoon Mr [Bro Bagster] Phillips and the Coroner for the district visited Miller's Court, and after the refuse had been passed through a sieve, it was subjected to the closest scrutiny by the medical gentlemen. Nothing, however, was found which is likely to afford any clue to the police.'[50]

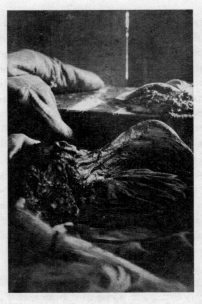

As I understand it, these two photographs are generally interpreted as depicting the crime scene, in other words what the police saw on arrival in Kelly's room. Palpably they are not. The differing positions of the body make this assumption impossible, proving that one or other of these photographs had to be contrived.

In the wider picture, Kelly's bed is pushed up against a wall. Next to her is a bedside table piled with her body parts, and this horror is the focus of the second picture. Common sense demands we immediately notice something iffy. The first and obvious inconsistency registers across Kelly towards the bedside table. The bed is against the wall, making this point of view impossible unless the bed has been moved.

For simplicity, I will call these two photographs the bed picture and the table picture. Consider the position of Kelly's arm/hand in the bed picture with the same arm/hand in the table picture. In the latter, the hand is about midway up the side of the table, but in the bed picture it is parallel with its front edge. This means either the table has been moved or the hand has been moved; it was probably both. These photographs do not agree with each other, and for want of a better word, one of them has been 'posed'. This presumption is important in respect of camouflaging the Ezekiel-motivated Masonic piss-take. Consider the position of Kelly's left leg in the bed picture, and now compare it with the leg in the table picture. In this, some part of the bone, like an arched knee, is visible, whereas in the bed picture it is not. In comparison with the right leg, this 'leg' has an almost ghost-like appearance, nearer to the camera but much less defined. In the (table) picture, the left 'leg' is more focused, but in a completely different position.

When these photographs were returned by their apparently anonymous donor, a part of Dr Bond's autopsy notes was included. Bond says Kelly was naked. Phillips said she was wearing a chemise. She wasn't, and as usual Phillips is dissembling.

Bro Dr Phillips made a significant slip of the tongue over Kelly at the inquest into another of the Ripper's victims. She was the headless and legless half-body of a woman found at Backchurch Lane (September 1889). Called 'the Pinchin Street Torso', it was written off by the police, as was the headless, blood-drained trunk in the cellars of New Scotland Yard, a.k.a. 'the Whitehall mystery'. The coroner presiding over the Pinchin Street mystery was again Wynne Baxter. During an exchange with Bro Dr Phillips, Bro Baxter blithely put up a question:

> BAXTER: I should like to ask Dr Phillips whether there is any similarity in the cutting off of the legs in this case and the one that was *severed from the woman in Dorset Street*? [My emphasis. 'Dorset Street' refers to Mary Kelly.]

To which Phillips replied:

> PHILLIPS: I have not noticed any sufficient similarity to convince me it was the same person who committed both mutilations.[51]

It's a revealing response. He doesn't say, '*What leg* severed from the woman at Dorset Street?' Implicit in his reply is that one of Kelly's legs *was* severed. Does that not explain the spectre-like appearance of the left leg in the wider picture? Bereft of injury, it looks like emulsion painted onto a negative to me; and if I am in error, what then is the footless leg with a viciously slashed thigh on the bedside table? Although the quality of the pictures is poor, Mary Kelly didn't have three legs. In the wider picture there's a length of cloth, absent in the table shot, covering her thigh joint and extending under her arm to obscure her shoulder.

Mr Philip Sugden says, 'Bond's statement that Mary's body was found naked was contradicted by Phillips's inquest testimony that she was clad in a linen undergarment. Phillips was right,' he asserts, 'because in a surviving photograph of the scene a puffed up sleeve of the garment is clearly visible about the top of Mary's left arm.'[52]

Mr Sugden is mistaken. Bond was right, and Bro Phillips wasn't telling the truth. He had occult reason for the porky: 'Gather the pieces thereof,' instructs Ezekiel, 'the thigh and the shoulder.' A glaring artifice is evident here.

I ask the reader to look closely at the photograph, and consider Mr Sugden's 'puffed sleeve'. Adjacent to it is Kelly's chest, her breasts removed, together with all the tissue down to the ribs. And yet this 'puffed sleeve' shows no apparent blood soaking. Could anyone imagine that this material was *in situ* when Jack carved her up? Flesh has been torn away at the inside of the 'puffed sleeve', a heart extracted, and a face hacked off.

In reality it isn't a 'puffed sleeve' at all, and nothing to do with an undergarment. What it is, is part of a carefully positioned cloth, covering her (missing) shoulder and extending down under her arm, where it abruptly detours in a connivance to cover her amputated leg at the thigh. Bro Phillips didn't care to admit that Kelly was 'desolate and naked' and boiled in the grate, because of the Biblical (Masonic) nut that comes to mind.

The historian Stephen Gouriet Ryan published an incisive essay on the events at Miller's Court, focusing on the Ripper's comprehensive 'desexing' of the victim: 'The Kelly mutilations have been seen as so much meaningless hacking and a frenzied wallowing in the entrails, in a paroxysm of sadistic impulses. But there was also a method in his madness, to demonstrate, in the most graphic, barbaric way, his absolute domination over, and rejection of, hated womankind.'[53]

Ten out of ten for the American journalist who could have known nothing of what Phillips actually saw. The Ripper hated like Ezekiel hated, and followed his instructions to the letter. 'On most of the New Testament,' writes theologian Lowther Clarke, 'Ezekiel has left little trace' – except, with dramatic exception, 'in the Book of Revelation of St John'.[54]

A psychopathic disciple, signing himself 'Revelation', followed up with a four-page snigger, mailed from 'America'.

Purporting to have been posted in 'Minneapolis Minnesota', it's dated 25 December 1888, and has nothing to do with Minneapolis, but is another tease bounced out of New York. We have no envelope, but precedent and the dates tell the story of the letter having undergone a twenty-three-day round trip before it was received by the City Police on 17 January 1889. It's the usual mocking ramble: 'I'll withhold my real name and just put a fictitious one, my name will be Revelation.' Referring to Revelation three times, he signs off with it – 'Respectfully Revelation'. Written in the margin, 'I do not wish my name to be published', and (with an 'f' for 's') 'A friend of mine Delia Bafs, 2323 Jackson St Minneapolis Minn can receive my.'

To accomplish his transatlantic trick, the letter's author would have had to be in Liverpool, where (M)inneapolis (M)innesota, also known as (M)ichael (M)aybrick spent Christmas 1888 as a guest of his brother. He would tell us so himself at the 'trial' of his sister-in-law, whose hospitality he was then enjoying. At Miller's Court he was killing her surrogate: the letters 'FM' – (F)lorence (M)aybrick – are visible on the wall behind Kelly, probably written in her blood.

In an interview with an American newspaper, Inspector Henry Moore said the assassin had 'hung different parts of the body on nails and over the back of chairs'.[55] A hundred years later, citing the incomplete report of Dr Bond, wherein such information is not to be found, Ripperology proclaims Moore's recollections must be 'treated with caution'.[56]

Caution against what? Doing a disservice to this fucking nightmare, or caution against thinking what might have motivated it? With a woman's leg on a bedside table, to what end might 'caution' be urged in respect of flesh over the back of a chair? Such parsimonious inhibition is what exasperates me most about Ripperology. It's always peering through a microscope, but blind to the bigger picture. Some bad-thinking man had been in this room hacking a woman to the bone, and the question isn't where he slung the flesh, but *why the authorities wanted to cover it up*.

'What,' asks Mr Tom Cullen, 'were the police trying to hide?'[57] The stupefying selfishness of the Victorian Establishment was in large part responsible for the picture above. Any smart copper could have stopped this catastrophe in its tracks.

The 'mystery' attached to Kelly is as sickening as it's artificial, a confection silencing the British press and initiating a tide of speculation that in our day is frankly ridiculous. In the opinion of *The News from Whitechapel*, a consensus of shock had muted Fleet Street. 'There was,' it surmises, 'an unspoken acknowledgement that the death of Mary Kelly went far beyond all that preceded it; a sense that some invisible dreadful line in murder news had been crossed.'[58]

This nonsense is straight out of the Macnaghten school of journalism, and about as intellectually astute as an episode of *Scooby-Doo*. Since when have newspapers, and particularly Victorian newspapers, ever had enough of blood and gore? 'If it bleeds, it reads' was the Street's historic dictum. Jack was money, and a lot of it, and there was no lack of reporters trying to get the lowdown on Miller's Court. We're looking therefore for a motive for this imposed silence, a motive superseding circulation wars and light years beyond rectitude.

It is of course an 'unspoken acknowledgement' of a ruling elite in the timeless business of saving their arses. I think a comment in the French press at the time of Cleveland Street is nearer the truth: '*La presse officiel s'est ligué pour cacher ces crimes et étouffer par un silence de mort cette grave question de moralité nationale.*'[59] (The official press are in league to hide the crimes and hush up with a deathly silence this serious question of national morality.)

As an addendum to the above, in reference to MacDonald's law-breaking haste, we read in *The News from Whitechapel* that 'Later writers have tended to view his actions with suspicion, but this shows a misunderstanding of Victorian inquests, which typically only ran for one or two sessions.'[60]

A critic of less generosity than myself might dismiss this as bollocks. Wynne Baxter held a total of fourteen sessions for his three victims – four for Nichols, five for Chapman and five for Stride. On that form, MacDonald might have pushed his enquiries somewhat beyond the recollections of a drowsy woman with a kitten on her tit. A nobbled coroner and a mute press are hardly the hand-maidens of justice. The Ripper made a mockery of a court, silenced Fleet Street, and brought about the dismissal of the Commissioner of Metropolitan Police.

Not bad going for a serial murderer.

The *Spectator* had a more plausible explanation for the press clam-up following Kelly and thereafter. Although itself of a conserv-ative bent, it wrote that British journalists 'are taught and tempted to seek rewards which limit their independence, fetter them in their work, and very often, we fear, will be found seriously to interfere with the acuteness of their judgement … the approval of a Premiere will be more than the approval of a people; and "good newspaper policy" will mean neither independence nor the adroit reflection of popular opinion, but careful attention to that which is known to be pleasing to the head of the Government, or to those who are believed to have influence on its decisions.'

Salisbury's government was putrid with self-interest, and serviced some of the fattest rats in the sewer. Just about everything to which the *Spectator* alluded was to be found daily in the house newspaper of the ruling elite, *The Times*. As far as it was concerned, the Ripper's expulsion of Warren constituted 'Loss of a valuable servant' (some-thing of an understatement). Entirely exonerating him for his comedic failure, it suggested that the prostitutes of Whitechapel were 'accessory to their own deaths', and at fault for not managing their own protection: 'It might have been supposed that they would have organised some system of mutual supervision and companionship in their dreadful trade. It is quite unreasonable to blame the police in such circumstances for failing to give protection, and hardly less unreasonable to condemn then for failing to detect the murderer.'[61] In other words, anybody who expected the police to catch Jack the Ripper was being 'unreasonable', and the homeless and penniless were to be blamed for not instituting their own police force.

After Kelly's murder the burlesque of pretending that Charles Warren was trying to catch the Ripper came to an end. This crisis of lying simply couldn't be sustained. Either Warren must go or the Ripper must. As it happened, both were to disappear, although in the case of the latter, only insofar as press coverage was concerned.

According to Macnaghten, Charlie was 'knocked out'[62] by Jack, and it's one of the only reliable things he had to say. Sharper minds at the Home Office were perfectly cognisant of the glaring symbiosis between this murderer and the Commissioner of Police. It looked as if any day now Jack was going to invite Warren out to dinner. The question that could no longer be avoided was, if Warren and his Freemasonry went, would the Ripper and his perversion of Freemasonry go too? Such a dilemma must have haunted many a discussion, although for public consumption the Home Office was obliged to behave like the worst of Ripperology: stumped, baffled, not a clue, etc.

Those who were Masons – and that's most of them – knew perfectly well what the symbolism of these crime scenes meant: from what had sprung Warren from his slumbers all the way down to why Kelly's kettle was melted in the grate. Attempting to navigate the atrocity at Miller's Court, a retrospective 'resignation' was cooked up to deny Jack yet another humiliating triumph. They would say that Warren had resigned the day before, on 8 November.

This shifty bit of calendar work didn't convince anybody, including even the *Tatler*. 'It was very curious,' it opined, 'that Sir Charles Warren should have sent in his resignation on the eighth, just one day previous to the latest murder by the Whitechapel maniac.'[63] Of course he hadn't, and once again it was the unfettered American press that was in charge of reality. 'The Whitechapel mysteries,' wrote the *New York Daily News*, 'have forced Sir Charles Warren, Chief of the Metropolitan Police, to resign. What other consequences will follow cannot be fully foreseen, but the resignation of the Home Secretary is highly probable and the overthrow of the Tory government is not an impossibility.'[64]

It quite seriously was not. On 11 November the *New York Times* explained:

> A motion to adjourn the House of Commons has been put down and a resolution attacking both Matthews and Warren will be moved. The division is regarded by some members of the government with apprehension. Urgent telegraphic whips have been sent to the Irish members who are still in Ireland, begging them to come over in time for this division, the effect of which may be to upset the Ministry or at least to sorely damage it. London members will vote almost solidly against Matthews, for their constituents are all up in arms against the existing police inefficiency.

But that's not the story the British got. For them, Warren's departure was nothing to do with a production line of corpses. It would be 'unreasonable' to blame the police for that. However, an excuse for his resignation was required to put before the public. They couldn't cite misfeasance of duty, because everybody had been living with that for the last four months. Plus, his 'occult motives' were taboo. What then was there? The Pecksniffs went to work, and dug out some arcane rule instituted (and forgotten) in 1879 that prohibited coppers from writing for the press without the prior consent of the Secretary of State. In October Warren had published an article of tranquillising tedium in a rag called *Murray's Magazine*. He made no secret of it, and nobody paid it any attention. If the Home Office felt like getting tetchy it could have reacted on 19 October, when the *Star* announced the piece's imminent publication:

<u>WARREN TAKES UP THE PEN</u>
The forthcoming issue of *Murray's Magazine* will contain an article upon the police of the metropolis by Sir Charles Warren.[65]

Nobody so much as blinked, but three weeks later it was elevated to an offence comparable to the claim that the Earl of Euston had fled to Peru. Warren had broken the rules, and would have to go. Never mind that he'd repeatedly broken the rules with similar articles in a variety of publications, most topically the *Contemporary Review*. As recently as 10 October 1888 he'd published an abbreviated but almost identical piece about the police in *The Times*. That was neither here nor there. It was the rule he broke nine days later that was unpardonable, and in the interests of democratic hygiene it must be adhered to. The 'rules' were the 'rules', and what does it matter that he broke every rule in Vincent's book when he destroyed evidence at Goulston Street?

Warren's exit was as farcical as the reason given for it. Nobody with a brain bigger than a currant could have believed it was nothing to do with Kelly. It was the *Pall Mall Gazette* that spoke up for reality with a front-page cartoon. Warren hasn't lost his mount jumping a wall called *Murray's Magazine*.

AT LAST.

In a risible attempt at diversion, Home Secretary Matthews threw the considerable weight of his legal department behind absolutely nothing. The upshot was the offer of a 'Pardon to any accomplice' of the murderer. This non-existent homicidal 'accomplice' was immediately elevated to a status beyond that enjoyed by the Insane Medical Student and the Nautical Man. Information on him was vague, but it can be assumed that he was less than five feet five inches tall, and was probably a cohabitant of the 'lair'. Needless to say, no accomplice came forward, but the police kept arresting people who looked like him.[66]

'Matthews' explanation of the rationale of a pardon offer is, quite frankly, unbelievable,' writes Mr Sugden, and once again I'm happy to agree with him. 'There was no evidence whatsoever that more than one man had been involved and Doctor Bond said so in his report.'[67] And so did internal (and secret) reports at the Home Office: 'It is generally agreed that the Whitechapel murderer has no accomplices that could betray him.' Matthews, as usual, was gulling the public.[68]

Meanwhile Warren clung on, and it wasn't until December that London was finally rid of him. The logistics of the buffoon's evaporation are of little interest. It's what came after him that compounds the misfortune. Any remote hope of apprehending the Whitechapel Fiend was now abandoned. A religious fanatic and a liar of incontestable talent was now in charge at Scotland Yard.

Robert Anderson didn't give a monkey's for catching Jack the Ripper, and said so. He claimed that on his return from his 'holiday in Paris' on 8 October 1888, Matthews had confronted him with 'We hold you responsible to find the murderer.' To which Anderson replied, 'I decline the responsibility.' Having established this novel attitude for a senior policeman towards a serial killer, Anderson went on (in echo of *The Times*) to remonstrate that current police attempts to nail the bastard were 'wholly indefensible and scandalous'. It was not the Ripper who should be arrested, but his victims. 'These wretched women were plying their trade under definite police protection. Let the police of that district, I urged, receive orders to arrest every known "street woman" found on the prowl after midnight, or let us warn them the police will not protect them.' It is no longer Jack who prowls looking for a victim, it is the victims who 'prowl', making themselves targets for the perfectly reasonable attentions of a psychopath with his knife. 'Though the former course [arrest] would have been merciful,' concluded the masterful detective, 'it was deemed too drastic and I fell back upon the second' – which, to reiterate, meant no police protection at all. This, then, was the stated policy (pre Kelly) of the incoming Boss of Metropolitan Police.[69]

16

'Red Tape'

Which way I fly is hell; myself am hell.

Milton

After the Kelly atrocity, all the police had to offer in lieu of investigation was lies. Jack's immunity was guaranteed by the state. They were never going to catch him, so they decided to make him dead.

Sir Melville Macnaghten later clarified the deceit in his book. 'In all probability', he wrote, the Whitechapel Murderer 'put an end to himself soon after the Dorset Street affair in November 1888'. A homely stab at psychoanalysis is then conscripted to colour the fantasy: 'After the awful glut at Miller's Court', Macnaghten concluded that 'his brain gave way altogether and he committed suicide; otherwise the murders would not have ceased'.[1]

Leaving aside the fact that the murders had not ceased, but were to escalate in their ferocity, the only substance underpinning Macnaghten's forensic breakthrough was an unidentified stiff hauled out of the River Thames. The corpse got the timing about right, but managed little else. His death certificate reads:

Unknown male, about 45 years, of unknown occupation. Died 24th November 1888 [in] River Thames off Hermitage Stairs, Wapping. Cause of death, 'Violent suffocation by drowning, evidence insufficient to show under what circumstances.'[2] (Wynne Baxter)

It isn't stated that he was wearing 'button boots and gaiters with white buttons', or a 'black tie with horse-shoe pin', as in the breakthrough supplied by Hutchinson, but it was apparently sufficient to qualify him as the Whitechapel Fiend? And if not him, there were others. Following Kelly the Thames bore a veritable flotilla of Jack the Rippers, including that sad little non sequitur, Montague J. Druitt.

In March 1889 a member of George Lusk's Vigilance Committee, Mr Albert Bachert, claimed that he was 'sworn to secrecy' by some unnamed officer in the Metropolitan Police. Once his secrecy was pledged he was told, 'The man in question is dead. He was hauled out of the Thames two months ago and it would only cause pain to relatives if we said any more than that.'[3]

Whether Bachert's story was reliable is anybody's guess, but my guess is that it is probably true. Police lies are an adequate provenance for police rumour. Thereafter the corpse attracted further credentials. A covenant of similarly questionable and hardly impartial authors were at their typewriters converting fiction into fact. Writing of his granddad, Bro Sir Charles Warren, Bro Watkin Williams has this: 'My impression is that he believed the murderer to be a sex-maniac who committed suicide after the Miller's Ct. murder – possibly the young doctor whose body was found in the Thames on 31 December 1888.'

Assistant Under Secretary at the Home Office, Bro Sir John Moylan, was happy to agree: 'The murderer, it is now certain, escaped justice by committing suicide at the end of 1888' – an opinion endorsed by the Assistant Commissioner of the CID Sir Basil Thompson. 'In the belief of the police,' he wrote in 1913, 'he was a man who committed suicide in the Thames at the end of 1888.' Thus the powers had spoken, and Jack the Ripper was officially no more – and you better believe it, because as Bachert was warned, 'His oath to secrecy was a solemn matter,' and 'Anyone who put out stories that the Ripper was still alive, might be proceeded against for causing a public mischief.'

Congratulations to the river for solving one of history's vilest mysteries. But strange it is that they all knew of the 'suicide' in 1888, yet in the official files (that were to remain closed for the next hundred years) there isn't a scintilla of documentation to support it. Not a paragraph, not a word. It was evidently so secret they kept it a secret from themselves.

In his memoir published in 1914, Macnaghten was one of the first to return public attention to it. When he arrived at Scotland Yard as Assistant Commissioner in June 1889, he recalled that he was confronted with a postbag that 'bulged large with hundreds of

anonymous communications on the subject of the East End tragedies'. Among them were one or two that caught his attention, probably because of the ditties composed by J.T.R.

> I'm not a butcher, I'm not a Yid,
> Nor yet a foreign Skipper,
> But I'm your own light-hearted friend,
> Yours truly, Jack the Ripper.[4]

'The above queer verse,' wrote Macnaghten, 'was one of the first
documents which I perused at Scotland Yard.' If Sir Melville was
with us now, I'm sure he'd wish he hadn't made it public. It was
Queen Victoria herself who suggested, in November 1888, that the
Ripper was perhaps a seaman from a foreign ship that periodically
visited London. Her letter was sent privately to the Home Secretary,
and remained classified for years.[5] For the Ripper to have knowledge of Her Majesty's correspondence meant, at minimum, that he
had access to the exchange of confidential gossip. As Mr Melvin
Harris writes, 'This could only have happened if the Ripper was
highly placed socially.'[6]

In other words, he was on the inside, and that is a proposition Mr
Harris doesn't like the sound of at all. Dismissing the 'Skipper' verse
as an irrelevance, he plunges forth with the usual bombast, berating
fellow Ripperologists for their infantile curiosity. For anyone to
believe the verse is anything beyond a common hoax is 'incredibly
naïve'. 'Oddly enough,' he adds, 'Colin Wilson, too, takes this seriously when he comments, "Queen Victoria had suggested that the
police should check on all foreign skippers coming ashore." This
was not public knowledge,' he agrees, while sermonising from
above, 'but a little extra thought would have shown that the verse
does no more than sum up speculations that were widely toyed with
at the time. Seamen, especially foreign seamen, were certainly
objects of suspicion, and if you want a nautical crew term to rhyme
with Ripper, what else are you going to choose but Skipper? It's as
simple and insignificant as that.'[7]

Except it ain't.

Wilson was right to be intrigued, and it's Melvin, with his self-
imposed myopia, who might have profited from 'a little extra thought'.
The association of Skipper and Ripper is not unique to Macnaghten's

stash at the Yard, and is not so easy to dismiss. Approximately three weeks after Victoria's confidential letter to Home Secretary Henry Matthews, preceding Macnaghten's postbag by seven months, somebody else posted a letter from Taunton, Somerset, in the south-west of England. Dated 4 December 1888, it's signed 'Jack The Skipper'.

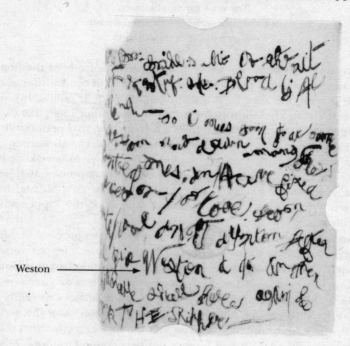

Weston

Although virtually unintelligible, this tangle of words would evolve into one of the most important letters Jack ever wrote. Only one word is clearly written, the word he intended to be understood. It is 'Weston', a coastal town in Somerset, and in a page or two its significance will begin to be explained.

Before attempting to make sense of this letter, we need to go back a couple of months and take a look at another. It was mailed out of Birmingham on 8 October 1888, addressed to 'the Detective Offices Scotland Yd', where it arrived on 9 October. It's another letter from on the road: 'I am as you see by this note amongst the slogging town of Brum [Birmingham].' The rest of the text rehearses his usual mirth at the expense of cruelty: '3 families will be thrown into a state of delightful mourning. Ha Ha. My bloody whim must have its way.'

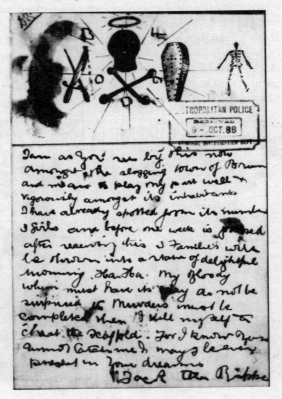

But this thing isn't about the text. Out of all the Ripper correspondence it is the most fastidious in its artwork. He sat down and bothered with it, using different-coloured inks. This macabre assembly meant something to its author, and was designed to mean something to its recipient. In my philosophy, it had to mean something to Charlie Warren.

When I first saw it I thought it was some kind of sneer at Freemasonry, the Brotherhood Jack abhorred. What makes it important is that (George Sims apart) there was never an inkling of Masonry in the newspaper reports of the murders, and no other so-called 'hoaxer' had ever made reference to it. So what was the catalyst for it now? What was it that stimulated the creation of this picture? It has many Masonic ingredients – a skull and crossed bones, a sword dripping blood, crossed with a poignard, an upright coffin with a cross and a heart on it, and a skeleton taking a stroll. The latter is unusual in the lexicon of Freemasonry, although it occasionally gets a look-in, and the rest are all common symbols. Yet, like 'Jack the Floater', there isn't the remotest suggestion of the significance of this letter to be found in the entire Metropolitan Police files.

Selective myopia is a scandalous alibi when you're chasing a serial murderer. One can only assume the police were all of a 'Melvin' frame of mind. 'Get thee glass eyes'; but they must have known that swaddling Jack and his perversion of Masonry meant that he would up the ante in his Funny Little Game, and hit back with something worse. Much worse.

The key to his next outrage, following Kelly, was, as I later understood, advertised in his Birmingham artwork. But at first I struggled to get traction on it. Everything about it said Masonry – except the letters around the skull and the halo above it, which are not Masonic. I didn't know what the letters meant, but I thought that one of them, like an 'F' on its back, might possibly be a crude representation of something called 'Dr Valpy's Crest', described by a not entirely reliable Victorian source, Mr Hargrave Jennings, as a 'Notable Cabbalistic & Rosicrucian emblem'.[8]

Birmingham letter

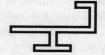

Dr Valpy's Crest

In the archetypal painting below we see a skull and crossed bones over the temple door, together with a sword crossed with a poignard. At the bottom left a Bible is open at St John. The text over the temple door, incidentally, '*In Hoc Signo Vinces*' (In This Sign Thou Shalt Conquer), is said to represent a cosmic hallucination of a fiery cross witnessed by the Emperor Constantine, causing him to convert to Christianity.

Even if Jennings was right – even if my interpretation was right – it didn't really get me anywhere. Beyond the obvious Masonic symbols, I couldn't see how it might relate to Warren. Then one winter's afternoon I ran into a bit of good fortune. My researcher Keith and I were in the library at Freemasons' Hall. One of the librarians introduced us to a fellow visitor who clearly knew his Masonic onions. I showed him the Birmingham artwork (shorn of its text) to see what he might make of it, anticipating that he would prop up my thinking by confirming it as a smirk at Masonry. But he didn't. He said, and I quote from my notes, 'It looks like something from the Golden Dawn.'

These were early days in my research, and at that time this meant absolutely nothing to me. I'd never heard of the 'Golden Dawn', and was then so innocent of my subject that I actually asked what the Masonic initials I.T.N.O.T.G.A.O.T.U. meant. He wouldn't tell me, and as we talked he seemed to become progressively less fond of my face. Nevertheless, he confirmed that the Birmingham drawing was some kind of aberrant visual derivative of the Golden Dawn.

There are a lot of 'world experts' in this caper. I didn't realise I was actually talking to one. I thought he was a devious Mason selling me a bum steer. It wasn't until I started swatting up on the Golden Dawn that I discovered he was telling the truth. Mr R.A. Gilbert is an authority on matters cabbalistic, and had written books on the subject that I was now reading.[9]

The Golden Dawn was the creation of a trio of occult obsessives by the names of Bro Dr William Robert Woodman, Bro Dr William W. Westcott, and a young weirdo, Bro Samuel L. MacGregor Mathers.

From its inception, 'the Hermetic Order of the Golden Dawn' was predicated on mysteriously faked documents and an equally phoney provenance, just as was MacGregor Mathers himself. He sold his act as that of a baronial Scot, when in reality he was the son of a West Hackney clerk. MacGregor wasn't even his real name. He was born Samuel Liddell Mathers, but adopted 'MacGregor' from the Scottish clan motto '*S Rioghail Ma Dhream*' (Royal is my Race).

When Woodman and Westcott first liaised with him, the Highlands were some way off: Mathers was living just outside Bournemouth. He joined Freemasonry at the age of twenty-three, initiated into the Lodge of Hengist (194) while working as a clerk at an estate agents, also in Bournemouth. As the history of Hengist remarks, it wasn't many years before S.L. MacGregor Mathers had become 'a shining light in Rosicrucian circles'.

Another was Dr William Wynn Westcott, also a bit of a Victorian weirdo. I don't necessarily mean that in a pejorative sense, but he kept a human hand as a paperweight, and his thinking was perverse even by the standards of esoteric Freemasonry.

Bro Woodman   Bro Westcott

Both Westcott and Mathers were Rosicrucians, and Dr Valpy and his crest were beginning to shape up. Westcott opened his first lodge of the Golden Dawn, called Isis-Urania, Temple No. 3, in London in 1888. That same year he opened his Osiris Temple at Weston in Somerset (8 October 1888), and Mathers his temple at Bradford, called Horus, the following day.[10] These dates are interesting, corresponding precisely with those of the Birmingham artwork, mailed from there on 8 October and received at Scotland Yard on 9 October 1888.

When Ripperology and its shadowy sidekick Freemasology run into any Ripper correspondence that might resist immediate dismissal as 'hoax', they move seamlessly into their second-favourite default position, 'coincidence'. Anything risking interpretation as evidence is branded thus. Well, let's see if these dates add anything like coincidence to the dates of the Golden Dawn.

Let us assume for a moment that the Masonic artwork was the spontaneous creation of some hoaxer in Birmingham, and then ask a very reasonable question. How did this Ripper wannabe know about the Golden Dawn, and understand a hybrid of Masonry that as yet was barely in existence? Seminars on the foundation of the Golden Dawn weren't held in the saloon bar of the Dog and Duck. It wasn't front-page news for some twerp in Birmingham to read. As a matter of fact, the first reference to its existence wasn't made until the following year. On 9 February 1889 it attracted a fleeting mention in Madame Blavatsky's short-lived occult periodical *Lucifer*, and that's it.[11]

Even the most virulent deviationist of the Melvin School would be hard put to deny the Freemasonic content of this drawing, and if he did he wouldn't be arguing with me, but with an acknowledged expert. Deferring to Mr Gilbert's unimpeachable scholarship *vis à vis* the Golden Dawn, it's clear that the creator of this artwork knew something about discussions held behind extremely closed doors. It seemed to me that something of importance was beginning to assemble itself. The question now was, what doors, and where?

Westcott's Osiris Lodge was situated in Weston, and perhaps here it's appropriate to return to the Ripper's 'Weston' letter. It was mailed out of Taunton, approximately twenty miles south of Weston, on 4 December 1888, arriving in London on 5 December (see opposite).

Once again, the dates are important in relation to the Golden Dawn. On 5 December 1888 the name for the lodge was finally chosen, and the 'Chiefs of the Second Order chartered the Osiris Temple No. 4 at Somersetshire'. The day before, someone signing himself 'Jack the Skipper' was little more than half an hour away, and apparently on the case. As has been mentioned, his letter of 4 December is extremely difficult to read, the only clear word being 'Weston'. But here's my shot at interpreting it:

Dear Boss ... sensible to wait ... try after blood ... so I was going to act soon ... some more ... down among the Counted ones ... and have fixed places or/or ... on Taunton ... After I'll pick Weston to do another Whitechapel ... shall hear again of JaCk THE Skipper

Most of it remains unintelligible, but it's clear that his homicidal interest is in Somerset, as he nominates two towns in that county. The curious assembly of words, 'down among the Counted ones', begins to make jocular sense in the context of Jack's jibes and Westcott's Golden Dawn.

The Westcott/Mathers Rosicrucian indulgence was predicated on the magic of numbers. Westcott actually published a book about this, *The Occult Power of Numbers*, and every experiment in the Golden Dawn's mystical canon referred itself back to numbers.[12] 'The absolute hieroglyphic science,' wrote Mathers, 'had for its basis an alphabet of which all the gods were letters, and all the letters ideas, all the ideas numbers, and all the numbers perfect signs.'[13]

Thus they all sat in the candlelit gloom of 'Osiris' at Weston and 'Horus' at Bradford, postulating astral formulations nobody in the room could understand, even though they were wearing the right hat.[14]

2 66 2	66 ▽	537 666	6B Gu	T·13 666	6 ·9
v-4 B	0 4 B B	B14 a	666 P·3·	6 GO	66 CV
8c 6	O-o 7 6 6	5	qq 6 3	q·9 B	L b 8
go 30 B	9·3 66	q q 5 66	d 6 6 A	7·2 6B	B B ·Λ· 8 3

2·6 6·3	G 66	J	B 22	24·6 666	66 L 6	B rog	B
8 6 6 6 2	66 8	G 6	GG 6	152 6	152	52 BBB	B B
q B q	6 o o	B 7	666 666 666	u B 5	6 6 6 6	66 6	6 8 6 3 6
66 66 66	6 6 6 6 6	6 M 166	7 66	6	c M	B	6 A 1556
6 1	B 2 3 123	6	6 T 6	4 B 9	BBB 6	66 72 F	6

The charts above are Golden Dawn, and the table below from *The Rosicrucian Cosmo-Conception*,[15] a baffling onslaught of numbers, but presumably something the adepts had 'counted'.

TABLE OF VIBRATIONS

WHOSE EFFECTS ARE RECOGNIZED AND STUDIED BY SCIENCE.

	Number of Vibrations per second.	
1st Octave	2	
2d "	4	
3d "	8	
4th "	16	
5th "	32	
6th "	64	
7th "	128	
8th "	256	Sound.
9th "	512	
10th "	1,024	
15th "	32,768	
20th "	1,047,576	Unknown.
25th "	33,554,432	
30th "	1,073,741,824	Electricity.
35th "	34,359,738,368	
40th "	1,099,511,627,776	Unknown.
45th "	35,184,372,088,832	
46th "	70,368,744,177,644	
47th "	140,737,468,355,328	Heat.
48th "	281,474,979,710,656	
49th "	562,949,953,421,312	Light.
50th "	1,125,899,906,842,624	Chemical Rays.
51st "	2,251,799,813,685,248	
57th "	144,115,188,075,855,872	Unknown.
58th "	288,230,376,151,711,744	
59th "	576,460,752,303,423,488	
60th "	1,152,921,504,606,846,976	X-Rays.
61st "	2,305,843,009,213,693,952	
62d "	4,611,686,618,427,389,904	Unknown.

I am of the view that the Golden Dawn became the motor of Jack's thinking, orientated around Westcott's Osiris Temple at Weston and Mather's Horus at Bradford. I don't want to get ahead of my narrative, but within thirty days of the 'Weston' letter, a little girl (as promised in Jack's December correspondence) had her throat cut and stomach slashed, literally outside Westcott's old family home in the remote Somerset village of Martock,[16] and a little boy (as promised in Jack's December correspondence) was killed in traditional Masonic style at Bradford. The child murdered at Martock had a cord fastened around her neck. But 'death was not caused by strangulation, and there was no mark left round the neck by the cord'.[17] Described as having a 'slip-knot',[18] this cord was no less Jack's calling card than anything he visited upon the unfortunate women in Whitechapel. It's a classic piece of Masonic symbolism, called a 'cable-tow'. 'Well known to every Mason' – and worn by all candidates at initiation – 'it is an emblem of death, symbolically fastened round the necks of captives to show that they were absolutely at the mercy of their conquerors.'[19]

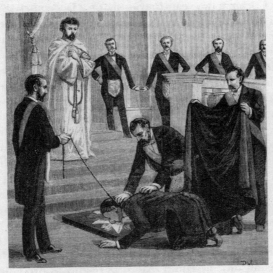

I think both the Martock and the Bradford atrocities fall within the parameters of the Fiend's Funny Little Game with Charlie Warren. So what was the connection between 'Charlie, Dear Charlie' and the Golden Dawn?

On the night before the murder of Mary Jane Kelly, 8 November 1888, a meeting of Warren's Quatuor Coronati Lodge was held at

Freemasons' Hall. Present that evening were about thirty members and guests, including some names of interest. A Founder Member, listed as second in seniority only to Warren himself, was William Harry Rylands, Past Assistant Director of Ceremonies, and Secretary of the Society of Biblical Archaeology at 9 Conduit Street – a street, it will be remembered, of no little importance to my candidate, and to someone signing himself 'Jack the Ripper'. One of Rylands' Biblical Archaeological members, and an officer of Michael Maybrick's 'Orpheus' Chapter, the Reverend Charles James Ball, was also present. As was yet another of Maybrick's Masonic intimates, William Matthew Bywater, an officer of 'Orpheus', and Number 11 on Warren's Quatuor Coronati roll-call. Maybrick had some pals inside Bro Warren's lodge.[20]

But there were more important faces present. Bro William Wynn Westcott, of the Osiris Temple at Weston, who had joined the Quatuor Coronati two years previously, on 2 December 1886, was to receive a distinction that night. He was appointed an officer of the Quatuor Coronati Lodge, and Bro MacGregor Mathers, of the Horus Temple at Bradford, was there to congratulate him.[21]

The first Grand Master and founder of the Lodge, Number 1, Bro Sir Charles Warren, was expected to attend, 'but was detained owing to the necessity of preparing for the Lord Mayor's Show' on the following day, 9 November[22] – which was to include the additional spectacle of the dismemberment of Mary Kelly (according to the instructions of Ezekiel) about twelve hours hence. Warren and Westcott were Masonically close, as were Westcott and Mathers, both of whom were familiar faces at Warren's lodge. If nothing else, this meeting of the Quatuor Coronati demonstrates an exclusive association between Westcott, Mathers and Warren, and by definition the latter's association with the Golden Dawn.

I think that when Warren saw the Birmingham artwork (initialled in the top left-hand corner by his 'eyes and ears', Bro Inspector Donald Swanson), he could read it as readily as Bro Gilbert, and that it was as clear to him as the writing on the wall. I think it must have smacked him around the head like a sockful of wet sand, because it would have shown him, unequivocally, that Jack the Ripper was on the inside.

From November 1888, the Ripper began to threaten the murder of children. He wrote that he was going to kill a little boy of about

Warren's disturbing-looking
Masonic associate, Bro S.L.
MacGregor Mathers, pictured here
in full 'Horus' rig, celebrating
'The Mass of Isis'

seven years, and in Bradford he killed a little boy aged eight. He wrote that he was going to kill a little girl, and in Somerset he killed a little girl aged ten.

It isn't surprising that the 'Melvin School' of Ripperology has kept well clear of the murders of Emma Davey and little Johnnie Gill. Bang goes the 'canonical', already risible after the Scotland Yard trunk. In the light of these murders, you'd have to share the cognisance of an earthworm not to abandon the 'hoax' routine in respect of Jack's mail. If they're hoaxes, they're written by a team of independent clairvoyants, predicting with uncanny accuracy the Ripper's itinerary over the next forty days.

On 14 November 1888 the Murderer to Her Majesty wrote, 'I am going to commit 3 more, 2 girls and a boy about 7 years this time,'[23] and on 20 November he threatens that his next job will be 'head off and legs off', adding, 'please will you pass this onto sir Charlie dear Charlie'.[24] On 26 November he will murder some 'young youth', and it will be worse than the women: 'I shall take their hearts, and rip them up in the same way'; and on 27 November, 'I shall give the police enough running around on Christmas,' a promise reiterated on 3 December in a letter signed 'Jack the Ripper' and addressed personally to Sir Charles Warren at Scotland Yard: 'I will send you something for a Christmas Box.'

Because the Ripper was a trash act, his melodramatic impulse never rises much above that of the spiteful child, and his thinking is therefore relatively easy to interpret. He was going to give 'Charlie' a dead boy for Christmas. If the coppers were stupid enough to be duped by their own propaganda, believing they had evaporated the bastard with 'suicide' after Miller's Court, the next outrage would surely disabuse them. Bro Jack was going to conjugate every insult in his Masonic death spree to assault Bro Warren's Freemasonry like a sledgehammer.

Following the murder of little Johnnie Gill, it is a bitter indictment that the Bradford press were able to comprehend something that was apparently far beyond the deductive competence of the Metropolitan Police. On Saturday, 5 January 1889, à propos of the little girl butchered in Somerset, the Bradford Daily Telegraph wrote: 'It is stated that the popular belief in the vicinity of the crime is that "Jack the Ripper" is on a murderous tour.' This assumption was echoed in the Bradford Observer of Tuesday, 8 January: 'People seriously maintain an impression that "Jack the Ripper" has visited Bradford in the course of a provincial tour.'

By extraordinary coincidence, Michael Maybrick was also on a 'provincial tour' in the autumn/winter of 1888–89. Like his aforementioned contemporaries Ada Crossley and Mr Durward Lely, he was city-hopping all over England, clocking up hundreds of railway miles every day. By way of brief example, on 20 November 1888 he was singing at the Free Trades Hall in Manchester,[25] from where, by extraordinary coincidence, Jack the Ripper mailed a letter: 'I am now in Manchester.' And the following night, 21 November, Maybrick was back in London, at St James's Hall.[26] The day after, 22 November, he was performing in Glasgow,[27] shifting east on 23–24 November to 'shout' at Edinburgh.[28] Then back to St James's Hall, London, on 26 November, travelling to Sheffield next day, 27 November,[29] and clattering back over the rails for St James's Hall again, singing in a concert there on 28 November.[30]

This endless criss-crossing of the Kingdom would of course provide excellent opportunity for anyone, should he be so inclined, to mail his childish insults from where he would – Birmingham,

Liverpool, Glasgow. At every terminus, at every change of trains, this compulsively itinerant 'team of hoaxers' on 'Her Majesty's Service' could pop another one into the box. Except they weren't a team, they were one and the same man, and he wasn't a 'hoaxer'. He was Jack the Ripper on a 'provincial tour'.

Mailed out of Glasgow on 19 November 1888, this collage prefaces the religious mania of the Alice McKenzie letter the following year (30 July 1889). Homicide is God's business there: 'that the

Lord hath designed it to do', and murder the Lord's mouthpiece here: 'THE LORD WILL DO HIS guaranteed WORK.'

Meanwhile the author is 'IN A FIRST CLASS [railway carriage] AT GOVAN', a borough south of the River Clyde just outside the municipal boundaries of Glasgow. The card is signed 'NO CLUE' – except that Michael Maybrick was habitually sitting in first-class railway carriages, and repeatedly in and out of Scotland, that same week. Hundreds upon hundreds of miles were travelled between venues. On 19 December 1888 a scrawl signed 'Jack the ripper' confided, 'I have come to Liverpool you will soon hear of me.'

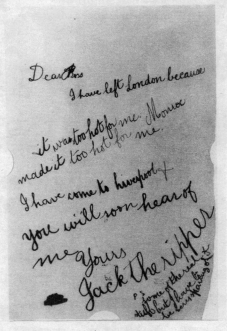

My candidate had also come to Liverpool, to spend Christmas with his brother James, his sister-in-law Florence and their kids. Michael Maybrick was now approximately one hour by train from Bradford, and Florence Maybrick was under the same roof as the most dangerous man in England.

Christmas at Battlecrease House must have been about as jolly as cancer. Despite the smiles and the presents, Michael Maybrick was preparing to bring catastrophe to this family. His homicidal plans were already well advanced, and were they not entirely justified? Dogs can't see in colour, and psychos can't see in human. Reducing those around the table to a psychopathic point of view, we have a fifty-year-old junkie and possible bigamist called James; his, wife, a twenty-six-year-old multiple adulteress, Florence; their two young children; and Bro Michael himself, a forty-seven-year-old serial killer with personal issues, and perfectly justified reasons for ripping out hearts.

Battlecrease, with its gardens, servants and cook, was a Victorian ideal, 'furnished with refined taste and elegance'. Within six months, Michael Maybrick would control and dispose of every stick of furniture in the place, from the Turkish carpets in the dining room to the Dresden candelabra hanging above them. Everything would be auctioned off, down to the last pathetic toy. Michael would own everything Florence Maybrick had ever had, including her husband, her children, and her freedom.

I can't be certain, but I am of the view that the children he was about to murder in Weston and Bradford were in some way connected in his head with Florie's kids, surrogates for them, just as the Whitechapel scum were surrogates for their mother. He certainly took pleasure in frightening them, regaling them with tales of ghosts and coffins under the bed.[31] The echo of screams rushing down the

Gladys and Bobo

stairs amused him, but as far as Florence was concerned he was a malign presence, a 'brute'.[32]

Florence was later to claim that from the day of her wedding, Michael had 'always had a spite against her'.[33] But she had underestimated the strength of his rage. It was hate. He hated her in her mortgaged silk frocks, and whatever was to happen to her, she brought upon herself. She was nothing more than a fourpenny whore, blackmailing his stupid brother with her cunt. It may well be that he had once been attracted to her himself, and that it was her adulterous relationships with his younger brother Edwin, and with James's handsome business associate Alfred Brierley, that finally triggered his murderous rampage.

Maybe he'd made a pass, and been rejected – 'Don't be so silly, Michael, you like boys.' Such a response, although no more than speculative, would be sufficient to snap the synapses in a diseased mind. Rejection of the great and famous man would threaten everything he was – his superiority, his masculinity and his money: and he'd lent the bitch a hundred pounds. Robert Ressler says the most dangerous trigger to a psychopath is an affront, or a perceived slight. She had fucked both his brothers, and said no to *him*? At *his* expense she was bleeding his drug-addicted idiot of a brother dry, and screwing Brierley, and she had the whore's brass neck to reject him?

I can't take the scenario further, because apart from what was about to happen, I have no ancillary evidence to support it. But nothing happens by accident, and it brings me back to the postcard out of London on 12 November 1888, with its inverted 'V's and signed by 'M Baynard'.

Who in Jack the Ripper's head was 'M Baynard'?

One of Michael Maybrick's greatest pleasures was reading[34] – he loved the 'great poets', he said. But this isn't a reference to Richard Crashaw, but like 'Andy Handy', a reference to a novel. M Baynard is, I believe, M[r] Baynard, a character from the epistolary novel *The Expedition of Humphry Clinker*, by the comic writer Tobias Smollett. Baynard is a desperate middle-aged man out of his sexual depth, married to a vivacious and beautiful wife who, by her youth and extravagance, is dragging him to ruin. She doesn't want to live in the sticks, she wants to live in the city. She doesn't want silver plate, she wants it solid, and her wardrobe refreshed constantly with the apogee of Parisian *haute couture*. The narrator describes the progress of this disintegrating marriage with both relish and alarm. He's a ruthless presence, taking pleasure above all in the knowledge that this young woman is 'driving on blindly to her own destruction'. In terms of what was on its way for Florence, you might want to call the Baynards' story prophetic.

Florence was 'driving on blindly to her own destruction',[35] and would get there with a little help from her brother-in-law. Everything was shaping up according to plan. Exploiting his brother's obsessive hypochondria, Michael had suggested that James should travel down to London to consult his physician, Dr Fuller, and an arrangement was made.[36] Thereafter, there were Judas kisses, coins for the kids, and the sweetest goodbyes for Florence.

One of the greatest difficulties in writing a story like this is the need to refer to events that haven't yet happened. Consolidation of the nightmare must wait until we get to the 'trial'. Meanwhile, in respect of the collusion against Florence orchestrated by Michael and his Establishment chums, a paragraph will suffice. It comes from a book published over fifty years ago, thirty years before the absurdly named 'Liverpool Document' was to emerge. But it sinisterly predicts it. And as we progress with the motive of the Ripper, it's worth bearing in mind.

The principal antagonist of Mrs Maybrick was her husband's brother, Michael. He had made up his mind that his brother was the victim of a designing and murderous woman. Only the sheer venom and spite of a man motivated entirely by hatred and antagonism can account for the way in which Michael Maybrick hounded his sister-in-law as closely as he could to the scaffold.[37]

On Christmas Day 1888, the Carl Rosa Opera Company left Liverpool on a specially hired train for a five-night engagement at Bradford.[38] Many of its stars were well known to Michael Maybrick, as he was to them – famous names performing a concert of sacred music that evening at the city's St George's Hall. I don't know if Bro Michael Maybrick hitched a ride with Bro Carl Rosa – a fellow member of the Savage Club[39] – but I do know with certainty that the Ripper also arrived at Bradford not later than Boxing Day, 26 December 1888.

Bradford's best hotel, the Alexandra, was attached to a theatre, the Empire. Built in 1877 and described by its architects as 'the finest and most expensive of its class', the Alexandra provided top-end accommodation for all itinerant thespians and concert singers who could afford it.

The hotel was managed by a gent of Italian origin, Mr Carlo Fara, a name of particular interest. Fara was a Freemason, a member of the Shakespeare Lodge (1018) around the corner in Darley Street, where he presided as Grand Master.[40] But more pertinently (and by what some would put down to extraordinary coincidence), he was also a founder member of the Golden Dawn in Bradford. It was actually in a room of the Alexandra Hotel that the Horus Temple was formally consecrated by Bro S.L. MacGregor Mathers on 9 October 1888.[41]

It was this hermetic ceremony that had inspired Jack's artwork of the same date. The nascence of the Golden Dawn and Warren's occult association with its founders had thrown up fertile possibilities for amusement in the disease of the Ripper's thinking. But this wasn't Whitechapel, and that would dictate a modification of approach. His choice of East End victims was entirely opportunistic. The logistics were crude, and apart from his ridicule of Freemasonry, and Warren along with it, there was no master-plan. If you were perceived as his kind of girl and were unlucky enough to run into him, you were dead. But with Mathers and Westcott in mind there was a change of narrative. These murders of children were not only specifically advertised, but the geography of their destruction was pre-planned. In that sense the crimes were more 'sophisticated', if such a word can be used in the context of such horror. His planning for the murder of the little boy required a secure environment where he wouldn't be discovered or disturbed.

Jack was therefore obliged to wander for a while, selecting an area that attracted him, and making a reconnoitre for some suitable premises. On the Thorncliffe Road he found what he was looking for. One of the houses was unoccupied, and had been 'locked up for some time'. It's likely this sombre residence was the referee of Jack's thinking. It was here that he would prepare and wrap up Charlie's promised Christmas present. The child, who as yet had no identity, was going to be murdered at Walmer Villas in the Bradford suburb of Manningham.

Christmas at the Alexandra was busy, especially with the influx from Liverpool who had come to perform, or perhaps to listen to Carl Rosa's American prima donna Miss Amanda Fabris. On the following night, 26 December, the hotel itself was to ring with music on the occasion of 'The Eighth Annual Boxing Night Ball'. 'The spacious entrance hall was tastefully decorated and arranged for dancing,' reported the *Bradford Telegraph*, congratulating the 'genial host, Mr Carlo Fara' for his stewardship. There was a supper for over two hundred guests, followed by speeches, before the band finally struck up, and 'dancing and merry-making were kept up with great zest until daylight dawned'.[42]

Among the revellers were a twenty-three-year-old tailor, James Cahill, and his twenty-six-year-old wife Elizabeth. In the wake of what was to transpire, Mr Cahill insisted that 'No one was aware of the fact they were going to the ball, except his employer.'[43] But without question, somebody else knew the couple were at the Alexandra Hotel, even though he couldn't have known who they were.

Maybe there was a guest list somewhere, maybe a raffle-board on which people had written their names and addresses? Or maybe a list of those invited to the reception, with the names and addresses of those who'd turned up ticked off? All we can be sure of – all Jack needed to be sure of – is that if the Cahills were at the ball, they couldn't be at home. Charlie's Christmas present was going to come with all the usual Freemasonic trimmings, and here was an opportunity for the mocking to begin.

It was probably some time after midnight that Jack left the hotel and climbed into a cab. The Cahills lived at 324 Heaton Road, Manningham, about two minutes from Walmer Villas.

The Cahills didn't get home until about ten o'clock on the following bitterly cold morning. It was Thursday, 27 December 1888. They had left their key hanging on a hook in a small outhouse just outside the front door, 'and found it there upon their return'. What they saw next comes from an important but rather lengthy report, published in the *Bradford Observer*:[44]

> Upon opening the door, Mrs Cahill was startled at the sight of her umbrella opened on the floor. Picking it up [Mr Cahill] noticed that it did not belong to his wife or himself ... looking into the living room he found a still more astonishing sight. His wife's dress was hanging from a hook in the ceiling over the table in the centre, and his first impression was that somebody was hanging ... On the table were a couple of drinking glasses which had apparently contained some spirit. But he had yet to see the most important and remarkable conditions of appearance which the room presented. On a table next to the front window were two knives, crossed, and with them was a card. Upon one side of this card were the words: 'Half-past nine. Look out, Jack the Ripper has been here.' Upon the other side were the words: 'I have removed down to the canal side. Please drop in. – Yours truly, SUICIDE.'

I'm reluctant to break into the report, which is far from finished. But this little jibe at the police can't be allowed to pass. By some occult intelligence the intruder is not only signing himself 'Jack the Ripper', he's also signing himself 'SUICIDE', and is clearly able to divine an association between the two. Once again we're looking at a little 'inside information', and it's less than eight weeks old. The convenient nonsense that the Ripper had committed suicide by drowning himself in the Thames after the murder of Kelly was cooked up in secrecy by worthless individuals in the Metropolitan

Police, but was not brought into the public domain for another ten years.[45]

But let us return to the Cahills and their discoveries:

> ... pen and ink were on the table but the words were written in pencil. A clock in the room had been set to the time stated on the card and stopped. Upon the table on which the knives were was a large tin basin with some water in it, and the top of the table was saturated with water. Another open umbrella was found behind the door leading from the room to the back of the premises ... No other room had been disturbed in any way, and nothing was missed from the house except a bottle of rum, and part of the contents of another bottle which had presumably been poured into glasses and consumed. Beyond the strange umbrella and the card there was nothing to afford a clue to the mysterious visitor or visitors.

Mysterious indeed – and the police wanted it kept that way. It wasn't until well after the discovery of the little boy's mutilated body that the mystery found its way into the press.

'A remarkable story came to light last night,' reported the *Bradford Observer*, 'which has been known to the Bradford Police for four days, but for some reason has been kept entirely secret by them.'[46] But now it was out it had to be trashed, and regurgitating police misinformation, the newspapers sank to the occasion. 'There is absolutely no foundation for the foolish attempt to connect the crime with "Jack the Ripper",' posited the *Bradford Telegraph*:

> The 'remarkable' and 'startling' story as to 'Jack the Ripper's' visit to a house in Heaton Road, Manningham, which is published in some of our morning contemporaries, has absolutely no importance whatever. It was fully investigated by the police on Saturday morning, and at once set down as a very coarse and foolish Christmas joke. There never was the slightest question after the first enquiries that it was anything else but a joke, and so little importance was attached to the matter that it was not even communicated to the Chief Constable.

Retracting its previous report, the *Bradford Observer* joined in: 'The supposed visit of "Jack the Ripper" to a house in Manningham, on Thursday morning last, and where a communication had been left purporting to be from that mysterious individual, is now known with certainty to have been a practical joke of a relative of the tenant.'[47]

Whoever this 'relative' was, was never discovered, and remained curiously unknown to either Mr or Mrs Cahill. The latter was so amused by the 'relative's joke', that she refused to live another day in the blighted property. 'It has taken such an effect upon his wife,' reported the *Bradford Observer*, quoting Mr Cahill, 'that he has been unable to persuade her to remain in the house alone, and has had to rent another house immediately, as she is afraid to live there.'[48]

So from whence came this seasonal comedian?

A question I would have liked to have asked in respect of the 'relative' – as mysterious as the intruder himself – is, did either of the Cahills have a 'relative' who was a Freemason?

I would have asked the question because only a Freemason could have conjured up such a 'joke'. A Masonic copper would have been able to read the Ripper's 'set-dressing' like a book – although, of course, no Freemason would ever read it out loud.

The ersatz ceremony Jack put together in the Cahills' parlour was a DIY rendition of a Knights Templar initiation known as 'the Fifth Libation'.[49] It required a couple of glasses, a bottle of alcohol (wine at the real thing, rum at the Cahills'), a pen and ink, a bowl of fresh water, a pair of crossed swords, and a skull and crossed bones (the latter not available for another hour or two).

At the lodge the Knights assemble under the instruction of the Grand Commander. Two rooms are required, and if only one is available it is divided by a veil (Mrs Cahill's suspended dress). One half is called the Assilum, and the other the Council Chamber. It's a convoluted ceremony, but in brief its mechanics are relatively straightforward. At the direction of the Junior Warden, the hood-winked Initiate is requested to sit at a table in what is called 'the Chamber of Reflection'. The explanation for the bizarre assembly at Heaton Road (specifically designed to mock the arcane procedures of Masonry) will now become self-evident. The candidate is told that on the table in front of him are a pen and ink and a sheet of paper, on which are written three questions. He must answer them yes or no, and sign his name after each. He will also discover a bowl of pure water (the large tin basin with water in it at the Cahills'). 'Wash your hands in the water,' instructs the Junior Warden, 'as a token of the purity of your intentions in the business in which you are engaged.' He then retires behind the veil (the dress) and the Initiate removes his blindfold. Apart from the pen and ink and the bowl of water, he's doubtless surprised to discover a human skull and crossed bones positioned on the table.

Assuming these present no problem, he washes his hands in the bowl, answers the questions, and the Warden reappears from behind Mrs Cahill's dress. A rather lengthy procedure ensues in which a year's pilgrimage is represented by a tramp around the room. The candidate then walks down an avenue of Knights forming an arch with their swords, arriving at the lower end of the Council Chamber, where he kneels at an altar (a table in the window) sporting an open Bible, upon which are a pair of crossed swords (crossed knives at the Cahills'). Oaths are now sworn: 'I do hereby and herein most solemnly promise and swear that I will always hail, forever conceal, and never reveal, any of the secret arts, parts or points appertaining to this Order of Knights Templars, etc.'

Once the oaths have been completed the Grand Commander takes over and the initiation comes to its point. He congratulates the Pilgrim, but requires 'some stronger proof of your fidelity to us'. Now the ceremony of the Five Libations begins. Alcohol is poured into a glass for each of them (two glasses in which rum had been drunk at Heaton Road), and here comes the First Libation: 'To the memory of Solomon, King of Israel, our ancient Grand Master.' Both drink, and then give the drinking sign by drawing the glasses across their throats. The Second and Third Libation follow, toasting Hiram King of Tyre and Hiram Abiff respectively. One or two selected verses of the Bible are then read (Matthew 26), until quaffing through the Fourth, they arrive at last in the Assilum, at the Fifth Libation. 'It is emblematic of the bitter cup of death,' intones the Grand Commander, and to show he's not messing about he pours booze into the human skull and drinks. He then hands it to the Initiate, who's also required to have one for the road. 'The Fifth Libation,' the Grand Commander says, 'is called the "Sealed Obligation",' and if the candidate doesn't like the sound of it he's threatened with a bristle of Knights' swords. Another oath to secrecy is sworn, 'considered by Knight's Templars, to be more binding than any obligation can be'. Both Charles Warren and Lord Kitchener had made these inviolable pledges, the latter, to Her Majesty's chagrin, grave-robbing and silver-mounting the Mahdi's skull for such a purpose.

The only thing missing from the Ripper's ceremony was the skull and crossed bones, which he intended to procure that very morning. He signed himself 'SUICIDE' in pencil. The unused pen and ink, like the basin of water, the empty glasses and the crossed knives, were set-dressing. To synchronise with the time written on his card, he reset the Cahills' clock to nine thirty. It was Thursday, 27 December, and Jack's promise to 'Charlie' was about to be fulfilled.

Neither the date nor the time were by idle happenstance, but were predetermined constituents of his homicidal muse. 27 December was St John the Evangelist's Day, of extreme Masonic significance, celebrated as the most important day in the Freemasonic calendar. St John is the patron saint of Freemasonry, and (incorrectly) credited as the author of that most important text amongst Masons, the Book of Revelation.

It was on St John's Day, 27 December 1813, that the disparate cadres of Masonry had at last been reconciled into one. Previous to this the 'Ancients' and 'Moderns' had given each other a rough ride, the former disinclined to be absorbed by the latter. This friction was damaging to both, and was resolved only when His Royal Highness the Duke of Kent was installed as Grand Master of the more progressive faction. 'It was then well nigh impossible,' recorded Bro John Lane in 1895, 'for Masonic rivalry to continue between two bodies about to be presided over by Princes of Royal Blood, so that eventually the unhappy differences were forgotten, and "The United Grand Lodge of England" was formed, to the great joy of both sections of the Fraternity.'[50]

This portentous ceremony took place at Freemasons' Hall, and was indelibly etched into the Masonic DNA. 'The Masters Wardens, and Past Masters, all dressed in black (regimentals excepted) with their respective Insignia and in white aprons and gloves, took their places by eleven o'clock in the forenoon.' 'The famous "Articles of Union" were finally adopted on December 27th 1813,' writes Bro Lane, 'having been duly signed by His Royal Highness The Duke of Sussex and His Royal Highness The Duke of Kent, as Grand Masters of the two organisations.' Warren's Lodge of Masonic Research, the Quatuor Coronati, celebrated the event thereafter with the issue of an annual card to its members, mailed to arrive on St John's Day, 27 December.

On Thursday, 27 December 1888, at some time in the forenoon, an eight-year-old boy named Johnnie Gill disappeared. Even the most rustic intelligence must surely find some resonance here. Six weeks earlier, the murderer had bragged that his next victim would be a seven-year-old boy. 'I shall give the police enough running around Christmas,' vowed the Ripper, and he was right. But they weren't running around in an effort to catch him, but to cover him up. How is it that a provincial newspaper is capable of deducing that the criminal is 'on tour', while the highest echelons of the 'baffled' police cannot?

Jack followed their shenanigans in the press with amusement and delight. One repetitive theme that took his fancy was Fleet Street's misguided obsession with attributing police worthlessness to 'Red Tape'. Something had to be responsible for reducing Scotland Yard to a confederacy of idiots, and a variety of newspapers put it down to the same thing. If it wasn't for the 'Red Tape', they opined, surely this bastard would be caught.

> Here's to the Scotland Yard Officials
> Goin' on in the usual way,
> As their heads are stuffed with sawdust,
> Is all that I can say,
> And what with Red Tape Matthews
> refusin' a hundred pound
> Of the British public's money,
> that the murderer may be found ...[51]

This sneer at Matthews (from the comic *Judy*) didn't go unnoticed by the Fiend, and was to become an inspiration. 'We do not intend to hold our hand,' barked the *Telegraph*, 'until a clean sweep of impotence and red-tape is made at Scotland Yard.' Such negative sentiment was echoed by the *Pall Mall Gazette*. 'Under these circumstances [at Scotland Yard] it is not very surprising that our detectives do not detect. Detection of crime under these conditions resembles a game of blind man's buff, in which the detective, with his hands tied and his eyes bandaged with red-tape, is turned loose to hunt a murderer through the slums of this great city.'[52]

PUNCH, OR THE LONDON CHARIVARI.—September 22, 1888.

BLIND-MAN'S BUFF.

(As played by the Police.)

"TURN ROUND THREE TIMES,
AND CATCH WHOM YOU MAY!"

'I think that unless those in authority take proper steps as advised and drop the red-tapism,' pronounced a Pecksniffian know-all by the name of Dr Forbes Winslow, 'such crimes will continue to be permitted in our metropolis to the terror of London.'[53]

'Permitted' is the salient word. The *New York Herald* headlined its report 'STEALTH VERSUS RED TAPE',[54] and another American newspaper, the *Tribune*, serves as good an example as any: 'In London the police remain bewildered and demoralised, their hands tied by traditional coils of red-tape, and their limited intelligence overtaxed by efforts to grapple with the mysterious madman.'[55]

A 'mystery' it certainly was, at least to Bro Warren, and subsequently to Ripperology. About one thing only does the latter display any certainty, and that is that the Bradford murder couldn't have been by Jack, because it's outside the stringent rules of the 'canonical'. And irrespective of that, Jack wasn't even a suspect, because he was already 'dead by suicide' and floating up the Thames.

Just before dawn on a harshly chill morning, exactly two days after Johnnie Gill was reported missing, a butcher's lad by the name of Joseph Bucke went as usual to the stables at Back Mellor Street, an unpaved lane in Manningham, to attend to his employer's horse. 'I took some manure out into the yard in front of the coach-house, where there is a manure pit. I had thrown the manure in, when I saw a heap of something propped up in the corner between the wall and the coach-house door. I could not make out what it was at the time, so I got a light.'

On closer examination and some probing with his pitchfork, he found it to be the body of a child 'that had been terribly mutilated, the legs having been cut away from the body, and the body ripped open. The legs were lying *on the trunk*, and the head resting on the left hand.'[56] (My emphasis.) Bucke ran in horror to a nearby bakery, where he got assistance from a young fellow named Teal. He in turn took off into Manningham Lane for a copper. PC Kirk was quickly on scene, followed by Dr Major and Mr Miall, 'who reside in the vicinity'. Soon after they were joined by Bradford's Chief Constable, James Withers, and his police surgeon, Dr S. Lodge.

Before the official imposition of the 'strictest silence' in respect of Bucke's discovery, there's an opportunity to record one or two first-sight impressions that did not appear in later press versions of the crime scene.

On that same day, 29 December, under the title 'A JACK THE RIPPER CASE', the *Leeds Evening Express* had this: 'The Bradford police [found the boy] with his legs, ears, and other members hacked off, the abdomen ripped open, the ears and other members thrust into the belly, the *legs placed on top*, and the whole tied together.'[57] (My emphasis.)

Excepting Teal and the freaked-out Bucke, these additional details could only have come from the police, who at this early hour were as yet unaware of their significance. That the legs were on top of the body is confirmed by the authoritative voice of the police surgeon, Dr Lodge. In similar innocence of its relevance, he made his first and last indiscretion, stating, 'The legs had been cut, or more properly termed, hacked, off, and *placed on the body*, with the thighs *protruding at each side of the head*.'[58] (My emphasis.)

These initial reports are significant, because later versions were tampered with. Within twenty-four hours (and subsequent to intervention by certain unnamed individuals in the Metropolitan Police) a news embargo was imposed by the city's Boss Cop, Mr Withers. 'Following the example of the Chief Constable,' reported the *Bradford Daily Telegraph*, 'the surgeons in the case maintain a strict silence in the matter of their discoveries.'

In the perfidious traditions of Scotland Yard, an artificial 'mystery' was already spawning, and its first task was to move Johnnie's legs from the top of his body to underneath it. Like Elizabeth Stride's wandering hands (in the effort to deny the grapes), Johnnie's limbs were also on the move after death, even the trunk itself involuntarily swivelling to comply with official requirements, being simultaneously both face-up and face-down.

Among the first uniforms on the scene was PC Haigh, and his evidence at the opening session of the coroner's court is illustrative of the above phenomenon. Haigh said he saw 'a bundle from which a human face protruded [and] put his hand on the face and felt it was cold'. Pulling off the top-coat that was covering it, he 'found the body of a boy in a nude state'. He also found a pair of braces, 'one of which was wrapped round the neck and thighs', securing the legs, which were 'cut off and placed under the chin'.[59]

In other words, if Haigh was able to see 'a face protruding' and legs 'placed under the chin', the body had to be on its back, with the legs on top of it, as both Joseph Bucke and Dr Lodge had described. Bucke did not turn the body over, but said it was ripped open.[60] But now, with no pause for breath, Constable Haigh says, 'The back part of the body was upwards. The face had gone.'[61]

Begging your pardon, but where had it 'gone'?

How a 'protruding human face' can suddenly vanish is not explained. How a head 'resting on the left hand', with legs 'placed under the chin', can similarly disappear is not explained either. But as will become apparent, this contradictory gobbledygook was a 'rehearsed mouthful', and but an early example of the scandalous bullshit yet to come out of the Bradford police.

It isn't much of a stretch to understand the copper's obfuscation, or indeed to extrapolate what the Masonic Joker had done to this poor little boy. The key, of course, is the missing element of the 'Fifth Libation' at the Cahills' home. Meanwhile, 'The police will not allow the body to be seen by anyone.'

'The extreme reticence of the medical gentlemen,' carped the *Yorkshire Post*, 'lends credence to the suspicion which is now widely entertained, that the whole truth has not been allowed to transpire.'[62] And guaranteeing it wouldn't be, there is this from the *Bradford Observer*. 'The inquest has been adjourned to the 11th inst, and so evident is the desire of the police to keep back the information, that it is not certain that the true state of the matter will be allowed to go forth even then.'

They were right. It wasn't.

Having got a murdered child, the police now needed a murderer. Sinister characters of the sort enjoyed by East Enders were naturally out of the question here. The Insane Medical Student, the Nautical Man and 'the Floating Ripper' could hardly have travelled to Bradford. Plus, they were all figments of police imagination. But London was pressing for a scapegoat. Someone arrestable was needed, and quick. So let us welcome to the team 'the Homicidal Milkman'.[63]

Little Johnnie Gill   William Barrit

William Barrit was twenty-three years old, recently married, and employed as a butter-maker and delivery man at Mr Wolfenden's dairy in Manningham Lane. Backing onto the premises was a maze of dingy alleyways, including Back Belle Vue, where Barrit kept his horse, and Back Mellor Street, where Johnnie was found.

At an early hour seven days a week it was Barrit's task to meet the milk train from Kildwick, where Wolfenden loaded the churns directly from his farm. Barrit would then drive back to the dairy, transfer the milk into cans and (at this time of the year) deliver them to his customers before daybreak.

Everyone thought highly of William Barrit, especially little Johnnie Gill.[64] Whenever he was able he was out of the house while the owls were still about, running to meet the milkman and his cart. It was 'a pastime in which he was accustomed to indulge very frequently', recorded the *Bradford Observer*, 'for he and the milkman appeared to be great friends'. On that last day of his life he had asked his mother to wake him at twenty to seven, and the last time she was ever to see him, she watched as Barrit picked up her son 'and the cart was lost in darkness'.

LOST, on Thursday Morning, BOY, JOHN GILL, aged seven [sic]; was last seen sliding in Walmer Villas at 8.30 a.m. Had on navy-blue top-coat (with brass buttons on), midshipman's cap, plaid knicker-bocker suit, laced boots, red and black stockings. Complexion fair. Home, 41, Thorncliffe Road.[65]

When Johnnie didn't come home his parents put the above ad in the newspaper. They searched for him everywhere, as did William Barrit, calling three times at his home the same day in the hope of news. Two days later, Johnnie's elder sister, thirteen-year-old Ruth, was on her way to work at the mill, and seeing a crowd of people around Back Mellor Street, asked a girl what the matter was. 'She told me my brother was dead. I think it was my little brother, Sam, who told my mother first of the affair. My parents knew nothing of the matter when I left. They had been very anxious, and had been up all night. I don't know exactly how my brother first came to know that Johnnie was dead, but presume that he had seen the crowd.'[66]

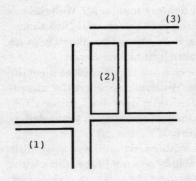

(1) Barrit's stable
(2) Body found
(3) Johnnie's home

X marks the spot

Johnnie's body had been found about a hundred yards from his home.[67] Later that day, 29 December, Chief Constable Withers arrested Barrit and put him up in front of the magistrates, charged 'on suspicion of having caused the death of John Gill'.

So preposterous was the accusation that they may as well have arrested his horse. Withers' sole evidence against the milkman was that he was the last person to be seen with the child. Predicated on such idiocy, PC Hutt, the copper who released Catherine Eddowes from her cell at Bishopsgate, should also have been arraigned for murder, he too being the last person to be seen with her.

Other than to claim that he'd dropped the boy off between about 8.30 and 9 a.m. outside Walmer Villas on Thorncliffe Road, Barrit made no defence. He said Johnnie was going home for breakfast, and heading that way he had fun sliding on the icy pavement. The magistrates remanded the prisoner into custody.

Withers then went about concocting a case on behalf of his Metropolitan associates. The rank and file of Bradford's police showed scant inhibition about plunging with their boss to the required levels of London degeneracy. As though bound by some zombie creed, they were either already irredeemably corrupt, or morons, or both. The cover-up and the frame-up were well under way. The Ripper was back amongst friends.

The mysterious visitor to the Cahills' home was resurrected, but his activities there were no longer a 'joke', and he was no longer a 'relative'. It was Barrit who had broken into the house to swill the rum, and never mind that he was a confirmed teetotaller.[68] It was he who had hung up the dress, crossed the knives and opened the umbrellas. He who had written the cryptic notes, and by definition, he who had signed himself 'Jack the Ripper' and 'Yours truly, SUICIDE'.

The make-believe behind the Chief Constable's forensic snooping was consolidated on the doorstep of Mrs Elizabeth Craggs. She claimed to have seen the milkman with Johnnie at 10.45 on that dire morning, 'in a great hurry, and smelling of rum'.[69]

Withers relished the remarkable olfactory talents of this woman, not only able to smell non-existent alcohol, but also to identify it as rum. Although Craggs was never heard of again, her toxicity lingered. Now that Barrit was safely in a cell, negative reporting against him began to appear. It was insinuated that there was 'insanity in the family', and that he was a man of 'strong animal passions'.[70] This twaddle emerged following a search of his house by detectives. In the kitchen they opened a drawer and found a bread knife. It wasn't an ordinary bread knife, but a 'very formidable bread knife', and what's more it was tellingly 'devoid of all traces of blood'.[71] It wasn't long before the indefatigable detectives had worked out why. It was because some unknown hand had washed it!

They seized the weapon and forwarded it to the medical men. There were two wounds in Johnnie's chest, considered to be the cause of death. The point of the bread knife, like the point of any other knife in England, fitted the wounds a treat. It was a break-through. This murderous blade, disguised as an innocent sand-wich-maker, had been cleansed of all incriminating stains, and craftily returned to a cutlery drawer where it had been camouflaged amongst a variety of knives and forks.

It was at this juncture that Barrit's legal representative, an able barrister from nearby Keighley, Mr J. Craven, demanded to see the doctor's notes. He also demanded that his own physicians, Drs Roberts and Hime, should be allowed to inspect the murdered boy, requests that Withers adamantly refused.[72]

Denied access, Craven and his legal partner William J. Waugh were all but reduced to scouring the newspapers for information. This wasn't as fruitless as it might appear. Now Withers had his man he'd slacked off on the censorship, and the press had become an increasingly useful (if selective) source. Doubtless hoping to get Barrit condemned in the public eye before the courts did it offi-cially, the constabulary were suddenly liberal with previously suppressed details. Among the most startling was this revelation from the *Bradford Telegraph*: 'The post-mortem (police say) leaves no room for doubt that the lad had been foully outraged before death, and with the exception of one portion of the body, which had been cut away with the object, it is believed, of removing all evidence of what was done immediately preceding death, they believe that the remainder of the mutilations were perpetrated chiefly with the object of throwing the public off the scent, causing them to lay the blame on the Whitechapel Fiend.'[73]

Poor Whitechapel Fiend. Although everyone else in Bradford was convinced he was the culprit, at least he could rely on Her Majesty's helmets. But the real news here is that Barrit, being a man of 'strong animal passions', is supposed to have sodomised Johnnie before killing him with the bread knife. 'The police also assert that it is impossible that the crime was the work of a stranger in the district, pointing out with unanswerable logic that if this had been the case, there could be no possible motive for running the risks inseparable from the removal of the body from the place where the crime was committed.'[74]

Withers had hypnotised himself into believing that this was Barrit's stable at Back Belle Vue. In they all went looking for blood, with no better success than had been achieved with the knife. Paving stones were lifted and they dug up a drain, finding nothing but some hairs that belonged to a horse. A broadening of enquiries led to the discovery of an insomniac in a nearby property who'd heard 'sawing' in the dead of night. 'Such was the feeling of uneasiness which it caused her that she sat up in bed.' That clinched it for Withers, and no blood was swapped for a sound of sawing. Nobody but Barrit had a key to get into the place, and thus it could only have been him. 'Yesterday evening,' reported the *Bradford Telegraph*, 'the Chief Constable informed our representative that the case was closing around Barrit.'

Apparently nobody had bothered to tell the fucking idiot that there was no evidence whatsoever of a saw being used in the process of Johnnie's dismemberment. 'The legs had been hacked off', reported the *Bradford Observer*, quoting Dr Lodge. 'The amputation was evidently the work of somebody who was quite inexperienced in an operation of this kind, for the flesh of the thighs was very much cut as if the murderer had had to search for the joints.'

Fortunately, more details were emerging in the press, and it became possible for Barrit's defence to assemble a reasonably accurate picture of the terrors endured by the little boy.

There was a gash in the front of the body extending from the bottom of the abdomen to the chest. The heart had been cut out, and was placed under the chin. Both ears had been cut off in an unskillful fashion and thrust into the gash in the abdomen. The face and neck were quite uninjured, and we believe the medical gentlemen who are concerned in the matter have not yet formed a definite opinion as to the extent to which the boy's suffering was prolonged. The condition of the clothing places beyond doubt the fact that the boy had been stripped before he was murdered, for there was not a spot of blood upon any of his clothing except his collar, which, strangely enough, in view of the entire absence of injury to the neck, was saturated with blood. There was no stain of

blood upon the body, it evidently having been well cleansed before
its removal to the yard where it was found. The legs, arms, and body
had been bound together in a compact parcel with the unfortunate
boy's braces.

Although the stable was a write-off to everyone but Withers, it was
irrefutable that Johnnie had been killed in a secure place. In this
respect the crime echoes the Kelly murder, clothes neatly folded
and carried out indoors at Jack's leisure. But in a variety of ways the
signature is more readily identifiable with the Scotland Yard Trunk.
In both instances the corpse had been tied in a bundle and carried
from the crime scene for deposit. In both, fragments of newspaper
were discovered inside the body cavity, and both bodies had been
comprehensively drained of blood.

In Johnnie's case, seventy-two ounces had been bled out of him.
He was 'blanched', as the doctors put it, Lodge having difficulty
finding enough blood even to take a sample. Thereafter the press
speculated on the obvious: 'It is suggested that the boy was decoyed
into a bathroom.'[75] As there was no bathroom and no blood in the
stables, it would have been wise for the police to check empty
houses. But they weren't wise, they were puppets of London, sharing
wilful blindness with the Metropolitan Police.

All will trust that this case will not lead to a lamentable miscarriage
of justice, nor yet into one of those unsolved mysteries which of late
have become far too numerous in the records of great crimes. Not
to mention the Whitechapel atrocities, to which the Bradford
murder bears such a close resemblance.[76]

Out of the darkness and from that very same Whitechapel came a
fraternal radiance to put their minds at ease. 'At the instance of the
Metropolitan Police authorities, and with the sanction of the Home
Secretary', Bro Dr Bagster Phillips pitched up from London on the
overnight express, bearing a letter from the Home Secretary to Dr
Lodge.[77]

It wasn't the first time Matthews had written to friendly gents in
Bradford. In the previous (Jubilee) year, he'd forwarded Her
Majesty's gratitude to the city's Freemasons, thanking them for their
supplications of loyalty, and he had Freemasons to thank now.[78] The

charade of Barrit's prosecution was orchestrated by Bradford's most eminent Mason, its Town Clerk, Bro William McGowan,[79] with assistance from his Treasurer to the magistrates, Bro Walter Firth, himself a member of the Golden Dawn.[80]

Bro William McGowan

At eleven o'clock on the morning of his arrival, and in company with Dr Major, Mr Miall, Dr Lodge and his son, Dr Lodge Jnr (but excluding Drs Roberts and Hime for the defence), Bro Dr Bagster Phillips was escorted to the mortuary, where he made 'a most careful and complete examination' of the body. It took him three hours, after which 'Phillips proceeded with Dr Lodge to the stable where it is supposed the body was cut up'.[81] The goon Withers then arrived, 'with whom he had a long conversation', and he subsequently wedged in a 'confidential chat with Chief Detective Inspector Dobson', an individual previously recorded in the equally confidential 'Bradford City Police Disciplinary Book' on 26 March 1888, 'for making a false charge and receiving cash, which he ought not to have received'.

Dobson's attraction to fiction seemed to enamour Phillips, who expressed 'a strong feeling of satisfaction at the manner in which the police are proceeding with their very onerous investigations'.[82] And he had fictions of his own. Predictably, as co-creator of 'the Womb-Collector', he now affirmed his conviction that this murder 'had no connection whatever with the series of fiendish crimes which have been perpetrated in the East End of London'. 'It is understood that he will make a full report of his examinations and observations to the London Police Authorities,' and that Withers would receive a copy 'within the next few days'.[83] Although Anderson would have read it, Withers did not, and 130 years later it still hasn't arrived.

Phillips's report remains a mystery. But irrespective of that, it's possible (as Barrit's defence surely did) to hazard an analysis of it. Before beginning his autopsy, Phillips would have learned something about the body's discovery. He would have examined police photographs (also suppressed) and read the doctor's notes. The child was propped face upwards, his heart under his chin, on top of his neatly folded clothes. The bundle was strapped with his braces, which included a sack imprinted with 'MASON – DERBY ROAD – LIVERPOOL'.[84]

Unarguably the Ripper had brought this sack with him, as he had furnished other teasing accessories that we will come to by and by. 'MASON' and 'LIVERPOOL' were evidently words of interest to Jack, and the coppers had originally hoped they would 'serve as a clue'.

How about a 'brother in trade', a Masonic drug-fiend resident of Liverpool, cuckolded by a slut-bitch of an American wife, whose whoring would drive any man to insanity?

Jack was motivated by grotesque hatred, and was intent on incriminating his *Mason* brother from *Liverpool* as similarly possessed. It's the reason he decorated his crime scenes with Masonic symbols, vandalising the Kelly and Gill corpses with ceremonious insults and laughing at Warren as he did it. 'Regretting you've been compelled to retire,' he sniggered at Charlie in a November scrawl – but never mind, he would still get his 'Christmas Box'.

Withers had ignored the abandoned house at Walmer Villas, where a 'blood stained bucket' was discovered some weeks later,[85] but it was almost certainly in the bathroom of this now demolished property that Johnnie was murdered. The press surmised that he was 'decoyed into a bathroom',[86] and that may well have been the case. A convivial smile followed by total physical control was Jack's game. Once inside and under his dominance, Johnnie was made to undress, or it was his murderer who stripped him. There was not the slightest evidence (shirt collar apart) of blood on his clothes, and no gash in his coat or shirt to match the wounds on his chest, where the boy had twice been stabbed. Once naked, he was raped, his assailant exalting in his victim's anguish. When he was finished, the time had come to kill him. Probably standing in the bath, he was carefully cut and bled like veal, still alive to facilitate the haemorrhage. 'The police have never supposed for a moment that the murder was the work of the same hand as the Whitechapel horrors; therefore they have never gone "on the wrong scent" in that direction. There's nothing in common with the Thorncliff Road affair and those in London.'

This house is full of godforsaken ghosts. Bro Warren is there, his face turned away, but he must turn back and look. He said he needed a 'scream' to catch this arsehole. Can he hear the screaming now? Can he hear this hysterical child screaming for his mother? Freemasonic Jack should have been arrested within days of the 'Double Event'. But you, you rotten little ghost, affected to be blind. I don't care what fancy-dress oath you ever swore, Warren, you belong with your monster in hell.

Subsequent to Gill's death, everything the Ripper did to his corpse was meticulously thought through. He cut him open from the lower abdomen to just below the chin. The left lung, heart and liver were removed, the ears cut off, and the arms and legs crudely hacked away. 'I am trying my hand at disjointing,' he had written on 4 December. The entire body was then washed inside and out, the liver also being washed before it was packed back into the carcass together with the lung, ears and boots. The whole hideous bundle was then secured with the child's braces.

Barrit was not only accused of the blood-letting and parcelling up, but by definition also of recreating esoteric details of a crime he'd probably never even heard of. Fragments of newspaper were found in the Scotland Yard Trunk, just as scraps of 'peculiarly shaped newspaper' were found in the entrails of Johnnie Gill. Moreover, the Homicidal Milkman must also have studied the psychological side of his supposed idol, because he was able to convincingly duplicate the Joker's style of humour.

It's established that the newspapers had made a song and dance over the redoubtable coppers being hindered by 'Red Tape'. If it wasn't for the red tape, they choresed, the Met would be standing tall. This horseshit amused the Fiend, and he decided to give them a bit more of it, coiling a length of red tape around Johnnie's intestines. This was inadvertently revealed in a coroner's court by Dr

Lodge, who had got himself into a bit of a fluster during cross-examination by Barrit's counsel.

Craven had never heard about 'Red Tape' before, and demanded to see the notes from which Lodge was unwittingly reading. The coroner replied: 'You are not entitled to them.' A brittle exchange followed. It was clear that Lodge was quoting from very different notes to those previously put before the court. 'Are these the first and original notes which you took?' asked Craven. They were, and the 'red tape' was meant to have remained a secret. The floundering doctor shoved the notes in his pocket and produced a different set that didn't impress Mr Craven.

'Then you have not previously been reading from the original notes you took?'

Clearly not.

'Now tell me which it is,' pressured Craven. 'Your pocket book, or the notes you have put into your pocket?'

'My pocket book.'

'Are these notes that you have put into your pocket [the red-tape notes] those which you used on a former occasion when you gave evidence on oath?'

'Yes, but I had not them with me, unfortunately.'

'Well, then, how could you use them?'

'Well,' flustered the Doc, 'I was taken suddenly, and I was very much interrupted.'

'Have you given on this occasion,' asked an icy Craven, 'very different evidence?'

'That I cannot allow,' said the coroner.

If Craven wanted the original notes he could apply for them. 'I cannot, sir,' snapped Craven. 'I have done my utmost to get that deposition, and I cannot get it.'[87]

Redirecting his frustration at Lodge, he said, 'Doctor, you have mentioned today that "red tape" was found in the remains?'

'Yes, didn't I say so before?'

'I will ask you,' insisted Craven, 'have you ever mentioned that before?'

'I'm sure I don't know. It was in my notes.'

Eyes detouring to the coroner, Craven said, 'I am going to put it very seriously to Mr Lodge, that he is giving a very different statement.'[88]

In this he wasn't unique. Everybody involved in the milkman's prosecution was giving a very different statement to the truth. Craven repeatedly complained of the 'determination of the police to make the crime fit the man',[89] and that anything that didn't do this was concealed. Suppression of 'red tape' and other essential evidence meant the authorities knew perfectly well that Barrit hadn't killed this boy, and perfectly bloody well who had.

'Mr Withers strives to be the Bench, Solicitor, and Jury,' quipped the *Yorkshireman*, sharing the opinion of an increasing variety of newspapers. 'Various parties,' wrote the *Bradford Telegraph*, 'have transgressed the bounds set by law.'[90] As Craven had consistently reiterated, 'The charge against Barrit was groundless,' adding that 'If the police had at the time of his arrest made the enquiries demanded in the interests of justice, they could easily have obtained proof of his absolute innocence.'[91]

But justice isn't what these boys were about. A Masonic oath was apparently inviolate, while an oath given in a court of law was not. Just as Jack was protected, Barrit was persecuted. At this point it's as well to explore what else these stooges covered up, these coroners and coppers, doctors and town clerks. What they were desperate to hide was the Freemasonry.

The Ripper's contempt for Johnnie Gill's body was manifest in an eclectic mix of Freemasonic, Rosicrucian and Golden Dawn symbolism. All the organs detached from the boy's corpse were replaced and accounted for except for his penis, which was taken away by the killer. This act had more significance than the collection of a trophy, as does the fact that he was sodomised.

I've explained my reasons for believing it was MacGregor Mathers' Horus Temple that brought the Ripper to Bradford. The Irish poet William Butler Yeats had the misfortune to briefly fall under Mathers' spell, although he later dismissed him, accurately, as 'half knave and half mad'.[92] Here he is in an anonymous and mocking caricature, perched in Horus mode under his occult umbrella:

In the mythology of Ancient Egypt, Horus was pre-eminent. He was god of the sky, his divine being represented by a falcon.

Horus (and Mathers) hold the Crux Anasta,
the symbol of eternal life

Horus was born to the goddess Isis, protector of the dead. It was a somewhat dysfunctional family. His father was the noble god Osiris, whose brother, Seth, was the personification of evil. Mythology has it that Seth clawed his way out of the womb. Sporting red hair and gnashing teeth, he's represented as having the features of 'a fantastic beast, with a curved snout, and stiff forked tail'. A disciple of Satan, if not a pre-Christian equivalent of Satan himself, he was uncle to saintly Horus.

He was also an inspiration to the Whitechapel Fiend. Just as Kelly was murdered according to the strictures of Ezekiel, so the legend of Horus was adapted to suit a new narrative of hate.

Seth subjected Horus to a violent homosexual attack, raping him while he was still a child. He visited a plague of iniquities upon the boy, including the cutting off of his hands. Horus's mother used her magic to restore them, and Horus then took revenge by castrating Seth. With no sorcery forthcoming to reinstate his nuts, and intoxicated with wickedness, Seth then murdered his brother, Osiris, dismembering his body and dumping his remains in a swamp. Isis was crazy with grief, but following the lucky discovery of the body parts she was able to reassemble him and restore him to life. Every limb and organ was accounted for except the penis, which was never seen again.

I don't know if my candidate was an active homosexual, but my guess is that he wasn't averse to the occasional bit of buggery. Jack sodomised a little boy and cut him to pieces (Seth), then reassembled his body (Isis) but stole his penis (Osiris). Thus, with Mathers in mind, an improvised rendition of the Horus myth was re-enacted, just as an improvised version of the Fifth Libation was enacted at the Cahills' earlier that same morning.

Much later, when Craven and his doctors were at last granted access to the original notes (but not the photographs), and Roberts and Hime were allowed access to Johnnie's body, the *Bradford Observer* of 13 March 1889 reported Craven as saying that certain undisclosed evidence 'would have astonished the public'.[93]

What exactly would have astonished them? The public knew that the boy had been sodomised, brutally murdered, disembowelled, had his arms, legs and ears cut off, and his penis taken away by his killer. They knew his heart had been propped under his chin, his boots stuffed into his abdomen, and that he'd been drained to his last drop of blood. So what else was there to be 'astonished' about?

The answer presents itself in the original reports of witnesses. 'The legs were lying on top of the body,' wrote Lodge, before he was corrected, 'with the thighs protruding at either side of the head.' What he was looking at was an extension of the ritual at the Cahills' house, where the only element missing was the skull and crossed bones. The Libation is a Knights Templar rite, and Jack had turned the boy into its most enduring symbol.

ORDER OF KNIGHTS TEMPLARS.

The above is a nineteenth-century Knights Templar logo, showing the skull and crossed bones. Not a mark was found on Johnnie's neck or face, but skulls don't have ears, so Jack cut them off.

'There was not a spot of blood upon any of his clothing except his collar, which, strangely enough, in view of the entire absence of injury to the neck, was saturated with blood.'[94] According to the *Bradford Telegraph*, it was 'perfectly soaked halfway up'.[95] This may have seemed strange to a provincial newsman, but in the context of the Ripper's set-dressing it wasn't strange at all. Bro Bagster Phillips would have recognised its significance instantly. In both Masonic and Rosicrucian ceremony the (crimson) collar is notable, and it wasn't random that Jack carefully steeped the boy's collar in his own blood. The Rosicrucians share their outfits with 'the distinctive sign of the Templars' (white chemise with a red edge). 'May its colour always remind you that it was tinged with innocent blood' (Grand College of Rites, Vol. 5).

Barrit was constantly in and out of court at the dictate of London, his jailers liaising regularly with the Met: 'The authorities are in communication with the London police, as it is thought probable that there is some connection between the crime and the Whitechapel murders' – and Withers actually travelled to Scotland Yard to coordinate strategy.[96] Bro McGowan kept shop while he was away, chaperoning the milkman's appearances before the Worshipful Justices – and Right Worshipful they were, including Bro Alderman Thomas Hill, Bro Alderman John Hill, Bro William Oddy, Bro John Ambler, and in the chair, Bro John Armitage. Complementing this lot was the Treasury Prosecutor, Bro James Freeman (Prince of Wales Lodge).[97]

Given the glaring innocence of William Barrit, and the evidence suppressed in respect of the Ripper, is it not an abiding scandal that this conclave of worshipful lackeys was allowed anywhere near a court of law? Would any citizen in control of their senses have considered this tribunal as worthy? Forget astonishment, the public would surely have been stunned had they known of the institution-alised criminality coming out of London. Even Bro McGowan was later to admit, 'It was London responsible for pressing the charges.'[98] I can hear the dirty little whispers of Robert Anderson.[99] But as will become apparent, Barrit was nothing more than a dry run for the prosecution of Florence Maybrick. In both conspiracies the Crown was seeking the ultimate penalty. Both Barrit and Florence were to suffer death as scapegoats for Jack.

Viscount Lord Salisbury had no problem hanging the occasional innocent Mick, and there was enthusiasm for his brand of justice in Bradford.[100] On 18 January 1889, the *Bradford Pioneer* reported Chief Constable Withers as relishing thoughts of the scaffold for Barrit, saying that he was 'weaving the rope'.[101] But the popular tide had turned in the milkman's favour, and the same newspaper referred to Withers' coppers as 'a shame throughout the nation':

The chief ground of complaint against the police consists in their studied attempts to manufacture evidence against Barrit and in their wilful withholding of facts which were sufficient at the outset to clear him. We have the fullest authority for saying that the police were in possession of knowledge which entirely removed suspicion from Barrit.[102]

It was this knowledge – the Freemasonic saturation, by way of example – that, like Bro Bagster's autopsy report, was ruthlessly suppressed, and remains unobtainable to this day. Fuck justice, fuck the law, fuck Johnnie Gill's devastated family, fuck his mother who took flowers to her child's grave every Sunday for the next thirty-seven years, and fuck the milkman, his wife and their baby; we're talking about a *threat to a system* here, all the way up to the Worshipful Grand Master and his Parisian fuck-chair. If you can frame a giant like Charles Parnell, what problem does a twenty-three-year-old provincial milkman with a horse and cart present?

Between the coroner and the magistrates, Barrit was hauled into court five times to listen to the ever-escalating inventions of the police. PC Arthur Kirk was one of the first helmets to attend the discovery of the corpse. He got off his 'burley' arse in front of the Worshipfuls to claim he'd patrolled the alleyway at Back Belle Vue and Back Mellor Street throughout the preceding night. He said he had tried Barrit's stable doors on many occasions, and found them locked. This was important, because Withers' deceit relied on the stable as the crime scene, from which his sleepless witness had heard the 'sawing' which could only have been the work of William Barrit, because only he had a key.

Craven was quick to prove that Kirk was lying through his teeth. He'd been nowhere near Barrit's stable that night, and he certainly didn't try its door. It couldn't have been locked, because the key to lock it had been lost weeks before.[103] Moreover, Craven proved that the spooky 'sawing' was the sound of Barrit's horse eating oats from its bucket, and scraping it along the stone floor.

Kirk had previous in respect of lying about his nocturnal rounds. He'd been admonished and fined for the same offence eighteen months before: he claimed to have been on his beat when in fact he was swilling booze in a pub.[104] It is curious, is it not, that on the former occasion he was punished, while in this instance, with a man's life in the balance, Withers didn't so much as peep?

Next up was Police Constable Haigh. Under interrogation, Craven brought him to the vital point of the 'thighs protruding' at either side of the head. 'Did not the legs protrude from under the top of the coat?' The stooge was on the spot, and contradicting Lodge, Bucke and himself, he replied, 'No, only the head.'

Craven was now in possession of the original notes, and of course he knew Haigh was lying. The next question would prove it, and there was a sudden rush of sweat to the helmet. Desperate to escape, PC Haigh decided to throw a fit. 'The witness was seized with illness during his examination,' recorded the *Shipley Times*, 'and had to retire.'[105] The justices then conveniently adjourned.

There was a similar fiasco at the concurrent coroner's proceedings, when a letter from Dr Hime brought the coroner, Bro John Hutchinson, into a comparable fluster. As yet unaware of its incendiary nature, Hutchinson had it read into the record, and very quickly wished he hadn't. Dr Hime offered to place evidence 'derived from his postmortem examination of the unfortunate little boy Gill', together with evidence 'from other sources', at the coroner's disposal:

> I feel the failure to bring the criminal to justice is no less a misfortune than the cruel murder he has perpetrated. Some of the evidence of Doctor Roberts and myself is in direct conflict with the medical evidence already laid before you in this case, and consequently opposes the conclusions founded on this portion of the evidence.[106]

What's all this 'bring the criminal to justice' nonsense? They had their criminal, with his milk cart, and were doing just that. Hime's letter was 'a very improper thing indeed. I'm surprised Doctor Hime should have so far forgotten himself to send such a letter.'[107] Hutchinson had it struck out. He was sure that 'the gentlemen to whom it had been read [the jury] would take no notice of it, and he regretted very much that Hime had sent the letter'.

What was denied to the jury found its way into the newspapers. In an interview with the *Yorkshire Herald*, Dr Roberts clarified various points of his associate's critique. He said their conclusions differed 'very materially indeed' from evidence given by doctors on behalf of the prosecution: 'There would have been a direct conflict,' he said, 'so far as the immediate cause of death was concerned. I am entirely at variance with Dr Lodge in his statements that two "stabs" to the chest were the cause of death. I do not consider them stabs at all, and am confident they were not given until after death.'[108] Rejecting Lodge's conclusions as make-believe, he continued, 'It would have been impossible for stabs to have been given in that position without cutting through the left lung, which was unhurt. They were simply cuts made through the integuements between the ribs for the purpose of reaching the heart.'[109] He further agreed with Dr Hime's assertion that the internal mutilations were inflicted with a small knife, such as a butcher might use on a sheep: 'It is inconceivable,' he said, prepared to swear it on oath, 'that the clumsy bread-knife which the police produced could have done them.'[110]

The physicians' intercession knocked on into the magistrates' court, and was found similarly offensive by the Crown Prosecutor Bro Freeman. Posturing in servility to his London puppet-masters, he squawked that 'On behalf of the Treasury [the Crown] he must protest against Mr Waugh, or Doctor Hime, or any other person seeing the witnesses for the prosecution.' To which Mr Waugh for the defence replied, 'He must protest against the action of the police in having obtained the evidence of one of the witnesses, and having given just so much as was against the prisoner, and kept back all that was favourable to the prisoner.'[111]

And so it went on, Waugh and Craven daily taking the prosecution to pieces. Freeman was running out of road, and forced into Withers' world of fantasy. Seeking the acquiescence of his fellow Bros on the bench, he requested their patience to allow him time to present a witness who would blow the defence out of the water.

Bro Armitage asked who the witness was, and what was the nature of his evidence. Like a sneak whispering in the toilets, Freeman said he 'would rather keep it a secret', and he 'could not disclose the name of the witness'.[112] Mr Waugh was getting angry, and asked that the name of the witness be given before the court adjourned. On Freeman's refusal, Waugh lost it. 'This conduct on behalf of the Treasury was the most extraordinary conduct he had ever seen in a court of justice.' He added that 'He would remind the Bench that this was not a Star-Chamber enquiry or an Inquisition, but a Court of Justice.' Unfortunately for Barrit and his counsel, a star chamber is precisely what it was. These geezers had nothing whatever to do with justice, and 'after conferring with Brother magistrates on the Bench', they decided in favour of Freeman and adjourned.[113]

Outside the court, Barrit had made a legion of new friends. His parish vicar, the Reverend J. Whitaker, had organised a defence fund, and a community that had little gave what they could. Its Chairman, Mr Morrison, set the tone of a packed meeting, describing the prosecution of Barrit as 'the most scandalous piece of injustice that had ever occurred in the history of England'[114] – which suggests he wasn't too familiar with English justice. In just a few months it would cast its putrescence over Mrs Maybrick.

Meantime, the Reverend Whitaker was on his feet attacking it. 'It was a downright sin and shame,' he said, 'to have put the Barrit family to the great amount of cost and suffering,' and he hoped they would make their voice heard throughout the kingdom, 'in order to show their abhorrence at these iniquitous proceedings. There was nothing against Barrit except that his wife had bought a new carving knife. They might as well come to any of their houses and say because they had their knives cleaned they had committed one of these dreadful Whitechapel murders. They had been disgusted with the Bradford police, who had spared no pains either in lying, nor prompting other people to lie.'

The Reverend was composing a letter to the government, demanding compensation for the milkman's unwarranted suffering and costs. 'The letter would be signed by himself and Mr Craven, and would be forwarded [via Morrison] to the Home Secretary.'[115]

I have some belated bad news for them. It was the Home Secretary, Henry Matthews, who was engineering the case against Barrit, and while he was at it, was sanctioning the Bradford police to commence proceedings against the Reverend Whitaker himself. Withers was taking care of it, while Barrit was a victim of Sir A.K. Stephenson KCB, Solicitor to the Treasury and Director of Public Prosecutions. It was Stephenson who made it an imprisonable offence to read Zola (and the milkman could have furnished the plot for one of his novels). Stephenson was at the epicentre of Matthews' legal shenanigans, a minion of executive corruption, dishing it out as required in the vernacular of autocratic pomp.

A correspondent by the name of William B. Gordon understood what was in progress and on 12 January 1889 wrote a damning letter to the *Bradford Observer*.

The public should now be informed, if they want to know how the institutions work for which they pay, what investigations the Public Prosecutor made of the statements laid before them by Mr Withers before he took on himself the responsibility of prosecuting. So far as has yet been shown to the public, the share of A.K. Stephenson in this abortive prosecution, has been to read the statement sent up by Mr Withers, and instruct Mr Freeman to prosecute. Had Sir A.K. Stephenson, on receipt of Mr Withers' statement, himself come down to sift the evidence in private, and ascertain its real bearing, it can hardly be believed that we should have heard anything of the charges against Barrit, who would therefore have been discharged without suffering as he has done in mind and pocket. As it is, not only has an innocent man been needlessly harassed, but the real murderer has had placed before him in public prints most valuable hints as to the best means of getting rid of any remaining traces of his guilt.[116]

The Ripper had all the hints (and help) he needed, thank you very much, and Mr Gordon was wasting his ink. Neither he nor Craven could have anticipated the depths to which the prosecution would sink – until the appearance of Withers' 'secret witness'.

John Thomas Dyer was an unemployed labourer, and literally a half-wit. Withers had to apply to three separate physicians in an attempt to get a certificate certifying he was competent to appear in court. Dyer could remember nothing, not even the date he was born, yet he had remarkable recall when it came to William Barrit. He claimed to have seen him in Back Belle Vue at 6.20 a.m. on Saturday, 29 December 1888, roughly an hour before the discovery of Johnnie's body.

'I went straight up Lumb Lane,' he said, 'and turned down the back of Belle Vue [where] I saw the milkman, Barrit. He had a parcel which he carried in front of him.' Hutchinson, the coroner, asked if he knew Barrit. He replied: 'Yes, I know him by his walk. He used to tease me on Manningham Lane, about the Salvation Army. When Barrit came out of the stable door he held the bundle under one arm and shut the door with the other. The bundle appeared to be a very heavy one. I did not notice the colour of the bundle, but it was wrapped up like a bundle of clothes.' Did he speak to him? 'Yes, I said, "Good morning, sir, Bless the Lord, Hallelujah," but he did not say anything and hung down his head.' Did he have any doubt about the man being Barrit? He did not, and was sure of it. Hutchinson then turned his attention to Withers, who wanted to present his 'certificates from the medical men' to the jury. A glance at the witness made them superfluous, and Craven stood to exploit the obvious.

In response to his opening question, Dyer said, 'I am twenty years of age, but do not know the year in which I was born.'

'Do you know how to get to know?'

'By going to the Register Office.'

'Do you know the year?'

'No, sir.'

No barrister willingly asks a question to which he doesn't already know the answer, and Craven's next was, 'Have you ever been in a court before?' Dyer confirmed that 'he'd been in a court four years ago, and also last year as a witness'.

'Do you remember having been there at any other time?'

'Yes, sir, eight years ago.'

'What were you there for then?'

'I was locked up for being with bad boys.'

Clearly he'd been led astray by the corrupted whispers of others. Craven established that he'd served two and a half years in a reformatory school, where they didn't teach him any figures, 'Because they could not teach me anything.'

How then could he be sure it was at 6.20 a.m. on Saturday, 29 December, that he'd seen Barrit? 'I'm sure it was,' said Dyer, 'because the same day I got three-pence as a Christmas Box.'

'Does anybody else tease you?'

'Lots of people.'

'Why?'

'Because they think I'm a bit silly.'[117]

Dyer's deposition was so transparently got-up it wouldn't have made it past the Mad Hatter. Withers applied for another adjournment, and the jury complained about the absence of the accused. To both points the coroner replied 'that he was loath to close the enquiry without having the subject thoroughly exhausted [but] he could not overlook the fact that already the case had been adjourned four times'. Withers finally won his adjournment, and minus Barrit, they were all back in the same seats fourteen days later.

During the hiatus, Hutchinson's opinion had swung decidedly in favour of Withers and his par-brained witness. Addressing the jury he said, 'He could scarcely find language in which to convey to their mind the importance of Dyer's evidence.' If it were true, 'then it became an important question whether or not it brought around Barrit an irresistible chain of circumstantial evidence which he was called upon to answer. If they believed Dyer, and the testimony which corroborated him [rubbish like the "sawing"], then it would be their duty to return a verdict of wilful murder against William Barrit.'[118] The jury duly returned such a verdict, and the milkman was committed for trial at the West Riding Assize Court at Leeds.

Having condemned their man, the authorities wasted no time in hastening him to the gallows. On the following day, 9 February, six weeks before he stood trial at the assizes, they deemed him guilty with a phoney entry on Johnnie's death certificate. Under 'Cause of Death' it reads: 'That William Barritt did feloniously wilfully and of malice aforethought Kill and murder the said John Gill.' It remains on the certificate to this day.

HC 802163

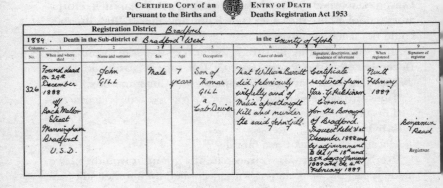

CERTIFIED COPY of an   ENTRY OF DEATH
Pursuant to the Births and   Deaths Registration Act 1953

	Registration District *Bradford*							
1889 .	Death in the Sub-district of *Bradford West*				in the *County of York*			
Columns:-	1	2	3	4	5	6	7	8	9
No.	When and where died	Name and surname	Sex	Age	Occupation	Cause of death	Signature, description, and residence of informant	When registered	Signature of registrar
326	Found dead on 29th December 1888 off Back Mellor Street Manningham Bradford U.S.D.	John GILL	Male	7 years	Son of Thomas GILL a Cab Driver	That William Barritt did feloniously wilfully and of malice aforethought Kill and murder the said John Gill.	Certificate received from Jas. G. Hutchinson Coroner for the Borough of Bradford. Inquest held 31st December 1888 and by adjournment to the 11th 18th and 25th days of January 1889 and the 4th February 1889	Ninth February 1889	Benjamin Read Registrar

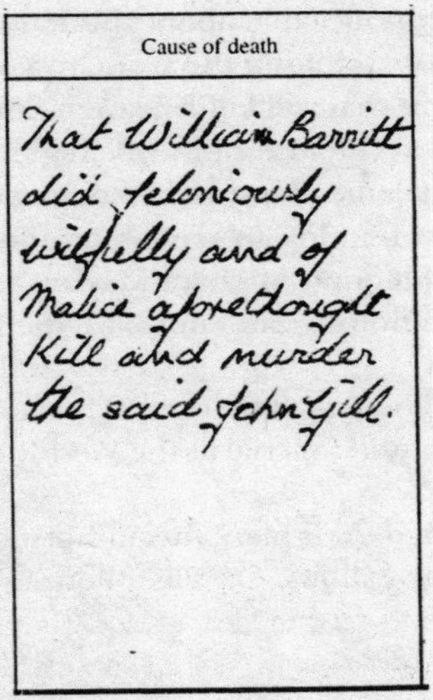

> Cause of death
>
> *That William Barritt did feloniously wilfully and of Malice aforethought Kill and murder the said John Gill.*

Dyer was put up to lie in service of an irredeemably corrupted executive who themselves were in service to a Freemasonic nightmare. The attempt to camouflage the Ripper behind Barrit exposes the mind-boggling duplicity behind the rest of the Scotland Yard walk-ons – Kosminski, Ostrog, Pizer, et al. – not to mention the ridiculous comedy turns from the non-existent Nautical Man, assorted short-arses, and the Fiend on the Float in the Thames. The police and politicians had murmured of an 'accomplice' when they were 'it', prepared to add Barrit to the roll-call of Jack's victims with a bit of judicial murder on his behalf.

Florence Maybrick too was soon to suffer their ceremonious perversions. Meanwhile, her brother-in-law wrote a letter from London:

Jany 16 88 [sic: 1889]

Dr Boss

… I am still in London after my trip to Bradford. I shall remain still for a time. I am preparing a draught that will kill & leave no marks those I shall give it to will fall in various places, either being run over or die from its effect for the future I am Scarlet Runner should you wish for particulars of the Bradford mystery give me a corner in the echo …[119]

What's immediately noticeable about this letter is that for the first time the Ripper is abandoning the blade in favour of poison. He's 'preparing a draught that will kill & leave no marks'. In view of the fratricidal scenario fermenting just off Regent's Park, we can say with hindsight that James Maybrick should never have made his forthcoming trip to London to see his brother's doctor. What he prescribed, or rather what Michael Maybrick sent in place of it, would later become notoriously known as 'the London Medicine'.

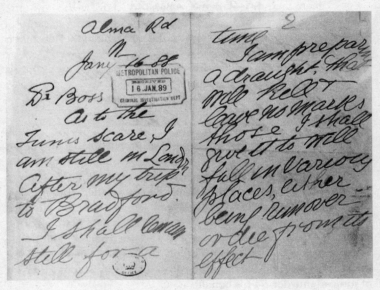

Meanwhile, Craven was engrossed in Barrit's defence. With admirable zeal he'd demolished every last fibre of the prosecution's case: 'We should have played havoc with their medical evidence,' said Hime. In respect of Dyer it emerged that he'd often 'given information to the police on other matters on previous occasions'.[120] A respected tradesman was prepared to testify that he'd seen Dyer in the street, and as a joke had said to him, 'Withers is wanting you to give evidence in the Barrit case.' 'I know nothing about the murder,' the imbecile had replied. Fortunately for Barrit the incident could be attested to by two others present.

Withers' star witness was beginning to look like no witness at all, and it didn't help that the defence had traced three workmen prepared to swear on oath that they were in Back Belle Vue at the time of Dyer's hallucination. 'A discussion took place,' reported the *Bradford Observer*, 'and two of them produced their watches to see the time, which therefore they could have fixed beyond all question.' It was precisely 6.20 a.m. 'After stopping together for about five minutes, two of them walked up Back Belle Vue, passed the stable, and went into Lumb Lane, and at that point heard the town clock strike 6.30.'

Needless to say, none of them saw Barrit, or more to the point the man who could have hanged him. This isn't surprising, because as his mother was to confirm, at 6.20 on the morning of 29 December, John Thomas Dyer was at home in bed asleep.[121]

Dyer wrote to the milkman while he sat in prison awaiting his fate. Enclosed in the envelope as a complement to the idiot's text was a Salvation Army tract titled 'Jesus Will be Our Judge'.[122]

> March 12 1889
>
> Dear Barrit
> My case has closed and your to, but the his day coming, that you and me will after stand on a better shore and we will after tille wath we hive done down here. But late salvation John Thomas Dyer will be him[?] him as he meats him on the greate with shrone and Jesus will be our judge and the Bad shall go to hell and There watch him save shall enter into a heavenly crown. But we do no for quite well and you too ... that hell his full of you no watch like them what was sent to prison a week or two agor. Dear sir, you cane not Blame for you been in prison, Because I did not go tille it in the twon hall. But I told a boy and he told it to police, and I was fast to tille wath I had see But the case his clear and I hope that if you are not the man God will bless you in all shapes and formes. But if you are mark my words you shall fall like snow worter. Now I will see you on the happy shore by and by and happy welkimming
>
> John Thomas Dyer[123]

Matthews was going to have to put this into a witness box, and without getting into the mechanics of his rarefied thinking, he decided to abandon the case. Bro McGowan was all sympathy for Barrit's terrible ordeal, though the law made no provision for compensation. At least Barrit was proved innocent, and walked free. But, hanged or not, he'd served his purpose by transporting the murder of Johnnie Gill into the comfortable world of bafflement.

'It was wrapped in the most profound mystery,' concluded the *Bradford Telegraph*, which on 13 March 1889 interviewed the Chief Constable. Withers was happy to agree. 'The case was as much a mystery as ever,' he said, 'and the Treasury had been as much puzzled at what course to adopt as the people in Bradford.'[124]

If crooks in the Treasury, and this numbskull in a helmet, had listened to the people of Bradford, the police would have been hunting a criminal who could easily have been caught. The people of Bradford knew on day one that the Ripper killed Johnnie Gill. I leave the last words of this chapter to him. With his characteristic sneer and in respect of his concern for the apprehension of the Fiend, he wrote pledging that he would 'turn in his own brother'[125] if necessary. And that is precisely what he did.

17

'The Spirit of Evil'

I pray that one day some-one will prove my innocence.

Florence Maybrick

Anyone who knew anything about James Maybrick knew two things. 1) He was a Freemason. 2) He was a junkie.

James ran on junk. His entire nervous system was wet through with arsenic. He put it in his wine, he put it in his tea, and he put it in his food. Maybrick's drug-taking was so well known amongst his contemporaries that it all but defined him. He swallowed arsenic like a condiment, and never said no to the occasional shunt of strychnine. Both were potentially lethal, but over the years he'd developed a gargantuan tolerance, and to kill him with either would have required enough to flatten an elk.

In loony paradox he was also a 'hypochondriac', in perpetual anxiety about his health while relentlessly doing everything he could to destroy it. After his death 163 medicine bottles were found distributed between his home and his office. There were fifty-one different medicines, both patent and prescribed, in his dressing room alone. 'He made a perfect apothecary's shop of himself,' said Baroness von Roques, 'as we all know.'

Everyone did know. A close friend and a captain in the cotton-shipping business, John Flemming, remembered Maybrick in action at his office in Norfolk, Virginia.

He was cooking in a small pan above an oil stove. I saw him deposit a grey powder in his food resembling light-coloured pepper.

'You would be horrified, I daresay,' said he, 'if you knew what this powder is.'

'There's no harm in pepper,' said Flemming.

'It is arsenic,' said Maybrick. 'I am now taking enough arsenic to kill you.'[1]

The minimum fatal dose of this colourless, odourless and tasteless metallic poison is two grains (about a match-head) for an adult human. Maybrick could swallow treble that and go back for a chaser. 'He used to call continually at my shop,' recalled a Liverpool pharmacist, Edward Heaton, 'sometimes four or five times a day, for what he called his "pick-me-up", but which was liquid arsenicalis.'[2]

Such statements about Maybrick were commonplace on either side of the Atlantic. Ten days before his death another seafaring friend, the aforementioned Captain P.J. Irving of the White Star Line, had come to dine with the Maybricks at Battlecrease House. His host was amiable enough, although Irving sensed something was amiss. Cornering Edwin after dinner, he asked why James was looking so quag. 'Oh, he's killing himself with that damned strychnine,' was the younger brother's reply.[3]

It didn't unduly surprise Irving to hear that Maybrick was poisoning himself, because 'everybody knew Jim was always taking some medicine or another. His office was more like a chemist's shop than anything else.' In a press interview published after the 'trial', Irving related how he had met Edwin and James that same day at the latter's offices in Knowsley Buildings, Liverpool West: 'He picked up a glass which he partly filled with water, and then pulled out of his breast pocket a small packet, the contents of which he emptied into the glass, and afterwards drank the whole concoction.'[4] It was probably strychnine.

But it wasn't strychnine or arsenic that killed James Maybrick. Arsenic was his drug of choice, and getting hold of enough of it was more often than not an ongoing obsession. Even by Victorian standards there were strict rules on its acquisition. Since the Poisons Act of 1851, arsenic was no longer sold raw, and even small quantities had to be mixed, by statute, with indigo, charcoal or soot. For a man with a habit like Maybrick's, these restrictions were an impediment, and so, like all addicts, he scored wherever he could.

In February 1889 he got lucky – more than lucky, he hit the jackpot. A young salesman by the name of Valentine Blake had come to Liverpool in hopes of revitalising ramine grass as a viable substitute for cotton. It was to be made by an entirely new chemical process, superior to anything preceding it, and as chance would have it, James was chosen to hear about it.

Like everyone else in cotton he despised ramine, but he became animated when he heard about the secrets of the new production method, which apparently involved copious amounts of the magic ingredient As_2O_3, or arsenic trioxide. Addiction took over, and thereafter the conversation turned on Blake's naïvety and Maybrick's craftiness. 'Maybrick asked me whether I had heard that many inhabitants of Styria, in Austria, habitually took arsenic internally and throve upon it?' When Blake acknowledged that he had, Maybrick then shifted his focus from the stoned-yodellers to an individual, in this instance one of the world's most notorious degenerates. Had Blake heard of Thomas de Quincey and his seminal work on junk, *Confessions of an English Opium-Eater*? Another confirmation stimulated further interest in Maybrick, and Blake must have wondered what had happened to the ramine. But, ever anxious to sell it, he played along with the de Quincey theme, speculating on how any man could possibly take nine hundred drops of laudanum a day.

'One man's poison is another man's meat,' retorted Maybrick, and then got down to it: 'There's a so-called poison which is like meat and liquor to me.' Dare Blake ask what that might be? 'I don't tell everybody,' said Maybrick, 'and wouldn't tell you,' but seeing it was Blake who had mentioned it, it was arsenic. 'I take it when I can get it, but the doctors won't put any into my medicine except now and then as a trifle, that only tantalises me. Since you use arsenic,' he continued, 'can you let me have some? I find a difficulty in getting it here.'[5]

The upshot was a *quid pro quo* deal. Maybrick would do his best with the ramine grass, and Blake would make a present of all the arsenic that was left over from his employer's now perfected experiments – in all, about 150 grains. Later that month Blake returned to Liverpool for further discussions and delivery on the agreement. That evening Maybrick walked through his front door with enough arsenic to slab the immediate neighbourhood.

Although he was considered so by himself and probably everyone else, Maybrick wasn't actually a hypochondriac at all. What he was, was sick from trying to stay well. He'd been swallowing poison for years, doubling the dose of anything prescribed, and then wondered why he felt ill. It was this insane cycle of drug-taking to ameliorate the effects of drug-taking that brought him constantly into the presence of doctors, and that Michael Maybrick saw over the Christmas of 1888 as an opportunity to exploit.

James travelled to London to see Dr Fuller at his brother's apartments on Sunday, 14 April 1889, and again on the following Sunday, 21 April, when he saw Fuller at his house. 'He was a man who seemed inclined to exaggerate his symptoms,' said Fuller; 'he complained of pains in his head and of numbness, and said he was apprehensive of being paralysed.' After an hour of examination Fuller could find little wrong with him: 'I told him he was suffering from indigestion, and that I was perfectly certain there was no fear of paralysis. He seemed a nervous man. It is almost impossible to say what is the cause of constant disturbances in the nerves.'[6]

How about strychnine, although James told Fuller nothing of that, or of the arsenic either. In ignorance of his visitor's pernicious 'pick-me-ups', Fuller prescribed two anodyne palliatives, 'one an aperient, and the other a tonic with liver pills'. Neither contained the remotest trace of anything poisonous, and whatever 'medicine' followed these visits (notoriously 'the London Medicine') was concocted and sent via the mails by Michael Maybrick.

Getting James down to London to see Fuller was part of an emerging strategy, a 'campaign' as the Ripper called it, of which Florence was already a part. Although neither of them could have known it, both were key protagonists in a miasma of wickedness which, from a psychopathic point of view, couldn't have looked rosier.

In the previous month, March 1889, Florence had also travelled to London, booking rooms in the names of 'Mr and Mrs Thomas Maybrick' at Flatman's Hotel, Henrietta Street. Flatman's was situated in one of the capital's most fashionable areas, and Mrs Maybrick wore her most *chic* of Parisian togs – staff at the hotel said they had never seen such pretty shoes. Florie had every reason to look her best. She was in town for two entirely different but organically interlocking reasons. The first was to seek legal advice on a separation from the fifty-year-old junkie, and the ancillary and primary reason for this was a consolidation of permanence with the man she loved.

How utterly tragic was this woman's fortune. She was a one-sided Romeo and Juliet. It was for a night in bed with Alfred Brierley that a senile judge was to sentence her to death.

In the shadows of Saturday, 23 March 1889, under the sobriquet of Thomas Maybrick, Brierley slipped into the hotel for some dick fun. Apparently it didn't go too well. Maybe he got the guilt in respect of his friendship with James; maybe he simply didn't love her. 'He piqued my vanity,' wrote Florence years later. But either way, she was never going to kiss Alfred Brierley again.

In the ordinary daylight came regret. He had told her that he loved another, and Flatman's had become a place where they rent rooms. Meantime, amidst her sorrow and putting on the pretty shoes, something sinister was in progress outside the hotel. Hostile eyes watched with interest. She and Brierley left Flatman's early on Sunday afternoon, agreeing that they should never meet in such circumstances again.

For the next three nights she stayed at Kensington Gardens with the family of John Baillie Knight, an intimate family friend who had known Florence since she was a little girl. The following day, Monday, 25 March, her ever solicitous brother-in-law Michael called at the Baillie Knight house in Kensington and took Florence out to dinner and a show. At least, that's what he claimed in a subsequent newspaper interview which appeared in the *New York Herald* after the 'trial'. He was trying to play the concerned relative, pretending that his sister-in-law's impending death sentence was nothing to do with him. 'Nothing would please me more,' he said (knowing nothing like it was going to happen), 'than to hear that the Home Secretary's decision is that Mrs Maybrick shall go free. It has been published that I never liked her, that I avoided her house. All this is untrue. My relations with her were always pleasant. Only three weeks before my brother died – the day after she was with Brierley in London, in fact – I took her to dine at the Café Royal in Regent Street, and took her to the theatre, does that look like I disliked and distrusted her?'[7]

No, it looks like lying. He was lying because it was he who had hounded her to the very steps of the gallows, and he was lying over this 'fantasy *soirée*' at the Café Royal. It was in fact not three but seven weeks before James was murdered; moreover, there was no way Michael Maybrick took Florence Maybrick or anybody else out to dinner on that last Monday in March 1889.

A Grand
SMOKING CONCERT
And ENTERTAINMENT
WILL BE HELD
ON THE EVENING OF MONDAY, THE 25TH INST
From 8.30 p.m. to 12.30.

Throughout the day and into the night of 25 March 1889, Michael was organising and later brown-nosing at a smoking concert he'd directed on behalf of the Artists Volunteers.

Florence returned to Liverpool on 28 March. It isn't known if she and Brierley met again during her London stay, or whether the Metropolitan Police were still watching her after she had left the hotel on Sunday the 24th. 'One of the strangest features of this strange case,' wrote the author Trevor Christie, 'was a subsequent article in the *New York Herald*'s London edition, to the effect that the police trailed Mrs Maybrick to the Hotel, and kept her under surveillance throughout her stay. The police saw her drive up to Chapel Place, and watched that part of the building. They were aware of "John's" having driven her to the Grand Hotel and the theatre, and they produced a photograph of that person which the Landlord of the House immediately identified.'[8] This was John Baillie Knight.

'The [Flatman's] waiter, Alfred Schweisso,' continued the *Herald*, 'who gave evidence for the prosecution at Liverpool, says he does not want to testify in any more criminal cases at Liverpool or elsewhere, as he wasn't treated well.' Schweisso had been bullied by the police, made to say what he knew was nonsense. It would be premature to get into the so-called 'trial' or its preliminaries. Suffice it to say that the Crown couldn't have got up its phoney and criminally wicked charges without a parroted testimony from this waiter.

So corrupt were these proceedings, so palpable the stitch-up, that in a remorseful confession Schweisso wrote to Alexander Macdougall,[9] a Scottish barrister who, with hopeless fortitude, was campaigning to prove Mrs Maybrick's innocence:

I should be too glad to do that which would be of assistance to your Committee in getting Mrs Maybrick released. I am very sorry that I did not act as I ought to have done, inasmuch as it was a matter of life and death. But I was really afraid of the consequences that might happen. I will give you an instance. When I arrived at the Coroner's inquest I met an Inspector. He said, 'Will you be able to recognise Mrs Maybrick?' I said I should not. He said, 'Keep with me, and I will take you so as you can see her, because you will be sworn, whether you can recognise her or not.' I saw her twice before I was taken to recognise her by order of the Coroner. You are aware that at the Coroner's Court the Coroner dealt chiefly on Mrs Maybrick's movements in summing up, and that it was published in the local papers that the case would be quashed up. I told the Inspector this. He said, I have seen it myself, but I have a different opinion, for it's going to end against her.

Anyone of a moderately enquiring mind might wonder how it was that this unnamed Police Inspector could know that.

Schweisso goes on to describe a matrix of chicanery holding this coroner's court together, concluding his letter with: 'I give you this statement voluntarily, to show you, as far as I'm concerned, that it was a regular got up case of the police.'[10]

A got-up case it was. It was a culmination of scheming instigated by Michael Maybrick; and with no shortage of informants inside the Maybrick marital home, he was well aware of the domestic ferment he was poised to walk into. The 'Whore' had inadvertently delivered herself into his hands at Flatman's Hotel, and he was almost ready to act. He would of course enjoy all the usual support from coroners, coppers and courts.

Anyone looking to cook up a motive for murder was spoiled for choice. Florence continued to supply all the ammunition needed. The day after her return from London, James took her to Aintree for the Grand National, the highlight of the racing year. At some point Florence was escorted arm-in-arm up the course by Alfred Brierley, and when they finally got home her husband freaked. 'I was expecting a tragedy in the family,' wrote one of the Maybricks' oldest friends, 'but I was looking at it from the other party. James had gotten wise to the Flatman's Hotel affair, and I was expecting him to plug Brierley at any time.'[11] Instead he took it out on his wife, smacking her in the face and telling her to get out. A servant girl called Brierley (no relation) was sent to fetch a cab. The fracas then moved into the hall, where Maybrick 'raved and stamped like a madman'. Another servant, Mary Cadwallader, was an eyewitness. 'She had on a fur cape. He told her to take it off as she was not going to go away with that on. He had bought it for her to go up to London in' (to see 'her aunt', the lying bitch).

Cadwallader attempted to intervene. 'Oh, master,' she begged, 'please don't go on like this, the neighbours will hear you.' He didn't give a fuck what the neighbours heard, and didn't want to hear her: 'Leave me alone, you don't know anything about it.' But Cadwallader was undeterred. 'Don't send the mistress away tonight. Where can she go? Let her stay until morning.' By now Maybrick was bellowing, 'By heavens, Florie, if you cross this doorstep, you shall never enter it again.' He became so exhausted, said Cadwallader, 'he fell across an oak settle and went quite stiff. I did not know if he was drunk or in a fit. I sent the cab away and we got Mrs Maybrick upstairs and Mr Maybrick spent all night in the dining room.'[12]

By morning the blow to Florie's face had matured into a black eye. She took it around the corner to show to a neighbourhood friend by the name of Matilda Briggs, seeking her advice about a separation. It was decided that she should see a solicitor, but first Mrs Briggs took her to see Florence's physician, Dr Hopper, who apparently had her trust. She told him that James had beaten her, that she couldn't bear him to touch her, that they slept in separate beds. Notwithstanding this, Hopper thought an attempt at reconciliation was the best option, and later that day he went to Battlecrease to have a go at it. Tragically, he succeeded. The couple agreed to try to forgive and forget, and James sealed the deal by consenting to pay Florie's debts. But the marriage was broken; she was an adulteress with little love for James, and ten weeks later he was dead.

Following her husband's murder, the machinery of state preservation, last visited upon a Bradford milkman, was now visited upon Florence Maybrick. The motive was precisely the same as with William Barrit: to blame anyone, destroy anyone, *hang* anyone, who might threaten Her Majesty's ruling elite. Jack was at the heart of it, and from the beginning Michael Maybrick knew he was on a win–win. He moved on his own family with the pleasure of Satan, accusing his brother of one horror, his brother's wife of another, and taking care of the documentation for both. There would be forged letters, phoney medical prescriptions, and a forged will. No one can lie like a psychopath, and nothing keeps its mouth shut like Masonry. The 'Mystic Tie' was its *raison d'être*, and having debased everything the Fraternity claimed to stand for, Michael now made it his servant.

Let me just stop and interview myself here. Are you saying that Michael Maybrick set James Maybrick up as Jack the Ripper, murdering him with the state's acquiescence, and blaming Florence Maybrick for the deed?

How about 100 per cent?

Michael had been whispering into receptive ears. No one can know exactly what came out of his mouth in respect of James, but the substance of it isn't difficult to construe. Certainly it is known what toxic murmurs he put about regarding Florence, and extrapolating from the one presents a useful idea of the other.

We will come to these accusations, and to Michael's 'regret' at having to make them, in due course. But make them he did, and was he not a man of unimpeachable honour? In the spring of 1889 the authorities had reason enough to believe that the nightmare who had been terrorising Whitechapel was in his grave. It was a welcome development, but there was a caveat. It was believed that Florence Maybrick had discovered the truth of a terrible secret. Most dangerously, she was now the guardian of a scandal that a legion of lickspittles, including the Commissioner of London's Metropolitan Police, had criminalised themselves to secure.

Masonic anxieties that Jack had generated in life were now transferred to the havoc he might wreak in death. At all costs, Bro James

Maybrick had to be disassociated from Freemasonry, and his wife permanently shut up. As a pillar of the Fraternity, a pillar of society, Michael Maybrick was only too ready to help. It goes without saying that in reality Florence knew nothing, because there was nothing to know. It was a lie within a lie. But that was all it took for the System to kick in – witness the cops at Flatman's Hotel – ultimately crushing her inside the well-rehearsed mechanism of an Establishment cover-up.

James Maybrick died in the arms of his best friend, George Davidson, on the evening of 11 May 1889. Thereafter, Florence was entrapped in the System, isolated and silenced. Virtually everyone had deserted her, but why had they deserted James? The only thing he'd done wrong was to get himself murdered, yet those who had been his intimates, particularly in Freemasonry, abandoned him. The nineteenth-century conventions of Masonic interment were quite specific, and there must have been those who wondered why tradition was flouted so brutally in respect of James. How was it that this hapless victim of homicide, a city worthy who counted so many of Liverpool's most prominent Masons amongst his business associates and friends, should go to his maker without a Masonic contingent present, much less a Masonic wreath?[13]

'There is no privilege appertaining to the Fraternity,' claimed a prominent Masonic periodical in 1882, 'of which Masons in general are so tenacious as the right of Masonic burial. So earnestly is this regarded that many, long before the approach of the dread messenger, request some brother, in case he should be the survivor, to see that this last token of respect to his memory be paid; and, in many instances, they select the Brother who is desired to officiate upon the solemn occasion.'

In this case, Bro Michael Maybrick.

'In view, therefore, of the value set upon this privilege by the great majority of Masons in deference to the feelings of the relatives and friends of the deceased, and with proper regard for the reputation of our craft before the public, no accessory which will lend dignity and solemnity to the ceremony should be neglected.'[14]

Sharing both blood and Masonic brotherhood with James, Bro Michael put himself in charge of the funeral. Surely of all people he should have assured Masonic solemnities for his wretched sibling. Instead he was secretly laughing at the graveside.

The vicar who buried James at Anfield Cemetery, the Reverend C.R. Hyde, had been his friend for twenty years, and was himself a prominent Mason. For a description of the funeral James should have had, we might do worse than turn to the *Liverpool Daily Post* of 12 February 1897, when Bro Hyde himself was interred.

> From the gates of the cemetery the cortege passed through a double line of Freemasons who flanked the road. The deceased gentleman was Chaplain of the Kirkdale Lodge (1756) and a considerable number from this Lodge were present, while Brethren from other Lodges were in attendance. The chief portion of the assembly at the graveside consisted of Freemasons.

Michael Maybrick denied his brother these solemnities. Apart from near family and a few friends, what James got was predominantly a contingency of the staff from Battlecrease. Among them was a twenty-eight-year-old nursemaid to Florie's kids by the name of Alice Yapp. She made no particular secret of her dislike for her employer. They were about the same age, probably as pretty as each other, but Yapp was a servant with nothing, and Florence her mistress with it all. I think it's indicative of the resentment Yapp felt that she would turn up at the 'trial' carrying one of Florie's Parisian silk parasols.

Raise your eyes across the grave and you're looking at another nasty piece of work, the counterfeit friend Matilda Briggs. Mrs Briggs was an intimate of the deceased, and like Yapp had personal reasons for despising Florence. She loathed her because she had been 'madly in love with James',[15] had made a desperate effort to marry him, and might well have pulled it off had not the adulterous little slut from Alabama turned up.

According to Florence Aunspaugh, both Briggs and Yapp 'hated Florence Maybrick', although Briggs camouflaged her bitterness behind a mask of saccharine benevolence.[16] Though of course ignorant of Michael's Whitechapel horror story, these two women were easy prey for a psychopath, predisposed in their animosity and only too eager to be walk-ons in his nightmare.

In a post-'trial' interview he denied any relationship with either, most particularly the accusation that Alice Yapp was acting as his 'spy' in the Maybrick household. 'There is not a shadow of truth in such a report,' he countered with commanding rectitude. 'Why should I want to have a spy upon Mrs Maybrick, I should like to know?'[17]

The question is answered with another. Why was Florence Maybrick not at her husband's funeral? Why was she semi-comatose in a stinking bed, abandoned in her own excrement, locked in a bedroom at Battlecrease House with no one in attendance?

Without Yapp and Briggs in the equation, it would have been infinitely more difficult for Michael to have got away with it. Without their willing acquiescence he might not have got away with it at all. Yapp was a harridan. In the context of such wickedness, to call her a mere 'spy' was a compliment.

Following her child's incarceration, Florence's mother, Caroline von Roques, wrote in her despair to the one individual whose Masonic clout she misguidedly imagined could help her:

TO HIS ROYAL HIGHNESS, THE PRINCE OF WALES

As the daughter and as the widow of a Freemason, and as an accepted member of the American Order for Women, the Eastern Lodge, I approach your Royal Highness with the entreaty that the [?] of my need, for the protective and fraternal respect of all Free and Accepted Masons and kindness of the Members of the Order. I now approach your Royal Highness under equally terrible conditions. The unjust and cruel punishment for an unproven offence has been the sentence to my young, delicate, well-born and innocent daughter, Mrs Maybrick. She has endured for 3 years a living death amongst the lowest class, taken from her family, her mother, her children, her station, deprived of all worldly interests, shamed and ruined, through the mere suspicion of her legal Brother in Law and treacherous friends – gossip of servants [?] [?] against her – a stranger, alone, friendless, brotherless, a mere girl, a widow, the daughter and the granddaughter, and the widow of a Mason.

All emphasis is hers. Baroness von Roques knew something that her son-in-law's Masonic contemporaries had mysteriously forgotten: that *James was a Mason*, and Florence 'the widow of a Mason'. What she didn't know was that Michael had fingered James as the Ripper, and that this functioned as an insurance policy for him to get away with anything he liked. The Victorian state had cast its mantle around the terrible secret, and as guardian of it Michael truly was 'On Her Majesty's Service'. He could snigger at their stupidity and relish the fun, indulging in the inevitable vaudeville of Her Majesty's 'justice'. A circus of bent coppers and zombie coroners was in his wake, and as with the milkman Barrit, the journalist Ernest Parke and the politician Charles Stewart Parnell, it was justice made into a mockery.

The imprisonment of Florence Maybrick represented a triumph of the rot. Totally framed and utterly innocent, she suffered '*an unjust and cruel punishment for an unproven offence*', predicated on nothing but the fabricated '*suspicion of her legal Brother in Law*', a serial killer called Michael Maybrick.

The desperation in von Roques' text tells us almost all we need to know about 'the Maybrick Mystery'. 'I appeal to your Royal Highness,' she continues,

> and plead as the Head and Chief of English Masons, mercy and justice and freedom where ever dispensed may be taken into serious consideration. Some months since the documents proving my rights to such considerations were shown to his Lordship the Earl of Lathom by a member of the Skelmersdale Lodge (1380). I had achieved through his influence to approach Her Majesty the Queen at a time when [my time?] when my awful sorrow as a mother and a grandmother. His Majesty's just heart has heretofore shown to the cause of mothers [brothers?] and children.[18]

It was like dropping a line to Adolf on behalf of Anne Frank. The well-being of this lot was precisely why Florence had been sentenced to life imprisonment. I naturally make no accusation against Fat Ed. He was as ignorant of Florence Maybrick as he was spared the bother of reading her mother's letter. It went to his private secretary, Bro Sir Francis Knollys, who forwarded it to the Masonic Secretary to the Prince and intimate pal of the Ripper, Bro Colonel Thomas Shadwell Clerke. Clerke dismissed it as a 'legal matter', and nothing further was ever heard of it.[19]

Nothing more was heard from the Earl of Lathom either. His lodge, the Skelmersdale, was but one of many at which this fabu-

Bro Colonel Shadwell Clerke   Bro the Earl of Lathom

lously wealthy aristocrat sat as Grand Master. His baronial heap at Ormskirk in Lancashire played frequent host to the masters of the state, Viscount Lord Salisbury among them.

This corpulent reprobate, England's Prime Minister, was well aware of 'the Maybrick Mystery', and it was he who recommended that Her Majesty should show no mercy in respect of the public agitation to free Mrs Maybrick. Salisbury was the boss cunt of his class, dominating the executive, and a 'dangerous leader to be placed in command of a body so easily influenced for evil'. Such was the opinion of his parliamentary contemporary Lord Rosebery: 'I hope the Noble Marquis will excuse me when I say that he is a little impetuous in the use of the weapon committed to his charge. If he is not hacking about and dealing death and destruction with it, he is always threatening with it.'[20]

But let us return to Salisbury's Liverpool host, the Earl of Lathom. Chamberlain to the Queen, Master of her Swans, he was Provincial Grand Master of Lancashire. Among his other lodges was the Liverpool Lodge of Harmony (32), in which James Maybrick was a fellow Companion, and the exclusive London chapter St George's

(42), where he enjoyed the company of Bros Colonel Shadwell Clerke and the serial killer Michael Maybrick.

42.

Members of the St. George Chapter, London.

St. George's Day (Inst.), and second Thursday in January and November.

Br. F. LEVICK, M.W.S.
,, EDWARD J. CASTLE, Q.C., Recorder.

Benson, George Vassall, *LL.D.*
Burroughes, James Samuel
*Castle, Edward James, *Q.C.*, late *R.E.*
†Clerk, Maj.-Gen. Henry, 33
→ †Clerke, Col. Shadwell Henry, 33
†Costa, Raphael, 33
*Davison, Frederic (*Treas.*)
*Gibson, John Thomas, 30
*Grisbrook, Edward, 30
Hay, Harry Parnell
Inskipp, George [30
*Kempster, Wm Henry, *M.D.*,
Kempster, Wm. Henry, *M.B.*
†Lathom, Rt. Hon. Earl of, 33 ←
Levick, Frederick
Marshall, Henry Darly
Maude, Rev. Samuel
*Maybrick, Michael ←
†Montagu, J. M. P., 33
†Philips, Capt. N. G., 33
*Read, John, 30
†Sandeman, Hugh D., 33
*Scamell, George, *C.E.*
*Steele, Joseph, 30
Veley, Arthur Curtis

Caroline von Roques didn't have a hope in hell, and neither did Florence. They were up against a government within a government, a judiciary within a judiciary, and a police force within a police force. Jack the Ripper was as much a part of the 'Mystic Tie' as its Grand Master, Bro the Prince of Wales himself.

Because the British state was rotten to the core, Bro Jack got away with it. Nothing could be allowed to threaten Masonry, because the whole venal dinosaur of the Victorian ruling elite couldn't function without it. If you wanted your bit of ribbon, you pressed your fingertips together and bowed out backwards like you were sucking on a gallstone.

In December 2013 the journalist Nick Cohen wrote a characteristically incisive piece in the *Observer*. What he writes of the English governing class and its Civil Service is as accurate now as it was 130 years ago: 'The best way to imagine the British Establishment, is to picture a committee that never meets. There is no chain of command, which might leave incriminating paper trails; no controlling intelligence. Its members do not need to wait for instructions from on high, they know what to do without being told.'

Three great corruptions were simultaneously in progress in 1889. They were the conspiracy to frame Charles Parnell, the conspiracy to bury the Cleveland Street scandal, and the conspiracy to hide Jack the Ripper. To this substantial list we can add another: the conspiracy to frame Florence Elizabeth Maybrick.

18

'The Maybrick Mystery'

Some men wish evil and accomplish it,
But most men, when they work in that machine,
Just let it happen somewhere in the wheels.
The fault is no decisive, villainous knife
But the dull saw that is the routine mind.

Stephen Vincent Benét, 1928

On 7 August 1889 a withered misogynist with animal hair on his head told Florence Maybrick that the state was going to take her from this place and break her neck. The place was a courtroom buried in St George's Hall in Liverpool, where for the previous eight days she had listened to a confection of invention and treacheries that were now to take away her life.

The man with the morbid tidings, Judge Sir James Fitzjames Stephen, was a sixty-year-old Queen's Bencher who was himself to die four years later in a lunatic asylum. Symptoms of his 'fatal affliction' developed after a fuse-out at the Derby Assizes in April 1885. The stroke – if that's what it was – had blown away the intellect but left a lot of the nasty stuff. Already suffering from the uglier excesses of hag-worship, he was a virulent monarchist whose conservatism was off the scale. 'It is highly desirable that criminals should be hated,' he wrote, 'that the punishment inflicted upon them should be so contrived to give an expression to that hatred.'[1]

To that end, and irrespective of any accompanying prison sentence, he was vociferously in favour of 'the increased use of physical pain by flogging, as a form of secondary punishment, with an enhanced degree of severity. At present,' he grumbled, 'it is little, if at all, more serious than a birching at a public school.'[2]

He had gone to Eton with Salisbury,[3] and if they didn't share such views as schoolboy contemporaries, they certainly did now. Both were into hanging, Fitzjames Stephen in terms of moral retribution, and the Prime Minister wherever death was expedient to the survival of his Queen and his class.

To Fitzjames Stephen, capital punishment was 'the keystone of all moral and penological principles', a novel attitude that his bigotry somehow conflated with the teachings of Jesus. 'Christianity has two sides,' he pronounced: 'a gentle side up to a certain point, a terrific side beyond that point.' In other words, the rope: 'No other way of disposing of criminals is equally effectual, appropriate and cheap. When a man (or woman) is hung, there is an end of our relations with him. There are many people, with respect to whom, it is a great advantage to society to take this course.'[4]

Law, wrote Fitzjames Stephen, was 'the organ of the moral indignation of mankind'. But not if the indignation came off the pen of Charles Dickens or Tom Paine. He published a tirade against Dickens's novels, his stupid invective reading like 'an indictment of a man guilty of sedition'. Oliver Twist was just another parasite on the take, better off in a pauper's grave. But his abhorrence of Dickens was as nothing compared to the violence of opinion he reserved for the revolutionary politics of Paine. The author of *The Rights of Man* brought him to boiling point: 'the wretched, uneducated plebeian', he raved, who 'dared to attack the Church and State'.[5]

The Church and state was what Sir James Fitzjames Stephen was all about. He was their Avenger, and together with his holiness Sir Robert Anderson, an exemplar of their religious propriety. As the great American poet Kenneth Patchen later described such crawling hypocrites, 'Behold, one of several little Christs.'

According to his brother and biographer Sir Leslie Stephen, Fitzjames Stephen was recognised amongst his peers by a 'spontaneous freemasonry' which apparently 'forms the higher intellectual stratum of London society'.[6] This presumably included that notable intellect the Duke of Clarence, whom Stephen's homosexual son tutored and probably buggered from time to time.[7] Such indulgences attracted severe penalty in Victorian courts, and his dad must have turned a blind eye. (It was after all, royal arse.) I don't know if Stephen was a practising Mason, but what's for certain is that, like his schoolboy chum in Downing Street, 'he was one of the most mordant and persistent critics of democracy'. This gallstone-sucker believed Liberalism would 'surely increase the power of the "popular voice"', threatening everything greed held dear, 'including the preservation of the British Empire'.[8]

This meant Ireland, but most of all India, a nation otherwise dismissed by Fitzjames Stephen as a place 'where we can work *and make money* [his emphasis], but for which no Englishman ever did, or ever will, feel one tender or genial feeling'.

It was doubtless in India, where (as a member of the Colonial Council in the early 1870s) he wrote his white law for the recalcitrant darkies, that he developed his taste for opium. At the time of Florence Maybrick's 'trial' he wrote to Lord Lytton, 'I do still now and then smoke an opium pipe, as my nose requires one occasionally, and is comforted by it.'[9] He must therefore be the only individual in pharmacological history who smoked dope to get his nose high. It's possible that this unique organ was intoxicated when he ladled out his unremitting hatred to those in the dock.

Apart from the class he represented, it's hard to work out who Fitzjames Stephen didn't hate. He had an organic antipathy towards the common man. 'The average level of the great mass,' as he perceived and expressed it, 'would fix the position and career of the nation at the level of a lowland, stagnant river.'[10]

A dozen of these stagnations constituted Florence Maybrick's jury. They were empanelled and respectively sworn as Thomas

Wainwright, a plumber – who was foreman – and the rest (one of whom couldn't read or write): a farmer, a grocer, a baker, and others of similar trade. Considering the case turned on the esoterica of forensics, the Crown had itself a perfect jury.

The Jury Which Decided The Maybrick Trial

This interesting picture reached the *Echo* following the recent interesting correspondence from Sir Samuel Brighouse and others. Left to right—Top: J. Taylor, W. A. Gaskell, W. Walmsley, A. Harrison, Thomas Ball, and Joseph Thierens. Below: John Bryers, J. Tyrer, W. Sutton, R. G. Brook, G. H. Welsby, and Timothy Wainwright.

I've tarried over the prejudices of this judge, and now come to the most egregious of them. Sir James Fitzjames Stephen had a bit of a problem with women – particularly young women – who had sex for any reason other than Christian procreation. If a woman should fornicate outside marriage, whore herself in that vilest of female sins, adultery, then you're looking at Ezekiel in a wig. Stephen told the jury, 'It is easy enough to conceive how a horrible woman, in so terrible a position, might be assailed by some fearful and terrible temptation.'[11]

James Maybrick wasn't murdered by adultery, wasn't murdered by arsenic either, but in the mire of this bigot's disintegrating cognisance, they were conflated as one. Florence Maybrick's night with Alfred Brierley at Flatman's Hotel became central to the Crown's case.

Fitzjames Stephen told the jury that she had acquired 'flypapers', and had soaked them in a bowl of water to extract the arsenic, referring to this domestic commonplace as a 'suspicious circumstance'.

'These papers,' he said, 'which nobody can have a proper occasion to use except it be to kill flies, were found soaking in water, and that water would become impregnated with arsenic, and might have been used for poisonous purposes.'

It 'might have been' if you were the umpire of a totally got-up judicial perversion, but arsenic was in fact one of the constituents of a mundane facewash. Together with benzoin, elderflower and other ingredients, such infusions containing a minuscule amount of arsenic were widely used by gentlewomen of a certain class, and like Florence, none of them were going to seek arsenic in a chemist's shop by proclaiming their acne. Like her, they'd say it was for flies.

Arsenic was widely present in the manufactured commodities of Victorian England – found in soaps, dyes, medicines – and not infrequently used by ladies to enhance their complexion. Fitzjames Stephen was either too ignorant to know, or so embroiled in the forthcoming deceit that it was beyond his reduced grasp to understand, that there was nothing 'suspicious' about a woman soaking flypapers. Florence had acquired them quite openly at a local pharmacy, around the corner from her home at 'Wokes & Co.', subsequently leaving these tools of homicide on a table in the hall of

Battlecrease House, where they were picked up in passing by her foredoomed husband, who showed scant interest, if any at all.

Florence had studied in Germany, where she'd learned the secrets of soaking flypapers as a pimple-killer from her student contemporaries.[12] They were soaking now in preparation for a night out to which the Maybricks had been invited. But with James too ill to attend, Florence had asked if his younger brother Edwin could escort her.[13] No problem with that, and aspiring to be *la belle de la nuit*, she went into *haute couture* mode, writing to her mother: 'We are invited to a Bal Masque which being given in Liverpool and the people provincials, I hardly think likely to be a success. A certain amount of "diablerie", wit and life is always required at an entertainment of this sort; and it will be quite a novel innovation, people will hardly know what is expected of them.'[14]

James Maybrick knew what the flypapers were for, even if Fitzjames Stephen didn't, and it's part of an almost unbelievable fraudulence that nobody told him. It was all the Crown had, but this flypaper bullshit was nothing less than absurd. To accuse Florence Maybrick of murdering her husband with arsenic was like accusing her of trying to murder an alcoholic with a teaspoon of gin. Had flypapers been an efficient and accessible source of arsenic, there would have been a weekly wholesale delivery of a dozen gross to the back door of Battlecrease House.

Maybrick's unrelenting addiction to various poisons was well established; a legion of family friends and associates could have testified to this as fact. Such evidence, of course, would have immediately destroyed the Crown's case, so no such witnesses were called. Vital depositions were suppressed, both by the prosecution and the treacherous 'defence', which colluded to present James Maybrick as a paragon of physical virtue who barely took anything beyond an occasional stomach sedative.

Had the jury heard the truth, Florence would have walked free. But the function of this 'trial' was to shut her up, and keep her shut up in perpetuity. Had not the whole base affair been bone-marrow corrupt, she would have walked within fifteen minutes. Instead, she was sentenced to death, later commuted to life imprisonment, which she was to suffer for fifteen years.

The tragedy of Florence Maybrick is mind-blowing. How could this perfectly innocent mother of two little children be snatched from her life and told she was going to die? The charges against her were fake – like those against an equally innocent Bradford milkman – with no explanation other than the wickedness of a System that would do anything to ensure its own survival. We have it from the Prime Minister's own mouth that he had no scruple about executing the odd innocent Irishman, so what problem presented itself with stringing up this Yankee whore?

When Florence heard that she was to be 'hanged by the neck until you are dead', it was out of the mouth of a System well summarised in the quote at the beginning of this chapter. She was within the wheels of a machine, serviced by 'routine minds' whose only business was the protection of the machine itself.

It's why their judicial contingency wore daft wigs, symbols of insult to a failed republicanism and to such counteractive voices as that of Tom Paine. Oliver Cromwell's Protestant thugs – the 'Roundheads' – cropped their hair short, while the King's men and his boys – the 'Cavaliers' – wore their locks long. When the Royalists hauled Cromwell from his grave to re-kill his rotten corpse, Charles II was back on the honeypot, sporting horsehair to disguise his billiard ball. Thus the wig represented royalty, the resurgent royalist state; and Sir James Fitzjames Stephen was but one of its walking-backwards mouths.

How stultified were these widow's men. Florence Maybrick had the unavoidable misfortune to be represented by one of their best, the famous 'silk' Sir Charles Russell QC.

The case was a pushover – any fledgling solicitor could have won it. So how was it that 'the greatest advocate of his age' lost it? The answer depends on who you think Sir Charles was working for. Apologists claim he failed to secure the freedom of his client through exhaustion engendered at the recent Parnell Commission. Fatigue had debilitated him, they say. I say, to the contrary, that in the framing of Florence Maybrick he displayed an energetic courtroom wizardry that has fooled the record for 130 years.[15]

Soon to be ennobled as Lord Russell of Killowen and promoted to Lord Chief Justice of England, this Belfast Judas was at the top of his game. He lost because it was predetermined that Florence Maybrick should go to the grave with her supposed secret, born from the hideous calumnies of Michael Maybrick.

Like Sir Charles Warren, Sir Charles Russell was an oft-time visitor to the glutton's palace at Sandringham, a personal friend of the monarch to be, and we need waste no time considering where his loyalties lay.[16] Russell had turned into a kind of Warren in a wig, prostrating his infinitely more sophisticated treacheries on behalf of the Crown. The buffoon Commissioner was required to pretend he was hunting the Ripper, while Russell was entrusted to put up a show of 'defending' Florence Maybrick. He was in fact fully committed to the prosecution, generous in the use of his skills to keep it on track. Russell had repeated opportunities to win this case, but either ignored them or turned them to Florence's disadvantage. Time after time he interceded on the Crown's behalf, dominating the courtroom and watching the bewigged back of 'Fat Jack', the Crown's inept prosecutor.

John Addison QC MP was an archetypical huckster of Victorian values, a barge of stale silk, able to lie with alacrity but as prone to blunder as that indentured chump Bro Wynne Baxter. On behalf of Addison's frequent errors, Russell was ever alert to intercede, correct, steer and suppress. He could see the mistake coming before Addison made it, and wasn't going to let his Honourable Friend botch the frame-up by default. Bro Russell was as much in the 'loop'

as Bro Charlie Warren, or for that matter Bro Michael Maybrick himself. Bro Jack had initiated much corruption in a variety of courts. But this was the big one. When Sir James Fitzjames Stephen slung a bit of black rag on top of his wig, it was the triumph of the Ripper's career. The state was now going to do his killing for him. These men were going to murder Florence Maybrick.

The previously mentioned barrister Alexander Macdougall described the intrigue against Mrs Maybrick as 'the Spirit of Evil'.[17] The British public must 'feel shame' he wrote, 'as long as a guiltless woman is passing a living death in our midst'.[18] Although in ignorance of the Crown's subplot, cooked up on behalf of a psychopath, Macdougall went on to demand 'the removal from office of all those who can be shown by their unconstitutional conduct to have been responsible for the miscarriage of justice that has taken place'. And further, 'the bringing to justice of any person who can be shown to have recklessly and maliciously put the charge of murdering her husband, upon Mrs Florence Maybrick'.[19] In other words, icons of the legal engine of Queen Victoria's Masonic state. A contemporary of Macdougall's possessing a similar independence of legal mind, the barrister J.H. Levy, wrote: 'A blush of shame ought to come to the cheek of every Englishman. The case is, in my opinion, one of the most extraordinary miscarriages of justice in modern times.'[20]

Neither Levy nor Macdougall knew about the fly in the gravy, thus both were mistaken. A 'miscarriage of justice' implies that justice was intended, but that some error had been made. But this wasn't an error, it was a predetermined conspiracy to keep the little flags waving, and protect those they were waved at.

Sir Charles Russell himself was later to describe the Maybrick trial as 'rotten', and of all people, he should know. 'The foundation on which the whole case for the Crown rested was rotten,' he wrote in 1896, '*for there was in fact no murder*'[21] (his emphasis). If he knew it was 'rotten' in 1896, he knew it was 'rotten' in 1889 when he and his pals orchestrated it. While the word 'justice' exists in the lexicon of human exchange, these sons of bitches can never be forgiven.

Russell was candid about the rottenness, but bashful with the truth about James Maybrick's demise. Unequivocally Maybrick was murdered, done to death by cruel poisoning – but it was never Florence Maybrick who administered it.

*

At about half past eight on the morning of Friday, 26 April 1889, the parlourmaid at Battlecrease House, Mary Cadwallader, took in a delivery from the postman. Postmarked London, it was a pasteboard box, which she correctly assumed contained a bottle. It was addressed to James Maybrick, who told her he'd been 'expecting the medicine for a day or two'.[22] This was six days after his visit to his brother's physician in London, Dr Fuller, and day one of Michael Maybrick's first homicidal move.

On the following day, Saturday the 27th, a date of dark import, James hauled out the cork. Within minutes he was heading for the bathroom to get his head in a sink. When the vomiting was over he came downstairs to tell Florence and Cadwallader that his legs had gone stiff as a pair of pokers, and that he couldn't feel his hands. This isn't surprising, because he'd just swallowed a savage dose of an alkaline toxin whose fearsome calling card he recognised at once. To crease Maybrick it must have been inordinately potent.

Whatever else may be said about this mysterious 'London Medicine', one thing is for certain, and that is that it had nothing whatsoever to do with Dr Fuller. Fuller's prescription had been made up at a nearby pharmacy, Clay & Abrahams, on 24 April.[23] There were three medicines in all. One was a harmless aperient (containing an unweighable trace of arsenic), and the second was a tonic (with a homeopathic-quantity dash of nux vomica, or strychnine). The third was a patent medicine called Plummer's Pills, whose main ingredient was antimony. Following the instructions, a ten-year-old could have safely swallowed the lot.

By mid-morning James had somewhat recovered, and despite continuing 'numbness in the legs' he got on his horse and left the house at about 10.30 to ride over to the Wirral races. Florence watched his departure with her usual trepidation, telling the ever-observant nanny Alice Yapp, 'Master has taken an overdose of medicine. It is strychnine and is very dangerous.'[24]

Meanwhile it was April in Liverpool, sky like a dustbin lid with intermittent heavy rain. By the time Maybrick arrived at the racecourse he was wet through to his boots. The umbrellas were up, and under one of them he ran into a friend from the Cotton Exchange, a Mr Morden Rigg, and his wife. Mrs Rigg picked up the concern where Florence had left it. She only had to look at the mauled face to know that James was sick. He told her quite openly that he'd taken an overdose of strychnine, information he shared with another associate from the Exchange, a Mr Thompson.[25] Maybrick must indeed have looked peculiar, judging by the way he was looking at them. Twenty-four hours later he told his local doctor, 'It was a peculiar feeling, although he knew they were still there, they appeared to be a long way off.'[26]

That night Maybrick dined with friends on the 'Cheshire Side', that is on the opposite bank of the River Mersey. At the table he could barely control his wine glass because of tremors, and he was worried his hosts might think him drunk. It was past midnight before he arrived back at Battlecrease, leaving his saturated clothes to the care of the kitchen staff.

Despite the ravages of the previous day, next morning James took another hit of 'the London Medicine'. To consume more of it was clearly crazy, but he was a junkie, and addiction is a kind of insanity. Predictably, the servants' bells were soon clattering. Florence didn't wait for anyone to answer, but ran downstairs, dispatching Mary Cadwallader to fetch the nearest doctor.

'Without waiting for him to arrive, she told Alice Yapp to be with her master, while she went downstairs and told the cook, Humphreys, to make up immediately some mustard and water, as the master had taken another dose of that "Horrid Medicine". She would not wait even for the cook to make it, or for a spoon, but stirred up some herself with her fingers, and rushed back into the bedroom with it,' *and as Yapp is her witness*, said, 'Drink this mustard and water in order to make you sick.' Until assistance arrived Florence could do little more, except confiscate what was left of the 'Horrid Medicine' and throw it down the sink. She later told the cook that if James had swallowed even another drop 'he would have been a dead man'.[27]

The above account is Alexander Macdougall's, gleaned from various transcripts. He makes it clear that Maybrick's reaction to the strychnine on Sunday morning was infinitely more severe than to the Saturday dose. In order to get an idea of what all or any of these reactions might have been, I quote from *Husband's Forensic Medicine*: 'The effects of the poison come on suddenly. The earliest symptoms are a feeling of suffocation and great difficulty in breathing. Twitching of the muscles rapidly passing into tetanic convulsions. The head after several jerks becomes stiffened, the neck rigid; the body curved forward, quite stiff and resting on the back of the head and heels.'[28]

All this is accompanied by staring eyes and an expression of 'intense anxiety'. It must have been shared by everyone in the room, who could only look on in alarm as Maybrick's spine rose in an approximation of the Sydney Harbour Bridge. 'During the intervals of the paroxysms,' continues Husband, 'the intellect is usually clear, and the patient appears conscious of his danger, frequently exclaiming, "I shall die!"'[29]

James Maybrick had probably swallowed enough strychnine to kill the entire household, horse thrown in, but it's testament to his elephantine tolerance that it didn't kill him. Although the stuff had all but murdered him and Florence had probably saved his life, the reality of this 'London Medicine' was to be distorted under the charlatan eyes of the Irish Judas, to her fatal disadvantage.

Russell was well aware of the strychnine incident, but conspired with no less a personage than Michael Maybrick to conceal it. Keen attention must be paid to Dr Fuller's so-called medicine. It was to become one of the principal ingredients in Russell's betrayal, confirming beyond doubt that he was treacherously active on behalf of Florence's prosecution.

By the time the doctor arrived Maybrick was on top of it, chronically poisoned but with the immediate crisis past. Dr Humphreys (no relation to the cook) arrived at Battlecrease House just after 11 a.m. He was hurried upstairs, where he 'found Mrs Maybrick at the bedside'. James was in it, looking like he was halfway to hell. Humphreys probably knew less about medicines than his patient. He certainly knew less about strychnine, and Maybrick didn't tell him he'd taken it.

'Mr Maybrick,' said Humphreys at the inquest, 'complained about some great fear and anxiety in consequence of a pain in the region of his left side, the region of his heart, and said he was frightened of dying. He further said he was afraid of paralysis coming on. I asked him when these symptoms began; he told me after breakfast, and he put it down to a strong cup of tea he had taken.'[30]

Whether Humphreys laughed out loud or not isn't known, but this rubbish was repeated in court without laughter, and puts the prosecution into perspective. Any problems with the flypapers, and they would have nailed Florence for a teabag.

'He showed me Dr Fuller's prescription,' said Humphreys, 'and had an idea the stiffness in his limbs was due to that. He was a man who prided himself on his knowledge of medicine. He said, "Dr Humphreys, I think I know a great deal of medicine."'[31]

'He deceived Humphreys,' wrote Macdougall, 'by attributing it to Doctor Fuller's tonic-medicine. He knew perfectly well what was the matter with him and that his illness was not due to that, but to an overdose of *strychnine*.'[32] (Macdougall's emphasis.)

Attributing Maybrick's symptoms to a tea attack, with associated indigestion, 'distress and palpitations of the heart', Humphreys told him to lay off the London brew, prescribing dilute prussic acid in its place. With a recommendation of bed rest for a day or two, the physician then bade him good morning.

Dr Humphreys had been in attendance at Battlecrease House once before, though not for James Maybrick, but for whooping cough in the kids. He could therefore have no idea of the maniac he was dealing with – or rather, he wasn't astute enough to put two and two together. On that occasion in early March, Florence had told him of her anxieties over her husband's surreptitious use of 'white powders'. 'She was alarmed about it,' he said, 'and didn't know what it was. She thought that possibly it was strychnine.' He clearly didn't take her too seriously, actually making a somewhat inopportune joke of it. 'Well, if he should die suddenly,' he said, 'call me, and I can say you have had some conversation with me about it.'[33]

I'm relieved this quack wasn't treating me. She *had* called him, reiterating her apprehension about the 'white powders', and with a prospective corpse upstairs, it's astonishing that strychnine poisoning didn't cross Humphreys' mind. The witless physician later claimed that he'd questioned James Maybrick on the topic, apparently eliciting a strong denial. 'I cannot stand strychnine,' was the answer, from which Humphreys 'drew the conclusion that he wasn't in the habit of taking it'.[34]

If Florence got nowhere with the doctor, she naturally fared no better with the psycho in London. In that same month she'd written to James's brother Michael expressing the anxieties she'd shared with Humphreys over 'white powders'. Considering it was Michael who was engineering the murder of James and the utter destruction of Florence herself, it was a wasted stamp, and the letter must have brought a smile to the bastard's face as he crumpled it.

How terrible were to be the coming weeks. How pathetic was this woman's fate. As Macdougall was to write of her accusers, who charged that it was on 27 April that she administered the first of a cumulative and ultimately fatal dose of arsenic: 'I cannot conceive how the conduct of Mrs Maybrick on that day leads to any other conclusion than innocence and anxious solicitude for her husband. A woman engaged in poisoning her husband with "arsenic" would not have rushed to give him an emetic to throw it up, or told Doctor Humphreys and Alice Yapp and the cook that it was dangerous medicine ["the London Medicine"] he was taking which had made him so ill on those two days, the 27th and 28th April.'[35]

James remained in bed, with two more visits from Humphreys. The first was that same night, Florence recalling him at about ten o'clock. In acute discomfort, Maybrick complained of 'stiffness in the lower limbs', which not everyone might interpret as an obvious symptom of dyspepsia. The bewildered doctor rubbed James's legs, bent them at the knee and changed the prescription, believing 'papine irridan' might hit the spot that prussic acid had evidently missed. He also prescribed a diet of coffee and bacon for breakfast, 'for luncheon he was to take some beef-tea with Arabica Revalenta (Du Barry's Food), and for dinner, on alternate days, a little chicken and fish'.

Next day James was well enough to sit up in bed and write a letter to his brother Michael. At least, that's what Michael was to tell Fitzjames Stephen and his conspirant wigs in secret conference. Dated 29 April 1889, it was addressed to 'My Dear Blucher':

Liverpool April 29th 1889

My Dear Blucher
I have been very seedy indeed. On Saturday morning I found my legs getting stiff and useless, but by sheer strength of will shook off the feeling and went down on horseback to Wirral Races and dined with the Hobsons. Yesterday morning I felt more like dying than living so much so that Florry called in another Doctor who said it was an acute attack of indigestion and gave me something to relieve the alarming symptoms, so all went well until about 8 o'clock I went to bed and had lain there an hour by myself and was reading on my back.

Many times I felt a twitching but took little notice of it thinking it would pass away. But instead of doing so I got worse and worse and in trying to move round to ring the bell I found I could not do so but finally managed it, but by the time Florry and Edwin could get upstairs, was stiff and for five mortal hours my legs were like bars of tin stretched out to the fullest extent, but as rigid as steel. The Doctor came finally again but could not make it indigestion this time and the conclusion he came to was the Nuxvomica [strychnine] I had been taking. Doctor Fuller had poisoned me as all the symptoms warranted such a conclusion. I know I am today sore from head to foot and layed out completely.

What is the matter with me none of the Doctors so far can make out and I suppose never will, until I am stretched out and cold and then future generations may profit by it if they hold a postmortem which I am quite willing they should do.

I don't think I shall come up to London this week as I don't feel much like travelling and cannot go on with Fuller's physic yet a while but I shall come up and see him again shortly. Edwin does not join you just yet but he will write you himself. I suppose you go to your country quarters on Wednesday.

With love,
Your affectionate Brother Jim.[36]

This letter has much to say for itself, and what it says reeks of deceit. Taken literally, it could have set Florence Maybrick free. Here we have James Maybrick accusing not his wife, but Dr Fuller in London, as his poisoner – 'Doctor Fuller had poisoned me as all the symptoms warranted such a conclusion.' Whether James believed 'the London Medicine' had come from Fuller or not, it is beyond conjecture that he and everybody else in the house (including Alice Yapp) knew it was a hotshot of strychnine. He swallowed it on 27 April 1889, the very day the Crown accused Florence of administering the first dose of arsenic. It was an absurd and wicked accusation. The revelation of this text, purported to have been written by the victim himself, would have constituted all Sir Charles Russell needed to secure the liberty of his client. Everyone in that rotten little cesspit of a court – Fitzjames Stephen, 'Fat Jack' Addison, and the Irish Judas himself – was only too aware of this letter, and it is a criminal obscenity that both prosecution and defence suppressed it.

Notwithstanding the state's filthy little secret, we're supposed to believe that a roaring hypochondriac in constant terror of the Reaper, who had told Dr Humphreys he was 'frightened of dying', should announce twenty-four hours later that he was perfectly gung-ho for a stretch on the slab, and only too delighted to be hacked to bits for the profit of 'future generations'.

James Maybrick suffered from a maniacal fear of death, and in my view is an unlikely advocate of his own posthumous butchery. Ripping up bodies was more in his brother's line. The last thing James wanted was his dick flopped out in a mortuary, and no way did he write this letter. It was faked by a man with 'many pens' who was proficient in various schools of handwriting. Michael Maybrick had been systematically poisoning James with pills he claimed were from Dr Fuller, but which in fact had no more to do with him than the postal hotshot of strychnine. The so-called 'Blucher' letter was composed to validate a variety of intentions. In the first place, it's probable that Michael thought his mystery brew might actually kill James, and this letter would then serve as his alibi; and second, had 'the London Medicine' done the trick, the letter would have vanished, and Florence would have been accused of murdering her husband with strychnine.

As with the unfortunate Bradford milkman William Barrit, malign articles began to appear in the press – the *Liverpool Post* of 15 May, by way of example: 'It is not impossible that some very startling revelations will be made. The suspicion of the police and of the medical gentlemen being that the deceased succumbed to poisoning by strychnine.' This calumny was enhanced by the *Liverpool Weekly News*: 'An extraordinary rumour prevailed yesterday to the effect that Mrs Maybrick has not lately been accountable for her actions, and that she is really suffering from some mania.' As far as certain sections of the Liverpool press were concerned, murdering husbands was a family trait. Florie's mother was forced into broadcasting a public disclaimer following accusations that she had disposed of not one but two of her previous spouses. 'These malicious rumours,' reported the *Liverpool Review*, 'without a particle of feasible evidence to support them, have been freely circulated in Liverpool, and have found their way into print in London.'

But it is the malicious journey of the 'Blucher' letter that takes precedence. Artfully abbreviated, it was to reappear, surfacing when it could do maximum damage to Florence, and then disappear when it could easily have proved her innocence.

On the day after he was supposed to have written it, James was feeling recovered, and returned to his business affairs in the city. That evening Dr Humphreys called at the house, and found him much improved. James told the doctor not to trouble himself further. If necessary, he would call on him.

It was a misguided forecast. The following day, on 1 May, James having forgotten to take his lunch to work, Edwin graciously volunteered to make the train journey to his brother's offices in the Knowsley Buildings with a ceramic jugful of the prescribed Revalenta. James ate it, complaining of the sherry in it, and was ill that evening. He was well enough to go in to his office the next morning, and again took a dose of Revalenta for lunch. Once again he complained of feeling ill that evening. At ten o'clock next morning Dr Humphreys was listening to tales of fresh gastric woe.[37]

'He said that he had not been well since eating lunch the day before,' recounted the doctor, who not knowing his diagnostic arse from his elbow, suggested a Turkish bath might tone James up. It didn't. At midnight the same day, Humphreys got another urgent summons. His patient had been vomiting – 'green bile' was mentioned – and suffering a 'gnawing pain that extended from the hips to the joints of his legs'. A morphine suppository went up, and Maybrick was back in bed. He would not get out of it until his corpse was carried away a week later in a coffin.

It was the Revalenta Edwin had brought to the office that had kicked off this new bout of illness. There's no doubt that somebody was poisoning James, and apparently no doubt who that somebody was. Mrs Maybrick had prepared the jugful that travelled to her husband's office that day. She had personally concocted it. James had eaten it. *Ergo*, she had poisoned him. This neat syllogism was presented by her prosecutors, ignoring one glaring ingredient: the jug of lunch on 1 May was carried from the kitchen of his home to the Knowsley Buildings by Edwin Maybrick.

Michael Maybrick was over two hundred miles away, but was fully in control of the evolving wickedness at Battlecrease House. He had his rats on leashes, and one of them was Edwin. It was Edwin, jilted by Florence in favour of Alfred Brierley,[38] who I believe put a little top-up into the jug on Michael's behalf. Like everyone else, he was totally subservient to Michael's will. Edwin's daughter Amy Maine was to write that her father 'couldn't buy a pair of shoes without referring the matter to Michael'. But this story isn't about shoes and boots (be they tight or not). It's about murder, and I'd be the last person to bring footwear into the equation as any credible explanation for the activities of Jack the Ripper.

On some midnight in late spring 1889, certainly after Edwin Maybrick had returned from America on 25 April, a twenty-year-old man was lurking about the shadows of downtown Liverpool. His name was Robert Edward Reeves, and it was his practice to lurk. He was a small-time felon, a deserter from Her Majesty's Liverpool Regiment, and perpetually on the lookout for an easy quid. Reeves had been in and out of jail since the age of fifteen, for theft in general, and this night he was sniffing around the columns of the Royal Exchange, looking for an unlocked door. He heard voices in the darkness, urgent whispers, and silent as the little thief he was, stopped to listen.

What he heard was Michael and Edwin Maybrick discussing the forthcoming murder of their brother James. 'They could not see me as I was behind a pillar,' said Reeves. 'I drew near as I could to hear what they were talking. One said to the other, "How will you manage this?" The other said, "I will manage that alright with the servant. I will get her to put a bottle of laudanum in Mrs Maybrick's drawers and leave one on the table just as if it had been used and we can get Mr Maybrick to go and have some drink with us tomorrow and you can engage him in talking about the business and I will slip a strong dose in the drink that will settle him by tonight."'[39]

Reeves's statement totally contradicts contemporary perceptions of Florence Maybrick's supposed infamy, and in that it is starkly correct. Michael murdered James with Edwin as his besotted assistant.

'Blame will fall on our sister,' said one of the two men. 'The other said, "What do that matter, you know she don't like Mr Maybrick and she is in keeping with that other fellow that she seems to like best. She will be glad to get him out of the way, you know that they can't prove it was her poisoned him, if they do send her away the whole business will fall to us you know and we shall be two lucky fellows, then it don't matter about getting rid of one or two out of this world, will you agree with me about it?"[40] Edwin agreed: "'Yes, you will see that that will manage this business alright." Then the other said, "It is settled." They then left their hiding place and went as far as the Merchant Tavern close by. I followed them. I could not go in as I had no money with me at the time, I was a deserter at the time, else I should have gone to Dale Street Police Court. I was afraid of getting taken back to my Regiment. I belonged to the Eight of King's Liverpool Regiment, my regimental number was 2955, at the depot at Warrington.'[41]

The absentee soldier went home 'to my young girls house, number 5 Vaughn Street, Toxteth Park, and told her brother John Crane, all I had heard them two young men say. He said, "Don't you have anything to do with it, you might get caught and taken back to your regiment." So I said nothing about it. Soon after I was taken by Detective Wilson in Manchester Street one night so soon after I heard how Mrs Maybrick poisoned her husband and was sent for trial. I didn't think it worthwhile to say anything about it, but it has been on my mind ever since, I even think of it at night when I lay awake, that such a thing could be done against a lady that is innocent.'[42]

Reeves was lying awake in a prison cell. He'd been slammed up for 'warehouse breaking' at Sussex Assizes and sentenced to five years' hard. He was guilty, but not as guilty as the insects who jailed Florence Maybrick. Reeves insisted on making his statement, but the venal crew suppressed it. It was to remain classified as a secret Home Office file for the next hundred years.[43]

Reeves's statement was smothered by the authorities as 'absurd'. But had he not heard what he claimed to have heard, how could he even remotely have known the secret of James Maybrick's murder? It's taken rather a while to uncover the truth about Bro Michael Maybrick, and by any objective view it is beyond incredible for a near-illiterate like Robert Reeves to have dreamed up so complementary a narrative, ad hoc, in a prison cell. Everything Reeves said is substantiated in its entirety by fact. Moreover, it is borne out by realities that were then unknown.

Before, during and after the 'trial', the press had saturated the public mind with sensation about arsenic. Mrs Maybrick was an 'arsenic poisoner'. That's what the judge said, and that is what was said in every newspaper from Liverpool to London. Yet Reeves dismisses this, and doesn't talk about arsenic at all. He says James Maybrick was murdered with laudanum (liquid morphia). If he was making it all up, why risk his credibility with unnecessary invention? A man telling an absurd tale would have surely kept within the 'known facts'.

Reeves's statement annihilates the rubbish underpinning Florence Maybrick's conviction. Had Alexander Macdougall been aware of it, I think it would have caused friction enough to ignite his pen. He didn't know about Reeves, but in his subsequent treatise of 1891 he set out his suspicions concerning laudanum. An empty bottle of it had been 'discovered' by Alice Yapp in a chocolate box inside one of Mrs Maybrick's trunks. It had clearly been secreted there to incriminate her, as is consistent with Reeves's statement: '"How will you manage this?" The other said, "I will manage that alright with the servant. I will get her to put a bottle of laudanum in Mrs Maybrick's drawers."'

Macdougall wanted to know where this bottle had come from, and why it was ignored by the police. 'There ought to have been no difficulty in the way of the police finding out whether she had been buying a bottle of a solution of morphia. And then again, why was the label, "Solution of Morphia", left on, and the name of the druggist scratched off? Solution of Morphia is a white liquid, which looks like water. If a person was engaged in crime, I can understand their taking off the words, "Solution of Morphia", but they were left on, and the chemist's name erased!'[44]

I suggest it was because the laudanum had been obtained in London, and its source erased precisely to prevent the cops from tracing it – not that they gave a toss for detection. Nobody apart from his murderers knew that James Maybrick had been dispatched with a hotshot of morphia – except this easy-to-dismiss convict Robert Reeves.

We come now to the last and most important of the soldier's revelations, a subterfuge not even Macdougall was ever cognisant of, and that is the theft of James Maybrick's business: 'the whole business will fall to us you know and we shall be two lucky fellows'.

James Maybrick's will, dated 25 April 1889, makes absolutely no mention of Edwin. He doesn't get a paperclip. James bequeathed 'all my worldly possessions, including life-insurances, cash, *shares*, property – in fact everything I possess – in trust with my brothers

Michael & Thomas Maybrick *for my two children*, James Chandler Maybrick & Gladys Evelyn Maybrick' (my emphasis).

It was a trust that wasn't honoured. On 14 October 1889, Michael handed over *all shares* in James's business to Edwin: 'Transfer of shares from James Maybrick (decd) to Edwin Maybrick.'[45] It was undoubtedly as reward for services rendered, but that isn't the immediate point. Unless Robert Reeves had somehow accessed the records of the Liverpool Cotton Brokers Association (while simultaneously serving five years in prison), there is no conceivable way he could have known what a 'lucky fellow' Edwin was to become other than in the way he described. Reeves was telling the truth about these toxic gentlemen, proving that it's not entirely beyond the realms of imagination for a Freemason like Michael Maybrick to indulge in a sideline of murder.

This might be a convenient point at which to note that while the Whitechapel Fiend was concentrating his attentions on a forthcoming homicide in Liverpool, his fan base of travelling 'hoaxers' were somehow aware of the interlude, and ceased to mail their letters. For some arcane reason, the team of provincial Jack the Rippers had fallen into group silence? Ha ha.

But let us return to the real thing. In hindsight the events unfolding at Battlecrease are as clear as day, but for those in that woeful house, most especially Florence, it must have seemed like the inexplicable progress of a blighted dream.

Dr Humphreys was in and out like he was paying rent. He was just one of many in attendance. Most frequently present were James's eternal friend George Davidson and another pal from the Cotton Exchange, Charles Ratcliffe, who he'd known since the Virginia days. They sat and listened, and were as baffled as the bedridden wreck himself. He complained incessantly of a phantom 'hair in the throat' that caused him to 'hawk'. Plus, he had a tongue like garbage. Humphreys stuck to his 'dyspepsia' theory, but clearly didn't have a clue. His patient had gone from sick to sicker, alternating the vomiting with bouts of diarrhoea. The consistently ineffectual physician decided the best way to stop both was to allow nothing in. Apart from an increasing variety of prescribed medicines, Maybrick was denied any liquids whatsoever, including even water. He could chew on a wet towel and suck an occasional ice cube, and that was about it.

His thirst became an ancillary torture. He begged the cook for some lemonade, which came up from the kitchen and was promptly confiscated by Florence.[46] Although she was only trying to follow the doctor's strict instructions, this prohibition was publicly used against her as an example of her heartlessness. Subsequent to her conviction, an anonymous letter signed 'Antifiction' appeared in the *Liverpool Courier*. It serves as an example of the malignancy directed at this woman, its author as sour with spite as he or she was well-informed: '... this confiding innocent wife could snatch from the hand of the nurse the lemonade that was to quench the parching thirst of her "darling" husband while in the agonies of death'.[47]

Such venom might well have spilled from what Charles Ratcliffe described as the 'Female Serpants'[48] in daily commute through Battlecrease House. Alice Yapp and Matilda Briggs, by way of example. Another bedside regular was of course Edwin, but there was no such press condemnation for him. Despite Humphreys' stringent ban on liquids, on 5 May Edwin pitched up in the sickroom bearing James a brandy and soda. We needn't speculate what was buried within it. The ricochet came within half an hour as Edwin was attempting to ply him with 'a dose of physic'. Because no one suspected him, Edwin proffered this information himself at the 'trial'.[49]

'I don't question the brother's actions at all,' said the Irish Judas, and no one did, except Alexander Macdougall. He wrote a blistering assault on Edwin's interference. 'It was an outrageous piece of presumption on his part, and might have caused his brother's death!'[50] Had he been aware of Reeves's statement, he would have known that such presumptions ultimately did.

On the following day, Humphreys pulled another bottle from his bag. What the hell, he'd tried everything else – this was good old Fowler's Solution, whose active ingredient was arsenic. A minute amount of arsenic, one tenth of a grain, was finally discovered in Maybrick's viscera, and this was probably its source. Whether it was or wasn't (he could handle fifty times more), the only certainty is that he wasn't getting dosed with arsenic by his wife, and she would never have been accused of it without the irredeemable wickedness of Briggs and Yapp. This pair shared a trade in whispers, knew everything, and what they didn't know they invented. 'The most pathetic part about it,' wrote Florence Aunspaugh, 'was that Mrs Maybrick did not have the brain to realise their attitude towards her.

Had she sensed their enmity and been more cautious, conditions would have been very different, and much better for her.'[51]

They were about to get very much worse.

Florence Maybrick wasn't stupid, but she wasn't particularly clever either. Even had she been the ace in the pack, I think it's unlikely she, or anyone else, could have been aware of the degree of raw evil about to be unleashed against her. It was driven by a psychopath whose *métier* was control. By stealth and force of personality he had assembled a formidable team, each with their individual motives for animosity towards Florence, that by his nature he was able to exploit. He chose Yapp for her spite, Briggs for her jealousy, and Edwin for his greed. Michael Maybrick himself constituted the binding ingredient, which was non-negotiable HATE.

He had further potent allies under his spell, not least the London and Liverpool police, including their coroners and courts. This was a state as sick as anything in *Gulliver's Travels*, its people, wrote Swift of his barely disguised kingdom of 'Tribnia' (Britain), made up of 'Discoverers, Witnesses, Informers, Accusers, Prosecutors, Evidencers, Swearers, together with their several subservient and subaltern Instruments', and 'all under the colours, the conduct, and pay of ministers of state'.

Sir Charles Russell QC was one such citizen, who suppressed vital evidence to the gross detriment of his client. A document that would have exonerated her never saw the light of day. Conversely, he sanctioned focus on a letter that by any equity should have been struck out as inadmissible. It was from Florence to Brierley, of counterfeit date but claimed to have been written on Wednesday, 8 May 1889. The prosecution rode in on the back of it. Written in pencil, it was spore for the ugly brain of Fitzjames Stephen, wherein it served to ferment his wild misogynies. I'll be taking a closer look at this letter, but for the moment restrict myself to its opening lines.

Wednesday

Dearest
Your letter under cover to John K— came to hand just after I had
written to you on Monday ...

'John K' was Florence's London friend John Baillie Knight, who in
March was acting as an intermediary for her illicit mail to Alfred

Brierley. While she was under sentence of death in Walton Jail, Brierley swore an affidavit on Florence's behalf. It was destined for the Home Secretary in expectation of a reprieve, and he was very frank: 'I never was improperly intimate with her until our meeting in London on 22nd March last. We parted abruptly at the Hotel in Henrietta Street on Sunday, the 24th March. When we so parted on the 24th March it was distinctly understood that we would not meet again except in public, and I for my part had finally resolved that I would not again be tempted into a similar position.'

Among other things pertaining to their defunct affair, *which was over on 24 March 1889*, Brierley wrote: 'If Mrs Maybrick wrote to me on Monday the 6th May, I never received it, and am informed and believe that the word "you" on the second line is a mistake for "him".'

In other words, he believes her letter originally read: 'Your letter under cover to John K— came to hand just after I had written to *him* on Monday.'[52]

Brierley was quite right, except that it wasn't a 'mistake'. Florence's letter to him of Wednesday, 8 May (which he didn't receive either) had been tampered with by an unfriendly hand. Somebody was trying to pretend that Florence was still embroiled in an adulterous relationship with Brierley. Before arriving at who this snake might be, we need to make a brief detour a few weeks hence, to an article in the *Liverpool Daily Post* of 3 June. Published under a bold headline, while Florence was being held in isolation on remand, it's a sniff of the rot to come. It's also the reason (were he not at the core of it) why Russell should have had all such correspondence struck out as inadmissible. 'It was bruited about in the course of Saturday,' reported the *Post* (one of Liverpool's most prestigious newspapers),

> that the police have resorted to an extraordinary stratagem, in order to procure evidence of a peculiar character, which they require in the case. The story goes that at their instigation a lady was employed to write a letter to a person well known in Liverpool, purporting to come from Mrs Maybrick. It is alleged that the writing so closely resembled that of the prisoner as to have deceived the person to whom it was addressed, and to have brought from him a response. This remarkable proceeding, we are informed, took place immediately prior to Mr Maybrick's death.[53]

If this were true – and it *was* true – it tells us all we need to know about the confederacy of gangsters operating out of Liverpool while disguised as policemen. 'It was a direct imputation of FORGERY against the Police,' charged Macdougall, 'engaged in getting up this case against Mrs Maybrick!!' That it was, and the police made no denial. 'Do the people of this country intend to allow criminal trials to be got up in such a way?' I'm afraid the answer was yes. Yes, when they all but hanged William Barrit; yes, when they bullied the waiter Alfred Schweisso into perjury; yes, when they were snooping about in the bushes outside Flatman's Hotel. The police in Victorian England were simply the thug-end of Victorian 'law'. They were accountable to no one but the System they serviced, and it was as corrupt as they were. A cartoon from the *New Statesman* of many years ago hits the nail on its head, and saves me writing a paragraph.[54]

TAKING LIBERTIES
John Griffith on law and the State
PLUS: Chancellor Nigel ● Bradford schooling ●
Greek elections ● Black publishing ● Arts

So who was it who was messing around with Florence Maybrick's correspondence? Who owned the deceitful pencil, and how could he/she have had such a familiarity with Florence's handwriting?

According to Florence Aunspaugh, Mrs Matilda Briggs had her snout into everything. When the Maybricks were out, Briggs was in, snooping into every corner and drawer of the residence. For one so minded, getting a sample of Florence's handwriting would be simple as a smile. 'She was supposed to be Mr and Mrs Maybrick's guest,' wrote Aunspaugh, 'yet she was on far more intimate terms with Yapp than she was with Mrs Maybrick.'[55]

In his account of the 'mystery', Trevor Christie writes: 'It is undoubtedly true, that an amorphous, loosely organised cabal was operating at Battlecrease House to snare Florrie in some misdeed that would break up her marriage and deprive her of her children; but, whatever its objective, it was certainly not to hound her to the gallows.'[56]

I agree with Christie *vis à vis* the domestic wipe-out, but I take a less sanguine view in respect of the noose. Michael Maybrick exploited Yapp and Briggs, offering certain base satisfactions. But they didn't know what was intended on his side of the deal. His hatred for Florence Maybrick was of a different order, and on Wednesday, 8 May 1889 he made his opening move.

On the previous day Briggs claimed he'd sent her a telegram, 'informing me that his brother was very ill and requesting me to go and see him'.[57] The next morning, she and her equally unsavoury sister, Mrs Hughes, turned up at Battlecrease House. Before they made it through the door, Yapp beckoned to them from across the lawn. 'Thank God, Mrs Briggs, you have come,' she said, 'for the mistress is poisoning the master.' Mrs Hughes was naturally taken aback, and asked what reason she had for making so dreadful an accusation. 'She then told us about the flypapers,' said Briggs, 'and how the food intended for Mr Maybrick had been tampered with by his wife. We were so shocked by what she said that we went up at once to his bedroom. Mrs Maybrick followed us immediately and was apparently angry, telling us we had no right to be there, but that if we would go downstairs she would let us know all about his symptoms.'[58] Briggs doesn't say whether she let Florence know about Yapp's accusation concerning the 'flypapers'.

Yapp's monstrous lie was to become one of the reasons Mrs Maybrick would spend the next fifteen years of her life in a prison cell. By what possible contagion of mind could Yapp have conceived such a charge? She doesn't even have herself as an alibi. Under cross-examination by Fat Jack for the prosecution, she was asked:

ADDISON: Did you suspect your mistress?
YAPP: No, sir.
ADDISON: When you saw the fly-papers, did you suspect her?

YAPP: No, sir.

ADDISON: When you did see them, what then?

YAPP: I did not think anything of them.[59]

So what the fuck are you talking about, Alice Yapp? These flypapers arrived at Battlecrease House on or about 24 April, and were seen soaking quite openly in Mrs Maybrick's dressing room. They were, as everyone in the house knew, a cosmetic preparation for the forthcoming *bal masqué* to which Florence would be escorted by Edwin on Tuesday, 30 April.

If Yapp thought nothing of the flypapers in April, why is she suddenly converting them into weapons of murder in May? She was in the house when the so-called 'London Medicine' that had practically coffined James arrived. When he was blasted with strychnine on 27 April, she assisted when Florence administered a mustard emetic to save her husband's life. Why did she not run round in circles then, yelling 'Poison!' at Mrs Briggs – 'Thank God you've come, Mrs Briggs, *someone in London is poisoning the Master*!'

How is it conceivable that she should tell Briggs that Florence was murdering James with flypapers, long since thrown away, when she had been a witness to the near-fatal effects of 'the London Medicine'? At a pre-trial hearing Alice Yapp's deposition was as near to the truth as she was ever going to get : 'I remember Mr Maybrick going to the Wirral Races, and after he had gone, Mrs Maybrick came to me and said: "Master has been taking an overdose of medicine. It is strychnine and is very dangerous. He is very ill."'[60]

Such evidence isn't what the Crown or the cops wanted to hear, and it would never be heard again. This so-called 'magisterial hearing' was a dry run for the rottenness that came after, giving the authorities a chance to rehearse and to correct any possible mistakes. Yapp's recollection was duly corrected. By the time of her appearance in the witness box at St George's Hall, she'd quite forgotten about the panicking bells and running up and down stairs in crisis, quite forgotten the strychnine James had taken, which had mysteriously transformed itself into brandy.

ADDISON: Do you remember the next day, Sunday the 28th of April? Did you on that day hear the bedroom bell ring?

YAPP: Yes, sir.

ADDISON: What was the next thing you saw?

YAPP: I was coming downstairs and saw Mrs Maybrick on the
landing. She came to the night-nursery door and asked if I would
stay with the master. He was lying on the bed with his dressing
gown on. My mistress came into the bedroom a few minutes after
with a cup in her hand. She said to her husband, 'Do take this
mustard and water; it will remove the brandy, and make you sick
again if nothing else.'[61]

And that was that for the strychnine. Under further examination,
Yapp revealed her benevolence towards the dying man, interspersed
with spiteful jibes towards his wife, who 'went shopping' while Yapp
sat at the bedside, 'rubbing his hands'.[62] The angel Yapp announced
that it was she who had advised Mrs Maybrick to call in another
doctor, which attracted the rebuke 'All doctors are fools.' She
described how she'd seen her mistress 'apparently pouring something out of one bottle into another'. What sort of bottles were they?
'Medicine bottles.'[63]

ALICE YAPP SAW HER MISTRESS POURING SOMETHING FROM ONE BOTTLE
INTO ANOTHER.

Further questioning brought her to the fateful afternoon of Wednesday, 8 May. Having accused their mother of murder that morning (of which she said nothing in court), she said she had been outside playing with the Maybricks' children. Yapp spent a lot of time in the garden that day. I don't say I believe a word of it, but this is how the story of that afternoon continues.

Alice Yapp was on the lawn with the children, and Dr Humphreys was upstairs with James. On the previous day he'd been joined by another physician, Dr William Carter, together with a professional nurse. Their presence tells the tale of James's continuing decline. It was somewhere during this traffic of bedpans and pails that Florence found a breather in which to write to Brierley. What she did next, if she did it, bears out Aunspaugh's assessment of her intellectual shortcomings, plus some. She took the letter into the garden and gave it to Yapp to post.

Barring Michael Maybrick himself, Yapp was the last person on earth to be entrusted with such a task. As soon as Florence's back was turned, Yapp opened the envelope. Apart from a few words that could be adjusted, it was what they were all waiting for.

> Wednesday
>
> Dearest
> Your letter under cover to John K— came to hand just after I had written to you on Monday. I did not expect to hear from you so soon, and had delayed in giving him the necessary instructions. Since my return I have been nursing M— day and night. He is sick unto death! The doctors held a consultation yesterday, and now all depends upon how long his strength will hold out! Both my brothers-in-law are here, and we are terribly anxious. I cannot answer your letter fully today, my darling, but relieve your mind of all fear of discovery now and for the future. M— has been delirious since Sunday, and I know that he is perfectly ignorant of everything, even as to the name of the street and also that he has not been making any inquiries whatsoever. The tale he told me was pure fabrication, and only intended to frighten the truth out of me. In fact, he believes my statement, although he will not admit it. You need not, therefore, go abroad on this account, dearest, but in any case please don't leave England until I have seen you once again. You must feel that those two letters of mine were written under circumstances

which must ever excuse their injustice in your eyes. Do you suppose I should act as I am doing, if I really felt and meant what I inferred there? If you wish to write to me about anything do so <u>now</u>, as the letters pass through my hands at present. Excuse my scrawl, my own darling, but I dare not leave the room for a moment, and I do not know when I shall be able to write to you again. In haste, Yours ever, Florie.

It is not unreasonable to describe this letter as toxic, both in provenance and content, and in how it arrived in the hands of Michael Maybrick 'that same night'. It was claimed under oath by Yapp that it was given to her at about three o'clock that Wednesday afternoon, in time to catch the 3.45 post. This is contradicted by the letter itself, and everything after is a Yapp invention. She said she gave it to the Maybricks' young daughter Gladys to carry, but that she dropped it in the mud. A fresh envelope was required, she said, but instead of asking for one in the post office, readdressing it and mailing the original in that, she opened Florence's letter.

In fact Yapp was nowhere near the post office, and the child had not dropped the letter. She opened it because she was a conniving little sneak, and everyone including Sir Charles Russell knew this 'mud' story was rubbish.[64] Nevertheless, it gave the Irish Judas an opportunity of showboating, which at the 'trial' served its purpose of looking like something to do with Florie's defence.

> RUSSELL: Why did you open that letter?
> YAPP: To put it in a clean envelope.
> RUSSELL: Why didn't you put it in a clean envelope without opening it?
> (No answer.)

He then demanded to know whether it was a wet or a dry day.[65] Again, no answer. He pressed her, and again received no answer. The Brierley envelope was produced, the address quite clear despite a water stain, and with no running of the ink.

RUSSELL: Can you suggest how there can be any damp or wet in connection with it without causing some running of the ink?

YAPP: I cannot.

RUSSELL: On your oath, girl, did you not manufacture that stain as an excuse for opening your mistress's letter?[66]

Yapp denied it, but the envelope didn't. That the ink hadn't run is a small but notable point whose subtext was missed by Russell. The letter was written in pencil, 'in haste' – so, in such haste, why bother to seek out a pen and ink for the address? In respect of 'adjustments' that were later made to the text, it crosses my mind that this wasn't the genuine envelope at all, but that it was part of an overall fabrication.

When Florence's mother, the Baroness, arrived at Battlecrease House from Paris on 17 May, to discover her daughter prostrate in a filthy bed and detained under police guard, she laid into Edwin Maybrick, demanding an explanation. According to her, he had a rather different story to tell regarding the letter's provenance:

Oh, I have been very fond of Florie. I would never have believed anything wrong of her. I would have stood by her, and did until a letter to a man was found. I said, 'Letter to a man! Do Edwin, tell me a straight story!' 'Why, to the man Brierley. She wrote him a letter and it was found.' I said, 'Who found it – you?' He said, 'Nurse.' I asked, 'Where?' He replied: 'She found it on the floor; it fell from her dress when she fainted and I carried her into the spare bedroom.' 'But,' I said, 'how did you know it was to Brierley?' He replied: 'It was directed to him, it was written in pencil; and it fell to the floor.'[67]

We can take our pick, Yapp or Edwin. Both are lying, but at least Edwin confirms that the address was written in pencil.[68]

As Russell charged, the mud-stained envelope was faked, a ruse to disguise the prying. From where they acquired this letter in truth remains unknown. So much sinister baggage is attached to it, it's tiresome to work out where to begin. Florence admitted to her mother that she had indeed written to Brierley, but because she never saw or was able to comment on the version of the letter that was used in evidence against her, she couldn't know what letter it was, or what the text actually said.[69] Looking at it from the point of view of Yapp's evidence (that it had been given to her in the garden at 3 p.m.) raises the first egregious inconsistency. Were this true, the line 'Both my brothers-in-law are here' is in want of explanation. At three o'clock only Edwin was there. Michael didn't arrive from London until about 8.30 that evening.

According to Edwin's more plausible version of the provenance, the letter didn't come into their possession until Florence had 'fainted' on Saturday, 11 May, the day on which James died, by which time both her brothers-in-law *were* there, and James truly was 'sick unto death'. This brings the date of Wednesday, 8 May into obvious question. Macdougall thinks the letter was forged, and so do I. 'I have my suspicions,' he writes,

> Nay! my doubts about the genuineness of some parts of that letter!! I do not doubt that the great bulk of it is genuine, but assuming it to have been written on Wednesday the 8th of May, I doubt the genuineness of some parts of it. I must recall one or two dates. Mrs Maybrick returned from her visit to London on the 28th of March. On the 29th of March Mr James Maybrick attended the Grand National and among his party were Florence and Brierley. Under such circumstances I think it inconceivable that the words, 'Since my return I have been nursing him day and night,' can be the genuine words which Mrs Maybrick would have written to Brierley on the 8th of May!!

Macdougall's argument is sound. Moreover, in his sworn affidavit Brierley states, 'I only met her once again after the Grand National races on 29th March, viz: on or about the 6th of April, when I met her in Liverpool.' This was a clandestine encounter of which the forger was ignorant, exposing the sentence 'since my return' in the letter as the counterfeit it was.

'It's written,' continues Macdougall, 'on the first piece of paper that came to hand, bearing the monogram of her mother, the Baroness von Roques. It purports to be dated, "Wednesday", and I call attention to the flourish under that word and invite my readers to compare it with the flourish under the signature "Florie". I appeal to my readers to share my doubt whether the same hand made that flourish under "Wednesday" as under "Florie".'

Unquestionably it's an iffy-looking 'Wednesday', but with or without it the text stands no scrutiny. It goes far beyond Brierley's point about 'you' for 'him', underpinning the certainty that whatever is genuine in this 'May 8th' letter had to have been written in *March*. John Baillie Knight was not forwarding letters 'under cover' to Florence in *May*. As Brierley had written, the affair was all over by 24 March. The question therefore is, to whom did this meddling hand belong? Could it be the same one the police had commandeered to cook up a letter from Florence, as reported without denial, in the Liverpool newspapers of 3 June?

The *New York Herald* wrote of Mrs Briggs that she 'constituted herself as a public prosecutor before Maybrick's death, and to that end was a most skilled traitress to Mrs Maybrick during all the time preceding'. I second that, and Macdougall seconds me in believing the Brierley text was amended by Briggs.

You don't have to be a conspiracy theorist to see the conspiracy here. Here was Briggs swapping telegrams with Michael Maybrick: 'Come quickly,' she wired. 'Strange things going on.' He claimed he received four telegrams from Briggs before she rushed round to Battlecrease House, barging into James's bedroom in a pantomime of neighbourly concern. Here was Yapp, whispering 'poison' in the morning – and it was pretty damned convenient that the incriminating 'love letter' should fall into her hands that same afternoon. And here comes Michael; having created the scene he now walked into it, all on that same Wednesday, 8 May. Macdougall says the 'accusing three', Yapp, Edwin and Michael, kept the letter secret for three days, but in my view this is incorrect. I don't think they kept it a secret because I don't think they had it yet. I don't think it was found until James was dead and Florence unconscious, and these three, abetted by Briggs and Hughes, ransacked the house.

Meanwhile, on his arrival at Battlecrease, Michael Maybrick had just put his bag down in the hall. No time was wasted with pleasantries. Within minutes he owned this place and everyone in it. He met Florence on the landing, and the pair of them went into James's sickroom. 'I was much shocked at my brother's condition,' Michael said in evidence at the 'trial'. 'Afterwards, downstairs, I told Mrs Maybrick I had very strong suspicions about the case. She asked me what I meant. I said my suspicions were that he had not been properly attended to, and that he ought to have had a professional nurse and a second doctor earlier. She said she had nursed him alone up to that point, and who had a greater right to nurse him than his own wife, or words to that effect. I then said I was not satisfied with the case, and that I would see Doctor Humphreys at once, which I did.'[70]

While he was popping round the corner, Edwin kept 'suspicions' on the boil: forbidding 'any intervention by Mrs Maybrick in the nursing or administration of medicine or food, I gave orders on Wednesday night to Nurse Gore, and repeated them on Thursday morning. I never mentioned Mrs Maybrick's name in the matter, but I told the nurses I should hold them responsible for all foods and medicines given to him, and that no one was to attend to him at all except the nurses, but I did not mention any names.'[71]

He admitted under cross-examination that he said nothing to Mrs Maybrick about any of this, but the infection was now abroad. Thereafter lies were dancing in the air like gnats.

Humphreys' doorbell rang at about 10.30 that Wednesday night. He could have had no idea of the wickedness motivating his visitor. In the bastard went, and the doctor listened while the most notorious killer in England aired his suspicions about the flypapers Mrs Maybrick had procured in some quantity before James's illness. Apparently they were a source of arsenic. It must have been heart-rending for Michael, so sensitive was the matter, but James was his much-loved brother, and he felt he had a duty to speak. Humphreys' reaction was far from what was hoped for. The quack was so shocked he went to bed.

Back at Battlecrease, Edwin's orders had been converted into whispers. Anyone who doubts a conspiracy was in progress might ask themselves how, that same Wednesday, Yapp and Michael came to the same conclusion about arsenic? Yapp told the court she didn't think anything of the flypapers, so how was it that Michael Maybrick was thinking of them 250 miles away? Who told him there were flypapers soaking in a bowl? Who told her they were 'suspicious'?

In March Florence had written to Michael expressing her concerns over the 'white powders' James was taking. He acknowledged receipt of her letter, but ignored it. 'I destroyed it,' he said. A month later, in the so-called 'Blucher' letter, James supposedly wrote to Michael about his overdose of strychnine and his desire to be cut up after death, and Michael ignored that too.

Thus 'strychnine' from his brother, and 'white powders' from his sister-in-law, were apparently of no consequence? Yet one whisper of 'flypapers' in a neighbour's ear, and he was running to Liverpool in perfect synchronicity with Alice Yapp? What did Yapp know that James Maybrick's relatives didn't? James was an *expert* on arsenic, and he said nothing of it. How is it credible that a servant girl knew more about arsenic than he did?

James had three days to live. On the first of them, 9 May, Michael made another move on the medical contingent, including Nurse Gore. If Dr Humphreys didn't want to hear it, Dr Carter was going to get it in no uncertain terms. He was considered one of the most distinguished physicians in Liverpool, a widely held misconception shared by Carter himself.

At about 4.30 that afternoon he arrived at Battlecrease, called in response to a telegram from Florence. Edwin, Yapp and Briggs all claimed to have been instigators of the visit, but this was a spiteful fabrication. Michael came immediately to the point, bearing down on Carter in his usual commanding manner. I leave it to the physician to describe the ensuing conversation in his own words:

'Now what is the matter with my brother, Dr Carter?' was a question put to me very abruptly in the presence of Dr Humphreys, before we had any opportunity for further conversation. I therefore simply repeated the opinion we had formed [on 7 May] and expressed then [acute dyspepsia]. 'But what is the cause of it?' demanded Michael, to which Carter replied, 'It was by no means clear. It could have been caused by many things.'

The conclusion the doctors had formed was that James 'must have committed a grave error of diet, by taking some irritant food or drink, so to have set up inflammation.' But Michael didn't want to know about diet.

Turning then sharply to Dr Humphreys, Michael Maybrick asked him, if he had informed me of the subject of their last night's conversation? Humphreys simply replied that he had informed me of nothing. All this was a matter of great surprise to me. I did not know until that moment that any conversation had taken place, and as I had had no communication directly or indirectly with Doctor Humphreys since the time it was said to have been held, I looked at the speaker wondering what would come next.

What came next was a reiteration of the previous night's accusations. Michael was talking flypapers and he was talking arsenic, and once again he spoke under the strain of cosmetic rectitude:

> It was made under the influence of great excitement, the speaker's mind evidently struggling under a conflicting sense of what was due to his brother on the one hand, and possible injustice to his brother's wife on the other. 'God forbid that I should unjustly suspect anyone,' he said, in reply to an observation made by myself, 'but do you not think that if I have serious grounds for fearing that all may not be right, that it is my duty to say so to you.'

The doctors concurred, agreeing it was quite right that he had told them. But what he told them betrays what he was really thinking. It was all accusation, and no cure. Any sincere actor would have put the patient first, or at least included him. If James was dying of arsenic, where was the antidote? At no time during his protracted journey to the grave did Michael raise the question of an antidote, and none was ever given.

'We heard all there was to say,' wrote Carter, 'that only so late as the middle of April the patient had been able to eat ordinary food at his [Michael's] house; that he had soon been subject to sick attacks after returning home; that this contrast between the condition of health while at and away from home, had been the subject of remark, and had been noticed before; that there had been a most serious estrangement between husband and wife; that the wife was known to have been unfaithful, and that just before the commencement of his illness, she was known to have procured many fly papers.'[72]

Not a word about 'the London Medicine', the 'Blucher' letter or the 'white powders' that had caused Florence to write to Michael in March. The bastard was laying his pipe. I think this deceitful conference affords an accurate template for something similar in respect of James. I don't know what words were whispered in London, any more than I know what was whispered between Michael and Yapp; but I know that similar covert accusations were made against James into equally receptive ears. Michael must have believed he was some sort of criminal genius. His plan had become the authorities' plan, and that was *to shut Florence Maybrick up* – he for his reasons, they for theirs: HATE and fear respectively. To be told (as he was forced to reveal with an unbearable sense of duty) that James was Jack, and that *she knew*, was all that was necessary.

The Whitechapel side of this scenario was of course kept secret at Battlecrease House, while the other was robustly promoted. Every move Florence made was watched by unfriendly eyes, and those so predisposed could see what Michael had told them to see. Even walking into another room had acquired connotations. As soon as you begin to spy on anyone they will begin to fulfil your expectations. If there's nothing to see, you will think you have missed it, and as with any paranoid state beguiled by its own propaganda, broaden your surveillance to spy more intently. Michael was whispering 'arsenic' into every ear but the most important of them all. To his beloved brother he said nothing. No way could he infect that ear with rubbish about flypapers, because if James had had the strength he would have laughed in his face. Such idiocy was left to the physicians to discount, and that's precisely what Dr Carter did. On the evening of 9 May he returned to his surgery with samples of James's excrement and urine. Both were subjected to scrutiny by means of a process known as the 'Marsh test' (see overleaf).

For those who knew how, it was simple and 100 per cent accurate. Had the slightest trace of metallic poison been present in either sample, a residual trace would have shown up on a piece of copper foil. Carter ran the test twice, and both times the results were negative. There was no arsenic in James's body, so the only certainty is that Florence wasn't killing him with incremental doses of it. Had this conclusive evidence – most vital to the proof of her innocence – been promoted in her defence, there would have been no case for the Crown to cook up. But evidence was incidental to

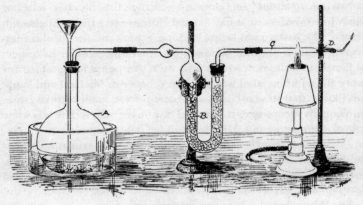

Marsh Apparatus

the trial's nefarious intention, and most unfortunately Michael had made Florence the poisonous star of the so-called 'Maybrick Mystery'.

It was either the Irish Judas or Carter himself who caused this testimony to be suppressed at the 'trial'. Somebody must have treated Carter to a whisper. Writing of him seventy years later, the historian Nigel Morland pre-empts my suspicion: 'Nothing is quite so peculiar in the Maybrick case as the behaviour of Dr Carter.'[73] He questioned why the physician kept his trap shut over the negative results of the excrement test, yet opened it wide in court over a positive show of arsenic in a bottle of meat juice. The bottle in question came out of Michael Maybrick's pocket, and it is interesting that both he and Mrs Hughes (Matilda Briggs's sister) knew it had been adulterated with arsenic before Carter or anyone else had even put it to the test.

ADDISON: Do you recollect that arsenic was traced and had been found in a bottle of Valentine's meat juice?

HUGHES: Yes.

ADDISON: When did you learn about the Valentine's meat juice? Was it from Doctor Carter you heard it?

HUGHES: No.

ADDISON: From whom?

HUGHES: Mr Michael Maybrick.[74]

Sir Charles Russell let this pass, but not so Alexander Macdougall. 'Now,' he asked, 'how came Michael Maybrick to know that arsenic had been found in the meat juice on Saturday? Doctor Carter had certainly not told him so. He had taken the bottle back with him on Saturday to test. He could not have told Michael Maybrick arsenic had been found in the meat juice because he didn't know it himself.' In reality, it wasn't until fourteen days later that the City Analyst confirmed it.[75]

So how did Michael Maybrick know there was arsenic in the meat juice? It's either a handy adjunct to the 'mystery', or the more cynical amongst us might think he put it in there himself. He and Edwin were constantly in and out of the sickroom, with as much opportunity to poison James as anyone else. The only difference is that they weren't suspected, and Florence Maybrick was. On Friday, 10 May, Michael walked into James's room and converted a perfectly blameless activity into a melodrama of the murderess caught in the act. Nurse Gore had been relieved by Nurse Callery, and had asked Florence to pour medicine from one bottle into another so it might be shaken. 'Florie!' Michael roared, doubtless barging in to snatch it, 'how dare you tamper with the medicine!'[76] Much was made of this incident at the 'trial', although her defence neglected to mention that Callery had asked Florence to do it to rid the bottle of sediment.[77]

Florence was utterly crushed, and downstairs in the kitchen she wept, her wretchedness compounded with the exhaustion of nursing James. 'I am blamed for all of this,' she said, in an agony to understand why. Comfort came from the cook, Mrs Humphreys, one of the few she could rely on for a sympathetic ear. 'She said her position was not worth anything in the house,' said Humphreys in evidence, 'that she was not even allowed to go into the master's bedroom to give him his medicine.'

Crying 'very bitterly for a quarter of an hour', Florence accused Michael of being the engine of it all: 'This is all through Mr Michael Maybrick,' she wept. 'He had always had a spite against her since her marriage.'[78]

ADDISON: Did it seem to you that she was attending to her husband?

HUMPHREYS: She seemed very kind to him and spent all her time with him.

ADDISON: And when she told you she had been blamed, you took her part?

HUMPHREYS: Yes I did, because I thought she was doing her best under the circumstances. She was very much grieved over it, and was very sorry. She was crying.

ADDISON: You knew she was set aside by her brothers and these nurses?

HUMPHREYS: Yes, she was set aside.

Neither Humphreys nor the parlourmaid Mary Cadwallader 'had the slightest doubt over Florence's innocence', wrote Macdougall after interviewing both, 'and do not believe and never did believe for one moment that Mrs Maybrick had a thought of compassing her husband's death'.[79]

As to the flypapers, Humphreys said, 'There had been joking in the kitchen about the fly-papers when Bessie Brierley came down and said there were some soaking in the bedroom, and joking going on between Alice Yapp and Alice Grant, the gardener's wife, about the Flannagan case,[80] but they thought nothing about it except as a joke.'

Here was the provenance, under Michael's tutelage, for the transformation of flypapers from banter into a means of murder. It was a kitchen nonsense. 'It was all done so openly,' continued Humphreys, 'and certainly no thought entered their minds of suspecting Mrs Maybrick till Michael Maybrick came to the house on the 8th of May and took control in the way he did.'[81]

That night Michael and Edwin went into James's bedroom and tried to bully him into signing some papers. Although near to death, James found the air to raise a shout that was heard all over the house. 'Oh Lord! If I am to die, why am I to be worried like this? Let me die properly.' His protests were 'very violent' and 'very loud'. Both Humphreys and Cadwallader saw Edwin come out of the room with a paper in his hand, and they said that Alice Yapp, 'knowing and hearing everything', told them that the brothers had been trying to get James to sign a new will.[82] Maybe this is correct, but I think it more likely they were after a sign-over of the company shares. Notwithstanding that, Michael was having difficulties finding the original will. Their other brother, Thomas Maybrick, had arrived from Manchester, and he told Humphreys that the 'Will had been left very awkward' – awkward, that is, for the murderous duo who were in the business of creating another one.

We shall be two lucky fellows ha ha.

Humphreys was not alone in balancing her dislike of Michael Maybrick with distrust. 'Michael, the son of a bitch should have his throat cut,' was the view of James's friend Charles Ratcliffe. In a letter to Florence Aunspaugh's father John, he described the evolving nightmare, conjured in raw wickedness, that was soon to swallow Florence: 'When Michael took possession and put Mrs Briggs in charge, she [Florence] was subjected to all kinds of insults and ill-treatment by Briggs and the servants. She was not allowed to have any visits from her friends. She was cursed and given impudent answers whenever she made a request of them.'[83]

Florence was isolated in a house full of people. Apart from her children, her only friend whose love was unequivocal was James. 'He wanted her with him always,' said Cadwallader, 'and asked for her when she was not.' No one had nursed him with more humanity than his wife, sitting with him night after night; and though she may no longer have loved him, she brought him comfort. It was this solicitude that Michael converted into her cunning.

By now there seemed no hope of recovery. Yet another uniform had arrived from the Liverpool Institute as a relief for Callery. Susan Wilson was perfect gas-lit casting, a carbolic presence, unpleasant as she was fat. Like her predecessor she would appear for the prosecution, but she had little to contribute, and I'd hardly trouble with her were it not for her name. Wilson had a brother called Harry, whose supposed death two years later is of interest to this narrative.

Michael was in and out of the sickroom, shuffling medicines around and confiscating a bottle of brandy that he gave to Carter for testing. This suggests that brandy was still being given to James, otherwise why hand it over for analysis? I think it was brandy that Edwin used to disguise hotshots of laudanum.

Having discovered nothing untoward in James's bedpan, it seems the physicians had satisfied themselves that Michael was mistaken, and not bothering to look for anything but arsenic, compounded their ignorance by picking up where they had left off. Between 27 April, when 'the London Medicine' arrived, and the expiration of their patient, the two quacks Humphreys and Carter had prescribed everything but motor oil and Vim from under the sink. In fourteen days they poured enough crap into James's gut to kill him, with or without the intercession of Michael and Edwin Maybrick.

Here's the menu: tincture of nux vomica (strychnine), Plummer's Pills (antimony), cascara sagrada, hydrocyanic acid (prussic acid), bromide of potassium, tincture of henbane, Seymour's papaine and iridan, morphia suppository, ipecacuanha (to stop sickness due to the morphia), Valentine's meat juice, Condy's Fluid, Fowler's Solution (arsenic), Brand's beef tea, Sanitas, antipyrine, tincture of jaborandi, chlorine water, bismuth, opium suppository, sulphonal, cocaine, nitro glycerine, phosphoric acid (and brandy and soda, given by Edwin).[84]

Handing Carter the brandy was a bit of a masterstroke. It proved to be unadulterated, so its presence was established as benign. The quacks may have missed Edwin handing out the drinks, but why didn't they suspect any other poison, even something as obvious as strychnine? 'White powders' had been the focus of Florence's anxieties, and she'd discussed them with Humphreys in March. It's notable that he confirmed such a conversation at the magisterial hearings, but said nothing of it at the 'trial'.

Nor was anything said of the will and James's torment at the threshold of death, or about Florence saving his life. In court 'the London Medicine' was redacted in favour of strong tea. Nobody spoke on behalf of this innocent woman, accused by a psychopath and framed by Her Majesty's men in wigs.

On the morning of Saturday, 11 May, the day on which James was to die, Florence poured her desperation into a letter to Dr Hopper. It was he who had effected the reconciliation between herself and James after the Grand National débâcle, and he was one of the few people she felt she could trust. Her text makes it clear that the physician knew everything about her and James's marital strife, including the adulterous liaison with Brierley at Flatman's Hotel.

Dear Doctor Hopper,

I am sure you must have heard of Jim's dangerous illness, and no doubt feel that I ought to have called you in to see him. My misery is great and my position such a painful one that when I tell you that both my brothers-in-law are here and have taken the nursing of Jim and management of my house completely out of my hands, you will understand how powerless I am to assert myself. I am in great need of a friend! Michael, whom Jim informed of the unhappiness existing between us last month, now accuses me as being the primary cause of Jim's present critical state, to which want of proper care from me as regards his nourishment and medical attention may be added. Michael hardly speaks to me. I am neither cheered nor told the worst. I am a mere cypher in my own house, ignored and overlooked. I am too utterly brokenhearted to struggle against myself or anyone else; all I want to do is die, too. I should like to see you – you as a medical attendant. Could you not call as a friend and ask to see me? I have not been to bed since Sunday, for although I may not nurse Jim, I will at least be near to him to see what is done. It is terrible. How shall I bear it? I have no one to turn to, and my husband's brothers are cold hearted and brutal men. Because I have sinned once, must I be misjudged always? Yours distractedly,

F.E. Maybrick.

Although mentioned by Hopper in his deposition at the 'trial', this text wasn't read into the record, and the letter itself disappeared for another forty years. It does nothing to support the veracity of Florence's 8 May letter to Brierley that was supposedly intercepted by Yapp, but rather buries whatever putative credibility that letter ever had. How is it remotely possible for Florence to write that James had told Michael everything in April, and then to write that James 'is perfectly ignorant of everything' in May? 'Because I have sinned once' must have been old news to Hopper, and cannot refer to walking up a racecourse with Brierley, but to the night spent with him in a London hotel.

Every anomaly in the Yapp letter is here explained. I don't believe for a second that that letter was written on 8 May, but on or about 29 March, when 'since my return' makes sense. Florence returned from London on 28 March, and I think she wrote the letter on 29 March, after the Grand National altercation, but that because of the reconciliation engineered by Hopper on the following day, it was never sent. Michael didn't mention it to Humphreys on 8 May, or to Carter on 9 May, when its impact would have enhanced the 'motive' he was trying to sell. He clearly didn't have it yet. I don't think it was found until Briggs & Company searched the house on 11 May, Mrs Briggs squatting to make her incriminating amendments before Michael handed it on to the police.

The substance of this Brierley letter was a vicious compilation, designed to ensnare Mrs Maybrick. Its provenance was faked, its contents were faked, just as the accusation of intent to murder with arsenic out of flypapers was faked. These charges were put up in an English court, not to determine justice – far from it – but to counter a perceived threat to a ruling executive which included Freemasonry and its Boss Apron the Prince of Wales. It was upon these two false charges that the Crown of England sought to put Florence Maybrick to death.

She never got the visit from Hopper. Later that day she fell into a 'mysterious swoon', and was carried into a bedroom by Edwin. A majority of authors, whether for or against her, believe something she had eaten or drunk was spiked with chloral hydrate, and I don't demur from that, but would add that anything in this house with the word 'mystery' attached is a cast-iron euphemism for 'deceit'.

Michael wanted Florence silenced so he and the coppers could get about the task of concocting 'evidence'. The trap had snapped, and she wouldn't get out of it until she was forty-one years old.

I've stayed away from the so-called 'Diary of Jack the Ripper'. I don't need it to make my case, and have purposely avoided it. My view of it remains the same as set out in an earlier chapter: don't try to prove it, see what it might prove. The last few minutes of James Maybrick's life present an opportunity for a brief reappraisal.

The 'Diary' accuses James of being Jack, and reeks of hatred for his whore-wife. At its ridiculous dénouement – its third act, if you like – it claims that she 'knows all' of his homicidal rampage, and asks that she might find the courage to kill him. Like the 'Blucher' letter and the 'Brierley' letter, it is a forgery, and the only question worth asking is, who forged it?

James Maybrick's death gives us a choice of Rippers. The first is a man in ruins, with a gutful of worthless chemicals, gagging at the air while his wife lies unconscious in a mysterious swoon in an adjoining room. She is innocent of poisoning him with flypapers, and ignorant of the wicked charges made against him in this document. She knows nothing of it, and never will.

And then we have a second Ripper, a commanding, handsome man, in total control of this house and everybody in it. He is my candidate, Michael Maybrick, watching his brother die with accusations of 'murderess' against Florence fresh on his lips.

To this we can add another voice, accusing the accuser. I concur with the absconding soldier Robert Reeves that together with his brother Edwin, Michael Maybrick is James Maybrick's murderer. I believe I've presented ancillary evidence in support of the imputation. Reeves said nothing of arsenic, but accused Michael of planning to use a rather different poison. It's an intent shared by somebody who mailed a letter to Scotland Yard claiming to have 'particulars of the Bradford murder', which itself shares calligraphy with that of the Liverpool Document.

My comment on it concludes with a reproduction from one of its pages in parallel with the letter in question. I know nothing of graphology, but that doesn't invalidate a comparison. On top is handwriting from the 'Diary', and below it the letter referencing the murder of Johnnie Gill.

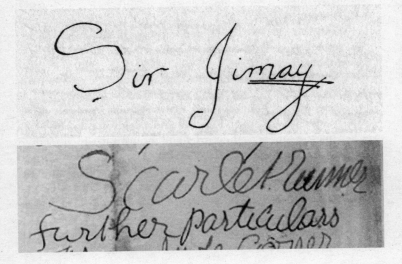

Both texts feature a spontaneous enlargement of the letter 'S'. This might legitimately be argued away as coincidence, but in context I think it cannot. 'I am preparing a draught that will kill & leave no marks,' brags the letter's author, and as far as James is concerned, it didn't. Yapp brought the children in for him to kiss, and he died at 8.40 that evening in a room stuffy with people. His pal George Davidson held him to the last, while Charles Ratcliffe looked on. His brothers Michael, Edwin and Thomas were there, as were Mrs Briggs, Mrs Hughes, Nurse Wilson and the attendant physicians.

It seems the doctors were prepared to nominate gastroenteritis as the cause of death; but Michael wasn't having any of that. 'Now wouldn't that cork you,' wrote Ratcliffe, 'a musical composer instructing a physician how to diagnose his case? Old Dr Humphreys made a jackass of himself. After James died he and Dr Carter expected to make out the death certificate as acute inflammation of the stomach [but] after Humphreys had a conversation with Michael, he refused to make a certificate to that effect, but said there was strong symptoms of arsenical poisoning, though Doctor Carter still insisted that it should be inflammation of the stomach.'[85]

RUSSELL: Had it not been for the suggestion of arsenic, were you prepared to give a certificate of death?
DR HUMPHREYS: Yes.
FITZJAMES STEPHEN: Then if nothing about poisoning had been suggested to you, you would have certified that he died of gastritis, or gastro-enteritis?
DR HUMPHREYS: Yes, my Lord.[86]

'Humphreys was afraid of Michael,' wrote Florence Aunspaugh.[87]

After their friend's death, Ratcliffe and Davidson quit the property, leaving the others to their grief and mourning, which focused on the traditional frenzy of ransacking the house in an attempt to flesh out evidence against the newly-made widow while simultaneously hunting for James's will. It's therefore apparent that the episode with the papers that had caused him so much vocal distress had nothing to do with it.

Florence was forced into brief consciousness. 'Edwin Maybrick was leaning over me,' she recalled many years later:

he had my arms tightly gripped and was shaking me violently. 'I want your keys – do you hear? Where are your keys?' I tried to form a reply, but the words choked me and once more I passed into unconsciousness. Consciousness came and went. During one of these interludes Michael Maybrick entered. 'Nurse,' he said, 'I am going up to London. Mrs Maybrick is no longer mistress of this house. As one of the executors I forbid you to allow her to leave this room. I hold you responsible in my absence.' Towards the night of the same day I said to the Nurse [Wilson], 'I wish to see my children.' She walked up to my bed and in a cold deliberate voice replied, 'You cannot see Master James and Miss Gladys. Mr Michael Maybrick gave orders that they were to leave the house without seeing you.'[88]

She was never to see them again. And no one was allowed to see her. 'My wife and myself called,' wrote Ratcliffe, 'and were told by Mrs Briggs that Mrs Maybrick was too sick to receive any company. Sutton and his wife called, Holloway and his wife, Hienes and his wife, and numerous others. They were all told the same thing. No one could see Mrs Maybrick.'[89]

Still in her dress, with neither food nor drink, Florence was left in her own filth. Although she could not know it, she was already serving the first of the five thousand four hundred and seventy-five days she was to remain in captivity.

On the third day she heard 'a tramp of many feet coming upstairs'. A crowd of men entered, one of them stationing himself at the foot of the bed. He was a policeman by the name of Inspector Isaac Bryning, and he addressed her as follows:

Mrs Maybrick, I am a superintendent of the police, and I am about to say something to you. After I have said what I intend to say, if you reply be careful how you reply because whatever you say may be used in evidence against you. Mrs Maybrick, you are in custody on suspicion of causing the death of your late husband James Maybrick, on the eleventh instant.[90]

She was charged with causing the death of 'Mr Maybrick's brother' – even this junk in subliminal subservience to Michael.

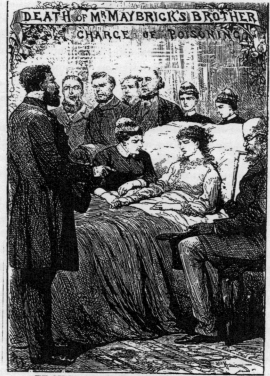

DEATH OF MR MAYBRICK'S BROTHER
A CHARGE OF POISONING

THE OFFICIAL VISIT TO THE WIDOW'S HOUSE, LIVERPOOL.

This foolish illustration appeared in the *Illustrated Police News* of Saturday, 1 June 1889. It depicts Nurse Wilson comforting Florence with a supportive holding of hands. Nothing could have been further from the truth. Wilson was in the league of hags, as treacherous a reptile as the Briggs sisters or Yapp.

While Mrs Maybrick was unconscious her enemies had searched the house, and the police had later searched it with them. From the moment Bryning stepped into Battlecrease House he was told who the perpetrator was, and thereafter investigation fizzled. He thought he had it nailed, and not an eyebrow was raised, nor a question asked of the squad led by the bereaved musician who were hauling arsenic out of wherever they looked and waving it in the air like a prize. Briggs, Hughes, Yapp and the Maybrick brothers (excluding

Thomas, who had left) were allowed free rein by the constabulary to 'find' what they liked and accuse who they liked – and all accused Florence Maybrick.

This was, supposedly, a crime scene, and the coppers stood about it scratching their nuts while 'evidence' was planted and evidence found. Yapp had found a packet of arsenic labelled 'Poison For Cats', and without further ado its owner was determined as the incapacitated widow. This was most unlikely. Florence was a lover of cats, owned three, doting on one which was her constant companion. Why would she want to poison a cat? While searching for keys to the safe (which hopefully contained the will), Briggs discovered a clutch of love letters from Brierley and Edwin,[91] and of course a packet of arsenic. Both became trophies.

The house was suddenly awash with arsenic. Where had it all come from? Any partially-brained copper in Liverpool could have traced it back to the corpse upstairs, and with a little effort, back to Valentine Blake and his gift in respect of ramine. They only needed to ask any one of James's pals at the Cotton Exchange to be told he was an arsenic head. But that wasn't the news they wanted to hear. Instead, they were operating under the instructions of a psychopath, and like a gang of animals destined to become mutton, they accepted every word out of his criminal mouth and arrested Florence.

An honourable Judge, Sir Edward Parry, a world away from the state lackey Fitzjames Stephen, later wrote: 'A very strong point in the prisoner's favour was that the Crown never proved that she had brought any powdered arsenic into the house. Why should she have purchased flypapers to procure an arsenic solution, either for cosmetic or for evil purposes, if she was already possessed of considerable quantities of powdered arsenic?'[92]

Ask Alice Yapp. Or better still, ask the Irish Judas who failed on this crucial point. Parry's comment was written in 1929. In 1926 the then Chief Constable of London gurgled up a bit of twaddle that would seem to discredit it. At the time of the Maybrick frame-up, Sir William Nott-Bower was Boss Cop of Liverpool. He was of the Anderson ilk of police, bedecked in the same helmet and similarly indifferent to truth. The only difference between them was that rather than do his lying in *The Times*, Nott-Bower published his in a book.

Describing it as 'a curious sequel to the case, not, I think hitherto known to the public', Nott-Bower writes that soon after Mrs Maybrick's conviction,

> a highly respectable Liverpool chemist, carrying on business in the centre of town, came to the police and said he wished to make a confession on a subject which he had come to the conclusion he should make known to them.
>
> He went on to say, that in the Spring of 1889, Mrs Maybrick drove up to his shop in a dogcart, and asked him for powdered arsenic to kill cats, and he supplied her with a considerable quantity which she took away with her.
>
> A week or two later she drove again to his shop, and told him she had lost the arsenic she had had from him, and asked for more, and he again supplied her. He was afraid to tell the police of this, as he feared the consequences to himself.
>
> The police subsequently compared the chemist's handwriting with the handwriting on the label – 'Arsenic – Poison For Cats' – upon the box, taken from the trunk belonging to Mrs Maybrick, and found the two handwritings to be identical.

> It afterwards came to my knowledge that the fact of the supply
> of this arsenic by the chemist was known to the *defence* at the time
> of Mrs Maybrick's trial.[93]

That this goon should be in charge of anything beyond a municipal urinal is extraordinary. How could he possibly be Boss Officer of Liverpool's police? His yarn is both fantastic and absurd, self-destructing in the first paragraph by an oxymoron he's too dim to understand. On the one hand he needs his phantom chemist to be 'highly respectable', so as to give credibility to his story; and on the other he tells us the man sold the arsenic outside the law. How respectable is that? Had he actually done it he wouldn't be respectable at all, but in prison.

Nott-Bower says the *defence* (his emphasis) was aware of this purchase of arsenic, which is baffling. Russell and his team falsely claimed to have had the utmost difficulty in finding anyone to attest to James Maybrick's gargantuan arsenic addiction, yet easily discover this chemist before he's reported himself to the police?

He says the chemist gave Florence two lots of arsenic because she had 'lost' the first. Where did she lose it? She's got two young children in the house whom she adores, and she 'loses' a package of deadly poison? She has a husband who scours Liverpool for arsenic – 'I find difficulty in getting it here,' he complained to Valentine Blake – yet she arrives at a random pharmacy and instantly scores? If such an obliging chemist had existed in the middle of Liverpool, James would have discovered it years before Florence turned up 'in a dogcart'. James was a junkie, on an eternal prowl for arsenic. In his zoo of medicine bottles the names of *twenty-seven* different pharmacies appear, and this idiot copper expects his readers to believe that he missed this one 'in the centre of town'?

Nott-Bower's tale is horseshit, every half-witted word of it, and the whole thing was later revealed as a scandalous invention. It seems a majority of the Victorian constabulary were good for nothing but lying. They were a kind of tea-brewing Cosa Nostra, as corrupt as anything in the slums of Naples. Its masters were degenerates like Charlie Warren, Robert Anderson, and that lamentable little moron running Bradford, James Withers. It was men like these, in association with a psychopath, who sacrificed Florence Maybrick's life.

Michael Maybrick's refusal of a death certificate led to an autopsy two days later in James's own bedroom. Drs Carter and Humphreys performed it under the guidance of Dr Alexander Barron, a professor of pathology at the Royal Infirmary. They removed various organs for analysis, *and no arsenic was found.*

Despite this negative outcome further inquisition was initiated, comprising of two magisterial hearings and the sitting of a coroner's court. 'The enquiry was opened by Mr Samuel Brighouse, the coroner of South West Lancashire,' reported the *Liverpool Mercury*, 'yesterday morning [14 May] at the Aigburth Hotel. The only witness was Mr Michael Maybrick of London, a brother of the deceased.'

We've become accustomed to the expedient of lying out of the mouths of coroners, and this one doesn't disappoint. Mr (later Sir) Samuel Brighouse and his acolytes were right off the pages of Swift. Brighouse hauled in a jury and told them: 'The result of the post mortem examination was that poison was found in the stomach of the deceased in sufficient quantity to justify further examination.' This was a lie, or as Macdougall put it, it is 'a matter for strong observation that this statement was a false one'.[94] *No poison* had been found in the stomach of the deceased.

'The appearances of the post mortem,' deposed Humphreys, 'were consistent with congestion of the stomach, not necessarily caused by an irritant poison.'[95] It was a prognosis supported by Carter and Barron. 'An irritant poison might be bad food or bad wine, or an indiscreet dinner,' said Barron; 'it might be bad tinned meat, bad fish, mussels, or bad food of any kind.'[96]

What it definitely *wasn't* was arsenic from flypapers. So, Robert Reeves aside, we're left with the rest. Was Florence discovered by Michael Maybrick stuffing corned beef into a medicine bottle, or known to have marinated putrid mussels? There *was* no arsenic, there wasn't even any rotten meat. A coroner's business was to determine cause of death, and now he had it, and Florence should have been free of all accusation that very day.

But that wasn't the business Michael and the bewigged minions were into. Following an adjournment, an extraordinary conversation ensued between Brighouse and the foreman of the jury. His name was Dalgleish, a Freemason and a close associate of James, and he had a statement to make. He said that, just prior to the

Wirral races, 'he had met James Maybrick, of whom he was a personal friend, in the train, and had seen him take a powder out of his waistcoat pocket and take it, and that he'd asked him what he was taking, and that he replied strychnine'.[97] Our noble coroner didn't want to hear anything about it, and summarily dismissed Dalgleish as foreman. It was a hooligan suppression of evidence. Had Russell known of this deposition, it would obviously have been of more than casual interest to the defence. It was another wide-open door for Florence Maybrick.

Russell *did* know of it, but like this whelp of a coroner, kept his trap shut. 'Not one word about this appears on the depositions,' writes Macdougall, 'nor was a word said about it either before the magistrates or the jury.'[98] On resumption of the inquest on 5 June, Russell's junior, Mr (later Sir) William Pickford, had got wind of Dalgleish's statement and interposed:

> PICKFORD: I understand a communication was made to you, Mr Coroner, on the first sitting by a gentleman, originally sworn in as Foreman of the Jury, and I should like to know whether it is proposed to call him.
> BRIGHOUSE: No.
> PICKFORD: I understand it was something so important that the gentleman thought he ought not to sit upon the jury? But should rather appear as a witness for the defence?
> BRIGHOUSE: I feel certain it is not relevant. The Foreman went to view the body, and then made a statement. I communicated it to Mr Steel, as acting for the relatives, and to Superintendent Bryning, and I said: 'If you think this statement is useful to you, and that it is evidence, and that the Foreman ought to appear as a witness, then I will discharge him.' They both thought it would be a better course to discharge him, and I did so.

Such incendiary evidence wasn't 'useful' to them at all. As Macdougall makes clear, 'Mr Dalgleish's statement that the man was physicking himself with strychnine immediately before his illness was, of course, not likely to be useful to the police or to Michael Maybrick.'[99]

They all concluded that a man self-dosing with deadly poison in a capital case of murder by poisoning was 'not relevant', as Mr

Brighouse so daintily put it. Needless to say, Dalgleish never appeared as a witness. Meantime, Pickford was still flapping about to try to discover what it was he'd said.

> PICKFORD: I rather gathered it had been a statement favourable to my client, Mrs. Maybrick, or contrary to the theory set up against her? Do you say it was a matter which you would not allow to go before the jury?
> BRIGHOUSE: I ought not to tell the jury. The gentleman [Dalgleish] called upon Mr Cleaver and gave his statement, and therefore it rests with Mr Cleaver or Mr Bryning to call him.

This was bullshit of a high order. The law required the coroner to examine 'all witnesses without distinction'.[100]

Notwithstanding that, we know who Bryning was, but who's this geezer Cleaver, and what might be his interest in hearing a statement so favourable to Mrs Maybrick? Well, actually not a lot, other than that he'd been appointed, or rather imposed, as the solicitor for her defence. When the horror bloomed, Florence had cabled her legal representatives in New York – at least she thought she had. The communication was intercepted by Michael, and held back until he could get his own man in. From the get-go it's apparent that Arnold Cleaver was 'in the loop', a member of a cabal Bro William Pickford was poised to join.

> PICKFORD: I understand it was a statement as to the cause of illness made to this gentleman, but whether it would be evidence as to the cause of death, I don't know. I confess I've not the knowledge you have as to what is evidence at investigations of this kind.
> BRIGHOUSE: I have ruled against it.
> PICKFORD: I say no more about it, if you do not think it right to go before the jury.

Someone was tugging hard at Brighouse's strings, and Pickford was in process of having his attached.[101] 'The coroner took it upon himself,' writes Macdougall, 'to keep this statement from the coroner's jury, because if it had been put before them, it is a fair presumption that they would not have exposed Mrs Maybrick to the expense and to the risk of trial. This incident illustrates the way in which these proceedings were conducted, and points to the conclusion that the provisions of our Law for the protection of persons against False Accusations were not observed by Mrs Maybrick's accusers, or by the officers of the Law, by whom these criminal proceedings were set in motion and administered.'

Brighouse took it upon himself to issue a verdict before the accused had got anywhere near a court. On 8 June he signed a death certificate for the already interred James. As in the bent certificate naming William Barrit as Johnnie Gill's murderer, Florence Maybrick was now officially the murderer of James Maybrick. Brighouse couldn't nominate arsenic as the offending substance, so we must suppose she offed him with a dose of meat.

CERTIFIED COPY OF AN ENTRY OF DEATH

GIVEN AT THE GENERAL REGISTER OFFICE

Application Number R000 250

	REGISTRATION DISTRICT	West Derby						
1889	DEATH in the Sub-district of	Wavertree		in the	County of Lancaster			

Columns:-	1	2	3	4	5	6	7	8	9
No.	When and where died	Name and surname	Sex	Age	Occupation	Cause of death	Signature, description and residence of informant	When registered	Signature of registrar
404	Eleventh May 1889 Battlecrease House Riversdale Road Aigburth	James Maybrick	Male	49 years	Cotton Merchant	Irritant poison administered to him by Florence Elizabeth Maybrick Wilful murder	[signature] Samuel his house Coroner for Liverpool Inquest held 28th June 1889	Eighth June 1889	James Mascie Registrar

Under 'Cause of death' this corrupt document says: 'Irritant poison administered to him by Florence Elizabeth Maybrick. Wilful murder.'

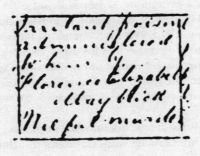

681

Were it not for the compromised sanctums in which these accusers and swearers of Queen Victoria's England grovelled for the Crown, such a monstrosity could never have got into a court.

Michael Maybrick was well aware of what any honest lawyer in America would make of it. On 3 June the *Liverpool Daily Post* had this: 'Considerable speculation was caused in the city by the telegram published from New York, to the effect that proof will be forthcoming of the deceased gentleman having been in the habit of taking arsenic in large quantities.' This was followed shortly after by an intercession from Florence's lawyer, Alfred Row of Manhattan. He made a statement to the press, reported in the *New York Herald* just before commencement of the 'trial': 'We have no doubt that she will be acquitted as the evidence against her amounts to almost nothing. Maybrick had been addicted to the use of arsenic for a number of years, and the evidence on which the prosecution is based is not worth a puff.'[102]

Further witnesses to James Maybrick's nasty habits came forward in the United States, including Edward Nacy, a past employee, and Archie Church, a former valet, both prepared to testify to his ravenous consumption of arsenic. It's clear as day that many in America knew of his addiction, and curious it is that Russell couldn't replicate such deposition in Liverpool. Neither he nor Cleaver could find anyone to attest to it, even when it came knocking on the fucking door.

If suppressing Dalgleish was an outrage, the same word might do for Morden Rigg. It will be remembered that it was he and his wife who had met James at the Wirral races, when he was deep into an O/D from 'the London Medicine'. Rigg recognised this as a potentially important contribution to Mrs Maybrick's defence, and like Dalgleish gave a statement to her solicitor: 'I knew Mr James Maybrick well. My general impression of him was that he was a man with a tendency to talk about his ailments, or fancied ailments, and to take various supposed specifics for them. I saw him on the course [on 27 April]. He turned round to my wife's carriage and told her he had taken an overdose of <u>strychnine</u> that morning and that his limbs were quite rigid. She is prepared to testify to this if necessary.'[103]

This went to Russell, and not another word was ever heard of it. Thus we have three crucial witnesses denied – Dalgleish and the

Riggs – any one of whom would have seen Michael's flypapers laughed out of Liverpool. But they were never called, and nor was anyone like them. Russell had 'reserved the defence', meaning everyone was ignorant of it. He proclaimed this as a strategy in his client's favour, when in reality it was a treachery on behalf of the prosecution. He knew that to ensnare Florence he had to avoid Maybrick's various addictions, and that if witnesses to arsenic-taking were advertised for, half of the Cotton Exchange would have been in stampede to the court.

Back at Battlecrease, Florence was allowed to speak to no one, and no one spoke to her but in insolence. Yapp was heard to say that she'd do anything to 'prevent the mistress from having her children back'. In despair, Florence turned to Briggs, an enemy who shared a mask of friendship with the Irish Judas. As she was later to admit in court, it was 'in sarcasm' that she suggested Florence should write to Brierley for help:

> I am writing to you to give me every assistance in your power in my present fearful trouble. I am in custody, without any of my family with me, and without money. I have cabled to my solicitor in New York to come here at once. In the meantime send some money for present needs. The truth is known about my visit to London. Your last letter is at present in the hands of the police. Appearances may be against me, but before God I swear I am innocent! Florence E. Maybrick.[104]

Like the cable, the letter went straight to the police. A quartet of helmets and nurses Gore and Wilson were on around-the-clock guard duty. It was into this environment that Florence's mother Baroness von Roques was hastening. Michael had sent a telegram to Paris: 'Florie ill and in awful trouble. Do not delay.' It was he who had delayed, not troubling to inform her of the situation until James was under the granite. By chance the Baroness had run into Michael at Lime Street station, on his way to London. 'Florie is very ill,' he said. 'Edwin will tell you every thing. It is a case of murder, and there is a man in the case.' She'd heard from Florence by telegram that 'James passed away on Saturday,' but what was this of murder? Plunged into the trauma of it all, she took a cab to Battlecrease, a residence she'd never visited before.[105]

In the vestibule Edwin gave her a lowdown on the Brierley letter and the manufactured intrigue that came with it. 'The police are in the house,' he said, a presence that was already evident. Hurrying upstairs, she passed two coppers outside the bedroom door, and on entry her reception was as hard as stone. Her first instinct was to embrace her still prostrate child, but Nurse Wilson interposed. The Baroness ignored her, and spoke to her daughter in French. 'You must speak only in English,' commanded one of the helmets. 'I must warn you Madam, I shall write down what you say,' and he proffered his paper and pencil to prove it.[106]

Later that evening, Florence had 'a violent fit of hysteria and crying'. Her mother rushed back into the room. 'Four policemen and the two nurses were holding her down on the bed. The men had hold of her bared arms and legs,' wrote the Baroness, 'and I was outraged. I pulled the fat nurse [Wilson] away, and ordered the men out, and said, "If you will let me hold her hand and speak to her, she will be calm."' The fat nurse was very insolent, and said 'she would put me out if I did not take care, she was in charge and should act as she thought best'. There was no way of having any private conversation with her daughter that night, nor the morning after: 'The police and nurses were listening, and they all had paper and pencil, and were always rapidly taking notes of heaven knows what, and whispering together.'[107]

Although the Baroness didn't realise it, it was her presence that freaked the authorities out. They were paranoid that Florence should have any external communication, that she might say something or hear something that could spring her from captivity. Now James was dead they were fearful she might squawk the 'secret' that she knew nothing of, but that traumatised them all. Keeping her mouth shut was what the intimidation was all about, and they decided to move her from the house immediately.

I do not say of course that the nurses or helmets were aware of 'the secret', but there were others who certainly were. Midway through that Saturday morning, following von Roques' arrival, thirteen men were milling about inside Battlecrease House. They included Florence's solicitors, Richard and Arnold Cleaver, who prior to their entry had held a brisk discussion outside with a magistrate called Colonel Bidwell, his clerk Mr Swift and Superintendent Bryning. Once in agreement, the conclave tramped upstairs into

Mrs Maybrick's bedroom. It was apparent to her mother that they were going to take Florence away, and she begged Bidwell for an opportunity to say goodbye. He refused, and instead initiated an impromptu court in the bedroom.

Bryning was back at the end of the bed. 'This person is Mrs Maybrick,' he said, 'wife of the late James Maybrick. She is charged with having caused his death by administering poison to him. I understand her consent is given to a remand, and therefore I need not introduce any evidence.' What did he mean, 'her consent'? Other than the slanders whispered by Bro Michael Maybrick, there was no 'evidence' against her. 'You asked for a remand of eight days?' enquired Bro Swift. 'Yes, that is so,' affirmed Superintendent Bryning.

> CLEAVER: I appear for the prisoner, and consent to a remand.
> BIDWELL: Very well. That is all.[108]

Her mother watched from an upstairs window as, too sick (or drugged) to walk, Florence was carried out of the house in a chair. Accompanied by Humphreys, Bryning and a nurse, she was put in a carriage and was on her way to prison.

The Baroness heard the twist of a key: someone had locked her in. It was probably Edwin, and the symbolism of the act was apposite. From that moment on her daughter would never again be allowed to speak openly to anyone but her jailers, her aberration of a solicitor, and the Irish Bastard betraying her.[109]

On the following day the Baroness was asked to leave, and a few days later Michael slammed the door on the lot of them. Retaining only Grant the gardener as caretaker, he dismissed the entire staff. Even Yapp was out, and Battlecrease was his. Over the following weeks he kept up the pressure, dissembling through magisterial hearings and manipulating the authorities to his will. His sister-in-law remained hermetically sealed in Walton Jail, represented by nothing but Russell's silence. At the 'trial' he was to call her 'this friendless lady', and Michael aside, he was first amongst her enemies.

Florence wanted the proceedings moved to London, and it was Russell who denied this. Years later she wrote: 'It was a mockery of justice to hold such a trial in such a place as Liverpool. The excitement ran so high that the Liverpool crowds even hissed me as I was driven through the streets.'[110] She wanted her mother to speak in her defence, but Russell denied that too, refusing to allow the Baroness anywhere near the witness box, or even to sit in the court. He knew only too well that she was a major threat to the frame-up, able to confirm the soaking of flypapers as the precursor to a common cosmetic, and more dangerous still, testify to James's habitual use of arsenic when he wasn't out of it on strychnine.

Baroness von Roques was locked out just as her daughter was locked in. So anxious were her accusers to enforce the isolation, they descended to trickery. The whole affair became like one of those old-fashioned roller towels in a municipal toilet: it went round and round, more soiled with every hand that touched it.

Coroner Brighouse was not only adept at lying, he proved his competence in deception. On 28 May he opened his inquest at the Wellington Rooms in the Liverpool suburb of Garston. The dirty-hands were naturally concerned about press interest, so the press were tricked *en masse*. On 29 May the *Liverpool Citizen* published an enraged complaint from one of the journalists who had been subjected to it:

THE MAYBRICK SCANDAL
A Pressman's Protest

That was a clever dodge of which the local Press representatives were the victims on Monday morning. It was a triumph of legal subtlety and police craft of which both Swift and Superintendent Bryning have every reason to be proud. From the very first discovery of the Maybrick cause celebre, all the ingenuity of the county coroner, county police, and county magistrates' clerks has been employed to prevent the press from obtaining the slightest information of the affair. The initial enquiry before Mr Coroner Brighouse was conducted in *private*, and strict injunctions having been issued that under no circumstances were the newspapers to be told the result.

It was another put-up job, like Bradford. Though his report is rather lengthy, it's worth hearing this journalist out:

The reporters had positively to organise a kind of secret detective service to fight this conspiracy of silence. The same tactics were brought into play at the County Police Court yesterday. The business of trying prisoners in this temple of 'county justice', always commences at eleven o'clock, and having taken their places, the reporters settled down to await the calling of Mrs Maybrick's case. But while they were thus waiting the advent of justice, the magistrate and his *swift* clerk were actually on their way to Walton Jail for the purpose of remanding the accused in secret. The learned 'beak' and his legal advisor, together with the astute Bryning and the irreproachable [Arnold] Cleaver, stole off to the prison, leaving the hoodwinked stenographers in ignorance of this remarkable skedaddle. It will scarcely be credited that the dispensers of justice should have deliberately given the slip to the public's representatives in this absurdly undignified and preposterously stupid manner. On learning that the trick had been played on them, one Pressman took a hansom to the jail but arrived too late. Mrs Maybrick had been tried clandestinely within the gloomy walls of the Walton Bastille, and the newspapers were again baffled by the agents of law.[111]

'The principle of trying a prisoner,' concludes the article, '(accused of the most terrible crime known to law), with the secrecy of the Inquisition is repugnant to modern ideas. Somehow people don't place much confidence in justice which hides its, head, throwing a black veil over its tribunal.'[112]

Michael Maybrick and his friends had been busy. On the same day, Brighouse suspended his inquest so that James's corpse could be exhumed. In my view this was just a bit of low theatre, designed to further titillate the public mind. Either way, the press made the most of whatever they could get, inventing a 'family vault' to fit the occasion. In reality there was no vault and no family skeletons, simply James's parents' names on a modest headstone.

The scene of the exhumation was one of the most ghastly that can be imagined. The body had been interred in a family vault not far from the catacombs, and covered with a large flat stone now much discoloured with age. Beneath this were two heavy flag-stones, and below the whitewashed brick vault, which contained not only the remains of the late Mr James Maybrick but also those of his mother and father.[113]

The account continues via 'the sickly glow of naphtha lamps', complemented with the steady rhythm of gravediggers' shovels. Why midnight should have been chosen to dig him out isn't explored, but Drs Barron, Humphreys, Hopper and Carter, plus a couple of police inspectors, were at the ready.

'There was scarcely anyone present who did not feel an involuntary shudder as the pale worn features of the dead appeared in the flickering rays of a lamp held over the coffin by one of the medical men.' Maybrick apparently looked rather healthy, and this was the topic of much remark. 'As the dissecting knife of Dr Barron pursued its rapid and skilful work there was, however, whenever a slight breath of wind blew, an odour of corruption.' Barron removed the lungs, heart, kidneys, and part of the thigh bone. 'Coming to the head, he cut out the tongue, and, opening the skull, removed one half of the brain. Whilst the dissection was going on those present discussed the evidence given at the inquest in the earlier part of the day.'[114]

During the inquest the matter of the will had arisen, Brighouse acquiescing to Michael's request to keep its contents secret. Before Florence had ever been found guilty of anything, Michael had registered the will in London. On 29 July 1889 he became master of everything she had ever owned.

While Florence was in Walton Prison, listening to the sounds of a gallows being erected, a reporter asked Michael, 'Did you think during the trial that she would be convicted?' 'No I did not,' he replied. 'I said to my brother [Edwin] after the case was closed that I believed she would be acquitted,'[115] which is presumably why he had auctioned off all her furniture and effects, and rented Battlecrease House to a man named Rogers.[116]

Were Messrs Cleaver and Russell worthy of their profession, they would never have allowed this. Coupled with the dramatics of the exhumation, emptying the house was psychologically disastrous in terms of the public perception of their client. If her own brother-in-law thought she was never going home, why should anyone else?

'The truth is,' Michael continued, 'I thought that no one connected with the case tried very hard to have Mrs Maybrick convicted. I know I tried my best to have the physician give a death certificate that would have prevented the trial entirely, but he refused to do so, and when the trial came I assure you I was a most unwilling witness.'[117]

One of the more egregious talents of the psychopath is this facility to lie. But so misconstructed was Michael Maybrick's ego, he finished with a statement that was breathtaking, even out of him: 'As for my scheming with Mrs Briggs and Miss Yapp against her, that is all nonsense. Why, after my brother's death, Mrs Maybrick thanked me for being so kind to her.'

She had just lost her husband, her children, her home and her liberty, and while lying incapacitated in her own shit, she looked up at the kindly Michael and 'thanked' him.[118]

By now the results from the graveyard were in. A Crown Analyst at Guy's Hospital in London, by the name of Dr Stephenson, had found minuscule amounts of arsenic in Maybrick's viscera. This isn't surprising, because Humphreys was giving him Fowler's Solution. To kill the average human at least two grains are required, and in James Maybrick's case you could safely double that. Negligible traces were found in the intestines and liver. Although barely enough to bother a rat (and a dose Maybrick wouldn't even have noticed), this would do nicely. They weren't actually concerned with quantity, it was the *word* they were looking for, and now they had it, and the press howled 'ARSENIC'.

Florence Maybrick was put on trial for fifteen 1,000th parts of a grain.

19

Victorian Values

He who holds the ladder is as guilty as the thief.

Traditional

At about ten in the morning of 31 July 1889, a pair of sheriff's heralds announced the arrival in court of Judge Fitzjames Stephen with a blare of trumpets, and the frame-up known as Regina vs. Mrs Maybrick was officially in progress.

Stephen took his Right Honourable seat on the bench accompanied by the High Sheriff, Mr Royds, various church officials, and the Earl of Sefton. Other than owning 23,000 acres in the vicinity (which may have qualified him for something or other), I can discover no explanation for Sefton's presence. Next on the bill was the court chaplain, anointing proceedings with Christian prayer. He was followed by Clerk to the Assizes, Bro Thomas Shuttleworth (Grand Steward to the Earl of Lathom's Liverpool Lodge 2229, thus sharing his Grand Master with Bro Michael Maybrick in London's St George's 42).

Shuttleworth addressed himself to the Chief Warder of Walton Jail, ordering him to 'Put up Florence Maybrick,' and she was duly brought up into the dock from a subterranean cell. Flanked by a male and a female warder, Florence was dressed in the black crêpe of a widow's weeds, black gloves, black bonnet and a transparent black mourning veil.

The court was airless and crowded, with many society ladies peering through opera glasses, and thousands more milled in the streets outside. There had been a vigorous black market in tickets, some paying a week's wages to get in. 'There have only been two celebrated trials in Liverpool in the last quarter of a century,' wrote the *Daily Post*, 'that have attracted anything like so much interest.'

The bewigged Freemason, a counterpart to Bro McGowan at Bradford, read out the indictment for murder and asked, 'How plead you?' Mrs Maybrick replied with one of the few truths to be heard in this place that day: 'Not guilty.'

The guilty wore the wigs. By that I mean there wasn't a man under one of them whose sole and primary interest was anything other than the protection of the elite they represented. Jack the Ripper was a stick of dynamite right up its arse, and thus justice didn't come into it. From the get-go it was apparent that Bro Russell was not only complicit on behalf of the prosecution, but actually the conductor of it.[1] Under any other circumstances this Houdini of the court-room would have had his client out of there in time for lunch. But these weren't any other circumstances, and it's surely a testament to his litigatory skills that he could 'pretend a defence' and pull off such a conjuring trick so publicly. The charge of murder by means of arsenic culled from flypapers was ridiculous. It was, as Russell said himself, 'rotten'. To defend it was a pushover – he could have phoned it in, but instead, by criminal dishonour, he contrived to lose it.

Addison was responsible for the first onslaught of lying. Clutching a wad of got-up rubbish, he stood to enunciate the prosecution's case. 'May it please your Lordship,' he intoned: 'Gentlemen of the Jury, it is my duty, in conjunction with my learned friends, to lay before you evidence in support of the indictment you have just heard read. Each and every one of you know that the charge against the prisoner at the bar is that she murdered her husband by admin-istering him doses of arsenic, and it would be idle in me to suppose that each and every one of you do not know some of the circum-stances of the case, either by means of the press or in other ways, and that probably you have discussed the matter, but I know equally well that ...'

It was here that Russell made the first of his many interventions. Less than a minute in, and 'Fat Jack'[2] had already strayed into hazardous territory. According to H.B. Irving's transcript of the trial, 'Sir Charles Russell leaned across and whispered to Mr Addison, who, nodding assent, said, "It has been suggested to me, and probably it is right, that, except the scientific witnesses, all the witnesses be requested to leave the court." The witnesses [and jury] then withdrew,' says Irving. This incidentally didn't include the scientific witnesses, because they were not yet in court. Out they all trooped, 'with the exception of Michael Maybrick who was allowed to remain'.[3]

Now, I don't know much about the protocols of Victorian courts, but is it not extraordinary that Mrs Maybrick's principal accuser should stay in his seat while confidential legalities were debated? What did it have to do with Michael Maybrick, and where were the principal witnesses for the defence? The latter part of the question has an easy answer: there weren't any. All dangerous voices – like that of Baroness von Roques, by way of example – had been kept out.

A huddle formed, and the whispering began. So what was it that these men in robes and Michael Maybrick secretly discussed? Irving skips over it, and gives no clue, and you can scour the Liverpool press without an answer. Whatever was debated *at Sir Charles Russell's request* was intended to stay unheard forever.

However, there's always a caveat, enshrined in my favourite ditty: 'No action whether foul or fair, is ever done but it leaves somewhere a record.' In this instance the honour falls to an American newspaper, published a day later in New York: 'The most important thing during the day,' it reported, 'was the production of the long rambling letter which Mr James Maybrick wrote to his brother Michael, on the 29th of April last, just eleven days before he [James] died.'[4]

What these bastards were discussing was the 'Blucher' letter, and it was *on behalf of the prosecution* that Russell caused it to be suppressed. He got a red light when Addison blundered into recent press reports in which a redacted version of the letter had appeared. Its full contents would of course have summarily destroyed the prosecution's case. Here was a man, supposedly murdered with incremental doses of arsenic, admitting that he was killing himself with doses of strychnine: 'The Doctor finally came again but could not make it indigestion this time and the conclusion he came to was the Nuxvomica [strychnine] I had been taking. Doctor Fuller had poisoned me as all the symptoms warranted such a conclusion.'

Far from his wife being the perpetrator, the deceased was accusing nux vomica, abetted by Michael Maybrick's London physician. This letter was the invoice to Mrs Maybrick's innocence, and could have paid for her liberty there and then. Michael had forged it as a cover for 'the London Medicine', and now it had come back with the potential to bite them right in their lousy arses. Russell should have waved it in Addison's face, but by suppressing it he became no less treacherous than Yapp.

Excerpts from the 'Blucher' letter had twice been published in the Liverpool press, timed on both occasions to inflict maximum damage on Florence. Its first outing in the *Liverpool Courier* of 3 June preceded the decision to prosecute at the coroner's inquest, and it appeared again in the *Liverpool Daily Post* on 31 July, coinciding with the opening day of Mrs Maybrick's 'trial'. The publication of 'Dear Blucher' on that day couldn't have been more damaging to Florence Maybrick. It was a redacted version, with references to strychnine and 'Doctor Fuller had poisoned me' edited out. The text of the original, which was presently in Russell's hand, would have set Florence free; the text as published condemned her.

ALLEGED REMARKABLE LETTER OF THE DECEASED

We have it on the authority of a gentleman who affirms that he saw the document that, prior to his visit to London in April last, the late Mr James Maybrick wrote to his brother, Michael, a letter, which in view of the present circumstances is extraordinary.[5]

Never mind that it was *post* his London visit and consultation with Fuller, the 'gentleman' in question can have been none other than Michael Maybrick, and this posed a dilemma for Russell. He needed to keep the jurors' minds well away from questions raised by the press, not least of which was who caused the 'Blucher' letter to be published? On 28 May Michael had given evidence before the coroner, and said absolutely nothing about it.

I'm not a Victorian barrister, but Alexander Macdougall was, and according to him the withholding of this letter from a coroner's jury was an act of 'criminal suppression'.[6] If it was an act of 'criminal suppression' before a coroner's jury, it had now become an act of 'criminal conspiracy' amongst the brigands in this court.

Not even Macdougall knew that this letter had also been withheld at the trial, but we know that the *full text* was the subject of debate, because it was copied simultaneously by Bro Swift and found its way into the Home Office files (HO 144/1639/A50678).

The craftily pruned article of 31 July continues:

He states that on returning home he was seized with a rigidity of the limbs and a general feeling of sickness which quite prostrated him. Proceeding to comment on the inability of the doctors to diagnose his complaint, he goes on to bitterly deplore their confusion of ideas, and to express an emphatic opinion that, 'this time Dr — cannot say that I am suffering from a violent attack of indigestion'. Towards the end of the epistle he again reverts to the strange malady which affects him, and adds that the medical men will perhaps be able to tell what is the matter with him when, for the benefit of future generations they have examined his remains.

'Every Juryman who took his seat that morning,' writes Macdougall, 'may be taken as having read this scandalous paragraph.'[7] Without the references to nux vomica and Dr Fuller, it reads as Michael intended it to read, i.e. that someone was poisoning his brother, and it was the woman standing in the dock.

The function of any judge is to appear for the Crown, and Fitzjames Stephen couldn't have done it better. Following this judicial interlude with Russell and his pal Michael Maybrick, the jury and the rest of the spectators were allowed to resume their seats.

À propos of that, and although I dislike the expression, what happened next beggars belief. Having just discussed James Maybrick's self-administered dose of *strychnine* on 27 April, and his conviction that *Dr Fuller was poisoning him with the London Medicine*, Addison was back on his feet, primed to reanimate his charlatan accusations: 'It was on the 27th of April that the first illness occurred, which we say was caused by arsenic. The illness he had that day was attributed to an overdose of medicine, but the doctor will tell you there was nothing put in the medicine to make him ill at all, but arsenic was later found in the medicine.'

This was a fiction, and Russell squatted there like the scoundrel he was and listened to it. *No arsenic* was found in 'the London Medicine', because Florence threw what was left of it down the drain and thereafter trashed the bottle. 'The next day was Sunday the 28th of April, at that time he was undoubtedly very ill, and the consequence was that Doctor Humphreys was seen, and he will tell you that Mrs Maybrick told him she attributed the illness to some bad brandy which her husband had at the races.'[8]

She said no such thing. And it was most certainly nothing to do with what he had at the races. It was pre the races, and it was Alice Yapp who converted the strychnine into brandy. What Florence said was that she believed it was the 'white powders' James was taking that might contain strychnine. Humphreys acknowledged this at the magisterial hearings, but by the time of the 'trial' he had quite forgotten it.

What Addison was doing, and Russell allowed him to do, was to artfully conflate Fuller's prescriptions, made up at Clay & Abrahams pharmacy on 24 April, with 'the London Medicine' that arrived by post at Battlecrease on 26 April.

On 1 August, the second day of the 'trial', Dr Fuller travelled up from London to appear in the witness box. His evidence is salutary, presenting the Irish Judas (should he remotely have cared for it) with yet another glaring opportunity to win his case. 'These prescriptions,' deposed Fuller, producing them, 'are the ones I prescribed on the 14th of April for him. The one is an aperient, and the other a tonic, with liver pills.' On the following weekend he saw James again: 'The dyspeptic symptoms of which he complained had partially disappeared. I therefore slightly altered the prescription and wrote another. None of the three prescriptions contained arsenic in any shape or form.'[9]

Because 'the London Medicine' and the 'Blucher' letter had been kept secret from both him and the jury, Fuller could have had no idea of the murderous brew (now ascribed to him) subsequently winging its way via the mails. Poisoning James was nothing to do with him, but get ready for this: 'Deceased told me he had been taking a pill which he said I had prescribed for his brother. This however was not the case. *I had not prescribed it.*'[10]

Had you not?

This was *a trial for murder*, with a potential rope at the end of it. It was a case of premeditated poisoning, and Florence Maybrick's defence counsel had just heard that Michael Maybrick was giving his brother 'pills' that he mendaciously claimed were prescribed for him by Dr Fuller. A chimp in a wig would have leapt on it. Any barrister worth the name would have put Michael Maybrick into the witness box post haste, demanding to know what these 'pills' were, why he had lied about them, and why he had attributed them to Dr Fuller. Instead, without the merest enquiry, Russell said, 'He told you he had been taking some pills you had prescribed for his brother,' and without waiting for an answer, cunningly buried that statement under another question, 'and you understand him to say that was the only medicine he had recently been taking?'

'Yes,' said Fuller, falling right into it, and from now on these unexplained 'pills' (and 'the London Medicine') went into the casual vernacular of the trial as 'Dr Fuller's Medicine'.

Had Russell wished to pursue these mysterious 'pills' (which of course he did not), he would have needed to look no further than a recent Liverpool newspaper. On 25 May the *Liverpool Weekly Post* had had this: 'Some weeks ago he [James] went up to London to consult a leading physician as to his ailments, and this gentleman, in addition to some other medicine, prescribed for him certain pills. Mr Maybrick took them (doubling the dose), and told a friend he had felt much worse for it. He made a second visit to London and on this occasion the physician told him he had done wrong because the pills consisted largely of strychnine. This story Mr Maybrick told to one or two of his friends on the Cotton Exchange, and doubtless led to the suggestion that he had overdosed himself with other dangerous medicines.'[11]

Here was another document Russell could have waved in the prosecution's face. His entire case could have been argued from the text of this one newspaper article. It was dangerous stuff, hence his intervention at Addison's clumsy mention of the press: 'The statement that Mr Maybrick was in the habit of taking medicine in which active poisons were an ingredient is confirmed by the opinions of other friends ... these confident statements as to the nature of the medicines taken by him point to the probability that the serious charge brought against Mrs Maybrick may be totally unfounded.'[12]

Unfounded they certainly were, but such reports raised questions that the court could well do without. Several of them spring easily to mind. Where were 'these men from the Exchange', and why didn't Russell produce them as witnesses? Why were not these 'friends' brought into court to make their confident statements? Where were the witnesses who could speak to the 'pills' that had made James ill (a precursor of the London hotshot, similarly raw with strychnine), which had been given to him under false pretences by his brother Michael Maybrick?

The defence didn't need Robert Reeves's statement. No eavesdropping required – it was said openly by Fuller, and confirmed in
a fucking newspaper.

What else do we need to know about the treachery of this
Hibernian pimp, Russell? He laboured to keep up a mask of
'defence', a running charade of advocacy. As a cover for James's use
of arsenic he managed to find a couple of irrelevancies in Virginia,
USA, both of whom acknowledged that about a decade ago he had
been known occasionally to take arsenic for medicinal purposes.
Apparently he took it for malarial fever, but beyond that the slate
was clean. One of these Americans, a Mr Thomas Stansell, had been
James's servant, and was black. 'His ebony skin and woolly head,'
commented the *Liverpool Review*, 'conjured up a host of recollections in one's mind. One thought of distant cotton-plantations, of
piccaninnies, of the hunted slave and the planter's whip.' And it was
precisely for these recollections that Russell had hauled him in.
Liverpool had prospered from shipping this kind of cargo, and
Russell wasn't averse to exploiting the city's shadow of prejudice.
Addison couldn't even bring himself to call Stansell by name, referring to him as 'the black man'. Whatever he had to say about his
master's former arsenic habits was regarded as little more than the
comic performance of a nigger minstrel. He said, 'Iss sar' for 'Yes
sir,' and all that was missing was a banjo.

Is it not remarkable that Russell could find such a witness on the
other side of the Atlantic, yet was incapable of accessing crucial
witnesses less than a mile away? The Cotton Exchange was crawling
with men like Mr Dalgleish and Morden Rigg, both of whom had
given written statements to Florie's solicitors Richard and Arnold
Cleaver, and both of whom were willing to appear in her favour and
give their depositions under oath. Apart from Rigg and his wife there
were a host of others who could have torn up the prosecution's case
like shit-paper. Where, by way of example, were Valentine Blake,
Charles Ratcliffe, George Davidson and Captain Irving? It was Ratcliffe
who wrote of James 'dosing himself as usual', and Irving who'd heard
from Edwin Maybrick that his brother was 'killing himself with that
damned strychnine'. But most important of all, where was Florence's
mother, Caroline von Roques, who could have confirmed flypapers
as a commonly used cosmetic, and who was as well apprised of her
son-in-law's addiction to lethal toxins as any of the rest?

However, none of these were in the scheme of things. Florence Maybrick had to be silenced. Sir Charles Russell had no more care for her innocence than Sir Charles Warren had for Jack the Ripper's guilt. They were myrmidons of a System that would descend to any misfeasance to preserve itself. If Russell was to lose on behalf of the prosecution, it was essential that he present Michael Maybrick as 'innocent' of his brother's arsenic addiction, and further that he represented James Maybrick himself as a mahatma of clean living who barely took any medicines at all.

Cross-examination of the Maybrick brothers established that they were probably the only men within a five-mile radius of the corpse who knew nothing of their brother's drug-taking. Edwin claimed complete ignorance of arsenic or anything else. During questions regarding Irving's dinner date at Battlecrease House he left out both the captain and the drugs. The reference to James 'killing himself with that damned strychnine' had entirely slipped his mind. 'I dined with him that evening,' he said, 'and he appeared to be in his usual health. So far as I knew my brother on the whole enjoyed very good health. From time to time he took ordinary liver medicine.'

'Any sort of arsenic?' asked Addison.

'No,' replied the perjuring pipsqueak.[13]

Before arriving at Russell's cross-examination of Michael Maybrick it's worth a moment to put these two into context. Both were celebrities on the same social circuit, both were members of the Savage, and shared intimacy with the same famous names. Russell lived at 86 Harley Street, all but next door to one of Maybrick's oldest friends, the musician and composer Wilhelm Ganz, who himself considered Russell an intimate. 'At that time,' wrote Ganz, 'Harley Street was not only a street of doctors, but my neighbours and friends included the Kendalls [famous actors], the Chappells [music publishers], Mr Gully [Speaker of the House of Commons], and Sir Charles Russell [Queen's Counsel, and liar, on behalf of the Victorian Establishment].'

Bro Gully

Bro Russell

These eminent men *were* the Establishment, at least the glittering manifestation of it, and Russell himself, was a frequent house-guest of the King to be. Shagger Ed's special friend was Russell's closest friend, the composer Sir Arthur Sullivan. Russell had defended Sullivan in a suit against the Comedy Company for illicitly performing his operetta *HMS Pinafore*, and they became firm friends, sharing an obsession with the card game bezique. 'Played Bezique with Sir C Russell (6 a.m.!),' wrote Sullivan, 'and won a hundred and two pounds!' They spent at least one Christmas together on the Riviera, at Sullivan's villa on the French side of the border with Monaco.[14] And Sullivan was equally no stranger to Maybrick. As far back as 1880 they had been co-instigators of a musicians' union to protect their respective copyrights.[15] Asked many years later who his 'best friends' were, Michael replied, 'Well, I practically knew everyone of note in the profession. Sir Arthur Sullivan took a great deal of interest in me, and I succeeded him as Freemasonry's Grand Organist.'[16]

That he did, Sullivan having succeeded Bro Wilhelm Ganz.[17]

Bro Ganz

Bro Sullivan

So when Michael Maybrick got into the witness box, the questioner and questionee enjoyed a much greater social interaction than was public knowledge. They were stars of the same circuit, sharing the same friends, and members of the same club.

> RUSSELL: I will ask you one or two questions about your brother. Was he a man rather fond of his appearance?
> MICHAEL MAYBRICK: He was particular about it.
> RUSSELL: Was he a man given to dosing himself?
> MICHAEL MAYBRICK: That I am not aware of. I never saw him. At times he took a little phosphorus I know.[18]

The above question was put by a liar to a liar with a lie as the answer. Predicated on secret discussion of the 'Blucher' letter and its strychnine, both were lying through their teeth.

> RUSSELL: Have you ever heard about his dosing himself?
> MICHAEL MAYBRICK: I never heard, except in a letter from Mrs Maybrick.
> RUSSELL: I should be glad to see that letter.
> MICHAEL MAYBRICK: Well, unfortunately, I destroyed it. I did not think it of any importance.

RUSSELL: Did she say she had seen him take a white powder on several occasions?

MICHAEL MAYBRICK: Yes, I believe she did say something to that effect.

RUSSELL: Did she say she herself had searched for the powder, and could not find any trace of the powder he took?

MICHAEL MAYBRICK: That I do not remember. I have no recollection of it.[19]

Victorian courts made no provision for the defendant to speak. Florence could neither contest nor contribute, but it is recorded that 'she studied Michael Maybrick the whole time he was in the witness box, her expression being one of "fascinated disbelief", almost of repugnance'.[20] She had to sit there and listen to these zombies lying her life away with no one to defend her but Russell, who was no defence at all. Did James take 'a little phosphorus' from 163 different medicine bottles?

At one point the prosecution required a confirmation of Mrs Maybrick's handwriting, and to obtain this Addison called upon the skills of a world-famous scribe and impartial graphologist: 'With your permission, my Lord, I should like to recall Mr Michael Maybrick to prove the handwriting of these letters before I put them in [as evidence].'

Back in the box, Michael studied the letters, including the 'Brierley text' that Mrs Briggs had adjusted on his behalf.

ADDISON: Will you look at those letters and tell me in whose handwriting they are.

MICHAEL MAYBRICK: Mrs Maybrick's.[21]

For Michael Maybrick the proceedings couldn't have been anything other than a daily jubilation. This wasn't a sudden flash of steel in gaslight, but an enduring torture. It would take a week in this pigsty, and another three after that, to murder Florence Maybrick. It was Whitechapel in slow motion. Everyone in this charade of a court knew they were going to nail the whore, which is why Clerk to the Assizes Bro Shuttleworth slept through most of it.

Sir Charles Russell QC, however, was wide awake, interceding once again as Addison blundered into dangerous territory. He was questioning the Maybricks' servant Mary Cadwallader about the arrival of the flypapers, and was about fifteen seconds from putting his foot in it.

ADDISON: Now, about those fly-papers. Did you and the servants talk about them at all?

CADWALLADER: Well, sir, they were mentioned one day.

ADDISON: Do you recollect if anyone suggested what they were used for?

CADWALLADER: Yes, the cook said they were used for cleaning silk.

ADDISON: Did you at that time think anything of consequence of them?

CADWALLADER: No.

ADDISON: Now, I want to take you to another thing in connection with the fly-papers. Do you recollect a Domino Party or Ball to which Edwin Maybrick escorted Mrs Maybrick?

She certainly did, and it was an alarm bell for Russell. Addison was about to associate the flypapers with the truth of them – that they were the ingredients of a cosmetic.

ADDISON: Do you recollect how long before that you saw these fly-papers in the hall?

CADWALLADER: About a week before ...[22]

That was quite enough of that, thank you very much, and the Irish Judas moved in to silence it. 'Sir Charles Russell,' records Irving's transcript, 'spoke to Mr Addison and the question was not pressed.'[23]

Yet again the defence had shut Addison down on behalf of the prosecution. Addison's charge against the prisoner was that she was a woman engaged in 'a murder founded upon adultery and profligacy, and carried out with a hypocrisy and cunning rarely equalled in the annals of crime'.[24] In fact the cunning belonged to the Crown, and it would never make its charges stick if flypapers were merely a primitive precursor to Max Factor. It was crucial that they remained the principal ingredients of murder, and that's why Russell interrupted Addison. He was desperate to avoid any mention of their function as a cosmetic because, apart from adultery, they were all the Crown had.

It wasn't by accident that Baroness von Roques was excluded from the trial, any more than that Dalgleish and Morden Rigg were kept out. Enquiry into these flypapers would raise very serious difficulties for Russell, and unless Addison were gagged, these were about to be presented to the jury on a plate. 1) Why hadn't he gone after the 'Domino Party' himself, broadcasting it, and its logistics, as an unarguable truth? 2) Why hadn't he brought in witnesses to testify that flypapers were ingredients of a widely used cosmetic? 3) Where indeed was Florence's mother, who could have proved they were intended to be used in a facewash, and who with scant effort could have produced prescriptions confirming it? Russell had managed to rake up some 'black' from the plantations, but was unable to procure easily available copies of prescriptions from Paris or New York?

'The question of calling the Mother of the Prisoner,' wrote Florence's solicitor Richard Cleaver in his subsequent deposition to Matthews, 'to speak of her knowledge of the use by her daughter of Arsenic for Cosmetic purposes was considered and abandoned on the ground that the value of such evidence did not appear to warrant the infliction of the pain of such an appearance.'[25]

Such solicitude for the anguish of a mother is difficult to construe as sincere in the context of her daughter's possible death sentence. This trash out of Cleaver/Russell elevates an appearance in a witness box as more trying than her child's broken neck.

Russell's farce in St George's Hall wasn't far removed from Warren's fiasco in Whitechapel. He was no less a servant of the psychopath's charms than the joke of the Metropolitan Police. Both had to pretend they were doing what they were not. *À propos* of that, Russell nearly blew it. He brought in two witnesses for the defence who weren't quite so easy to handle as 'Fat Jack'.

They were Charles Tidy and Rawdon Macnamara, professors of forensic medicine and probably the world's pre-eminent living authorities on irritant poisons. The evidence of either should have seen Florence reunited with her children, and together these gentlemen constituted Russell's biggest headache.

The prosecution (and defence) were relying on the toxicological expertise of Doctors Humphreys and Carter, neither of whom had the first idea of the pathology of poisoning by arsenic or how it could be determined from an autopsy.

> RUSSELL: You have never assisted at a post-mortem examination
>   of any person supposed to have died from arsenical poisoning?
> DR HUMPHREYS: No.
> RUSSELL: I think I might also ask you whether you have ever
>   assisted at a post-mortem where it was alleged that death was
>   caused due to irritant poisoning?
> DR HUMPHREYS: No.[26]

Professor Tidy, by contrast, had conducted something short of a thousand autopsies, forty of which were due to arsenical poisoning. He introduced himself to the jury as a 'Bachelor of Medicine, Master of Surgery, and an Examiner of Forensic Medicine at the London Hospital'.[27] Within minutes of cross-examination his credentials were manifest. He knew everything there was to know about the ravages of arsenic, from kidneys to liver, via petechiae of the stomach, all the way up to bloodshot eyeballs. On pre- and post-mortem evidence, James Maybrick failed on all necessary criteria.

> RUSSELL: You say undoubtedly that these are not the symptoms of
>   arsenical poisoning?
> TIDY: Certainly not.
> RUSSELL: But as regards the symptoms?
> TIDY: There is an absence of three or four of the leading
>   symptoms, and if I had been called upon to advise, I should have
>   said it was undoubtedly not arsenical poisoning.[28]

No counsel for the defence could have asked for anything better, because the one thing Charles Tidy was absolutely certain of is that whatever killed James Maybrick, it wasn't arsenic.

ARSENICAL POISONING.	MR. MAYBRICK'S CASE.
Countenance tells of severe suffering.	Not so described.
Very great depression an early symptom.	Not present until towards the end.
Fire-burning pain in stomach.	Not present.
Pain in stomach increased on pressure.	Pressure produced no pain.
Violent and uncontrollable vomiting, independent of ingesta.	"Hawking rather than vomiting"; irritability of stomach increased by ingesta.
Vomiting not relieved by such treatment as was used in Mr. Maybrick's case.	Vomiting controlled by treatment.
During vomiting burning heat and constriction felt in throat.	Not present.
Blood frequently present in vomited and purged matter.	Not present.
Intensely painful cramps in calves of the legs.	Not present.
Pain in urinating.	Not present.
Purging and tenesmus an early symptom.	Not present until twelfth day of illness, and then once only.
Great intolerance of light.	Not present.
Eyes suffused and smarting.	Not present.
Eye-balls inflamed and reddened.	Not present.
Eye-lids intensely itchy.	Not present.
Rapid and painful respiration an early symptom.	Not present.
Pulse small, frequent, irregular and imperceptible from the outset.	Not so described until approach of death.
Arsenic easily detected in urine and fæces.	Not detected, although looked for.
Tongue fiery red in its entirety, or fiery red at tip and margins, and foul towards base.	Tongue not red; "simply filthy."
Early and remarkable reduction of temperature generally.	Temperature normal up to day preceding death.

The above is taken from *The Maybrick Trial: A Toxicological Study*, a pamphlet published by Tidy and Macnamara in 1890, following Mrs Maybrick's conviction. It does Russell no favours.

We will return to Professor Tidy in a moment, but first let us hear it from his associate, Professor Rawdon Macnamara.[29]

> RUSSELL: You have heard the description of Dr Humphreys of pains in the thighs. Have you in your experience known that in connection with cases of saturation or over-saturation with arsenic?
> MACNAMARA: Never.
> RUSSELL: Now, bringing your best judgement to bear upon the matter, you have been present at the whole of this trial, and heard the evidence. In your opinion was this a death due to arsenical poisoning?
> MACNAMARA: Certainly not.[30]

And there you have it, gentlemen of the jury. You have heard the evidence of two of the leading experts of our day, men whose reputation is revered far beyond these shores, and both are categorical in their certainty that James Maybrick did not die of arsenical poisoning. Any honourable defence counsel would have been on his feet to remind the jury of the prosecution's charge '*that she murdered her husband by administering to him doses of arsenic*'. Except she didn't, and two of the most eminent toxicologists in England said she didn't. The flypapers relied upon by the prosecution had become an irrelevance, a mere concoction of this innocent woman's cosmetic, and anything beyond that was the unfounded charge of Michael Maybrick and the spite of a servant.

The case was 'rotten', predicated on malicious gossip, police corruption and false accusation. Russell had everything he needed to kick this rubbish out of court, and after the appearance of Tidy and Macnamara the press thought so too. 'As far as I could gather from the hundreds of people I heard speak of the case,' wrote the *Liverpool Review*, 'opinion was unanimous on the subject. I can solemnly swear that I have not heard one man, woman, or child, who has not said positively that they were absolutely certain that the prisoner would get off. After Dr Tidy's evidence, these people dropped saying get off, and took the more important phrase "Not Guilty".'[31]

The Crown's case had imploded, game set and match, and it would take every sinew of Russell's duplicitous tongue to revitalise it. Without arsenic Mrs Maybrick was free, but the function of this gang was to manufacture a conviction. Just as Russell had to keep arsenic away from the jurors' ears in respect of James Maybrick, it was equally vital to keep arsenic as a live issue in respect of his wife. But there was no arsenic, it was a dead duck, and it was with escalating incredulity that Tidy sat there and listened to Charles Russell reintroduce it.

The next witness up was Dr Frank Paul, Professor of Medical Jurisprudence at University College, Liverpool, and Examiner of Forensic Medicine and Toxicology to the Victoria University. Dr Paul was there to support the defence, but Russell craftily destroyed any chance of that, and nobbled him in his tracks. Rather than welcoming his evidence as a supplement to that of Macnamara and Tidy, he sabotaged it from the outset, catching Paul off guard by dragging back the glazed pan from which James had eaten his office lunch. It was a dastardly long shot, and nothing less than treachery, but this glazed pan was the only possible source from which Russell could reanimate the arsenic.

By casual stealth – 'There are one or two smaller matters I must ask you about' – he asked Paul if he had examined any such pan. A positive answer developed Russell's line of questions, which didn't take a minute to arrive at the possibility of arsenic being present in the glaze. Did the doctor have any such pan in court? On being told that he did not, Russell called it a 'great pity', and wondered out loud whether any such pan could be obtained. When told it would take about fifteen minutes, Russell asked, 'Can anyone go and bring it here?' and looking directly at him said, 'Perhaps Doctor Tidy would go for it?'[32] The professor stared back with a mix of astonishment and rage. The only reason he might oblige would be in order to shove the glazed pan down Russell's throat. Was he purposely intimidating Tidy, converting him into some kind of court usher, and making it clear that he held both him and his evidence in contempt?

The case was won, *and it didn't include arsenic*. It was obvious to Tidy that Russell was in the business of unwinning it by sneaking arsenic back in, and he couldn't have been more right.

In the ensuing cross-examination Russell set about deconstructing his own certain victory and replanting the virus of arsenic in the jurors' minds. Launching forth with redundant questions about copper foil, hydrochloric acid and the irrelevant analysis of some unspecified person's urine, he escorted Paul through details of the Reinsch test (an alternative to the Marsh test for arsenic).

RUSSELL: Just tell us, what was the experiment?

DR PAUL: I experimented with various quantities, and found 1-200th of a grain to one ounce, which would readily be detected by a person, scientific or otherwise, who saw the test; 1-1000th of a grain would readily be detected in this way.

Readily detected for what reason? Arsenic didn't kill James Maybrick, so they may as well have been talking about a non-existent bullet-hole. This was nothing to do with Maybrick, but the pathology of a jug. And whose urine was it? What it wasn't was James Maybrick's. For all Tidy knew, it could have been from someone who took a piss round the back of a pub.[33]

RUSSELL: Now, I wish just to follow that to thousandths of a grain. What I want to ask you is this. You can reduce that to proportion between the arsenic and the urine in which it was placed? [He could.] And how many times was there the quantity of urine that there was of arsenic?

DR PAUL: About fifty five thousand.

RUSSELL: That would be 1 to 55 thousand?

DR PAUL: Yes.[34]

And two pages later:

RUSSELL: Taking altogether what was found quantitatively, 88-1000ths or 92-1000ths, would you explain to the jury what that quantity would represent?

DR PAUL: A thousandth of a grain would be, I suppose, barely visible.

FITZJAMES STEPHEN (writing): The 76 thousandths of a grain of arsenic ...[35]

Every question was designed to confuse the guileless mind, and every answer was another shovel of earth on Mrs Maybrick's grave. By now Fitzjames Stephen was in the swing of it, asking how long the doctor had boiled his urine, and over what sort of flame.

The boys were back in business.

Tidy was 'extremely angry', and at the earliest opportunity he left the court to engage with Russell in his allocated chambers. A barrister at law himself (Lincoln's Inn), Tidy wanted to know what the fuck Russell thought he was up to. Florence Maybrick was innocent, the trial was a stitch-up, and even the previously hostile press agreed.

Russell couldn't give a monkey's for the press, but he had to hear it from Tidy. 'Any more extraordinary line of argument,' protested his own expert witness, 'can scarcely be imagined. The post-mortem appearances were those of inflammation,' insisted Tidy, 'but not consistent with arsenical poisoning.' In respect of Drs Humphreys and Carter he said, 'They do not think it worthwhile to examine the urine, which would have set the question at rest, save on one occasion, when they found *nothing*. Nor do they attempt any antidotal treatment, seeing there was *nothing* to indicate such remedies being required.'

This would have been music to the ears of any honest advocate, but Russell wasn't an honest advocate; he was a shyster, playing off the downside of his rented tongue, 'overbearing in his manner, and to his clients contemptuous, even offensive'. Russell was in 'one of his moods, and treated the scientist's view with the utmost contempt'. He 'scarcely listened to him, in fact would listen to no one but Sir Charles Russell'.[36]

What Tidy didn't know was *who* Russell was defending. They would have hanged this woman a dozen times to protect their East End psychopath, or rather to protect themselves.

With arsenic back on the slate, this mockery progressed towards its foregone conclusion. At times Russell's deceit was all but overt, particularly in respect of who was and who wasn't the toxicological expert around here. Marginalising Professors Macnamara and Tidy, he championed Humphreys. 'Of course,' he told the jury, 'the most valuable witness on that head is Dr Humphreys, because he was in charge of the case from the 28th April, at its beginning, until it closed with the death of James Maybrick.'[37] Such a distortion would have been ludicrous out of Addison's mouth, let alone that of the counsel for the defence.

Although in the matter of arsenical poisoning, Russell seems to have forgotten his own cross-examination, it's worth revisiting to gauge the breadth of Dr Humphreys' expertise. Russell asked: 'Did it in any way occur to you that there were symptoms present during life of arsenical poisoning?' There is no recorded answer to this. Russell continued:

RUSSELL: When was it that the idea was first suggested to you?

DR HUMPHREYS: I think on Thursday, or on the Wednesday night, when Michael Maybrick came to see me.

RUSSELL: From a communication made to you by Mr Michael Maybrick?

DR HUMPHREYS: Yes.[38]

And that's how much of an expert Humphreys was. The expert was Michael Maybrick. Or in other words, it was Michael Maybrick who had diagnosed arsenic. Thus, via Humphreys, Russell was sidelining Professors Tidy and Macnamara in favour of the Crown's chief accuser. Quite an achievement for a man purporting to be counsel for the defence. He was investing a pea-shooter with the hitting power of a Sherman tank, and it laid pipe for the mad old bigot on the bench. Fitzjames Stephen went for it like a red rag.

'I venture to say,' wrote Alexander Macdougall, 'that the records of criminal trials would be searched in vain for a parallel example of a judge thus interfering with the functions of a jury, or attempting to obtain a verdict for the prosecution. He had got it into his own head that Mrs Maybrick's story of a mislaid prescription for an arsenical facewash was a lie, and he was determined that the jury should not be left to their own conclusions about it, but driven to adopt his own.'[39]

'About the fly-papers,' hawked Fitzjames Stephen, 'there is some kind of evidence, though I must say it is very insufficient, about some of these things being used for cosmetic purposes ... it is a singular thing that, if this is a fact she has stated, there should be no witnesses to prove it ... why are there no witnesses here to prove it? If she knew her young friends were in the habit of using things of this kind, why was it more difficult, or why could it take more time or money to get witnesses from Germany?'[40]

By any objective analysis he was right. Sir Charles had managed to track down a 'niggra' from the Virginia sticks, but he couldn't get a girl on a train from Berlin: 'This is a thing which might have been done, but it has never been done.'[41]

It wasn't done because it would have gone a long way to substantiating Florence Maybrick's innocence. Russell could have brought these friends from Germany and accessed copies of prescriptions with ease. Instead he crammed such attestations in at the end of the trial, when any value in them was spent: 'She was in the habit of using a face-wash prescribed by Dr Briggs of Brooklyn, which prescription she says she lost.'[42]

'Why is there no evidence?' continued Fitzjames Stephen. 'Why is the matter brought forward at the last moment in this way, when it is no longer possible to test it in any other way? Where is her mother? Why is her mother not called if she knew this? If she knew that Mrs Maybrick had been in the habit for many years of using an arsenical cosmetic? *It is certainly very strange that there is no evidence of this matter in the defence.*'[43]

It's my emphasis but Stephen's invective, and once again he was right. Russell was the smartest bastard in the business, so 'strange' isn't the right word – rather it was treachery.

'I was ready and willing to be called as a witness at the trial,' protested Baroness von Roques in her petition to Home Secretary Matthews, 'to speak of the circumstances within my knowledge, but I was not so called, and it was not till after the said trial that I became aware that, in the opinion of the learned judge, as expressed in his summing up, the absence of my evidence was an important factor in the issue left to the jury to determine, nor was I permitted to be present during the said trial.'[44]

Russell kept her out like he kept Dalgleish out, like he kept Mr and Mrs Morden Rigg out, together with a host of others whose evidence would have seen Mrs Maybrick acquitted. That Russell conspired to lose his case is perfectly evident from his suppression of the 'Blucher' letter, backed up by Richard Cleaver's notes. They'd banged her up, effectively silencing her, but didn't necessarily require her to be hanged. In a deposition after the conviction, this individual calling himself a solicitor also wrote to the Home Secretary:

I admit that I have, perhaps wrongly, never attached great importance as to the evidence of the fly-papers, certainly at the outset very little, because I considered

a) That the circumstances attending their purchase and subsequent soaking of them precluded the presumption of guilty use of them.

b) That such a clumsy expedient for obtaining arsenic was inconsistent with the theory of the prosecution of knowledge by her of the arsenical contents of the house.

c) That the use of arsenic and of solution of fly-papers as a cosmetic was notorious and that formal proof would hardly be requisite.[45]

'Hardly be requisite'? I beg your pardon, Mr Cleaver, but flypapers were the only 'clumsy expedient' the Crown had upon which to hang its rotten hat. Was there ever such rottenness from the pen of a solicitor? The prosecution *had nothing but flypapers*? Every word exiting Fitzjames Stephen's throat had relied on arsenic soaked out of flypapers. They were what animated that vile little creature Alice Yapp, and sent Bro Michael Maybrick scurrying with his rubbish to Dr Humphreys' house.

Russell had supplied everything this relic of a judge needed to pursue his harangue, and in his summing-up Fitzjames Stephen got stuck into it with relish: 'Evidence was given with regard to the purchase of fly-papers; that although Mrs Maybrick had a bill running at each of these shops [Wokes & Co. and the chemists Hanson] she paid for the fly-papers out of her own pocket, and, of course, the suggestion would be that she had been actuated in doing so by the desire to avoid detection.'[46]

No such thing had been suggested or proved. The argument was so ridiculous that even the prosecution objected, Addison stating, 'I studiously avoided making any such suggestion.'

Any dispassionate observer might have thought it was Sir Charles Russell's duty to intervene, but he kept his trap shut, and the apology went to the Crown.

FITZJAMES STEPHEN: I am quite aware of that, Mr Addison. I know perfectly well that you avoided it, and that you avoided it wisely and properly, but it was brought out in evidence, and I think you will agree with me in what I have said, because this is not a vindictive, cruel, or unfair prosecution, and I think I have seldom heard of such a thing in my life. I have instanced this to show you what a foolish argument that would be, a very unjust argument to be advanced in such a serious question as one of life or death – it is so foolish an argument that I just mentioned it – I do not say that any kind of weight attaches to it.[47]

This is a classic example of paralipsis, of pretending to deny what you're saying by saying it. It's the oldest trick in the book. For example: I do not say that this voluptuous female with pert tits, high heels and a provocative mini-skirt was inviting rape, far from it, but I will say, etc. etc.

Fitzjames Stephen continued: 'I now come to other points. A question always gone into in matters of this nature is the question of motive. I shall say absolutely nothing upon that subject.'[48] Except of course an earful about Florence's dirty little night at Flatman's Hotel, 'where she did about the latter part of March, carry on an adulterous intercourse with this man Brierley'. He didn't think it was necessary, he said, to mention the mysterious 'second visitor to the Flatman's Hotel, a Mr John K' – an old friend of the Maybrick family, but here presented by Fitzjames Stephen as another customer with an urgent hard-on:[49]

It is not my business to speak as a moralist, but there is one horrible and lamentable result of a connection of that sort, which renders it almost a moral necessity, it furnishes the strongest possible provocation, the strongest possible inducement, for entering upon a system of the most disgraceful intrigue and telling a great number of lies.[50]

In contradiction of his previous statement he said, 'Gentlemen, I am on the question of motive, and I point out to you a motive which I feel to be my duty not to overlook.'

Adultery then temporarily took the place of arsenic – the indulgence of one necessitating recourse to the other. In other words, it was Florence's sexual rapaciousness, her desire for the younger man, that mutated into the decision to bump the older man off. *Ergo*, James Maybrick was murdered by adultery. 'It is a sad and terrible case,' said Stephen, 'and I ask whether the matter I now suggest is not supported by terrible evidence.'[51]

In this instance the terrible evidence was James Maybrick smacking his wife in the face. 'A blow, a black eye, a half-leaving the house, a consultation with Dr Hopper, and then a complete reconciliation for the sake of the children? Do you believe that?' he hawked. 'Do you believe that a quarrel of that sort can be made up by a family doctor?'[52] It was left to the 'stagnations' to answer for themselves.

On and on he sawed, seasoning his prejudice with endless error, reading in a letter which had not been presented as evidence, and confusing the sequence and dates of domestic events which he sold to the jury as substantiating this 'black eye'.

> ADDISON: May I point out to you, my Lord, in favour of the prisoner, that the Grand National was on the 29th of March, and the reconciliation took place on the 30th.
> FITZJAMES STEPHEN: You are quite right.
> ADDISON: The only assignation after that is a letter in which she says she would like to see him.
> FITZJAMES STEPHEN: You are quite right. I have made a mistake, and I am sorry I have done so in a case of this importance.[53]

Is it not extraordinary that once again it was left to the prosecution to interrupt, and that it was not Sir Charles Russell who pointed out these calumnies?

It was not until after the event that Russell spoke out. In a memorandum to Home Secretary Matthews he wrote 'a forceful censure of Fitzjames Stephen's conduct', pointing out that the judge had 'passionately invited the jury to find a verdict of guilty. He made suggestions that were untenable and had never been advanced by the prosecution, and went out of his way to make misleading references.' (So why the silence in court?)

It was a little late in the day to retrospectively try to rearrange the case in Mrs Maybrick's favour, but a majority of the press agreed and took up the argument, most notably the great W.T. Stead, who poured anger into his *Review of Reviews*: 'I cannot resist the criticism that the case is so scandalous an illustration of the very worst sides of the British judicial system and the British character. No Englishman can feel otherwise than ashamed of having to defend the manner in which she has been dealt with by our Courts and our Government. A sorrier exhibition of all that is worst in the blundering, wrong-headed illogical side of John Bull [England] has seldom or never given occasion for his enemies to exult and his friends to wince.'

Fitzjames Stephen harangued the jury for twelve hours over a period of two days, and on the second day it might as well have been Bro Michael Maybrick sitting there in a wig. 'Some malign influence seems to have possessed or obsessed him,' wrote Stead; 'he raged like a violent counsel for the prosecution, leaving no stone unturned to excite prejudice against the unfortunate woman in the dock. The fact is that the case was decided not in the least upon the evidence of experts, but solely upon the prejudice imported into the case by the judge on that last day of his summing up.'[54]

Russell had given Fitzjames Stephen his arsenic back, and although it never killed James, it fed the judge's senile frenzy. Error after error came out of his mouth. So egregious were his mistakes that some have ascribed them to misprints in the transcript, but the culprit was Fitzjames Stephen's clapped-out brain. Addison joined Shuttleworth in the Land of Nod: 'During a good portion of the time,' reported the *Liverpool Review*, 'Mr Addison fell fast asleep with his head lying on the desk before him.'[55]

They were hours into it, with hours to go, and here come the flypapers and blah blah blah ...

What did it matter what Florence Maybrick had bought flypapers for? It was immaterial whether she had bought a ton of the bastards from every other pharmacy in Liverpool. Professors Tidy and Macnamara had demonstrated beyond reasonable doubt that James Maybrick *did not die from arsenical poisoning*, and at the very minimum Florence should have been given the benefit of that doubt. But Fitzjames Stephen was giving nothing, and jawed himself into a repudiation of any such dilemma. At the end of it the jury took thirty-eight minutes to reach a verdict of guilty, and Stephen duly sentenced Florence Maybrick to death.

The nightmare engendered by Michael Maybrick at Battlecrease House had sustained itself into another place. Florence was taken to a gaslit cell in Walton Jail to await her execution.

Any thoughts of cheating the gallows (which were in loud construction in the yard outside her cell[56]) by suicide were precluded by the presence of two female warders, who were not allowed to speak to her. Her only conversation was during a single visit from her equally tortured mother: 'Florie was sitting in a chair with her face in her hands crying bitterly. She cried incessantly, begging in vain to see her children and was in the most agonising distress about them ... if there is anybody on earth who hates my daughter I wish they could have seen her there.'[57]

Bro Michael would have been only too delighted. The Masonic psycho, now temporarily decamped to the Isle of Wight, relished everything he'd achieved. What he'd wanted was revenge, and he'd got it. But it came with a backlash. Five thousand people had massed outside St George's Hall on the day of the jury's verdict, and most of them didn't like what they heard. Public antipathy towards Florence was now entirely reversed, and she was cheered as the police took her away in a prison van.[58] The public's rage now fell upon those who had convicted her. Fitzjames Stephen was heckled and booed as his carriage tried to escape the attentions of an angry mob, 'hooted in the streets by Irishmen', according to the Solicitor General and Tory QC Bro Sir Edward Clarke.[59] Those without transport had to risk it on foot, the Flatman's Hotel waiter Alfred Schweisso copping an unwarranted punch in the chops that cost him a couple of teeth.[60] Florence's supposed friend Matilda Briggs and the nursemaid Alice Yapp were similarly unpopular, running a gauntlet for shelter at Lime Street railway station under the protection of a bunch of Her Majesty's vilified helmets.[61] 'I do not remember any case,' wrote Stead, 'in which the public protested so vehemently against the decision of a court.'[62]

The hostility of the crowd found expression in headlines all over the world, and the men in wigs weren't able to hide this one behind the Micks. The verdict went down particularly ill in America. 'If the trial had happened in the United States,' reported one correspondent, 'the judge would have been impeached.'

Whether true or not, the general view of the American press was one of suspicion. 'The curious facts and strange motives which underlie this case from beginning to end are something amazing,' wrote the *Washington Evening Star*, 'and the half of it has not been told.'[63] You can say that again, and a variety of the US papers' correspondents did. Both in America and England a torrent of letters filled the press, by far the majority in Mrs Maybrick's favour. I select but one, which resonates with the outrage of many. On 15 August 1889 the *Manchester Courier* published a letter from a Mr R.F. Muckley, his observations preceding whatever I might write about the murderous Mr Michael Maybrick by 126 years:

> Sir – There remain yet a few circumstances in this case that have had very little airing, and which at least admit of some notice from those who have a penchant for reflection and the solution of conundrums.

1: Who had great antipathy to Mrs Maybrick?

2: Who had as much or more access to Mr Maybrick about the period of his violent attacks than anybody else?

3: Who had as much chance as anyone else of adding extra 'condiments' to Mr Maybrick's food or medicine? [An extraordinary point, considering the eavesdropping statement by Robert Reeves wouldn't be made for another four years, and remained secret for another hundred.]

4: Who, on one occasion, administered a pill to Mr Maybrick, causing him illness?

5: Who made a mistake in stating that the pill[s] administered was 'written upon' by a doctor?

6: Who administered a pill[s] that was not written upon by a doctor to Mr Maybrick, which pill[s] caused illness?

7: Who takes charge of the bulk of the deceased's property? Query: Why is Mrs Maybrick charged with murder any more than he whose name forms an answer to all the above questions? Why?

R.F. Muckley. Hope Road, Sale, August 14 1889.

The questions were never answered. Bro Maybrick threatened to sue, and Muckley backed off.[64] But a disturbed and substantial tide of public opinion did not, and neither did Alexander Macdougall. He never knew, nor ever met, Florence Maybrick, but he articulated the affront to justice on her behalf, and organised it into a nation-wide protest. Petitions demanding an immediate reprieve were signed by thousands up and down the kingdom. One of the first signatories was Thomas Maybrick, who travelled to London to do so, while his recalcitrant brothers kept their heads down at Michael's holiday rental on the Isle of Wight.

'Nothing would please me more,' said the instigator of her tragedy, 'than to hear that the Home Secretary's decision is that Mrs Maybrick shall go free.'[65]

Ha ha.

Macdougall's British endeavour was replicated in the United States, coordinated there by a stringent activist by the name of Helen Densmore, an academic and writer with some distinguished connections which she would relentlessly exploit, all the way up to the President himself.

Meanwhile, she and Macdougall and their allies were beset with the same urgency to save Mrs Maybrick's life. The decision to hang or not to hang fell upon that most notable of inadequacies, and guardian of Her Majesty's ever-clogged judicial latrine, Home Secretary Henry Matthews.

After the uproar following Mrs Maybrick's conviction, and in an effort to discredit her by association with 'hooting Irish supporters', Matthews caught it square in his Right Honourable neck during an exchange on the affair in Parliament. A Liverpool newspaper reported: 'When the Home Secretary stated that the prisoner was cheered, the jury who found her guilty hissed, and Her Majesty's Judge mobbed and hooted, Mr O'Connor (Home Rule) arose to remark that such scenes often occur in Ireland, and when they do the mob is made to suffer. "Had the Honourable Gentleman heard," asked Mr O'Connor, "whether on this occasion the police on duty had either batoned, or bayoneted, or shot any of the crowd?" Mr Matthews,' continued the *Lancashire Advertiser,* 'made no reply, but sat down hurriedly.'

Matthews had made his discredited name with obfuscation over the Ripper, the pen of the journalist George Sims summing the worthless lackey up: 'He is probably the most exasperating person who ever reigned at the Home Office. In the art of rubbing up the people in the wrong way he never had an equal.'

And here he is again, featuring in one of the most remarkable illustrations yet of Her Majesty's legal pantomime. Matthews is presented as if in some sort of dilemma. On the left, wielding his blade, is Jack, wanting the 'wanton' hanged, and on the right the blindfolded damsel with the sword, known as 'Justice'.

The caption reads: 'ATTEMPTED MURDER OF FLORENCE MAYBRICK – "SAVE HER" MR MATTHEWS'. This picture is a graphic representation of what Alexander Macdougall called 'the Spirit of Evil'. To me it is the apogee of what Thatcher called 'Victorian values'. 'The mystery of Jack the Ripper' and 'the Maybrick Mystery' were one and the same – the one protected, the other persecuted, and for the same reason – and by some extraordinary intuition this forgotten artist seemed to be aware of it.

In reality there was no deliberation worth the word. Mrs Maybrick was innocent, and the zombies knew it, and if they didn't, they were about to find out. Matthews' senior civil servant at the Home Office, an aristocrat called Hamilton John Agmondesham Cuffe, had written to William Swift, Clerk to the Justices at Liverpool, requesting a copy of the 'Blucher' letter. It arrived on Matthews' desk on 20 August 1889, one week before Mrs Maybrick's scheduled murder at Walton Prison on 27 August.[66]

Cuffe's request poses one or two questions, does it not – not least of which is, how did he even know about the letter? Russell had caused its suppression at the 'trial', to the fatal detriment of his client. Following the secret conclave with Michael Maybrick, it was not admitted as evidence, and there is not the slightest mention of it in any of the transcripts. Yet in the present shenanigans it has apparently acquired a relevance? The Home Office's interest in this document found its way into the press, and once again it was cynically manipulated to Mrs Maybrick's disadvantage. The crucial phrase 'Doctor Fuller had poisoned me' was of course expunged, and the rest presented as a potent ingredient of Henry Matthews' quandary: 'A most important piece of testimony for the prosecution was kept back at the trial, simply because there was some doubt as to whether it would technically rank as evidence ... this was a letter written by Mr Maybrick to his brother just before he died, in which he said, "I am being poisoned ... When I am dead you must open my body."'[67]

'Blucher' was in fact a most important piece of testimony for Mrs Maybrick's defence, but it was twisted here to represent a reason for the tormented Home Secretary to have her executed. The above report is from the *Manchester Courier* on 22 August, and its theme was picked up by the *New York Herald* on the same day. Confirming that the 'Blucher' letter was in Addison's brief, it wrote: 'but it could not be produced on trial because there was a technical objection to it as evidence'.[68]

What technical objection was that? Alexander Macdougall described the withholding of this letter as a 'criminal conspiracy', and it was a conspiracy still in progress. Although 'Blucher' was leaked to the newspapers, the Home Office minute referring to it was not, and it demonstrates the criminality underpinning this Victorian charade.

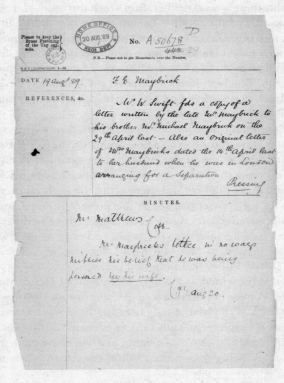

MINUTES

Mr Maybrick's letter in no ways implies his belief that he was being poisoned by his wife.[69] [Home Office emphasis.]

That's what Russell, Michael Maybrick, Fitzjames Stephen and Addison knew, and shared in whispers on the opening day of the 'trial'. Coupled with the expert testimony of Tidy and Macnamara, it blows the prosecution to pieces. The Crown's case was that Mrs Maybrick began her poisoning campaign with *arsenic* on 27 April, and here is her supposed victim, two days later on 29 April, accusing Michael Maybrick's doctor of poisoning him, and stating that the offending agent is *strychnine*.

There was nothing for Matthews to fret over. Florence Maybrick was innocent as daylight. It was Bro Michael who was poisoning her husband with his 'London Medicine' and phoney pills, and Mr Muckley couldn't have been the only one who knew it. Following the conviction a torrent of depositions materialised that Russell could and should easily have accessed before anyone ever thought of accusing Florence. Russell was good with letters, and during the Parnell frame-up he had busted the squalid forger Richard Pigott with one of them. If 'Blucher' could save Mrs Maybrick's life after conviction, why not before it? If it added resonance to calls for her reprieve, why wasn't it used as a reason not to prosecute her in the first place?

By now, thanks to the efforts of her ostracised mother, the New York prescription for the facewash had turned up, accompanied by a report from Liverpool's City Analyst, Mr Davies, who had ransacked

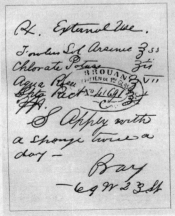

James Maybrick's intestines for any indication not of arsenic, but for microscopic fibres of the flypapers it was imagined to have come from. There was no trace of them whatsoever.[70]

An ancillary report commissioned by Alexander Macdougall from two of the nation's foremost analytical chemists (Coats and Clayton) confirmed Mr Davies' findings, or rather the lack of them. 'It is, I believe, a fact beyond contradiction,' wrote Dr Coats, 'that in the Maybrick case fly-papers could not have been used. It is almost impossible for anyone not skilled in analysis to have got rid of the woollen fibres.'[71] This judgement was reiterated by Mr Godwin Clayton:

> *It is next to impossible* [his emphasis] for any person without opportunities for, and knowledge of, chemical manipulation, to make or procure an aqueous infusion of the fly-papers without signs of the addition being evident on microscopical examination, in the shape of characteristically coloured fibres and hairs derived from the fly-papers. The only method by which it is possible, even in the chemical laboratory, to obtain an infusion of these papers free from coloured fibres of cotton and woollen hairs, is filtration through filter paper of good quality. I consider it in the highest degree unlikely that an ordinary individual would think of employing such a process, or would even contemplate attempting to eliminate the fibres from the infusion.[72]

Curious it is that the redoubtable Inspector Bryning overlooked Mrs Maybrick's 'laboratory' when he and his pals searched her house. If Charles Russell QC had been an honest broker he would have hired these chemists on day one, perhaps wedging their deposition between those of Dalgleish and Baroness von Roques.

But Russell wasn't an honest broker, and neither was Matthews. He was joined in his deliberations by a variety of gents under horsehair whose inclination was to travel up carpets in reverse. James Fitzjames Stephen was reanimated for consultation, abetted by the Dionysus of Cleveland Street's upmarket buggers and the kingdom's most senior officer of the law, Bro Lord Halsbury.

According to a contemporary effusion, the Bro Lord Chancellor was responsible for 'the efficient and harmonious working of the entire judicial system of Great Britain. As the First Great Officer of

State, he takes rank immediately after the Monarch Herself. His designation of "Keeper of The Royal Conscience"[73] is in itself a testimony of the great influence which has always attended the position.' 'Keeping the Royal Conscience' was a medieval euphemism for keeping the peasants in awe of it. The Lord Chancellor *was* the law, and by holding his own laws in contempt Halsbury was to be the last grotesque turn in the Jack the Ripper Show.

Their problem wasn't whether they were going to hang Mrs Maybrick or not, but how they were going to keep her in prison if they didn't. She had been convicted of murdering her husband by the administration of arsenic. She was either guilty of it or she was not. If guilty, the death penalty was mandatory; if innocent, she must be set free.

The latter wasn't an option. Since Florence's arrest in her bed at Battlecrease House the state had managed to isolate her, convinced she was in possession of a terrible secret that would have shafted them all. At all costs she must be kept incommunicado. So they came up with a compromise that was as unprecedented as it was iniquitous. Two days after receipt of the 'Blucher' letter, Matthews and his chums announced that there was a reasonable doubt that James Maybrick hadn't died from arsenical poisoning, but that there was no doubt that Mrs Maybrick would have poisoned him with arsenic if she could have: 'Although the evidence leads clearly to the conclusion that the prisoner administered and attempted to administer arsenic to her husband with intent to murder, yet it does not wholly exclude a reasonable doubt whether his death was in fact caused by the administration of arsenic.'[74]

In other words, James Maybrick may have died of gastro-enteritis (or indeed a hotshot of laudanum delivered by his brother). Notwithstanding the alternatives, the Keeper of the Royal Conscience concluded: 'The Home Secretary, after fullest consideration, and after taking the best legal and medical advice that could be obtained, has advised Her Majesty to respite the capital sentence on Florence Maybrick and to commute the punishment to penal servitude for life.'[75]

It was as stupefyingly crooked as that. If James Maybrick had died from a plateful of contaminated oysters, his wife was to take the rap and spend the rest of her life in prison. But let me not argue against this Victorian monstrosity. I prefer to leave it to Thomas Crispe QC, a barrister and contemporary of Bro Halsbury: 'The position in regard to the remission of the death-sentence resulted in a scandalous anomaly: the prisoner is charged with murder. It is doubtful whether murder has been committed at all – the death may have been from natural causes – therefore we will not hang her. Ergo, on that charge she is innocent. But inasmuch as there was evidence which led to a conclusion that she *attempted* to murder, she shall have penal servitude for life, *although that charge was not preferred against her*[76] [his emphasis].'

Thus Florence Maybrick 'endured punishment for a crime for which she was not charged'.[77]

Matthews' judgement was greeted with as universal an uproar as had been the original death sentence itself. The consensus was that if there was 'reasonable doubt', there was no legal reason not to consider Mrs Maybrick as innocent. 'If that doubt existed,' continued Crispe, 'it existed at the trial, and if the matter had been treated in the way it ought to have been, the jury would have given the prisoner the benefit of that doubt.'[78]

He was pointing a finger at Charles Russell QC. Having ensured Mrs Maybrick's conviction, he would spend the rest of his life maintaining her innocence. 'She is suffering imprisonment,' he asserted, 'on the assumption of Mr Matthews that she committed an offence for which she was never tried by the constitutional authority, and of which she has never been adjudged guilty.'[79] If she wasn't guilty, Russell sure as hell was. He knew perfectly well that she was in prison because he'd put her there.

Matthews dispatched a messenger to Liverpool with word of the commutation. He arrived at Walton Jail at about 1.30 in the morning. Those who needed to be were woken up, including the prison Governor Mr Anderson and his chaplain the Reverend Morris, who hurried together to Mrs Maybrick's cell. 'Mrs Maybrick was undressed and in bed,' recounted the Religious Gent. 'She made no sign as we entered. She merely turned her eyes and looked at us. She was very weak and had the listless air natural to her constitution.' On hearing of her reprieve she said nothing. 'She merely lifted her left hand and stretched it out to take that of the Governor. That was all that was said.'[80] Her constitution was hardly in a fit state to accommodate good news. Escape from the hangman meant little more than a migration from Hell Central into one of its suburbs.

A few days later, dressed in a brown uniform marked with arrows and escorted by Walton's chief warder and a female counterpart, Florence was driven by cab to Lime Street railway station. Here they boarded a specially reserved third-class carriage with the blinds pulled down. She was on her way to incarceration for life at Knaphill Prison at Woking, in the county of Surrey.

On arrival, Florence had 'her lustrous blonde hair hacked off by some heavy-handed harsh-voiced woman'. She was then stripped, weighed, measured and thrust into a shapeless dress, branded with the broad arrow of the convict, a red star for her classification as a first offender, and her personal identification as 'LP29': 'L' for life imprisonment, 'P' for the year of her conviction, and '29' as the twenty-ninth prisoner of the year. She was then locked in a cell, seven feet by four, 'containing only a hammock and three shelves'.[81]

'Oh, don't put me in there! I cannot bear it!' she wrote a ruined life later. 'There was nothing to sit upon but the cold floor. I sank to my knees. I felt suffocated. It seemed that the walls were drawing nearer and nearer together, and presently the life would be crushed out of me. I sprang to my feet and beat wildly with my hands. For God's sake, let me out!' But as regulations stipulated, this was to last for nine months, Florence and her fellow inmates stitching cotton in silence and 'marched once a day like dumb cattle to the worship of God'.[82] 'Solitary confinement,' she wrote, 'is by far the most cruel feature of English penal servitude. It inflicts upon the prisoner at the commencement of her sentence, when most sensitive to the horrors which prison punishment entails, the voiceless solitude, the hopeless monotony, the long vista of tomorrow, tomorrow, tomorrow, stretching before her, all filled with desolation and despair.'[83]

Florence Maybrick spent fifteen years behind bars, first at Woking and then at Aylesbury, also in Surrey. A few months after her imprisonment a penman with an apparent interest in her predicament sent a letter to the City of London Police.

And verso:

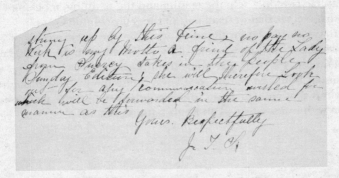

The text is the customary fight between an ego demanding to be heard and an intellect struggling to hide itself. Its author signed himself not 'Jack the Ripper', nor 'Jack the Skipper', but referring back to a previous letter with the initials 'J.T.S.'. On 22 June 1889 a correspondent signing himself 'Jack the Snicker' had written of his travels taking him to the Isle of Wight – which, by bizarre coincidence, is where Michael Maybrick had a house. In May 1890, following Mrs Maybrick's imprisonment at Woking in Surrey, 'Jack the Snicker' wrote another letter, rehearsing some familiar themes: Battersea (Lily Vass), 'the Whitehall mystery' ('the Scotland Yard Trunk'), an obsession with one hundred pounds, conflating them all with 'the Lady from Surrey' (Mrs Maybrick).

I decline to transcribe the opening claptrap, but here is where the ego takes over:

J.T.S. Alias the Lady from Surrey would come forward, but in the interests of justice, it is best for her to remain in incognito for the present – as there are other mysteryes being solved from ocular demonstrations in my possession. if father Matthews had offered publickly £100 reward he would have had the Whitehall Mystery cleared up. possibly the man strung up by this time, no pay no Work is my Motto A friend of the Lady from Surrey takes in the people Sunday Edition, she will therefore look out for any communication wished for which will be forwarded in the same manner as this.

Yours Respectfully
J.T.S.[84]

Michael Maybrick was sailing close to the wind, but was also driven by it. He couldn't help the teasing and the taunting, mocking with abstruse clues that were all part of the 'Funny Little Game'.

In an earlier letter, timed to arrive on the opening day of Mrs Maybrick's 'trial', he wrote an archetypical sneer to the Lord Mayor of London. Purporting to come from Washington DC, the letter was as usual bounced out of New York. Some might have thought it curious that an 'American' correspondent shared the same obsession with transvestism as an English murderer.

My Lord

Motto

All is possible in this world even the most incredible!
I am very sorry that I must address Your Lordship once more, but I
remembered that I forgot yesterday by reason of that be in the
business, (with old silk Lady sufferer, a very poor one) – a <u>third
possibility</u> – Perhaps it may appear to your Lorship like insane, but
the <u>story of the human sex (In) show us with surprises!! For: why
can that formidable brute of a beast never be surprised – by that
good police of London?! ?! ! !</u> ... – He <u>must be sheltered by his
dress</u>, and if <u>it is not a dress of a woman, – shouldn't it be the
uniform of an officer</u> ...

Echoing Florence Maybrick's description of her brother-in-law, the
writer calls the Ripper a 'brute'. The rest is a tedious descant of glee
at the notion of policemen dressed as women. But let me stay with
the 'Funny Little Game'. 'I forgot yesterday,' he writes, 'by reason of
that be in the business, (with old silk Lady sufferer, a very poor
one)'.

Only a ferocious ego could have risked something like this. The
writer was indeed 'in business' with an old silk suffering a lady. The
'business' can be encapsulated in the 'Blucher' letter. The lady was
'the Lady From Surrey', a.k.a. Florence Maybrick, and the old silk
was Sir Charles Russell QC.

This isn't the Enigma code. It's the spite of a cruel child out of a
rubbish brain. Who did the police think was writing these letters?
After the murder of Alice McKenzie on 17 July 1889 (about a week
before the beginning of Mrs Maybrick's 'trial'), even the dimmest
twat on the block must have realised they'd been duped.

'My brother in trade' was dead. No way did Bro James Maybrick
kill Alice McKenzie. The 'Snicker' says, 'if father Matthews had
offered publickly £100 reward he would have had the Whitehall
Mystery cleared up'. And in a letter dated 23 October 1888, Jack the
Ripper said, 'I lent three women from London about a hundred
pounds sterling'. Michael lent Florence £100, and it gnaws at both
Jack the Ripper's and Jack the Snicker's psyche. There's a Freudian
slip from the Snicker. Corroborating my point about the grown-ups,
he calls Home Secretary Henry Matthews 'father Matthews', a daddy
figure – and he hates the dads, like he hates the police, and hates

the Freemasons. But not as much as he hated Florence Maybrick. He wanted her hanged, and struggled to achieve it, but was ultimately satisfied with her life imprisonment.

Underlined and overlined on the envelope of a Ripper letter, it's as well to bear this arsehole's 'HA!' in mind.

Over the following months a formidable engine of dissent evolved in Mrs Maybrick's favour, most notably in the United States. There was a lengthy petition from 'The Women of America', and even the American Freemasons had taken up the case. Bro John Vincle, Grand Secretary of the Grand Lodge of Missouri, had exchanged letters with a British counterpart, which he proposed should serve 'as a basis for action by the Masonic Fraternity of the United States, who expect to reach the Queen through the Prince of Wales'.[85] It was an expectation shared by the Baroness von Roques; but like her, they got nowhere.

Alexander Macdougall and Helen Densmore remained indefatigable, the latter attracting an equally zealous convert to her cause. The public first heard of him in the columns of a British magazine called the *Hawk*. 'Who is Gail Hamilton?' it asked. 'He is indeed a very impudent fellow.' This view was predicated on an article published in the *North American Review*, which Hamilton had the brass Yankee neck to call 'An Open Letter to the Queen'. 'In terms of easy familiarity,' reported the *Hawk*, 'he requests Her Majesty to release Mrs Maybrick. A formal petition to that effect bearing the signatures of many influential Americans, has already been received by the Sovereign.'[86]

Received with disdain. Her Majesty didn't care for it any more than she was charmed by the man who organised it.

'Mr Gail Hamilton,' continued the *Hawk*, 'addresses the throne with an air of easy patronage, saucy to such a degree that were he to display his ill-breeding this side of the herring pond, he might be subjected to disagreeable consequences.'

One such disagreeable consequence now stuck his oar in. 'Taking the most lenient view which the facts proved,' warbled Prime Minister Salisbury, 'and known to Her Majesty's Secretary of State admit: the case of this convict was that of an adulteress attempting to poison her husband under the most cruel circumstances, while she pretended to be nursing him on his sick bed. The Secretary of State regrets that he has been unable to find any grounds for recommending to the Queen any further act of clemency towards the prisoner.'[87]

Had Hamilton been English, he would probably have got a dose of the Ernest Parke treatment. But he wasn't English, and he wasn't Mr either. She was in fact a Miss Hamilton, whose real name was Mary Dodge. Like Helen Densmore, she was a writer and feminist firebrand who had honed her campaigning skills fighting for the abolition of slavery, from which she graduated to become one of America's loudest mouths championing women's suffrage. Together with Densmore she would organise the Women's International Maybrick Society, whose president, Caroline Harrison, was wife of the President of the United States. 'No mountain of opposition was too high for these feminine Zolas to scale,' wrote Trevor Christie, 'no pit of apathy too deep for them to scour in their zeal for their heroine.'[88] This was a powerful, well-connected bunch of women, driven by a stubborn anger for justice, and neither the British government nor *Hawk* magazine had heard the last of them.

Although first greeted with ridicule, Mary Dodge had a foot in the door at the *Hawk*, and with initial reluctance and then intrigued acceptance, it published her letters. Alexander Macdougall added his voice, and over the weeks there was an extraordinary turnaround in the magazine's attitude. 'Certain events,' wrote its editor, Augustus Moore, 'tend to induce me to keep these columns open for some time to come for the possible elucidation of what is unquestionably shrouded in mystery.'[89]

This was immediately countered by a letter from Macdougall. 'Why not leave the word "mystery" out,' he asked, 'and confirm any discussion that might take place to the hard dry facts (1) Did James Maybrick die of arsenic? (2) If so, was the arsenic of which he died administered to him by Mrs Maybrick?'[90] Following in the footsteps of Mr Muckley, Macdougall and Mary Dodge were dragging Michael Maybrick back into the light.

'After several weeks' publication of letters relating to Florence Maybrick's case,' opined Moore in an editorial,

> wherein a decisive authoritative statement should be made upon the cumulative evidence which has been brought forward by 'Gail Hamilton', Mrs Maybrick's champion in the U.S.A. and by Mr Alexander Macdougall, her counsel and staunch defender in England. In a former issue, I appealed to the Messrs. Maybrick [Michael and Edwin], to state in these columns whatever information they might desire to make public in reference to the very pointed allusions contained in Gail Hamilton's résumé of the case, as well as Mr Macdougall's letters. They did not deem it fit to make any reply to what was considered by some as a challenge on my part to them, to clear the atmosphere of mystery which apparently surrounds the inmate of Woking. However, better counsels have prevailed, and for the first time since the close of the trial, Messrs. Maybrick have volunteered to me directly, with a view of its being published in the columns of The Hawk, the information *that all and every statement which refers to themselves,* and which has appeared in print, *is absolutely without foundation,* and further, that they are prepared at any time to show me documents, which might prove of an *extremely interesting character.*[91] [Emphasis in original.]

What these documents were wasn't disclosed, but Moore acquiesced at the threat of them, publicly declaring a complete *volte-face.* There would be no more of Mrs Maybrick in his magazine: 'I practically close any further discussion until hypothesis and conviction have given way to facts.'[92]

It was an onslaught of irrefutable facts that had aroused Moore's interest in the first place. Surely the offer of sensational evidence countering all that had preceded it in the *Hawk,* and settling 'the Maybrick Mystery' forever, would have been embraced and published with enthusiasm? But Moore didn't want to know.

Whether by the Maybrick brothers or some other clandestine intercession, he and his magazine had been shut up.

Such an unexpected change of mind was greeted with dismay on both sides of the Atlantic. 'This is, to say the least, a most surprising denouement,' wrote Helen Densmore. She questioned how it was that after so many weeks of silence the brothers had finally deigned to give information, and without the production of any of it, it was accepted unreservedly by the editor of the *Hawk*: 'It will occur to the thoughtful mind to ask what bearing the Maybrick brothers' denial has upon the many facts that have no relation to any statement said to emanate from them, or about them; and why, when demanding "facts" for Mrs Maybrick, the Editor of the *Hawk* so freely accepts the unsupported denial of these gentlemen. The Editor ignores the fact that, before the public, the Maybrick brothers are quite as much on trial as Mrs Maybrick.'[93]

Any traction Florence Maybrick's supporters had achieved in the *Hawk* was over, and by the winter of 1892 (with one dramatic exception) virtually all the British press had closed ranks against them. They persevered with the struggle, but were like flies that didn't understand the windowpane. They could buzz up and down and squabble about forever, but they were never going to get through.

What Miss Densmore didn't know, and Alexander Macdougall didn't know, and the American Freemasons didn't know, was what this was all about. The English Establishment had a full-blown psychopath still active in their midst – but no problem, they could cope with the odd dead kid or two, even more with the odd dead whore. Their only problem was that if he got caught they all got caught, all the way up to the Grand Glutton. How could this profligate prance about in his pinafore when he shared one with Jack the Ripper?

Bro Edward enjoying family life in Paris

The winter of 1892–93 was not the best of times for the supporters of Florence Maybrick. In August 1892 there had been a change
of government, as a result of which Henry Matthews was replaced by
Herbert Asquith, a heavy-drinking, highly intelligent Liberal who
was Russell's junior counsel during the Parnell frame-up. At first the
new Home Secretary appeared to look favourably upon Mrs
Maybrick's plight. The petition dismissed by Salisbury, it was
announced, would now receive 'due consideration'. But within
weeks Asquith had made as sudden a turnaround as Augustus

Moore. If anything, his point of view was now more draconianly negative than that of the Tories.

On 10 December 1892, about a week before Moore slammed his door at the *Hawk*, the British government announced a cessation of all diplomatic exchange with the US government in respect of the Maybrick case. As was reported in the *New York Herald* on 11 December, the Brits were attempting to play the victim: 'There is a general feeling here that Asquith should not go out of his way to release Mrs Maybrick just to oblige the United States government. The only explanation for this is that they feel that England has been treated cavalierly by the United States.'

The explanation, for what it was worth – and it was worthless – fell back behind the predictably moth-eaten camouflage of Ireland. 'England,' continued the report, quoting an unnamed politician, 'is constantly held up to ridicule and contempt to please the Irish, yet your people ask us to release legally committed convicts for no other reason than that they are Americans.' By this facile casuistry, Mrs Maybrick must remain incarcerated because of American support for Home Rule.

Concurrent with this, Asquith revoked what meagre concessions Florence was allowed. 'The only result of Mr Asquith's appointment,' wrote the barrister J.H. Levy, 'was the curtailment of a few privileges, as to the reception of visitors, etc., which had been conceded by Mr Matthews.'[94] There were to be no more conferences with her mother, and excepting the Bible, no further access to any printed material. The prisoner who was already incommunicado was now doubly so. 'Mr Asquith never gave any reason for this action,' continued Levy, at a loss to understand. Like everyone else struggling to free Mrs Maybrick, he'd anticipated progress from a Liberal Home Secretary. To get the opposite was inexplicable as the pirouette at the *Hawk*.

In respect of the latter, it's apparent that the *Hawk*'s editor had indeed been warned off, rather as Muckley and his publisher had been silenced in Manchester. Macdougall however was made of different stuff, and wasn't going away. His charges of misfeasance were escalating into specific accusation, and his penultimate letter to Moore might well have been the clincher. Published on 6 December 1892, it was an openly provocative attack on the Maybrick brothers:

They could not dispute or deny what are simple plain facts which are both incontroverted and incontrovertible. The arsenic was not found by the police, but was produced to them by the five persons who put the charge of murdering her husband upon Mrs Maybrick. These five people – the Maybrick brothers, Yapp, Briggs, and Mrs Hughes – said they had found it after the death of James Maybrick, while Mrs Maybrick was lying in her mysterious swoon, and before they called the police. Neither the police nor anybody else produced any evidence as to where this arsenic had been procured, or who had procured any of it, as to where and by whom it had been introduced into the house.

Although Macdougall left it at that, at least for the time being, it's worth one last reiteration of the obvious: if Florence Maybrick was in possession of enough arsenic to wipe out a street, why bother to soak fifteen one thousandths of a grain of it out of a bloody flypaper?

In her evidence at the inquest, when these 'criminal instruments' were fresh in her memory, Bessie Brierley described their discovery: 'On going into Mrs Maybrick's bedroom,' she said, 'I noticed a small basin with a towel over it. I lifted up the towel and looked under it. There was a <u>fly-paper</u> under this.' Coroner Brighouse immediately converted this solitary flypaper into a plural. 'What did you see in the basin beside fly-papers?' In answer she said she found 'some bits of fly-paper in the slop-pail'. In other words, there was *only one*, and this was the *only* occasion on which a *single flypaper* was ever seen soaking in Battlecrease House.

'So far as evidence has been adduced, there has been no proof that the cause of death was arsenical poisoning,' wrote a correspondent to the editor of the *Daily Post*. 'The whole case is about the most mysterious and extraordinary in judicial records.'

Does this flagrant entrapment of Florence Maybrick merit the word 'mysterious'? After the 'trial' various statements were made that are very material to the question. In an interview with the *Liverpool Daily Post*, Mrs Briggs was asked, 'When did you first hear anything about the letter opened by Alice Yapp?' To which she replied, 'I knew nothing about it until it was publicly mentioned, and I was perfectly ignorant of Mrs Maybrick's intrigue with Brierley.'[95]

In respect of Alfred Brierley, she's lying through her teeth. The intercepted letter wasn't made public until 28 May, when it was revealed at the coroner's inquest. If Briggs had no knowledge of Mrs Maybrick's affair until then, how was it that she could suggest, in self-admitted sarcasm, that a desperate Florence should write to Brierley for assistance on 14 May? She clearly knew all about the adultery long before the newspapers got hold of it. Notwithstanding that, Briggs's claim that she had no knowledge of the intercepted letter was certainly true. It was true because it hadn't yet been concocted. On that Wednesday morning, she and her sister went barging into Battlecrease House at Michael Maybrick's request. In her evidence at the inquest, Briggs deposed: 'On Wednesday May 8th I went to Battlecrease. When I got there Alice Yapp said something, and in consequence I went into Mrs Maybrick's room.'[96]

Alice Yapp *said something*? Something about what? What happened to 'Thank God, Mrs Briggs, you have come, for the mistress is poisoning the master'? Given the circumstance of her mission, it's hardly something the prying old ghoul would be likely to forget. Yet Briggs didn't regurgitate this indelible exclamation at the coroner's court, and neither did she speak of it at the 'trial'.[97] She said absolutely nothing about it, and the reason was because Alice Yapp had never said it. It was a subsequent invention, designed to inflict further injury upon an innocent woman whose hours were already an anguish. Briggs's statement – or rather, slander – about the poison was first made to a newspaper on 14 August, while Mrs Maybrick waited under sentence of death.

'On Tuesday May 7th,' she said, 'I received a telegram from Mr Michael Maybrick, informing me that his brother was ill, and requesting me to go and see him. On the following day my sister and myself went to his residence. Nurse Yapp beckoned to us across the lawn, and said to me, "Thank God, Mrs Briggs, you have come, for the mistress is poisoning the master."'

Not according to Alice Yapp she didn't. On 20 August Yapp told the same newspaper, 'I never said to Mrs Briggs as she has stated, that the mistress is poisoning the master.'[98] This was consistent with her evidence at the trial, where she denied any suspicion in respect of the flypapers. As Macdougall was later to write, 'It is clear that one or the other of these women is a liar,' and equally clear which one of them it was.

Had Alice Yapp really said it, Briggs and her sibling could have bolted up the stairs and saved James Maybrick's life. Both Edwin and

Dr Humphreys were in the house, and with the briefest of conferences Briggs could have solved James Maybrick's mysterious illness there and then. Wednesday, 8 May could have been the end of 'the Maybrick Mystery' rather than the beginning of it.

But flypapers were not yet in the equation, and saving James wasn't part of Michael Maybrick's plan. The crucial day in the frame-up was this monstrous Wednesday, when Michael Maybrick arrived from London. More interested in chauffeuring than attending to his dying brother, Edwin picked Michael up at Edge Hill railway station at about 8.15 that evening. It isn't difficult to imagine their conversation in the cab. It probably went something like the whispers overheard by the absconding eavesdropper Robert Reeves. Michael would have wanted to know which of his instructions were in progress, what Briggs was up to, and where his 'servant girl' was at. Yapp claimed in her cross-examination that she'd given the intercepted letter to Edwin earlier that afternoon. But for some mysterious reason he'd neglected to bring this most incriminating of documents with him. Asked in forthcoming questions at the 'trial' whether he had read the letter during the drive, Michael replied, 'No, I was told about it.' His memory fails him. On its production at the inquest, he identified the letter, 'which Edwin had given him on his arrival from London'.[99]

This testimony was a lie, of course, because they didn't yet have the letter – at least not a useful version of it. It wasn't until three days later, when Michael and his cohorts ransacked the house, that Mrs Briggs got her pencil out to forge it. The accusations on which the Crown relied were got up by Michael Maybrick on the evening of his arrival. At risk of repetition they were: 1) murder by arsenic obtained from flypapers; and 2) a letter intercepted by Alice Yapp that would 'prove' a continuing adulterous relationship between Mrs Maybrick and Brierley. Once he'd got his story straight and drummed it into his co-conspirators, Michael took the lethal package around to Dr Humphreys.

On the following day he repeated it to Humphreys in the presence of Dr Carter. Saturating his fictions with arsenic, he said, 'Mrs Maybrick's infidelity to her husband is positively known.'[100] How did Michael know that? Who told him that? In his evidence at the 'trial' the bastard said:

SIR CHARLES RUSSELL: You were aware, of course, were you not, of a dispute having arisen to this man Brierley?

MICHAEL MAYBRICK: I did not hear the nature of the dispute. I had heard there had been a dispute.

SIR CHARLES RUSSELL: As far as you are aware, your brother died entirely in ignorance of the guilty meeting in London?

MICHAEL MAYBRICK: Yes, I am convinced of it.[101]

To borrow an expression of disbelief from Charles Ratcliffe, doesn't that exchange just cork you? How could any counsel for the defence, never mind a man of Russell's experience, use the word 'guilty' in respect of his client? All the Crown desired to prove was arsenic and adultery, and with the 'guilty meeting in London', the Irish Judas had just conceded them half of their case.

Russell should have torn Maybrick's tongue out by the root, but he didn't, electing to suppress what everybody knew. If James knew nothing of the affair with Brierley, who told Michael Maybrick? It wasn't Florence, and it wasn't Brierley, so we're left with Briggs, or the helmets in the hedge outside Flatman's Hotel. Did the police tell him, or did he tell them? Like his godforsaken associates, Michael Maybrick spat nothing but lies. Everybody, and most especially James, knew about Florence's adultery. Dr Hopper knew about it. John Baillie Knight knew about it. Charles Ratcliffe knew about it, writing to John Aunspaugh, 'James had got wind of the Flatman's Hotel business.' But Michael had to deny that James had any such knowledge, because it would have exposed the infamous letter to Brierley for the forgery it was. 'Jim informed Michael last month,' wrote Florence in her letter to Dr Hopper, admitting once again that she 'had sinned'. The point is an important one, and worth reiteration: no way could she have written to Brierley in May that 'he [James] is perfectly ignorant of everything', when James had told Michael all about it in April. And curious it is that along with 'Blucher' this letter to Hopper was yet another text denied to the gentlemen of the jury.

The ability to manipulate comes with the credentials of a psychopath, and this can clearly be read in the behaviour of those converted into heartless automatons at Battlecrease House. It wasn't too much of a challenge. All stood to gain from the indulgence of Michael's hatred, which according to Florence Aunspaugh was primed for just such a trigger. Briggs hated the slut because she'd purloined James and then run off to fuck some other wretch. She had fucked Edwin, fucked some solicitor in London, and now Briggs was going to fuck her.

Yapp's share of the hatred was similarly primitive. She hurled insults at the helpless woman as she lay abandoned in her own filth. A request for water was met with, 'Get up and get it yourself.' Yapp was as pitiless as her homicidal mentor, and flaunted her reward: 'She has made good use of her position to possess herself of many of Mrs Maybrick's dresses and such like, and in court, she actually had with her an umbrella which was the property of Mrs Maybrick.'[102]

And what of James's clothes? In the prosecution's quest for arsenic (no matter how insignificant), inordinate effort was made to exhume various body parts from six feet under. But what of such enterprise of the defence? What of half a dozen waistcoats hanging in James Maybrick's closet? If the City Analyst could paw his way through jars of the deceased's viscera looking for arsenic, could not the indefatigable Irishman have spared a glance into one or two of his pockets? It was a waistcoat pocket that was specifically referred to by Dalgleish in his deposition to Coroner Brighouse. Both the Cleaver brothers and Sir Charles Russell were well aware of it, but had no more interest in arsenic (or arsenic residuals) than they had in Dalgleish himself.

Such scandalous insouciance did not apply to the *New York Herald*. In a series of questions to Home Secretary Matthews, it had asked, 'Do you know where Mr Maybrick's clothes are? Do you appreciate the tremendous importance of these clothes in this case? Do you know that one white powder (or perhaps fifteen thousandths of a grain of one) would have saved Mrs Maybrick's life?'

It was the usual waste of ink. Matthews wasn't going to trouble himself with facts. The pleas and petitions for Mrs Maybrick's release, and the presentation of fresh evidence that should have secured it, hit a wall as impenetrable as the granite incarcerating her. It didn't matter what the newspapers wrote, what Macdougall wrote, or what the wife of the President of the United States wrote – they believed this innocent woman was all there was between themselves and an Establishment catastrophe. Cleveland Street was a pleasure in comparison. Thus, nothing made any impression on Her Majesty's henchmen, or on Michael Maybrick either. They kept this young woman in hell so this old woman could get on with the grinning.

In 1892 Henry Matthews moved his worthless arse out of the Home Office, and Michael Maybrick also moved house. He relocated from his apartments at Clarence Gate, Regent's Park, to a snazzy residence half a mile north, at 52 Wellington Road, St John's Wood, Marylebone. Not long after the move (with an apparent loss of interest in Whitechapel but referencing Maybrick's new postal district), the Ripper mailed one of his now infrequent scrawls.

Its receipt was reported by *Reynold's News*: 'An unstamped letter, for which 2d had to be paid, was received at Marylebone Police Court on Wednesday, addressed to The Boss, Police Court, Marylebone. Its contents were as follows: "March 21st, Jack the Ripper – I am just about to commence my tricks at Regent's Park, and will give myself up when I've finished."'[103] In other words, the letter refers to the neighbourhood Maybrick had just left and the one he had just moved into – Regent's Park and Marylebone respectively.

Meanwhile, the famous composer must have looked about his new property with a good deal of satisfaction. It was a large villa in one of London's most salubrious quarters (Santley lived just around the corner), and he was making shedloads of money. This was in fact the year he hit the really big one. With 'Nancy Lee' in 1876 and 'The Holy City' in 1892, we can bookend the Weatherly/Adams partnership. The first made Maybrick a star. With the second he'd put down a score that was to become the single most popular song of the nineteenth century. 'The Holy City' outsold all the rest of his compositions put together; in sheet music alone it sold over a million copies, leaving Sir Arthur Sullivan and the rest staring after it. 'Though I must not boast of such things,' boasted Maybrick, '"The Holy City" has had as large, if not larger, sale of any contemporary song ever written.'[104] It filled the Boosey coffers, and Maybrick's ego was on afterburn. He was a man at the summit of fame, basking in radiance – or as his niece chose to put it, 'raised to the celestial plains'.

And then he disappeared.

Michael Maybrick went up the gangplank with the velocity of Lord Arthur Somerset at the height of the Cleveland Street scandal. Apart from a couple of abortive appearances in 1893, he bailed out of London, slammed the door on his gilded high life, and crept away to marry a forty-year-old butcher's daughter from Hammersmith.

No beauty, but he didn't care for that sort of thing in women anyway, or much for the rest of it. They married on 9 March 1893 in a register office in Marylebone, with Dr Fuller and his wife (who now fostered Florence's kids) as witnesses. Laura Withers had been Michael Maybrick's housekeeper in a house she would never get to live in as its mistress. The newlyweds had already set up home at a spread called 'Lynthorpe' on the Isle of Wight, where Maybrick would live in self-imposed exile for the remaining nineteen years of his life.

Sounds a bit odd, don't it? Especially for a man who liked lime-light and arse? It was as if McCartney had vanished into wilful obscu-rity after 'Yesterday' or 'Hey Jude'.

But something more extraordinary yet was simultaneously in progress. Everyone who knew him forgot that they ever had. Even his most enduring friends were struck with a stultifying amnesia concerning the name Michael Maybrick. It was stripped from the corporate memory. A most intriguing facet of this phenomenon was Maybrick's own participation, because he enabled it, actively going about the business of shedding his name like a serpent sheds its skin. Just as Bro James was relieved of his Freemasonic past, so too was Bro Michael extirpated from his musical world.

This wasn't just leaving London. It was a rout from his association with everything in it. Within a very few weeks he had detached the name Maybrick from every aspect of his social, musical and Masonic affiliations, resigning from the Artists Volunteers, the Savage Club, the Philharmonic Society, the Arts Club, and the Orpheus and St George's chapters. The shouting was over. At the apogee of his triumph with 'The Holy City', Michael Maybrick transformed himself from a celebrity as hot as Sullivan into an anonymous recluse married to a fat woman on the Isle of Wight.

Odd, ain't it?

Some might even call it a mystery, but I think it more likely to be an extension of the 1892 shutdown. The *Hawk* didn't bolt its door by accident; Asquith didn't deny Mrs Maybrick's meagre concessions by accident, any more than the British government terminated all further diplomatic exchange with the USA in respect of her imprisonment.

I was of the view that these sanctions were somehow connected with Maybrick's concomitant and summary evaporation. In short, I didn't believe it was Michael Maybrick who had disappeared into obscurity, but Bro Jack the Ripper. I thought that something had spooked them,* and that the System that had formerly been so accommodating now had urgent reason to see the back of him.

Miss Fanny Davies, the pianist and regular amongst those who performed at Toynbee Hall, took over Michael's lease and moved into the house at St John's Wood. Apart from entries in forgotten rate-books there is little now to remember it. The house is long since demolished, and there is no record of Michael's sojourn there, who he entertained, or indeed what its interior looked like. But I got luckier with the house on the island. A distant relative of Laura Withers had been traced to Connecticut, and thanks to her generosity I was able to acquire photographs of the interior of 'Lynthorpe'.

The picture opposite was taken in the 1920s, after Maybrick's death. His widow had wired the place for electricity, but in Michael's day it was lit with oil lamps and candles. At intervals these glum rooms were underscored with the resonance of an organ. Michael kept it in his study, and kept his study door locked. Apart from the sombre music, virtually nothing was heard of Michael Maybrick for the next seven years.

---

* See Appendix II, 'A Very Curious Letter', page 791.

Michael's brother Edwin's daughter, Amy Maine, supplies one of the few insights into life at Lynthorpe that we have. As a little girl she was sent there for her summer holidays, and dreaded every moment of it. 'Michael wasn't fond of children,' she said, 'and didn't want anything to do with them.' Children were to be seen (as infrequently as possible) and never heard.

Amy's bedroom in the attic was above Michael's, and if she arose too early and made a noise on the floorboards, 'my Aunt came up in her dressing gown and very upset because she said I must go back to bed at once or it would wake my Uncle and he'd be upset for the whole day'. Her memories of Laura were scant. Once attractive, or so Amy had been told, she was now hefty, with khaki-coloured hair. 'She was of a very ordinary family, really,' and definitely not the kind of date Michael would have been comfortable with at the Café Royal. Amy was allowed bread and jam, or bread and butter at tea-time, but never bread, butter *and* jam, and that just about sums this place up. 'All the Maybricks were very cold,' said Amy, 'very formal.' The house itself was cold, 'heated in winter by an oil-stove of some kind in the dining room'. She remembers her uncle as 'vain, arrogant, dictatorial' and bereft of friends. Maybrick spent most of the day in his study, and she doesn't recall any visitors. He was a member of a local cycling club but didn't own a bike, a member of the yacht club but didn't have a boat. He never talked about his past, his interest in the Artists Volunteers or his life as a singer, and never spoke of Freemasonry.

As the lamps were lit, more often than not there was an after-dinner ritual, when all would troop into the hall to listen to Michael's choice of music. 'He was one of the first people on the island to own a gramophone. He was sent one by Boosey's because he wrote to them complaining that some of his songs had been recorded out of context. To pacify him they gave him a very beautiful gramophone, and he would bring records out in the evening, and we sat in the sort of alcove in the hall, and he played these records – very, very long pauses between, while he dusted each record with a silk hand-kerchief or a camel-hair brush. It all had to be very proper. My aunt lay on the couch and went to sleep. She wasn't musical at all.'

It is a portrait of excruciating stagnation: a provincial *Hausfrau* dozing in her bulk, a bored little girl on a chair, and a forlorn murderer dusting off his Mozart through endless Victorian evenings, gramophone records his only friends.

'Michael is an enigma,' writes Shirley Harrison. 'He is hardly ever mentioned in the diaries or reminiscences of many of his famous contemporaries.'[105] I think Mrs Harrison may well have invented a new definition for the word 'understatement'.

It might be argued that hardly anybody in our day has ever heard of other celebrated Victorian performers like Santley, Ganz or Frederick Weatherly. The difference between them and Michael Maybrick is that if you want to discover them, you simply have to look. There are comprehensive archives. All have written books or had books written about them.

Michael Maybrick wrote nothing, and nobody wrote anything about him. The nearest we get is a memoir by Weatherly, written thirteen years after Maybrick's exit, wherein a lifetime of associa-tion merits little more than a page. The Trinity College of Music has never heard of its former Vice President: 'There is nothing in the Jerwood Library, including the Mander and Mitchenson Theatre Collection, on this singer/composer, and we have no record of the Maybrick (Ballad) Prize.'[106] Not a scrap either in the National Archives: its collection of 'Opera Singers, Vocalists, Singers, in the P.R.O. Archive of Photographs (1863/1913)' doesn't have a scintilla of Michael Maybrick. Ditto the three-volume *Two Centuries of Music in Liverpool*. You may as well look in the non-record records of the Arts Club, or for that matter the nothing at Toynbee Hall.

I've wasted more hours than I care to mention searching for the elusive name, returning time after time to the archives of great and insignificant libraries, scouring the indexes and peering past closing time into the footnotes of Christ knows how many thousands of books. I wasn't alone. I had endless assistance, most notably from an insider at the greatest library on earth. My contact at the British Library went way beyond the call of duty. He trawled the collections, accessed avenues of shelves, hunting for the name Michael Maybrick. But he found just about nothing. 'It's been a virtually fruitless task going through the various memoirs we have here,' he wrote, making the point with an awesome list of titles. 'George R. Sims' *My Life* was the only book in which I found any mention of Michael Maybrick.'[107] Bro Sims sets a very low standard and precedent for the rest. He remembers Maybrick, but only as some sort of transient at a funeral in 1877. It was reminiscent of James and his Freemasonry; or if you will, James and his arsenic. Sir Charles Russell could discover no one beyond the 1870s who would confirm he even took it, and I could find no one beyond that same decade who would admit to knowing Michael Maybrick.

Stuck in the same time-warp, Russell's buddy Bro Ganz does no better, blacking out in 1876. His autobiography *Memories of a Musician* was published in 1913. Although it overflows with anecdote for everyone in Maybrick's circle – Santley, Sims Reeves, Sullivan et al. – the best he can do for the man himself is to rake up a forty-year-old memory: 'I was first to accompany him,' he recalls, 'at a concert at Stratford in Essex.'[108] The song was 'Nancy Lee', and that's it for Bro Ganz. It seems to have entirely slipped his mind that he was one of Maybrick's closest friends, accompanying him at innumerable concerts throughout the 1880s, most especially at St James's Hall in London.

It had also slipped his mind that he was an enthusiastic member of Orpheus Lodge, where on Saturday, 30 October 1880, Michael Maybrick was installed as Worshipful Master. Among those present were some of Maybrick's dearest, including Masonic Secretary to the Prince of Wales Colonel Thomas Shadwell Clerke, William Hayman Cummings (of whom more in a moment), and the absent-minded Bro Wilhelm Ganz. Ganz was yet another groupie of the Prince, 'a personal friend', according to Bro T.G.E. Sheddon, 'and of the Royal Family, many of whom he taught at St James's Palace … He was the accompanist par excellence of his day and played for all the best singers'[109] – which, at risk of a lousy segue, puts him back on stage with his pal Michael Maybrick: 'Bro Wilhelm Ganz's Matinee Musicals were held at the Marlborough Rooms on Tuesday last [in July 1882] the attendance being such as might be expected on such an occasion. Madame Antoinette Stirling, Miss Santley, and Bro Michael Maybrick were principal vocalists, Bro Ganz [accompanying on] piano.'

Ganz and Maybrick were used to sharing applause. The quotation above is from *The Freemason*, and below is a programme from one of the many concerts in which they performed together at St James's Hall.

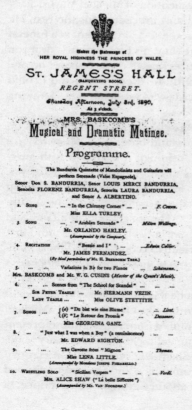

Although Ganz runs into a mental block after 1876, his recollections of Michael Maybrick are positively encyclopedic compared to everyone else's. We get glimpses at the peripheries from the likes of George Sims, but never a whisper from the insiders. Bro Sir Charles Santley (fellow member of the Savage, knighted in 1907) is a classic example, as close to Maybrick's publisher, John Boosey, as he was to the star himself. 'I had many spars with J. Boosey,' he writes, 'but we never quarrelled; we were very intimate friends; both personally and professionally.'[110] He could have said the same for his friend Michael Maybrick, but he didn't.

Featuring the biggest names of the day, the picture below appeared in *Sphere Magazine* in 1892. The great baritone Sims Reeves stands at its centre, Maybrick to the left of him on piano, and Santley to the right, above Madame Patey's fan.

Santley wrote two autobiographies, *Student and Singer: The Reminiscences of Charles Santley* and *Reminiscences of My Life*.[111] Neither so much as mentions Michael Maybrick. You don't have to grow up in the same city, share the same teachers (in Liverpool and Milan), get a hit song dedicated to your daughter and another to yourself, and sing on the same stages for twenty-five years, to remember a man as famous as Michael Maybrick.

Yet he apparently made no impact on Santley. Maybrick described Santley as one of his bedrock friends, 'of whom he cannot say too much', and peculiar it is that Santley has nothing to say about him.

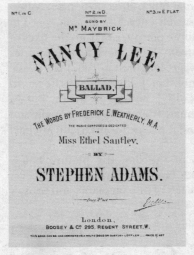

It's the same story in Santley's archive at Liverpool. A lifetime of programmes and press cuttings and *soirées* with the Queen at Buckingham Palace, but not a scrap refers to the singer born next door and who until the sudden exit lived two streets away in St John's Wood.

He does no better with Sims Reeves. 'I take the opportunity to testify to the merits of that great artist,' says Maybrick. And now let's hear what Reeves has to say about him. Nothing. Two autobiographies and a definitive *Life* by Charles Pearce contain not a word about the composer whose songs Bro Reeves sang so often.[112] Bro Arthur Sullivan also falls victim to the same uncompromising amnesia. Wheelbarrows of books exploring every facet of Sullivan's life are completely in ignorance of his friendship with Maybrick. A cynic might find that somewhat incomprehensible, what with the two men being Masonic Grand Organist almost back to back. Some might wonder what it was about Maybrick that annulled the Masonic memory.

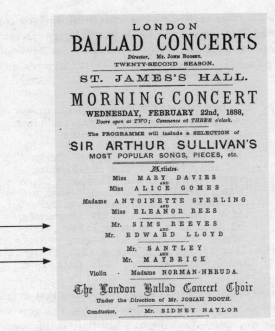

It's with Frederick Weatherly that history runs out of excuses. His archive is housed at the British Library, and it would take a more acquiescent point of view than mine not to feel a trifle suspicious of the thirty-eight folios evidencing his life. Once again the name Michael Maybrick is nowhere to be discovered. There is of course a collection of Weatherly/Adams song-sheets, but not a single reference to the name behind the sobriquet. The only hint we get is an oblique mention in 'Friend o' Mine', a lyric Weatherly wrote in 1913, which he sent 'to the man I loved, a lifelong friend', who predictably remains anonymous. 'Stephen Adams' was Weatherly's collaborator, but it was Maybrick who was the lifelong friend, a fellow he saw 'constantly, usually at his own house in Wellington Terrace'.[113]

How intriguing it is that a relationship lasting over forty years is not worthy of a single mention in Weatherly's archive – not a letter, not a card, not a name scribbled in the margin refers to Michael Maybrick. Like Gilbert without Sullivan, Lennon without McCartney, Weatherly is without Maybrick. If you didn't know better you might imagine that Weatherly was a one-man band, and you could hardly be blamed. Never mind Maybrick, by 1911 even 'Stephen Adams' had disappeared, *Black's Musical Dictionary* elevating Weatherly from lyricist to actual *composer* of all Maybrick/Adams's most famous songs.

> **WEATHERLY (Frederic)** composed numerous popular songs, including " Nancy Lee," " The Holy City," " When We are Old and Grey," " Bid Me Good-bye," " London Bridge," " Danny Boy," " The Midshipmite "; wrote " Musical and Dramatic Copyright," books for children, poems, etc. Educated at Brasenose College, Oxford; M.A., then a coach at the University, he became a barrister, 1887; celebrated his jubilee as a song writer, Dec. 11, 1919; *b.* Oct. 4, 1848, Portishead, Somersetshire; *Add.* Bath, Eng.

Needless to say, neither Maybrick nor Adams gets an entry, his hit compositions now credited to someone else. This is probably what Mrs Harrison means by 'enigma'. Nowhere is this more startling than in Maybrick/Adams's absence from Sir George Grove's *Dictionary of Music and Musicians*. This four-volume, 2,444-page shelf-bender references practically anyone who ever whistled through his teeth. But you will look in vain for the superstar who created some of the most celebrated music of the Victorian epoch.

At first glance this seems incomprehensible, because Maybrick's soulmates Bro W.H. Cummings and Bro Sir Arthur Sullivan were contributory editors to Grove, and are named as such in all four volumes. How this Fraternal duo could have overlooked their equally famous contemporary might be regarded as 'a bit of a mystery' by those who indulge in such conundrums.

Sir Arthur Sullivan was one of Sir George Grove's special friends – 'perhaps his best friend', according to one of his biographers – with the two men enjoying a more enduring relationship than that Sullivan shared with Sir Charles Russell. Sir George of course was on more than cordial terms with Bro Sir Charles Warren, mentoring him through his scrapes with the Palestine Exploration Fund, as he would later mentor the career of Bro William Hayman Cummings.

It was Sir George who had secured Cummings' appointment as Principal of the Guildhall School of Music.

Cummings began his rise to fame in opera, singing with the best of them at Covent Garden, Drury Lane, and many of the kingdom's principal festivals. He and Maybrick first performed together in 1876 in the Three Choirs Festival at Hereford. Thereafter their paths followed an intersecting lattice. Cummings was a director of the Philharmonic Society, of which Maybrick and Ganz were associates, together with their ubiquitous hero Sullivan, who was a guarantor. Bro Cummings was a founder member of Orpheus, and like Maybrick and Ganz a member of the Savage and the Arts Club, the latter that exclusive rendezvous at the end of Conduit Street. Frederick Weatherly was also a member, as was W.H. Thomas, the fellow Artists Volunteer who taught the lads to sing at Toynbee Hall.[114] Notwithstanding that some of his closest friends are listed as members in 1888, Maybrick's blatant clear-out is again starkly in evidence. Club records purport to show that he never joined in the fun until *1896*, and was only briefly a member before resigning in 1900.

Give me a fucking break.

Whoever cooked this up wasn't as adept at meddling with documents as some of the competition. Maybrick actually resided at the Arts Club in 1884, and was a regular throughout that decade. His unctuous interrogation, published in the *World* magazine in 1890, is worth reiteration: therein he's either doing his manly things – riding, rowing, etc. – 'or enjoying the conviviality of the Arts Club'.[115] Before Jack the Ripper took to the streets with his blade, Michael Maybrick can readily be found at the Arts, but after 1892 he's apparently still four years away from joining?

So what reason can be divined for this erasure from the picture as surely as Trotsky was airbrushed out of history in Stalin's Soviet Union? Michael Maybrick vanished with a similar alacrity to Lord Arthur Somerset. The noble faggot went to France, Maybrick to the Isle of Wight. Somerset was protected by the System, 'men of rank', as a previously quoted newspaper put it, who 'stand by scoundrels of their order, no matter what their crimes are'.

I think we're looking here at an explanation for the Fraternal amnesia. The answer is that Sir Charles Santley, Wilhelm Ganz, Sims Reeves, Col. Sir Robert Edis, Sir Frederick Leighton, William Cummings, Sir Frederick Weatherly and Sir Arthur Sullivan were all Freemasons, most of them intimates of the Bro King to be (as was Sir Charles Warren, husbanding his aproned police), and that's why you won't find Bro Michael Maybrick in their archives or books. Freemasonry was holding the ladder.

Weatherly didn't get into Grove either, manifestly because of his association with Maybrick. You can't have Tweedledum without Tweedledee. Maybrick betrayed the lot of them, but they didn't dare betray him. He was too strategically positioned in the house of cards.

At the opposite end of the metaphor was of course the torture of Florence Maybrick. Trading an innocent life for their own survival wasn't a proposition worthy of the Establishment's consideration. LP29 was a convict the authorities would have been pleased to forget. But not so her brother-in-law, whose hatred had migrated with him to the Isle of Wight. Although Florence was permitted almost nothing in her prison cell – even looking at freedom beyond the walls was punishable – Michael Maybrick's unquenchable 'spite' against her managed to find a way in.

During her early years at Woking, James Maybrick's brother Thomas wrote friendly letters with news of the children, and every year he sent their photographs, which Florence was allowed to keep in her cell for twenty-four hours on Christmas Day. To look at them through tears and kiss their ghosts was as close to them as she would ever get. Then, without explanation, the photographs ceased. Sacrificing one of her precious letters out, she wrote to Thomas to ask why, to which he replied that 'Mr Michael Maybrick refused to permit it.' Moreover, Michael wrote to the governor of the prison 'to inform me that my son did not wish either his own or his sister's photograph to be sent to me'.[116] James Chandler Maybrick was twelve years old.

Whether or not she was immediately aware of Michael's letter to the prison, Florence was suffering no delusions about who had put her into it. In 1895 a fellow inmate was released on a 'ticket of leave', and the whispered intimacies she had shared with Mrs Maybrick found their way (via Macdougall) into the press. 'The principal topic of her conversation when talking of her case,' reported the ex-prisoner, 'was Michael Maybrick. She often used the expression that he was her "bitter enemy", and said that he had always acted as a bitter enemy to her. He was her accuser, and it is her contention that it was in consequence of the charge he put upon her of poisoning her husband that she is in prison.'[117]

Florence had been incarcerated for seven years, with another seven to go. But neither Alexander Macdougall nor Helen Densmore ever lost hope, the latter motor-driven with rage. Macdougall had published his treatise on the case in 1891, supplemented thereafter with ever more ferocious attacks on the British Establishment from Densmore:

> Mr Asquith, the successor of Mr Matthews, from first to last was invulnerable to any plea for her release, and yet Mr Asquith pardoned during his term 166 women for whom no claim of innocence was made. This is only another evidence that there exists some subtle reason that does not appear why such strenuous care is taken that this one woman should be held so firmly behind bars. The [British] press has been closed fast as a door at midnight against discussion of the facts … whether or not Mrs Maybrick shall end her unhappy life in prison, it is certain that some time the facts will be known, and her trial and condemnation and the refusal to investigate her case will make a dark page in the history of English criminal jurisprudence.

Accusing an 'insane judge' of being responsible for Florence's conviction, Mrs Densmore then turned her ire on the police, 'who were among the active conspirators against her. Mrs Maybrick is the victim, not only of legal injustice, but of a conspiracy formed at the time of her arrest, which has followed her through the trial and pursued her to the Home Office when the case was being considered there. Its venomous trail has been seen during all these years of her imprisonment, wherever and whenever an effort has been made for her release.'

Diplomatic exchange between Britain and the US in respect of Mrs Maybrick remained stalled until 1895. It then reanimated as if it had never gone away. In June that year the Conservatives were returned to power. Salisbury was back as Prime Minister, with a new installation as Home Secretary who was as slippery a piece of work as Matthews. He was Bro Sir Matthew White Ridley, Provincial Grand Master of Northumberland, and owner of an estate in that county of 10,000 acres.

It was Ridley's turn to field the ceaseless barrage of criticism and petitions on Mrs Maybrick's behalf, including yet another entreaty from Macdougall, published in 1896 as 'Three Letters Addressed to Sir Matthew White Ridley, Bart'.[118] These 'letters' were about a hundred pages apiece, and like everything else they were curtly ignored. In response to a question from an Irish Member in Parliament, the recalcitrant Bro 'gave the usual evasive reply that he could give no hope of a speedy release. No reason; no explanation; and with an attitude that says, "We have the power to keep her, and we neither intend to release her, nor give any reason thereof."'

By now even the press were beginning to believe something peculiar was going on. 'The public cannot help feeling that the shadow of a great wrong is over us,' wrote the *Daily Mail* in August 1896, echoed that same month in the *Blackpool Times*: 'The impression grows with increasing strength that there is some mystery about the continued imprisonment of Mrs Maybrick.'

It was an opinion widely shared in America. 'Some influence which does not appear on the surface was responsible for her continued detention,' was the view of the *Brooklyn Eagle*, and it attracted some potent support. 'Among them,' writes Mr Trevor Christie, 'was Clerk Bell, a leading attorney who was president of the New York Medico-Legal Society. Although he had never met Florence or her mother, he took up the cudgels with boundless energy, and on the tenth anniversary of her imprisonment became Chairman of the Maybrick Memorial Committee. He addressed new petitions to the Home Office and the State Department, and journeyed to Europe in the summer of 1898 to try and unravel the enigma.'

He got nowhere. It didn't matter what the argument was or who it came from, the government were as deaf to it as the coppers had been blind in Whitechapel. And it was for the same reason.

'It must have been a very strong influence that operated to induce the English Government to refuse the request of President McKinley,' recorded Clerk Bell in his *Medico-Legal Journal*. 'Sir Matthew White Ridley's recent statement in the English Parliament shows that this official is under some peculiar restraint in his action in this matter. Some very deadly hostilities against this unfortunate exist which seem not only all-powerful but controlling on the Home Secretary.'

The all-powerful element was complicity between this exalted elite and a Freemasonic monster. No policeman dared to touch him, and no politician either. They were sick men. They were Jack's whores. 'My contention is that Mrs Maybrick has fallen a victim to this political disease,'[119] wrote J.H. Levy, and like the rest of her allies, he was right.

Another question, by another Irish Member, was put to Ridley in the House of Commons. T.P. O'Connor, the editor of the *Star*, challenged the Home Secretary with yet another appeal for clemency. He received the usual evasive reply, but it was inadvertently more revealing than any answer preceding it. Ridley intimated that the Home Office was in possession of a 'secret dossier' on Florence Maybrick, proving her guilt. Thus, Mrs Maybrick was being held captive for life *not* because of the evidence that supposedly convicted her, but because of a 'secret dossier', suppressed at her 'trial', and so incendiary that it was 'impossible for him to make it public'.

In other words, 'the Maybrick Mystery' wasn't a mystery at all, but rather 'the Maybrick secret'. What was the 'secret' that this Freemason knew, and by definition shared with Salisbury and his mob? Was the secret the reason Florence Maybrick was framed in one of the most despicable got-up outrages ever to poison an English court? Sixty-five years after it, a barrister of the Inner Temple gave his view of these proceedings. 'Mr Justice Stephen,' he wrote, 'was regarded as the greatest authority on our criminal law. But, since the evil that men do alone lives after them, he is best remembered today as the judge who, more than any person, even her vindictive brothers-in-law, was responsible for the absurd conviction of Mrs Maybrick.'[120]

The British use a euphemism for corruption, called tradition – which brings us back to the Establishment and its bewigged 'secret'. Was this 'secret' the reason James Maybrick was stripped of his Masonry in death? Was it the same 'secret' that corrupted every coroner presented with it, and turned the Metropolitan Police into a herd of idiots?

Was Bro Jack the Ripper the secret?

'The case of Mrs Maybrick is a most important one,' argued J.H. Levy in his important book *The Necessity for Criminal Appeal* (1899). 'When it is realised by the British public that Mrs Maybrick has been doomed to life-long imprisonment on the strength of a "secret dossier", for a crime for which she has never been publicly tried, and on a warrant for an offence of which it is admitted she may be innocent, the result will be a revulsion of feeling such as has not been experienced in England for many a long day.'[121]

Justice was not something in which these morally disabled men had any interest. One hundred and thirty years later this bullshit of a so-called 'secret' still festers – our startlingly obvious Whitechapel Psychopath continues to attract a miasma of misguided protection from the Ripper industry. I don't blame those who feel thus obliged, but at the end of this long toil, I rather pity them. Is Freemasology going to try to sustain its loony-tune 'secret' for the next 130 years?

History is a long time.

James Maybrick's family crest, which he acquired in 1881, bears the legend '*Tempus Omnia Revelat*' – 'Time Reveals All'. It features a falcon (Horus the sky god) holding a sprig of acacia in its beak, in deference to the memory of Masonry's first Grand Master, Hiram Abiff. After murdering James, Michael stole the crest for his carriage door on the Isle of Wight.

'Time Reveals All', and time's up for Michael Maybrick. Jack the Ripper was a Victorian psychopath, he belongs to them, and posterity – for want of a word – should rejoice to be rid of him.

'Truth is the Law of God,' wrote Confucius. 'Acquired Truth is the Law of Man. Being indestructible it is eternal. Being self-existent, it is infinite.'

For myself, I haven't got much of a God, and certainly no religion. Crack open a falcon's egg and that slime knows all the laws of aerodynamics a thousand millennia before Christ. Is that God? I really couldn't say. But I hope there's a deity somewhere, some indestructible truth, that these men who countenanced such evil might face the justice of the angels.

Appendix I

The Parnell Frame-Up

Although born in Dublin, Robert Anderson despised the Irish, or rather any Irishman who wasn't a Conservative Unionist. 'He belonged to one of those Irish Protestant families who had the fiercest hatred and dread of the purposes of the majority of their countrymen.' He was the younger son of a family 'who for at least two generations had given their zealous and effective support to the open and secret forces that were arrayed against the Nationalists and the Nationalist Party'. Anderson wanted to be an Englishman, and the closest he could get was slavish subservience to English interests. 'No one could suppose,' he wrote, '[that] the United Kingdom will tamely consent to be swamped by a horde of [Irish] paupers and agitators.'

His father was Crown Solicitor at Dublin, his brother Samuel a solicitor in the Crown Prosecution Department, and Anderson himself a rising star in the political police. All three operated out of Dublin Castle, which throughout Victoria's reign was one of the world's great citadels of despotic repression. It was from the Castle that Anderson ran his network of intrigue, agents provocateurs and coppers' narks.

Business was always brisk. Over a million Irish people had died in the great famine of 1846, and three million had been forced to emigrate. 'Ireland is boiling over and the scum flows across the Atlantic,' was a typical comment from the British press of the day. They took their tears and their hatred with them, and occasionally they came back with dynamite. The British had created what they most feared. Half of Ireland's population were now out of their control. In the slums of Baltimore and Boston young Irishmen with revenge in mind formed secret societies. Wilful government blindness empowered these 'Fenian' outrages, when the solution was timeless, universal, and simple: if you want to stop terrorism, get out of their fucking country.

Ireland was an imperial adjunct in a state of permanent defeat; law was whatever came out of a soldier's mouth. What resistance there was, was quelled without quarter, its patriots arrested, incarcerated, sometimes tortured and not infrequently hanged. Since the time of Oliver Cromwell, Ireland had been a *de facto* police state. Nascent hopes of independence were crushed in an 'orgy of corruption' when in 1800 the Irish were traduced into an act of permanent union with Great Britain. Byron called it 'the Union of a shark with its prey', and half a lifetime later Prime Minister William Gladstone agreed: 'There is no crime recorded in history which will compare for a moment with the means by which the Union was brought about.' Thereafter cordial relations were sustained by the enduring presence of 35,000 British bayonets.

For most of his political career Gladstone had supported the imperial presence. But in 1886 he had a change of mind and declared himself in favour of Home Rule (i.e. the government of Ireland by the Irish). A frisson of horror ran through the moneyed classes, their anguish in direct correlation to their wealth. Salisbury called it 'the greatest threat to Empire since Napoleon', and Victoria fouled her corset. The name of the game was acquiring countries, not giving them up. Gladstone was 'plunging a knife into the heart of the British Empire'. She already loathed him – 'a dangerous old fanatic' – and since the Fenians had tried to dynamite a statue of her dead husband in Dublin, she similarly despised the Irish. 'No one would go to Ireland,' she gawped; 'people only go there when they have their estates to attend to.'

Her point of view was precisely the Irish point of view, but from a rather different perspective. Over the centuries land grabs had created vast estates, with palatial houses built for migrating English aristocrats. They stole the best of it. The Irish got the rocks and the bogs. No one had ever pretended any subtlety of intention: rip off the real estate, then rent an acre or two to the people who had owned it – and if they couldn't pay, or wouldn't pay, kick their arses off, demolish their hovels, and let them starve. 'I have seen the Indian in his forest, and the Negro in his chains,' wrote a French traveller, Gustave de Beaumont, 'and I thought then I beheld the lowest terms of human misery, but I did not know the lot of Ireland.'

A minute more of the British was a minute too many, and for the first time in decades there seemed to be a reason for the Irish to hope.

The Act of Union had furnished seats in the Westminster Parliament for Irish Nationalists. In 1886 there were fifty-seven of them, led by a forty-year-old enigma called Charles Stewart Parnell. Resistance to British rule was defined by this indefatigable Irishman. His political genius was acknowledged by all, but fathomable by nobody. 'He achieved his unique success by the possession of a unique capacity of holding his tongue,' was the judgement of W.T. Stead. Parnell was a man sparse of words, 'but when he spoke he was obeyed'.

Parnell put an end to Fenian violence, depriving his Conservative opponents of a staple of condemnation. He fought the Rt Honourable Gents on their own terms. In debate he was 'Invincible', wrote the Irish historian Shane Lesley: 'more than a politician, he was a Principle, and Principles are not easily broken'.

The fifty-seven Nationalist MPs held the balance of power in a precarious Parliament, and Parnell made no secret of his indifference to the asinine squabbling of British party politics. He would side with anyone, Tory or Liberal, if there was a deal to be done on the side of Ireland. His association with Gladstone over Home Rule was a catastrophe for the Conservatives. The London Stock Exchange lost a quarter of its value, bleeding £4 million, an astronomical hit for the 1880s, but mere pocket money compared to the £100 million sterling the City and its bandits had leaning on the security of Irish real estate.

Salisbury, who replaced Gladstone as Prime Minister in July 1886, knew very well that he couldn't counter Home Rule by parliamentary means. Forget democracy – democracy wasn't up to the crisis. Voting was all very well when you knew you were going to win, but worthless in these circumstances. Something more exotic was required. They were going to have to devise a way to eradicate the mad old idiot Gladstone, and to neutralise Home Rule in the process. In short, they were going to have to fit Parnell up.

By now Anderson had quit Dublin, and was operating out of London. He'd brought his Bible with him. When he wasn't pawing through it he was preaching from his local pulpit, putting himself about like some sort of secretary to the late Jesus Christ. Years later, when he was finally rumbled for the viper he was, the contemporary verdict was harsh. He had 'violated the traditions of the high position he held', and was a man of 'violent political prejudices' so all-consuming 'that they often blind him to the difference between what is right and what is wrong'.

The Right Hon. Viscount Lord Salisbury had once remarked, 'Ireland awoke the slumbering genius of British Imperialism.' It was wide awake now, and seeing it controlled a quarter of the land surface of the earth, Charles Parnell was about to discover that he had something to worry about.

On 21 December 1886, somebody placed an advertisement in *The Times*:

AUTOGRAPHS WANTED – TEN POUNDS will be given by the advertiser for a collection of not less than TWENTY AUTOGRAPHS of distinguished PARLIAMENTARY LEADERS ... To include: Mr Gladstone, Lord Hartington, Sir William Harcourt, Mr Bright, Mr Chamberlain, Lord Salisbury, Lord Randolph Churchill, Mr Parnell, Mr Sexton, and Sir M. Hicks-Beach, must be supplied within the next fortnight.

This seemingly innocuous ad was in fact the precursor of one of the filthiest conspiracies in British parliamentary history. Every department of state was marshalled as required in the plot against Parnell, and that included the Criminal Investigation Department at Scotland Yard.

Throughout the latter period of 1888, the government conspiracy ran in parallel with the Ripper – uncannily so, almost on a day-to-day basis.

Anderson had 'gone on holiday' on the day Polly Nichols was murdered, and returned to London on the day of the 'Double Event'. Anyone who believed he was genuinely vacationing in France might not quite have a grip on what was going on. The two chiefs of Metropolitan Police, (Sir) Robert Anderson and Sir Charles Warren, were respectively concocting evidence in order to destroy Parnell, and destroying evidence in order to protect the Ripper.

In both cases the motivation of these God-sodden zealots was to safeguard the perceived interests of Her Majesty's ruling elite. The House of Commons looked like what it was, a museum of Conservative well-being. Indifferent to anything but its own self-interest, Parliament belonged to wealth and was rotten to its sanctimonious marrow. Arthur Balfour, promoted by his uncle, Salisbury, to Secretary of State for Ireland in 1887, famously said, 'It doesn't matter which party is in office, the Conservatives are always in power,' and nobody was arguing with that.

Balfour quickly established his credentials as a dictatorial bitch. Known in some quarters as 'Pretty Fanny', he soon acquired a change of name in Ireland, where he was known as 'Bloody Balfour'. His complicity in the Parnell conspiracy was already well advanced. Most of it was conducted in secret, but as an overt element, he was poised to introduce a new 'Coercion Act' that would practically make it illegal to be Irish, or more specifically, an Irish Nationalist. Under these new statutes, any person could be arrested for any reason, or without any reason, and imprisoned indefinitely without trial. Protest was irrelevant, as the protection promised in Habeas Corpus was no longer applicable. Viscount Salisbury had written, 'A more arbitrary government, that was not squeamish about forms of law, or particularly about hanging the wrong man occasionally, might succeed where previous legislation has failed.'

Cunningly synchronised to coincide with the introduction of 'Fanny's Act', something of equal odium was on its way out of Fleet Street. On 18 March 1887 *The Times* printed the first of a series of seven articles titled 'Parnellism and Crime'. Authored anonymously with escalating venom, and published between March and May, their litany of accusation caused the required sensation, stunning Parnell's friends and delighting his foes. It was no accident that *The Times* had been selected as the vehicle for the destruction of the Irish leader. If something was in 'the world's greatest newspaper' it had to be true, and on that chill London morning as Parliament assembled, it looked as if the game for Home Rule was up.

Parnell's domestic organisation was known as the Land League, and out of it had evolved the Plan of Campaign. Both outfits were dedicated to ameliorating the lot of Ireland's agricultural workers, resisting the imposition of punitive rents and summary evictions (by the thousands) of those who couldn't pay. Both were popular with the people, and although they achieved only minimal reform, they were rather too successful for those with their hands in the Irish till. With spectacular hypocrisy, Balfour declared the Plan of Campaign a 'criminal conspiracy', then nipped down to Fleet Street to organise his own. The first instalment of 'Parnellism and Crime' was an omen of the ill to come. Dismissing whatever legitimate advances the Land League had made, *The Times* put its spite in like a hooligan's boot. It was a tirade of libel designed to force Parnell into one of Salisbury's courts. If he sued, he'd lose; if he didn't, he was guilty: 'Be the ultimate goal of these men what it will,' squawked *The Times*, 'they are content to march toward it in the company of murderers. Murderers provide their funds, murderers share their inmost councils, murderers have gone forth from the League offices to set their bloody work afoot and have presently returned to consult their constitutional leaders in the advancement of their cause.'

Over the next eight weeks 'Parnellism and Crime' continued to bludgeon the public with ever more ferocious propaganda. It would accuse Parnell of every conceivable felony; every violence he abhorred and struggled to rectify he was now blamed for, impugned as its instigator down to the last renegade bullet. 'That worthless man,' Victoria called him, 'who had to answer for so many lives lost' (indifferent to the million Irish dead on her own rap sheet).

Yelling 'Murderer' in Parnell's face and goading him to sue, *The Times* was anxious to keep a focus on the slanders. 'Unless further steps are taken to bring the matter before a court of law,' it proclaimed with bogus rectitude, 'it is difficult to see what more we can do to prove our own good faith, and the charges we believe to be true.'

No deal from Parnell, who would put the faith of a tapeworm before that of *The Times*, knowing full well that in respect of Ireland there wasn't a judge in the kingdom who wouldn't pimp for Salisbury and his government.

Lack of traction caused *The Times* to change tack, switching from Ireland to the supposed terrorist contacts Parnell maintained in the United States. The last three articles in the series were titled 'Behind the Scenes in America', and were compositions of unleashed bigotry. When the first of the articles appeared it was accompanied by the facsimile of a letter, claimed by *The Times* as part of its as yet unpublished evidence, 'which has a most serious bearing on the Parnellite conspiracy. We publish one such document in facsimile today, and invite Mr Parnell to explain how his signature has become attached to such a letter … written a week after the Phoenix Park murders, excusing his public condemnation of the crime, and distinctly condoning if not approving of the murder of Mr Burke.'

The assassination of Thomas Burke, together with Lord Frederick Cavendish, in Phoenix Park, Dublin, on 6 May 1882, was one of the most infamous murders in all Ireland's history. Burke was Permanent Under Secretary at Dublin Castle, and had acquired the hazardous reputation of being 'a devoted and most fearless servant of the Crown'. It was for precisely that reason that an extreme faction of the Fenians known as 'the Invincibles' had an 'order of execution' on the 'Castle Rat'. The unfortunate Cavendish, who had been newly appointed Viceroy, happened to be walking with him as the Invincibles struck. Both were slashed to pieces with surgical knives. What made the event particularly tragic, and fuel for the screech of the newspapers, was that Cavendish was a benevolent and compassionate man, whose plans for reform would have brought glad tidings to Ireland. Instead the nation stood accused, energising Conservative fury for ever more repression. With customary venom *The Times* sank to the occasion, recommending that the innocent Irish population of England 'should be massacred', and Irish leaders blamed for an outrage at which they despaired.

Although Parnell was in prison under Gladstonian edict at the time of the murders, he was blamed then, and in *The Times*'s rhetoric five years later, he was guilty of complicity now. Repackaging him with the Invincibles, who incidentally spat the name Parnell, condemning his constitutional efforts as a waste of air, 'Parnellism and Crime' all but put a bloody knife in his hand.

Such outrageous accusations had been rebutted by Parnell as 'a cold and frigid lie'. But *The Times* didn't want denials, it wanted him in court, and claimed that its latest public fiction, substantiating the facsimile letter, was 'in harmony with the language of some of his allies beyond the Atlantic': 'We have in our possession several undoubted examples of Mr Parnell's signature [obtained by means of the cunning ad requesting autographs] and there can be no doubt of the genuineness of the letter ... If these charges are false, Mr Parnell and his friends can resort to an easy and effectual remedy. The courts of law are open to them [and] they would have an opportunity of proving that the whole story of their association with [various Fenians here named] had been fabricated in the offices of this journal.'

At least something these hyenas wrote was accurate. The whole story had essentially been fabricated in the offices of *The Times*. It's easy to forget that this rubbish had little to do with Irish terrorism, and everything to do with British cash. Meanwhile, its mouthpiece Salisbury was on his feet taunting Gladstone at a Conservative assembly, informing his audience that from the dawn of Parliament they would never find a prime minister countenancing an ally 'tainted with a strong presumption of connivance at assassination, which has been accepted by Mr Gladstone'. His speech was made within twenty-four hours of publication of the facsimile letter, and is as apt an explanation as any of why Parnell would not bring an action in an English court.

If the Prime Minister had already expressed his conviction of Parnell's guilt, what hope did he have in front of one of those carcasses from the Athenaeum? But so far so good for the government. By now various Irish

MPs were in prison for sedition, and Parnell's political stock was crashing. He had but one defence, of scant consequence to the conspiracy mobilising against him, and that was the truth.

The facsimile letter was a forgery, and as always the ominous presence of Robert Anderson was in the vicinity. He had had a clandestine hand in framing some of the 'Coercion Acts', underpinning much of the venom that went into 'Parnellism and Crime'. But it was this counterfeit letter that rose above the general feculence. The letter and a dozen like it had been procured via the services of an 'intimate personal friend' of Anderson with whom he was oft to pray. His Christian sidekick was a young Dublin journalist and son of a prison officer called Edward Caulfield Houston. As manic as his pal in the political police, Houston was secretary to 'the Irish Loyal and Patriotic Union', an ultra-conservative outfit that, according to one contemporary observer, was 'composed of the lineal descendants of degenerates who had betrayed their country for peerages and monetary reward, of grasping lawyers on the make, and academic gentlemen on the look out for jobs'. Considering this was the opinion of William Joyce, a police official at Dublin Castle and ostensibly on the same ticket, these anti-Home Rule fanatics were unquestionably bad news.

The higher echelons of the ILPU had much reason to wake up sweating in respect of Parnell. Its half-dozen presidents were among the biggest landowners in Ireland. It was from their sacred fields that Houston, indirectly, got his finance. The brief was simple enough. Anything, anywhere incriminating Parnell – here or in the US – that facilitated the *Times*/Salisbury conspiracy was the order of the day.

Relishing his task, Houston went about it, procuring the services of a fifty-two-year-old Dubliner by the name of Richard Pigott. This fat little parasite could not have been a more perfect choice for the intended business. Formally a journalist, now derelict, when he wasn't power-begging he got by on fraud, busted for setting up a charity and stealing the donations, and you wouldn't want to trust him dead. Well known in publishing circles and the courts alike, he was a dealer in pornography and a liar of repute, and therefore ideally suited for the chore in hand.

Paid a pound a day to dig dirt on Parnell, Pigott found nothing and so forged it, his sausage-like fingers tracing incendiary falsehoods as required. A dozen months of subterfuge followed, featuring liaisons in ill-lit hotels which for the most part, for reasons of security, were conducted in Paris. At one such rendezvous Houston pitched up with a co-conspirator named Dr Thomas Maguire. Virulent in his enmity towards Irish self-government, Maguire was an academic at Trinity College Dublin, periodically contributing royalist tosh via a rag called the *Union*, and was there to authenticate the letters.

Pigott concocted an outlandish provenance for his merchandise, false as the correspondence itself. There were mysterious 'black bags, mislaid by revolutionaries', wherein Fenian epistles from Parnell and his bloodthirsty mates were discovered. But nobody really cared where they came from, and that was certainly the case when Houston sold them on to *The Times*. The world's worst newspaper was later to claim that it had never heard of Richard Pigott, a man everyone in Dublin had heard of, and especially the cops. *The Times* would have needed to look no further than its own indexes (as I did) to discover articles referencing Pigott's career in misfeasance and four months in jail. Failing that, it could have asked Anderson, who was in regular contact with both the forger and *The Times* itself.

1887 turned into 1888, and *The Times* persisted in its onslaught, republishing 'Parnellism and Crime' in pamphlets and later as pocket-sized books. It couldn't go on, and it didn't. Parnell finally threw in the towel, not to the courts, but to Parliament. Denouncing his accusers in the House of Commons, he demanded a parliamentary inquiry into the articles and letters, and the source of the inquisition against him. It was like asking his torturers for an aspirin. The Leader of the House, W.H. Smith, wasn't interested. Himself a member of the ILPU, he proposed instead a Parliamentary Commission, inadvertently letting it slip in debate that it was in fact a political trial.

Parnell was out of options: either that or destruction by a thousand cuts from *The Times*. At last Salisbury had him where he wanted him. Under his administration the law had visibly decomposed into what it actually was, a brazen instrument of the ruling elite. His understanding of justice was at the discretion of his prejudice, thus in matters Irish (or East End), truth didn't have a chance. The judges selected for the Commission were all appointed by his government, all members of his club, the Athenaeum, and all vigorously opposed to Irish self-government. Maintaining continuity with the judicial shenanigans of Cleveland Street, Bro Sir Richard Webster was chosen to appear on behalf of *The Times*.

Not everyone in the Establishment, however, was as bereft of integrity as the Prime Minister. Although the 'Commission Bill' had been bullied through Parliament using an arcane device called 'Closure' to shut everyone up, in the House of Lords Salisbury ran into a dissenting voice. It belonged to an excellent gent by the name of Lord Herschell, who got to his feet on 10 August 1888: 'Charges of the gravest character are made against those taking an active part in political life. To test these charges and inquire into them a tribunal has been appointed at the absolute discretion of their most vehement political opponents, who have always been bitterly opposed to them, and those who entertain these feelings towards them have also determined what shall be the limit and scope of the enquiry, as to which they have listened to not one word of remonstrance or protest whatever.'

During this Salisbury had gone temporarily deaf. He had an unwholesome view of parliamentary democracy, and would have been just as jolly presiding over a land fit for nothing but royals, bankers and riot police. He didn't care if 'Parnellism and Crime' was without substance or whether the letters were fake. To him law was no different to propaganda – no right, no wrong, only what it wanted – and he wanted Parnell politically dead. The Irish Nationalist leader was charged with conspiracy by a conspiracy. These were the same politicians, in the same Parliament, with the same policemen, who were supposedly trying to catch Jack.

A comparison of the attitudes towards the Purger's correspondence and that forged by Pigott is salutary. On the one hand the Establishment was exerting itself to prove Pigott's letters genuine, while on the other it was dismissing Jack's letters (Moab excepted) as 'hoaxes'. Reality insists the opposite. Anyone who knew anything about Pigott knew his letters were forgeries, and anyone who didn't could have read it.

Eighteen months earlier, Henry Labouchère's magazine *Truth* had blown the scam. On 21 April 1887 it wrote that the first facsimile letter 'was obtained from a person by the name of Pigott'. Did nobody at *The Times* see this? Could not the most humble office boy have pointed it out? Are we to believe that Robert Anderson's secret police, charged with gathering intelligence into the activities of Irish desperados, were incapable of picking up a popular twopenny magazine?

What *Truth* published was indeed the truth, and what followed was a judicial atrocity evolving in extraordinary parallel with the Ripper. Let no one imagine this befoulment of police and politics spontaneously converted itself into the trade of saints when the topic turned to Whitechapel. Of what interest were a handful of murdered whores compared to the financial threat looming over Ireland? The Commission was gearing up for what Gladstone's biographer described as 'one of the ugliest things done in the name of law in this island during the century'.

Welcome to 'Victorian values'.

At Dublin Castle the police administrator, William Joyce, was instructed to clear his desk, the authorities decreeing that he should act as 'Chief Agent' on behalf of the government in surreptitiously procuring such evidence and materials as would enable *The Times* to sustain, if that were possible, the accuracy of the allegations in 'Parnellism and Crime'. Such instruction was echoed in London: 'all the resources of the Home Office and Scotland Yard were at the disposal of *The Times*'.

Anderson and his detectives were suddenly very busy. The logistics of accruing 'evidence', often to include the bribing or blackmailing of witnesses, took up Anderson's every minute throughout the autumn of the Whitechapel terror. Pigott is quoted as claiming 'incessant journeys backwards and forwards to Paris', and it is of course pure coincidence that he happened to be in the French capital in October 1888, when the Chief of the Criminal Investigation Department was also in Paris 'on holiday'.

Outside of the ruthlessly duped Victorian public, only the cerebrally unfortunate could have countenanced this nonsense. After eighteen months of scheming and plotting and forging, we are invited to believe that Anderson was squatting on some boulevard with a croissant when the prize was finally in his grasp.

By the time Anderson left for Paris, his duplicity was approaching the industrial. His co-conspirator, Prime Minister Viscount Lord Salisbury, had said that 'if secret service evidence comes naturally into our hands – and still more clearly fixes someone's guilt, we shall be fulfilling an obvious and elemental duty in facilitating the proof of it before the Commission'. This raises the question, how could it have come *un*naturally into their hands? Was it borne on a breeze through an open window? Who was the secret service working for and supplying information to if not Salisbury's government, and the despicable old bastard was passing every tittle of it on to *The Times*.

It is, I think, significant that government files relevant to police activities during this period are closed to public scrutiny for perhaps another thousand years. In 1888–90 these documents were proscribed under the hundred-year secrecy rule, but one hundred years later they were reclassified in perpetuity, turning on its head the oft-heard bleat of the common parliamentary oaf, 'If you've got nothing to hide, you've got nothing to fear.'

Salisbury's government had everything to hide, as apparently did the government a century later. Anderson actually admitted, 'We did a lot of illegal things,' but so scandalous must be the content of these files that the British people are still not permitted to see what their politicians and policemen were up to 130 years ago.

The Special Commission began its hearings on 17 September 1888, nine days after the murder of Annie Chapman, and thirteen days before the 'Double Event'. Anderson may well have heard that there had been a murder or two in London's East End, but the business of destroying Parnell allowed little time for distraction, especially in respect of those forsaken sluts whose ritualised deaths, according to him, were their own fault. Parnell was the only 'murderer' of interest. Unable to cripple him by means of the niceties of Parliament, the government had created existential 'crimes' on his behalf, and was engaged in nothing less than prosecuting him for its own inventions.

The Irish leader had sought to clear his name, but now, together with sixty-four members of his party, he found himself on trial, charged with 'a conspiracy seeking absolute independence of Ireland from England, that they had promoted an agrarian agitation against the payment of rent with a view to expelling from Ireland the "English Garrison", and, most important, that by their speeches and money payments they incited persons to sedition and the commission of crimes, including murder'.

In other words, it was a legalised rendition of the lies serialised in *The Times* and the newspaper proclaimed it as such: 'The Special Commission

Bill was adopted by Parliament with the object of instituting a thorough enquiry into the whole of the "charges and allegations" embraced in our articles on "Parnellism & Crime".' The whole lousy charade should have been thrown out on day one. Question one from the judges should surely have required the identity of the accusers. Yet the authors hid in secrecy.

So here were the Irish and their leader, democratically elected Members of Parliament, subject to a criminal inquisition, predicated on anonymous slanders in an English newspaper. Much of the American press looked on open-mouthed. 'Respect for *The Times*,' commented the *Nation*, 'without regard to the kind of men who are behind it [i.e. the entire British state], is really a discredit to a civilised nation in our day.'

What this was was a classic example of the aggressor presenting itself as victim, throwing its autocratic weight about in time-honoured fancy-dress tradition. Paradoxically, the government's biggest cannon was also its weakest point. Everything hinged on the letters, and thus Webster stalled for time. Forgeries or not, his intention was to postpone the day of reckoning, anticipating that by then the damage to the Nationalist cause would be so catastrophic as to render it beyond repair. Time favoured such a scenario. Over the next sixteen months the judges would sit for 128 sessions, during which 150,000 questions would be asked of 445 witnesses.

To plunge the depths of Anderson's input would mean kicking in the door to another book. It would be a startling volume, exploring a long career in serial hypocrisy and dazzling misfeasance. His chicanery on behalf of the 'Commission' is well represented across a spectrum of crooked enterprises, but nowhere with more dishonour than in the matter of HM Prisons. Wearing a different hat, Anderson was Secretary to the Prison Board, a title and office he had imported from Ireland. Irrespective of his function as a Commissioner of Metropolitan Police, this put him in charge of everyone Her Majesty locked up, most specifically 'political opponents', i.e. the Irish.

Without access to documents the government fears to show us, it's impossible to fully assess the degree of official felony. However, we get the gist of the rot on the rind from a retired detective by the name of Patrick McIntyre, who described himself as 'Late of the Political Department of Scotland Yard'. Between February and May 1890, McIntyre published a series of reminiscences in *Reynold's News*. In the introduction he kicks off with 'I propose to compare the old detective system with the new Criminal Investigation Department' under honest Bob; 'my account of the secret service will give me a good opportunity of revealing how bogus conspiracies are got up'.

Even by the flexible standards of our day, McIntyre's revelations are staggering. Barring one, he writes: 'In the whole series of dynamite plots, the hand of the spy, or agent provocateur, is clearly visible.' His account records a catalogue of such police conspiracies, reserving special approbation for undercover coppers who had infiltrated the Land League: 'It is distinctly creditable to the young Irishmen in the League, that they held themselves aloof from outrage when they were being egged on by men who only joined The League for the purpose of associating it with dynamite conspiracies and other criminality.' McIntyre then turns his attention to the more primitive of our species, that popular police employee the coppers' nark, men who would sell Ireland for a £5 note: 'These people see their opportunity when any government is in a perturbed state of mind. They seize the "flowing tide that leads to fortune". Their intrigues produce conspiracies. What does the provoking-agent do when he finds the prevailing danger is diminishing in quantity? He manufactures more "danger"! Not a single plot in England,' asserts McIntyre, 'had not been incited by the police.' Such an allegation would be incredible were there not copious evidence supporting it, and none more noxious than in the case of a man called John Daly.

Daly was an active Irish Nationalist, fitted up with explosives by Special Branch at Birkenhead Docks in Liverpool in 1883. The police's motive, as proclaimed by Sir Edward Jenkinson, was to put the fear into Daly's associates and the public alike, as 'obtaining a conviction would have more effect on the public mind than prevention of an outrage'. In other words, a PR exercise that Jenkinson admitted took three attempts before the bombs were successfully planted.

Daly was followed and arrested in Birmingham, where the cops gilded the sting with Fenian romance. The nub of it was that Daly 'planned to hurl the grenades from the Strangers Gallery in the House of Commons'. Forestalling this fiction by no means denied the politicians its propaganda value. If he'd had the bombs (which he hadn't), and if he'd thrown them into Parliament (which he didn't), Matthews would have had his own head blown off, with the unwished-for loss of Parnell's head as well.

Because Daly had not brought such atrocity to the House of Commons, the Home Secretary decided to stage a facsimile of the event on his behalf. A set was built at Woolwich Arsenal and a bunch of tailors' dummies were cast as politicians. The Right Honourables sat around a table while a grenade was detonated in their midst. Needless to say, these dummies were all killed stone dead, one of them receiving as many as forty-seven shrapnel wounds to his stuffing. Only an Irishman could have done such a thing, and Daly was duly sentenced to prison for life.

Incarceration in a British jail, in this case Chatham, was especially harsh for Irish political prisoners. They were kept in isolation and subjected to constant brutality. McIntyre informs us that Daly was so badly beaten by warders 'that the very walls were painted with blood'. He was one of many of his nation's patriots – some guilty, but just as many not – who saw their futures mocked by those same indifferent walls. Contact with relatives was vindictively proscribed, one letter in and one out were allowed every six months, and strictly no visitors.

Had Daly's niece Kathleen Clarke written of all Ireland's outrage it would not have survived the censor. I quote from an account published years later in her book *Revolutionary Women*: 'The Birmingham Chief of Police,' she wrote, 'lay dying, and in a statement to the press confessed that John Daly had been convicted on perjured [police] evidence, and that he could not die in peace with the knowledge of it on his mind.'

This news wasn't rushed to the gates of Chatham prison. Daly heard nothing of it, and four more years went by. One morning in the autumn of 1888, the fifth year in which he'd been confined in silence, a warder appeared, informing him he had a visitor and instructing him to follow him to a designated room. Trying to get into a Victorian prison was sometimes almost as difficult as getting out. Relatives would have to petition for months for the briefest of visits, and only under exceptional circumstances would permission be given.

The visitor who awaited Daly was Richard Pigott, now employed in the blackmail department of Metropolitan Police. Here was the very icon of government duplicity offering his fat little forger's hand. He and Daly had known each other in Dublin in the old republican days. It must have been a joy for Daly to see him, but not to hear what he had to say. He was empowered, he said, to offer Daly his freedom in exchange for the betrayal of Parnell. If Daly would give evidence he would in return 'have liberty, protection, and an income for life'.

Daly didn't have a clue what was happening in the world outside his cell, and with sickening lies, Pigott moved in to exploit his ignorance. 'Parnell,' he said, 'has attributed the Phoenix Park murders to the Fenians. He is lying against you and your organisation.' Don't accept the offer, continued the wretch, 'because you want to betray him for money, but because you want to vindicate yourself against his calumnious slanders'.

Every dirty mischief of Salisbury's regime was encapsulated in that moment. They had robbed Daly of his life when it suited, and now they offered him his life back when it suited them differently. Daly told Pigott to fuck off. He would rather rot in an English hell than mortgage his freedom to such dishonour. Who had sanctioned this visit? How was Pigott able to swan in and out of prisons at will? Somehow Parliament got wind of it, and there was a hoo-ha on the opposition benches. Only two men in the kingdom could have authorised it, and an irate Member asked the Home Secretary if it was him. Matthews gave a categorical denial, and that left only the Secretary to the Prison Board, Robert Anderson. Time after time Anderson denied any association with either the Commission or *The Times*, raising the question, how did that newspaper's solicitor, Mr Soames, also gain access to Chatham jail with similar bribes and then threats to Daly? The prisoner's intransigence caused Soames to freak. If Daly didn't want his freedom, he'd get worse treatment in his cell: 'Severe punishment will follow,' Soames vowed, Daly's incarceration graduating from the terrible to the intolerable.

No deal, but the visitors just couldn't keep away. Apparently Anderson was in complete ignorance of any of them. Dipping his pen for one of his more extravagant lies, he wrote: 'Scotland Yard had no part whatever in the conduct of the case. I had never received even a hint that the government wished me to assist *The Times*, and I had never been as much as asked a question as to what I knew of the matters involved in the enquiry.'

Meanwhile, Chief Inspector Bro John George Littlechild, head of Special (Irish) Branch and thus second in seniority only to Anderson himself, had paid his rail fare and was on his way to Chatham jail. If Anderson hadn't authorised it, we must assume that Littlechild got out of bed one morning and, for reasons best known to himself, decided to pop down to Chatham to have a go at trying to bribe John Daly. Obviously this impulse had come into his head via some sort of telepathic transmutation. He'd been subject to the phenomenon on various occasions, with a variety of Irish prisoners.

The room selected for his Chatham visit was made cosy with a blazing fire, a pint of whisky on the table, and Littlechild playing uncle at the other side of it. What was left of Daly was escorted in, and the man from the Yard came to his purpose: 'They've sent me down to see you,' he said, doubtless offering a slug of Scotch, 'to give you a chance of appearing in the witness box for *The Times*.' He didn't specify who 'they' were, but Daly wanted nothing to do with them or their newspaper, and responded by heading for the door. 'Wait,' insisted Littlechild, gesturing back to the chair. 'Sit down and let us talk things over.'

Daly sat and listened to a predictable supplication on behalf of those who'd put him where he now was. 'Here you are,' reasoned the friendly copper, 'associated with the worst class of criminals, treated worse than they are, shut out from God's free air and sunshine, and yet you propose to spend the rest of your life here? You may not be aware of it, but you are merely a tool in the hands of others, others on the outside with plenty of money in their pockets, thinking no more of you and your sufferings than if you were a disgrace to them.'

In evident indifference to the cruelty of his pitch, the Inspector went on to conjure up an unnecessary picture of the miseries of prison life, contrasting it with the joys of freedom, and ending up by proclaiming Daly an 'infernal fool' if he didn't avail himself of the opportunity now offered for release.

'You know my answer.'

'Very well,' said Littlechild, retrieving his unopened bottle. 'When you go back to your cell and think things over, you'll probably change your mind. If you do write to me, the Governor will give you a pen, ink and paper.' Bidding his farewell, he made a most intriguing remark that remains a mystery to this day. 'Scotland Yard will find me,' he said. It must have been a slip of the tongue. After all, his boss had repeatedly assured anyone craven enough to believe it that Scotland Yard had nothing whatever to do with *The Times.*

Anderson wasn't chosen as chief of CID by accident, but because of his qualifications. He was a 'professional liar' and a moral degenerate, and John Daly was a man of infinitely more virtue than the entirety of those abetting his persecution. This noble Irishman was to remain Her Majesty's prisoner for another ten years.

Those less choosy over whose coin they took were presently lining up wholesale on behalf of the Commission, the business of which was now in full odorous bloom. Week in and week out the judges heard from whoever the authorities could gather. A majority came from the Irish countryside, some stammering their evidence in Gaelic. The Hibernians had been temporarily redesignated as allies. It didn't matter much what they said, as long as Bro Richard Webster and his acolytes could manipulate it into condemnation of the Land League, and better still of Parnell. 'In truth', declared the Liberal MP John Morley, the whole despicable construct was 'designed for the public outside the court, and not a touch could be spared that might deepen the odium'.

But no matter how they argued it, it was Ireland as always that emerged as the ultimate victim. On 9 November 1888, the day Mary Kelly entered the realms of 'insoluble mystery', a correspondent for the *Daily News* concluded his report with: 'Lawyers may wrangle and differ, but underneath all their differences lies this fact, which none can dispute – that Ireland is wretched, miserable, demoralised, sick unto death. This is a legal trial, and it is also a history of a people, one of the dreariest, saddest histories in the world. And when one listens to it, one feels with something like despair, how little Englishmen know of this mournful island, which is only twelve hours' journey from London.'

All too aware of his nation's plight, Parnell paid small attention to any of it. It was a 'show trial' on behalf of spiteful Wealth, worthy of any rotten dictatorship. To the annoyance of his counsel and fellow Irishman Sir Charles Russell, Parnell rarely visited the court. He knew none of it had any significance in comparison to the issue of the forged letters, and despite Webster's obfuscation and verbiage through fifty-three sessions, he knew that at last they would have to come to them.

On 21 February 1889 a court usher called the name Richard Pigott. This was the only name Parnell had been waiting for. In attendance that day, it must have been with a certain satisfaction that he watched Russell do what he had declined to do on behalf of Mrs Maybrick. He destroyed Pigott with a forensic onslaught that left the prosecution in pieces. The inquisition continued for two days, and was apparently torturous to watch. 'Some miscalled the scenes drastic,' wrote Morley. That is hardly the right word for the merciless 'hunt of an abject fellow creature through the windings of a thousand lies'.

Pigott had run out of lies to tell, and the only thing that came out of his face was sweat. Once the government's greatest asset, he had become its greatest liability. Every question tore through the falsehoods and into the conspiracy itself. He had to be shut up. A third day of interrogation was scheduled, but when his name was called, there was no answer. Pigott had disappeared.

There was champagne in the Parnell camp and almost universal press condemnation for *The Times* – excepting of course from *The Times* itself. Attempting to present itself as a fellow victim, it wriggled in the ooze: 'Our desire is simply to express deep regret for the error into which we were led.' It unconditionally withdrew the forged letters, 'which we cannot continue to maintain'. A curt apology was issued in court by Bro Webster that in its meanness of spirit did nothing to lessen the condemnation from Fleet Street. *Reynold's News* published a lengthy denunciation that in tone might serve for all:

> With the flight of Pigott and the downfall of *The Times*' huge superstructure of fraud and villainy, the real work of the Commission has only begun. Behind Houston, who hired the forger, are a number of men who determined to ruin the political party to whom they were antagonistic and who stopped at nothing to compass their shameful ends. These men must not be allowed to skulk behind while their tools are being made the scapegoats. Who would care to see Pigott or Houston in the dock if their high-placed, titled, and wealthy employees are allowed to go scot-free?

The invective swells through further furious paragraphs:

> This is no ordinary offence. It was an impeachment by one of the leading journals of the country, backed by the government, and warmly supported by one of the great parties of the state. It was made with every pomp and circumstance that the support of the government could give it, and the legal officials of the state were permitted against all precedent to press it home. Behind it are men of great wealth, some of whom are associated with it in responsibility for this gigantic fraud ...

Pigott's escape from London was apparently baffling to both the police and press alike: 'How the author of the forged Parnell letters managed to slip past the surveillance and vanish, not only from London, where he was known by all, but from England without trace, is a total mystery.' Or if you prefer, the continuation of a conspiracy. Pigott was too dangerous a mouth to remain in the metropolis, so Anderson let him go, Scotland Yard facilitating his exit. Only a day before, two Irish detectives had stood before the Commission and sworn on oath that they were 'protecting Pigott'. What happened to these guardians of justice? Maybe they'd had a Guinness too many, and didn't notice the most recognisable crook in London tiptoe out of his hotel's front door.

Pigott should have been more cautious of the friends he chose. He was now in a dangerous wonderland. On the afternoon of 1 March 1889 he was shot dead in a hotel room in Madrid. Dates in respect of this event are crucial. On Sunday, 3 March, *Reynold's News* published the following report:

> Reynold's Newspaper Office, Saturday 4 a.m.
> Reuters Telegrams, Etc
> REPORTED ARREST AND SUICIDE OF PIGOTT
> Madrid, [Friday] March 1st
>
> This afternoon the police went to the hotel des Ambassadeurs for the purpose of arresting an Englishman who had arrived there, and who gave the name of Roland Ponsonby. The officers entered his room, and took him into custody; but taking advantage of a moment when the attention of his custodian was diverted the man drew a revolver, and shot himself in the head. Death was instantaneous. The cause of the arrest is not stated, but it is believed that it was effected under an extradition warrant.
>
> Madrid, March 1st, 11.30 p.m.
>
> It is believed that the so called Roland Ponsonby was no other than Mr Richard Pigott. He arrived from Paris yesterday morning [Thursday, 28 February], and was accosted at the railway station by the hotel interpreter, who eventually conducted him to the Hotel des Ambassadeurs. Here he gave his name as Roland Ponsonby. Acting under instructions from the authorities, a police inspector went to the hotel at five this afternoon, and was taken to Mr Ponsonby's room, an interpreter accompanying him. The Englishman came out and asked what was the object of the inspector's visit. The interpreter explained that the officer had come to arrest him. The Englishman thereupon asked permission to fetch his hat and went into his bedroom where he opened a bag. Taking out a revolver, he pointed it at his mouth and fired. He fell to the ground and was found to be quite dead.

He was very dead indeed, and here's where it starts to get a little sinister. On the day before his 'suicide', Thursday, 28 February, *The Times* itself had reported:

> THE ABSCONDING OF PIGOTT
>
> At midnight last night the police had not succeeded in tracing the where-abouts of Pigott. A news agency says that there is very little doubt that the fugitive made his way to Paris, where he stayed but a short time, afterwards

proceeding to some other part of the Continent calculated to conceal him better.

It was later discovered that Pigott left Paris on an overnight train, arriving in Madrid about eight o'clock on the morning of Thursday, 28 February, and checked in as reported to the Hotel des Ambassadeurs (also known as the Hotel de los Embajadores). On that same day he is purported to have sent a telegram to a lawyer in London called Mr Shannon, which immediately found its way into the hands of *The Times*'s legal heavy, Mr Soames. *The Times* of 4 March 1889 reported the proceedings:

> It is stated that on Thursday afternoon [28 February] a telegram was received by Mr Shannon as follows:– 'Please ask Mr S. to send me what you promised, and write to Roland Ponsonby, Hotel Embajadores, Madrid.'
> Immediately upon its receipt Mr Soames telegraphed to Chief Inspector Littlechild as follows:– 'Have news for you. Call at once.'

Littlechild personally called on Soames that day, and *The Times*'s solicitor handed him the telegram received by Shannon:

> At the same time Inspector Littlechild requested Mr Soames *not to disclose to any person, under any circumstances, the receipt or the contents of the telegram,* lest the ends of justice should be defeated … [My emphasis.]

Rather than replying by telegram, Inspector Littlechild asked that 'a letter should be sent, with the object of detaining Pigott in Madrid until he could be arrested'.

Twenty-four hours later Pigott was dead, and it is here *The Times*'s story begins to disintegrate. Let me ask, and try to answer, a few questions. If Pigott had vanished from Paris and arrived in Madrid on the morning of 28 February, how by the following day did the Spanish police know more about his location than the British? The only policeman in England who knew of Pigott's whereabouts was Littlechild, and he wanted them kept a closely guarded secret, requesting Soames, according to Soames himself, not to disclose them 'to any person, under any circumstances'. Littlechild said nothing about informing the Spanish police, rather the opposite: he wanted a letter sent as a delaying tactic, since it would take two or three days to reach Madrid.

So the question is worth repeating. If Pigott's address and alias were known only to Littlechild (via the telegram received on 28 February), how did the Spanish police come by this secret information the following day, 1 March? How did the Spanish policeman know that 'Roland Ponsonby' was Richard Pigott? And what precisely was this Iberian copper supposed to be arresting 'Roland Ponsonby' for? Pigott's alias was as yet unknown beyond Littlechild and Soames. Reuters reported on Friday, 1 March that the arrest was believed to have been 'effected under an extradition warrant'. In which case it would have been made out in the wrong name, and miraculously procured overnight. By whom was it supposedly issued, and in respect of what country? I claim no knowledge of the procedures of extradition, but common sense suggests that this 'document' is a figment of someone's imagination. It is true that an extradition treaty existed between Spain and England – signed, as fate would have it, on 22 January 1889, a mere five weeks and two days before Pigott pitched up in Madrid. But as I understand it, extradition can be a protracted process, requiring at a minimum the name of the country in which the person sought has taken refuge, and that person's correct name. Both were supposedly Littlechild's secret.

The question of how the 'Spanish' police were so quick off the mark is inexplicable, except to *The Times*. With its usual predilection for making things up, it attempted on 7 March to dismiss the conundrum with a revisionary bit of twaddle that wouldn't persuade a cartload of imbeciles:

> A great deal has been said about the extraordinary activity of the Madrid police in discovering and effecting the 'capture' of the deceased in so short a time after his arrival [in Madrid]. As a matter of fact no such discovery was made at all, and no search was necessary. A full description of Pigott and the name under which he was staying and his exact address, was telegraphed from the Foreign Office to the British Embassy, with instructions to the effect, that if a man staying at the Hotel de los Embajadores, under the name of Ponsonby answered the description given, Sir Clair Ford should ask the Spanish authorities for that man's provisional arrest according to the custom in such cases.

What custom, in what such cases? The treaty had been ratified only thirty-seven days before – hardly time to establish a 'custom'. We're asked to swallow that the Foreign Office telegraphed Madrid on the very afternoon (28 February 1889) that Littlechild had issued his fervent plea to Soames 'not to disclose to any person, under any circumstances, the receipt or the contents of the telegram'. If we're to believe *The Times* of 7 March, it means Soames paid no attention whatsoever to Littlechild, and contacted the Foreign Office as soon as the bastard walked out the door.

There are two conflicting reports to consider, and I believe neither. I don't think Scotland Yard needed a telegram from Madrid to know where Pigott was, because I think they knew all the time, and these *Times* articles are a shoddy camouflage.

I stay with *The Times*, because if this scandal belongs to anyone it is to that newspaper and Scotland Yard. The paper's official history states unequivocally that it was 'Anderson's emissaries' who caught up with Pigott at the Hotel de los Embajadores on 1 March 1889. There is no mention of ambassadors, interpreters or Spanish policemen, which I consider all so much invented crap. Given *The Times*'s topical reputation and felonious association with Scotland Yard, I prefer to believe the dispassionate accounts of the Spanish press. Therein the 'mysteries' of how Pigott managed to escape his police guards in London, and of how Anderson's detectives were able to arrive with such jet-propelled velocity in Madrid, are simply explained.

On 3 March 1889 a Spanish newspaper called *La Vanguardia* wrote: 'Pigott was being followed by two officers of the English Secret Service and one from the Irish police. The latter was staying, for good measure, at the same hotel as Pigott.' Thus Anderson's emissaries didn't need a tip-off directing them to Madrid. They were already there. I can conceive of no reason for a Spanish newspaper to make this up. What I believe *was* made up was *The Times*'s contradictory tale about Littlechild on the one hand, and the British Ambassador on the other. The British police had no authority to arrest Pigott in a foreign country, hence the invention of the unnamed and never subsequently questioned Spanish cop. Whatever Anderson's detectives were in Madrid for, it couldn't have been to make an arrest. In my view it's implausible that secret service agents would allow some random Spaniard and his interpreter to breeze into Pigott's hotel room. I give no credibility to this 'suicide'.

Those closer to the coalface of Anderson's Scotland Yard hazard a similar view. William Joyce, the police administrator at Dublin Castle, is quoted to that effect by the Irish historian Leon O Brion in his account of the Parnell conspiracy. 'When Pigott ran away,' he writes, 'the question was asked whether he had really died by his own hand or had been assassinated.' Joyce was emphatic that 'Soames got Pigott away, helped by one of the law-agents and by the Royal Irish Constabulary officials who had surveillance over Pigott.' This substantially corroborates *La Vanguardia*'s claim that an Irish copper was staying with Pigott in the same hotel. 'He [Joyce] adds that in government circles a sigh of relief went up when Pigott's death was made public. If he had lived, he might have opened his mouth too wide.'

Richard Pigott was a big-mouth who knew everything and would have sold it to anyone at the right price; and failing that would have shopped the fucking lot of them to save his own skin. He and Thomas Maguire had the goods on Anderson and his chums, and within twenty-four hours of each other both were dead.

REYNOLD'S NEWS – MARCH 3 1889
MYSTERIOUS DEATH OF A TIMES WITNESS – Dr. Maguire, of Dublin, whose name had often been mentioned in the course of the investigation before the Parnell Commission, died suddenly and mysteriously the other

day [Saturday, 2 March] in London. It was stated in evidence that the deceased accompanied Mr Houston to Paris to obtain the letters from Pigott, and advanced money for their purchase. There were two medical examinations of the body at 72, Eaton Terrace, and the medical gentlemen stated that they found the death due to natural causes.

This naturally wasn't accepted by anyone who could count recent corpses. In Parliament, an Irish MP by the name of Thomas O'Hanlon was inquisitive, and put a question to the Home Secretary: 'Owing to the fact that Doctor Maguire may have had poison administered to him, will the right hon. gentleman see that a post-mortem examination is held?'

Hansard records: 'No answer was given to this question.'

This put no end to the suspicion over the Maguire/Pigott deaths. Many years later, when at least a part of Anderson's criminal input was revealed, the journalist George R. Sims taunted in his column, 'Now that Robert Anderson is becoming so communicative with regard to the mysteries of the past, he may, perhaps, in a future statement, tell us the true story of the death of Pigott?'

Again, no answer is recorded.

It was Sims, incidentally, who received one of those beguiling bum steers so beloved of Ripperology. Like 'the Swanson Marginalia' and 'the Macnaghten Memorandum', it is reverentially referred to as 'the Littlechild Letter'. The copper who never caught the Whitechapel Fiend, and squandered no time trying to, is now thrashing away on his Underwood with a solution. While his letter has charm as memorabilia, it's worthless as anything else.

Bro Littlechild (Zetland Lodge 511) introduced another non sequitur into the Ripper jamboree with the name of Dr Tumblety, a candidate so silly I'm not even going to bother to dismiss it. The rest of the text (presumably in expectation of Sims tossing a quote into his column) plunges into fantasy. 'With regard to the term "Jack the Ripper",' writes Littlechild, 'it was generally believed in the Yard that Tom Bullen [sic] of the Central News [Agency] was the originator.' Oh, really? It was certainly Bulling who made useful adjustments to Jack's 'Moab' letter, but to credit him with 'Dear Boss' is expecting a little too much servitude from ink.

Meanwhile, drama was unfolding at the Commission. Parnell's counsel, Sir Charles Russell, had demanded that the books and accounts of the Irish Loyal and Patriotic Union be presented in evidence. But the judges refused. It was apparently acceptable to present forged letters and the bitter fictions of 'Parnellism and Crime' on behalf of the prosecution, but documents vital to the defence were out of bounds.

These records contained, and of course could prove, the complicity of every Right Honourable shithouse in the book responsible for the financing and framing of Parnell. They represented precisely the scandalous head-count that Pigott and Maguire knew only too well – or rather, knew until they terminally forgot.

Truth couldn't quite cope with these ILPU records, and the judges' refusal to allow them as evidence caused Russell and his team to walk out. The Commission then collapsed in everything but name, Her Majesty's judges being obliged to sit through six more months of this junk on their own. Her Majesty's opposition went through the usual sham of outrage, promising a full inquiry on their return to power, with sonorous commitments to a full exposure of whoever was behind Pigott. By tradition, nothing came of it; there was no revelation of the guilty, presumably because nobody wanted to arrest themselves. Lessons would naturally be learned, of course (the standard mantra of the culpable), but no lesson would ever be taught.

And what of 'Parnellism and Crime'? The public now knew who had faked the letters, but who had cooked up the articles on which this conspiracy was forged? Russell had repeatedly asked representatives of *The Times* who wrote the poisonous rubbish, and Soames and James Cameron MacDonald, the paper's manager, just as repeatedly denied any knowledge of his identity. From this miasma of perjury a name was at last to emerge. The son of an Irish judge, John Woulfe Flanagan, was finally admitted as the penman of 'Parnellism and Crime', although his co-author, responsible for 'Behind the Scenes in America', remained a mystery. Among the principal actors behind the government's now seized machine there were many who could have resolved it, but none more qualified than Robert Anderson. However, the Chief of Police was never asked, nor did he ever appear before the Commission. 'In view of all this,' he later wrote, if 'the reader expects me to solve the mystery why I was not a witness at the Special Commission he will be disappointed. The more I review the circumstances, the more impenetrable does that mystery become.'

It was Anderson's kind of 'mystery', just as Bro Jack was Warren's. But 'mystery' is a misuse of language: the salient word is 'conspiracy'. Not my choice in this instance, but that of Lord Chief Justice Coleridge, who wrote to Sir Charles Russell two days after Pigott's 'suicide': 'My Dear Russell. I can't help writing you a line to congratulate you on your part in the destruction of what you quite properly described as a "foul conspiracy".'

A knighthood for Robert Anderson, and another twenty-one years, were to pass before more of the odour seeped out. 'It was a foul, terrible, subtle, and powerful conspiracy,' declared T.P. O'Connor in Parliament, 'which was woven around our liberties, our characters, and perhaps our lives.' He was referring to 'Parnellism and Crime', and then more specifically to the lies called 'Behind the Scenes in America': '… seeking to blast the reputation of the Irish leader and the Irish party by charging them with association with crime, to organise these crimes, and to endeavour to entrap the labour leaders in America into conspiracy of the same character'.

APPENDIX I

So who exactly was the author of 'Behind the Scenes in America', a unique felony constituting 'one of the greatest scandals ever known in police administration in this country'?

Please step forward our old God-stained friend and chief of the Criminal Investigation Department at Scotland Yard, the Christian Charlatan and Pulpiteer himself, SIR ROBERT ANDERSON. Anderson had written 'Behind the Scenes in America', and then went about the business of prosecuting Charles Parnell for its content. Could anything be more corrupt? Could anything be more disgusting than this confederacy of bewigged pimps and their craven little minions in helmets? Most certainly yes. It was called 'the trial of Florence Maybrick'. Anderson had concocted his American fictions in association with his buddy Edward Caulfield Houston. In court, *The Times*'s manager MacDonald repeatedly denied that he knew the author's name. 'It was the work of several writers,' he insisted, and he hadn't the vaguest idea of who they might be. It had obviously slipped his mind that he'd written to one of them only a few weeks before. On 10 January 1889, fourteen days after the Ripper had made one of his more egregiously Masonic hits in Bradford, MacDonald wrote: 'Dear Mr Anderson, if your man is not available as quickly as steam can carry him the case will have been virtually concluded & that section of it embraced in *your articles* no longer needful to be gone into.' My emphasis, but Anderson's 'articles'. MacDonald continued with an urgent plea for the immediate importation of one of Anderson's American-based narks: 'That immediately upon his arrival in England he shall make in writing and sign a complete full statement of everything and every circumstance within his knowledge which shall substantially prove when given in evidence the several statements and allegations contained in XXXX [sic] or alleged in several articles published in *The Times* newspaper in the year 1887 entitled "Behind the Scenes in America".'

I think even the most dispassionate observer would conclude that MacDonald had known for at least two years who was the writer of 'Behind the Scenes in America'.

Sometimes I left my typewriter feeling bilious after a day with these people. The whole damned lot of them, beginning with Robert Anderson, should have been slung into prison. A farce it may have been, and owned by the elite it was, but this was the 'law in action' at the time of the 'Parnell Commission':

1) The fabrication of false evidence with intent to mislead a judicial tribunal is an indictable misdemeanour punishable with imprisonment.
2) All acts which are calculated to interfere with the course of justice, are misdemeanours at the common law, punishable with imprisonment.
3) A conspiracy to prevent, obstruct, pervert or defeat the course of justice is a criminal conspiracy [in respect of] wilfully producing false evidence

to the court or by publishing information that may prejudicially affect the minds of the jurors [in this case judges]. A conspiracy to charge a man falsely with a crime, also falls within this category. And any combination which has for its object the perversion of true justice is a criminal conspiracy and indictable as such.

But only if you were Irish.

The man MacDonald and his newspaper were anxious to rush before the Commission went by the name of Major Henri Le Caron.

Le Caron was a kind of fleshless Pigott with an American accent, and plying similar wares. He'd been exchanging secret correspondence with Anderson for twenty-five years – virtually all of it dross, but lapped up by his paymaster, who converted it into a permanent terrorist threat. It was from these dispatches that 'Behind the Scenes in America' had been culled.

Like all con artists, Le Caron was a good actor, and he saw Anderson as an easy touch. Substantial amounts of cash found their way into the little spy's bank account at Braidwood, Illinois. On occasion these sums were so huge they attracted the attention of the local Sheriff and Postmaster. 'He frequently received large British money orders from England,' said the Sheriff, 'and in addition to this received large bank drafts from time to time through the Braidwood Bank. He said it was the rent from estates owned by him.'

All of this was actually secret and unauthorised money literally embezzled from the British state. Le Caron had been duping Anderson for a quarter of a century, and thus by osmosis duping the British people who had to pay for his fabrications. 'But he would not touch Fenian money,' was Anderson's later bleat. In fact Le Caron took $179 a month from those he spied on, as a 'Major and Military Organiser of the Irish Republican Army'. Apart from blood money and barrowloads of cash from the British, he was also on the take from the Canadian government. It's indicative of his crippled morality that he took his sobriquet of 'Major' from the Irish Republicans. US Army records reveal a less glamorous truth.

According to these documents, Le Caron was born in Paris in 1841, of French parents, and served on the Union side in the American Civil War as a hospital orderly and bugler. The same records describe him as a 'mutineer' who 'refused to march' before the battle of Merfreeborough, and ended up in jail at Nashville because of it. Imprisonment didn't seem to affect his subsequent promotion, and by the war's end he'd ascended to the rank of Second Lieutenant.

In reality, Le Caron wasn't a major, wasn't French, and his name wasn't even Henri Le Caron. When he got into court, Sir Charles Russell called him a 'living lie', ridiculing him with disparaging emphasis on his true name. It was *Thomas Beach* (Russell's emphasis), and he was born at the aspirant edge of the lower middle class in Colchester, Essex. In his early teens he split for Paris, travelling on money he'd stolen from his sister's charity collection box. From France he shipped to the United States. If we're to believe what came to be known as 'Anderson's Fairy Tales', Beach wrote to his father in the 1860s condemning the burgeoning movement of Irish/American nationalism. His letter was apparently forwarded by his dad, circuitously finding its way to Anderson, and the Major's career in 'espionage' began.

About twenty years later in London, Anderson introduced Beach to Houston, 'a man he could trust implicitly'. The trio then went about the business of selecting the most damaging 'evidence' they could discover against Parnell from the vast archive of mail accrued over years of exchange between himself and Anderson. 'Apart from the Le Caron disclosures,' wrote Anderson, 'I repeat I had nothing to do with *The Times* case [and] I must premise that Le Caron's evidence was my only point of contact with the case for *The Times*.'

Notwithstanding these astronomical lies, about a hundred letters were chosen and organised for the coppers' nark to take before the Commission. Le Caron, or *Beach*, as Russell spat it, was undoubtedly the best witness the Crown could muster, but it was to no avail. In the wake of Pigott, a celestial intervention couldn't have saved the government's case, and neither could the Major. The *New York Times* put the final nail in:

> For all its avowed and immediate purposes the testimony [of Beach] is a complete failure … so far from showing that PARNELL or his associates in parliament were privy to the dynamite plots on this side of the water, it furnishes evidence as strong as negative evidence can be made that these plots were undertaken without any connivance or any knowledge on the part of the Irish parliamentary leaders. A spy who had been on intimate terms with the plotters for twenty years was not able to adduce any testimony that raised a reasonable suspicion of their complicity. The spy's testimony really disposes of *The Times*' charges against PARNELL.

Beach's fee was ten grand, and Houston got thirty thousand. Added to this were enormous legal costs of over £200,000. It was a 'foul conspiracy' that all but bankrupted *The Times*. For a nation given to bragging about the superiority of its judicial institutions, it's a task to believe this could have happened; and it couldn't have happened had not those same institutions, including Scotland Yard, been irrefutably corrupt.

There are two theories of history, the 'cock-up' and the 'conspiracy'. This was both. It was a conspiracy that cocked up. A majority of Ripperologists don't care much for the word 'conspiracy', fearing, I suspect, mission-creep into the unfathomable purity of 'the mystery of Jack the Ripper'. But one day, even if it takes a thousand tomorrows, they're going to have to come to terms with 'the Conspiracy of Jack the Ripper'.

Two thoughts occur. The first is the laughable prattle put about at the time of Warren's 'resignation'. It will be remembered that he was accused of having 'broken the rules' by writing for the press, a dispatch about as controversial as a twelve-month warranty for a garden rake. And second, a comparison between that and Anderson's contributions to *The Times*. Lying if he was awake, Anderson was unworthy even to look at a policeman's badge. 'He had made many statements,' said T.P. O'Connor, 'calculated to interfere with the course of justice. I regard him as the symbol and outcome and the standard bearer of a bad and false and rotten system.'

It was Sir Robert Anderson, KCB (Knight Commander of the Bath) LL.D (Doctor of Laws), who gave Ripperology one of its most cherished candidates: the Generic Jew. 'In saying that he was a Polish Jew,' wrote the Pulpiteer, 'I am merely stating a definitely ascertained fact' – or put another way, merely lying through his teeth. For years Ripperology interpreted this balls as referring to Aaron Kosminski, then when that fell to pieces it widened the debate to include another nutty Yid called David Cohen. I'll leave it to them and Anderson. His explanation of why this 'definitely ascertained' Polish Jew wasn't arrested is even more ridiculous. 'The only person who ever had a good view of the murderer,' he wrote, 'unhesitatingly identified the suspect the instant he was confronted with him; but he refused to give evidence against him.'

That must have been annoying. What an obstreperous cad. Maybe the police should have pleaded, taken him out for a slap-up dinner, whisky on the house? Failing that, they could have applied the law. As a 'Doctor of Laws', Anderson should surely have known what the law was. Anyway, what the hell, he was only chief of CID, and apparently no one bothered to tell him there were harsh penalties for denying the cops such evidence. It's a little late in the day, but here it is, Chapter III/(3) under 'Stephen's Commentaries on the Laws of England':

An accessory AFTER the fact is one who knowing a felony to have been committed, receives, relieves, comforts, or assists the felon. To make such an accessory, it is in the first place requisite, that a felony has been committed, and that it was committed, to the knowledge of the accessory, by the party in question. Any assistance whatever makes the assistor an accessory. [Under] the 'Accessories and Abettors Act, 1861', accessories after the fact, in the case of murder, may be punished by penal servitude for life.

What an awful pill it is that Anderson didn't apply the law. We'd have all known who the Ripper was 130 years ago. Except it was all so much Anderson bullshit, and the only surprise is that he didn't accuse Charles Parnell. In reaction to his half-witted imputations, the *Jewish Chronicle* wrote: 'I fail to see upon what evidence, worthy of the name, he ventures to cast the odium for this infamy upon one of our people.' It's called 'anti-Semitism'. There was no evidence. Anderson was playing it for the gullible. Apart from inventing this Kosminski nonsense and lying about 'Israel Schwartz's' appearance at a coroner's court, Anderson's participation in attempting to interrupt the career of Jack the Ripper was zero.

Ireland and the Ripper remain amongst the foulest stains on the nation's officially secret underwear. It was to be another twenty years before Anderson's leading role in the Parnell conspiracy was finally made public. Curiously, the revelation came from his own pen. In a series of self-congratulatory articles published in 1910, wherein he and Le Caron are elevated to the status of unsung heroes, he claimed that his involvement in the scandal had never really been much of a secret – 'all of Fleet Street knew'. He added that his then superior at Scotland Yard, James Monro, had approved of his concoctions known as 'Parnellism and Crime'.

Monro found the energy to disagree. All but bedridden, and on his way out in Scotland, he wrote from Aberdeen to his protégé Sir Melville Macnaghten, himself now Assistant Commissioner of Metropolitan Police, dismissing Anderson's disclosures as yet another example of the man's self-serving fictions: 'the alleged statement of Anderson that it was agreed between him and me that he should write the letters & that they should be offered to *The Times* as the best medium for their publication is *absolutely incorrect*'.

Monro is here confusing Anderson's articles with Pigott's letters, a conflation that isn't far off the mark, as they were virtually one and the same. Either way, he insisted he had nothing to do with any of it, and was prepared to get out of his sickbed to prove it: 'I am willing to place myself at the disposal of the Home Office and give the fullest explanation of my action in the matter.' The Home Office had no choice but to agree, calling Anderson's revelations 'a public scandal' – not so much for having done it, but for having made it public.

A young Liberal Home Secretary, called Winston Churchill, declared that had the government known (as if they didn't) about his activities, Mr Anderson would have been 'instantly dismissed'. And a previous Home Secretary, the Gladstonian Sir William Harcourt, spoke for most in Parliament that session when he said with some acrimony, 'Anderson should not have been running Scotland Yard.'

But between 1888 and 1901 the man who should not have been running Scotland Yard *was* running Scotland Yard, and to the great satisfaction of Salisbury's government. An Irish Nationalist MP by the name of Jeremiah McVeagh put the scandal into perspective, regretting 'that the circumstances of the case compel us tonight to deal with a miserable creature like Anderson, instead of with some of those more sinister figures which are lurking in the background of this black plot'. Dismissing Anderson as 'one of the villains of the piece', he said that the Police Commissioner was in fact merely a 'pivot around which the whole conspiracy turned'.

In terms of evolving nineteenth-century democracies, the British ruling class had pulled off a formidable oxymoron. Its democracy remained feudal. There was no constitution, the country was a 'Constitutional Monarchy'. The dukes, earls, barons and others sagging under regal anointment continued to own it. Fewer than five hundred families owned half of Scotland. At the system's apogee was the worshipped royal family, without which none of the panto could exist. Its nearest contemporary comparison, perhaps, is the royal house of Saud in Saudi Arabia, where a succession of kings and their issue replace each other in perpetuity as hereditary heads of state. In the British example this was supplemented with an Anglo version of the Mullah, a confederacy of non-elected men in weird religious costumes, and others with an affection for wearing weasel fur (ermine) called the House of Lords.

The day a state becomes sick is the day it considers the protection of itself more important than the protection of its people. It conflates the protection of the people with a camouflaged reality of the protection of itself. It usually tells the people to be afraid of something or other, in direct proportion to its own interest. In this case it was Irish earth, engendering 'Irish Terrorism', and that is what it sold in its propaganda.

PUNCH, OR THE LONDON CHARIVARI.—May 20, 1882.

THE IRISH FRANKENSTEIN.

"The baneful and blood-stained Monster * * * yet was it not my Master to the very extent that it was my Creature? * * * Had I not breathed into it my own spirit?" * * * (Extract from the Works of C. S. P-RN-LL, M.P.)

THE NEMESIS OF NEGLECT.

" THERE FLOATS A PHANTOM ON THE SLUM'S FOUL AIR,
SHAPING, TO EYES WHICH HAVE THE GIFT OF SEEING,
INTO THE SPECTRE OF THAT LOATHLY LAIR.
FACE IT—FOR VAIN IS FLEEING
RED-HANDED, RUTHLESS, FURTIVE, UNERRING.
'TIS MURDEROUS CRIME—THE NEMESIS OF NEGLECT!"

'The Irish Frankenstein' and 'The Nemesis of Neglect' were opposite sides of the same coin. They were society's most dreaded bogeymen. But what the public didn't understand was that, although of a vastly different dynamic, both represented an equal peril to the British ruling elite. Both were egregious players in the same Establishment nightmare, but an entirely contradictory approach was taken to the two threats. Every imaginable conjugation of law and state violence was evoked to suppress Ireland, while Jack was menaced by not so much as the distant echo of a police whistle. While infantry and riot police were the order of the day in Dublin, bent coroners' courts and wilfully blind coppers constituted the state contingency in Whitechapel. The Micks got bullets, and Jack bafflement. Beyond a mystified Freemasonic Police Commissioner with a waterlogged sponge, Jack got no policing at all. This wasn't by accident. It was by design. Concurrent with Anderson thrashing out his filthy articles for *The Times*, Irish journalists faced summary incarceration for having the temerity to publish an alternative point of view. Mass arrests of Irish MPs and their 'terrorist' countrymen continued throughout Bro Jack's homicidal reign, but under no circumstances could there be an arrest of a psychopathic Freemason terrorising the people of London. Sir Charles Warren couldn't have caught the Ripper in a hundred years, and neither could Sir Robert Anderson. That isn't what they were there for.

Appendix II

A Very Curious Letter

Within days of assuming his tenure as Home Secretary, Asquith was in receipt of a letter from W.T. Stead, now the editor of a relatively new monthly magazine, the *Review of Reviews*:

> Dear Mr Asquith, I have received a very curious letter from the Transvall [sic], which seems to me to be genuine. It purports to be the death-bed confession of a man of the name Harry Wilson, who accuses himself, and either his sister or wife (Elizabeth Wilson) of introducing the arsenic into the Maybrick House, in order to avenge themselves on Mrs Maybrick.
>
> The man who made the confession died in Mashonaland, requesting with his dying breath that this letter should be sent to Sir Charles Russell. As Russell did not move in the matter he sent it to me. I feel that this letter imposes upon me a responsibility which I would very gladly hand over to you in case you are disposed to take the same view of it as myself.
>
> As I shall probably publish the confession in the next number of REVIEW OF REVIEWS, I should be very glad to hear from you [as] there is no disposition on my part to do anything that would be contrary to your wishes, or your judgement as to what would be fit and proper under the circumstances.

Whether Asquith replied or not isn't known, at least not by me. Six weeks later Stead duly published 'Harry Wilson's Confession' in the October issue of his magazine. The article, for which the 'confession' was a catalyst, was a brilliant supplication on behalf of Florence Maybrick. It was titled 'OUGHT MRS MAYBRICK BE TORTURED TO DEATH?', and once again 'the Maybrick Mystery' was back on the boil. Stead rehearsed what he'd already told Asquith: that he'd received a letter from the Transvaal Republic, bearing the postmark of Krugersdorp, franked with four penny stamps, and dated 19 July 1892.

About twenty miles west of Johannesburg and nearly six thousand miles from London, Krugersdorp was a small coalmining town, and 'of all places in the world' the last anyone would have expected to hear anything of the name Maybrick. 'On opening the missive,' wrote Stead, 'which reached me August 15th or 16th, I found it was dated "Rithfontein, July 10th 1892." The

791

extraordinary spelling, due to the effort of a South African Dutchman to spell English as he pronounces it gave the communication an unmistakable stamp of authenticity.' I'll skip the cod Dutch ('yor Walubele and waid Rede Peper'), reminiscent of the phoney illiteracy in the scrawl to George Lusk, and go directly to Stead's translation:

> Mr. Stead.
>
> Dear Sir
>
> Please will you insert this in your valuable and widely read paper, in justice to a poor woman, who is still in prison for a crime another person has committed. It is about five months ago since (I was) in company with Harry Wilson from Mashonaland to the Transvall. He was sick with fever and at last died on January 14th, 1892. Before he died he made the following confession, which he instructed me to send to Sir Charles Russell, barrister-at-law, London, England.
>
> There were four of us who started back, and all three died from fever except myself. And as nothing has been done in the matter – Sir C. Russell has not moved in the matter, I hope that you, loving justice to your fellow men, will move in the matter. He died on the Limpopo flats on January 14th 1892, and was buried by me, and what is the worst part I was the only one of the four left to hear that miserable confession.
>
> Trusting that you, loving justice, will take this into consideration, I will subscribe myself your most humble servant,
>
> MOREAU MASINA BERTHRAD NEUBERG

Included with the letter was Mr Neuberg's transcribed copy of Wilson's 'confession'.

Confession of Harry Wilson

> He stated that he, in conjunction with a woman by the name of ____ ____, tampered with medicine which was intended for Mr Maybrick, put arsenic into the ____. He said because Mrs Maybrick and he could not agree, and he had a grudge against her. There was also another woman, he called her Sara, but I don't remember the other name.
>
> It was somewhere near Manchester, some time ago, and she is still in prison. He told me to send this statement to Sir Charles Russell, Barrister at Law.

Stead immediately contacted Russell, who forwarded him Neuberg's earlier letter. Unfortunately it was without an envelope, and with no postmark there was no way of establishing an indisputable date or from where it was actually posted. However, the text was headed 'Johannesburg' and dated 25 March 1892. Once again, the 'Dutch' is rendered into English by Stead.

APPENDIX II

Sir Charles Russell.

Sir, – A man of the name of Henry Wilson made a confession to me in my tent at Mashonaland that he put arsenic into some medicine for the purposes of revenge on Mrs Maybrick, near Manchester, some years ago. She was convicted of the crime of murder and sent to prison for life, and he wants me to write to you his confession of the crime. He died, and was buried on the Limpopo River, near the drift crossing to the Transvaal.

'CONFESSION OF HENRY WILSON'

He said he wanted to be revenged on Mrs Maybrick. He with a servant girl tampered with the medicine for Mr Maybrick, and put arsenic into it, but how much I could not get to know as he was delirious for fourteen days. He died and I buried him on the Limpopo Flats on the other side of the Transvaal two months ago. Trusting you will interest yourself on behalf of the woman Mrs Maybrick, I remain, your most humble servant,

M. M. BERTHRAD NEUBERG.

This is written on arrival from Mashonaland. I am sorry there is not another witness to this miserable statement, – M.M.B. NEUBERG.

'Mr Neuberg was evidently profoundly convinced of the serious importance of the case,' wrote Stead. 'He seems to have written to Sir Charles Russell as soon as he got within range of a Post Office.'

Except he didn't, and it's at this point that Mr Berthrad Neuberg's correspondence begins to look decidedly iffy. In fact this whole South African fraudulence is so transparent I can't believe Stead gave it a moment's credibility. But believe it he did, and so did Helen Densmore. I can only imagine that their desperation over Mrs Maybrick's plight, combined with an ignorance of the locality the letters refer to, was the reason for their unaccountable naïvety.

This correspondence can be attacked from whatever angle one chooses. Let us start with the geography. The principal crossing of the Limpopo River out of Mashonaland into the Transvaal was at Baine's Drift. Two hundred miles south of it was Pretoria, a city of 22,000 Boers and the capital city of the Transvaal. It was well served by post offices. Yet Mr Neuberg didn't report anything untoward to the authorities there, or post his apparently vital letter either. Instead he kept travelling south for another thirty-five miles to Johannesburg. In all he has covered 235 miles from the Limpopo, where he supposedly buried Wilson on 14 January. Even at a snail's pace of five miles a day, he would have arrived in Johannesburg on 1 March, more than three weeks before the date of his letter.

Thus he had time on his hands, certainly enough of it to seek assistance from those fluent in English to help him with translation – he couldn't have wanted the contents of his letter kept secret, because he asked Stead to insert it in his 'valuable and widely read paper'. How did Berthrad Neuberg know that the 'Reweu of Reweujs' – whose name he couldn't even spell – was widely read? The *Review of Reviews* was published in America, Australia and England, but not in South Africa, and was definitely not widely read there. From whence did this semi-illiterate Dutchman acquire such insight into a foreign publication? We live in the age of the internet, but I couldn't name a single periodical in Holland, much less a widely read one whose editor was a 'lover of justice'.

Stead wrote that it was impossible to refuse to look into the matter, but unfortunately he was looking in the wrong direction. He might have asked, by way of example, why Berthrad Neuberg didn't report his recent misfortunes to the police, or at least to the coroner's office either in Jo'burg or Pretoria. Admirable as was Mr Neuberg's concern for an unknown woman in a prison six thousand miles away, what about his dead companions up the track on the Limpopo Flats? Did none of them have a name, outside of Henry, or Harry, Wilson? Who were these men? Did no one miss them? Did no one report them missing? Did they not have wives, sisters, mothers, families of their own, and did not Mr Neuberg salvage what he could of their possessions, or perhaps a last dying message, to pass on to their loved ones? For a man of such Christian tenacity, he seems to have acted curiously out of character in respect of his deceased friends.

Neuberg claims he saw three of them into their graves, the last of them, on 14 January, being Wilson, who he says 'was buried on the Limpopo Flats, near the Drift crossing to the Transvaal'. This returns us to Baine's Drift, and Neuberg is lying. I quote from John Wellington, Professor of Geography at the University of Witwatersrand, Johannesburg: 'In the dry season this part of the course contains but a feeble stream a few inches deep, or there may be no flow at all, but just a series of pools on the rocky bed.' This however is not the case in the rainy season, which reaches its peak in January. In that month the Limpopo explodes, surging over its banks and having been recorded, according to Professor Wellington, as reaching a level of twenty-six feet above its bed. The Flats are inundated, and the Drift quite impassable. In short, if Moreau Masina Berthrad Neuberg had buried Wilson on the Flats at the Limpopo crossing, he would have had to be wearing some sort of underwater respiratory apparatus.

Ernest Hemingway wrote, 'All writers need a cast-iron bullshit detector,' or words to that effect, and I could smell bullshit. Something was staring me in the face, some kind of riddle, some hidden conundrum, but I couldn't see it. I had to step back, and keep stepping back, until I could.

It's fortuitous that Stead printed a facsimile of the 'confession'. I read it repeatedly before I actually started to look at it. I'll get to the text by and by, but first let us consider this document without bothering with the words. What I noticed was that Moreau Masina Berthrad Neuberg and Jack the Ripper shared the curious idiosyncrasy of spontaneously enlarging their handwriting at the end of their text.

I thought I might well be looking at an element of the 'Funny Little Game', and that the key to it might be hidden in the 'confession'. For reasons best known to himself, Stead had redacted a name from its text that he'd revealed in his letter to Asquith. It was Elizabeth Wilson. Originally the opening line of the confession read: 'He stated that he, in conjunction with a woman by the name of Elizabeth Wilson, tampered with medicine which was intended for Mr Maybrick.'

The only Wilson in Battlecrease House was Michael Maybrick's harsh little sidekick, Nurse Susan Wilson. She was present from 9 May until 18 May, and indeed had a brother called Henry, who was born in Doncaster, Yorkshire, in 1862. But unless Henry was ensconced in some convenient cupboard, or perhaps concealing himself behind the curtains, he was never at Battlecrease. Maybrick died about forty-eight hours after Nurse Wilson arrived, and so tight a schedule would have presented Henry with a bit of a problem developing his grudge.

'He said because Mrs Maybrick and he could not agree,' explains the confession, 'and he had a grudge against her.'

This bullshit invites another question. If his grudge was so extreme that he would poison James Maybrick in order to frame Florence, why not simply poison *her*? With the kind of access his sister enjoyed, he could just as easily have slipped Florence Maybrick a dose. The reason he didn't is because he was a hundred miles away, and had never heard of her. In 1891 Henry Wilson was living with his parents in Doncaster, and he is recorded in that year's census as a commercial painter. When he married in 1901 he was still living in Doncaster, and still up a ladder with a pot of paint. Goodbye Henry, it wasn't you buried on the Limpopo, and neither was anyone else.

The question therefore isn't who was Henry Wilson, but who was Moreau Masina Berthrad Neuberg? A dictionary of Dutch names tells us who he wasn't, or rather what he wasn't, and that was Dutch. Neither 'Moreau', nor 'Masina', nor 'Berthrad' appears, and neither does 'Neuberg', which if anything is German.

What interests me about this 'confession' is that via a surrogate (Henry Wilson) it describes precisely what I believe went down at Battlecrease House. It shares its narrative with the statement of the eavesdropping soldier Robert Reeves. Both Reeves and Wilson refer to a 'servant girl' as co-conspirator and vehicle by which the poison could be administered. Is it remotely conceivable that these two separate entities, one in prison in Brighton, England, and the other under fifteen feet of water in Mashonaland, could have independently come up with the same extraordinary story? Reeves got it because he'd overheard it, and the non-existent 'Wilson' got it from the same fucked-up brain. Only three people knew how James Maybrick had been murdered: Michael Maybrick, Edwin Maybrick and Robert Reeves. Reeves didn't write this letter from South Africa, he was in a cell in Sussex. That leaves Edwin and Michael. It was Michael Maybrick who had a grudge against Florence (she called it a 'spite'), and only Michael knew that Florence had been framed, because it was he who framed her.

Wilson's 'confession' continues with further reference to a secret that nobody but an absolute intimate of James Maybrick could have known. Navigating the phoney Dutch syntax, here it is in English: 'There was also another woman, he called her Sara, but I don't remember the other name.'

She was Sarah Ann Robertson, James Maybrick's mistress, with whom he is reputed to have fathered five children. At Florence's insistence, and in deference to the reputation of her deceased husband, the name was never publicly mentioned. Wilson couldn't have known it, even if he'd been real. But Mr Moreau Masina Berthrad Neuberg certainly did.

In 1892 it took about three weeks by ship and the new railway to get from England to Johannesburg. Named after its founder, a surveyor called Johannes Rissik, it was a city that appeared out of nowhere, and whose language was gold. In 1886 the richest seams of gold on earth had been discovered at Witwatersrand in the Transvaal. It was a motherlode stretching for fifty miles, and it would make multi-millionaires of men like Sir Cecil Rhodes. But for those who lived there it wasn't the best of tidings. The Boers (indigenous Dutch) had farmed the Transvaal, in harmony with its endless horizons, for almost three hundred years. Gold wasn't what these simple God-fearers were about, and they tried to keep it a secret – not because they wanted to harvest it, but because news of it would mean certain war with England. That came fifteen years later, with its hooligan destruction, burning of farms, public hanging of prisoners, and recourse to Britannia's new invention of the concentration camp, where 26,000 Boer women and children were starved to death.

The poet and traveller Wilfrid Scawen Blunt described it as a 'gangrene of Colonial rowdyism', and it was everything the Boers had feared. 'Johannesburg at present has no politics,' wrote the journalist Flora Shaw in 1892; 'it is much too busy with material problems. It is hideous and detestable; luxury without order, sensual enjoyment without art; riches without refinement; display without dignity.' The riff-raff of the world descended upon the city, its population swelling by about 20,000 a year. Almost everyone but the Boers, the blacks and the unlucky hit the jackpot. Johannesburg was, said one of its burgeoning oligarchs, 'Monte Carlo superimposed upon Sodom and Gomorrah'. Grandiose buildings went up, plush hotels, a stock exchange, and theatres to entertain the new rich. 'Much of Johannesburg's social life revolved around theatre and music hall, and some of the biggest names in contemporary entertainment found their way to the dusty, untidy settlement.' They included some of England's greatest stars, among them many of Maybrick's chums. His lifelong friend Charles Santley sang there, as did Lionel Brough and Signor Foli (both performers at the concert Maybrick had organised on behalf of the Artists Volunteers in March 1889).

They were easy to find, but tracing Maybrick was of a different order. He may have been there for the nightlife, but he wasn't there to sing. Like his co-existent celebrity 'Jack the Snicker', he was a frequent long-distance traveller. In a letter to the City Police dated 21 June 1889, the 'Snicker' writes of excursions to Spain, America and the Isle of Wight.

In 1884 Maybrick toured the USA, but comprehensive searches of passenger lists failed to turn up his name, and I knew I wasn't going to find him on the extant itinerary of any steamer bound for South Africa. 'I always go abroad as a private gentleman,' Maybrick laughed, 'for I wish to thoroughly enjoy myself.' In 1892 there were no passports, no 'security', and no questions. You could get on a ship with one name and get off it with another. Plus, Maybrick was used to using sobriquets, composing as Stephen Adams, performing as Michael Maybrick, and killing with another appellation that dwarfed the pair of them in its fame. Anyone concocting 'Moreau Masina Berthrad Neuberg' could dream up any phoney name he liked. 'Rithfontein' was bogus, and as a postal address it didn't exist. There was a 'Rietfontein' about five miles north-east of Krugersdorp, and another ten miles south, but they were nothing more than fields, prospectors' mining claims (numbers 84 and 48 respectively), and barely a name on the map.

'What is this "Cock and Bull" story,' asked the *South African Empire* on 15 October 1892, 'that Mr Stead has received from South Africa concerning the death of Mr Maybrick?'

One Harry Wilson, while on his way from Mashonaland to the Transvaal, falls ill with fever and dies on the road. His sole surviving travelling companion is a Mr M.M.B. Neuberg, and before Wilson passes from this world to the next, he narrates in his agonies how, having a grudge against Mrs Maybrick, he with a servant girl, tampers with the medicine for Mr Maybrick by putting arsenic into it, with the sole object of bringing Mrs Maybrick into a murderer's dock. Neuberg says:– 'I am sorry there is not another witness to this miserable statement.' It certainly is regrettable, seeing that no one, unless it be Mr Stead himself, is likely to give any credence to the so-called confession. One is tempted to ask why Neuberg, on his arrival in the Transvaal, did not make known the story to the local press. It would have put pounds in his pocket. Was Harry Wilson known to anyone in the Transvaal? Did he die with any papers about him, and where are they? These and other questions naturally suggest themselves in connection with the elucidation of the mysterious death of Mr Maybrick. Mr M.M.B. Neuberg may have taken down the statement correctly as delivered by the dying man, but who would believe the story of such a deep-dyed villain as Harry Wilson wished to make himself out to be without any confirmatory proof of his guilt? Cannot Mr Neuberg give any reference as to his standing and respectability in South Africa?

The answer to that question is no, because the whole scenario is fake. Thus I was looking for a person (Michael Maybrick) whose pseudonym I didn't know, and another (Harry Wilson) who didn't exist. Plus, it was six thousand miles away and 130 years ago.

Before even thinking about Maybrick in South Africa, I had to eliminate him from England. No point trying to nail him on the veldt if he was provably in this country during the summer of 1892. I don't know where or on what date Russell's 'Johannesburg' letter was mailed, and I believe it was back-dated anyway (using his well-worn trick of the ship's letterbox). As he quit the boat in Cape Town his fraud was already poised to return home. But because of Stead's postmark I was obliged to accept that 'Neuberg' was probably in Krugersdorp on or about 19 July (although the letter is back-dated 10 July).

The effort to reduce Michael Maybrick's British whereabouts to a simple list was an endless slog. But after protracted effort a schedule emerged. The last known date when he was *definitely* in London was Wednesday, 16 March 1892, when together with Charles Santley he sang his stuff at a concert in St James's Hall. Another star who appeared on the Johannesburg stage, Madame Neruda, played the violin. Add to this the Ripper letter posted to the police in Marylebone five days later, and we get a marker at 21 March 1892.

The next date up was another Wednesday, 4 May 1892, when Maybrick was on the slate to attend a meeting of 'The Supreme Grand Chapter of Royal Arch Masons'. His friend and Grand Master Bro Letchworth 'announced that he had received a communication from Bro Michael Maybrick, Grand Organist, apologising for his inability to be present in Grand Chapter'. He never showed, and he never showed for his next engagement either. On 31 May the *Pall Mall Gazette* publicised a charity concert to be performed in aid of St Mary's Hospital Fund, billed for 9 June at the Haymarket Theatre. Some of the biggest names in the business had promised to donate their talents. Maybrick was among them, but again he didn't turn up. It wasn't until a meeting of the Royal Society of Musicians on 11 July that Maybrick was unequivocally in London. There are therefore about 115 days – between 17 March and 10 July 1892 – that are unaccounted for. He could of course have had his feet up in Regent's Park; or, if you were as certain as I was that 'Mr Neuberg' was in reality Michael Maybrick, he could equally well have travelled to South Africa.

The fastest ship on the route at that time, the *Scot*, made the trip from England to Cape Town in sixteen days. The conductor Sir Charles Hallé and his wife Wilma (stage name Madame Neruda) sailed on it. 'We shall leave Cape Town on September 11th,' he wrote to his son, 'and be in London on the 27th.'

But let us assume Maybrick wasn't aboard the *Scot*, and took something lazier. Allowing a generous twenty-one days out and twenty-one days back, that's still seventy-three days available to waddle about the Transvaal and manipulate his fraudulent letters from Neuberg. Even if he hadn't posted Russell's letter from the ship but actually from Johannesburg, he could have been there to do it in the first week of April. Back-dating his text by nine days would have raised no questions, any more than Stead questioned his nine-day back-dated letter out of Krugersdorp.

In the American edition of *Review of Reviews*, W.T. Stead published a codicil to his plea for Mrs Maybrick: 'The case has, from the first, aroused the most intense interest; and it has created much bitter indignation against the British Government for its denial of palpable justice to an American woman.' A month later, 'indignation' had found a focus, as was reported in the British edition: 'The United States Government has telegraphed to its Consul at Cape Town to take immediate steps to ascertain further particulars of the alleged confession.' The Yanks were going to investigate, probably sending detectives into the Transvaal, and I think this put the wind up the British. If the Americans had found Michael in Johannesburg, the Maybrick scandal might well begin to unravel. Michael Maybrick was at the fulcrum of London Society, a man who knew the men. Many of them must have known he was out of town, and not a few must have known where he was; that, I think, is what spooked them, initiating Mr Asquith's inexplicable shutdown.

Everything in South Africa that was feasible to research was researched, every extant newspaper, magazine and microfilm. It cost endless hours, without success. One last hope was the Government House (GH) archive at Cape Town, whose inventory was enormous.

- GH 1/454 General despatches June – December 1892
- GH 4/21 Confidential despatches January 1889 – July 1893
- GH 15/43 General and confidential minutes January 1892 – December 1892
- GH 18/79 Communications from private individuals 2 April – 18 June 1892
- GH 18/80 Communications from private individuals 26 June – 22 September 1892
- GH 18/81 Communications from private individuals 24 September 1892 – 29 December 1892
- GH 23/39 General despatches January – December 1892
- GH 32/30 Draft general and confidential despatches 1890 – 1898

But unfortunately there is a gap in these records at just the wrong year. Everything to do with diplomatic traffic (be it British or American) for 1892 is missing. Apologists will say the file simply went missing sometime in the last 130 years, while the more cynical might say that the file was pulled. Predicated on the cheats and deceits of the British authorities during the Ripper scandal, I am of the latter school.

After months of research I was left with the impossible coincidence of Robert Reeves and Harry Wilson attributing Mrs Maybrick's frame-up to the same 'servant girl'. I had the secret of 'Sara' and a Harry Wilson alive in Doncaster. But it wasn't enough, and I couldn't prove who 'Neuberg' actually was.

By now I had been researching Bro Michael Maybrick for rather a while, and considered myself somewhat *au fait* with the way he thought. He was a Mason and a murderer, described by Florence as a 'brute'. He was a smartarse, smarter than everyone else, and was amused by the stupidity of his targets. Everything to do with his correspondence required thinking sideways, like him. He enjoyed the risky stuff – the Women of Moab, the Lady from Surrey, Yack and May-bee, to recall but a few. He was playing his Funny Little Game, and knowing his affection for puns and conundrums, I wondered if the bastard had tried his hand at an anagram. I couldn't find Michael Maybrick in South Africa, but I still had the puzzle of Moreau Masina Berthrad Neuberg.

MOREAU/MASINA/BERTHRAD/NEUBERG

I BEGAN A BRUTE MASON MURDERER HA

Acknowledgements

It's been a long haul, and there are many to thank. First in line is my friend and researcher, Keith Skinner, who was there at the beginning of this book, and still there, fifteen Christmas trees later, at the end of it. Keith can work an archive like a bee in a meadow, and not a few of the names that follow come courtesy of his expertise. They are in no particular order, of no specific association, and apologies to anyone I've left out. Richard Booth and all at Booth's Books, Hay-on-Wye. Derek Addyman and Anne Brichto at Addyman Books, and George at Greenway Books, and the Cinema Bookshop, all at Hay-on-Wye. Derek Warman (Isle of Wight), Tracy Steinback (USA), Anne Clarkson (South Africa), Frank Rickarby (The British Library), Trevor Glover and A.P. Pool (Boosey & Hawkes), Sir David Ramsbotham, Anne Graham, Andrew Birkin, James Scott (Madrid), Caroline Morris, Kate Clarke, Robert Gilbert, Caleb Carr, Dr Bruce S. Fisher (USA), Melissa Strickland and Pam de Montmorency (USA), Damian Russell, Terry Wilde, Paul Robinson (Freemasons' Hall, Liverpool), Ian Sanderson (St George's Lodge of Harmony, 32, Liverpool), Peter O'Toole (Artists Rifles), Liz Calder (Bloomsbury Publishing), Lord David Puttnam, Shirley Harrison, Robert Smith, Marie Campbell (Bradford), Rebecca Coombes and all at the library of Freemasons' Hall, London, Stewart Evans, Paul Begg, Don Rumbelow, Susannah Garland, Johnny Depp, Norman Healy (Ireland), Lindsay Siviter, Caroline Morris, Andy and Sue Parlour, Alistair Owen, Caitlin Zenisek, Coral Atkins, Mick Brown, Will Self, Clare Reihill, Robert Lacey, Stephen Guise and everyone else at HarperCollins, including Minna. David Nochimson, Ed Victor and most of all Rand Holston, my agent, who has given me unceasing enthusiasm, wisdom and support. And finally, I want to use the last line I will ever write in this book to thank my beloved family, Sophie, Lily and Willow.

Sources

Chapter 1: All the Widow's Men

1. 'The British Opium Trade in Asia', *Review of Reviews* (American edition), Vol. VI, August 1892/January 1893
2. *Scotland Yard Case Book*, by John Lock, Robert Hale, London, 1993 (p.131)
3. 'The Maiden Tribute of Modern Babylon' 1885
4. *The Case of Eliza Armstrong*, by Alison Plowden, British Broadcasting Corporation, 1974 (p.134)
5. *Salisbury: Victorian Titan*, by Andrew Roberts. London, 1999 (pp.470–1)
6. Letter of Eleanor Marx, 23 June 1888. 'In the East End 1888' by W. J. Fishman, Duckworth, London, 1988 (p.22)
7. *The London Handbook*, The Grosvenor Press, London, 1897 (p.146)
8. *Review of Reviews*, Vol. xiv, New York, July 1896, No. 1 (p.77)
9. Ibid. (p.78)
10. *The Letters of Queen Victoria*, edited by George Earle Buckle. Second Series, Vol. 3 (p.38)
11. *Queen Victoria*, by Sidney Lee, London, Smith, Elder & Co., 1903 (p.495)
12. *W. H. Smith*, by Viscount Chilston, Routledge & Kegan Paul, London, 1965 (pp.276–7)
13. Ibid. (p.277)
14. *Bygone Punishments*, by William Andrews, William Andrews & Co, London, 1899 (p.14). Note: The Punishment of multilation was uncommon before the reign of Henry VIII, but introduced by statute 33, Henry VIII, c. 12 (p.137)
15. *The Age of Sex Crime*, by Jane Caputi, The Women's Press, 1987 (p.7)
16. *The Green Bag* vol.1, Boston, January 1889
17. Ibid.
18. *The Criminal*, by Havelock Ellis, Walter Scott, London, 1890 (p.93)
19. Ibid. (p.90)
20. Ibid. (p.20)
21. *Vital Force or Evils and Remedies of Perverted Sexuality*, by R. B. D. Wells, n. d., circa 1880 (p.7)
22. Dr Bond's Report to Robert Anderson, submitted 10 December 1888
23. A Solution of Arsenic and Potash, or Soda. Dr Humphreys' evidence at the 'trial' of Mrs Maybrick, Irving (p.132)
24. *Jack the Ripper and the London Press*, by L. Perry Curtis Jr., Yale University Press, New Haven and London, 2001 (pp.257, 272)
25. *Oliver Cromwell: The Man and His Mission*, by James Allanson Picton, 2nd edition, Cassell, Peter, Galpin & Co., 1883 (p.290 et seq.)
26. *Review of Reviews*, Vol. XV, 1897 (p.236)
27. *Review of Reviews*, Vol. II–9 September 1890 (p.235)
28. *Review of Reviews* Vol. XII, July/December 1895 (p.218)
29. *The African Dream*, by Brian Gardner, History Book Club, 1970 (p.176 et seq.)
30. *Kitchener*, by Philip Magnus, John Murray, London, 1985 (p.62)
31. *The African Dream*, by Brian Gardner (p.148)
32. *General Gordon, a Christian Hero*, by Seton Churchill, James Nisbet & Co., London, 1904 (p.271)

33. *Real Soldiers of Fortune*, by Richard Harding Davis, Collier & Son, London, 1906 (p.107)

34. *Lord Kitchener of Khartoum*, by the Author of *King Edward the VII*, James Nisbet & Co., London, 1914 (p.46)

35. *Kitchener: Portrait of an Imperialist*, by Philip Magnus, John Murray, London, 1958 (p.133)

36. Ibid. (p.135)

37. *Days of My Years*, by Melville Macnaghten, Edward Arnold, London, 1914 (p.62)

38. *Today*, edited by Jerome K. Jerome, Vol. 1, 20 January 1894 (p.13)

39. *I Caught Crippen*, by ex-Chief Inspector Walter Dew, Blackie & Son, London, 1938 (p.132)

40. The Grosvenor Press, 1897 (p.130)

41. *New York World*, 18 November 1888

42. *The Freemason*, 16 February 1889 (p.98)

43. *The Freemason*, 14 January 1888

44. *The 19th Century*, July 1891, and *Review of Reviews* Vol. III, No. 18 (p.77)

45. *The Rough Ashlar*, Virginia Grand Lodge, USA, September 1891 (p.42)

46. The Masonic Constellation Grand Lodge of Missouri, USA, July 1891 (p.3)

47. Ibid.

48. *The Freemason*, 8 June 1889

49. *Blotted 'Scutcheons*, by Horace Wyndham, Hutchinson & Co., London, circa 1920 (p.110)

50. *The Freemason*, 6 February 1889

51. *The Freemason*, 22 October 1887 (p.568)

52. Masonic Biography (Freemasons' Hall, London)

53. *The Origin and Progress of the Preceptory of St. George 1798–1895*, by C. Fitzgerald Matier, Spencer & Co. London, 1910

54. *The Cleveland Street Scandal*, by H. Montgomery Hyde, W. H. Allen, London, 1976 (p.24)

55. Ibid. (p.25)

56. Ibid. (p.55)

57. *Evening Star*, Washington DC, 2 December 1889

58. *The Clan-Na-Gael and the Murder of Dr. Cronin*, by John T. McEnnis, Boston, 1889 (p.75)

59. *Evening Star*, Washington DC, 18 November 1889 (p.6)

60. Ibid.

61. *Evening Star*, Washington DC, 19 November 1889

62. *Clarence: The Life of H. R. H. the Duke of Clarence and Avondale*, by Michael Harrison, W. H. Allen, London, 1972 (p.30 et seq.)

63. *The Earl of Halisbury*, by A. Wilson Fox, Chapman & Hall, London, 1929 (p.126)

64. *Conversations with Max*, by S. N. Behrman, Hamish Hamilton, London, 1960. 'Max began talking about King Edward VII: "He spoke English with a heavy German accent"' (p.85). See also: *A History of the Artists Rifles 1859–1947*, by Barry Gregory, 2006. 'What struck me most was the strong guttural accent, he rolled his "r"s like a German' (p.155)

65. *Victoria: The Widow and Her Son*, by Hector Bolitho, D. Appleton Century Company, New York, 1934, (p.273)

66. *Washington Evening Star*, 2 January 1890

67. *Star*, Monday, 1 October 1888

68. *Washington Evening Star*, 10 January 1890

69. *The Cleveland Street Scandal*, by H. Montgomery Hyde (p.84)

70. *Truth* reported in *North London Press*

71. 'Having let Hammond run for it, Detective Inspector Abberline was publicly accused of perverting the cource of justice at Bow St Court.' *The Times*, Friday, 24 January 1890

72. *North London Press*, Saturday, 16 November 1889

73. *The Hawk*, 28 January 1890 (p.99)

74. *Some Victorian Men*, written and illustrated by Harry Furniss, London, John Lane, 1924 (pp.123–6)

75. *The Poor Man's Court of Justice*, by Cecil Chapman, Hodder & Stoughton Ltd, London, n. d., circa 1920 (p.14)

76. *The Cleveland Street Scandal*, H. Montgomery Hyde (p.156)

SOURCES

77. Hansard, 28 February 1890 (p.1556)
78. Ibid. (p.1548)
79. Ibid.
80. Ibid.
81. Ibid.
82. Ibid. (p.1571) See also: *Washington Evening Star*, 5 March 1890: '... odds are freely offered in club circles that Mr. W. H. Smith will receive a peerage for his cool, not to say brazen, defense of Lord Salisbury. Mr. Smith's career has been an illustration of the success which rewards adroitness and subserviency in a country like England.'
83. Hansard (Lords), 3 March 1890 (pp.1618–19)
84. *The Story of My Life*, by the Right Honourable Edward Clarke, K. C., John Murray, London, 1923 (pp.112–13)
85. *Light Invisible: The Freemason's Answer to Darkness Visible by 'Vindex'*, The Regency Press, London, 1952 (p.34). See also: *Freemason's Chronicle*, 6 February 1892: 'Masons are especially loyal to the Royal Family, not only as Englishmen, but also on account of that mystic tie which joins them in a brotherhood.'
86. *Guardian*, 11 November 2003
87. *More About King Edward*, by Edward Legge, Eveleigh Nash, London, 1913 (p.162)
88. *England's Masonic Pioneers*, by Dudley Wright, George Kenning & Son, London, 1925 (pp.62–3)
89. Prince of Wales's Lodge No. 259, privately printed, 1910 (pp.81–3)
90. *The Times*, Wednesday, 29 November 1893 (p.10)
91. *Blotted 'Scutcheons*, by Horace Wyndham (p.126)
92. *Glasgow Mail*, reported in *Evening Star*, Washington DC, 5 March 1889

Chapter 2: A Conspiracy of Bafflement
1. In 1888 there were 2,235 Masonic lodges in England. *The Freemason*, 7 January 1888
2. 'Perhaps the most incompetent General of the war.' *Salisbury, Victorian Titan*, by Andrew Roberts (p.752)
3. Ibid. (p.227)
4. 'Grave differences of opinion' between Warren and Monro caused the latter to resign on 16 August 1888. *Fenian Fire* by Christy Campbell, HarperCollins, London, 2002 (p.302)
5. *The Recovery of Jerusalem*, by Capt. Wilson, Capt Warren, Richard Bentley & Son, London, 1871
6. *The Life of General Sir Charles Warren*, by Watkin Williams, Basil Blackwood, Oxford, 1944 (p.41)
7. Freemasonry defines itself in a series of degrees that predicate on the number of vertebrae in the human spine. There are thirty-three of them. The first three degrees – Entered Apprentice, Fellow Craft and Master Mason – (beyond which most Masons don't aspire) are secular, the Brethren meeting together at a Lodge. Thereafter (British) Masonry jumps directly to the 18th Degree, which is strictly Christian, conducting its business at assemblies called Chapters. It is in these higher Degrees (18th to 33rd) that we find the rulers of the Craft, and indeed the rulers of Victorian England.
8. *The Story of the Temple*, by Robert J. Blackham, Sampson Low, Marston & Co., London, n. d., circa 1930
9. Wallace McLeod, *Ars Quatuor Coronatorum*, Vol.99, 1986 (p.183)
10. Ibid.
11. Robert Morris: 'A well known American Masonic lecturer and poet, born in 1818 and Grand Master of the Grand Lodge of Kentucky in 1858. He died in 1888.'
12. *Freemasonry in the Holy Land*, by Robert Morris, Masonic Publishing Company, New York, 1873 (p.462)
13. Ibid. (p.464)
14. *The Keystone*, Saturday, 15 March 1884 (p.292)
15. *Freemasonry in the Holy Land*, by Robert Morris (pp.461–5)
16. Ibid. (p.463)
17. Ibid.
18. Ibid. (p.465)
19. *The Builders: A Story and Study of Freemasonry*, by Joseph Fort Newton,

807

Macoy Publishing, New York, 1951 (p.123)

20. *Who Was Hiram Abiff?*, by J. S. M. Ward, The Baskerville Press, Ltd, London, 1925 (p.2)

21. *Richardson's Monitor of Freemasonry*, 1860 (pp.10–11, 21, 30)

22. Lodge Quatuor Coronati (No. 2076), London

23. The mechanics are complex. Knight was building on research initially instigated by the BBC

24. *Ars Quatuor Coronatorum*, Vol. 99, 1986 (p.183)

25. 'It was found that beyond doubt the piece of apron corresponded exactly with the part missing from the body of the murdered woman.' Inspector Donald Swanson's report, Scotland Yard, 6 November 1888.

26. *Ars Quatuor Coronatorum*, Vol. 99, 1986 (p.184)

27. *Ars Quatuor Coronatorum*, September 1986 (p.172)

28. *Ars Quatuor Coronatorum*, Vol. 100, 1987, published November 1988 (pp.109–12)

29. Ibid.

30. Notable anti-Masonic writers

31. *Ars Quatuor Coronatorum*, Vol. 99, 1986 (p.184)

32. On 5 July 1974 Knight signed an agreement with Scotland Yard in respect of his book, agreeing 'to submit the final manuscript to the Commissioner of police of the Metropolis for approval prior to publication'. (Stephen Knight Collection)

33. *Evening Standard*, 12 August 1960

34. *Jack the Ripper: A Bibliography and Review of the Literature*. Contains a piece by Colin Wilson dated 1972 (p.14, et seq.)

35. Reviewed in *Books and Bookmen*, December 1972 (pp.92–3). And see: *Jack the Ripper, Summing Up and Verdict*, by Colin Wilson and Robin Odell (p.206)

36. *Edouard VII*, by Philippe Jullian, Hachette, Paris, 1962

37. *The Criminologist*, November 1970, Vol. 5, No. 18

38. *Sunday Times*, 1 November 1970

39. *The Centenary History of Cornubian Lodge (450)*, by Thomas E. A. Stowell, circa 1948 (p.186)

40. *Police and Public*, by Maurice Tomlin, Formerly Assistant Commisioner Metropolitan Police, John Long Limited, London, 1936 (p.232)

41. During the Ripper outrages Monro had resigned as Commissioner, and wasn't reinstated until 7 December 1888

42. *The Story of Scotland Yard*, by Sir Basil Thompson, Grayson & Grayson, London, 1935 (p.178)

43. Police Orders 1888 (p.1190)

44. *Scotland Yard and the Metropolitan Police*, by J. F. Moylan. C. B., C. B. E., Receiver for the Metropolitan Police District and Metropolitan Police Courts, G. P. Putnam's Sons Limited, London & New York, 1929 (pp.48–9)

45. Tomlin (p.233)

46. *Ars Quatuor Coronatorum*, Vol. 99 (p.186)

47. Ibid. (p.179)

48. See Chapter 12, 'The Mouth of the Maggot'

Chapter 3: 'The Mystic Tie'

1. 'You Are Now A Master Mason.' Respectfully and dutifully dedicated to R. W. Bro Sir John Corah, Provincial Grand Master for Leicestershire and Rutland. (For private circulation only. Keep this report under lock and key.)

2. Maybe he was thinking along the same lines as the *Star* newspaper: 'surely Jack the Ripper is not to be our modern John the Baptist' (Freemasons' Patron Saint). *Star*, Friday, 5 October 1888

3. In their *News from Whitechapel* (McFarland & Co., 2002) Chisholm, DiGrazia & Yost attempt to explain this away with a footnote: 'This does not demonstrate a lack of knowledge on his part. Contemporary police policy prohibited Abberline from giving out such information' (p.67). This is nothing less than nonsense. Abberline couldn't say because he didn't know, and his ignorance

wasn't unique. Five days later Dr
Bagster Phillips tried every which
way to withhold such evidence from
Wynne Baxter and his jury at the
coroner's court. *Daily Telegraph*, 20
September 1888

4. *Public Opinion*, 28 September 1888
(p.385)

5. *The Story of John George Haigh*, by
Stafford Somerfield, Hood Pearson,
Manchester, 1950 (p.84)

6. *The Complete History of Jack the Ripper*,
by Philip Sugden (p.131)

7. *Evening Express*, Monday, 12
November 1888

8. *The Lancet*, 20 September 1888
(p.637)

9. *Truth*, 4 October 1888 (p.581)

10. Sir James Risden-Bennett, letter to
the *Evening Standard*, Tuesday, 22
October 1888

11. *The Lancet*, 29 September 1888
(p.637)

12. Ibid.

13. *Standard*, Friday, 15 October 1888

14. Sugden (p.133)

15. Despite his lunch with Wilson, and
an article written by him in *The
Criminologist*, Stowell published a
letter in *The Times* of 9 November
1970 denying that he had ever
accused Albert Victor, the Duke of
Clarence.

16. *Bradford Observer*, 27 September
1888

17. Ibid.

18. *New York Herald*, 1 October 1888

Chapter 4: The Funny Little Game

1. *The Builders: A Story and Study of
Freemasonry*, by Joseph Fort Newton
(p.27)

2. Reported by Alfred Long, PC254A,
6 November 1888. Note: Despite
Crawford hammering home the
spelling of 'Juwes' at the inquest,
both Long and Arnold revert to the
incorrect spelling 'Juews'.

3. *The Bible and Modern Criticisms*, by
Sir Robert Anderson, K. C. B.,
Hodder & Stoughton, London,
1902 (p.17)

4. Police Constable Long at the
Eddowes inquest, 4 October 1888

5. *Daily News*, 1 October 1888

6. *The Times*, Friday, 5 October 1888
(Bond said Phillips was there about
2.30 a.m.)

7. *From Constable to Commissioner*, by Sir
Henry Smith, KCB, Chatto &
Windus, London, 1910 (p.152)

8. Signed Jas McWilliam, Inspector,
City of London Police, 27 October
1888 (Stamped HO, 29 October
1888 Dep #) A4930186.

9. Home Office, 6 November 1888
(93305/28)

10. 'A good schoolboy's round hand.'
Halse's deposition at Eddowes'
inquest. *Daily Telegraph*, 12 October
1888

11. Superintendent Arnold's report to
Home Office, 6 November 1888

12. *Lloyd's Weekly*, 9 September 1888

13. *Public Opinion*, 11 September 1888

14. *East London Observer*, 10 November
1888

15. Sir Charles Warren letter to the
Home Office, Confidential Letters
Book, 6 November 1888 (p.7/180)

16. Ibid. (p.4/177)

17. Letter from Charles Warren to the
Right Hon. Godfrey Lushington,
Permanent Under Secretary at the
Home Office, 11 October 1888.
Metropolitan Police Office of the
Commissioner, Letter Books
MEP01–48

18. Martin Fido, 'Case Book Message
Boards', Thursday, 27 June 2002

19. 'Freemasonry and the Ripper', by
Bro Dennis Stocks, Kersting, 2006,
and Barron Barnet Lodge of
Research (Lodge 146)

20. *Jack the Ripper: The Uncensored Facts*,
by Paul Begg, Robson Books, 1988
(pp.127–8)

21. See also: *The Masonic Why and
Wherefore*, by Bro J. S. M. Ward, 1929
(p.67), and *Masonic Problems and
Queries*, by Herbert F. Inman, 1950
(p.127), where the three Assassins
are referenced

22. *Jack the Ripper: The Uncensored Facts*,
by Paul Begg (p.183). Note: Mr
Sugden may consider Mr Begg as a
'reliable student', but I do not. In
the acknowledgements to his book,
Mr Begg references Bro J. M.
Hamill (WM of the Quatuor

Coronati Lodge) as his Freemasonic source. Ergo, Begg quotes Hamill and Mr Sugden quotes Begg, which is presumably why both are so dramatically in error. (See Bro Mendoza, pp.109–11, *Ars Quatuor Coronatorum*, Vol. 100, for the year 1987)

23. Palestine Exploration Fund, Quarterly Statements for 1875 (p.227)

24. *The Bible and Modern Criticism*, by Sir Robert Anderson. 'The Name Jehovah', 1902 (p.87)

25. Written by the librarian at Freemasons' Hall, London, on behalf of Bro Hamill, 6 July 1992 (p.3). Archive at Freemasons' Hall.

26. *The Complete History of Jack the Ripper*, by Philip Sugden, 1994 (p.112)

27. Home Office 93305-28 (pp.174–81)

28. Sugden (p.185)

29. *Morals and Dogma of the Ancient and Accepted Scottish Right of Freemasonry*, prepared by Albert Pike, Charleston, A. M. 5641 (p.82)

30. *The Grand Master, Commentary on the Masonic Legend of Hiram Abiff*, by Dr Bruce S. Fisher, Prescott, Arizona, 1996

31. *Pall Mall Gazette*, 8 October 1888

32. Ibid.

33. Ibid.

34. Ibid.

35. *Pall Mall Gazette*, 12 October 1888

36. Ibid.

37. Ibid.

38. Ibid.

39. *A Police Code and Manual of the Criminal Law*, by C. E. Howard Vincent, Cassell, Petter, Galpin & Co., London, 1881

40. Ibid.

41. *The Star*, Saturday, 12 October 1888

42. *Sir Evelyn Ruggles-Brise*, compiled by Shane Leslie, John Murray, London, 1938 (p.59)

43. *The Star*, Saturday, 10 November 1888

44. *Pall Mall Gazette*, 8 October 1888

45. *Pall Mall Gazette*, 12 October 1888

46. Superintendent Arnold's statement to the Home Office, 6 November 1888

47. *Pall Mall Gazette*, 12 October 1888

48. Sugden (p.254)

49. Anderson was appointed Assistant Commissioner of Police for the Metropolis on Saturday, 2 September 1888 (Police Orders Book, p.878)

50. *From the City to Fleet Street*, by J. Hall Richardson, London, 1927 (p.217)

51. *Daily Chronicle*, 1 September 1908

52. In the *Daily Chronicle* of 1 September 1908, Anderson incorrectly refers to Sir William Harcourt as being Home Secretary at the time of the Ripper

53. Letter received on 14 October 1896, at H Division, Whitechapel. Chief Inspector Moore submitted a report on the letter on 18 October 1896

54. Macnaghten (p.55)

55. There are many versions of this oath; this example is from *A Ritual of Freemasonry* by Avery Allyn, Boston, 1831

56. George Oliver (1782–67), known as 'the Sage of Masonry', was one of its earliest and most prolific writers

57. *New York Tribune*, Sunday, 11 November 1888

58. Letter signed 'R. Fairfield, 64, South Eaton Place (London) S. W.', *The Times*, 1 October 1888

Chapter 5: The Savages

1. *A Dictionary of Historical Slang*, by Eric Partridge, Penguin Books, 1977 (p.271)

2. *The Age of Sex Crime*, by Jane Caputi (p.33)

3. Sixty-three handwritten pages in what appears to be an old scrapbook, from which the first forty-eight pages have been removed with a knife. Traces of gum and card show they once held pictures or photographs. The writing, signed 'Jack the Ripper', purports to be a record of the Ripper's activities from about April 1888 to May 1889. Internal evidence proves beyond doubt that the author is intended to be James Maybrick.

According to ex-scrap-metal-dealer Mike Barrett, he was given the scrapbook by a friend named Tony Devereux (now deceased), who told him nothing beyond assurances that it was genuine. In April 1992 Barret took the document to the Robert Crew Literary Agency in London. Thereafter Shirley Harrison was commissioned to research and write a book. *The Diary of Jack the Ripper* was published by Smith Gryphon, Ltd, London, in 1993. Arguments over provenance have continued ever since.

On 27 June 1994 the *Liverpool Daily Post* reported Mike Barrett's claim to have forged the journal using a scrapbook bought from auctioneers. At the same time he claimed to have only days to live and said he'd 'worked on the diary for five years'. The following day, the confession was withdrawn by his solicitors, who said that he was not in full control of his faculties when he made that statement, which was totally inaccurate and without foundation.

The above is an abbreviated version of the entry referencing the MAYBRICK JOURNAL from *The Complete Jack the Ripper A to Z*, by Paul Begg, Martin Fido and Keith Skinner, John Blake Publishing, Ltd, London, 2010.

In *Mapping Murder* (Virgin Books, 2003), England's leading practitioner of geographical criminal profiling, Professor David Canter, argued that the Maybrick journal was either genuine, or the work of a literary genius.

4. *Tyler's Book, Records of the St. George's Lodge of Harmony, Liverpool*, Liverpool City Library
5. *The Story of Government*, Henry Austin, editor, A. M. Thayer & Co., Boston & London, 1893
6. Mr Martin Fido, speaking on the BBC Radio 4 arts programme *Kaleidoscope*, 9 September 1993. Reported in *Jack the Ripper: The Final Chapter*, by Paul H. Feldman, Virgin Books, 1997 (pp.82–3)

7. Referring to Stride and Eddowes, it references the latter's empty tin matchbox. *The Diary of Jack the Ripper*, by Shirley Harrison (p.282)
8. *Lloyd's Weekly*, Sunday, 30 September 1888. See *My Life's Pilgrimage*, by Thomas Catling, John Murray, London, 1911, for a description of visit of Dr Gordon Brown to Mitre Square (pp.183–5)
9. *Lloyd's Weekly*, Sunday, 30 September 1888
10. *A Savage Club Souvenir*, privately printed, 1916 (p.83)
11. Ibid. (p.67). It's worth noting that Thomas Catling and George Sims (who wrote of 'The Firm of Assassins') were socially and Masonically close. See *My Life's Pilgrimage*, by Thomas Catling (p.287)
12. *The Freemason*, 7 February 1891 (p.71)
13. *The Freemason*, 2 November 1889
14. *The Freemason*, 5 May 1888
15. Bro Shadwell Clerke died in 1892, replaced as Grand Secretary to the Prince of Wales by Sir Edward Letchworth, who, continuing the fraternal tradition, was described as one of Michael Maybrick's 'most intimate friends'. *The Freemason*, 30 August 1913
16. *More About King Edward*, by Edward Legg (p.180)
17. *The Freemason*, 11 February 1888
18. *Jack the Ripper: The Final Chapter*, by Paul H. Feldman
19. *The Diary of Jack the Ripper*, by Shirley Harrison

Chapter 6: On the Square
1. *The Times*, Wednesday, 3 October 1888
2. *The Yorkshireman*, Tuesday, 2 October 1888
3. *The Corporation of the City of London*, edited by Alfred Arthur Sylvester, London, 1897 (p.111)
4. Ibid. (p.109)
5. *Daily Telegraph*, Friday, 5 October 1888
6. Home Office Minute Sheet: A49301/86

7. *Evening News*, 1 October 1888
8. Sugden (p.247)
9. Report to Home Office by Donald Swanson, 19 October 1888
10. Letter from Sir Charles Warren to Commissioner of City Police, Col. Sir James Frazer, 3 October 1888, MEPO1/48
11. *Evening News*, 12 October 1888
12. *Daily Telegraph*, Friday, 12 October 1888
13. *The Ripper File*, by Elwyn Jones and John Lloyd, Arthur Barker Limited, London, 1975 (p.132)
14. *Jack the Ripper: The Uncensored Facts*, by Paul Begg (p.127)
15. *The Freemason's Chronicle*, 27 April 1889
16. *The Freemason*, Saturday, 14 January 1888
17. *Light Invisible by 'Vindex'* (p.34)
18. *New York Tribune*, 13 November 1888
19. *The History and Practice of the Political Police in Britain*, by Tony Bunyan, Julian Friedmann, London, 1976 (p.196)

Chapter 7: The Ink-Stained Hack

1. *Our Conservative and Unionist Statesmen*, Newman, Graham & Co., London, n.d., circa 1899, Vol. 2 (p.129)
2. *Victorian Titan*, by Andrew Roberts (p.451)
3. *Police*, Charles Tempest Clarkson and J. Hall Richardson, Field & Tuer, The Leadenhall Press, London, 1889 (p.278)
4. Document written by Sir Charles Warren appointing Donald Swanson as his 'eyes and ears', drafted 15 September 1888
5. Ibid.
6. Ibid.
7. Swanson joined the Grand Lodge of Scotland on 21 September 1885, and St Peter's Thurso Lodge, No. 284, on 12 August 1886
8. *Jack the Ripper: The Uncensored Facts*, by Paul Begg (p.127)
9. Ibid.
10. *Evening News*, 2 September 1888
11. *Daily Telegraph*, 4 October 1888
12. *The Ripper File*, by Melvin Harris, W. H. Allen, London, 1989 (p.58)

13. *Life and Death at the Old Bailey*, by R. Thurston Hopkins, Herbert Jenkins, Ltd, London, 1935 (p.201)
14. 'Dear Boss' was preceded by a letter addressed to Sir Charles Warren with 'on her majesterys service' gracing the envelope. Date stamped 'Received Metropolitan Police. 25 Sept 88'
15. *The Lighter Side of My Office Life*, Sir Robert Anderson, Hodder & Stoughton, London, 1910 (p.138)
16. Ibid.
17. Ibid.
18. Sugden (p.268)
19. Ibid.
20. Eddowes inquest: Thursday, 4 October 1888
21. *The Detection of Forgery*, by Douglas Blackburn and Waithman Caddell, Edwin Layton, London, 1909 (p.11)
22. *Evening Post*, Monday, 1 October 1888
23. Letter published in *The Times*, 2 October 1888
24. Letter from Sir Charles Warren to the Chairman, Board of Works, Whitechapel District, 3 October 1888
25. Ibid.
26. Ibid.
27. 'I had served in two provincial police forces for thirty years and though I had known wrongdoing, I had never experienced institutionalized wrongdoing, blindness, arrogance and prejudice on anything like the scale accepted as routine in the Met.' *In the Office of Constable* by Sir Robert Mark, Collins, London, 1978 (p.124)
28. Letters from Sir Charles Warren to the Chairman, Board of Works, Whitechapel District, 3 October 1888
29. *The Ripper Legacy*, by Martin Howells and Keith Skinner, Sidgwick & Jackson, London, 1987 (p.194)
30. *The Letters of Queen Victoria*, edited by George Earle Buckle, John Murray, London, 1930, Vol. 1 (p.449)
31. *East London Observer*, 15 October 1888
32. Ibid.

33. *The Echo*, Monday, 10 September 1888
34. Home Office A49301C/10. 27 October 1888
35. *East London Observer*, 6 October 1888
36. Report by Superintendent Thomas Arnold, H Division (Whitechapel), dated 22 October 1888
37. *Bradford Observer*, 15 September 1888
38. Metropolitan Police Orders, 1888 (pp.874–1114)
39. Ibid. (pp.480–1, 797)
40. 'Every single article in the Queen's possession had been photographed from several points of view,' resulting in an encyclopedic set of specially bound volumes, cataloguing Her Majesty's possessions. Opposite each article, be it a Van Dyke or a stuffed dachshund, 'an entry was made, indicating the number of the article, the number of the room in which it was kept, its exact position in the room, and all its principal characteristics'. *Queen Victoria*, by Lytton Strachey, Chatto & Windus, London, 1921
41. Whitehall, 17 September 1888, A49301/3
42. *The Story of Scotland Yard*, by George Dilnot, Geoffrey Bles, London, n. d., circa 1925. Note: 'After I became a member of the permanent staff of the Yard and received such gratuities as I earned, I reckoned them to be worth half the amount of my pay to me taking the year all round' – Detective Inspector Meiklejohn. Meiklejohn was betrayed by his criminal associates and kicked out of the Metropolitan Police, attracting two years' hard labour.
43. Home Office, 7 October 1888. HO 144/220/A49301B
44. Ibid.
45. Ibid.
46. HO 144/220A 49301B f180–1 (See Dr Gordon Brown/Eddowes inquest, *The Times*, Friday, 5 October, and Dr Bond, HO 144/221–A493 01C f220–3)
47. *The Star*, Saturday, 10 November 1888
48. *The Times*, Thursday, 27 September 1888
49. *Kenning's Masonic Cyclopaedia*, 1878 (p.476)
50. Sugden (p.94)
51. Ibid. (pp.109–10)
52. *From Constable to Commissioner*, by Lieut. Col. Sir Henry Smith (pp.147–8)
53. *The Times*, 19 July 1889
54. Police Orders, Thursday, 23 August 1888 (p.850)
55. *East London Advertiser*, 15 September 1888
56. *The Jack the Ripper A to Z*, Headline Book Publishing, 1994 (p.372)

Chapter 8: The Double Event: Part Two

1. *East London Observer*, 13 October 1888
2. *East London Advertiser*, Saturday, 6 October 1888
3. *I Caught Crippen*, by Walter Dew (p.141)
4. *Daily News*, Monday, 1 October 1888
5. *Daily Telegraph*, Monday, 1 October 1888
6. *Evening News*, 1 October 1888
7. Ibid.
8. Ibid.
9. Sugden (p.227)
10. *Forensic Medicine*, by Keith Simpson, Edward Arnold & Co., London, 1951 (p.7)
11. *Principles of Forensic Medicine*, revised by William R. Smith, Henry Renshaw, London, 1895, 7th edition (pp.288–9)
12. *Daily Chronicle*, Monday, 1 October 1888
13. *Illustrated London News*, 30 October 1888
14. 'On arrival of the Superindendent from Leman Street Police Station, which took place almost simultaneously with that of the divisional sergeant'. *Daily News*, Monday, 1 October 1888
15. Crime Department's Special Branch Ledger, Special Account, commencing 1 February 1888
16. *Reynold's News*, Sunday, 7 April 1895
17. *Daily News*, 1 October 1888

18. *Jack the Ripper: Scotland Yard Investigates*, by Stewart P. Evans and Donald Rumbelow, Sutton Publishing, 2006 (p.101)
19. *Observer*, 30 September 1888
20. Evans and Rumbelow (p.101)
21. *The Unpublished Memories of James Monro*, April 1903 (p.77)
22. *Evening News*, 1 October 1888
23. Ibid.
24. Ibid.
25. Diemschutz was sentenced to three months' imprisonment with hard labour, and Kosebrodski sentenced to pay a fine of four pounds or to be imprisoned for one month. *The Times*, 26 April 1889
26. *I Caught Crippen*, by Walter Dew (p.141)
27. London Report for the *Te Aroha News* (New Zealand), 12 December 1888
28. *Daily Telegraph*, 1 October 1888

Chapter 9: Rotten to the Core
1. Criminal Investigation Dept, Scotland Yard, 4 October 1888 – reference to papers 52983
2. Metropolitan Police H Division, 4 October 1888 – Reference to papers 52983
3. Before PC White was kicked out of the police force for drunkenness, we find he was 'severely reprimanded and cautioned'. Police orders, Friday, 23 November 1888
4. *Stephen's Commentaries on the Laws of England*, 18th edition, Vol. IV, Butterworth & Co., London, 1925 (p.220)
5. *East London Advertiser*, 28 July 1888
6. *The Times*, 8 October 1888
7. Memo by J. S. Sandars, Assistant to E. J. Ruggles-Brise, who himself was the private secretary to the Home Secretary, Henry Matthews, 19 September 1888
8. *Evening News*, Monday, 1 October 1888
9. Robert Anderson to the Home Office, 23 October 1888: A49301/60
10. It is of note that Sergeant White does not give 'evidence' at the Stride inquest. Yet it was he who made 'a house-to-house search of

Berner Street', and supposedly interviewed Packer. Calling White to the inquest would of course mean calling Matthew Packer.
11. *The Star*, 4 October 1888
12. *Jack the Ripper: Scotland Yard Investigates*, by Stewart Evans and Don Rumbelow (p.107)
13. Ibid. (p.108)
14. Sugden (p.227)
15. Ibid.
16. Ibid. (p.228)
17. *Daily Telegraph*, Saturday, 6 October 1888
18. Ibid.
19. Ibid.
20. *East London Advertiser*, Saturday, 6 October 1888
21. *Manchester Guardian*, Monday, 8 October 1888
22. *Jack the Ripper: The Facts*, by Paul Begg (p.145)
23. Le Grande briefly reappears as a 'witness' in the Parnell frame-up
24. Donald Swanson's report, Metropolitan Police, 19 October 1888
25. Sugden (p.225)
26. *Jack the Ripper: The Facts*, by Paul Begg (p.147)
27. Ibid. (p.144)
28. *The Star*, 1 October 1888
29. Ibid.
30. *Evening Post*, 1 October 1888
31. Report to Home Office by Chief Inspector Donald Swanson, dated 19 October 1888
32. Ibid.
33. Ibid.
34. *The Trials of Israel Lipski*, by Martin Friedland, Macmillan, London, 1984 (p.187)
35. Metropolitan Police Office, Police Orders, Thursday, 13 December 1888 (p.1215)
36. *The Yorkshire Pioneer*, 5 October 1888
37. *The Yorkshireman*, 11 September 1888
38. *The Standard*, 1 October 1888
39. *Daily News*, Monday, 1 October 1888
40. Swanson's report to Home Office, 19 October 1888
41. Draft letter to Home Office from Robert Anderson, 5 November 1888 (3/53983/1119)

42. *The A to Z*, 1996 (p.388)
43. Ibid.
44. Report from Sir Charles Warren, confidential letter dated 6 November. Stamped Home Office, 7 November 1888
45. *East London Advertiser*, 6 October 1888

Chapter 10: 'They All Love Jack'
1. *Tatler*, 30 March 1889 (p.90)
2. *The World*, 15 January 1890 (p.8)
3. *Hymns Ancient and Modern*, by Jimmy Glover, Fisher Unwin Limited, London, 1926 (p.92)
4. *New Era*, 14 September 1878 (p.3)
5. *Sir Charles Santley*, John Newburn Levin, n. d., circa 1927 (p.7)
6. *New Penny Magazine*, Vol. VIII, Cassell & Co., 1900
7. *Memories, an Autobiography*, by Walter Macfarren. The Walter Scott Publishing Co. Limited, London & New York, 1905 (pp.1, 4, 6–7)
8. *Musical World*, 6 December 1884 (p.766)
9. 'The Regimental March "They All Love Jack" was a composition of one of our celebrated officers of later days, Capt. Michael Maybrick, who wrote under the name of "Stephen Adams", and was adopted by the corps as their capital Regimental march in the 80s.' *Memories of the Artists Rifles*, by Colonel H. R. A. May, 1929 (p.13)
10. *The World*, 15 January 1890 (p.8)
11. Internet profile of British composer Stephen Adams, by Derek Strahan
12. *Once an Artist Always an Artist*, by Capt. C. J. Blomfield, Page & Co., London, 1921
13. Records of the Artists Volunteers, 26 February 1886. 'Michael Maybrick, Gent, to be Lieutenant (Supernumerary),' 6 February 1886
14. *The Criminal*, by Havelock Ellis, 1890 (p.94)
15. *New York Daily Tribune*, 11 November 1888
16. *Whoever Fights Monsters*, by Robert K. Ressler and Tom Shachtman, St Martin's Press, New York, 1992 (p.63)
17. *Beside Me*, by Ann Rule, W. W. Norton & Co., New York and London, 1980 (p.31)
18. Ressler (p.64)
19. *Vanity Varnished*, by P. Tennyson Cole, Hutchinson, London, 1931 (p.88)
20. Letter to Trevor Christie from Florence Aunspaugh, n. d., circa 1942
21. *The Star*, 1 October 1888. 'He gave his name and address, but the police have not disclosed them.'
22. *Sunday Times*, 11 November 1888
23. *Evening News*, Saturday, 20 October 1888
24. *Evening News*, Friday, 19 October 1888
25. *The Criminologist*, Spring 1989, Vol. 13, No. 1 (pp.12–15)
26. Thomas Horrocks Openshaw, Hotspur Lodge No. 1626. Initiated 27 April 1882, aged twenty-six. Archive at Freemasons' Hall, 9 May 2007
27. *From Constable to Commissioner*, by Lieut. Col. Sir Henry Smith (p.154)
28. Ibid. (p.155)
29. *Sunday Times*, 21 October 1888
30. Report of Chief Inspector Donald Swanson. A49301C/8c. Stamped: Home Office, 6 November 1888. See: City Report, signed Jas. Inspector McWilliam, City of London Police 27 October 1888, who gives the correct date Tuesday, 16 October 1888.
31. Donald Swanson Report to Home Office, 6 November 1888
32. *From Constable to Commissioner*, by Lieut. Col. Sir Henry Smith (p.154)
33. *Sunday Times*, 21 October 1888
34. *A Treatise: Bright's Disease*, by James Tyson, M. D., P. Blakiston's Sons & Co., Philadelphia, 1904 (p.101)
35. Report to Home Office, Donald Swanson: A49301C/8c
36. City of London Police: Stamped: Home Office, 29 October 1888. Dept. No. A493018b
37. *The Star*, Wednesday, 17 October 1888
38. *The News from Whitechapel*, by Alexander Chisholm, Christopher-Michael DiGrazia and Dave Yost, McFarland & Co., Jefferson, North

Carolina, and London, 2002
(p.189)

39. *Sickert and the Ripper Crimes*, by Jean
Overton Fuller, Mandrake, Oxford,
1990 (p.128)

40. Philip Sugden (p.275). Based on
Thomas J. Mann, 'The Ripper and
the Poet, a Comparison of
Handwriting', *Wade Journal*
(Chicago) Vol. 2, No. 1, June 1975
(pp.1–31)

41. *The True History of the Elephant Man*,
by Michael Howell and Peter Ford,
Penguin Books, London, 1980
(pp.18–19)

42. *Round London*, by Montagu Williams
QC, Macmillan & Co., London and
New York, 1892 (p.8)

Chapter 11: On Her Majesty's Service

1. *The Monster of Dusseldorf: The Life
and Trial of Peter Kurten*, by Margaret
Seaton Wagner, E. P. Dutton & Co.
Inc., 1933 (p.141)

2. *The Unknown Murderer*, by Theodor
Reik, Prentice-Hall, Inc., New York,
1945 (p.86)

3. Jack the Ripper letter, 23 October
1888

4. To the Under Secretary of State,
from Charles Warren. Stamped
Home Office, 10 October 1888,
A49301C

5. *The Life of General Sir Charles Warren*,
by his grandson, Watkin W.
Williams, Basil Blackwell, Oxford,
1941 (p.222)

6. Home Office, 10 October 1888.
Dept. No. A49301B/8

7. 'The Police of the Metropolis',
Murray's Magazine, November 1888
(p.16)

8. *Days of My Years*, by Sir Melville
Macnaghten (p.54)

9. *The Story of John George Haigh*, by
Stafford Somerfield, Hood Pearson
(p.67)

10. *Cassell's Saturday Journal*, 26
December 1900 (p.310)

11. *Life and Letters of Sir Charles Hallé*,
edited by his son, C. E. Hallé,
Smith, Elder, & Co., London, 1896
(pp.117–18)

12. *The Nation*, 16 August 1888
(p.127)

13. *The Post Office and its Story*, by
Edward Bennett, Seeley, Service &
Co., Ltd, London, 1912 (p.73)

14. Letter sent by Jack the Ripper to
Metropolitan Police, 8 October
1888

15. *Truth*, 18 October 1888

16. *The Post Office and its Story* (p.213)

17. Letter from Jonathan Hopson,
National Art Library, Victoria &
Albert Museum, London, 8
February 2001

18. *Masonic Problems and Queries*,
compiled by Herbert F. Inman, A.
Lewis (Masonic Publishers) Ltd,
London, 1950. Note: A Lodge is
'squared' during the actual
progress of a ceremony, when
'squaring' is symbolical. To be a
Mason is to be 'On the Square', as
Masons nominate themselves.
(p.217)

19. *Handy Andy: A Tale of Irish Life*, by
Samuel Lover, Milner & Co., Ltd,
London (p.1)

20. *Chief Men Among the Brethren*, by Hy
Pickering, Pickering & Inglis,
London, n. d., circa 1900 (p.211)

21. *Robert Anderson, K.C.B.L.L.D. and
Lady Agnes Anderson*, by their son, A.
P. Moore-Anderson, Marshall,
Morgan & Scott Ltd, London, 1947

22. Amy Maine interview, conducted by
Roger Wilkes (p.7)

23. *Fifty Years of Music*, by William
Boosey, Ernest Benn Ltd, London,
1931 (p.18)

24. Copied from a letter to Trevor
Christie from Florence Aunspaugh
(n. d., circa 1942)

Chapter 12: The Mouth of the Maggot

1. *An Inquiry into the Age of the Moabite
Stone*, by Samuel Sharpe, Watson &
Co., London, 1896. Note: The
stone bears an inscription, which
purports to have been written
about 850 BC by Mesha, King of
Moab, who lived in the reigns of
the kings of Northern Israel. In its
subject matter, its language and its
characters, it is most interesting to
the student of the Bible.

2. *The Life of General Sir Charles Warren*,
by Watkin W. Williams (p.70 et seq.)

3. Ibid. (p.73)
4. Ibid. (p.74)
5. Palestine Exploration Fund quarterly statement for 1876 (p.137)
6. *Ars Quatuor Coronatorum*, March 1887 (p.37)
7. Ibid.
8. Ibid. (pp.41–2)
9. *The Religion of Ancient Palestine in the Second Millennium B.C.*, by Stanley A. Cook, Archibald Constable & Co., London, 1908 (p.39)
10. *Bible Side-Lights: A Record of Excavation and Discovery in Palestine*, by R. A. Stewart Macalister, Hodder & Stoughton, n.d., London (p.72)
11. *Punch*, 14 August 1886 (p.75)
12. *The Echo*, Wednesday, 3 October 1888
13. *The Times*, 9 October 1888
14. Ibid.
15. Ibid.
16. Ibid.
17. *The Times*, 4 October 1888
18. *The Times*, 9 October 1888
19. *Bradford Observer*, 13 September 1888
20. *Bradford Observer*, Thursday, 4 October 1888
21. *New York Herald*, 2 October 1888
22. *The Echo*, Monday, 1 October 1888
23. *The Times*, 9 October 1888
24. Ibid.
25. Ibid.
26. Ibid.
27. Ibid.
28. Ibid.
29. Ibid.
30. Ibid.
31. Ibid.
32. Ibid.
33. *Public Opinion*, 12 October 1888
34. *The Echo*, Wednesday, 3 October 1888
35. *Bradford Observer*, Monday, 8 October 1888
36. Ibid.
37. Reported *Bradford Observer*, Thursday, 13 September 1888
38. *New York Herald*, 2 October 1888
39. JTR letter, 22 October 1888
40. *History of the Royal Engineers*, by Whitworth Porter, 1889, Vol. 2 (p.66). See also *The Life of Sir Charles Warren*, by Watkin W. Williams (p.139)
41. Home Office Minutes, 24 October 1888. No. A49301/E/3
42. *Illustrated Weekly Telegraph*, Bradford, 3 November 1888
43. *Evening News*, 18 October 1888
44. *Evening News*, 19 October 1888
45. *The Times*, 18 October 1888
46. *Jack the Ripper and the London Press*, by L. Perry Curtis 2001 (pp.180–1)
47. *The Times*, 20 October 1888
48. *Maggots, Murder and Men*, by Zakaria Erzinclioglu, Harley Books, Colchester, 2003 (p.69)
49. *The Encyclopedia of Forensic Science*, Brian Lane (ed.), Headline Books, 1992
50. *The Times*, Register of Events in 1888, Saturday, 29 September (p.157)
51. Dr Mark Benecke, 'The Great Maggot Detective,' *Sunday Telegraph Magazine*, 6 March 2003 (p.22)
52. *Casebook of a Crime Psychiatrist*, by James A. Brussel, with an introduction by Gerold Frank, Dell, 1968 (p.12)
53. Ibid. (p.149 et seq.)
54. *The Times*, 23 October 1888
55. Ibid.
56. Ibid.
57. Ibid.

Chapter 13: A Gentleman's Lair

1. *The Toynbee Record*, December 1888 (p.31)
2. Fifth Annual Report (Toynbee Hall), 1889
3. *Canon Barnett by His Wife*, John Murray, London, 1921 (p.161)
4. Ibid. (p.479)
5. *Toynbee Hall*, by J. A. R. Pimlot, J. M. Dent & Sons Limited, London, 1935 (p.82)
6. *Canon Barnett by His Wife* (p.694)
7. Robert K. Ressler was a supervisory Special Agent with the FBI. He has served as an instructor and criminologist at the FBI's training academy since 1974, and is on the faculty of the FBI Academy in the Behavioral Science Unit. Robert D. Keppel is the Chief Criminal Investigator for the Washington

State Attorney General's Office. He has a Ph.D in criminal justice from the University of Washington and has been an investigator or consultant to over 2,000 murder cases and over fifty serial murder investigations.

8. *New York Herald*, 19 July 1889
9. *Mapping Murder*, by Professor David Canter, Virgin Books, 2003 (pp.92–3)
10. *The Windsor Magazine*, Ward, Lock & Co. Limited, London, 1898 (p.541). See also: *Quintin Hogg: A Biography*, by Ethel Hogg, Constable & Co., London, 1904
11. *The Story of My Life*, by the Right Honourable Sir Edward Clarke, K.C., John Murray, London, 1923 (p.29)
12. *Casebook of a Crime Psychiatrist*, by James A. Brussel (p.12). This is actually in the introduction to his book, written by Gerold Frank
13. *The Freemason*, 6 February 1892 (p.67)
14. *East London Observer*, 7 February 1885
15. *The Toynbee Record*, October 1888 (p.11)
16. Joined in 1879 and 1882 respectively
17. *Men and Memories: Recollections of William Rothenstein*, Faber & Faber Limited, London, 1932 (p.30)
18. *Memories of the Artists Rifles*, by Colonel H. A. R. May, Howlett & Son, London, 1929 (p.260)
19. 'He would kidnap his victims from the parking lot of a restaurant and transport them elsewhere for rape and murder. Unlike many organized offenders, he would leave the bodies in locations that were only partially concealed, and then would call the police and report seeing a body. As the police rushed to the location of that body, the offender rushed back to the hospital, so that when the call from the police came to the hospital for an ambulance to be dispatched, he would be in a position to answer that call.' *Whoever Fights Monsters*, by Robert K. Ressler and Tom Shachtman (p.120)

20. Ibid. (p.116)
21. 'Most serial killers have been living with their fantasies for years before they finally bubble to the surface and are translated into deeds.' Robert D. Keppel (p.7)
22. *East London Observer*, 11 August 1888
23. Ibid.
24. *Days of My Years*, by Sir Melville Macnaghten
25. *Pall Mall Gazette*, 31 March 1903
26. *The Times*, 19 July 1889
27. *Ars Quatuor Coronatorum*, March 1887 (p.37)
28. Macnaghten (p.62). Simon Pure: the real man. In Mrs Centlivre's *Bold Stroke for a Wife*, a Colonel Feignwell passes himself off as Simon Pure, and wins the heart of Miss Lovely. No sooner does he get the assent of her guardian than the veritable Quaker shows himself, and proves, beyond a doubt, that he is the real Simon Pure. (Source: M. N. Brewer, *Dictionary of Phrase and Fable* (p.1144)
29. *Morals and Dogma*, by Albert Pike (p.75)
30. *The Times*, Thursday, 15 August 1889
31. *Isle of Wight Observer*, Saturday, 20 September 1913
32. Crashaw was popular with the Victorians. His poems are reviewed alongside those of Frederick Weatherly in *The Times* of 23 December 1884, the pair of them appearing in the same article, entitled 'The Poets of Christmas'.
33. *The Meaning of Masonry*, by W. L. Wilmshurst, Bell Publishing Company, New York, 1927 (pp.167–8)
34. *The Jack the Ripper A to Z*, by Paul Begg, Martin Fido and Keith Skinner, 2010 (p.64)
35. *New York Herald*, 17 July 1889
36. *New York Tribune*, 11 November 1888

Chapter 14: 'Orpheus'

1. Deposition of Mr Edward Garnet Heaton, Pharmacist, at Mrs. Maybrick's trial. *The Trial of Mrs.*

Maybrick, edited by H. B. Irving, William Hodge & Co., London, 1912 (pp.192–4)

2. Inscribed 'on her birthday', 2 August 1865. *Jack the Ripper: The Final Chapter*, by Paul Feldman, Virgin, London, 1997 (p.123)

3. 'There is a woman – who calls herself Mrs. Maybrick, and who claims to have been James Maybrick's real wife. She was staying on a visit at a somewhat out of the way, at 8, Dundas St, Monkwearmouth, during the Trial.' Alexander Macdougall (pp.20–1)

4. Evidence of Elizabeth Humphreys, at the trial of Mrs Maybrick, Irving (p.83)

5. *Review of Reviews*, edited by W. T. Stead, Vol. VI, July–December 1892 (392)

6. Michael Maybrick interview, *New York Herald* (London edition), Wednesday, 21 August 1889

7. Part II of Longfellow's 'Christus: The Golden Legend'

8. *Orpheus from Consecration to Jubilee*, by Bro G. T. E. Sheddon, 1977 (p.1)

9. Letter from the Library and Museum of Freemasonry, 29 October 2001

10. *Royal Arch Working Explained*, by Ex. Comp. Herbert F. Inman, Spencer & Co., London, 1933 (p.170)

11. *Constitutions of Free and Accepted Masons, United Grand Lodge of England*, by Colonel Shadwell H. Clerke, London, 1884 (p.viii)

12. *The Cotton Trade of Great Britain*, by Thomas Ellison (first edition 1886) (p.258)

13. Letter from myself to the Supreme Council, 10 Duke Street, London, 7 March 2002

14. Reply from Supreme Council 33° (Ref 2412/nrb), 8 March 2002

15. It's one thing to clutch at straws and another to clutch at water. While it is true that the so-called 'diary' passed through Mike Barrett's hands on its journey to the light, it is equally true that he had absolutely nothing to do with the creation of it. If Barrett was the author of this document, why is its provenance protected by the Metropolitan Police?

In 2009, under provisions of the Freedom of Information Act, Keith Skinner made an application to obtain what is known of the provenance of this 'diary'. The request was refused by the Metropolitan Police, on grounds that most certainly did not include the authorial fantasies of Mr Michael Barrett.

'Freedom of Information Request No: 2009080005788

Dear Mr. Skinner, I respond in connection with your request for information dated 19/08/2009, which was received by the Metropolitan Police Service (MPS) on 24/08/2009. Decision: In accordance with the Freedom of Information Act 2000 (the Act), this letter represents a refusal notice for this particular request under Section 17(4). No inference can be taken from this refusal that the information you have requested does or does not exist.

Yours sincerely Ben Sayers Specialist Crime Directorate SCD Senior Information Manager'

In other words, the provenance of this document, which either does or does not exist, must remain a 'mystery'. Put that in context with the rest of the 'Mystery of Jack the Ripper', and we get a pretty good idea of what the 'mystery' is.

In my view this 'diary' was not written by Michael Barrett but by Michael Maybrick, and it is consistent with the rest of the poison he disseminated in an attempt to implicate his brother James as the Ripper. I believe this example of it was concealed at Battlecrease House, where it remained undiscovered for about a hundred years. I don't need it to bust Michael Maybrick, but it gives me a perverse satisfaction to know that this repugnant criminal ended up busting himself.

16. Also reported in the *Pall Mall Gazette*, 12 October 1888

Chapter 15: 'The Ezekiel Hit'

1. Jack the Ripper letter to Central News, 19 October 1888
2. Note: Hutchinson added further invention to his description, including 'his watch chain had a big seal with a red stone hanging from it'. *The Times*, Wednesday, 14 November 1888
3. Ibid.
4. *The Globe*, Friday, 9 November 1888
5. *The Graphic*, 17 November 1888
6. *Manchester Evening News*, Friday, 9 November 1888
7. 'Sir C. Warren arrived at a quarter to two in a hansom cab.' *Manchester Evening News*, 9 November 1888
8. *Daily Telegraph*, Saturday, 10 November 1888
9. Ibid.
10. *Daily Telegraph*, Thursday, 20 September 1888 (4th session of inquest into the death of Annie Chapman)
11. *The Times*, Thursday, 11 October 1888
12. *St James's Gazette*, 10 November 1888
13. *Evening Express*, 12 November 1888
14. *Pall Mall Gazette*, 10 November 1888
15. *Manchester Evening News*, 9 November 1888
16. *Yorkshire Post*, 10 November 1888
17. *Evening News*, Monday, 12 November 1888
18. *The Times*, Monday, 12 November 1888
19. *Evening Post*, 9 November 1888
20. Report from Dr Thomas Bond, requested by Robert Anderson and submitted 10 November 1888, HO 144/221/A49301C/ff217-232
21. According to Sydney Smith (Professor of Forensic Medicine at the University of Edinburgh), 'rigidity is present to a quite definite extent, four or five hours after death; it is usually present in the muscles of the lower jaw in three hours or even earlier' (p.19). Dr Bond reported that 'rigor mortis had set in but increased during the process of examination'. Bond arrived at 2 p.m. into a still-warm room ('the police say that when they entered the room it was quite warm', *The Star*, Monday, 12 November 1888). 'Rigor is delayed by cold, accelerated by heat,' writes Professor Smith. Thus, extrapolating from Smith would give a probable time for Kelly's death at between nine and ten o'clock that morning. *Forensic Medicine*, by Sydney Smith, J. & A. Churchill Limited, London, 1938
22. Addressed to 'Dear Boss, Lemen [sic] Street Police Station'. In this letter the author again threatens to kill Matthew Packer: 'I mean to kill Packer, the fruiterer in Berner St, he knows me too well.'
23. 'Some Medical Observations on the Ripper Case', by Nick Warren, *Ripperana*, No. 18, 19 October 1996
24. 'The Millers Court murder/A disgusting affair/Done by a Polish Knacker rather fair/The Morn (of the murder) I went to the place–/Had a shine but left in haste'. This crass verse was mailed on the eve of the anniversary of the Kelly murder at Miller's Court, to which it refers. 'Had a shine' means to masturbate. Signed J. Ripper, November 8, 1889, addressed to Superintendent of Great Scotland Yard, London.
25. *Pall Mall Gazette*, 12 November 1888
26. *Autumn of Terror*, by Tom Cullen, The Bodley Head, London, 1965
27. Ibid. (p.191)
28. *Police*, by J. Hall Richardson, London, 1889 (p.277)
29. *The Globe*, Monday, 11 November 1888
30. 'During the course of last evening Dr. G. B. Phillips visited the House of Commons, where he had a conference with the Under-secretary of the Home Office, Mister Stuart-Wortley.' *Daily Telegraph*, 10 October 1888
31. Sir Richard Webster, Hansard, 28 February 1890 (p.1555)
32. *Jack the Ripper: The Final Solution*, by Stephen Knight, David McKay Company, New York, 1976
33. *Jack the Ripper: The Definitive History* (p.248)

34. *Portrait of a Killer*, by Patricia Cornwell (p.349)
35. *New York Daily Tribune*, 10 November 1888
36. *New York Daily Tribune*, 14 November 1888
37. *New York Daily Tribune*, 11 November 1888
38. Ibid.
39. *New York Times*, 14 November 1888
40. *New York Daily Tribune*, 11 November 1888
41. *The World*, New York, 10 November 1888
42. *New York Herald*, 18 July 1888
43. *The Referee*, 2 December 1888
44. Sugden (p.314)
45. *The Ritual of Transcendental Magic*, by Eliphas Levi, translated by Arthur Edward Waite, reprinted Bracken Books, London, 1995 (p.334)
46. *Morals and Dogma*, by Albert Pike (p.321)
47. *Scintilla-Altaris, Being a Pious Reflection on Primitive Devotion*, by Edward Sparke, Preacher at St. James Clerkenwell, London, 1660 (p.97)
48. 'The author of Revelation calls himself John the Apostle, and addresses the Seven Churches of Asia; as he was not the Apostle John, who died perhaps in Palestine about [AD] 66, he was a forger.'
    'Since the year 1892, we have been in possession of a large portion of an Apocalypse attributed to St. Peter, discovered in Egypt six years before this date, together with the gospel known as that of St. Peter. It is derived from popular Jewish and Greek sources, and shows striking analogies with the Orphic doctrines. The author was an Egyptian Jew, of Hellenistic tendencies and some erudition. This Apocalypse was probably produced in the same literary factory as the two letters of St. Peter and his Gospel, which are also Greco-Egyptian forgeries.' *Orpheus: A History of Religion*, by Salomon Reinach, Horace Liveright, Inc., New York, 1930 (p.261)
49. Revelation, Chapter 17 – Numbers 4 & 16
50. *Evening Standard*, Saturday, 12 November 1888
51. *The Thames Torso Murders of Victorian London*, by R. Michael Gordon, McFarland & Co. Inc., North Carolina and London, 2002 (p.163)
52. Sugden (p.315)
53. 'Another Look at Mary Kelly's Heart', *The Criminologist*, Winter 1998 (p.245)
54. *Concise Bible Commentary*, by Lowther Clarke, SPCK, London, 1952 (p.568)
55. *Pall Mall Gazette*, 4 November 1889
56. *The Jack the Ripper A to Z*, by Paul Begg, Martin Fido and Keith Skinner (p.214)
57. *Autumn of Terror*, by Tom Cullen, The Bodley Head, London, 1965 (p.191)
58. *The News from Whitechapel*, by Alexander Chisholm, Christopher-Michael DiGrazia and Dave Yost (p.195)
59. *La Lanterne*, Paris, 19 January 1890
60. *The News from Whitechapel* (p.194)
61. *The Times*, 13 November 1888
62. Macnaghten (p.62)
63. *Tatler*, 17 November 1888 (p.195)
64. *New York Daily Tribune*, 13 November 1888
65. *The Star*, 19 October 1888
66. 'Absurdly ineffectual arrests have been made.' *New York Herald*, 11 November 1888
67. Sugden (p.322)
68. 'It is generally agreed that the murderer has no accomplices who could betray him.' Home Office, 10 September 1888. No. A49301B/
69. *The Lighter Side of My Official Life*, by Sir Robert Anderson, Hodder & Stoughton, London, 1910 (p.136)

Chapter 16: 'Red Tape'
1. *Days of My Years*, by Sir Melville Macnaghten (p.61)
2. Death Certificate received from Wynne L. Baxter. Inquest held 26 November 1888. Death Certificate No. W145516 – see *The Times*, 5 January 1889

3. *The Identity of Jack the Ripper*, Donald McCormick, Jarrolds, 1959 (p.156) and *Unsolved Victorian Murders*, by Jonathan Sutherland, Breedon Books, 2002 (p.41)

4. *Days of My Years*, Macnaghten (p.54)

5. *The Letters of Queen Victoria*, Third Series, edited by George Earle Buckle, three volumes, Vol. 1 1886/1890, John Murray, London, 1930 (p.449)

6. *Jack the Ripper: The Bloody Truth*, by Melvin Harris (p.119)

7. Ibid. (p.120)

8. *The Rosicrucians. Their Rites and Mysteries*, by Hargrave Jennings, London, 1887

9. *Revelations of the Golden Dawn*, by R. A. Gilbert, Quantum, London, 1997

10. *Ars Quatuor Coronatorum*, Vol. 100, 1987, published November 1988, article 'William Wynn Westcott and the Esoteric School of Masonic Research', by Bro. R. A. Gilbert, 19 February 1987 (p.14)

11. *Lucifer: A Theosophical Magazine*, edited by H. P. Blavatsky and A. Besant, Vol. 3, 1889

12. Theosophical Publishing Society (1911)

13. Mathers was quoting Eliphas Levi's *Histoire de Magie* (translated from the French by A. E. Waite, circa 1920)

14. *Real History of the Rosicrucians*, by A. E. Waite, 1887 (p.424)

15. *The Rosicrucian Cosmo-Conception or Mystic Christianity*, by Max Heindel, London, L. N. Flower & Co., 1911 (p.254)

16. *Evening Post* (Somerset), 22 August 1888

17. *Bradford Observer*, Tuesday, 8 January 1889

18. *Western Advertiser*, 9 January 1889

19. *The Masonic Why and Wherefore*, by W. Bro. J. S. M. Ward, London, 1929 (pp.5–7)

20. *Ars Quatuor Coronatorum*, Vol. 1, 1886–1888 (p.198)

21. Ibid.

22. *The Freemason*, 17 November 1888

23. Found at Cage Lane, Plumstead, London

24. Mailed from Paddington to Commercial Street police station, Whitechapel

25. *Manchester Courier*, 20 November 1888. Note: On the following day a young woman passed a threatening letter she'd received to the Manchester Police. Signed 'Jack the Ripper' and 'couched in the usual language', its author claimed immunity from arrest because he had 'squared the police'. This was either another remarkable telepathic communication between the Ripper and his provincial fanbase, or it was penned by the same correspondent who about a month before had written to Superintendent Foster of the City Police: 'Has it not occurred to you that your men are unable to find "Jack" because he "Mitre Square'd" them?' (16 October 1888)

26. Ballad Concert, St James's Hall, London (programme singing with Sims Reeves). *The Times*, Wednesday, 12 November 1888

27. *Glasgow Herald*, Friday, 23 November 1888

28. *Edinburgh Evening News*, Wednesday, 21 November 1888 (announcing concert)

29. *Sheffield & Rotherham Independent*, Thursday, 22 November 1888 (announcing concert)

30. London Ballad Concert programme, St James's Hall, 28 November 1888

31. Amy Maine interview (aged ninety-one), recorded July 1985 by Roger Wilkes (p.4). 'He used to tell little anecdotes about staying [in] a place where there was a coffin under the bed with a body in it.'

32. *Etched in Arsenic: A New Study of the Maybrick Case*, by Trevor L. Christie, George G. Harrap & Co., London, 1969 (p.63)

33. *The Maybrick Case*, by Alexander William Macdougall, 1891. Evidence of Elizabeth Humphreys at the 'trial' (p.351)

34. *Isle of Wight Observer*, Saturday, 20 September 1913, and *Great Thoughts*

From Masterminds, Vol. 5, 1913 (p.393)

35. *The Expedition of Humphry Clinker*, by T. Smollet M.D., Cochrane & Pickersgill, London, 1831 (p.338)

36. *The Trial of Mrs. Maybrick*, edited by H. B. Irving (p.31). 'I mentioned it at Christmas time, when I asked him to come up to London to see Dr. Fuller.'

37. *Great True Crime Stories*, selected and edited by Pamela Search, Avco Publications, London, 1957, Vol.2 (p.133)

38. *Illustrated Weekly Telegraph*, Saturday, 29 December 1888

39. *The Savage Club*, by Aaron Watson, T. Fisher Unwin, London, 1907 (p.307)

40. *Bradford Post Office Directory*, 1894 (p.39). Carlo Fara joined the Shakespeare Lodge on 8 April 1885

41. *The Magicians of the Golden Dawn, 1887–1923*, by Ellic Howe, Routledge, Kegan Paul, London, 1972 (p.54)

42. *Illustrated Weekly Telegraph*, Bradford, Saturday, 29 December 1888

43. *Bradford Observer*, Tuesday, 1 January 1889

44. Ibid.

45. *Mysteries of Police and Crime*, by Major Arthur Griffiths, Castle & Company, London, 1902, Vol. 1 (p.35). This is generally considered its first appearance in print, but see *The Referee*, 22 January 1899: 'Almost immediately after this murder he drowned himself in the Thames.'

46. *Bradford Observer*, Tuesday, 1 January 1889

47. *Bradford Observer*, Wednesday, 2 January 1889

48. Ibid.

49. *Richardson's Monitor of Free-Masonry*, by Jabez Richardson, Dick & Fitzgerald, New York, 1860 (pp109–10). See also: *Ritual of Freemasonry*, by Avery Allyn, Boston, 1831 (p.223 et seq.)

50. *Masonic Records 1717–1894*, by John Lane, F.C.A., Freemasons' Hall, London, 1895 (p.22)

51. *The Judy*, 3 October 1888

52. *Pall Mall Gazette*, 8 October 1888 (p.3)

53. *New York Herald*, 10 November 1888

54. *New York Herald*, 1 October 1888

55. *New York Daily Tribune*, 18 September 1889

56. *Bradford Citizen*, Saturday, 5 January 1889

57. *Leeds Evening Express*, Saturday, 29 December 1888

58. *Bradford Observer*, Monday, 31 December 1888

59. (Bradford) *Herald*, Friday, 4 January 1889

60. Bucke did not turn the body, meaning he was looking at the front of it

61. (Bradford) *Herald*, Friday, 4 January 1889

62. *Yorkshire Post*, Tuesday, 1 January 1889

63. The name is spelled BARRIT in the 1881 census, and also on his gravestone. He died aged sixty-two on 26 September 1927

64. *West Yorkshire Pioneer*, Friday, 4 January 1889

65. *Leeds Mercury*, weekly supplement, Saturday, 5 January 1889

66. *Bradford Daily Telegraph*, Monday, 31 December 1888

67. *Bradford Daily Telegraph*, Saturday, 29 December 1888

68. *Otley News*, Friday, 4 January 1889

69. (Bradford) *Herald*, 14 January 1889

70. *Yorkshire Post*, Wednesday, 2 January 1889

71. *Illustrated Police News*, Saturday, 5 January 1889

72. *Bradford Observer*, Monday, 7 January 1889

73. *Bradford Daily Telegraph*, Tuesday, 1 January 1889

74. Ibid.

75. *Keighley Evening News*, Saturday, 12 January 1889

76. *Bradford Telegraph*, Monday, 31 December 1888

77. *Bradford Observer*, Thursday, 3 January 1889

78. *History of the Royal Yorkshire Lodge* (Minutes of 1 August), 19 July 1887 (p.50)

79. William Thomas McGowan, Bradford Lodge of Hope, was

THEY ALL LOVE JACK

Senior Warden in 1883. Lodge records (p.20)

80. *The Magicians of the Golden Dawn*, by Ellic Howe (p.111)
81. *Bradford Observer*, 3 January 1889
82. Ibid.
83. *Illustrated Weekly Telegraph*, Bradford, Saturday, 5 January 1889
84. *Illustrated Police News*, 5 January 1889
85. *Bradford Daily Telegraph*, 28 February 1889
86. *Bradford Observer*, Thursday, 8 January 1889
87. *Keighley News*, 19 January 1889
88. Ibid.
89. *Bradford Daily Telegraph*, Thursday, 17 January 1889
90. *Illustrated* (Bradford) *Weekly Telegraph*, 19 January 1889
91. *Bradford Daily Telegraph*, Wednesday, 16 January 1889
92. *The Great Beast: The Life of Aleister Crowley*, by John Symonds, Rider & Company, London, 1951 (p.24)
93. *Bradford Observer*, Wednesday, 13 March 1889
94. *Bradford Citizen*, Saturday, 5 January 1889
95. *Bradford Daily Telegraph*, Tuesday, 14 March 1889
96. *Leeds Evening Express*, Saturday, 29 December 1888
97. i) Bro Alderman Thomas Hill: Past Grand Warden Scientific Lodge No. 439 (*Centenary History of the Scientific Lodge*): *Bradford Telegraph*, 7 November 1885, and Worshipful Master, Bradford Lodge of Hope, 1883 (obituary in *Bradford Observer*, 2 October 1891)
   ii) Alderman John Hill: unknown whether he was a Freemason
   iii) Bro William Oddy: listed as a visitor to Acacia Lodge, No. 2321 (*The Freemason*, 12 November 1892); his grave at Undercliff Cemetery, Bradford, is engraved with the Freemasonic symbol of the compass and the square
   iv) Bro John Ambler: Bradford Lodge of Hope (Lodge records, p.20)
   v) Bro John Armitage: Bradford Lodge of Hope, and its Worshipful Master in 1894 (ibid.)

vi) Bro James Freeman: Past Master, Prince of Wales Lodge, No. 1648 (*Bradford Contemporary Biographies – Legal*, circa 1890, Keighley Public Library, p.221)
98. *Otley News*, 4 January 1889: 'The Bradford and London police have been in active communication.'
99. Home Office Confidential Entry Books, 1 November 1887–30 November 1890 (p.407: 'Murder of J. Gill at Bradford')
100. *Salisbury: Victorian Titan*, by Andrew Roberts (p.448)
101. *Bradford Pioneer*, Friday, 18 January 1889
102. Ibid.
103. *Shipley Times*, Saturday, 12 January 1889
104. West Yorkshire Archive, Wakefield: A250/4 1859–1898. *Disciplinary/Defaulters Book, Bradford City Police*. PC171, Arthur Kirk, was fined two shillings for the offence.
105. *Shipley Times*, 12 January 1889
106. Hand-delivered letter to the coroner, *Bradford Daily Telegraph*, 25 January 1889
107. Ibid.
108. *Keighley Herald*, 15 March 1889
109. Ibid.
110. *Bradford Daily Telegraph*, Monday, 18 March 1889
111. *Bradford Observer*, Thursday, 10 January 1889
112. *Bradford Observer*, Friday, 11 January 1889
113. Ibid.
114. *Keighley Gazette*, Thursday, 17 January 1889
115. *Keighley News*, Saturday, 12 January 1889
116. *Bradford Observer*, Monday, 14 January 1889
117. *Bradford Daily Telegraph*, Saturday, 25 January 1889
118. *Keighley News*, 9 February 1889
119. (JTR Letter) Sent from Alma Road N. Jany 1888 [sic: 1889]
   Note: On 15 January 1889, Jack the Ripper wrote, 'I ripped up/ little boy in Bradford,' signed Jack Bane. ('Bane' means ruin, death, or destruction – Anglo-Saxon, *bana*, a murder)

120. *Bradford Daily Telegraph*, Thursday, 14 March 1889
121. Ibid.
122. *À propos* of his membership of the Salvation Army, Dyer had sent a letter to the *Bradford Observer* on 13 February 1889 (p.7):

'On Monday last, we published a statement from a correspondent to the effect that the man Dyer, a witness in the Manningham murder case, was not connected with the Salvation Army. This has drawn forth the following extraordinary communication, which reached us last night:–

"Dear Captan of the salvation Army, I ham so glad that you have put in the paper that I never was a member of your Low lot of people only if captan hagget was her he would have no me. But it will save Late salvation John Thomas Dyer a lot of Penny and shillins in his pocket and it will make me into a gentleman and the money that I youst to give to keepe Black pudin Lucey and orane harert and Big Lazy follows of Captons and Low peple it will take me to Liverpool from a week or tow.

From the Late Salvation Jony Thomas Dyer

Think of me on the happy shore by and …"'

123. *Keighley News*, 30 March 1889
124. *Bradford Daily Telegraph*, Wednesday, 13 March 1889
125. (JTR) Letter to City Police Office, 18 October 1888. Police Box 318. No. 215

Chapter 17: 'The Spirit of Evil'

1. Post-trial affidavit of John Flemming, in *The Necessity For Criminal Appeal as Illustrated by the Maybricks Case*, edited by J. H. Levy, London, P. S. King and Son, Orchard House, Westminster, 1899 (p.484)
2. Evidence of Edward Heaton – p.192, *The Trial of Mrs. Maybrick*, Irving, 1912 (Heaton's shop was opposite the Cotton Exchange, now 'right across the street'; reported in *New York Herald*, 21 August 1889)
3. *The Maybrick Case*, by Alexander William Macdougall, Baillière, Tindall & Cox, London, 1891 (p.76)
4. *Liverpool Daily Post*, 8 September 1889; also Macdougall (p.75)
5. Affidavit of Valentine Blake, J. H. Levy (pp.477–84)
6. *The Trial of Mrs. Maybrick*, Irving (p.58)
7. *New York Herald*, Wednesday, 21 August 1889
8. *New York Herald*, Wednesday, 14 August 1889
9. A barrister since 26 January 1871, practising out of Lincoln's Inn, London. *The Lawyer's Companion and Diary*, 1890 (p.65)
10. Letter from Schweisso to Alexander Macdougall, London, 19 January 1890, Macdougall (pp.16–17)
11. Letter from Charles Ratcliffe to John Aunspaugh, 7 June 1889 (Trevor Christie Collection)
12. Evidence of Alice Yapp at magisterial inquiry, Macdougall (p.503), Irving (p.64)
13. In the weekly *The Freemason* for 28 December 1889 is an end-of-year round-up of all Freemasons who died between January and December 1889. James Maybrick is not included in this list
14. *The Keystone*, a Masonic weekly newspaper published in Philadelphia, USA, 30 September 1882
15. Letter from Florence Aunspaugh to Trevor Christie (Trevor Christie Collection)
16. Ibid.
17. *New York Herald*, Wednesday, 21 August 1889
18. Letter from Caroline, Baroness von Roques, to the Prince of Wales. Dated 15 May 1891 (Courtesy of the Library of Freemasons' Hall, GBR 1991 FMH HC9/C/31a-d)
19. Letter from 'Marlborough House' to Shadwell Clerke, 16 May 1891. Return letter from Colonel Shadwell Clerke, dated 21 June 1891 – 'Matter a legal one in which it's impossible that H. R. H. can interfere.'

20. *The House of Lords*, by Thomas Alfred Spaulding, T. Fisher Unwin, 1884 (p.123)

Chapter 18: 'The Maybrick Mystery'

1. *Sir James Fitzjames Stephen*, by Leon Radzinowicz, Bernard Quaritch, London, 1957 (p.30)
2. Ibid. (p.33)
3. *The Marquis of Salisbury*, by Frederick Douglas How, Isbister & Co. Limited, London, 1902 (p.20)
4. Radzinowicz (p.35)
5. Ibid. (p.8)
6. *The Life of Sir Fitzjames Stephen*, by his brother, Leslie Stephen, Smith, Elder & Co., London, 1895 (p.302)
7. *Prince Eddy and the Homosexual Underworld*, by Theo Aronson, Barnes & Noble Books, New York, 1995
8. Radzinowicz (p.15)
9. *Politics and Law in the Life of Sir James Fitzjames Stephen*, by John Hostettler, Barry Rose Law Publishers Ltd, Chichester, England, 1995 (p.243)
10. Radzinowicz (p.15)
11. Sir Fitzjames Stephen, Summing up to Jury, Irving (p.352)
12. *Washington Evening Star*, 20 August 1889
13. 30 April 1889, Macdougall (p.73)
14. Ibid. (p.74)
15. *The Life of Lord Russell of Killowen*, by R. Barry O'Brien, Smith, Elder & Co., London, 1902. O'Brien writes, 'When the Pigott [Parnell] crisis was over, I called on Russell. He was a new man. All traces of stress and anxiety had disappeared. He looked happy and joyous' (p.243)
16. *The Life of Edward VII*, J. Castell Hopkins, 1910 (p.209)
17. Macdougall (p.410)
18. Ibid. (p.576)
19. Ibid.
20. *The Necessity for Criminal Appeal as Illustrated by the Maybrick Case*, by J. H. Levy, P. S. King & Son, London, 1899 (p.vii)
21. Sir Charles Russell's letter to Sir Matthew White Ridley, 21 November 1895. Received Home Office 26 November 1895. HO code: A50678D-267
22. Evidence of Mary Cadwallader, Macdougall, 1891 (p.480)
23. Macdougall (p.469)
24. Evidence of Alice Yapp, given at the magisterial inquiry, Macdougall (p.477)
25. Macdougall, 1896 (p.118)
26. Ibid. (p.123)
27. Macdougall, 1891 (pp.476–7)
28. *The Student's Hand-Book of Forensic Medicine and Medical Police*, by H. Aubrey Husband, E. & S. Livingstone, Edinburgh, 1877 (pp.287–8)
29. Ibid.
30. Dr Humphreys' evidence at inquest, Macdougall, 1896 (p.123)
31. Macdougall, 1891 (p.53)
32. Macdougall, 1896 (p.19)
33. Macdougall, 1891 (p.54)
34. Ibid. (p.72)
35. Macdougall, 1896 (p.121)
36. Stamped: Received, Home Office, 20 August 1889: A50678D
37. Edwin gave evidence that the only days lunch was taken to the office were Wednesday, 1 May and Thursday, 2 May. Macdougall (p.78)
38. Her affairs with Edwin Maybrick and Williams (a London lawyer) were not made public as was that with Brierley. Letter from Florence Aunspaugh to Christie (Trevor Christie Collection)
39. Statement by Robert Edwin Reeves (Convict 289) given at H.M. Prison, Lewes, Sussex, on 27 January 1894. Stamped: Home Office, 1 February 1894. HO 144/1639/A50678
40. Ibid.
41. Ibid.
42. Ibid.
43. Home Office: 30 January 1894. HO 144/1638 A50678D/16
44. Macdougall, 1891 (p.241)
45. Records of Liverpool Cotton Association Limited. Board Meeting: 'Transfer of shares from James Maybrick (decd) to Edwin Maybrick.' (Board Minute Book/Vol.2/6 Dec 1888–15 Oct 1894)
46. Dr Humphreys in his evidence said, 'If Mrs Maybrick said her husband was not to take any drink, except as a gargle, she was carrying out my orders.' Macdougall, 1896 (p.188)

47. *Liverpool Courier*, 29 June 1889
48. Letter from Charles Ratcliffe to John Aunspaugh, 7 June 1889
49. Macdougall, 1891 (pp.315–17)
50. Ibid. (p.82)
51. Letter from Florence Aunspaugh to Trevor Christie, circa 1942 (Trevor Christie Collection)
52. Affidavit of Alfred Brierley, n. d. but August 1889. Macdougall, 1896 (p.221)
53. *Liverpool Daily Post*, 3 June 1889
54. Cover of *New Statesman* magazine, 15 March 1985
55. Letter from Florence Aunspaugh to Trevor Christie (Christie Collection)
56. *Etched in Arsenic* by Trevor Christie, 1968 (p.56)
57. *Liverpool Daily Post*, 14 August 1889 (See Macdougall, 1896, p.78). Note: In his evidence at cross-examination, Michael Maybrick said the opposite, claiming, on Wednesday, 8 May, that Mrs Briggs had sent *him* a telegram (Irving, p.24). Who informed Michael Maybrick that his brother was 'very ill' on Tuesday, 7 May? In evidence given at the 'trial', Dr Humphreys deposed: 'on Tuesday (7 May) I saw Mr. Maybrick in the morning and he appeared better. He said, "Humphreys, I am quite a different man all together today."'
58. *Liverpool Daily Post*, 14 August 1889
59. Irving (p.72)
60. Yapp's deposition at magisterial hearing. Macdougall, 1896 (p.41)
61. Alice Yapp's evidence at the 'trial'. Irving (p.66)
62. Ibid.
63. Ibid.
64. Accusations that Yapp was spying on behalf of Michael Maybrick are plausible. Nurse Over, who preceded Yapp as the children's nanny, speaks of her as '"of an exceedingly prying nature, and says that on several occasions the cook, Humphreys, said that she opened letters, and that as soon as Mrs. Maybrick's back was turned, she was prying about in her room. The letter Mrs. Maybrick sent for reference for the girl Parker, she held over a kettle, steamed it, and opened it so as to know what she had said." Over's impression of Alice Yapp is confirmed by a Mr M. R. Levy, who has made a statement, which is interesting in view of the increasing public interest in Alice Yapp. He says: "Last October I went to Battlecrease to see Mrs. Maybrick and found she had gone to Southport. I asked if I might write a letter to her, and was shown into a room for that purpose. I wrote the letter supposing I was alone in the room. Just as I had finished something caused me to turn, and I found Alice Yapp leaning over my shoulder and perusing the letter. It made me so angry that I struck her."' *New York Herald*, Sunday, 18 August 1889
65. There had been a 'violent rain storm' on the previous day. 'Notes on the Maybrick Trial, by Dr. William Carter', *Liverpool Medical Chirurgical Journal*, 1890 (p.121)
66. Evidence of Alice Yapp, Irving (pp.70–1)
67. Letters to Sir Matthew White Ridley, Macdougall, 1896 (p.236)
68. Florence 'fainted' on 11 May, meaning Yapp couldn't have been given the letter on 8 May
69. Macdougall, 1896 (p.232)
70. Evidence of Michael Maybrick at the 'trial'. Irving (p.24)
71. Irving (pp.50–1)
72. This evidence wasn't given at the 'trial', but was written up later by Dr Carter. 'Notes on the Maybrick Trial, by Dr. William Carter', *Liverpool Medical Chirurgical Journal*, 1890 (pp.124–5)
73. *This Friendless Lady*, by Nigel Morland, Frederick Muller Limited, London, 1957 (p.57)
74. Evidence of Mrs Martha Louisa Hughes at the 'trial'. Irving (p.45)
75. Edward Davies was given the bottle of meat juice on the night of Saturday, 11 May by Dr Carter. It wasn't tested until the following day, on Sunday morning, but no 'quantitative analysis' was made

until 23 May, when 'half a grain of arsenic was found in the solution'. Macdougall, 1896 (p.112)

76. See Macdougall, 1896, where Michael Maybrick is quoted as saying, 'Florence, or Flory, how dare you change the medicine from one bottle to another' (p.100)

77. Evidence of Margaret Jane Callery at the magisterial inquiry. Macdougall, 1896 (p.182): this evidence was withheld at the 'trial'

78. Evidence of Elizabeth Humphreys, Irving (p.83)

79. Macdougall, 1891 (p.219)

80. A Liverpool cause célèbre. Between 1880 and 1883, sisters Mrs Flannagan and Mrs Higgins poisoned four of their relatives, including Higgins's husband Thomas, with arsenic, believed to have been boiled out of flypapers (the plan was to collect on life insurance policies). On 14 February 1884 they were found guilty of wilful murder at Liverpool Assizes, and were hanged at Kirkdale Prison a few weeks later.

81. Post-trial deposition from Cadwallader and cook Humphreys given to Macdougall. Macdougall, 1891 (pp.219–20)

82. Post-trial statement given to Macdougall by Elizabeth Humphreys and Mary Cadwallader. Macdougall, 1896 (p.183)

83. Letters from Charles Ratcliffe to John Aunspaugh, 7 June 1889 (Trevor Christie Collection)

84. Macdougall, 1896 (pp.201–3)

85. Letter from Charles Ratcliffe to John Aunspaugh, 7 June 1889 (Trevor Christie Collection)

86. Irving (p.98)

87. Letter to Trevor Christie from Florence Aunspaugh, circa 1942 (Trevor Christie Collection)

88. *Mrs. Maybrick's Own Story: My Fifteen Lost Years*, by Florence Elizabeth Maybrick, Funk & Wagnalls Co., New York and London, 1905 (p.23)

89. Letter from Ratcliffe to Aunspaugh, 7 June 1889

90. *Mrs. Maybrick's Own Story* (p.26)

91. They found in Mrs Maybrick's writing desk thirteen love letters from Edwin Maybrick, seven from Alfred Brierley, and five from lawyer Williams of London. Michael Maybrick suppressed Edwin's letters, and also made an arrangement with lawyer Williams that he would return his (Williams's) letters to him if he would not assist in any way with the defence. Florence Aunspaugh's letters to Trevor Christie (Trevor Christie Collection)

92. *The Drama of the Law*, by Sir Edward Parry, Ernest Benn Limited, London, 1929 (p.101)

93. *Fifty-two Years a Policeman*, by Sir William Nott-Bower, Edward Arnold & Co., London, 1926 (pp.131–2)

94. Macdougall, 1896 (p.25)

95. Dr Humphreys' evidence at the inquest, Macdougall, 1891 (p.59)

96. Dr Barron's evidence at the inquest, Macdougall, 1891 (p.60)

97. Statement of Dalgleish to Coroner Brighouse, 28 May 1889, Macdougall, 1896 (p.26)

98. Macdougall, 1896 (p.26)

99. Ibid. (p.27)

100. 'FOR DEFENCE – As there are no parties, no distinction should be drawn before verdict between evidence for and evidence against the crown. See Rex V. Scorey (1748), 1 Leach C. C. 43, and the C. A. 1887, s. 4(1), which requires all witnesses to be examined without distinction' (p.19). 'A Jury man may be sworn as witness' (p.58). *A Digest of the Law and Practice Relating to the Office of Coroner*, by Sydney Taylor, Horace Cox, London, 1893

101. Bro William Pickford, later the Right Honourable Lord Sternsdale, was initiated into Freemasonry on 10 November 1870 (Apollo University Lodge No. 357). *The Freemason*, 1903, and in 1892 the Northern Bar Lodge No. 1610. *History of the Northern Bar Lodge*, G. V. D., privately printed, 1976. Knighted in 1907, Pickford became a High Court judge that same year

102. *New York Herald*, 28 July 1889
103. Macdougall, 1896 (p.23)
104. Ibid. (p.237)
105. Baroness von Roques' account in a letter to Alexander Macdougall. Macdougall, 1891 (p.9)
106. Ibid. (p.10)
107. Ibid. (p.11)
108. Ibid. (p.8)
109. Ibid. (p.12)
110. *Mrs. Maybrick's Own Story* (p.51)
111. *Liverpool Citizen*, 29 May 1889
112. Ibid.
113. *Liverpool Daily Post*, 1 June 1889
114. Ibid.
115. *New York Herald*, Wednesday, 21 August 1889
116. 'Sale of Mrs. Maybrick's Furniture', *Liverpool Citizen*, 10 July 1889 (p.9). Note: Fletcher Rodgers replaced Dalgleish as foreman at James Maybrick's inquest. He rented Battlecrease House, where he died in December 1891
117. *New York Herald*, Wednesday, 21 August 1889. Note: It was Michael Maybrick who refused the death certificate: see Dr Humphreys' cross-examination at the 'trial', Macdougall, 1896 (p.153)
118. *New York Herald*, Wednesday, 21 August 1899

Chapter 19 Victorian Values
1. *The Freemason*, 19 November 1892
2. 'There are few more genial fellows than "Fat Jack," as he's called, and one cannot meet him, without thinking of Falstaff or Friar Tuck.' *The Man of the World*, 10 August 1889 (p.8)
3. *The Trial of Mrs. Maybrick*, Irving, 1912 (p.3)
4. *The World*, New York, Thursday, 1 August 1889
5. *Liverpool Daily Post*, 31 July 1889
6. Macdougall, 1896 (p.152)
7. Ibid. (p.32)
8. Addison's opening address for the prosecution, *The Trial of Mrs. Maybrick*, Irving (p.12)
9. Evidence of Dr. Fuller, Irving (p.58)
10. Ibid.
11. *Liverpool Weekly Post*, 25 May 1889
12. Ibid.

13. Irving (p.47)
14. *Arthur Sullivan, a Victorian Musician*, by Arthur Jacobs, Oxford University Press, 1984 (p.246)
15. Ibid. (p.139)
16. *Isle of Wight Observer*, Saturday, 20 September 1913
17. Ganz was G.O. in 1871 and 1873. Sheddon (p.27)
18. Irving (p.30)
19. Ibid. (p.36)
20. *This Friendless Lady*, by Nigel Morland, Frederick Muller Limited, London, 1952 (p.121)
21. Irving (p.129)
22. Ibid. (p.77)
23. Ibid.
24. Closing words of Addison presenting case for the Crown, Irving (p.273)
25. Affidavit to Home Secretary Matthews from Richard Cleaver, 11 August 1889 HO: A50678D-15
26. Irving (p.98)
27. Ibid. (p.198)
28. Ibid. (p.201)
29. Macnamara was fellow and former President of the Royal College of Surgeons of Ireland, and its representative on the General Medical Council of the United Kingdom, Doctor of Medicine of the University of London, Professor of Materia Medica at the Royal College and author of a standard work on the action of medicines. Irving (p.211)
30. Irving (p.212)
31. *Liverpool Review*, 10 August 1889 (p.15)
32. Irving (p.216)
33. What it wasn't, was James Maybrick's urine
34. Irving (p.216)
35. 'It is difficult to distinguish between the blunders of counsel or the judge ... of course the quantity here was not 1/76,000 of a grain, but 76/1000; and a few lines before, it was not 1/26,000 or 1/27,000, but 26/1,000 or 27/1,000. This is one of the ways in which a case may be prejudiced by trial before a physically incompetent judge. Probably if the

notes were published, they would be found to contain dozens of errors, some of them of an important character. On the only occasion that they were referred to during the trial they proved to be wrong.' Footnote on Stephen/Russell, *The Necessity for Criminal Appeal*, J. H. Levy (p.205)

36. *Reminiscences of a K.C.*, by Thomas Edward Crispe, Matthew & Co., London, 1909 (pp.102–3)

37. Sir Charles Russell's closing speech for the defence. Irving (p.242)

38. Irving (p.98). Immediately after this disclosure, 'The Court adjourned.'

39. Macdougall, 1896 (p.58)

40. Ibid. (pp.58–9)

41. Ibid.

42. Ibid.

43. Ibid.

44. Affidavit of Baroness von Roques to Home Secretary Henry Matthews. Stamped: Home Office Received, 15 August 1892. A50678D/92. H. Levy (pp.475–6)

45. Cleaver's petition to the Home Office, 11 August 1889. Home Office: A50678D

46. Irving (p.325)

47. Ibid. (pp.325–6)

48. Ibid.

49. 'Mr. John Baillie Knight, when he found what use Mr. Justice Stephen had made of his not being called, at once communicated to [Home Secretary] Mr. Matthews, all he knew about what Mrs. Maybrick did while in London, but I venture to think it would be more satisfactory to the public, and more fair to Mrs. Maybrick, that he should publicly clear up the mystery which Mr. Justice Stephen made about him …' Macdougall, 1896 (p.21)

50. Irving (p.328)

51. Ibid. (p.332)

52. Ibid.

53. Ibid. (p.333)

54. *Review of Reviews*, W. T. Stead, Vol. 6, July–December 1892 (p.393)

55. *Liverpool Review*, 10 August 1889 (p.4)

56. 'The carpenters were, in fact, engaged in erecting the gallows, and Mrs. Maybrick could hear them raising her own death scaffold.' Macdougall, 1896 (pp.231–2)

57. *Eched in Arsenic*, by Trevor L. Christie (p.166)

58. *The Umpire*, Sunday, 11 August 1889

59. *The Story of My Life*, by Sir Edward Clarke, John Murray, London, 1923 (p.280)

60. *New York Herald*, 14 August 1889

61. *Pall Mall Gazette*, 8 August 1889

62. *Review of Reviews*, W. T. Stead (p.393)

63. *Washington Evening Star*, 13 August 1889

64. To the editor of the *Manchester Courier*. 'Sir, – Referring to my letter of the 15th inst. Relating to the above case, I have, since writing the same, learnt that the suggestions made therein are not correct, and hereby beg to tender apologies to Messrs. Michael and Thomas Maybrick for causing same to be published. – Yours, etc, R. F. Muckley. Malvern, August 26, 1889.' *Manchester and Lancashire General Advertiser*, Wednesday, 28 August 1889

65. *New York Herald*, Wednesday, 21 August 1889

66. Stamped: Home Office: A50678D.29

67. *Manchester Courier and Lancashire General Advertiser*, 22 August 1889

68. *New York Herald*, 22 August 1889 (i.e. Bro Sir Charles Russell)

69. Minute to Henry Matthews. Stamped: Home Office, 20 August 1889. No. A50678D

70. Macdougall, 1896 (p.53)

71. Dr Coats' report to Macdougall, 1896 (p.249)

72. Mr. E. Godwin Clayton's report, Chemical Laboratory, 43 & 44 Holborn Viaduct, London, E.C., 2 May 1890. Macdougall, 1896 (p.257)

73. *Our Conservative and Unionist Statesmen*, London, Newman, Graham & Co., n.d., circa 1890, Vol. 2 (p.72 et seq.)

74. Henry Matthews announcement, 22 August 1889, Irving (p.xxxvii)
75. Ibid.
76. *Reminiscences of a K.C.*, by Thomas Edward Crispe (pp.102–3)
77. Ibid.
78. Ibid.
79. Letter from Sir Charles Russell to Sir Matthew White Ridley, 21 November 1895. HO 144/1640/A50678(D)
80. *Etched in Arsenic*, by Trevor Christie (p.169)
81. Ibid. (p.173)
82. *Mrs. Maybrick's Own Story* (p.67)
83. Ibid. (p.75)
84. Letter to City Police, Date stamped, 22 May 1890. Police Box 321 No. 332
85. *New York Times*, 11 October 1891
86. *The Hawk*, 13 September 1892 (p.3)
87. Ibid.
88. *Etched in Arsenic*, Christie (p.190)
89. *The Hawk*, 6 December 1892
90. *The Hawk*, 13 December 1892
91. *The Hawk*, 20 December 1892 (p.11)
92. Ibid.
93. *The Maybrick Case, English Criminal Law*, by Dr Helen Densmore, London and New York, December 1892 (p.127)
94. Levy (p.470)
95. *Liverpool Daily Post*, 14 August 1889
96. Macdougall, 1891 (p.333)
97. Ibid. (pp.536–7)
98. Ibid.
99. Ibid. (p.524)
100. Macdougall, 1891 (p.221)
101. *The Trial of Mrs. Maybrick*, Irving (p.31)
102. *New York Herald*, Monday, 19 August 1889
103. *Reynold's News*, Sunday, 27 March 1892
104. *Isle of Wight Observer*, Saturday, 20 September 1913
105. *The Diary of Jack the Ripper*, by Shirley Harrison, London, 1993
106. Letter from Dr Rosemary Williamson, Chief Librarian, Trinity College of Music, 22 November 2001
107. *My Life, Sixty Years' Recollections of Bohemian London*, by George R. Sims, Eveleigh Nash, London, 1917 (p.149)
108. *Memories of a Musician: Reminiscences of Seventy Years of Musical Life*, by Wilhelm Ganz, John Murray, London, 1913 (p.102)
109. *Orpheus, From Consecration to Jubilee*, by Bro T. G. E. Sheddon, 1977
110. *Reminiscences of My Life*, by Charles Santley, Sir Isaac Pitman, London, 1909 (p.34)
111. *Student and Singer: The Reminiscences of Charles Santley*, Edward Arnold, London, 1892, and *Reminiscences of My Life*, Santley
112. *Sims Reeves: Fifty Years of Music in England*, by Charles E. Pearce, Stanley Paul, London, 1924
113. *Piano and Gown*, by Fred E. Weatherly, G. P. Putnams Sons, London & New York, 1926
114. *The Arts Club and its Members*, by G. A. F. Rogers, Truslove & Hanson, London, 1920 (p.99)
115. *The World*, 15 January 1890 (p.8)
116. *Mrs. Maybrick's Own Story* (p.223)
117. *Manchester Times*, 25 October 1895
118. *The Maybrick Case: A Statement of the Case as a Whole*, by Alexander William Macdougall, Baillière, Tindall & Cox, London, 1896
119. Levy (p.19)
120. *Eight Studies in Justice*, by Jack Smith-Hughes, Barrister-at-Law of the Inner Temple, Castle & Co. Limited, London, 1953 (p.209)
121. Levy (p.vii)

Picture Credits

Page 18: Universal History Archive/UIG via Getty Images
Page 152: Private Collection/©Look and Learn/Illustrated Papers
  Collection/Bridgeman Images
Page 166: Hulton Archive/Getty Images
Page 176: Private Collection/©Look and Learn/Illustrated Papers
  Collection/Bridgeman Images
Page 183: Stephen Barnes/Religion/Alamy
Page 338: © The Royal London Hospital Archives & Museum
Page 366: TopFoto
Page 444: Gregory S. Paulson/Corbis
Page 563: akg-images
Page 651: New Statesman
Page 740: Hulton Archive/Getty Images

The following images are reproduced courtesy of the London
Metropolitan Archive, City of London: page 75 (original held at the
Royal London Hospital Archives & Museum); page 120 (original
held at the Royal London Hospital Archives & Museum); page 182
(original held at the Royal London Hospital Archives & Museum);
page 382 (top and bottom); page 385; page 388 top and bottom;
page 390 (original held at the Royal London Hospital Archives &
Museum), page 391; page 458; page 459; page 466; page 467; page
468 left and right; page 475; page 477; page 726; page 727, page 728.

The following images are reproduced courtesy of the Metropolitan
Police Service, via the National Archives, Kew: page 145, MEPO 3/142
Pt 2 (302, 303 reverse); page 163 left and right, MEPO 3/140; page
334, MEPO 3/142 Pt1 (137, 138, 139); page 336 top, MEPO 3/142 Pt1
(137, 138, 139); page 349, MEPO 3/142 pt 1 (94v-95v); page 350,
MEPO 3/142 Pt1 (96); page 354, MEPO 3/3157; page 355, MEPO
3/142 Pt2 282, 283 reverse); page 369 left, MEPO 3/142 Pt2 (282, 283
reverse); page 369 right, MEPO 3/142 Pt2 (282, 283) page 370, MEPO

3/142 pt 1 (128-130); page 371 top, MEPO 3/142 Pt1 (131, 132, 133 reverse); page 371 bottom, MEPO 3/142 Pt3 (483, 484, 485 reverse); page 372, MEPO 3/142 Pt3 (545, 546); page 373 top, MEPO 3/142 Pt3 (517, 518, 519 reverse); page 373 bottom, MEPO 3/142 pt 2 (240-242); page 374 top, MEPO 3/142 Pt2 (333, 334, 335, 336); page 374 bottom, MEPO 3/142 pt 1 (5); page 375, MEPO 3/142 Pt3 (503, 504, 505, 506 reverse); page 378, MEPO 3/142 pt 1 (90-91); page 384 bottom, MEPO 3/142 Pt3 (526); page 387 bottom, MEPO 3/142 Pt2 (293); page 389, MEPO 3/142 Pt3 (520, 521 reverse); page 394, MEPO 3/142 Pt3 (514, 515); page 395, MEPO 3/142 Pt2 (192, 193, 194); page 398 top, MEPO 3/142 Pt2 (340); page 398 bottom, MEPO 3/142 Pt2 (339, 341, 342); page 430, MEPO 3/142 Pt3 (491); page 457 top, MEPO 3/142 Pt2 (339, 341, 342); page 457 bottom, MEPO 3/142 Pt2 (340); page 460, MEPO 3/142 Pt1 (179, 180, 181, 182 reverse); page 472, MEPO 3/3155; page 511 top, MEPO 3/142 Pt1 (149); page 511 bottom, MEPO 3/142 Pt1 (149 reverse); page 512, MEPO 3/142 Pt2 (269, 270, 271); page 513, MEPO 3/142 Pt2 (269, 270, 271); page 514, MEPO 3/142 Pt3 (556); page 533 top, MEPO 3/142 pt 1 (14-15); page 533 bottom, MEPO 3/142 Pt3 (500, 501, 502); page 538, MEPO 3/3155; page 540, MEPO 3/3155; page 543, MEPO 3/3155; page 554, MEPO 3/142 pt 1 (124-127); page 555, MEPO 3/142 pt 1 (160-162); page 561, MEPO 3/142 pt 1 (124-127); page 567 top, MEPO 3/142 Pt1 (74); page 567 bottom, MEPO 3/142 Pt1 (74 reverse); page 568, MEPO 3/142 pt 1 (121-123); page 570, MEPO 3/142 Pt3 (520, 521 reverse); page 608, MEPO 3/142 Pt2 (268); page 671 bottom, MEPO 3/142 Pt2 (266, 267); page 730, MEPO 3/142 Pt2 (272 reverse); page 795 top left, MEPO 3/142 Pt2 (298, 299, 300, 301); page 795 bottom, MEPO 3/142 pt 1 (82-84); page 801, MEPO 3/142 Pt2 (272 reverse).

The following images are reproduced courtesy of the National Archives, Kew: page 659 left, HO 144/1640-A50678/272; page 659 right, HO 144/1640-A50678; page 720, HO 144/1638-A50678 (D29); page 721, right HO 144/1639-A50678/202.

The author and publishers are committed to respecting the intellectual property rights of others and have made all reasonable efforts to trace the copyright owners of the images reproduced, and to provide appropriate acknowledgement within this book. In the event that any untraceable copyright owners come forward after the publication of this book, the author and publishers will use all reasonable endeavours to rectify the position accordingly.

Index

Aarons, Joseph 236, 291, 337, 341, 352

Abberline, Detective Inspector Frederick 31, 38, 46, 59, 105–6, 128, 315, 342, 352, 474, 521, 523, 527, 539

Aberdeen 364, 376–7, 787

Abiff, Hiram 70, 76, 77, 78–80, 406–10, 535, 578

Abrahams, Maurice 235

Adams, Stephen *see* Maybrick, Michael

Addison, John QC 634, 641, 652–4, 664, 666, 691, 692, 694, 695, 697, 701–3, 712, 714, 715

Albert Victor, Prince, Duke of Clarence 206, 462, 629
  connection to the murders 81–3, 85–6, 92, 93–5, 98–9, 109–10, 164, 215
  as Freemason 177, 179
  involvement in high society scandals 30–1, 35, 36, 38, 39–40, 42, 46, 56, 57, 142

Alexandra, Princess of Wales 329

Allen, Oswald 243

Allyn, Avery 158

Alma-Tadema, Lawrence 329, 451

Alpass, Horace Seymour 179, 506

Ambler, John 599

Anatomy Act (1832) 344

Anderson, Samuel 725, 761

Anderson, Sir Robert
  as corrupt 292, 320–1, 440, 486, 507, 521, 550, 629, 764, 767, 769–70, 773–5, 776–7, 781, 782–8
  nicknamed Handy Andy 392–3
  and the Parnell case 434, 474, 761, 763, 764, 766, 769, 782
  and the Ripper case 14, 15, 81, 82, 97, 117, 126, 141, 152–5, 160, 210, 218, 227, 232, 238, 293, 414, 440, 486, 496, 507, 521, 550, 769

Andrews, Walter 128

Armitage, John 599

Arnold, Superintendent Thomas 35, 126–7, 128, 129, 130–2, 133, 134, 143, 151, 152, 227, 232, 252, 256, 277, 467, 521, 527

Ars Quatuor Coronatorum journal 87, 90–1, 98, 122

Arthur, Sir George 28–9

Artists Volunteers *see* 20th Middlesex (Artists) Rifles

Artists' Royal Gala (1889) 462

Ashanti 20–1

Ashworth, Edmund 172

Asquith, Herbert Henry 734–5, 744, 755, 791, 796

Aunspaugh, Florence 333, 648, 651–2, 655, 739

Aunspaugh, John 739

Austin, Henry 60, 164, 167

Aylesbury Prison (Buckinghamshire) 726

Bachert, Albert 552

Baden-Powell, Robert S. 20–1

Balfour, Sir Arthur 764, 765

Ball, Rev Charles 401, 564

Barbados 19

Barnett, Henrietta 449–52, 486

Barnett, Rev Samuel 249, 449–52, 462

Barratt, Mike 507

Barrett, William Alexander 498

Barrit, William 585–9, 593–5, 599–606, 608–10, 623, 642, 651

Barron, Dr Alexander 678, 688

Batchelor, J.H. 281–2, 288, 289, 290, 291–3, 296, 297, 302, 304, 306, 307

Battersea, Lady Constance de Rothschild 451

Battlecrease House, Aigburth (Liverpool) 489, 568–72, 612, 632, 636, 637, 647–8, 652, 659, 660, 661, 674, 675, 683, 685, 688, 723, 737, 739

Baxter, Wynne 3, 199, 203, 246, 247, 249, 254, 315, 545
  presides over Chapman's inquest 104, 107, 110–17, 186, 258–9, 545
  presides over McKenzie's inquest 474–5

Baxter, Wynne (cont ...)
  presides over Stride's inquest 258–9,
    260–78, 280, 298, 300, 302–3, 317–19,
    545
Beach, Thomas *see* Le Caron, Major Henri
Beaumont, Gustave de 762
Beaumont, Lord 37, 39
Bechuanaland Protectorate 61
Beck (policeman) 527
Begg, Paul 139, 140, 198–9, 215, 305,
    309–10, 530
'Behind the Scenes in America' 765,
    782–4
Belgium 45
Bell, Clerk 757
Benecke, Dr Mark 444
Benn, Anthony Wedgwood 56
Berkowitz, David 15
Berlin 38
Besant, Walter 89
Best, J. 310
Best, W.T. 325
Bianchi, Kenneth 163
Bidwell, Colonel 684
Birkett Committee 209
Birmingham 554, 772
Birtles, Sergeant 68
Black Hole of Calcutta 3–4
Blackham, Colonel Robert 66
Blackwell, Dr William 252, 255, 265, 266,
    269, 270, 309
Blackwood's Magazine 153
Blair, Tony 240
Blake, Valentine 612–13, 675, 677
Blavatsky, Madame 560
Blücher, Gebhard Leberecht von 396–7
Blunt, Wilfrid Scawen 797
Board of Works 246
Boer War 17
Bond, Dr Thomas 15, 239, 414, 415, 417,
    423, 424, 438, 441, 442–5, 483–4, 522,
    524, 542, 544, 549
Boosey, John 326, 376, 386, 457, 742, 746,
    749
Boulogne 47
Bournemouth 558–9
Bowyer, Thomas 520
Boy Scouts 20
Boy's Own Paper 23
Bradford 236–7, 562, 563, 565, 569, 572
  Alexandra Hotel 572, 573–4
  Back Belle Vue 589, 600, 604, 609
  Back Mellor Street 582, 585, 600
  Empire Theatre 572
  Heaton Road (Manningham) 574–6
    murder of Johnnie Gill in 484, 582–95,
      597–610
  St George's Hall 572
  Walmer Villas (Manningham) 573, 592
Bradford Daily Telegraph 566, 573, 588, 589,
    595, 598, 610
Bradford Observer 232, 566, 574, 575–6, 585,
    589, 597, 603–4
Bradford Pioneer 599
Braidwood, Illinois (US) 784
Brassey, Lady Sybil de Vere 451
Brassey, Lord Thomas 451
Brierley, Alfred 490, 570, 614–16, 618, 643,
    649–50, 655–9, 668, 669, 683, 736–9
Brierley, Bessie 736
Briggs, Matilda 490, 648, 649, 651–2, 659,
    661, 664, 667, 670, 672, 674, 716, 736–8
Brighouse, Samuel 678–81, 687, 736, 740
British Medical Journal 259
Bromley (Kent) 512–15
Brooklyn Eagle 757
Brough, Lionel 797
Brown, Dr Frederick Gordon 35, 120–1,
    123, 127, 130, 168–71, 177, 184–6, 202,
    220–2, 239, 341, 342, 345–6, 352, 522
Brown, James 273, 301
Brown, William 413, 414, 421, 441
Browning, Robert 451
Brussel, Dr James 446, 459
Bryning, Superintendent Isaac 673, 674,
    680, 684–5, 687, 722
Bucke, Joseph 582, 600
Budden, George 414, 421, 441, 445
Bulling, Thomas J. 430–2
Bundy, Ted 331–2
Burke, Thomas 765–6
Burma 40
Butt, Clara 365
Byng, Rev Francis 206
Byron, Lord George 762
Bywater, Witham Matthew 401–2, 564

Cadwallader, Mary 618, 636, 637, 666, 667,
    702–3
Cahill, Elizabeth 573–8, 587
Cahill, James 573–8, 587
Cain, Tubal 77
Cairns, Lord 41
Callery, Nurse 665, 667
Cambridge University 41
Canter, David 456–7
Cape Town 800
Caputi, Jane, *The Age of Sex Crime* 9–10, 15
Carmichael Bruce, Alexander 212, 232,
    293–9, 307

Carnarvon, Earl of 35, 174, 203
Carter, Dr William 655, 661, 662, 663–4, 665, 668, 670, 678, 688, 704, 709, 738
Cassell's Saturday Journal 365–6
Catling, Thomas 137, 169–70, 171, 177
Cavendish, Lord Frederick 765–6
Central News Agency 212, 216, 217, 219, 223, 272, 416, 429, 430
Chandler, Halbrook 487
Chandler, Inspector 103
Chandler, Raymond 165
Chandler, William 487
Chapman, Annie 12, 14, 82, 135, 160–1, 227, 232, 241, 242, 243, 244–5, 418, 454, 497, 770
  discovery and 'Masonic' mutilations 102–8, 203, 230
  inquest 108–18, 203, 246, 266
  missing rings 102, 386
Chatham prison 772, 773, 774
Christie, Trevor 616, 652, 731
Church, Archie 682
Churchill, Randolph 35
Churchill, Winston 24–5, 787
City of London Police 120, 127, 128, 130, 133, 134, 136, 139, 155, 183, 186, 188, 190, 191, 192, 200, 208, 224, 228, 235, 238, 308, 346, 458, 475, 798
Clarke, Sir Edward QC 716
Clarke, Kathleen, *Revolutionary Women* 773
Clayton, Godwin 722
Cleaver, Arnold 680, 684, 685, 687, 688, 697, 740
Cleaver, Richard 684, 697, 703, 711–12, 740
Clerke, Colonel Thomas Henry Shadwell 57, 173–7, 204, 408, 624, 625, 747
Cleveland Street scandal (1889) 31, 33, 35, 36–53, 58, 81, 436, 529, 544, 626, 740, 768
Coats, Dr 722
Cohen, Nick 625
Cole, Tennyson 333
Coleridge, John, Lord Chief Justice 210, 385, 782
Coles, Frances 107, 474
Collard, Inspector 129, 130, 133, 184
Collins, Police Constable H. 274, 276
Confucius 759
Contemporary Review 547
Conway, Thomas 201
Corah, Sir John 105
Cormac, John 337, 338
Cornwell, Patricia 530

correspondence
  American letters 377–83, 490–1, 492–3
  analysis of 358–65, 368–404
  Birmingham letter 554–60
  Bradford Suicide card 574, 575, 578, 587
  Bromley letter 512–15
  child-killing letters 564–6
  Conduit Street letter 397–8, 400–4, 457
  'Dear Boss' letters 145–6, 212–24, 236, 299, 370, 374, 375, 429, 492–3, 512–14, 517–18, 607–8
  Edinburgh letters 467–8, 510–12
  Folkestone card 460–1
  From Hell letters (Lusk and West Ham) 338–40, 346–50, 351
  Glasgow letter 567–8
  House of the Lord letter (McKenzie letter) 475–85
  Jack the Snicker letters 726–30, 798
  Liverpool fanatic letter 508–10
  Manchester 566
  Moab letter 431–3, 439, 480, 781
  money owed letters 490–1
  Openshaw letter 352–7
  Packer letter 333–6
  'Saucy Jack' letter 219–24, 299, 429
  Stoke-on-Trent letter 466–7
  Westcott/Taunton letter 554, 560–6
  Whitehall mystery letters 429–33
  Whittington letter 459–60
  Wilson/Neuberg letter 791–801
Craggs, Mrs Elizabeth 587
Crane, John 645
Crashaw, Richard 571
  'Sancta Maria Doloroum' ('The Mother of the Sorrows') 480–1
Craven, J. 588, 594–5, 597, 600, 601, 602, 603, 608
Crawford and Balcarres, Earl of 35
Crawford, Henry Homewood 184–6, 188, 189–90, 191, 192–3, 194–202, 203, 204, 279, 300, 308
  A Statement of the Origin, Constitution, Powers and Privileges of the Corporation of London 184
Cream (Ripper suspect) 164
Criminologist magazine 94
Crispe, Thomas QC 724
Cromer, Lord 26
Cromwell, Oliver 18, 19, 633, 761
Crook, Annie 82, 83, 85, 86
Crook, Stanley 410
Crossley, Ada 365–6, 461, 566
Crow, Albert 470–1

Crusades, Crusaders 65, 66
Cuffe, Hamilton John Agmondesham 38, 719
Cullen, Tom 526–7, 544
Cummings, William Hayman 498, 747, 752–3
Cunard Line 379
Cutbush (Ripper suspect) 164

Daily Chronicle 150, 228, 229, 256, 292, 425
Daily Mail 757
Daily News 62, 104, 106, 214, 254, 257, 775
Daily Post see Liverpool Daily Post
Daily Telegraph 102, 105, 106, 116, 123, 217, 230, 242, 243, 245, 252, 254, 259, 264, 266–7, 275, 291, 300–2, 304, 305, 317, 333, 337, 340, 343, 345, 348, 351–2, 434, 509, 520, 521, 529, 580
Dalgleish, Mr 678, 679, 682, 697, 703, 711, 722, 740
Dalton, John Neale 41
Daly, John 772–4
Davey, Emma 565
Davidson, George 620, 647, 672, 697
Davies, Fanny 451, 744
Davies, Mr 721–2
Davison, Frederic 498, 501, 504
Densmore, Helen 717–18, 730, 733, 755–6, 793
Der Arbeter Fraint (The Worker's Friend) 261
DeSalvo, Albert (aka. Boston Strangler) 446
Dew, Inspector Walter 28, 250, 252, 253, 254, 268, 298, 310
Dewer, Mr 91
Dhiban 406
Dickens, Charles 8, 628
Dictionary of Music and Musicians 64
Diemschutz, Louis 119, 251, 252, 253, 254, 255, 263–4, 265, 266, 268, 269, 270, 278, 298
DiGrazia, Mr 352, 420
Disraeli, Benjamin 37, 49
Dobson, Chief Detective Inspector 591
Dodge, Mary (aka. Gail Hamilton) 730–2
Dolden, Police Constable 285, 318
Doncaster 796, 801
Double Event (Stride/Eddowes murders) 123, 133, 146, 162, 168, 233, 235, 251, 292, 332–3, 364, 411, 446, 764
Dover 54
Downes, Detective Constable 130, 133
Druitt, Montague J. 164, 474, 485, 552
Dublin Castle 761, 767, 769

Dudley, Earl of 3
Dyer, John Thomas 604–7, 609

Eagle, Maurice 251–2, 263
East London Advertiser 249, 302, 311, 315
East London Observer 134, 229, 237, 249, 471
Echo newspaper 230, 292, 413, 425, 426, 438
Eddowes, Catherine (aka 'Kate Kelly') 82, 168, 177, 332
  anti-Semitic connotations 132–3, 149, 153–4, 193, 195–9, 202
  arrest and release from prison 162–3, 587
  empty tin matchbox and Maybrick association 167–70, 390
  inquest 184–203, 239, 264, 279
  Masonic connections 74, 121–5, 138–45, 154–60, 183, 199, 203, 342, 536
  missing apron 123–4, 125, 127–30, 133, 138, 143, 144, 152, 157, 183, 186, 193–4, 202, 216
  missing kidney 339–48, 385, 389
  murder and discovery of 88, 119–29, 163, 181–3, 225, 256, 282, 296, 361, 415, 454
  Warren's interest in 131–61
  writing on the wall 88, 124–5, 130–54, 156, 186, 195–201, 257
Edgbaston 326
Edinburgh 467–8, 566
Edis, Colonel Robert W. 206, 329, 463–4, 504, 754
Edward, Prince of Wales (later Edward VII) 93–4, 172, 329, 622–3, 625
  involvement in high society scandals 3, 30–6, 38, 41–2, 50, 54, 57
  Masonic connections 58, 60, 142, 167, 174, 175, 206, 530
Egypt, Egyptians 24–5
Eliot, George 21
Elizabethan Literary Society 450–1
Ellis, Havelock, *The Criminal* 11
Errant, George 441
Evans, Stewart 258, 259, 263, 297–8, 528
Evening News 188, 190, 191, 193, 194, 197, 215, 220, 223, 252, 253, 254, 263, 264, 267, 275, 280–1, 283, 284–5, 286, 287, 291, 292, 295, 299, 302, 305, 308, 309, 347–8, 415, 416, 429, 430, 434, 437
Evening Post 225
Evening Standard 48, 93, 115, 254, 539
Evidence Act (1843) 308
Ezekiel theory 532–9, 542, 543, 597

Fabris, Amanda 573
Fara, Carlo 572, 573

Feldman, Paul 168, 178
Fenians 761, 766, 768
Fido, Martin 138–9
Fildes, Luke 329
Firth, Walter 591
Fisher, D.B. 144
Fitzroy, Henry James, Earl of Euston 36–9,
   43, 46, 47, 48, 57, 58, 65–6, 92, 328, 547
Flanagan, John Woulfe 782
Fleming, John 611
Foli, Signor 325, 797
Folkestone 460–1
Ford, Peter 356
Foreign Office 779
Foster, Frederick (architect) 184
Foster, Superintendent 130, 133, 388–9
Foulton, Sir Forrest 58
Franklin, Mr 441
Frazer, Sir James 193, 194
Free Trades Hall (Manchester) 566
Freeman, James 599, 602
The Freemason 40, 62, 171, 172, 462, 500,
   748
Freemason's Chronicle 203
Freemasons, Freemasonry
  American 730, 733
  and Annie Chapman's mutilations 102–8,
   116, 117
  and Catherine Eddowes' murder 121–5,
   130, 138–45, 154–60, 183, 199, 342, 389
  and Catherine Stride's murder 259
  devotion to the Crown 206
  Jerusalem excavations and symbolism
   63–80, 409–10
  Maybrick connection 165–80
  membership and influence 33–5, 37,
   55–8, 329, 754
  Ripper connections 59–60, 84–101, 215,
   240, 241, 419, 432–3, 446, 475–9, 492,
   496–508, 530, 532–9, 546, 555–60,
   563–6, 572–3, 576–9, 591, 592
  Tyler's books 506–8
Friedland, Martin, *The Trials of Israel Lipski*
   316
Frith, William Powell 329
Fuller, Dr 571, 614, 636, 638, 639, 641, 642,
   693, 694, 695–6, 743

Gabe, Dr 522
Galashiels 376
Ganz, Wilhelm 175, 326, 327, 698, 746–9,
   753–4
  Memories of a Musician 747
Gardner, John 310
Gaskell, James 179, 506

George, Duke of York 5
George, Sir John 206
Gibraltar 66
Gilbert, W.S. 326
Gill, Johnnie 671
  discovery of his body 582–3, 586, 592
  Masonic connections 592
  media reports 583–4, 585, 588, 592, 593,
   595, 601, 603–4, 610
  murder and mutilation of 147, 473–4,
   484, 533, 565, 566, 573, 580, 582, 583–4,
   589–90, 592–3, 597–8
  suspected murderer arrested, put on trial
   and hanged 585–9, 593–5, 599–606,
   608–10
Gill, Lieutenant William 434
Gilles de Rais 84
Gladstone, William 22, 23, 42, 54–5, 762,
   763, 766, 769
Glasgow 376, 566, 567–8
Globe newspaper 249–50, 254
Glober, Jimmy 324
Godfrey de Bouillon 65, 66
Golden Dawn *see* Hermetic Order of the
  Golden Dawn
Goldstein, Leon 319–20
Gordon, Charles George 21–3
Gordon, William B. 603–4
Gordon, W.S. 26
Gore, Nurse 660, 661, 665, 683
Gorst, Sir John Eldon 206
Gosse, Edmund 451
Gower, Lord Ronald 37, 39–40
graffito 13–14, 15, 16, 88–9, 131, 147, 151,
   156
Grand, Mr *see* Le Grande, Charles
Grant, Alice 666
Grant, Mr (gardener) 685
Graphic magazine 206
Greatorex, Rev Dan 231
Green Bag journal 10
Grossmith, George 176
Grosvenor Press 4
Grove, Sir George 64, 407
  Dictionary of Music and Musicians 752, 754
Grover, Mr 437
Gull, Sir William 82–3, 85, 86, 93, 164
Gully, William 698

Hahn, Louis 288
Haigh, John George 108, 364
Haigh, Police Constable 600–1
Hall, J. 229
Hallé, Sir Charles 365
Hallé, Charles Edward 365

Halsbury, Hardinge Stanley Gifford, Lord 44, 58, 60, 177, 722–3, 724

Halse, Detective Constable 128, 129, 130, 133, 154, 195–8, 201

Hamill, J.M. 98, 142, 154

Hamilton, Dr Alan 428

Hamilton, Gail *see* Dodge, Mary

Hamilton, Lord George 35, 58, 206

Hammond, Charles 38, 45–6, 52, 53, 527

Hannah, Father 91

Hansard 781

Harcourt, Sir William 237, 787

Harlech, Lord 35

Harris, Henry 187, 192

Harris, Melvin 154, 167–8, 215–20, 222, 247, 553

Harrison, Caroline Scott 731, 740

Harrison, Shirley 746, 752

Hart, Lydia (Pinchin Street Torso) 455, 474

Hart-Dyke, Sir W. 35

Hartstein, Eva 254

Hawk magazine 47–8, 730–5, 744

Hawkins, Sir Henry 'Hanging Hawkins', Lord Brampton 48–50, 207, 297

Hayter Lewis, T. 80, 408

Heaton, Edward 612

Hedge, Ernest 422, 425, 440, 442

Helson, Detective Inspector Joseph 105, 106–7

Hemingway, Ernest 794

Hermetic Order of the Golden Dawn 558–64, 572, 591, 595

  Horus Temple (Bradford) 559, 561, 562, 572, 595

  Isis-Urania, Temple No.3 (London) 559

  Osiris Temple and Lodge (Weston-super-Mare) 559, 560, 561, 562, 564

Herschell, Lord 768

Hertford, Marquis of 35

Heshburg, Abraham 188–9

Hibbert, Dr Charles 415, 417–18, 420, 423–4, 443

Hicks Beach, Sir Michael 35

Hienes, Mr & Mrs 673

Higman, Bro 91

Hill, Alderman John 599

Hill, Alderman Thomas 599

Hime, Dr 588, 591, 597, 601, 602

Hogg, Quintin 458–9

Holloway, Mr & Mrs 673

Home Office 31, 45, 148, 149, 183, 188, 191, 230, 234, 236, 238, 300, 306, 311, 320, 343, 413, 415, 529, 532, 549, 645, 693, 756, 758, 769, 787

Hopkins, Gerard Manley 492

Hopkins, R. Thurston 217

Hopper, Dr 618, 668–9, 670, 688, 713, 739

Horus myth 596–7

Houston, Edward Caulfield 767, 768, 783

Howell, Michael 356

Hughes, Mrs 652, 664, 672, 674, 736

Humphreys, Dr 638, 642, 643, 647, 648, 655, 660, 661, 662, 668, 670, 672, 678, 688, 689, 694–5, 704, 709–10, 712, 738

Humphreys, Mrs (cook at Battlecrease) 637, 648, 665–6

Hunt, Detective 129, 130, 133

Hunt, William Holman 451

Husband's Forensic Medicine 637

Hutchinson, George 518–20, 525, 528

Hutchinson, John 601, 606

Hutt, Police Constable 587

Illustrated London News 29, 176, 256

Illustrated Police News 674

India 20, 40, 629

Ireland 18–19, 317, 629, 718, 761–89

Irish Home Rule 18, 762–4, 767

Irish Loyal and Patriotic Union (ILPU) 767, 768, 781–2

Irish Nationalists 762, 763, 769, 772

Irving, Captain P.J. 380, 612, 697

Irving, H.B. 691, 703

Irving, Sir Henry 329

Isenchmid (Ripper suspect) 164

Islam 67, 70

Isle of Wight 328, 427, 451, 498, 715, 717, 727, 744

  Lynthorpe house 743–5

Isle of Wight Observer 480

Izzard, Inspector 133, 137

The Jack the Ripper A to Z 127, 188, 222, 223, 246, 247, 321, 339, 411, 429

Jackson, A.C.F. 98

Jenkinson, Sir Edward 292, 772

Jennings, Hargrave 557, 558

Jerusalem 63, 405–6, 410

  Qubbat as-Sakhra (Dome of the Rock) 66–7

  Solomon's Temple 64–7, 69–71, 73, 75–8

  Temple Mount 66

Jervois, Colonel 38

Jerwood Library, Greenwich (London) 746

Jewish Chronicle 786

Johannesburg 791, 792, 793, 794, 797, 799

Johnson, Edward 265, 269

Jones, Mr QC 58

Joyce, William 767, 769, 780
Jubelo, Jubelo, Jubelum (Three Ruffians or Three Assassins) 78–80, 88, 89–90, 100–1, 118, 139–41, 144, 215, 419
Judicature Acts and Rules 107
Judy 580
Julian, Phillip 93–4
Juwes message 71, 85, 88

Karamelli, Mr 315
Kay, Dr 265
Keighley 588
Keir Hardie, James 56
Kellie, Lawrence 328
Kelly, John 201
Kelly, Kate *see* Eddowes, Catherine
Kelly, Mary Jane 147, 775
   investigation and inquest 109, 239, 263, 400, 516, 518–20, 522–33, 539–44
   Masonic connection 512, 535, 536, 592
   murder and mutilation of 15, 80, 100, 234, 432, 453, 454, 473, 485, 497, 517–18, 520–2, 525–6, 536, 537–9, 540–3, 563, 574
   removal of evidence 239, 361
   as royal nursemaid and potential blackmailer 82
Kenning's Cyclopaedia of Freemasonry 140
Kent, Duke of 578, 579
Keppel, Robert 453
Keyser, Sir Polydore de 171, 206
the Khalifa 25
Khartoum 21–3
Kidney, Michael 275–6
Killeen, Dr T.R. 453, 471
Kipling, Rudyard 176
Kirk, Police Constable Arthur 582, 600
Kissinger, Henry 240
Kitchener, General Herbert 24–7, 578
Klein, Frederick Augustus Klein 405–6
Klosowski (Ripper suspect) 164
Knaphill Prison, Woking (Surrey) 725, 727
Knight, John Baillie 615, 616, 649–50, 659, 739
Knight, Stephen 84–7, 91, 92, 93, 95, 98, 104, 289, 527, 529
   Jack the Ripper: The Final Solution 81–2, 94, 98
Knights Templar 37, 65, 66, 70, 578, 598
Knollys, Sir Francis 54, 57, 176, 623
Kosebrodski, Isaac 252, 253, 254, 263, 264, 266, 268, 270, 298
Kosminski, Aaron 14–15, 81, 82, 164, 218, 429, 474, 485, 486, 607
Krantz, Philip 261, 262

Krugersdorp, Transvaal Republic 791, 798
Kumasi 20–1
Kürten, Peter 359, 360

La Grange (Kentucky) 71
La Vanguardia 780
Labouchère, Henry 19, 40, 45–6, 50–1, 53, 56, 769
Lamb, Police Constable Henry 137, 252, 253, 254, 264, 265–6, 267, 268, 269, 274, 276, 298
Lancashire Advertiser 718
The Lancet 114, 259
Land League 764, 765, 772
Lane, John 579
Lang, Andrew 451
Langham, S.F. 183, 186, 189, 194, 201–3, 239
Langtry, Lillie 34
Lathom, Earl of (Lord Skelmersdale) 35, 57, 172, 176–7, 203, 204, 206, 504, 623–5
Law, John 356
Lawende, Joseph 187–90, 202, 203, 264, 275, 279, 280, 308, 310, 321, 337, 430
Lawley, Detective Superintendent 129, 130, 133
Lawrence (carpenter's labourer) 441
Le Caron, Major Henri (aka. Thomas Beach) 784–5, 787
Le Grande, Charles 281–2, 288–93, 296–8, 302, 304, 306, 307
Le Grande Starkie, Colonel 58, 172, 504
'Leather Apron' *see* Pizer, John
Leeds 459–60, 467
Leigh-Pemberton, E. 236–7
Leighton, Sir Frederick 34, 35, 64, 167, 175, 176, 206, 328, 451, 465, 469, 754
Lely, Durward 367–8, 566
Leopold, Prince, Duke of Albany 29
Lesley, Shane 762
Letchworth, Bro 799
Levy, J.H. 635, 735, 758
Levy, Joseph 187, 188, 189, 192, 310
Lewes (Sussex) 107
Lewis, Maurice 524, 525
Limpopo River 793, 794
Lincoln, Abraham 385
Lincoln, Robert 385
Lipski, Israel 250, 314–17, 320
Littlechild, John George 99, 774, 778, 781
Littler, D.R. QC 58
Liverpool 164–5, 166, 172, 175, 178, 325, 379, 380, 488, 489, 492, 497, 568, 572, 612, 613, 616, 658, 661, 750

Liverpool (cont ...)
  Aigburth Hotel 678
  Aintree Grand National race 618, 668, 669
  Birkenhead Docks 772
  Clay & Abrahams pharmacy 636, 695
  Flatman's Hotel 616–17, 618, 651, 668, 713, 716, 739
  Hanson (chemists) 712
  Knowsley Buildings 643
  Manchester Street 645
  Merchant Tavern 645
  St George's Hall 627, 653, 703
  Vaughn Street (Toxteth Park) 645
  Walton Jail 685, 687, 688, 690, 719, 725
  Wokes & Co. pharmacy 631, 712
Liverpool Citizen 686–7
Liverpool Cotton Brokers Association 505–6, 647
Liverpool Cotton Exchange 675, 683, 696, 697
Liverpool Courier 648, 693
Liverpool Daily Post 220, 650, 682, 690, 693, 736
Liverpool Document 165, 167–8, 169–70, 177, 571, 671
Liverpool Echo 508–9
Liverpool Mercury 678
Liverpool Post 642
Liverpool Review 697, 706, 715
Liverpool Weekly News 642
Liverpool Weekly Post 696
Llewellyn, Dr 107
Lloyd, Edward 325, 326, 327
Lloyd George, David 322
Lloyd, Sir H. 58
Lloyds Weekly Newspaper 133, 168–9, 322, 438
Lockwood, Sir Frank QC 58
Lodge, Dr S. 583, 589, 590, 594, 598, 600
Lodge Jnr, Dr 591·
Londesborough, Earl of 35
London buildings and institutions
  Argyle Rooms (Piccadilly) 329
  Blind School (Lambeth) 419, 420
  Brick Layers Arms (Settles Street) 310
  Britannia pub (Whitechapel) 525
  British Library 747
  Buckingham Palace 161, 750
  Café Royal (Regent Street) 324, 616
  City Mortuary (Golden Lane) 183–4, 282, 296
  Covent Garden Opera House 325, 753
  Freemason's Hall 37, 173, 178, 498, 558, 564, 579

George Yard Buildings (Whitechapel) 455
Guildhall School of Music 462, 753
Guy's Hospital 689
Harrods (Knightsbridge) 1
Haymarket Theatre 799
Holborn Restaurant 171
Houses of Parliament 7, 50, 161, 413, 772
Imperial (Duke Street) 187, 275
Inns of Court 57, 66
International Workingmen's Educational Club 250, 251, 256, 257, 261, 277, 304
London Hospital (Whitechapel Road) 341, 352, 356
Marlborough Rooms 748
Merchant Taylors' School (Goswell Street) 459
Millbank Street mortuary 415
Newgate Prison 316
Old Bailey 51
Police Museum, New Scotland Yard 218
Queen's Head (Whitechapel) 518
Royal Institute 324
St George's mortuary (Dutfield's Yard) 256, 419
St James Church (Piccadilly) 489
St James's Hall 326, 566, 747, 799
St James's Palace 40, 744
St Jude's Church (Whitechapel) 452
Sessions House (Westminster) 421
Shoreditch Town Hall 527
Society of Biblical Archaeology (Conduit Street) 400–4, 564
Swan & Edgar (Piccadilly) 3
Toynbee Hall (Whitechapel) 206, 249, 330, 449–58, 461–5, 467, 469–71, 520, 753
Vestry Hall, Cable Street (St George in the East) 260
Woolwich Arsenal 772
Working Lads' Institute (Whitechapel) 108
Young Men's Christian Institute 'the Polytechnic' (Regent Street) 457–9
London clubs
  Arts Club, Hanover Square (Mayfair) 328, 329, 451, 462, 744, 753
  Athenaeum (Pall Mall) 1, 34, 35, 44, 45, 48, 50, 92–3, 161
  Brook's (St James's Street) 29
  Carlton (Pall Mall) 44
  Pratt's, Park Place (St James's) 34
  Savage, Lancaster House (Savoy) 169, 171, 175–7, 360, 367, 396, 744, 753
  United Services (Pall Mall) 396
  White's (St James's Street) 34

London Post Office Directory 289–90
London Stock Exchange 763
London streets and areas
  Alderny Road (Whitechapel) 337
  Arlington Street 35
  Backchurch Lane 311
  Berner Street (Whitechapel) 252, 257,
    260, 262, 264, 271, 275, 277, 281, 285,
    301, 304, 308, 310, 312, 314, 320, 335,
    422
  Buck's Row (Whitechapel) 13, 105, 454
  Carlton Gardens 459
  Castle Alley (Whitechapel) 400, 454,
    472–3
  Castle Street (Whitechapel) 187
  Church Passage 188
  Clarence Gate (Regent's Park) 327, 335,
    741
  Commercial Road 285, 312, 318
  Commercial Street 234, 274, 318, 453
  Conduit Street 397–8, 400, 432, 753
  Duke Street 187
  Dutfield's Yard, off Berner Street
    (Whitechapel) 119, 127, 134, 137, 143,
    188, 194, 249–50, 251, 254, 255–6, 258,
    259–62, 266, 276, 280, 291, 292, 298,
    313, 454
  Eaton Place 161, 225
  Ellen Street 314
  Fairclough Street 273, 280
  Fashion Street (Whitechapel) 181–2
  Finsbury Circus 184
  Fleet Street 216
  Goulston Street (Whitechapel) 13, 62, 71,
    88, 108, 124–5, 128, 129, 130, 131, 134,
    137, 140, 144–5, 150, 156, 188, 192, 200,
    202, 248, 257, 343, 419, 434, 455, 520
  Hanbury Street (Whitechapel) 102, 112,
    114, 227, 242, 243, 454
  Harley Street 698
  Hyde Park 234, 435, 438, 521
  Jubilee Street (Whitechapel) 337, 343
  Kensington 615
  Lambeth 419–20
  Leman Street 125–6, 127, 129, 150
  Mile End Road 230
  Miller's Court (Dorset Street) 454, 519,
    520, 524, 526, 539, 540–1
  Mitre Square (Aldgate) 120, 127, 128,
    129, 135, 137, 170, 182, 187, 194, 197,
    202, 277, 308, 310, 345, 389, 430, 454
  Old Brown's Lane (Spitalfields) 13
  Peckham 420–1
  Petticoat Lane 139
  Phillip Street 314

  Pimlico 420, 421, 426, 443
  Pinchin Street 314, 455
  Plaistow 512, 513
  Poplar 512, 513
  Regent's Park 170
  St George's Yard (Whitechapel) 451, 455,
    470
  St John's Wood 451
  Sealcott Road (Wandsworth Common)
    427
  Settles Street 310
  Spitalfields 106, 227
  Wellington Road (St John's Wood) 741,
    744, 750, 751
  Westow Hill Market (Crystal Palace) 251
  Whitechapel 28, 81, 227, 240, 331
  William Street, off Cannon Street Road
    (Whitechapel) 261
Long, Police Constable 125, 126–7, 129,
  131, 152, 193, 194–8, 196, 197–8, 199,
  200, 256, 300
Longfellow, Henry Wadsworth 494, 501
Lopes, Mr Justice 2
Lott, Edwin 171
Lucifer periodical 560
Lumholtz, Charles 19–20
Lushington, Sir Godfrey 45, 306
Lusk, George 230–1, 235–6, 237–8, 247,
  288, 289, 290–1, 337–41, 343, 351,
  352–4, 389, 530, 552
Lytton, Lord 629

Macdonald, John Cameron 783, 784
MacDonald, Dr Roderick 522, 523, 526–9,
  651
Macdougall, Alexander 617, 635, 637, 639,
  640, 646, 658, 659, 665, 678, 679, 680,
  693–4, 710, 717, 720, 722, 730, 736, 740,
  755
McFarren, Walter 326
McGowan, William 591, 599, 609, 691
McIntyre, Inspector Patrick 257, 771–2
McKenzie, Alice 107, 234, 242, 381, 400,
  453, 454, 497, 567, 729
  murder and inquest 472–3, 474–5,
    478–80, 482–6
Mackey, Albert, *Lexicon of Freemasonry* 144
McKinley, President William 757
McLeod, Bro 69–71, 87, 88–9, 91–2, 94,
  101, 103, 139, 152, 155
Macnaghten, Sir Melville 14, 15, 27, 99,
  156, 218, 219, 234, 239, 363, 473, 474,
  478, 485, 531, 551–4, 787
Macnamara, Rawdon 704–6, 709, 715, 721
McVeagh, Jeremiah 787–8

McWilliams, Inspector James 128, 130, 131, 133, 134, 154, 183, 200, 346
Madrid 778, 779, 780
Maguire, Dr Thomas 767
the Mahdi 21, 22, 25–7
Maine, Amy Maybrick 644, 745
Major, Dr 582, 591
Malcolm, Mrs Mary 271–2, 295, 298, 302, 317
Manchester Courier 716–17, 719
Manchester Guardian 303
Manchester Weekly Times 479
Mander and Mitchenson Theatre Collection (Bristol University) 746
Mann, Thomas 353
Mark, Sir Robert 226–7
Marriot (police officer) 133
Marsh, Emily 337, 338, 340, 343
Marshall, Detective 414, 424, 426, 440, 442
Marshall, William 271–2, 301
Martock (Somerset) 563
Marx, Karl 62
Masonic Constellation (1891) 33
Masonic Lodges and Chapters 33, 37, 76, 78, 158, 178–9
  Athenaeum Lodge (1491) 166, 462
  Bramston Beach Lodge 37
  Chancery Bar 58
  De La Pre Lodge 37
  Doric Lodge (993) 530
  Fitzwilliam Lodge 37
  Foxhunter's Lodge 37
  Grafton Lodge and Chapter (London) 37
  Grand Lodge of England (No.1) 33, 90–1, 171, 203
  Grand Lodge of Missouri (US) 730
  Guildhall Lodge (3116) 203
  Hengist Lodge (194) 558–9
  Liverpool Lodge (2229) 690
  Lodge of Fidelity 37
  Lodge of Masonic Research (Quatuor Coronati Lodge) 80, 89, 98–9, 151, 400–2, 408–10, 481, 563–4, 579
  Military Lodge 37
  North and Hunts Master's Lodge 37
  Orpheus Lodge and Chapter (1706) London 171, 497–506, 564, 744, 747, 753
  Pegasus Lodge 37
  Prince of Wales Lodge 599
  Reclamation Lodge of Jerusalem (Warren's Masonic Hall) 69–70, 71, 73–4
  Rose Croix Chapter (19) Liverpool 494, 504–5, 506
  Royal Alpha Lodge 37
  Royal Arch chapter, Jerusalem (32)
    Liverpool 172, 494, 504, 505, 624, 799
  St George's Chapter (42) London 172, 173, 624–5, 690, 744
  St George's Lodge of Harmony (35) Liverpool 494, 495–6
  St Peter's Lodge (284) 37, 213
  Savage Club Lodge (2190) 169, 171, 177
  Shakespeare Lodge (1018) Bradford 572
  Skelmersdale 623
  Stour Valley Lodge 37
  Studholme Chapter (London) 37
  Studholme Lodge 37
  United Grand Lodge 203, 579
  Westminster and Keystone Lodge 502–4
  Zetland Lodge (511) 781
Mathers, Samuel L. MacGregor 558–9, 563, 564, 572, 573
Matthews, Henry QC 31, 35, 38, 45, 60, 148, 150, 230, 235, 237, 238, 240, 290, 300, 306, 316, 419, 435, 549, 550, 554, 603, 609, 703, 711, 714, 718, 724, 729, 740, 741, 773
Maxim, Sir Hiram 25
Maxwell, Mrs Caroline 524, 525
May, H.R.A. 464
Maybrick, Doris 383
Maybrick, Edwin 333, 488, 490, 612, 632, 643, 644–6, 647, 648, 649, 653, 657, 658, 660, 665, 666, 668, 672, 684, 685, 697, 698, 796
Maybrick, Florence Elizabeth Chandler 482
  affair with Brierley 490, 570, 614–16, 618, 668, 669–70
  apparently poisons her husband using flypapers and arsenic 164–5, 175, 316, 380, 474, 507, 630–2, 640, 641, 643, 645, 647–9, 652–4, 662, 666
  and the Brierley letter 649–52, 655–9, 669, 670
  charged with her husband's murder 673, 675, 685
  falls into a swoon 670–3, 674, 689
  framed by Michael 177, 381, 614, 619, 626, 663, 738–9, 796–7
  letter to Dr Hopper 668–9
  meets and marries James 164, 487–90, 618–19
  Michael spends Christmas with 568–72
  Michael's dislike of 490–1, 570, 615–16, 619, 633, 652, 665

obtains arsenic from chemist 676–7

public support for 716–22, 730–4, 740, 756–7

receives photographs of her children 754–5

sentence of death commuted 715–16, 724–7, 755

trial of 493–4, 496, 508, 599, 603, 607, 617, 627–8, 629–37, 645, 653, 656–7, 664, 666, 672, 685, 689, 690–724, 737–40

visited by her mother while held in her own home 683–5

visitors refused access to 673

writes to Michael concerning her anxieties about 'white powders' 639, 660–1, 668

Maybrick, Gladys Evelyn 489, 569–70, 647, 656, 673

Maybrick, James 222, 333, 380, 608

apparently poisoned by Florence 164–5, 175, 316, 380, 474, 507, 630, 630–1, 636–43, 645, 647–9, 652–3

beats Florence 618

body exhumed 687–8, 689, 722, 740

death and burial 620–1, 658, 671, 672, 678, 683

and Diary of Jack the Ripper 164–70, 504, 507–8, 670–2

as drug addict 165, 488, 490, 493, 496–7, 611–14, 632, 636–9, 677, 679, 682–3, 697

family crest 759

framed by Michael 493, 496–7, 508–15, 619–20, 622–3

inquest 638–9, 678–83, 686–9, 736–7

maniacal fear of death 642

Masonic connections 166–8, 172–3, 174, 177–80, 204, 492, 494–6, 501–6, 620, 622, 758, 759

meets and marries Florence 164, 487–90, 618–19

Michael spends Christmas with 568–72

no arsenic found during autopsy 678

will of 646–7, 666–7

writes the 'Blucher' letter 640–1, 642–3, 692, 695, 711, 719–20, 721, 723, 739

Maybrick, James Chandler 489, 569–70, 647, 673, 755

Maybrick Memorial Committee 757

Maybrick, Michael (aka Stephen Adams) 222, 451, 469

anagram as Ripper proof 801

at Florence's trial 692, 695, 698, 700–1, 738–9

at James's inquest 678–9

attends James in his final days 659–68, 667–8, 671, 672

disappears into obscurity 742–54

dismisses staff and keeps Battlecrease for himself 685

disregards James's will 647, 688

exploits Yapp and Briggs 652

frames James 493, 496–7, 508–15, 619–20, 622–3

hatred of Florence 490–1, 570, 615–16, 619, 633, 652, 665, 685, 754, 796–7

joins the Artists Volunteers 328–30

loans Florence money 490–1

manipulates evidence 638, 688–9, 692–3, 719, 721, 738–9

marries his housekeeper 742–3

Masonic connections 169–77, 180, 204, 206, 327, 401–4, 497–8, 501, 504, 534–5, 625, 699

moves to the Isle of Wight 743–4

musical career 171, 176, 323–30, 367, 462, 465, 488

organises James's funeral 620–1

plots with Edwin to kill James 496, 643, 644–6, 665

possible visit to South Africa 796–7, 799–801

refuses death certificate for James 678

as Ripper candidate 330–1, 333–8, 359, 376, 380, 480–1, 564, 566–72, 671–2

as Ripper letter-writer 383–404, 459–61, 468–93, 508–15, 607–8

spends Christmas with James and Florence 568–72

Maybrick, Sarah Ann Robertson 488, 490

Maybrick, Thomas 488, 672, 717, 755

The Maybrick Trial: A Toxicological Study (1890) 705

Maynard, M. 390

Medico-Legal Journal 757

Mendoza, Harry 90–1

Merrick, Joseph 356

Methuen, Lord Paul 463, 464, 465

Metropolitan Police 11, 14, 34, 35, 44, 60, 82, 95, 105, 126, 130, 131, 136, 137, 139, 140, 146, 183, 190, 191, 196, 197, 201, 202, 210, 213, 219, 223, 229, 235, 249, 266, 269, 283, 288, 297, 308, 336, 362, 428, 552, 590, 773

A Division (Westminster) 414

H Division (Stepney) 95, 105, 126, 232–3, 234, 260, 267, 521, 527

J Division (CID) 105

Miall, Mr 582, 591

Millais, John Everett 329, 451
Moab 404, 405–8, 410, 419, 431, 432–3, 434, 439, 446
Monro, Assistant Commissioner James 62, 96–8, 228, 234, 237, 259–60, 264, 484, 787
Montagu, Samuel 237
Moore, Augustus 731–3, 735
Moore, Frederick 416
Moore, Chief Inspector Henry 59, 128, 155, 219, 283–4, 286–7, 544
Morland, Nigel 664
Morley, John 775
Morning Advertiser 254, 291
Morning Post 222, 236
Morris, Robert 69, 71, 73
Morrison, Mr 603
Mortimer, Mrs Fanny 252, 254, 255–6, 263, 266, 270, 298, 313, 319, 320
Moulton, Lord Justice 175
Mount Edgecombe, Earl of 35
Mowbray, Sir John 35
Moylan, Sir John F. 552
  Scotland Yard and the Metropolitan Police 97
Muckley, R.F. 716–17, 735
Murdoch, Rupert 8
Murray's Magazine 148, 548
Musical World 327, 329, 367, 515
Mylett, Rose 107

Nacy, Edward 682
National Archives (Kew) 87, 242, 746
Nava, Geatano 325
Neruda, Madame 799
Netley (a driver) 83, 87
Neuberg, Moreau Masina Berthrad 791–801
Neville, Dr 416–18, 424, 443
New Era magazine 324
New Scotland Yard 218, 224, 300, 410–20, 438, 441–5
New Statesman 651
New York 379–83
New York Herald 118, 234, 344, 419, 428, 453, 455, 486, 581, 616, 659, 682, 719, 735
New York Medico-Legal Society 757
New York Times 425–6, 531, 785
New York Tribune 160, 209, 486, 531, 532, 581
New York World 39
Newlove (a postboy) 38
The News from Whitechapel 351–2, 544, 545
Newton, 52
Newton, J. Fort 74, 122

Nichols, Mary Anne 'Polly' 82, 103, 107, 135, 244, 266, 454, 497, 764
Norfolk Cotton Exchange (Virginia) 488
Norfolk, Virginia 611, 647
Norman Shaw, Richard 413
North London Press 44
Northcote, Sir Stafford 21–2
Notes on Ritual and Procedure (1976) 89–90
Nott-Bower, William 675–7

Observer newspaper 114, 258–9, 625
O'Connor, T.P. 44, 47, 52, 718, 758, 782
Oddy, William 599
Official Secrets Act 210
Oliver, Rev George 158
Olsson, Sven 271
Omdurman 25
Onion, William 461
Openshaw, Dr Thomas Horrocks 341–2, 345, 352, 354, 355–6
Ormskirk (Lancashire) 172, 624
Orpheus document 497–506, 508
Ostrog, Michael 164, 429, 474, 485, 607
Ottolenghi, Salvatore 12
Ouida (Marie Louise de la Ramée) 5–6
Outram (police officer) 133

Packer, Matthew 267, 268, 272, 275, 277, 280, 281, 283–7, 289, 290, 291, 292, 294–311, 313, 317–19, 321–2, 333, 335–7, 377, 519–20
Packer, Mrs 287
Paine, Tom 633
  The Rights of Man 628
Palestine Exploration Fund (PEF) 64, 71, 407–8, 434, 752
Pall Mall Gazette 2, 144–7, 148, 150, 151, 193, 243, 316, 356, 434, 475, 548, 580, 799
Palmer, Professor Edward 434
Palmerston, Henry John Temple, Lord 1
Paris 41–2, 434, 487, 769, 778
Parke, Ernest 43, 44, 47–8, 49–50, 86, 92, 207, 240, 623, 731
Parnell, Charles 51, 55, 210, 434, 529, 600, 626, 721, 761–89
Parnell Commission 633
'Parnellism and Crime' 765–9, 781, 782, 787
Parry, Sir Edward 675
Partridge, Detective 46–7, 53
Patchen, Kenneth 629
Patey, Madame 749
Paul, Dr Frank 707–8, 708
Pax Britannica 16–27

Pearce, Charles E., *Sims Reeves: Fifty Years of Music in England* 750
Pember, E.H. QC 58
Penzance 364
Peter the Hermit 65
Petermann, Dr Heinrich 71, 406, 407
Philadelphia 377–83
Philadelphia Keystone 73
Philbrick, F.A. QC 58
Philharmonic Society 744, 753
Phillips, Dr George Bagster 125, 127, 300, 302, 342, 346, 435, 474, 496, 590
and murder of Johnnie Gill 591, 592, 600
and murder of Kelly 521, 522–3, 532, 540–3
and murder of Stride 252, 254, 256, 265, 266, 267–70
presents findings on Chapman's mutilations 103, 105–12, 475, 521, 528
withholds evidence concerning McKenzie's murder 475, 479, 482–4
Phillips, Captain N.G. 498
Phoenix Park murders (Dublin, 1882) 765–6, 773
Pickford, Sir William 679–80
Picton, James Allanson 19
Pigott, Richard (aka. Roland Ponsonby) 721, 767–9, 773, 775–81, 782
Pike, Albert 144, 537
Morals and Dogma 144, 478
Pinchin Street Torso *see* Hart, Lydia
Pizer, John 'Leather Apron' 13–14, 15, 81, 132–3, 149, 164, 245–6, 256, 257, 316, 343, 428, 607
Poisons Act (1851) 612
Police Gazette 190–2, 279, 317
police stations
  Arbour Square (Whitechapel) 234
  Commercial Road 125, 131, 143, 150, 198, 234, 303
  Gerard Row 416
  Great Marlborough Street 38
  King Street 414
  Leman Street 125–6, 127, 129, 143, 150, 200, 202, 233, 252, 256, 311, 319, 343, 427
  Old Jewry 238
  Pimlico Road 416
Ponsonby, Roland *see* Pigott, Richard
Pool, Sir James 505
Portland, Duke of 35
Poses Plastique *see* Cleveland Street scandal
Press Association 291
Probyn, Sir Dighton 45, 53–4, 57
Public Opinion 133

Pullen, Hyde 498
Punch magazine 228–9, 392, 412, 788, 789
Purdie, Ferguson 29, 30

Quincey, Thomas de, *Confessions of an English Opium-Eater* 613

Rader, Dennis 155
railways 376, 566–8
Ratcliffe, Charles 647, 648, 667, 672, 697, 739
Reed, F.S. 341, 352
Reeves, Mr 291
Reeves, Robert Edward 644–6, 647, 648, 678, 697, 796, 800
Reeves, Sims 325–6, 367, 749, 750, 754
Referee 104
Reid, Inspector John 59, 134, 242, 243, 244–5, 250, 260, 262, 266, 275, 277–8, 280, 283, 521
Reik, Theodor 359
Ressler, Robert 163, 331, 453, 570
Revelation, Book of 536–9, 543
Review of Reviews 6, 714, 791, 794, 800
Reynold's News 49, 227–8, 741, 771, 776, 777
Rhodes, Cecil 5, 20, 797
Richardson, J. Hall 527
Richter, Hans 325
Ridley, Sir Matthew White 756–7
Rigg, Morden 636, 682, 697, 703
Rigg, Mrs Morden 636–7, 711
Roberts, Andrew 53
Roberts, Dr 588, 591, 597, 601
Roberts, Lord Frederick 17
Roques, Baron Adolph von 487, 722
Roques, Baroness Caroline von 487, 622–3, 625, 642, 657, 658, 683–4, 685–6, 686, 697, 703, 711, 715
Rosa, Carl 326, 572
Rosebery, Archibald Primrose, Lord 624
Rosenfield, Mrs 254
The Rosicrucian Cosmo Conception 562
Rosicrucians 481, 482, 557, 559, 562, 595, 598
Rothenstein, William 463
Rough Ashlar (Freemason tract, 1891) 33
Row, Alfred 682
Royal Irish Constabulary 780
Royal Society of Musicians 799
Royds, Mr 690
Ruggles-Brise, Evelyn 149, 435
Rule, Anne 331
Rumbelow, Donald 167, 170, 258, 259, 263, 297–8

Russell, Sir Charles QC 35, 43, 52, 175, 207, 633, 634–5, 638, 641, 649, 650, 656–7, 665, 672, 677, 679, 682–3, 685–6, 688, 691, 692–3, 695–712, 715, 721, 722, 724, 739, 740, 747, 752, 775, 781, 782, 792–3

Ryan, Stephen Gouriet 542–3

Rylands, William Harry 400–3, 564

St Mary's Hospital Fund 799

Salisbury, Robert Cecil, Lord 7, 24, 26, 35, 43, 45, 47, 50, 53–5, 61, 172, 210, 428, 434, 529, 599, 624, 628, 731, 734, 756, 762, 764, 766, 768–70

Salsotto, Giovenale 12

Salvation Army 609

San Francisco 46

Sandeman, Hugh 172

Sandringham, Norfolk 31, 206, 634

Santley, Charles 325, 326, 367, 488, 742, 746, 749–50, 754, 797, 799

Reminiscences of My Life 749

Student and Singer: The Reminiscences of Charles Santley 749

Santley, Miss 748

Saturday Review 49

Saunders, Mr 315

Schwartz, Israel 311–15, 317, 318, 320, 321, 335

Schweisso, Alfred 616–17, 651, 716

Scotland Yard 11, 29, 45, 47, 48, 86–7, 92, 95, 103, 114, 131, 133–4, 135, 146, 149, 155, 157, 192, 212, 216, 218, 230, 238, 286, 293, 296, 302, 311, 333, 336, 340, 343–4, 362, 430, 434, 474, 607, 769, 779, 787

Criminal Investigation Department (CID) 14, 97, 98, 105, 109, 126, 148, 152–3, 230, 283, 303, 763, 769, 771

Special Branch 97, 257

Scotland Yard Trunk mystery see Whitehall mystery

The Scotsman 425

Sefton, Earl of 690

Sequeria, Dr 168–9

Sheddon, T.G.E. 498, 500, 748

Sheffield 566

Shelton (in Coroner's Office) 186–7

Shipley Times 601

Shuttleworth, Thomas 690, 701

Sickert, Joseph 84

Sickert, Walter 83, 95, 164

Simpson, Sir Keith 255

Simpson, William 400–1

Sims, George R. 104–5, 435–6, 718, 749, 781

My Life 747

Sisters of Jesus 3

Skelmersdale, Lord see Lathom, Earl of

Smith, Sir Henry 119, 123, 127, 129, 130, 133, 135, 154, 183, 224, 228, 231, 244, 299, 343, 345, 352

Smith, Kate 36

Smith, W.H. 53, 768

Smith, Police Constable William 274–8, 280, 295, 301, 308, 309, 318

Smith, Dr William R., The Principles of Forensic Medicine 255

Smoker (dog) 437, 438, 442

Smollett, Tobias, The Expedition of Humphry Clinker 571

Soames, Mr 773–4, 778–9

Society of Medical Jurisprudence and State Medicine (New York City) 531

Somers Vine, J. 176

Somerset, Lord Arthur 'Podge' 31, 36–7, 39, 45, 46, 47, 51, 54

Somerset, Henry 31

South Africa 16, 17, 791–801

South African Empire 798

Special Commission 770, 782

Special (Irish) Branch 774

Spectator 545

Speth, G.W., Builders' Rites and Ceremonies: The Folk Lore of Masonry 409–10

Sphere Magazine 749

SS Baltic 487–8

SS Republic 380–1

SS Scot 799

Standard Bible Dictionary 64

Stansell, Thomas 697

Star newspaper 44, 47, 150, 157, 223, 227, 231, 240, 251, 296, 299, 302, 311–12, 348, 350, 417, 758

Stavely Hill, Alexander QC 58

Stead, William Thomas 2, 316, 434, 714–15, 762, 791–4, 800

Stephen, James Fitzjames 31, 32, 35, 286, 316, 628–9, 630–1, 631, 632, 633, 635, 641, 690, 694, 708, 710, 711, 712–15, 716, 721, 722, 758

Stephen, James Kenneth 31–2

Stephen, Sir Leslie 629

Stephenson, Sir A.K. 603

Stephenson, Dr 689

Stirling, Madame Antoinette 748

Stocks, Dennis 138–9

Stoke-on-Trent 466–7

Stone, Marcus 329

Stowell, Thomas Eldon 92–3, 94–5, 98, 109, 142, 179, 486